CAMBRIDGE LATIN AMERICAN STUDIES

EDITORS
MALCOLM DEAS   CLIFFORD T. SMITH   JOHN STREET

18

POLITICS ECONOMICS AND SOCIETY IN ARGENTINA IN THE REVOLUTIONARY PERIOD

THE SERIES

1. SIMON COLLIER. *Ideas and Politics of Chilean Independence, 1808–1833*
2. MICHAEL P. COSTELOE. *Church Wealth in Mexico: A study of the Juzgado de Capellanías in the Archbishopric of Mexico, 1800–1856*
3. PETER CALVERT. *The Mexican Revolution, 1910–1914: The Diplomacy of Anglo-American Conflict*
4. RICHARD GRAHAM. *Britain and the Onset of Modernization in Brazil, 1850–1914*
5. HERBERT S. KLEIN. *Parties and Political Change in Bolivia, 1880–1952*
6. LESLIE BETHELL. *The Abolition of the Brazilian Slave Trade: Britain, Brazil and the Slave Trade Question, 1807–1869*
7. DAVID BARKIN AND TIMOTHY KING. *Regional Economic Development: The River Basin Approach in Mexico*
8. CELSO FURTADO. *Economic Development of Latin America: A Survey from Colonial Times to the Cuban Revolution*
9. WILLIAM PAUL MCGREEVEY. *An Economic History of Colombia, 1845–1930*
10. D. A. BRADING. *Miners and Merchants in Bourbon Mexico, 1763–1810*
11. JAN BAZANT. *Alienation of Church Wealth in Mexico: Social and Economic Aspects of the Liberal Revolution, 1856–1875*
12. BRIAN R. HAMNETT. *Politics and Trade in Southern Mexico, 1750–1821*
13. J. VALERIE FIFER. *Bolivia: Land, Location, and Politics since 1825*
14. PETER GERHARD. *A Guide to the Historical Geography of New Spain*
15. P. J. BAKEWELL. *Silver Mining and Society in Colonial Mexico, Zacatecas 1546–1700*
16. KENNETH R. MAXWELL. *Conflicts and Conspiracies: Brazil and Portugal, 1750–1808*
17. VERENA MARTINEZ-ALIER. *Marriage, Class and Colour in Nineteenth Century Cuba: A Study of Racial Attitudes and Sexual Values in a Slave Society*

POLITICS ECONOMICS AND SOCIETY IN ARGENTINA IN THE REVOLUTIONARY PERIOD

by

TULIO HALPERÍN-DONGHI

Professor of History, University of California, Berkeley

Translated by Richard Southern

CAMBRIDGE UNIVERSITY PRESS
Cambridge
London · New York · Melbourne

Published by the Syndics of the Cambridge University Press
The Pitt Building, Trumpington Street, Cambridge CB2 1RP
Bentley House, 200 Euston Road, London NW1 2DB
32 East 57th Street, New York, N.Y. 10022, USA
296 Beaconsfield Parade, Middle Park, Melbourne 3206, Australia

© Cambridge University Press 1975

Library of Congress Catalogue Card Number: 74-79133

ISBN: 0 521 20493 3

First published 1975

Printed in Great Britain
at the University Printing House, Cambridge
(Euan Phillips, University Printer)

CONTENTS

Preface	page vii
Acknowledgement	xi
List of abbreviations	xii

PART ONE: THE BACKGROUND

1 The River Plate at the beginning of the nineteenth century	3
The stability of the Interior	6
The rise of the Littoral Provinces	16
Buenos Aires and mercantile expansion	29
A society less reformed than its economy	40
2 Revolution and the dislocation of the economy	65
The mutilation and fragmentation of the Viceregal economic territory	65
The increasing burden of the State	72
The breakdown of the pre-Revolutionary commercial structures	81

PART TWO: FROM VICEROYALTY TO 'UNITED PROVINCES OF THE RIVER PLATE'

3 The crisis of the Colonial order	111
The War and the weakening of Imperial ties	111
The British Invasions and the institutional crisis	124
The Revolution	150
4 The Revolution in Buenos Aires	158
The birth of political life	158
The crisis of the bureaucracy	176
The Revolutionary leaders, the Army and the urban socio-economic élite	190
The end of the Revolution and the beginnings of order	226
5 The Revolution in the country as a whole	239
The Interior	239
The Revolution as a social revolution: Upper Peru	241

Contents

Revolution in stability: Tucumán and Cuyo	page	245
Salta and 'Güemes's System'		264
The other Revolution: Artigas and the Littoral		269
6 The dissolution of the Revolutionary order		308
Political fragmentation (1819–21)		308
Buenos Aires in 1820: political ruin and reconstruction		331
The 'fortunate experience' of Buenos Aires		345

PART THREE: CONCLUSION

7 The legacy of the Revolution and the war, and the political order of independent Argentina 377
    The 'barbarisation' of politics: the militarisation and ruralisation of the bases of political power 377
    The holders and the administrators of power 382
    The search for a new cohesion 390

Notes to the text 402
Bibliography 415
Index 421

PREFACE

This book is, primarily, a political history. Even though it begins with an examination of the economy and society of the River Plate area in the period of transition towards Independence, this is because it appeared to us impossible to leave out of account the effective dimensions of the collective political entity of which this book attempts to trace the history. Its theme is not, therefore, very different from those which absorbed the attention of the founders of Argentina's tradition of historiography; that is to say, the growth of a centre of autonomous political power, controlled by a well-defined group of men, in an area where the very notion of political activity had been unknown to almost everybody until a short time before. Our greatest historians, however, did not state the problem in exactly these terms. As far as Mitre was concerned, the rise of this centre of power was merely the obvious outward sign of a change much broader in scope: the rise of a new nation within the frontiers of the territory which had been mysteriously predestined for that purpose. The men and the groups which took part in that process appeared to be connected, not so much by definable ties of affinity or hostility – of which, however, the historian did not fail to take account – as by their common participation in the building of a future which none could foresee and which all were preparing, and which provides the perspective from which the historian of later times considers and judges the participants.

López, in more than one respect, represents a diametrically opposite approach. The rôle of the historian of the rise of a new nation was of less interest to him than the nostalgic evocation of a liberal élite based on Buenos Aires, the destiny of which was, not so much to prepare the ground for the creation of a more broadly based national community, as to fill the gap left by the continuing absence of such a community, and to govern the area which destiny had placed in its charge in accordance with the rules of an art of politics and administration learned in the school of that finest of all sovereigns, Charles III. Nevertheless, he was in agreement with Mitre in considering the entire process of the foundation of the nation from the point of view of a development, with the fundamental characteristics of which he strongly sympathised: the consolidation of a sharply defined national state, bounded by frontiers that had not been in any way pre-determined by the pre-Revolutionary political order, and governed in a

Preface

particular style and with particular objectives, appeared to him, as it did to Mitre, a sufficient retrospective justification of a historical process, though he took care to emphasise the darker side of the latter.

This outlook, shared by the greatest founders of Argentina's tradition of historiography, was, of course, related to the peculiar positions held by both men in the life of the nation. Even when both of them, when they wrote their most mature historical works, had already been excluded from the politically dominant faction, their allegiance to the basic principles underlying the political order in force in the country more than outweighed their differences with the group enjoying political control. Moreover, that order appeared to them more fragile and less securely consolidated than it does to the retrospective observer. The contingent elements of the historical process which they evoked appeared to them to have relevance for their own day and age. Their adherence to a particular concept of Argentina as a nation and to the historical process which gave rise to it was not so much a gesture of posthumous approval of an already irreversible development as a polemical stance *vis-à-vis* the present and the future. Of course, neither Mitre nor López would have gone so far as the alarmed José Posse, who from his native city of Tucumán proclaimed in 1879 the ultimate failure of the attempt to build a new nation, in which seventy years of effort appeared to have been wasted. It is, nevertheless, significant that both men were writing at a time when such thoroughgoing pessimism was still possible. Even though they fortified themselves against that attitude by affirming their faith in the destiny of the nation, the temptation to surrender to pessimism perhaps explains why the expression of that faith was so vociferous and frequently reiterated. Although the development, of which they fundamentally approved, appeared to them not as one of the many possible outcomes of the process initiated in 1810 (a particular outcome arrived at, by no means inevitably, as a result of a chain of historical events characterised by sharp fluctuations of fortune), but as the fulfilment of a destiny mysteriously foreordained from the beginning of time in the body and soul of the new nation, this was precisely because they felt the need for this over-emphatic justification in order to silence the doubts to which the fragility of the prevailing political order still appeared to give rise. Similarly, their hostility towards the supporters of political solutions other than the one which actually prevailed was not a merely posthumous condemnation: the virulence with which it was expressed would not be explicable if the defeat suffered by those supporters had really been considered as definitive.

This complex network of sentiments and attitudes which inspired our early historians is not, of course, capable of evoking a comparable response in historians of the present day. The political outcome, from the standpoint of which they judged the past, today appears both less threatened and less admirable. Rather than making another devout pilgrimage along that

Preface

highway followed by the new nation in its historical development, historians are increasingly coming to prefer the sympathetic exploration of those alternative paths which were not taken, but at the end of which it is permissible to envisage a present very different from that which most present-day scholars – albeit from often conflicting motives – agree to be intolerable.

Having made these brief observations, we must point out that the purpose of this work is much more limited: its aim is to trace the vicissitudes of a political élite created, destroyed and then created again by war and revolution. This involves the consideration of a whole series of problems: what were, in the complex of social relationships existing before the rise of political activity, in the strict sense of the term, the relationships that were to provide a context for that new activity? What was the relationship between the political élite created by that process of social specialisation and the social and economic élites whose position and attitudes were, inevitably, seriously affected by the very changes that made the area both the scene and the subject of political struggles? How did that political élite use its recently acquired power to redefine its relationship both with the other sectors of the élite and with those popular groups without whose activity it would never have risen to power, but with which it was often reluctant to share the political influence it had acquired? Here, then, is a whole complex of problems, the importance of which is undeniable. The examination of them involves the exploration of fields which have been dealt with by previous historical research in extremely varying degrees of detail, and this factor has inevitably influenced the present work. Occasionally, it has been found impossible to submit certain aspects, and not always unimportant ones, of the general theme to an investigation sufficiently detailed to offset, to a satisfactory degree, that long neglect on the part of historians. At times, a more detailed investigation appeared to threaten the entire structure of the work: thus, the finances of the Revolutionary régime have been the subject of a separate study, the results of which I hope to publish in the near future.

It remains for me to add a few remarks concerning the origin of this book, for the circumstances of this origin have played some part in determining the final shape of the work. In 1957 I was invited by Don Arnaldo Orfila Reynal to write a history of Argentina in the first eighty years of the nineteenth century. I was soon to discover that I had been imprudent in accepting this offer with such alacrity. For over ten years – during which I was, moreover, busy with other work and with academic activities as time-consuming and disturbed as they would be in the unsettled Argentina of those years – I did my best to fulfil that commitment in which my ignorance and lack of caution had involved me. Eventually I realised that, in the form in which I had originally approached it, the task was impossible: I

Preface

had neither the time nor the resources needed to deal with the questions which, in my view, required an answer if one were to write a history of that stage of Argentina's development on the basis of a unified and systematic approach to the problems involved. The present work is, therefore, one of the unexpected fruits of that prolonged and perplexed effort. In publishing it, I would like to express once again my thanks to Don Arnaldo Orfila for his initial confidence in me and his sustained patience. I would also like to thank all those who – often unknowingly – have helped me to formulate the thoughts expressed in this book – some of them were my colleagues and students in the Universities of the Littoral and of Buenos Aires, at a time which now appears to me almost as remote as that discussed in this book – and also those with whom, in so many other places, I have conversed about these matters.

T.H.-D.

ACKNOWLEDGEMENT

The English edition of this book is being published by the Cambridge University Press in its Latin American series, thanks to the initial suggestion of Dr John Street, who subsequently lent his painstaking support to the book during the successive stages leading to its publication. In the early stages great help was given by the late Professor David Joslin, and I cannot fail to pay tribute here, with feelings of admiration and gratitude, to the friendship, generosity and intelligence which he displayed to every Latin American scholar who had the good fortune to cross his path. Were this a more appropriate place to do so, one might also recall the debt, of a less personal character, which Latin American studies in Great Britain owe to his unassuming but highly influential activities. I would also like to express by gratitude to the employees of the Cambridge University Press, especially Mrs Patricia Skinner. Finally, my heartfelt thanks are due to Dr Richard Southern, whose skill and patience have been responsible for the accuracy and style of the English version of this book.

T.H.-D.

ABBREVIATIONS

A.G.N. Archivo General de la Nación, Buenos Aires
BIIH   *Boletín del Instituto de Investigaciones Históricas*
F.O.   Foreign Office Papers (Public Record Office, London)

NOTE

All books, articles and MSS. cited in the footnotes are also included in the checklist of sources (p. 415). In the footnotes, the full name of the author or authors and the full title of the document are given when it is referred to for the first time, and thereafter it is referred to by the author's surname or surnames and, where necessary, by an abbreviated form of the title.

PART ONE:
THE BACKGROUND

1 THE RIVER PLATE AT THE BEGINNING OF THE NINETEENTH CENTURY

On the map of South America the Viceroyalty of the River Plate, created in 1776, was a cohesive, compact territory which, from the Amazon Basin to Tierra del Fuego, and from the Pacific and the Andes to the River Plate and the Atlantic, included all the Spanish lands in this Southern corner of the Continent. It would be futile to look for such a coherent and compact structure in the actual geography of South America. On the contrary, if we were to trace the profile of the territory effectively governed and populated in this Southern outpost of the Spanish Empire, we would find a fragile and disjointed picture, in which the vicissitudes of two and a half centuries of colonisation were reflected. Of these, the more important were those that occurred at the beginning of the process. From that initial moment the River Plate region preserved characteristics which it was only to abandon very slowly, as a result of major structural crises, in the course of the nineteenth century. In the River Plate area, as throughout America, Spanish colonisation was superimposed on pre-Hispanic populations of sedentary agriculturalists, on the basis of which it was possible to erect a society both rural and hierarchical, following the model which the metropolis – in common with almost all Europe – was to adopt with increasing thoroughness in the course of the sixteenth and seventeenth centuries.

This tendency coincided with the exercise of a more strictly geographical option. In the greater part of Spanish America, lying in the Tropics, European immigration was on the whole orientated towards the high-altitude territories, where the climate was less adverse. In the River Plate region this geographical consideration was of less relevance. The existence of a settled native population was enough to lend the demographic – and consequently, the social and economic – structure of the region characteristics which it was only to lose in the course of the nineteenth century. There were two zones in the River Plate region where this first condition obtained: the vast interior, of extreme geographical complexity, and the Guaraní lands of Paraguay, Upper Paraná and Uruguay. In both these areas there arose centres of culture strongly marked by the admixture of Indian with Spanish traits, and differing from one another considerably.

Between these two areas of settlement stretched the Chaco and Pampa plains, and to the South the tableland of Patagonia. Both were populated by tribes of nomadic hunters. This central belt, which dominated the access to the immense River Plate system, came to constitute, for those Argentines who from the mid-nineteenth century became accustomed to thinking that geography imposed its influence on history, the 'natural' nucleus of the territory and of Argentine nationhood. However, this nucleus remained unpopulated for a long time. Of its extent, the Spaniards controlled only the territory necessary to maintain communications between Paraguay, the Interior and the Atlantic. From Córdoba, by way of the 'Santa Fe isthmus' and the 'Buenos Aires corridor' – expressions coined by two historians with a realistic outlook, Juan Álvarez and Emilio Coni, and which we may use to describe the Argentina of the first half of the nineteenth century – the narrow strip of effectively dominated lands included Buenos Aires ('the Port'), founded where Pedro de Mendoza found, in 1536, the first high ground on the swampy right bank of the River Plate. Buenos Aires had river communications along the Plate and the Paraná with the Northern nucleus of Asunción, Corrientes and Misiones. On the right bank of the Paraná, Santa Fe was the staging-post for direct trade between the Guaraní area and the Interior. Both navigation and trade were hazardous, and were not free, until well into the nineteenth century, from the attacks of the hostile Indians living on the right bank of the river North of Santa Fe.

To the East of the Paraná, Spanish rule was established late and with some difficulty. In Upper Paraná and Uruguay the Jesuit missions were a bulwark which, although obliged to yield gradually to Portuguese penetration, prevented a total collapse. Further South the Portuguese established themselves opposite Buenos Aires, in Colônia do Sacramento, which, for over a century of hazardous conflicts and truces, constituted an element of disintegration in the flank of the Spanish Empire.

This demographic structure concentrated on the high lands and the steppes of the Interior was reflected in an economy also orientated not towards the Atlantic but Northwards, towards the nucleus of Spanish power in South America – Peru. Buenos Aires, Colônia do Sacramento, Misiones and the Interior at first organised their economy to satisfy the requirements of Potosí, where there had arisen beside the mountain of silver, in a bitterly cold desert, one of the biggest cities in the world. For Potosí the Interior and Paraguay produced their cotton cloths, the Interior its wool, Paraguay and Misiones their *yerba mate*, and Buenos Aires, Santa Fe and the Interior their mules – to satisfy the insatiable demand of the mountain roads and the mine workings. Buenos Aires began life as a clandestine port for the silver of Potosí, as a miserable village through which a part of that wealth sought an illegal outlet to Europe; and when it began, Colônia do Sacramento aspired to become the centre of this forbidden trade.

This demographic and economic structure was challenged in the eighteenth century. The decay of Upper Peru as a silver-mining centre, the fall in the price of silver itself, as gold – which was again beginning to come in from Brazil – recovered its position as the dominant medium of exchange, had less influence on this crisis than did the consequences of the appearance of new economic and financial centres in Europe. These consequences were, above all, the destruction of the previously existing economic equilibria in the territories dominated – or about to be dominated – by European influence in America, Africa and Asia. Spanish America had achieved, although at the cost of maintaining an extremely slow rhythm of production and trade, a unitary structure, in which the inter-regional economic ties possessed a certain stability. The increased pressure from Europe dislocated this structure. The eighteenth century already saw the beginning of the phenomenon that was to reach its fullest manifestation in the following century: the disintegration of Spanish America into one-crop zones comparatively isolated from each other, with a producing and consuming market in Europe. Except in the regions that were capable of adapting themselves to this change, the consequences were bound to be either relative or absolute decline.

In the River Plate region it was the coastal lands which were the most liable to prosper in this new economic climate, and they did in fact experience a phenomenal boom. Thus circumstances suddenly became favourable to the Littoral, which had been relegated to obscurity and poverty for two centuries. The Interior, on the other hand, was less capable of adapting to the new economic climate. Its diversified and technically backward production was finding it increasingly difficult to retain its outlet in Upper Peru. Another market had appeared to complement the traditional one: that of Buenos Aires, now a populous and wealthy city. But in Buenos Aires, from 1778 onwards, it was to encounter competition from the traditional agriculture of Southern Europe, and, very soon, from the new European industries. The last decades of the eighteenth century, therefore, were an epoch of rapid rise for the Littoral region, of only partial and moderate rise, accompanied by painful readjustments, for the trade and the craft industry of the Interior, and for the latter's agriculture one of unalloyed disaster.

This inter-regional imbalance was only beginning. In any case, a general war and an interruption of Atlantic trade would be enough for the economic climate of the preceding age to be temporarily restored, for the economy of the River Plate region to seek again, spontaneously, trade with the North, for the old road – its route shown by ill-defined cart-tracks on the plains, and continued by mule-trains in the valleys and highlands – for the road that ran from Buenos Aires through Córdoba, Santiago, Tucumán and Salta, as far as Potosí and Lima, to become once again the vital artery of the region.

This slowly increasing imbalance, however, was only the initial moment of an irreversible process, which in the course of the nineteenth century was to reshape drastically the very fabric of the nation, and provide one of the keys to its tormented history: the rise of an Argentina based on the Littoral region, and the decline of the regions which, for two and a half centuries, had been the centre of Spanish life in this part of the Americas.

THE STABILITY OF THE INTERIOR

At the beginning of the nineteenth century there appears to have been – thanks to the circumstances of the world war – a truce in the incipient rivalry between the Littoral and the Interior, in a climate of moderate prosperity that affected, though in differing degrees, both regions. But the Littoral and the Interior only appear as homogeneous entities when we contrast one with the other; examined separately, they manifest both variety and internal fissures, minor contradictions within the major one.

The Interior is the vast zone stretching to the East of the Andes, from the tableland of Upper Peru to the point where the Southern and Eastern outcrops of the Pampa range are lost in the plains. This region, more uniform than unified, spreads Northwards into the Humahuaca Valley:

> This is really the frontier of Peru: whereas one side of a mountain is bare of all vegetation and has all the appearance of solitude and aridity typical of Peru, the other side is covered with greenery...Everything seems to portend a very different country to that which one has left.[1]

But the principal characteristic of the Interior is not fertility. In its mountains, valleys and plains the fertile zone is limited to that irrigated by the streams and rivers which come down from the mountains, and indeed the broader plains are really steppe-land, with large stretches of desert. This barely remediable sterility was hardly noticed by the observers of the first half of the nineteenth century, for the limitations imposed by the scarcity of human and technical resources distracted attention from those imposed by Nature.

In the North the parallel mountain chains stretch between the Atacama tableland, a continuation of the Upper Peruvian plateau and a complete desert, and the Chaco plain. Between these two features the mountain ranges enclose long parallel valleys. To the East, the descent towards the Chaco plain consists of well-watered slopes, the settlement of which was then only just beginning. This was the jurisdictional area of Salta, the geographical uniqueness of which was accompanied by a social structure with characteristics also unique in the River Plate area. A *mestizo* (of mixed Indian and Spanish blood) lower class, identified as Indian by the criterion in force in Colonial Spanish America, which superimposed and confused racial and social characteristics, was ruled by an arrogant and wealthy aristocracy, which lent the city of Salta a splendour unknown in the rest of the River Plate area. This aristocracy owned the land, which was divided into great estates, devoted in the low-lying areas to wheat-growing and viticulture and on the high ground to livestock-raising. Still preserving the same characteristics, Salta spread outwards towards the Chaco plains. Orán was founded and became the nucleus of a settlement that necessitated a stubborn defence against the displaced Indians. Behind the line of forts, on the hillsides sloping down to the Chaco, tropical crops were grown, principally sugar which, tried unsuccessfully in the seventeenth century in the lowlands of Jujuy, enjoyed a boom from 1778 onwards. Sugar from the valley of San Francisco de Jujuy, within the jurisdiction of Salta, figured as early as 1805, together with Brazilian sugar, in the import and export statistics of Tucumán.[2]

Between the desert plateau and the tropical lowlands stretched the estates of some of the big landlords of Salta. The inventory of the possessions of one of them, Don Nicolás Severo de Isasmendi,[3] gives us a clear idea of a great Salta estate at the beginning of the nineteenth century. It included five big landholdings, of which the biggest, Calchaquí, had a soap-factory, warehouses and wine-presses, a still for the manufacture of *aguardiente*, two mills, 3,700 vines, storehouses with 1,400 yards of shirting material imported from Peru, 480 bushels of wheat and 350 of wine. Surrounding the landlord's domain were the lands of the Indians, with 70 tenants. Three of the landholdings, situated in the mountains instead of in the valley, were devoted to stock-raising: the hunting of vicuñas, guanacos and deer, and the raising of cattle and sheep. The landlord's house at Calchaquí, with its chapel, stood in its own square. Around it a small village had grown up, and in the house, as a discreet symbol of the landlord's power, there were 'a pair of handcuffs and a chain with two shackles'. The town house, as was frequently the case among the wealthy classes of Salta, had damask hangings and furniture inlaid with silver and gold.

This landowning aristocracy also dominated Salta's trade. At the edge of the city there was held an annual mule fair, 'the biggest in the world' according to Concolorcorvo,[4] who was able to see it before the caste war in Peru provoked a decline from which Salta only recovered at the beginning of the nineteenth century. Through it passed the mules of the old-established breeders of Buenos Aires, and those of newer ones of the Interior. They spent the winter season in the pastures near the city, before embarking on the final stage of the journey. The mule-market of Salta, which before the rebellions witnessed the passage of 70,000 mules a year, began to recover around 1795. During the following five years there was already an annual average of 30,000 mules being traded in Salta, and in 1803 the figure was 50,000.[5] This recovery, both hesitant and slow, provoked by the increased demand from a Peru that had lost its entire stock of mules, kept prices unusually high. The local consequence of this fact was the increasing prosperity of the cattle-dealers of the city, 'the Saravias, the Arias, the Castellanos and the Puchs'.[6]

These are the very names that we find in the registries of landed

The background

property in Salta. The Salta aristocracy thus enjoyed a concentration of economic power unequalled in the River Plate region, and counted among its numbers the richest man to be found on the route between Buenos Aires and Lima, the Marquis of the Valle de Tojo. This prosperous sector had only recently reached its zenith. It had been the reorientation towards the Atlantic of the entire commerce of Spanish South America that had increased the commercial importance of Salta, and more than one of its great families would have been unable to trace its origin beyond the second half of the eighteenth century, when that reorientation took place. It was the Basque, and generally Northern Spanish, dynasties, which were to play such an important part in the history of Salta in the nineteenth century: the Gurruchagas, the Uriburus, the Puchs, the Gorritis.[7]

The process of ascent of these families followed a remarkably uniform pattern. The founders of those dynasties, who had arrived in Salta either as government officials or as merchants, generally all became merchants anyway. The acquisition of land was almost always achieved by marriage with women from older families. It is, furthermore, significant that the latter were always so ready to intermarry with upstart Spanish immigrants. Doubtless mercantile wealth contributed thus to activate the rhythm of exploitation of rural Salta.

This dominant group of such recent formation nevertheless conceived of itself as being ancient and well consolidated. Its economic hegemony was accompanied by a social prestige that appeared unshakable. Social differentiation was based – in Salta more systematically than in the rest of the River Plate region – on ethnic differences. If the *mestizo* lower class appeared to be characterised by a resigned and blinkered obedience, the white aristocracy viewed with still greater suspicion the few border-line figures which the urban structure allowed, despite every precaution, to rise in the social scale. It attributed to them a servile origin, perpetuated by the inheritance of African blood, which in the absence of other more visible signs would always manifest itself in a secret mark preserved by even the lightest-skinned mulattoes. The aristocracy of Salta made successful efforts to defend itself from the 'red-tails' and their attempts at social-climbing. A hidden tension was the result of this excessively polarised social structure: in Salta, before it happened in any other area of the River Plate, and with more intensity than anywhere else, the revolution against the King acquired the characteristics of a social struggle. It was a struggle, however, with ephemeral results: in the mid-nineteenth century – without quoting more recent testimony – Salta was again a province where 'there are no masses';[8] the tribute-paying *mestizo* lower class simply did not count.

The territory of Salta ended where the Andean foothills joined a massive range, that of Aconquija, a chain separating Tucumán and Catamarca. This mountain chain, with its high snow-capped peaks, provided Tucumán with an exceptionally rich and dense river network, which had

8

created a subtropical oasis of long-standing prosperity, based principally on commerce and craft industries. The city of Tucumán was the nerve centre of the route between Buenos Aires and Peru, and a prosperous group of merchants owed its wealth to this decisive factor. It was they who acquired the greatest prestige in a region where ownership of the land was comparatively widely distributed. The city contained a large number of craftsmen, who used as material the hard woods that the zone produced naturally in its virgin forests (whereas on the steppes and in the temperate oases, as also in the Littoral region, the trees tended to be of softwood) and manufactured carts, used on the highway at the side of which the city had grown. More typical of the countryside was tanning: in the smallholdings the proprietors installed tanneries for the hides of their own cattle and of those which they went to fetch from other regions on behalf of the dealers, the principal merchants of the city. Thus this activity, which brought in an income of thirty thousand pesos a year, was controlled by 'ten or twelve individuals', and of that income, only seven thousand pesos found their way into the hands of the 'poor tanners'.[9] Livestock-raising (cattle, horses and mules for Peru) and agriculture (rice, exported to the entire Viceroyalty) were orientated towards trade, as was a small tallow and soap industry. Domestic weaving, the occupation of the peasant population, did not satisfy the local needs even of ordinary cloth, which was partly imported from Peru.

Such an economic structure guaranteed the social hegemony of those who controlled the marketing of products and were able to make the necessary financial advances to maintain production. It is no coincidence that twelve years after the Revolution one of the political leaders of Tucumán, Javier López, who was, besides, owner of land that gave him influence over the mountain populations of the West, should proclaim himself ready to 'leave the counter to unsheath the sword', or that – even thirty years later – the province was still governed by an oligarchy whose members were identified by their ownership of shops in the main square.[10]

To the South-East of Tucumán, Santiago del Estero was an extremely poor region: an American Galicia, as miserable and dirty as the Spanish one, in the words of General Iriarte.[11] Like Galicia, Santiago was, within the demographic equilibrium of the River Plate region, a kind of inexhaustible centre of high pressures. As temporary or definitive emigrants, the people of Santiago were an indispensable human base for all the agricultural enterprises of the Littoral region. In their inhospitable land, formed by two long and narrow parallel oases – those of the River Dulce and the River Salado – which separated the steppe from the Chaco forest, they had to defend against the Indians an over-extended frontier, inadequately protected by a sparse line of forts. In the city and on the farms beside the rivers the dominant activities were commerce and agriculture. The latter was divided between maize for local consumption, and wheat for shipment to other more prosperous regions with a higher demand. A very backward form of cattle-raising went on on the steppes, while to the East and West, in the Chaco forest and in the desert strip, an unstable population lived by collecting wild honey and beeswax in the forest (products that counted for more than one would expect today, at a time when sugar was expensive and scarce, and religious worship played such an important part in the life of the community), and cochineal from the desert. The first two products were primarily for export, while the third was mostly destined to be used as a dye for the woollen fabrics produced in the region.

In this desperately poor region domestic weaving flourished. While the men abandoned the land, the women wove wool on domestic looms. In the case of local consumers and also of sales to the Littoral, geographical proximity, as well as the prevailing poverty, made it possible for Santiago – and for the highlands of Córdoba – to compete in this market with the products of the Peruvian Indian workshops, offering to the poorest customers cloth and ponchos of which the principal merit was their low price. This production, like honey, beeswax and cochineal gathering in the border areas, was entirely dominated by the merchants of the city of Santiago, who were frequently proprietors in the irrigated zones, where, however, property was too widely distributed for a hegemonic landed class to emerge. Moreover, these merchants received the greater part of the income, modest enough if compared with other cities on the same route, but substantial in the local context, derived from Santiago's situation on the road to Peru.

To the South of Santiago the road led to Córdoba. Founded in the place where the foothills give way to the fertile Pampa, the city extended its jurisdiction Northwards and Westwards, through a land of steppe, valley and mountain, and (more hesitantly) Southwards, towards the Pampa, a region which it had to conquer from the Indians and subsequently defend against their counter-attacks. Córdoba had a long agricultural past, which went back, strictly speaking, to the pre-Hispanic period, but at the beginning of the nineteenth century it was affected by an offshoot of the stock-raising boom that was causing a profound transformation of the Littoral area. The upper class was closely connected with this expanding economic activity. Their lands were to be found less in the South and East, whose possibilities were only discovered in the second half of the century, than in the plains and steppes of the North. The rise of the stock-raisers did not signify a division within the oligarchy which dominated the city and the region, but it was, rather, a reorientation of the economic activities of its members, who came to prefer stock-raising to the more traditional urban commerce. The latter was not, however, neglected; the bulk of the income of this sector appears to have been derived from the hill region – where property was more divided, and more orientated towards agriculture and minor stock-raising – and domestic weaving offered an additional source of income to the destitute rural population, which subsisted thanks to the advances of the merchants, who went the rounds of the 'hills and dales' selling to the weavers on credit, and collecting their debts when the work had been done. In their reports to the *consulado* (official guild of merchants) in Buenos Aires these 'merchants and promoters' continually speak of their rural expeditions to encourage 'the manufacture of cloths for ponchos, coarse friezes, cloaks and blankets'.[12] On another page of the same ledger we find one of these self-sacrificing paladins acting with extreme harshness against three supposed debtors, old peasant women who had not delivered him the cloth demanded in payment of monetary advances (which were, in any case, only vaguely described).

The hill-country of Córdoba was – like Santiago – a land from which people emigrated. We find people of that origin throughout the rural areas of Buenos Aires, both in the villages where the cart-drivers lived and also in the agricultural centres.

The upper class which dominated the hill-country through its control of commerce, and owned the best stock-raising lands on the northern steppes, was also predominant in the city. The rival families vied with each other tenaciously for the highest secular, ecclesiastical and academic appointments, and they involved Intendants and bishops in a complex network of intrigue. This hegemony became even more firmly established after the expulsion of the Jesuits. There is no doubt that the other Orders were, as a result of that measure, rescued from total insignificance, but their rise was not enough to fill the void left by the expelled Jesuits. Their absence provoked a particularly marked decline of large-scale agricultural exploitation effected with adequate resources, which they had carried out on their estates with large numbers of slaves. The expulsion thus anticipated changes which in other parts of the country took place only later: the existence of a ruling class that was simultaneously very rich and very poor – rich in land, poor in money – which a present-day scholar, H. S. Ferns, considers to be one of the most original features of Argentine history of the nineteenth century, and which was in fact to lend a peculiar tone to the stock-raising Littoral, was already noticeable in Córdoba.

At this point the Peruvian route at last enters the Littoral area. That route, and the traffic along it, were what gave birth to this Eastern sector of the Interior. In so far as that commerce was able to continue in the face of the economic restructuring provoked by the introduction of 'free trade'* into the Spanish Empire, this area maintained its prosperity intact until 1810. Obviously, this continuity was unable to conceal the symptoms of future danger. The commercial Interior was increasingly becoming an intermediary between Peru and the Atlantic port. The export and marketing of local products was given an increasingly lower priority, and free trade was partly responsible for the acceleration of this process. But there appears to be no doubt that at the same time free trade intensified inter-regional

* That is, open trade between all parts of the Spanish Empire.

The background

commerce, and therefore, in the short term, guaranteed a new lease of life to that sector of the Interior so closely connected with that trade.

One should not, however, over-emphasise the detrimental consequences of the new system of free trade – limited though it was – established in 1778. Above all, it does not seem that this measure threatened the craft-industry structure of the region. For a time imports from overseas consisted chiefly of fine cloths, which did not compete with the crude local weaving industry. The latter was more threatened, and had been for some considerable time, by the textiles from Upper and Lower Peru, the cheapness of which was due to the miserably low standard of living of the Indians, which more than offset the high freight costs. As is shown by the lists of current prices kept by the *Consulado*, cottons and shirting material from Cochabamba, Cuenca and Arequipa were sold in Tucumán, Córdoba and Mendoza in competition with local cloth. Even in the case of wool, which was more effectively defended against Peruvian competition, the latter was strong enough for Tucumán wool to find its way to the Indian looms of Peru, returning to its place of origin in the form of coarse cloth.[13]

The consequences of free trade were very different in the Western part of the Interior, which consisted of a chain of agricultural oases at the foot of the Andes and its foothills. Here Spanish settlement had established small replicas of Mediterranean agriculture: vines, wheat and dried fruits. Among local products, only wheat was to remain comparatively sheltered from the consequences of the new commercial system. The high costs of sea transport were to keep its highly protected consumer market safe from European competition. On the other hand, the latter had devastating effects on other and more profitable products of the agriculture of the Eastern slopes of the Andes: wine from Catalonia, and oil and dried fruits from all over Spain were cheaper in Buenos Aires than the products of that remote region of the Viceroyalty. And not only in Buenos Aires: the entire Interior, and even Upper Peru, was deluged with products that provoked a catastrophic fall in prices. The ruthless competition between the different Andean regions, all struggling to retain a market which had suddenly shrunk, seemed to offer a prospect of irremediable decline.

The Northernmost sector of the Andean Interior was Catamarca, a complex of parallel valleys with poor communications between them, wider than those of Salta, and consequently with wider semi-desert strips between the narrow areas irrigated by the rivers and the mountain-slopes. The biggest of these valleys gave its name to the whole region, but even this valley was small in extent and had been devoted, since pre-Hispanic times, to agriculture. It maintained an exceptionally dense population, occupied in market-gardening and viticulture. In the smaller valleys (Santa María, Andalgalá and Belén) and at higher altitudes, wheat and stock-raising – the stock being kept in pens in the winter – were of greater importance. For the agricultural production of Catamarca virtually the only market was Tucumán; the small Western oases supplied wheat to the Tucumán plain, where more profitable crops were grown, and from all over Catamarca wine was sold to the neighbouring region, where proximity helped to defend it against the competition of its more Southerly rivals, San Juan and Mendoza. *Aguardiente*, of which the Catamarca variety was unrivalled, reached more distant markets, although with increasing difficulty. Another product of the principal valley still partly preserved its former importance: in Catamarca cotton was still being grown, whereas in the rest of the Interior this product failed to survive the demographic collapse of the seventeenth century. Catamarca cotton, in the form of cloth for everyday use by the very poorest, found a market in the Interior and the Littoral as late as 1810. The exiguous production did not, of course, threaten the predominance of Peruvian textiles, but managed to co-exist with them without difficulty. The cotton crisis did not occur until 1810; those affecting wine and *aguardiente* happened thirty years earlier, and led to the collapse of the traditional commercial structure. In order to survive in the new economic climate, it was necessary to sell at increasingly lower prices, and it was the producers themselves who, making increasingly long journeys, delivered their wines and spirits to the customers. In this area, the disappearance of the old hegemonic group did not open the way for a new group consisting of landowners. In the over-populated valleys, property was too subdivided for such a thing to happen. The life of Catamarca was dominated by a wealthy and respected institution: the Franciscan Order, established at the time of the Conquest after an ephemeral missionary effort on the part of the Jesuits, and represented by an ancient and illustrious convent in the provincial capital and by a shrine already famous throughout the Interior, that of the Virgin of the Valley.

The Catamarca Valley gradually widens towards the South until it becomes an increasingly broad plain, bordered on the West by the Sierra de Velasco and on the East by the central ranges of Córdoba and San Luis. In the middle of this plain an isolated mountain massif, which appears in the landscape like a gigantic fortress, has created a multitude of tiny oases principally devoted to stock-raising. These are the Rioja Plains, a territory inhabited from the earliest times, which also benefited from the beginning of the nineteenth century from the stock-raising boom, and to an even greater extent from the increased traffic in the Interior. Settlers came here from the neighbouring agricultural areas; an immigrant from nearby San Juan was destined to become one of the biggest landowners of the region and the father of its greatest *caudillo*, Facundo Quiroga. The land became settled and more prosperous, and to the sheep and goats raised throughout the Interior there was added the breeding of mules, some for export to Peru and Chile, but mostly used by the carriers of the Plains region, who journeyed throughout Tucumán and Cuyo with their mule-trains, were familiar with the roads to Chile and Peru, and even reached Buenos Aires.

The background

On the Eastern slopes of the Sierra de Velasco, facing the Plains, was La Rioja, a lifeless village, a staging-post on the way to an entirely different region, Western Rioja, a land of valleys bounded by the foothills of the Andes, with tiny oases devoted to agriculture, mostly the cultivation of alfalfa for winter pasture. This mountainous part of La Rioja was socially more archaic than the Plains. Its agricultural valleys were for the most part still populated by Indians, grouped in villages and subject to tribute. The differentiation from the neighbouring white villages, which had ceased to be based on ethnic or cultural differences, nevertheless had important judicial and social consequences. But even those who were by law Spaniards and white men free of tribute were, in La Rioja, harshly oppressed by their overlords. The entire region is one of big landed estates. Whereas on the Plains the more dynamic rhythm of the economy and a complex of economic activities less directly connected with the land made the predominance of the landlords more tolerable, in the Western Rioja region the latter was an intolerable burden on the submissive lower class. The limited prosperity of the ruling class prevented the occurrence in this locality of the contrasts so characteristic of Salta, but as late as the mid-nineteenth century the life of the peasants of Western La Rioja was harsher than that of those of Salta. Local history, which was turbulent even in Colonial times, is a chronicle of the rivalry between landlords; urban structures were weak; the provincial capital was considered wretched even by those whose only standard of comparison was the neighbouring cities, which were hardly worthy of that name. The possibilities of advancement of Western La Rioja were closely connected with the region's miniature Potosí – Famatina. But only slowly, in the course of the nineteenth century, would there arise a centre of mining activity at Chilecito, and the latter was never destined to fulfil the hopes that it had inspired since the Revolution.

To the South of La Rioja, the hills of Córdoba and the Plains region blend into those of San Luis. Stock-raising, which provided meat for the neighbouring areas of San Juan and Mendoza and exported some hides to the Littoral, the widespread domestic weaving industry, and small-scale market gardening comprised the economic activities of this region, which were insufficient to maintain even a declining population. San Luis, therefore, like Córdoba and Santiago, supplied emigrant workers to the expanding Littoral area.

Between San Luis and the Andes, San Juan and Mendoza were to become – as the most illustrious citizen of San Juan proudly expressed it – 'the only two agricultural provinces in the country'. Nestling beneath the highest peaks of the Andes, not separated at this latitude from the Littoral plain by any significant hills, and therefore giving rise to bigger rivers than those of the foothills and the Pampa region, the nucleus of the Mendoza and San Juan areas consisted of two oases much greater in size than those found in the Pampa and Pre-Andean ranges. These oases were devoted to the growing of irrigated crops, and had been so since pre-Hispanic times. Mendoza, on the road from Buenos Aires to Chile, on which, at the beginning of the nineteenth century,[14] 1,200 carts travelled every year, was an important commercial centre, which was better able than its Northern neighbour to resist the consequences of the viticulture crisis. Wine, however, was not the only product of Mendoza: there was also cereal-growing, and stock-raising designed not so much for production as for the fattening of cattle for local consumption and for export to Chile. All these activities took place under the direction of a dominant group of merchants and transport contractors, which managed to offset the losses caused by free trade to local agriculture by the advantageous position created by the reorientation towards the Atlantic of the economy of Chile.

It has already been observed that San Juan was not so fortunate. This city, which had been the most important in the region of Cuyo, suffered an accelerated decline from 1778 onwards. Before the advent of free trade, neither its distance from roads on which carts could travel – which made it necessary to employ mules for San Juan's commerce – nor geographical distance had prevented the *aguardiente* and wine of San Juan from finding outlets in Upper Peru, Tucumán, Córdoba and Buenos Aires. After the collapse of prices provoked by free trade, the only possibility left was commerce on a small scale exercised, with very small profit-margins, by the producers themselves, who travelled round the centres of consumption, as far as Salta, carrying with them the water necessary for a forty-day journey across the desert, Potosí, Tucumán, Santa Fe and Buenos Aires, where the San Juan mule-drovers opened improvised shops, to the considerable consternation of the inland revenue authorities, who had no idea exactly what taxes they should collect from them.[15]

Wine and, above all, *aguardiente resacado* (that is, double-distilled) constituted almost the entire wealth of San Juan. With the profits of this it was necessary to buy meat (from Mendoza), wool and hides (from Córdoba and San Luis), and even mules for the transport of goods. San Juan provided an extreme example of the results of a situation systematically unfavourable to the agriculture of the Interior, resulting from free trade. The measures taken to stave off the decline were fruitless: San Juan was slowly withering. Of that decline of an exceptionally mature style of Colonial life, which withered away when it came into contact too suddenly with the outside world, Sarmiento has left us an unforgettable picture in his *Recuerdos de Provincia*. One sees the old ladies of illustrious but impoverished families, consoling themselves for their penury by accusing the less impoverished of lack of racial purity, and the family of the author himself, all of them related to the best families of San Juan and reduced to a hand-to-mouth existence. The old wine-growing and commercial aristocracy, amid the general collapse, still maintained its comparative pre-eminence. The Del Carrils, owners of so many vineyards in the surrounding countryside, were

The background

still able every year to take out of their coffers their tarnished coins of silver and gold and spread them in the sun in the courtyards of their houses before the goggling eyes of the local urchins. But even their wealth was fast diminishing; only slowly was there arising an economic activity to replace the traditional viticulture: that of providing fodder for the herds of cattle driven through the area in search of pasture. But the change was not destined to restore San Juan to its lost prosperity and, in any case, it took a long time to mature. Only the expansion of mining in Northern Chile, after Independence, was definitely to establish this new cattle-raising economy, and by that time the San Juan whose death-agony Sarmiento had been able to witness in his youth had died.

THE RISE OF THE LITTORAL PROVINCES

Like the Interior, the Littoral area which was destined to form part of Argentina was by no means a homogeneous entity; its structure bore the traces of a complex history. In the North-Western corner of the region the Jesuits had their most extensive Spanish American possession, that 'empire' which fascinated so many European observers in the seventeenth and eighteenth centuries – the Guaraní missions where it was thought that Plato's Republic had been constructed in real life. But the Missions were only one aspect, though no doubt the most important one, of a structure that extended beyond their boundaries. Cotton, *yerba mate* – which the Jesuits, with unyielding determination, spread throughout South America as far as the Kingdom of Quito, thus creating a source of wealth from a hitherto despised wild shrub – and its cattle, which increased from the eighteenth century onwards, all found markets in the Interior via Santa Fe, which owed its prosperity to this situation as an unavoidable intermediary between Misiones and the Interior, rather than to its situation as an intermediary between Paraguay and Buenos Aires. This entire structure was beginning to break down even before the expulsion of the Jesuits: the centre of gravity of the Misiones territories was being displaced southwards, from the cotton and *yerba mate* fields to the cattle lands of Uruguay. Santa Fe, in the mid-eighteenth century, was ceasing to be the key port for the trade along the Paraná. Both in Misiones and in Santa Fe a complex and diversified structure was giving way to a simpler and, in a sense, a more primitive one: an economy dominated by stock-raising. This is one aspect of the process that affected the entire Littoral, a process even swifter where there were no inherited structures to stand in the way of the rise of stock-raising induced by current circumstances. Buenos Aires, as the capital of the whole Littoral area, and – what was even more important – the port for the entire Southern sector of the Spanish Empire, enjoyed rapid progress. Its hinterland, however, populated a long time previously, advanced much more slowly than the areas recently opened to colonisation, which were free of economic and human hindrances. The land-mass of Entre Ríos, enclosed between the Paraná and Uruguay Rivers, the Banda Oriental (East Bank) of the River Uruguay to the North of the River Plate, were the zones where progress was most rapid: they constituted a kind of Wild West of reckless and turbulent prosperity that suddenly arose beside the older settled centres of the Littoral.

These centres, apart from the most ancient of all, Asunción, which was destined to follow its own orbit after 1810, were three in number: Corrientes, in the North, where the River Paraguay joins the Paraná, Santa Fe, on the right bank of the latter river, half way between the River Plate and the Northern centres, and Buenos Aires, established in the place, very near the mouth of the great river, where the marshes of the right bank give way to low hills.

Of these settlements the most poor and rustic was Corrientes, the centre, virtually in name only, of a vast rural area which was rapidly being opened up for grazing. The entire history of Corrientes around the beginning of the nineteenth century can be summarised as the futile and stubborn efforts of the city to achieve effective control over its surrounding territory. But the latter, except for a diminutive agricultural area that was close to the provincial capital and had been settled for a long time, led a life of its own and – despite the sporadic repression carried out by the Intendency authorities, and the bitter complaints of the city merchants – continued to do so independently of the city, and even outside the bounds of the law. While the big landowners lived in the city, on their estates the foremen, peons and slaves traded in a stock of cattle which was increasing rapidly in numbers. Traffickers in hides used to travel through the rural area of Corrientes. In the upper reaches of the Paraná every place could become an improvised port, and fragile craft, filled to overflowing (and sometimes capsizing as a result) carried to Buenos Aires the hides acquired in the course of a successful expedition. Within this basic framework of life in rural Corrientes, there was infinite variety. An entire mass of humanity living outside the law can be discerned in those foremen and peons who were not always excessively loyal to their masters: the forests and swamps offered refuge to bandits and runaway slaves.[16]

However, although the city of Corrientes did not control the stock-raising wealth that was accumulating in the surrounding rural areas, it had some share in it. Not only did the biggest landowners live in the city, but there were also tanneries to process the hides produced in the countryside. The principal activity of the city, however, was commerce and navigation: its shipyards – in conjunction with those of Asunción – built not only all the ships sailing on the Paraná and the Plate, but also some that faced the crossing of the Atlantic.[17] The shipwrights became increasingly important in the life of Corrientes: one of them, the Irishman Peter Campbell, was to become the leader of Artigas's party in the city. Another, Don Pedro Ferré,

The background

was to symbolise for twenty years the stubborn resistence of Corrientes to the hegemony of Buenos Aires. Corrientes also carried on a very active commerce: after the expulsion of the Jesuits, Corrientes merchants competed with remarkable success with those of Asunción in the trade of *yerba mate* and cotton from the Misiones area.

In the latter area the disappearance of the Jesuits caused the way of life which they had instituted to suffer rapid disintegration. In theory, the expulsion did not imply any change of régime, but in practice, the activities of administrators bent on making quick profits from an extremely harsh way of life which was no longer being endured at the behest of any Divine mandate caused the régime to survive principally as a medium of massive exploitation. The system of communities established by the Jesuits on the basis of pre-Hispanic institutions was maintained in order to prevent individual possession by the Indians of their lands and harvests, but these communities were systematically looted by their administrators.

At the same time, the isolation of the population of Misiones was breaking down. The Indian villages were opened up to shady traffickers from Asunción and Corrientes, who – with the well remunerated complicity of the administrators – acquired a monopoly of the acquisition of cotton cloth. As a result of this contact, the Indians became rapidly Europeanised in dress and customs. The creation of new necessities, calculated to put them even more at the mercy of the traders, was undertaken by the latter with tenacity.

It is hardly surprising, therefore, that the Guaranís chafed with increasing impatience at the régime of communities, which barred the way to individual prosperity and only preserved the unfavourable aspects of the Jesuit disciplinary system. The population of Misiones was suffering a swift collapse. Jesuit rule had guaranteed in this area, sheltered as it was from the demographic collapse of Spanish America – and not only of Spanish America – in the seventeenth century, an exceptionally high density of population. Now this population was to overflow into the cattle-raising lands which had just been opened to the South of Misiones, and the growing harshness of the treatment which they were receiving in their villages only partly explained this process, which had already been noticeable before the expulsion of the Jesuits. The entire Littoral was to know the Guaraní Indians from Misiones: first the Jesuit estates of the Upper Uruguay, then all Entre Ríos and the Banda Oriental, those lands so hungry for labour.

Whereas in Northern Misiones, where agricultural life required the hard labour of an abundant population, the Guaranís were undisputed owners of the land, and continued to grow their *yerba mate* and their cotton and to weave their cloth, in Southern Misiones, on the River Uruguay, Guaraní expansion soon clashed with Spanish expansion. Despite all the prohibitions, the mission territories were populated by landowners from Buenos Aires and Montevideo who cut out for themselves, in those vast lands, enormous cattle-ranches. Here we find the typical social climate of the Littoral region at the beginning of the nineteenth century: an accelerated economic expansion taking place too fast for judicial institutionalisation to keep pace with the rise in population. A confused and turbulent mass of humanity was the inevitable result of this situation.

Santa Fe was, in the Littoral, another element in the Jesuit system, and as such it had faced a crisis in the mid-eighteenth century. Declining as a centre of land and river trade, Santa Fe did, however, experience a growing prosperity thanks to stock-raising. In the diminutive town there was still no craft industry at all. Despite the high prices being paid for wheat and maize, there was scarcely any agriculture in its jurisdictional area. Commerce – except in stock, and this was in the hands of the breeders themselves – brought neither great wealth nor great prestige: it provided a living for ten or twelve Spanish shopkeepers and some Indian and Negro minor shopkeepers, more numerous but doing business on a very small scale.[18] This was one aspect of the increasing ruralisation of Santa Fe's life; another consequence of it is to be found in the fact that the citizens themselves, while becoming increasingly prosperous, were now less prepared to spend money on the education of their children. For Santa Fe was becoming richer. After the war with Britain began, and the River Plate region was cut off from its European markets, trade in hides was interrupted, which meant that slaughtering was suspended, and the cattle, left to their own resources, multiplied extremely quickly; but Santa Fe, taking advantage of its relative proximity to the Interior and the old routes that linked the city with that region, enriched itself by the breeding and sale of mules, which the big breeders took for sale, in immense droves, as far as Salta and Potosí. Such were the activities that dominated the commerce of Santa Fe, and the biggest of the landowner-merchants, Candioti, was to govern the province in its first experience of autonomy, after the Revolution. But as a substratum beneath the new structure based on stock-raising, Santa Fe preserved the memory of what it had once been. The Church in Santa Fe had an influence which she was not to wield in the Littoral areas of more recent settlement, and Santa Fe, which had a community of interest with these areas, felt another more tacit solidarity with the areas of older settlement – a factor which would contribute to the peculiar behaviour of the province in the period of Independence. Another important element in the life of Santa Fe was the military force which, in the North, defended a line of forts against the Indians, who were dangerously close to the city.

To the South of Santa Fe, on the right bank of the Paraná and the Plate, was the rural area of Buenos Aires, which a recent offensive had cleared of Indians as far as the River Salado. To the North of the capital stretched the rolling plain, crossed by many streams. To the South lay the absolutely flat Pampa, dotted with numerous swamps and lagoons. To these geographical differences the pattern of settlement added others. The countryside of

The background

Buenos Aires province bore the traces of the long process by which it had been populated: to the North (San Nicolás, San Pedro, Pergamino, Areco, and other places) medium-sized estates were established, where agriculture was combined with stock-raising (the evidence available to us in the account-books of ecclesiastical property – confirmed by other more impressionistic sources – refers to typical rather than special cases). In the Western zone (Morón, Luján and Guardia de Luján) agriculture predominated and property was generally more widely distributed, as was, of course, the exploitation of it. To the South-West (Lobos, Navarro and Monte) there was a zone of transition towards forms of mixed exploitation, in holdings more extensive than those in the North, while in the South (San Vicente, Cañuelas and Magdalena) cattle-raising predominated. These differentiations are made, of course, speaking in general terms: they constitute a tendency towards local differentiation rather than outright contrasts. In any case, the greater size of the landholdings in the South was evidence of more recent settlement, although a current of equally recent settlement extended the pattern of small agricultural properties Westwards, beyond Luján. The Northern zone was a land with less possibilities of expansion, with a population more settled and more resistent to innovation.

In the face of these differences, the official colonisation campaign was intended to act as a levelling factor. This, from 1782 onwards, established a belt of settlements designed by their founders for agriculture, by means of which it was thought to guarantee the frontier line against Indian attacks. This campaign, continued beyond the Paraná and the Plate, brought Spanish labourers – at first assigned to an abortive colonisation project in Patagonia – to the River Plate area. But although the settlements thus founded were destined to enjoy a long and often prosperous life, very often they did not possess an agricultural character even at the outset. The relationship between agriculture and stock-raising was in fact too complex for any action on the part of the political authorities to influence it decisively. Although the efforts to extend agriculture were fruitless, the latter nevertheless showed an unexpected vigour in the area where it had become established. Observers at the beginning of the nineteenth century sadly announced the disappearance of agriculture in Buenos Aires province. But that prophecy was never fulfilled, and only in the middle of the century two new factors – the competition from American flour, and the expansion of sheep-raising and dairy-farming – were to set limits to the predominance of agriculture in the West of rural Buenos Aires. The centre of agriculture was, in fact, in the Western districts, except for a few isolated pockets, such as San Isidro, for example, to the North of the capital and on the bank of the River Plate, a wheat-growing zone that was very important in the late eighteenth century. The small farmers had to cope with very serious difficulties. Not all of them were proprietors: writers at the beginning of the century accepted as a valid generalisation the assertion that the farmers of land relatively close to Buenos Aires were all tenants; this generalisation appears, however, to be too sweeping.[19] Even the proprietors were obliged to surrender a considerable percentage of their harvests in the form of tithes and first-fruits. They also needed temporary help for sowing and harvesting, and labour was scarce, expensive and inefficient, consisting as it did of peasants who arrived every year as temporary migrants from Santiago del Estero, Córdoba and San Luis, day-labourers from the capital, and unemployed workers and vagrants forcibly recruited by the police.[20] This was a constant feature of life in the Littoral rural areas: wage-labour played a necessary part in the economy, even in the case of the poorest proprietors. The high cost of land and the high cost of labour were two major difficulties, but even more important was the shortage of money. The latter problem was particularly serious because the Littoral – even the agricultural part of it – belonged, albeit precociously, to a market economy. Although it might be thought that the small farmers fed themselves from their own resources rather than with purchased food, not only was the greater part of their production destined for urban consumption but – in the unfavourable situation in which they found themselves *vis-à-vis* the merchants – a system of purchasing in advance and of sales on credit of seeds for sowing was incorporated into the productive process itself, placing the farmers in the same position as were the tanners and weavers of the Interior *vis-à-vis* the merchants. An aggravating factor was that here only day-to-day consumption remained outside the market economy. The clothes the farmers wore and the extremely simple goods and implements for the household and for work had to be purchased with money. Even though the greater part of the farmers were immigrants from the Interior, their womenfolk all too soon abandoned weaving. Production for the market, with its hazards unfairly biassed as a result of the dependence of the producers on the marketers, constituted almost the entire activity of the farmers. Within the framework of this economy they sought relief from their penury by taking up carting as a complementary activity. The agricultural centres of the West – Luján, Pilar, Guardia de Luján, and later Chivilcoy – were villages of carters. This duplication of functions was due, according to a perceptive contemporary observer, to the low yields from agriculture. In contrast to what happened in the Interior, where transport was in the hands of the richest proprietors and merchants, who owned veritable fleets of wagons, in Buenos Aires there was a swarm of carters, each possessing two or three vehicles, which took to the city the substantial harvest of cereals, and even ventured out onto the Northern road.

Agriculture, therefore, survived only with difficulty: dominated by dealers in grains and flour who were much addicted to speculation, the market was, moreover, upset by violent crises of scarcity or abundance, caused by its dependence on one consumer, the city of Buenos Aires, the capacity of consumption of which was very inelastic. In these circumstances, the stabilising measures taken by the Cabildo to regulate cereal agriculture, measures taken more to assure the prosperity of the producers than to keep prices at levels acceptable to the consumers, had only a limited success. The measures taken were the traditional ones available to the Spanish and Colonial administrations: the prohibition of exports, the strict regulation of transactions, the prohibition of the sale of wheat outside certain localities and to persons other than millers and bakers, and so forth. *Pace* certain perhaps excessively cautious writers on this subject,[21] it appears that these prohibitions failed to satisfy the tacit aspirations of the grain-dealers. But in the new intellectual climate created by the Enlightenment, there was a tendency to view the measures with hostility. Freedom to export, which would guarantee constantly high prices, would favour an expansion of agricultural production and a hitherto unknown abundance of grain. Some also employed the argument which, on the basis of the economic theory then in vogue, was used against any policy of low and stable prices: that the inevitable consequence would be scarcity and high prices.

But the more clear-headed advocates of the new economic theory knew that things were not as simple as that.[22] River Plate wheat was too expensive, because rural wages were exceptionally high, for it to be exported except in exceptional circumstances. The result of free exports would, therefore, be an accentuation rather than an attenuation of the imbalance of the local cereal market. Events – after the Revolution had conceded freedom to export – were to confirm the predictions of Vieytes. For decades local cereals were unable to compete with the foreign product, and a place for them in the domestic market could only be maintained by means of import restrictions.

Anyway, agriculture survived in spite of so many disadvantages, and there were easily understandable reasons for this. The exploitation of the cattle resources had at first been purely destructive. Around 1750 the very success of the raids on the ownerless herds made necessary a new type of exploitation based on round-ups carried out on each estate. But after the declaration of free trade, the domesticated cattle suffered a process of exploitation reminiscent of that which had exterminated the wild ones. By 1795 there were reasons for believing that there would soon be a shortage of cattle in Buenos Aires. This system of exploitation has been strongly criticised, over a century after the event, by twentieth-century scholars, and there is no doubt that in it one can detect an extremely dangerous tendency to regulate the rhythm of production in accordance with that of an extremely variable foreign demand. In these beginnings of a River Plate economy open to the world market, the coming dangers were already apparent.

But there were other reasons for this suicidal policy: the stock-raising industry of rural Buenos Aires was beginning to suffer severe competition from Entre Ríos and the Banda Oriental. In the latter areas there were still ownerless herds, and they were lands free from the legal and economic controls which two centuries of settlement had created on the right bank of the Paraná and the Plate. At the end of the eighteenth century Francisco de Aguirre was able to observe the predominance of the Banda Oriental in the production and marketing of hides and to remark that the countryside of Buenos Aires was 'poverty-stricken in comparison with that of Montevideo'.[23] The shortage of wood and fresh water, the reasons which Aguirre adduced to explain this comparative poverty, were doubtless not the only ones. Be that as it may, rural Buenos Aires was no longer the most favourable area for cattle-raising.

Around 1795 the situation changed. The war dislocated the export of hides, and put a brake on the expansion of stock-raising. The hazards of years of frantic exporting, calculated to take advantage of the ocean route, an opening that was known to be ephemeral, and those of years of closure, when the piles of hides overflowed the warehouses and were stacked in the open air to fatten whole armies of rats – such fluctuations were better resisted by the cattle-raising industry of the new lands than by that of Buenos Aires. In the latter place, as in Santa Fe, the breeding of mules, which required less labour and land than did cattle-raising, tended to expand faster than the latter. At the same time, the war left, isolated by the circumstances of the times, tropical regions which were heavy consumers of cereals. Though not entering the markets of India, as Lastarria desired,[24] River Plate wheat discovered those of Cuba, Brazil and Mauritius. Here, then, were some good reasons for the survival of an agriculture which condemned those engaged in it to extreme penury.

But even in these unfavourable circumstances, cattle-raising continued to be the centre of the economic life of rural Buenos Aires. The *estancia* was the nucleus of cattle production, and almost everywhere combined this activity with cereal-growing. From the already mentioned Church properties in the North to the more recent settlements in the chain of lagoons North of the Salado, in Navarro and Monte, the extent of sown land increased on the *estancias,* following a trend which as early as 1790 had been denounced by the *Cabildo* (City Corporation) as dangerous to the survival of cattle-raising. On the *estancia* a labour-force brought together only by the opportunity of finding work, without family ties or a settled abode – accommodation was in any case scarce – was engaged in tasks which it considered as light. The work on a primitive *estancia,* with the exception of certain opportunities for extra work established in its simple calendar, did not in fact require very prolonged physical effort. But such special tasks, for example the breaking-in of horses and the rounding-up of stray cattle, were usually entrusted to respected experts who travelled the countryside from one *estancia* to another and received wages far higher than those of the established peons. This itinerant population had very little in common with the despised agricultural labourers.

The background

The peons shared the work with Negro slaves, who were often in charge of agricultural exploitation, under the command of foremen who – demonstrating thus their ties with the more settled slave population – were usually mulattoes or occasionally free Negroes. It has already been pointed out that the labour-force necessary for cattle-ranching was small: according to contemporary reports, one man was enough to look after a thousand head of cattle.[25] Soil conditions, however, imposed more stringent limitations to the expansion of the *estancia*, for the streams and, in the South, the lagoons were used not only for watering the livestock but also for cornering the herds during rounding-up.

In addition to the *estancia* there was a form of livestock raising on a smaller scale, carried out by the owners of flocks and sheepfolds only partly subsisting on their own lands, who made a living by renting or occupying waste land. This small-scale stock-raising was viewed with great suspicion by the big landowners and the authorities: it was regarded as a legal façade masking robbery and contraband.[26] A further reason for the hostility was that it provided a centre of attraction for labour, which was excessively scarce and therefore expensive. This was evidence of an enduring trend in the rural areas of the River Plate region: the land-hunger of the big landowners and their attempts to consolidate a monopolistic position was based not so much on the desire to acquire ever bigger properties as on the sustained endeavour to cut off alternative outlets for the labour force, which they thought to be already placed in an excessively favourable position. This attitude was also reflected in their predilection for the projects based on forced labour, disguised to a greater or lesser degree, of which writers on economic conditions in the River Plate region at the beginning of the nineteenth century provide abundant examples.

The situation described above has little in common with the traditional image of the carefree prosperity of rural Buenos Aires and of the abundance reigning there in the midst of a primitive way of life still untouched by progress. In actual fact, this area developed more slowly than did the newly settled lands beyond the Paraná and the Plate. The severe economic competition from the latter areas as they were opened for settlement contributed to tensions and difficulties in the life of rural Buenos Aires.

Beyond the Paraná there survived, in a new economic climate, the circumstances which had prevailed in Buenos Aires up to 1750. There the rounding-up of domesticated cattle and the hunting of wild ones still went on simultaneously. In those ownerless lands great estates could be carved out: on the Eastern bank of the Paraná it was the Santa Fe proprietors who took possession of the land around the Bajada, opposite Santa Fe itself; on the Western bank of the River Uruguay the majority of the proprietors came from Buenos Aires, while settlement organised from Madrid introduced new colonists of Spanish origin.

Between the two rivers that bordered Entre Ríos a vast stretch of woodland – the Montiel Forest, of which only scattered traces remain today – crossed the centre of the province from North to South. It was a land of hills and streams where stock-raising was introduced only slowly. In the Banda Oriental the pattern was more complex. In the South the authority of Montevideo was recognised over a zone of market-gardening and, more rarely, farms, and *estancias* raising domesticated cattle. To the West the lands which belonged to the mission settlements of Soriano and of the Jesuits (governed somewhat loosely from Yapeyú, on the Western bank of the River Uruguay) were a source of trouble for the citizens of Montevideo. In this area there prevailed a more primitive style of exploitation, accompanied by widespread slaughter of wild cattle. The permanent settlers suffered greatly under the persecution of those landowners who used their properties only nominally as *estancias* for the rounding-up of cattle, but in fact as slaughter-houses for ownerless cattle and bases for smuggling the produce into Brazil. In contrast to what was happening in Buenos Aires, where only the small stock-raisers resorted to destructive exploitation of cattle, in the Banda Oriental the same type of economy enriched the big landowners of the North and, above all, several of the bigger merchants of Montevideo. It is not, therefore, surprising that it was better able to defend itself against the timid measures taken by the political authorities, forewarned by those who – with some justification – feared the total extermination of the herds. Not even the advent of war interrupted the slaughter: the hides accumulated in Montevideo – immense piles of them in every corner – while the little town rapidly changed in aspect, its huts being replaced by houses with tiled roofs.

The primitive structure of stock-raising life in the Banda Oriental was accompanied by a technical progress greater than that of Buenos Aires. On the Northern bank of the River Plate, near Colônia do Sacramento, which had now been definitively seized from the Portuguese, there was established the first salting-plant of the region, that of Colla, the property of Francisco Medina, and it was quite a big business. It was followed by others on the Rivers Uruguay and Plate, established by merchants from Montevideo and Buenos Aires. As did agriculture on the West bank, so on the East bank the meat-salting industry benefited from the war, which isolated the tropical centres of consumption from their traditional European sources of supply. But – in contrast to what happened in the case of cereal-growing – the production of salted meat enjoyed too many local facilities for its initial expansion, caused by exceptional circumstances, not to give rise, on a permanent basis, to a solidly established industry. Moreover, the meat-salting industry progressed not only by consuming domesticated cattle; its appearance gave fresh encouragement to that old-style destructive cattle-hunting, which enjoyed in the Banda Oriental a last and ephemeral surge of prosperity, and established new ties between the more primitive parts of the

The background

countryside and the businessmen who dominated the economic life of Montevideo.

This was the origin of an incipient tension between the city and the more advanced parts of the rural areas, which were inadequately satisfied in their demands for more effective law and order in the countryside – law and order that could only be enforced by a civil authority that was too closely connected with the principal beneficiaries of disorder. But even the *estancia* region of the South did not find the disorder entirely prejudicial: even though its inhabitants may have detested the destructive exploitation which did not always distinguish between domesticated and wild cattle, and sometimes got completely out of control and took the form of sacking the settled estates, on the other hand it was able to perceive advantages in the existence of a strong current of contraband traffic with Brazil, carried on by that same semi-nomadic population whose depredations were so deplored. Mules from the Banda Oriental played their part in Brazil's mining expansion. In the middle of the Napoleonic Wars, while the hides piled up in Montevideo, the ports of Southern Brazil kept the sea-route to Britain open. The existence of these outlets proved much stronger than any preventive legislation, and clandestine trade with Brazil was already – as it was to be for a long time – one of the bases of the economy of rural Uruguay.

There were other reasons for the comparative isolation of Montevideo within the Banda Oriental. The city partly owed its development to the establishment of a base where the Spanish naval forces of the South Atlantic were concentrated. It was a fortified city and a garrison city, and had an exceptionally numerous Spanish population, which depended for its subsistence not on the local economy but on the ability of the Imperial administration to pay its salaries. In Montevideo – as happened at the same time in San Juan, Puerto Rico, another Spanish naval base in the Atlantic – this factor isolated the city from its hinterland, and was the beginning of a divergence which would have a marked effect on the history of Uruguay up to 1851 and, less openly, until more recent times.

The city, isolated from its hinterland, influenced it very little: the Banda Oriental, like Entre Ríos, therefore maintained in its rural areas a primitive life-style reminiscent of that of the entire River Plate region before 1750, but now accompanied by a frantic acceleration of the rhythm of economic activity which, however, accurately reflected the new relationship between the zone and its commercial metropolises. This accelerated and unbalanced development had its effects on the entire life of the area, so that extreme insecurity of life and property prevailed everywhere. In the lands which had belonged to the Jesuits, all the settlers were, strictly speaking, squatters on the lands which nominally belonged to the Indian communities. Although in other zones there was a possibility of securing legal title to property, there was little interest in doing so, and in any case property was mainly interesting as a means of indulging in fringe activities such as the slaughter of wild cattle, which hardly constituted examples of respect for the legislation currently in force.

But this insecurity affected the whole of life. An abundance of opportunities which attracted a heterogeneous population, in which, however, the Guaranís from Misiones were the dominant element, and the lessened significance of those elements which had lent solidity to the old Colonial culture (one need only reflect on the insufficiency, more serious here than in other areas, of the ecclesiastical organisation), gave the social structure which came to be established in this zone a greater dynamism than that which potentially existed in other areas of the River Plate region, and this difference was to be observable throughout the Revolutionary process.

This discrete human mass gathered together by the economic progress of Entre Ríos and the Banda Oriental was related to that other mass which, apparently unconnected with that economic progress, lived a life totally outside the law. In the Banda Oriental, in the eighteenth century, one already finds the *gauchos*, a pejorative term applied to the thieves and cattle- and hide-smugglers, and, by the city-dwellers, to countrymen in general; a term to which the Revolution – deducing a local interpretation from the egalitarian creed which it proclaimed – would sometimes lend a eulogistic connotation. Besides the gauchos there were the Indians, Chanás and Charrúas, who rebelled against domination by the settlers but not against contact with them. So deeply affected had they been by this contact that, by the end of the eighteenth century, they had forgotten their original languages and had, in many cases, adopted the Guaraní language spoken by the immigrants from the Misiones region.[27] Gauchos and Indians were able to subsist outside the normal economic process, because parallel with the latter there was developing another process which, as has been pointed out above, combined destructive activities with the task of keeping the route to Brazil open; and this route was vital to the economy of the Banda Oriental. Through this medium fruitful contacts, and not merely commercial ones, were established between the Banda Oriental and Rio Grande do Sul. The Rio Grande landowners, with lands in Uruguay and smugglers in Uruguay, and who were enemies and sometimes blood-relations of the Uruguayan landowners, were an element which the Portuguese and subsequently the Brazilian government had to take into account when pursuing its complex policy in the River Plate region. It was a determining factor in that policy until the Paraguayan War, and was even more noticeable in the day-to-day life of those territories.

On the other bank of the Plate the system implanted by Spain also had a kind of back door, more burdensome but less economically significant than that of the Banda Oriental. From 1750 onwards, the Indians were bringing implacable pressure to bear on the Spanish lands. For them, as for the settlers, the extermination of the herds of wild cattle made necessary a total change in their way of life. At the same time there appeared in the far Interior the Chilean Araucanians, who possessed a stronger political structure, both in peacetime and wartime, which they did not abandon when they reverted from agricultural to pastoral activities. This superiority allowed them to achieve rapid predominance over the earlier Indian inhabitants of the Pampa, whom they united in vast confederations. The defence of the frontier, from Buenos Aires to Mendoza, became one of the most urgent tasks of the Colonial government.

To achieve this object, the military organisation of the rural areas was reformed, and new guard-posts and forts were established. By the beginning of the nineteenth century it could be said that the situation had been stabilised, after many years had passed without any major Indian incursion. But cattle-rustling and the kidnapping of people continued to be part of the Indian way of life, hardly varying even after the fruits of looting came to be complemented by the receipt of official subsidies. A more serious factor was that the Indian threat increased, rather than diminished, as the Indians assimilated cultural usages adopted from the white settlers. Indeed, such usages involved the creation of new needs which only robbery could satisfy. Such robbery was, moreover, supported by the complicity of certain sectors of the white population, ranging from those landowners from Chile, Córdoba and Mendoza who made large-scale purchases of stolen cattle, to the traders and squatters of the frontier region who acquiesced in – and, according to their accusers, often encouraged – the Indian incursions, in return for a share of the booty of hides. Thus there grew up on the Frontier a system inimical to the maintenance of orderly production on the *estancias*, and marked by a great degree of complicity with the incursions. It was, particularly, the marginal population – Indians living outside the tribal structure, and sometimes converted to Christianity, and whites who had been prepared to settle on frontier lands which for others would have been too dangerous and which were populated by them, often on extremely weak legal grounds, without their title ever being disputed – which maintained this slow haemorrhage of the cattle-raising economy. For this reason, whereas the existence of the Indian frontier opened up a second outlet for trade with Chile, this did not have for the general economy of rural Buenos Aires the beneficial consequences which the Brazilian route brought to the Banda Oriental, and in any case an excessively high price was paid for this dubious service.

Simultaneously with these relationships of hostility, the Indians maintained with the white lands other relations not necessarily so hostile, although the latter were reproached, not without some justification, with lending support to the former. For example, together with the products of looting, the Indians sold the fruits of hunting: ostrich feathers, sea-otter furs, and those strange animals with which the fauna of the River Plate region appears to caricature that of past geological eras, the *quirquinchos*, *mulitas* and *peludos*. And not all the hides were stolen; in Indian territory, too, there were round-ups. Finally, the peasant of the Littoral, whose wife – if he had one – hardly ever wove cloth, esteemed above all others the textiles from the Indian lands, woven by the patient Araucanian squaws. The Pampa poncho was preferred to the heavier and less warm one produced in the Interior, and would in the future be preferred to that made from British wool, the only merit of which was its low price.

BUENOS AIRES AND MERCANTILE EXPANSION

Thus even the Indian territory had ties, at least economic ones, with the rising Littoral. The capital of the latter was Buenos Aires, the seat since 1776 of a Viceroyalty, and the protagonist since the early years of the eighteenth century of a progress that was never to be arrested. In the last years of that century Buenos Aires was already comparable to a Spanish city of the second rank and was very different, therefore, from the village of straw and adobe that it had been half a century before. This growth – accompanied as it was by a rapid increase in population – was not based solely on the economic rise of the Littoral; it was a consequence of the promotion of Buenos Aires as the principal centre for overseas trade for the extreme South of the Spanish Empire. Thus the prosperity of the port was more closely connected with the maintenance of the Imperial structure than its beneficiaries realised.

Buenos Aires was at the time, fundamentally, a commercial and bureaucratic city, with complementary economic activities (both craft and primary) geared to satisfying the demand created, above all, by those engaged in administration and commerce. The commercial importance of Buenos Aires dated from before the reforms of the 1770s, which established exemption from duty for goods shipped to Chile and Peru, and free trade with the most important ports of Spain. Even the commercial correspondence of Anchorena[28] provides evidence, throughout the preceding decade, of connections with almost all the areas which those reforms were to transform into the economic hinterland of the capital of the new Viceroyalty. But there is no doubt that the reforms consolidated and accelerated the commercial rise of Buenos Aires. They facilitated the establishment of a nucleus of powerful merchants which was soon to acquire a position of hegemony in the economic system of the entire Viceroyalty.

This nucleus reflected the economic development of Spain during that phase of expansion which occurred in the second half of the eighteenth century. The appearance of pockets of modern industry was accompanied in the Peninsula by a shifting of the economic centre of gravity from the South to the North, particularly to Catalonia and the Cantabrian regions. Although the Andalusian ports – above all, Cádiz – did not lose their pre-eminence in the commercial traffic with the Americas, they were to a

The background

great extent transformed into intermediaries of the newer and more vigorous economic centres. In the course of the second half of the eighteenth century the representatives of that reinvigorated Spain made their appearance in Buenos Aires: the Catalans Larrea and Mateu, the Basque-Navarrese Anchorena, Álzaga, Santa Coloma, Lezica, Belaústegui, Azcuénaga, and the Galicians Llavallol and Rivadavia. Their rise to fortune had been comparatively recent: the list of the richest citizens of Buenos Aires in 1766[29] includes only two of their names – Lezica and Rivadavia; but by the end of the century the Anchorena fortune was already almost legendary, partly owing to the precautions which its owner took to conceal it. This fortune had been made by exercising a form of commerce that owed nothing to innovation and was reluctant to take big risks. Most of the Buenos Aires merchants were agents for Spanish firms, and in more than one instance were relatives of the Spanish businessmen whom they represented or with whom they maintained close commercial ties. An example of this was Domingo Mateu, who established himself in Buenos Aires and represented his brothers who had settled in Guatemala and Manila, all of them maintaining ties with the parent firm in Barcelona. But even those who did not limit their operations to acting as agents for Spanish business houses engaged in business transactions without difficulties or risks. It is enough to examine the correspondence of Anchorena to observe to what extent his rôle was limited to that of intermediary between Spain and the ever-growing hinterland of Buenos Aires.

This routine-bound commercial way of life was bitterly denounced by Argentine economists of the Enlightenment. According to one famous characterisation, for these merchants who set the tone of Buenos Aires life business was just a matter of 'buying for two and selling for four'. In more modern terms, this pejorative characterisation has been repeated in recent times: in so far as they were merely acting on a commission basis for Spanish businessmen, the Buenos Aires merchants linked to the Cádiz route played no important part in the process of capital-accumulation which was to be the indispensable basis for the subsequent development of the local economy. However, this assertion is somewhat dubious. Indeed, in spite of the lack of detailed studies of this matter, it is safe to assert that this agency business was a source of high profits to the local agents concerned. Their rapid enrichment is a ready proof of it, and it is not difficult to give an explanation of the process. Sheer distance, and the ignorance as to the movements of the local market which this necessarily provoked, put the Spanish principals at the mercy of their local agents. Even a small-scale merchant such as Santa Coloma was in a position to give only vague answers to the specific and urgent questions raised by the Spanish owners of the goods he held in his shop: sales had fallen, and prices had been cut, because times were bad; anyone not satisfied with this reply could simply try to find another agent, without any guarantee of finding a better one.

This free-and-easy relationship with the Spanish principals coincided with a much stricter control over the commercial agents in the Interior. In this case contacts were much more frequent, and more complex types of association made possible a more effective vigilance. This was especially true of the biggest Buenos Aires business houses: the Anchorenas, for example, had agents established in the cities of the hinterland, from Santa Fe as far as Peru, and also had itinerant salesmen working on commission, who would set off with a fleet of wagons to sell goods on behalf of the Buenos Aires parent firm. Both sources supplied, independently, information as to the state of the market. In this way, the distribution of commercial profits favoured the Buenos Aires firms both at the expense of their Spanish principals and at the expense of the smaller commercial firms of the hinterland. This process was also self-sustaining: the possession of capital allowed the Buenos Aires merchants to complement their agencies for Spanish goods with direct purchases, not to mention extremely varied intermediate forms of transaction, and thus achieve an increasing autonomy *vis-à-vis* their original Spanish headquarters. Similarly, this capital made it possible to give credit in the hinterland, and occasionally to effect cash purchases from producers, by-passing the local distributors, as happened, for example, in the case of the purchase of hides in Corrientes and Entre Ríos.

Thus the big business firms of Buenos Aires had greater freedom of manoeuvre than their function as local agents of the Cádiz merchants would lead one to suppose, and they enjoyed the high profits which that freedom made possible. But this prosperity was not accompanied by the fulfilment of any dynamic function in the local economy. True, the merchants established in Buenos Aires did not, of course, disdain to engage in the export of hides, by means of which they channelled into their pockets a good part of the profits of the most dynamic sector of the Viceregal economy. The greater part of their business, however, consisted of the distribution of European imports which were paid for in cash. In neither field do the Buenos Aires merchants appear to have discovered the advantages of a progressive increase in throughput at the cost of a small decrease in profit-margins. On the contrary, their business dealings, not unjustly accused of being routine-bound, were maintained at a low level and guaranteed high profits.

This reproach has frequently been levelled at those people, who were observed to be enriching themselves by using, somewhat mechanically, their privileged position in commercial circles. The reproach was, perhaps, somewhat unjust: in 1826, in the Constituent Congress, the Salta deputy Gorriti was to express an eloquent refutation[30] (he was referring especially to the mule trade, but his arguments were susceptible of general application) of the new-fangled belief that the cheapening of goods by the renunciation of high profit-margins or the decrease of high excise dues

The background

would provoke an increase in demand which would eventually offset the losses of the businessmen and the exchequer. On the contrary, Gorriti observed, at the time mules were being bought by those who could not do without them and were in a position to pay high prices. In order to add to these wealthy purchasers a new market among the poor Indians of Upper Peru, so marked a reduction of prices would be necessary that it would not merely be a case of sacrificing profits and exchequer revenue, but even of selling at a loss. For those Indians, mules selling at fifteen pesos would be as far beyond their reach as mules selling for twenty pesos. This was one of the reasons for the comparative inelasticity of demand in the Colonial economic structure.

As was the case with the mules, for the overseas goods the greater part of the hinterland of Buenos Aires, including the Interior and Upper Peru, from which the greatest return in money was expected, was sharply divided between the small sector of *gente decente* (the rich), who were consumers, and a lower class which a cheapening of products by the sacrifice of the high profits of the importers could not possibly incorporate into the market. It is, therefore, probable that, in insisting on high profits and refusing to expand the market, the Buenos Aires merchants showed more knowledge of their business than did their subsequent critics. But, whoever was at fault, the fact is that this commercial sector, the hegemony of which over the Viceregal economy became ever more solidly established, did not fulfil a dynamic role; its success was due to the fact that it satisfied a demand which it believed to be irremediably static. This somewhat undynamic character of the Viceregal economy as a whole was reflected in another significant fact: the comparatively low rate of interest in force during Viceregal times and even in the first decade after the Revolution. The usual rate of interest on commercial transactions during that period was 6 per cent per annum, comparable to that in force in Spain and very much lower than the rates current after 1820, which even in times of slackening demand were to be more than double those in force previously.

But it was not only commerce with the Interior and Upper Peru, which consisted of the sale of fine and medium quality textiles and some hardware, for payment in cash, that took place in conditions which made dynamic expansion impossible. Even in the commercial relations between Buenos Aires and its immediate zone of influence in the Littoral one observes trends which had the same effect. Of course, the export of hides, which was for three quarters of a century the principal contribution of the River Plate region to the world market, did not encounter in the limitations imposed by world consumption any brake on its expansion. But the production of hides was not the only rural activity of the Littoral. In Santa Fe, Western Entre Ríos and Buenos Aires mule-breeding received a fresh stimulus, whilst in Buenos Aires, with the presence of a strongly consumption-orientated urban centre, meat for human consumption played an important part in the development of cattle-raising, which was comparatively slow in this part of the River Plate region. Both types of stock-raising were orientated towards somewhat inelastic markets. We have already observed how one of the causes of the prosperity of the mule-trade consisted in the limitations placed on dispatches of droves towards the North, which kept prices at a high level. As for the consumer market, it was a well known fact that those who controlled it were more afraid of abundance than of scarcity.

But even the production of hides failed to play a dynamic role. Of course, exports rose, and very swiftly, but this rise was not continuous. For an excessively long period overseas exports suffered the consequences of the world war situation, and the oscillation between years of stagnation and brief flurries of frenzied exporting continued. In the case of the hides, too, the immediate search for high profits, guaranteed by purchasing at low prices, and the storing of the hides in expectation of better times, was of more interest to the merchants than was the encouragement of a regular growth of production by increasing the profits of the stock-raisers.

Even less favourable to a sustained expansion were the prevailing business practices applied to the agricultural production of the Littoral. Marketing, in normal times, was almost entirely outside the control of the big merchants of Buenos Aires. A more restricted commercial circuit, in which the traders of the rural zones dealt with the lower-level urban sectors, grain-storers, millers and bakers, was geared to commercial practices even more markedly orientated towards scarcity and high prices. This was particularly evident in the case of the Littoral: in a market with an exceptionally rigid capacity of consumption, any overproduction, however small, was likely to cause catastrophic falls in prices, whereas any scarcity, even a mild one, caused extremely sharp price increases.

The basic principles of this method of doing business, which implied a resigned acceptance of a fundamentally static situation and an ability to take advantage of it, were not affected by the expansion of stock-raising, orientated towards the export of hides, which appears in retrospect to be the most potentially lucrative innovation of the Viceregal era. They were more directly affected by the war and the confusion which this provoked in commerce. The continually changing circumstances favoured those who were prepared to abandon the routine-bound practices to which the commerce of Buenos Aires owed its first phase of prosperity and instead display audacity and versatility. Besides the merchants concerned with the trade-route from Cádiz, the war raised to a level of prosperity others who were prepared to use more varied routes: those via Cuba, Brazil and the United States; that of neutral Northern Europe, which opened the door to France, which was an ally but semi-isolated, and to Britain, which was an enemy. (These were the years of the rise of Hamburg in the Buenos Aires trade.) Then there was the Indian Ocean route, with its reservoir of slaves in Mozambique and its sugar islands, where the need for grain was so great that they were prepared to buy River Plate wheat at the prices which the high costs of production and transport made inevitable.

This new commercial sector, which had come to the fore all of a sudden, naturally displayed an increasing impatience with the legal restrictions with which its commercial practices were hedged round. During the final years of Spanish rule it came out, together with the landowners, in favour of the liberalisation of trade undertaken by the Crown. This was not enough to give it a modernising role in the strictly economic field; or, to put it more exactly, one fails to recognise in its attitudes the style of modernisation which the new economic theory propounded, even though this sector was beginning to hint at innovations which independent Argentina was to know only too well.

What in fact happened was that this new sector replaced the routine exploitation of a privileged position in business with a tendency towards sheer speculation, and this tendency was, of course, represented, with some pride, as progressive in comparison with the previous situation. Tomás Antonio Romero, the most powerful of the new-style businessmen, was to point out the contrast between the 'sedentary and passive' commerce which formerly prevailed and the new commerce which 'discovered provinces, colonies and realms hitherto unknown'[31] and which he himself practised. But this new-found audacity was not rewarded – indeed, it could not be in the troubled times that world trade underwent during the revolutionary and Napoleonic wars – by the enduring conquest of new trade-routes and new markets. The new road to prosperity consisted of enjoying a series of successful coups, using the versatility necessary in a situation that was essentially unstable. We find something of this in the complex dealings of Romero himself: he imported slaves, exported goods to the Indian Ocean, and carried out such specialised operations as the – theoretically illegal – introduction of Brazilian tobacco, the cultivation of which was prohibited, and he was able to do this because he enjoyed the open support of the Viceregal authorities.

One must emphasise that it would be absurd to read into the above character-sketch a kind of posthumous reproach. Just as their predecessors who worked the Cádiz trade-route had done, these new merchant-venturers were working in the context of a situation which they could not ignore without risking ruin. As it happened, the business practices evolved by them were ultimately responsible for their eventual decline, just as they had been responsible for their previous prosperity. The commercial expansion which they brought to Buenos Aires was, in fact, ephemeral, and when the cycle was completed, they showed even less ability than the merchants accustomed to using the Cádiz trade-route to survive the changes brought about by free trade with overseas and by the Revolution.

The River Plate at the beginning of the nineteenth century

The fragility of their fortunes was a direct result of the situation from which they arose: the creation of a centre of autonomous commercial life in Buenos Aires was due to the simultaneous decline in the ascendancy of the European centres on which Buenos Aires depended. At war first with France and then with Britain, Spain saw threatened and later destroyed its ties with its overseas territories. A whole corpus of emergency legislation arose, designed to find palliatives for this situation, conceding commercial liberties that previously had been stubbornly denied. This legislation implied a recognition of the swift disintegration which was afflicting the economic unity of the Empire. These concessions – which were by no means spontaneous gestures of liberalisation – included authorisation to import slaves in ships owned by Buenos Aires merchants (1791), authorisation to accord naturalisation papers to ships with the same objective (1793), authorisation of exports to and imports from other nations' colonies (1795), authorisation for River Plate ships and merchants to intervene actively in trade with the Peninsula (1796) and authorisation of trade with neutral countries (1797). They were rescinded as soon as they ceased to be unavoidable, as was the case with the most important concession, regarding trade with neutrals. These measures were, undoubtedly, less influential in the rise of an autonomous commercial nucleus in the River Plate region than was the existence of an international situation which obliged the metropolis to follow this new policy because the commercial structure of the entire world had been dislocated.

The crisis not only diminished the pressure from Spain, but it also removed from the River Plate scene the most solidly established commercial powers, which were replaced by others which took advantage of a situation favourable to them. Buenos Aires was now to see the merchant ships of the United States, the Hanseatic cities and the Scandinavian countries, and even Turkey. But these new powers were a poor substitute for those which were no longer able to fulfil their traditional role, and Buenos Aires was to build up its own merchant fleet by the seizure of ships lying at anchor in the port when war broke out, and also by means of shipbuilding in the Corrientes and Paraguay yards, accustomed to building smaller craft for river trade. By this means, the Buenos Aires merchants reached the new markets of Europe, North America, Africa, and the sugar islands of the Indian ocean. For a city used to thinking of itself as being in the uttermost part of the earth, this was a heady experience. Normally cautious observers spoke of the city as being the 'centre of the commercial world'.[32] And in that world transformed by the semi-withdrawal of its European centre Buenos Aires came to occupy, if not the centre, at least an important place. The process was accelerated because the semi-isolation was financial as well as commercial: thanks to the situation, there had arisen in New England, on a relatively weak financial base, a naval and commercial centre which was to be one of the world's foremost. Thanks to it, there arose in Buenos Aires a centre that was no doubt less important, but which would in any case have been unthinkable without that vacuum of naval, commercial and financial power.

But the autonomous commercial development arising from this vacuum was of necessity ephemeral. Before the conclusion of the cycle of wars of Europe, the peace between Spain and Britain was to give the Americas a commercial and financial metropolis fully capable of fulfilling its functions. The repercussions of this new arrangement were to reach the River Plate as early as 1809, when commerce with the new ally was authorised. From then on, Buenos Aires would again be relegated to the periphery of the commercial world, and years were to go by before the full consequences of this new position were to be recognisable.

Is it possible to make a quantitative analysis of this frenzied commercial development? In order to do this, it would be necessary to undertake an inevitably tedious and lengthy search of the sources, which are abundant in quantity but in which the relevant information is sparse, and which are, moreover, dispersed in many locations, from the customs records of Buenos Aires and Montevideo to the various registers of taxes on internal trade. Research of this dimension could only be undertaken by a team of workers. In the absence of this, it is, nevertheless, possible to establish certain precise facts relating to the fundamental aspects of commerce in the last years of the Viceregal period.

In the first place, and despite the expansion of stock-raising in the Littoral, the principal export during this period was still precious metals. The proportion of total exports constituted by these varied, and in any case are not exactly known. According to data elaborated by Fischer,[33] in 1796, out of total exports of 5,058,882 pesos, gold accounted for 1,425,701 and silver for 2,556,304; that is, precious metals constituted 80 per cent by value of total exports. It would, of course, be wrong to extrapolate the figures valid for that year, in which exports of all products reached exceptional levels, to the period as a whole. But it is enough to bear in mind that the principal export item of the Littoral stock-raising industry – hides – only in exceptional years reached a total of one million units (of fluctuating value, but very roughly calculable as one peso per unit), to realise that the data for 1797 were in no way anomalous. The other export items were much less important than hides: the value of dried and salted meat can be calculated, for the quinquennium 1792–96, at around sixty thousand pesos a year; ten years later, the export of those products had increased markedly – in the second half of 1803 they were over 120,000 quintals, with a value that could be calculated as between 150 and 180 thousand pesos; in the following years, no figures as high as this were recorded; the figure for the whole of 1804 was 70,000 quintals, and for 1805, 60,000. The average annual values were under $100,000. In any case, the expanding salted meat industry only accounted for a very minor part of the River Plate's exports. Agricultural exports accounted for even less, and only occurred in exceptional years.

The primacy of precious metals among exports was, therefore, unquestioned. Through Buenos Aires there passed every year a quantity of silver that equalled the total amount minted in Potosí. Of course, a high proportion of Upper Peru's silver never found its way to the mint, but even so the rôle of Buenos Aires as the South American extreme of a mechanism for sucking precious metals out of the Americas is quite evident. How was Buenos Aires able to fulfil this rôle? Of course, a part of the silver that passed through the port was outside the commercial process altogether: this was the Crown's share of mined and minted silver. But the latter was comparatively small, and most of Upper Peru's precious metals, and of those of Lower Peru attracted to the Potosí mint, had to be attracted to Buenos Aires by the functioning of certain commercial mechanisms. This functioning is even more difficult to understand if one bears in mind that during the early phase of the Viceregal period the trade of the River Plate was certainly not in deficit. How, therefore, was it possible to extract from that region, as happened in the period 1792–96, four million pesos per year by value, of which at least two-thirds consisted of precious metals, in exchange for goods to the value of around two million pesos? Only the existence of an exceptionally expensive commercial system could guarantee an equilibrium. Such a system had the effect of levelling out in the centres of production, above all Upper Peru, what in Buenos Aires appeared to be in such pronounced imbalance.

This necessarily approximate analysis of the commercial equilibrium existing in the River Plate region brings us back, therefore, to the same conclusions obtained by our examination of society in the Viceregal period: the hegemony of the commercial sector appeared to be imposed by the very nature of things, and was a necessary aspect of the Colonial order. The prosperity of Buenos Aires, and that of the more modest of the centres of commerce and transport on the Peru route, was fundamentally derived from its participation, although in a subordinate position, in the advantages which that order gave to the marketers – the local emissaries of Spain's economy – over the producers.

Here, of course, we find one of the reasons for the suspicion with which the mercantile sectors were to face the Revolutionary crisis. Denunciations of the monopoly of Cádiz not only aroused misgivings owing to the ties of economic dependence which they maintained by means of that monopoly. The mercantile hegemony of Cádiz was only one aspect of a system of commerce which included the hegemony of Buenos Aires as a secondary metropolis, a position which was guaranteed, less by any gravitational impulse, than by political decisions taken by the Crown. The biggest business in the River Plate area – the export of Spanish products to Tucumán, Cuyo and Upper Peru, to be exchanged for precious metals –

presupposed the maintenance of the Colonial order. The business of exporting hides and jerked beef might well be an attractive complement to the former business, but as a substitute it would be ruinous.

The exports of precious metals were valued in millions, and those of the products of the Littoral stock-raising industry were around one million pesos a year. If we leave aside these two dominant nuclei of the Viceregal economy, and consider the nuclei subordinate to them, we find much more modest figures.

Let us first examine Tucumán, of which the commerce in 1805 was described in an admirable report by the deputy Salvador de Alberdi to the Buenos Aires Consulado.[34] Tucumán was importing annually goods to a value of 140,000 pesos, of which two-thirds were products of Castile, textiles which found consumers not only among the upper sectors but also, in this exceptionally prosperous region, even among the people of the countryside, who 'kept Castilian cloths and linens for the days when they dressed up'. Imports from Chile and Peru were of the order of ten thousand pesos; from the Andean area twenty-four thousand pesos. As an importing centre Tucumán was more closely tied to the metropolis than to the neighbouring and poorer regions.

Its exports were more complex: the principal item was the carrier business, which brought in seventy thousand pesos; the principal destination of goods was the Littoral. The second most important item was cattle on the hoof, to the value of 53,000 pesos, exported to Upper and Lower Peru. Thirdly, there were tanned shoe-soles and hides, to the value of thirty thousand pesos, which found a consumer-market in the Littoral and Córdoba. There was a more widely dispersed consumer-market for rice (seventeen thousand pesos), finished wooden goods (nine thousand pesos) and saddlery (three thousand pesos). Here too, however, the most important items were orientated towards the economically dominant zones, Buenos Aires and Upper Peru. Orientated as it was towards the more prosperous zones, the commerce of Tucumán was also linked to the socially dominant sectors; it was the satisfaction of their needs that accounted for the greater part of imports. In this respect, it is enough to compare the ninety thousand pesos' worth imported from Castile with the six thousand pesos' worth of ordinary textiles (raw cotton from Catamarca, to the value of 4,000 pesos, and coarse cloth from Cochabamba to the value of 2,000 pesos) to recognise to what extent luxury goods enjoyed a dominant share of imports.

Within the Interior Tucumán was a privileged area. San Juan was, however, as we have observed, the Andean zone which constituted the purest model of a one-crop economy based on viticulture suffering the impact of free trade with Spain. San Juan had an annual production of from nine to ten thousand *arrobas* of wine (from 2,250 to 2,500 mule-loads of four *arrobas*), and from fourteen to fifteen thousand *arrobas* (from 3,500 to 3,750 mule-loads) of double-distilled *aguardiente*. The sale prices in the place of destination varied: sixty pesos for a mule-load of double-distilled *aguardiente* in Salta, fifty-five in Tucumán, forty-four in Córdoba (all these figures refer to the year 1806). But of these prices, the greater part was made up by transport costs and taxes collected at the point of sale. According to José Godoy Oro, if one calculated a cost in San Juan of twelve pesos per mule-load, the profit was, in nearly all the points of sale, around ten pesos per unit. That is to say, that San Juan was bringing in 82,500 pesos annually for its *aguardiente*. As for wine, the first effect of free trade was to banish it from the market. The isolation after 1805 again allowed it access to the consuming-centre of Buenos Aires. Although overseas competition had made the price drop from 30–36 pesos per two-*arroba* cask to 10–12 pesos, isolation brought the price up again to 20 pesos. But of these prices, seven or eight pesos were taken up by the freight between San Juan and Buenos Aires, and then there were also the taxes on internal trade. In such conditions, it does not seem unduly hazardous to attribute to wine a revenue comparable to that produced by *aguardiente* only when war eliminated European competition, but in more normal times the wine-trade hardly covered its costs.[35]

San Juan was unable to show the same commercial surplus as Tucumán. The difficulties faced by its principal consumer product were not the only drawback; another, and no less important, one was the need to import the most essential supplies. San Juan was, therefore, less closely tied to the commerce of Castile, which was fundamentally a trade in luxury goods. With Buenos Aires it had an annual turnover of fifteen to twenty thousand pesos, which not only covered its small consumption of overseas goods, but also that of *yerba mate* and slaves. The remainder of the imports was principally made up of livestock: mules and donkeys for transport over short distances, horses, cattle for consumption, and even locally-manufactured products for consumption by the poor: ponchos, goat's-hair cloth, and tanned goatskins from Córdoba. San Juan was, therefore, an extreme example of an area almost independent of the important local currents of commerce, and from their increasing difficulties in inserting themselves into a mercantile structure based on the tremendous imbalance of economic potential and organised to perpetuate it. The solution to its problems could be found by reducing the costs of transport and marketing: that was what was desired by José Godoy Oro, deputy of the Consulado and author of the admirable 1806 report, through the reforms he proposed. But such a solution was unattainable within the Colonial order, and was also to prove unattainable, for virtually the same reasons, in the post-Revolutionary situation.

It was unattainable because the Colonial order was characterised by the rigid separation between a very small sector incorporated into a large-scale economic system, and much bigger sectors with an economic life carried on on a more reduced scale. As arbiter between one and the other there were those who dominated the marketing processes and used them to maintain this differentiated structure, which guaranteed them an exceptionally high proportion of the profits.

The period of dislocation of world trade, therefore, did not betoken any fresh prosperity for Buenos Aires. The prospects of commercial independence that were opened were not a valid substitute for the guaranteed profits assured by its enjoyment of a privileged position in the Imperial commercial structure, reformed for Buenos Aires's benefit. The new trade was a welcome complement; it was, above all, the result of necessity. But even though these prospects were in the long run deceptive, they contributed to weakening the resistance of the dominant commercial sector to the possibility of more far-reaching changes, towards which they were impelled, in the first place by outside pressures, and secondly by those exercised by the producers of the expanding Littoral, who were prepared to open up a broader road towards the overseas consumer markets. Even though, around 1810, Buenos Aires was still basically a silver port, the fluctuations in fortune caused by the world war situation were no less important for being ephemeral. Because of them Buenos Aires was able to face light-heartedly the crises which the Revolution necessarily was to bring in its train, and renounce the advantages which the Colonial order guaranteed it, with the conviction which the new situation had implanted in the heads of her wiser sons: placed there in the 'centre of the commercial world', the Tyre of the New World did not need the protection which the Imperial order provided. By gaining independence from this decrepit order, it hoped to embark on a new phase of life marked by unbounded prosperity.

A SOCIETY LESS REFORMED THAN ITS ECONOMY

The River Plate area experienced, during the years of the Viceroyalty, the beginning of a profound transformation of its economy. It has already been observed that this had less effect, even in the economic sphere, than might have been supposed; the repercussions of these changes on other aspects of Colonial life were even more attenuated. Society and the way of life remained substantially unaltered, even in Buenos Aires, and many of the changes attributed to the reforming influences that were beginning to make themselves felt could, on the contrary, be traced back to the earliest stages of Spanish settlement in the Americas.

Society in the River Plate region still conceived of itself as being divided along ethnic lines. In the Littoral the institution of slavery placed almost all the inhabitants of African descent in a special legal status; in Buenos Aires in 1778, Negro slaves dominated that sector of activities which may – not without some danger of anachronism – be classified as lower-class.[36] But even there, where the black population was due to a more recent immigration, there already appeared, when the Viceroyalty was established, Negroes who had reached higher social levels as craftsmen and merchants, sometimes owning slaves themselves. In the Interior, as has already been observed, a large part of the African population had managed to emancipate itself from slavery. In that region of longer-established prosperity, where Negroes had been in demand since the seventeenth century to fill the void left by the demographic collapse of the indigenous population, one sees a more advanced phase of the process which in the Littoral was only beginning. In both regions, it was evident that the existence of slavery was not sufficient to restrict the Negroes to the socio-occupational levels to which they were originally destined.

This did not mean that the slaves, through emancipation, entered a society open to further ascent. On the contrary, once they were free, they found themselves incorporated into a social structure organised, according to the highly significant expression that it applied to itself, into *castes*. On the one hand there were the Spaniards, the pure-blooded descendants of the Conquistadors, and on the other the Indians, the descendants of the pre-Hispanic population. Both groups were, in law, exempt from the limitations affecting the other castes, although their legal status was different, since Spaniards were not subject to tribute, from which in Spain only the nobles were exempt, and their real status was even more so. The rest, free Negroes, *mestizos*, Mulattoes and *zambos*, classified in minute gradations by a collective consciousness that was increasingly aware of ethnic differences and distinguished no less than thirty-two separate gradations between pure Spanish and pure Indian blood, lived in submission to legal restrictions of varying gravity. In schools, convents and army regiments the caste-differentiation made itself strongly felt: the descendants of the Conquistadors fully intended to reserve for themselves the highest offices in the State.

But the rigidity of these caste-gradations was of comparatively recent origin. In the seventeenth century they carried more weight than in the sixteenth century, and in the eighteenth century they became still more significant. The consequence of this was that the legal status of a Spaniard was not always accompanied by an ethnic origin as pure as the legally valid definition would require. It is not surprising, for example, that travellers at the end of the eighteenth century were to find in Buenos Aires a higher proportion of *mestizos* and Mulattoes than the census records would lead one to expect.[37] Another consequence was that the usurpation of the caste-status, and to a lesser degree the legal status, of the Spaniard, was still possible. The first of these was simply achieved by moving to a place where the migrant's origin was unknown. According to sources whose veracity we have no cause to doubt, this expedient was used fairly frequently, especially by light-skinned Mulattoes. The practice itself is a demonstration of the

The background

efficacy of the barriers established by the caste system. The legal acquisition of superior caste-status was obtained by means of a legal certificate which, above all, cost money for the proceedings, which were in themselves costly, and for the witnesses, who had to be people of a certain social prestige, who declared that they knew the petitioner and could testify to his pure origin. Such measures did not, however, guarantee the successful petitioner against further hazards; it was always possible that subsequent denunciations of mixed parentage – often only too well founded – would serve to ruin a public or professional career based on an insufficiently strongly founded claim of purity of origin.

The latter was confused with the legal status of *hidalgo*. In the first place, judicially: it has already been observed how all the Spaniards in the Americas were exempt from tribute, and such exemption, in Spain itself, was the distinguishing mark of *hidalgo* status. Just as in the Basque country, in the Indies it was considered licit to deduce that all those exempt from tribute were in fact *hidalgos*. This is one aspect of what has been called the democratisation of Spanish society in the Indies – another was the extreme popularisation, and eventual devaluation, of the title *don*. But this 'democratisation' was ambiguous: it created a more extensive socially superior class than that of metropolitan Spain, but it did not diminish the social distance between that sector and the rest of society. In Spanish America, more so than in Spain itself, a concept of nobility based fundamentally on the notion of purity of blood arose in contrast to one which reserved the title and status of nobles to an inevitably small number of families whose members had in the economic system and in society very clearly defined functions.

This concept, therefore, placed in the highest category an exceptionally numerous group of the population (in the Interior it was around one-third of the whole; in the Littoral region the proportion was even higher). This sector classed itself as noble, and considered itself to be so. The very use of such a self-characterisation was to be a long-lasting relic: we find it as late as 1836, used by the judiciary of La Rioja in the proceedings against those who had taken part in an anti-Rosas conspiracy. The use of the term in bureaucratic language was to be even more long-lasting; again in La Rioja, a visitor of the 1860s was to speak of the *Rosista* ex-governor Bustos as the 'only noble' in the province.[38]

This dividing line, theoretically the most important in Viceregal society, does not appear to have been threatened by any upward pressure on the part of those legally considered as Indians. Of course, the division of the rural areas into 'Indian' and 'Spanish' villages – a distinction maintained from Jujuy to Córdoba and Cuyo – although it had important judicial effects, bore little relation to the ethnic origin of the rural population. In almost all cases, it bore even less relation to cultural differences. Save in the extreme North, the 'Indian' villages, inhabited by *mestizos* like the neighbouring 'Spanish' villages, preserved very little of the pre-Hispanic legacy (the widespread use of native languages – Quechua in Santiago del Estero, Guaraní in Corrientes and Northern Entre Ríos – must not be allowed to mislead the reader on this point). In any case, this differentiation was staunchly preserved in the collective consciousness. Several decades after the suppression of caste differentiation by the Revolution, the parish priest of Santa María, in Catamarca, made a note almost surreptitiously (in the margin and in pencil) of the 'castes' of the infants he baptised; and in La Rioja, in the second decade after the Revolution, the British traveller French made a careful distinction between the 'Spanish' and 'Indian' villages through which he passed. In the 1860s, also in La Rioja, the Federalist leader Chumbita was universally regarded as an Indian, as were the majority of his followers, coming as they did from the old 'Indian' villages of Famatima.

There is no doubt that the structure of the 'Indian' villages faced a crisis in the eighteenth century. There remains in the archives more easily perceptible evidence of this crisis than of that encountered by the rural areas of the Interior inhabited by those who were legally Spaniards. In the former case, the pressure for change conflicted with a pattern of legislation which tried to maintain the native communities as semi-isolated entities within the Viceregal economic framework, and to preserve for them – partly for their protection – a communitarian structure which in any case did little to satisfy the appetites which the creation of a new economic system was awakening even in the most remote corners of the Viceroyalty.

The crisis faced by the 'Indian' villages – which was very clearly evident in Santiago del Estero, where the depopulation undergone by Misiones was repeated on a smaller scale – had two phases: their incorporation, despite all the prohibitions, into the same commercial circuits employed by the Spaniards, and, quite often, the emigration of a part of their inhabitants, as an indirect consequence of that very incorporation, which revealed the existence of fresh needs that could not be satisfied by the local economic system.[39] But the Indians who left their villages were incorporated into Spanish society at a very low level. They had no opportunities, nor, apparently, any desire to ascend. The barrier of 'nobility' was not threatened by any pressure from this group: we have already observed that, on the contrary, it was less easily defended against the pressure of the emancipated Negroes. The reason for this is easy to understand: even as slaves, the Negroes developed a series of socio-economic activities more favourable to upward social mobility than did the Indians, who worked lands that were almost always marginal. The Negroes formed a predominantly urban group, employed in domestic service or as craftsmen. Only in certain areas of concentrated wealth – almost always on ecclesiastical properties – was it possible for landowners to use slave-labour; this happened in Córdoba and in some parts of Northern Buenos Aires Province. Even slavery did not prevent the Africans from mixing their blood with others of the urban lower classes, and eventually, the Mulattoes were to become, almost everywhere, the most serious external threat to that social organisation based on castes which was supposed to be the prevailing system.

The principal threat, however, came from within the ruling caste. The latter was, in fact, too numerous for social superiority always to be accompanied by a corresponding economic and functional superiority. The ambiguity of this situation was particularly pronounced in the Interior, where caste-differentiation was more firmly established independently of economic differentiation (in the Littoral region the main function of the former was to justify the latter). The 'noble' class, which described itself as *gente decente*, included a vast semi-impoverished sector which affected its prestige. The maintenance of it in situations becoming to its status was considered a social necessity and tended to be guaranteed by the civil and ecclesiastical authorities; for example, by the endowment of dowries by the Cabildos to enable girls who were 'poor, but of good family' to find husbands, by exemption from payment of the novice's dowry in the case of girls of similar status who preferred the monastic life, and even by other measures less obviously designed with this end in view and which were, moreover, destined to last well into the Independence period – such measures as reserving minor civil service posts for members of that social sector, and other forms of ill-disguised charity such as the distribution of franchises for the sale of lottery-tickets.

But the lot of the distressed gentlefolk was extremely hard. Even though, for their own benefit, the more prosperous among the 'nobility' took measures to save such people from a poverty so excessive that they ran the risk of becoming confused with the lower orders, this did not mean that their attempts at upward social mobility were looked on with favour. Within the *gente decente*, therefore, there was another differentiation, unsystematised and based purely on economic differences: to defend this barrier when it appeared threatened, recourse was had to the general dividing-line which separated the 'nobility' from the great mass of the lower orders. Against the poor *gente decente* who, if they enriched themselves, aspired to other signs of superior social status, it was usual to employ accusations of lack of racial purity. Such accusations, which could, strictly speaking, have been levelled at the entire class that was legally Spanish, were particularly dangerous for those whose over-rapid ascent caused irritation among those previously situated at a superior level. Even when the legal effects of lack of racial purity had been abolished, the accusations were still used as a weapon. Thus, in Tucumán, they were levelled against the Governor Heredia who, despite his belonging to one of the richest and most illustrious families of the province, was still called 'the Indian Heredia', whilst in Santiago del Estero in the 1870s the victims were those who replaced in power the Taboada family, whose African blood was denounced by the partisans of the recently deposed leaders.

In Colonial times, such accusations could still have legal effects, for even though the latter only very rarely took concrete form (the law behaved with its customary delay in resolving questions of 'noble' descent), they were supplemented by the resistance of the *gente decente*, which displayed an aggressive solidarity in the face of pressure from below. There are numerous examples of this: Mulatto girls from Córdoba being punished for wearing clothes too fine for those of their caste; another Mulatto girl who caused unrest in her convent in Buenos Aires, whose sisters in religion split into two groups, one of which wanted to keep her, while the other – on the grounds of her ethnic impurity which was, in any case, far from proved – wanted to expel her; and applicants for admission to the University of Córdoba being rejected for the same reason.[40]

In spite of this internal barrier, the solidarity of the *gente decente* was very marked in the Interior. Even those who only just belonged to the group displayed a solidarity with it which social resentment only interrupted, but never destroyed. The most illustrious of the offspring of this sector of impoverished *gente decente*, Sarmiento, who came from San Juan, was to display throughout his life, in the course of a career which was to lead to the Presidency of the new Republic, an ambiguous attitude towards this group to which he only half recognised himself as belonging. He was not ignorant of its defects, and he abominated it, but in spite of everything he still considered it to be the group destined to govern the province and the country as a whole.

Even leaving aside this poorer sector, the *gente decente* were hardly a homogeneous group. Closed though it was – at least in intention – to upward pressure from below, it was, however, very open to fresh influxes from Spaniards and even from foreigners, who automatically complied with the requirements of ethnic 'purity' and were, moreover, placed from the moment of their arrival above the destitute sector. This openness is worth emphasising; we have already observed how even in Salta – probably the region of the Interior where there was, from the seventeenth century onwards, the most powerful upper class – the composition of the latter was fundamentally altered in the second half of the following century by the massive incorporation of officials and merchants from Spain; and how even some of the merchants began their rise in Salta society as employees of the Royal administration. Even there, where the hegemony of the *gente decente* had a strong local economic basis, its dependence on the Viceregal economic system was evident. In other less prosperous regions of the Interior, the monopoly of public office played an even more important part in the maintenance of this hegemony. A necessary consequence of this was that the hegemony of the *gente decente*, in places where its local economic basis was weak, depended above all on the solidity of the administrative system inherited from Colonial times. It is not surprising that it was ill able to face the crisis provoked by the Revolution. Another consequence was that the dividing-line between the classes, superimposed on that constituted by ethnic differences, was determined less by wealth than by education. It is dangerous to apply to the Interior of Argentina in the first decades of Independence the interpretation, which was no doubt valid for nineteenth-century Europe, according to which the emphasis on keeping political power in the hands of the most educated really concealed the intention of preserving it for the rich. In that Interior region, where old-established wealth had been, from the beginning, very scarce, and where Revolution and free trade dealt a harsh blow to inherited economic structures, where newly-enriched sectors tended to be overwhelmingly rustic, where political power depended on military power and the latter was based on the rural militias, the supposed need for political life to be dominated by the most educated was really a new formulation of the claims of that group of *gente decente* whose hegemony had been assured since Colonial times by the existence of an administrative and ecclesiastical apparatus with bases wider than purely local ones, and which desired to return to that order once the Revolutionary turmoil had passed.

However, this divergence between inherited social hierarchies and the economic differences in force was only to become firmly established after the Revolution. Before 1810, even though it was not possible to identify absolutely the *gente decente* with the economically dominant sector, the latter played a predominant role within the former. Within this hegemonic group – a minority within the minority constituted by the *gente decente* – the local roots of power and those derived from links with the administrative and ecclesiastical apparatus were inter-connected to a degree that varied according to place and circumstances. We have observed above how in Salta – and similarly in Córdoba, where, however, the monopoly of public offices played a more decisive part – the power-basis of this sector was land (large landholdings throughout the Salta area and the big *estancias* of Northern Córdoba). In Cuyo and Tucumán, in addition to landowning, it was commercial wealth that was complemented by participation in local administrative power. The latter not only conferred prestige and set the visible seal of approval on the privileges accorded by wealth, but it also helped to multiply the latter. Corruption, aggravated by the difficulties inherent in controlling from so far away the functioning of the administrative apparatus, was no longer a facet of anecdotal history, and deserves consideration on other grounds than purely moral ones. It doubtless facilitated simultaneously the enrichment of the Spanish officials and their rapid incorporation into the locally dominant sectors, with which they no doubt entered immediately into a complex web of complicity.

For the leading local inhabitants, too, participation in the administrative apparatus offered advantages. When, from the end of the eighteenth century onwards, the Interior was infected by this same impatient attitude towards the acquisition of wealth which in the Littoral took the form of audacious commercial and speculative ventures, this aspiration was satisfied in a different way, which showed all too well to what extent the decisive factor in this area was participation in the political and administrative apparatus. The archives of the Consulado are full of evidence of this new attitude and its curious consequences, evidence often manifested in the complaints of the victims. There are several examples of this. In Salta an old and illustrious family, the Saravias, proposed to build a fountain for the city; this generous offer failed to conceal their ulterior motive – in exchange for the fountain they wanted the concession of a monopoly of the import of coca from Upper Peru. The merchants of Salta supported the application, and explicitly called attention to the social prestige of the petitioners. There was good reason for this support. At the time the import of coca was prohibited, and was carried on by smugglers of very low social status, who were unable to make their voice heard in the local committee of the Consulado.[41] In Tucumán two prosperous merchants, Huergo and Monteagudo, arranged with the Cabildo, over the members of which they had firm control, for the collection of the excise tax on imports of *aguardiente* from the Andean areas. The skilful manipulation of the advantages which this situation gave them *vis-à-vis* the other importers – in addition, if we are to judge from complaints, to an adequate amount of intimidation – allowed them to monopolise not only the import but also the sale of that spirit, by opening their own retail shop and ruining the small shopkeepers who were unable to compete with the people who were supposed to be their suppliers.[42] In San Juan, the methods employed by the *fiel ejecutor* (municipal inspector of weights and measures) Pedro del Carril were more openly expoliatory: he fixed at will fines on merchants who competed with him. Installed in his office in 1792, he bequeathed it in 1804 to his brother-in-law Francisco de la Rosa. The deputy of the Consulado, José Godoy Oro, was also his brother-in-law and, according to his adversaries, accorded him favourable treatment.[43]

Such incidents were nothing new in the history of Spanish America: the inventiveness displayed in increasing personal wealth by the abuse of a person's legal and social position was, from the earliest times, one of the most alarming characteristics of the hegemonic groups in that region. Also in accord with the traditional situation was the decisive importance which the utilisation of political power played in these schemes of rapid self-enrichment through methods more akin to rapine than to commercial speculation. These archaic patterns are a faithful reflection of the less dynamic character of the situation in the Interior at the turn of the century. In the Littoral region, on the other hand, even before the Revolution, economic innovations

The background

were beginning to transform, albeit slowly, the pattern of social relationships.

We have already pointed out one of the reasons why, in the Littoral, the division between Spaniards and half-castes did not have the importance that it retained in the Interior. In the former case, Spaniards formed the bulk of the population, there were scarcely any Indians, at least in the towns, and almost all the Negroes were marked off from the rest by the institution of slavery. Even though caste-differentiation was lacking – or was operating very deficiently – urban society in the Littoral differed less than might be supposed from that of the Interior. Here also, we find an upper sector of dignitaries and big merchants, closely linked together, and we also find intermediate sectors, also connected with administrative and commercial life, in a situation of dependence. Up to this point the model corresponds quite closely to that of several urban centres of the Interior. The difference begins to be perceptible – at least as regards the most important of the Littoral cities, Buenos Aires – owing to the numerical importance of this dependent sector, which was much greater than was usual in the Interior. A further difference, also perceptible above all in Buenos Aires, consisted of a numerically large independent intermediate sector composed of craftsmen. In this case, the difference was not merely one of proportionately greater numbers: the situation of this craft sector within urban society was also different to that prevailing in the Interior. In the latter area, only a minute fraction of the products of craft industries was destined for the local market. Their activities, orientated as they were towards a wider consumer market, not only were concentrated on a relatively small range of products, but also depended, to a greater degree than was the case in Buenos Aires, on the goodwill of the marketers. The latter, who controlled access to the remote markets, also made monetary advances which were indispensable for bridging the time-lag between production by the craftsman and purchase by the consumer. In both ways, the independence of this craft sector was seriously restricted. In Buenos Aires – thanks to the existence of a local market that was wider and had more differentiated needs – the craft sector was able to subsist by means of direct contact with the consumer public. Not only was this sector numerically larger than that of the Interior, but its independence was less illusory.

Moreover, the complexity of the upper sectors was in fact greater. Of course, commerce of an increasingly speculative nature as imposed by the situation in Buenos Aires required greater benevolence on the part of the political authorities. However, this benevolence, due in some cases to connections of very varied origin, and in others more directly purchased, did not mean that the links between the economically dominant sectors and the highly placed officials of the administration were as close as was the case in the cities of the Interior. As beneficiaries of the general policy of the

Crown from 1777 onwards, the Buenos Aires businessmen had less need than did those of the Interior of the influence which the direct exercise of political and administrative power afforded.

This upper commercial sector in Buenos Aires found ways to affirm its presence in another field which was also less dependent on the administrative structure. The sons of the rich merchants turned, with a frequency already noted by contemporary observers,[44] to the liberal professions, principally that of the law: at first remote Charcas and Santiago de Chile, and later Córdoba, which was nearer, were the educational centres for those sons who desired something more than the increase of inherited wealth. One of them, destined for subsequent fame, Manuel Belgrano, followed this typically Spanish-American course of study in Salamanca.

But a law degree did not attract only the sons of upper-class families; the intermediate groups, too, had similar aspirations, because it was a highly effective instrument of upward mobililty. In Buenos Aires in the last years of the Viceregal period, the possession of an academic degree had become perhaps the most indisputable sign of incorporation into the ruling class. A symptom of this esteem is the contemptuous manner in which a graduate born of a family of minor civil servants, Mariano Moreno, thought fit to express himself when referring to Bernardino Rivadavia, who was the son of one of the wealthiest men in Buenos Aires and who through his father's influence had already found a place among the dignitaries of the Cabildo, but who was not a 'doctor'.

Equally peculiar to Buenos Aires was the structure of the lower sectors: the proportion of slaves among those who devoted themselves to the activities typical of this sector was overwhelmingly high. The numerical importance of the slaves was also felt in the intermediate craft sector. It caused recurring crises in the organisation of the guilds, which even before the Revolution were beginning to decline in importance. The presence of this vast mass of slaves doubtless contributed to the preservation of a sector of poor and unemployed whites; this trait, which was common to the cities of the Littoral and those of the Interior, was perhaps more pronounced in the former. In spite of their having a more dynamic economic life, the cities of the Littoral in fact appear to have been less capable of guaranteeing work for all their population. In this area characterised by the predominance of cattle-raising the urban population was, in both relative and absolute terms, too large, and this widely recognised phenomenon was criticised by Argentine economists of the Enlightenment as a waste of the labour force and by equally perceptive Spanish observers as a potential danger to the Colonial political order.

In the Littoral – in contrast to what happened in the Interior – that part of the urban population which was not integrated into the new market economy did not manage to develop activities outside it. One searches in vain for a domestic weaving industry, for example. The unemployed masses

The background

consumed very little and produced nothing, which caused justified alarm, but proved difficult to remedy. In addition to the low prestige accorded to subordinate positions within a trade – because these were identified with slave-labour – there was the comparative easiness of life, which made it possible to subsist from hand to mouth if one renounced the satisfaction of needs other than elementary ones.

This abundance of unemployed poor – a characteristic of Buenos Aires and of almost all the urban centres of the Littoral – resulted in fairly widespread criminal activities, which it was always feared would get out of control in times of crisis. This fear of the urban masses, which were still unruly rather than downright rebellious, was the cause of several of the precautionary measures taken by the Cabildo. The masses were thus sharply distinguished from the *gente decente*, and this dividing-line was more important than that between those of European and those of Indian or African descent.

Although the caste system did not function perfectly in the Littoral, social differentiations were, however, less affected than one might expect by the incipient economic changes; urban society conserved definitely hierarchical characteristics. Here, as in the Interior, the new elements which were incorporated into the upper sectors usually came from outside, that is from Spain; economic and social ascent within the local structure was, however, extremely difficult. Moreover, even though these elements were, in the Littoral, more independent of the Viceregal administrative structure, their attitudes were basically conservative. Only a limited sector, as we have observed above, displayed innovatory tendencies, but this sector, the long-term weakness of which has already been noted, was also lacking in prestige, and for a good reason – it was too closely connected with a spirit of commercial adventurism which had already attracted to Buenos Aires more than one foreign merchant with a dubious past.

In the Littoral rural areas, on the other hand, the newly forming society was more influenced by economic innovations. Above all, the new cattle-raising zone bore the mark of this influence. In this zone the fundamental unit was the cattle-ranch, an entity incompatible with family structures of a solidity comparable to the European model or even to that prevailing in the Interior. The nucleus of workers on the ranch was overwhelmingly male, and it possessed little stability. Relations between the sexes bore the mark of this economic atmosphere; even an impious old bachelor like Don Félix de Azara felt moved to express his consternation at the prevailing promiscuity and the precocious and varied – though not always pleasant – experiences undergone by the few girls who grew up in this masculine atmosphere.[45]

Even less resistent than the family structure was the complex system of social differentiation which – in full force in the Interior – survived in the cities of the Littoral despite its lack of compatibility with a more modern economic system. Azara himself discovered, among the cattlemen of the

Pampas, a total indifference to ethnic variations which, whether they were real or purely nominal, formed the basis of social differentiation in the rest of the region. This was inevitable in a situation where quite often, in the absence of the boss, the highest authority on a cattle-ranch was exercised by a Mulatto or freed Negro foreman, and when the daughters of such a foreman, a stable inhabitant of the ranch, were sought after by the permanently employed peons with an earnestness provoked not only by the scarcity of women but by the social prestige of those particular women. But the cattle-ranch did not establish the only valid social hierarchy in that area of turbulent progress: marketing systems which frequently incorporated illicit commercial practices and even banditry gave rise to other still less institutionalised systems. Wealth and personal prestige outweighed considerations of lineage in that area which was at the same time the most modern and the most primitive in the River Plate region.

In comparison, the cereal-growing and small stock-raising zones appeared much more orderly and traditional. Agriculture in the Littoral derived originally from that of the Interior. The types of crop, and even the dimensions of the cultivated area, reflected in those vast unpopulated lands the model evolved in the small irrigated oases of the inland provinces. There were very good reasons for this: the first was the difficulty of fencing off agricultural land, and the even greater difficulty of defending it in any other way from the depredations of cattle; this made necessary a reduction in the extent of the cultivated area. The shortage of wage-labour influenced the system in the same direction. Its cost was high enough, and its productivity low enough, for landowners with the resources to buy slaves to prefer that method, even up to a few years before the Revolution; in such a situation, the only recourse for the small cereal-growers was to reduce the need for labour to the minimum by reducing the cultivated area.

Another factor which influenced them in this direction was the fact that the people concerned brought with them the experience of the system of agriculture prevailing in the oases of the Interior. The cereal-growing areas of rural Buenos Aires received a continuous flow of immigrants; as late as 1868 Bartolomé Mitre, addressing the settlers of Chivilcoy and conscious that he was saying something pleasing to their ears, was to evoke the memory of the first man to sow wheat in Buenos Aires province, saying that he was doubtless a 'poor man from Santiago'.[46] Nor did the newcomers find anything novel in their relationship with those who controlled the marketing of products: as in the Interior, the latter completely dominated the cereal-growing areas and the comparatively small stock-raising areas in rural Buenos Aires.

This hegemonic sector, therefore, not only exercised a stabilising influence in the economic sphere (here, as has been observed, its predominance was based on the existence of a comparatively stable consumer market, that of Buenos Aires). Its hegemony also contributed to lend society in these rural areas both a more urban and more traditional character than would have been expected. A sketchy but sufficiently clear picture of the upper strata of that society has been left by the Scotsman Alexander Gillespie, who – a prisoner since 1806 – was successively imprisoned in San Antonio and Salto de Areco, in the North-Western corner of Buenos Aires province. As an officer, he was accommodated in the better-off houses, and in San Antonio was quartered in that of a merchant and warehouse-owner. In Salto he was quartered in the house of the deputy *alcalde,* who owned a shop, and then in the house of another shopkeeper, this time a Portuguese. The description of the social relationships formed by Gillespie in the rural upper sectors was equally revealing: his most frequent contacts were with a prosperous miller and with another Portuguese merchant who had grown rich through somewhat dubious transactions with the Indians. This circle also included junior officials who used their position to obtain extra income by the regular practice of commerce, and also clergymen, some well educated and others who appeared less so.[47]

Here, as in the cities of the Littoral, social hierarchy did not correspond exactly to caste differences. They were, however, only slowly affected by the process of economic modernisation, the incidence of which was, in any case, very variable. On the contrary, its very persistence contributed to the restriction of that modernisation to superficial levels. Here, as in the Littoral cities, the crisis of the social order based on the hegemony of the mercantile groups was only to take place after the Revolution had consolidated the effects of free trade.

A social hierarchy based on castes in the Interior and a system of social stratification little affected by economic changes in the Littoral, except in the new stock-raising zone, appear, therefore, to define the entire panorama of the River Plate region. Is this a complete picture? At first sight, it does not appear to coincide very closely with observations which have been made with the object of identifying, in Colonial society, not only the tensions which would lead to the Revolutionary crisis, but also certain characteristics which anticipated, in that society, egalitarian tendencies proper to the future Republican order. And there is no doubt that those characteristics appear to be confirmed by particularly perceptive observers during the last years of the Colonial period. Azara insisted on the egalitarian sentiments in force among all the Whites of the River Plate area, sentiments which overrode economic differences, and emphasised the absence of a titled aristocracy, or even of a landowning class endowed with long-standing prestige and which would fulfil an analogous rôle. Such observations, which refer to the Littoral, and especially to the more recently populated zones, can, nevertheless, be compared with other comments made by Azara himself and showing the tensions created by a rigid system of inequality in a society which was at first sight egalitarian. There is no doubt that the newly

The River Plate at the beginning of the nineteenth century

settled cattle-raising areas displayed a more authentic equality than did the areas of earlier colonisation. In such places, of course, caste differences counted for nothing and economic differences were not yet sufficiently institutionalised and were extremely fluid. But not only was that zone relatively marginal, and not only did it contain only a small part of the population of the River Plate region, but also the equality which prevailed there was that of a pariah-class: all the inhabitants were universally despised by the inhabitants of areas with a more firmly consolidated social order. After the Revolution the image of the rural political leaders of the newly-settled cattle-raising areas of the Littoral disseminated by public opinion in Buenos Aires was to be an accurate reflection of the misgivings which they aroused. Artigas, son of a highly-placed official who owned lands and herds, was described as a bandit who enjoyed looting because he had nothing to lose; Ramírez from Entre Ríos, a landowner, son of a landowner and subsequently stepson of a prosperous merchant was, according to his enemies in Buenos Aires, a starveling ex-carpenter's mate who was trying to rise in the world. Such denigratory myths fully demonstrated the extent to which the social hierarchies improvised by wealth and power in the new cattle-raising zones, which were still comparatively accessible to those who knew how to take advantage of the opportunities afforded by new lands being opened up to exploitation, remained unrecognised by those who could appeal to older-established and deeper-rooted social superiority.

In the areas which had been colonised earlier, however, the social order was marked by the existence of inequalities which increased the existing tensions. In the last years of the colonial period, such tensions led to an impatience, also increasing in scale, with another system of differentiation which, even though it was not incorporated into a social structure universally esteemed to be valid, was beginning to acquire such weight that it was becoming unbearable. This was the line of demarcation between the European-born and the American-born. The former were often accused of monopolising administrative and ecclesiastical appointments, and of excluding those born in the country from access to the highest offices in the State.

Such accusations were to be made repeatedly by the leaders of the Revolution. It would, of course, be unwarranted to accept as irrefutable evidence their impassioned harangues against the Spaniards' greed for office. Even if the part played by Spaniards in administrative and ecclesiastical life in the Americas increased in the course of the eighteenth century, this rise was far from dramatic. However, it was precisely the importance of the Church and, above all, of the administrative bureaucracy, which had increased enormously in the course of that century. The reforms of Charles III had led to the creation of a real corps of government officials for the Americas, and within this corps, the part played by the Spanish-born – although to a lesser extent than Revolutionary propaganda suggested – was preponderant.

At the same time the economic resurgence of Spain – limited in extent, but nevertheless of real significance – had the effect overseas of establishing new and rapidly enriched commercial sectors, the interests of which were closely bound up with the maintenance of the Colonial connection and the members of which achieved economically dominant positions shortly after their arrival in the New World. Such positions, in several cases, were acquired and consolidated thanks to the help received from government officials who were also Spanish-born.

Here, then, were very good reasons why the local upper classes, the Creole clergy, and the lower-level officials who were recruited locally and found their opportunities of promotion blocked, united in an increasing hatred of the Spaniards. But this sentiment was too sparsely diffused, and affected too low a level of society, for it to be explained by the effective consequences of the privileges which were implicitly accorded to the European-born. It appears, rather, that other forms of tension, provoked by very varied situations, tended to find expression in the hatred of the Spaniards. This appeared, especially, to be increased by the resentment provoked by the scarcity of opportunities in Viceregal society for maintaining one's position or bettering oneself in the middle and upper sectors.

This society was linked to an economy which – except for certain sectors destined to a great expansion in the future, but for the moment still not dominant – was less renovated than one might have expected. Moreover, the system of caste differentiation obtaining in the Interior and the rigid social structure in the cities of the Littoral placed comparatively numerous groups at levels where they could not maintain their standard of living. The impoverished *gente decente* of the Interior, anxious not to lose, by intermarriage with the lower castes, the last vestiges of their superiority, and the poor freemen of the Littoral cities, hemmed in by competition from slave-labour, were the most obvious examples of a situation which recurred in a less evident way on the other internal frontiers of Viceregal society. And in the transition from one generation to the next the problem was to recur, in a more acute form. Not only did it affect those who were only just managing to maintain themselves at the lowest level of respectability, but also merchants who occupied the highest level in Buenos Aires society, with regard to their children. Such difficulties perhaps explain the marked predilection for a legal career and the distaste for other professions more closely dependent on official favour.

This hatred of the Spanish-born – whose presence was one of the most harshly felt consequences of colonialism – was, therefore, evinced by very extensive social sectors. It was felt with particular intensity at the lower levels, which did not possess that interest in the maintenance of the Colonial connection which would impel them to silence or at least moderate their resentment. Azara clearly saw it as dominant in those overnumerous marginal sectors which the Littoral cities contained. To find work for them, to overcome what Spanish observers saw as an inborn propensity to idleness,[48] was, therefore, essential in order to ensure their wavering loyalty. But it was precisely the Colonial system that was incapable of assigning to them precise functions, and in such conditions, enmity towards the Spanish-born, whose privileges were not officially consecrated by the social order universally esteemed as valid, persisted in full virulence.

The society of the River Plate area was, therefore, less transformed than might be supposed by the modernising impulses which were felt in its economy. Culture and the general way of life were even less affected: the rigid image which River Plate society maintained of itself was only one aspect of its adherence to a way of life that was still substantially Baroque. Even the new institutions created by the reforms of Charles III were imbued with this hierarchical concept of society, which was reflected in a rigid system of etiquette deliberately designed to emphasise that hierarchy. An example of this was the judicial demand formulated by the Intendant-Governor of Salta against certain officers, requiring them to present their respectful greetings to him every Sunday in what he called his palace. In giving his decision, the Viceroy, while reminding the Intendant that, after all, his Court at Salta was not that of Madrid, nevertheless advised the officers that, as an act of subordination that, while not obligatory, was certainly highly advisable, they should go and pay their respects weekly as demanded.[49] In this way the officials of enlightened despotism cheerfully lost themselves in a labyrinth of precedence, preferential placement in processions and ceremonies, and the right to wear embroidered clothing, all of which it would be wrong to consider as nonsensical, for if it were, it would hardly have been able to arouse such passions in men who were often intelligent and active. This labyrinth of ritual ceremonies was a late reflection of the Baroque taste for display, which was itself a consequence of a very well-defined image of the entire social universe.

Religious piety in the River Plate region remained completely faithful to this Baroque tradition, despite intensive participation by ecclesiastics in the renovatory trends of the Enlightenment. The Church played a very important part in local life. Of course, the expulsion of the Jesuits signified an important change in this situation; the consequences, however, are more easily observed by the historian at two centuries' remove than they were by contemporary witnesses. In spite of that event, the Church and the religious Orders were still powerful organisations. The Orders, owing to the avidity with which they established themselves in the vacuum left by the expelled Jesuits, managed to inherit a part, albeit a small one, of their power and prestige. It is, moreover, enough to recall the testimony of a most perceptive observer of Buenos Aires life in the first decade of the nineteenth century (who, having known it from inside, already observed it from the perspective afforded by the post-Revolutionary process of secularisation), to notice how the essentially ecclesiastical tone of public life as a whole remained unchanged up to the Revolution. *Fiestas* and processions continued to determine the annual rhythm of social life, and the election of superiors of convents excited the passions of entire quarters of the city. Even though a more peaceable ideal of piety had replaced the blood-spattered flagellants, the taste for sumptuous spectacles persisted intact, and girls dressed as angels, 'in the way that dancing-girls dress nowadays', walked through the streets in the processions, to the delight of their mothers, and families spent more than they could afford on such functions. Church ceremonies, too, were enriched by an imagination addicted to the ostentatious and the astonishing. False clouds of cotton and cloth opened to reveal to the faithful the living figure of an angel, draped in gauze and wearing filmy artificial wings, perilously suspended from the roof of the church. Such *coups de théâtre* were appreciated by a public accustomed to them, and the name of the ingenious and devout lady who devised them achieved a lasting celebrity.[50]

In such circumstances, only a strict adherence to the style of authoritarian devotion established by the Counter-Reformation can explain the fact that the Church supervised the observance of its devotions with a rigour which the enthusiasm, at once devout and profane, of its faithful made unnecessary. In any case, a discreet though complicated system of certificates and receipts made it possible to ensure that everybody fulfilled their Easter obligations.

In addition to this prestige, the Church possessed considerable economic and social power: rural properties – chiefly in the Interior, but also in Santa Fe and Buenos Aires – and urban and suburban estates which required large numbers of slaves for their upkeep (in the city of Córdoba the Orders were the biggest slave-owners) gave such ecclesiastical bodies an unquestioned importance within the Viceregal economic system. To this they also owed part of their social influence: around the convents there was a numerous plebeian clientèle, not necessarily destitute, but often in close touch with, or indeed immersed in, criminal activities. The possession by the Orders of legal immunities, which were nearly always only vaguely defined and occasioned endless disputes with the civil authorities, but guaranteed a relatively efficient protection *vis-à-vis* the latter, helped to maintain the cohesion of these groups.[51]

Thus, in this rigidly hierarchical society, the Church and the Orders ensured an unexpectedly close contact between the highest and lowest rungs of that hierarchy. This plebeian counterface of late Colonial River Plate society was also typically Baroque: the disorderly style of popular life and, chiefly, the insolence of the urban plebs were traits which the metropolis knew only too well and which in the cities of the Littoral were accentuated, because the extreme easiness of life made the lower classes less dependent on the more prosperous sectors, and allowed them a freer enjoyment of their situation as pariahs who accepted their destiny. It was among this motley unemployed crowd, among the women who did not, as did the women in the North, weave wool and cotton, but also lived on the streets, this horde of vagrants and itinerant vendors which pullulated in the dry moats of the fortress of Buenos Aires, that His Excellency the Viceroy tried as best he could to reproduce the style of the Court at Madrid. This surplus humanity, over-numerous and living in cities which were themselves too populous for their functions, caused justified alarm – as we have already observed – both to zealous officials of the Crown and to the earliest Argentine economists. But excessive urban concentration, which was in any case a characteristic of societies based on stock-raising, became in this Southerly corner of the globe a very Hispanic panorama of a ragged, carefree and cheerful multitude.

Thus, even in the Littoral cities most affected by economic renovation, the latter still appeared incapable of provoking far-reaching changes in society and the style of life. Nevertheless, economic factors did have an influence, albeit an imperceptible one, in these changes. It was the growth of ever-increasing economic opportunities, offered to a rural population incapable of growing at the same rate, which forced that population to expand increasingly in an excessively vast territory, which it was occupying increasingly sparsely. Sixty years before Sarmiento proposed the first classic formulation of the effects of the sparseness of the population on the River Plate way of life, the Bishop of Córdoba, San Alberto, reached conclusions which, in their essence, foreshadowed those of *Facundo*: the lack of population density was leading to a sort of breakdown of social bonds, the consequences of which alarmed him, especially in their political and religious aspects.[52] The Bishop of Córdoba was thinking above all of his own diocese, the rural population of which was denser than that of the Littoral. It was in the rural areas of the latter where the sparseness of population and the speed of economic progress combined to produce the most extreme effects.

We have observed above how these factors affected sexual customs in the stock-raising Littoral; in fact, the traditional Spanish family structure – and also that which prevailed in the Interior, of which we know very little – was impossible to maintain in those human groups gathered in so unstable a manner around the *estancia*. One consequence of this was the more masculine character of Littoral society compared to that of the Interior. Perhaps because of the Indian heritage, perpetuated owing to the participation of women in economically important activities, in agriculture and above all in domestic crafts, the life of the Interior had a more marked feminine influence than that of the capital. The War of Independence and the subsequent civil wars were to show examples of women commanding battalions and leading armies of peasants, even though they never became, on a permanent basis, provincial political leaders.[53] Such active participation in public life was a prolongation of their traditional rôle in economic life. A search of the notarial registers of that remote corner of Catamarca, Santa María, reveals that there ownership of land, especially among the poorest smallholders, was predominantly in female hands. As late as the mid-nineteenth century that excellent observer, Martin de Moussy, was to notice how, as he progressed towards the Interior, he increasingly found women serving in the shops. There was an evident progression from predominantly masculine Buenos Aires towards Santa Fe, Córdoba and Salta.

In the Littoral one finds nothing of this. There the women of the people did no spinning or weaving, and in the rural areas they were, moreover, extremely scarce. But this masculine predominance, connected on the one hand with a more assured incorporation into the market economy, which displaced craft activities destined for domestic consumption, and on the other hand with the grouping of the inhabitants in accordance with the immediate needs of the stock-raising economy, was perhaps the least important of the visible peculiarities of the Littoral, especially in the rural areas.

To an even greater extent than the family structure, the ecclesiastical structure was weakened by this territorial expansion taking place on an inadequate demographic base. It is true that the criticisms levelled at an ecclesiastical system that concentrated efforts in places where circumstances were easier but the needs less urgent, that is, around the Cathedrals and their dependent benefices, and in the urban convents, were a repetition in the River Plate area of similar criticisms frequently made in Spain. But in the Littoral the situation in this respect was particularly serious. Observers drew attention to the natural devoutness of the herdsmen of the Pampa, but emphasised that this survived independently of any ecclesiastical organisation, and that resentment was felt at this state of affairs.

This situation was destined to continue, despite the efforts of successive independent governments to extend the Church's activities in the rural areas. In that complex picture of the stock-raising society as it existed around 1870 which appears in *Martín Fierro*, whilst the State and its agents already dominate the scene with their sinister power, the ecclesiastics are entirely absent. Indeed only one churchman appears, mentioned indirectly and that, characteristically enough, by the Negro, who belonged to the group which in the stock-raising countryside had the closest contacts with urban life. We have here an extreme example of a situation which was already to be found at the time of the Conquest of America, and the significance of which during that initial period has been emphasised by Marcel Bataillon; the breakdown of Spanish social bonds which took place in America in the sixteenth century led to a diminution in the prestige of the collective beliefs prevalent in the conquering power, Spain, and reflected, for example, in the many instances of spontaneous atheism, uninfluenced by impious beliefs stemming from erudite sources, found in the records of the Inquisition.

But in the latter period the breakdown was much more serious, and the loss of a cultural tradition affected unexpectedly deep strata of human life. Azara has left us a particularly impressive picture of this life reduced to the most primitive and elemental level. This 'primitivism' of the Littoral stock-raising area was not – as pejorative interpretations tend to suggest – a relapse into barbarism: being the result of contact between a region exceptionally poor in human resources and an industrially and commercially developed Europe, the organisation of the stock-raising areas was – as we have seen – at the same time very primitive and very modern. There was, then, a lack in this area of that variegated wealth of popular culture which less hostile observers have learned to discover when examining situations described as barbarous. The primitive nature of the stock-raising areas was contemporaneous, and not merely by chance, with that which arose in the new industrial centres of Europe: a phenomenon which included, for example, an unexpectedly abstract conception of nature, structured according to economic criteria. Amado Alonso has found traces of this attitude in the language used in the more traditional stock-raising areas of Buenos Aires Province, around 1930. It also includes, as a consequence of the absence of an authentically vigorous popular culture, an extreme permeability to innovation. Again, the language conserves traces of this, and the observations of Alonso can be completed in this respect with retrospective testimonies that confirm them. This openness towards innovation doubtless explains in part the rapid politicisation of the Littoral stock-raising zone. The ease with which the people accepted the new image of themselves which the Revolution provided was doubtless connected, in the stock-raising areas of the Littoral, with the absence of a previously established and satisfactory one.

The Littoral stock-raising zone, therefore, offers us the most extreme example of the changes in the prevailing life-style imposed by economic modernisation, both directly and as a result of the redistribution of the population. But it would be unjustified to suppose that the situation in these areas was identical to that in the entire River Plate region. Despite favourable circumstances and the attraction of immigrants from areas of earlier settlement, only comparatively small groups of the population were incorporated into the stock-raising economy of the Littoral plain. It would be even more hazardous to interpret this differentiation, provoked by the devastating pressure of the new economy on traditional cultural patterns, as the point of departure of a divorce between the civilised city and the barbarous countryside – this is a particularly deplorable consequence of the identification of stock-raising life with primitive barbarism, first suggested by Sarmiento and still implicitly accepted today, with a mere change of evaluative terminology, by several of those who imagine they have rejected the heritage of his thought. On the contrary, the great landowners of the Pampa were destined to come from the city, where their wealth had originated before the expansion of stock-raising and had given them access to ownership of land; and even when they became assimilated to rural life, they did not for that reason cut off all their links with urban life. This relationship was all the more close in so far as the group of big landowners was open, and accepted a continuous influx of men who had recently acquired wealth in the city. This process, which has continued to the present day, acquired special intensity during the first three decades of the nineteenth century. And ownership of land, ownership of those centres of rural social life constituted by the *pulperías* [stores] (and which very often, though managed by a foreman, were the property of some big landowner) were phenomena that had effects beyond the field of strictly economic relationships.

Such interpenetration between sectors was accelerated by economic modernisation but it was, in fact, evident at an earlier date. In contrast to what might be supposed, judging from too rigid an image of traditional society, the very technical insufficiencies of the latter made necessary the existence of a vast itinerant population: the difficulty of moving things made it necessary to move people. Transport consumed much human effort. In Mendoza, at the beginning of the nineteenth century, the carters formed one-tenth of the population;[54] in other Andean areas, muleteers predominated. And the most varied trades were, surprisingly enough, affected by the need to make long journeys: the tanners of Tucumán went to buy their hides in the poorest lands of the Andean zone; the small-holders of San Juan – in accordance with a custom which Juan Antonio Carrizo found still being followed around 1930[55] – went to collect fertilizer for their lands from the sheep-folds of the La Rioja plains. And there were entire categories of employed people who had no fixed abode, such as the makers of adobe bricks, the builders of adobe walls and the cereal-harvesters. The expansion of stock-raising and the rise of the Littoral not only brought to the fore other itinerant trades, which soon acquired prestige – for example the breakers-in of horses, and the branders – and not only did it attract to the agricultural zone serving the steadily growing needs of Buenos Aires ever increasing numbers of temporary immigrants from Córdoba, Santiago and San Luis; it also inaugurated a flow, which was henceforth never to be interrupted, of permanent immigrants from the Interior, based on agriculture and craft industries, to the rising Littoral. Thus, the scarcity of manpower began to affect the Interior, and to be felt especially in all the localities where there was a degree of local expansion, for example in the case of the cattle-raising lands of the La Rioja plains settled by the father of Juan Facundo Quiroga, with men from San Juan, Córdoba and Catamarca. The hunger for manpower was not confined to the White territories: pagan Indians from the Chaco, incorporated only temporarily into

Spanish life, contributed to making possible the navigation of the Paraná, and sometimes, after serving the Christians for several years, they would take up again the spear that they had left stored when they entered the colonised lands, and would be reintegrated into their tribe. (Sometimes, more expeditiously, they returned to savage life by murdering the boatswain and disappearing with the cargo entrusted to their care).[56] In Salta, Jujuy and the settled lowlands right along the frontier line, Chiriguano and Chané Indians would come out of the Chaco jungle every year to work in the harvesting and milling of sugar, and when the work was over they would return to their homes, 'swollen with sugar like bees', as a French traveller described them a century and a half later.[57]

These Indians were pagans, and there were also pagan Indians, although in lesser numbers, on the *estancias* and even in the city of Buenos Aires. This situation reflected an abandonment of that evangelising mission which Spain had undertaken when she conquered America, and which scarcity of men had obliged her to carry on in a more gradual and peaceable manner. The most scandalous case was, without a doubt, that of the Payaguás established in Asunción. These fishermen and canoers from the Chaco, who were most useful for river navigation, had established themselves in the Paraguayan capital from 1740 onwards. Until 1790 they were not baptised, and in the meantime they celebrated annually a bloodthirsty orgy, the 'June *fiesta*', which drew fascinated spectators to see the naked and blood-spattered dancers.[58]

However, even though they were better utilised thanks to internal redistribution, human resources were still scarce. Moreover, this redistribution did not keep pace with the economic transformations. As late as 1810, the Interior still had a more numerous population than the rising Littoral. Data which it would be imprudent to use without taking into account that they are very approximate give, for the Interior in the 1770s, a total population of 200,000 inhabitants; that of the Littoral could be estimated as a little more than a quarter of this figure (37,000 for Buenos Aires and the surrounding rural area, and 5,000 and 6,000 for Corrientes and Santa Fe respectively). In the decades between this date and the Revolution, the rise of the Littoral was, of course, more rapid than that of the Interior; the urban population of Buenos Aires around 1810 was 40,000, and that of its surrounding countryside may be estimated as about the same. Even though Santa Fe had made little progress, the opening up of new lands had made its consequences felt in Entre Ríos, Corrientes and the Banda Oriental. For the region as a whole, the population could be estimated as 160,000. At the same time the population of the Interior had grown, in some cases – such as that of Córdoba – so rapidly that one is led to suspect that, in fact, the registers were being kept more accurately. It does not appear excessive to attribute to the whole region 300,000 inhabitants at the time of the Revolution.[59] Despite this increase in the Littoral, the scarcity of population was then making itself felt there more seriously than in the Interior. Despite the nature of this increase, certain differential traits of the ecological distribution in the Littoral were maintained, albeit in an attenuated form. The most important of these was the high proportion represented by the urban population. The persistence of this trait shows how the demographic progress of the Littoral region was connected with its new mercantile position as well as with the expansion of its stock-raising.

This increase in population, insufficient though it was, was made possible both by natural increase and by internal migration. There were also other factors: immigration from Spain and the importation of slaves.

Immigration – almost entirely spontaneous – no doubt contributed to the increase of population in the Littoral. Its influence is not easy to measure since, in the first place, a high proportion of the immigration was clandestine and, secondly, the registers did not usually distinguish, until after 1810, between Spaniards and the American-born. Impressionistic observations reveal not only Spanish immigration flowing towards the urban mercantile and bureaucratic sectors, but also another current, consisting of deserters and vagrants, which preferred to avoid the comparatively strict vigilance in the city, and was channelled towards the suburbs or the open country. It is not easy to estimate the size of this current, and furthermore, it was only an anticipation of another current destined to be maintained throughout the nineteenth century and to cause concern to the representatives of more than one country with active commerce in the River Plate region, formed as it was by deserting seamen of very varied origin. This current does not, however, appear to have had any considerable influence on the demographic growth of the province.

Of greater numerical importance was, undoubtedly, the introduction of slaves. This was the preferred solution in the late Colonial period to the problem created by scarcity of labour. It is usual to point out the reasons which, in the River Plate region, prevented the system of slavery from acquiring the magnitude and intensity which it reached in the plantation colonies. In this region, of course, there were no plantations, and slavery was more an urban than a rural phenomenon, and moreover, the type of activities in which the slaves were engaged in the cities made their masters less interested in the maintenance of the institution itself, which doubtless explains the frequency of manumissions.

These observations – which are mostly valid – should not, however, lead one to forget the importance of the entry of black slaves as a means of obtaining manpower which the sparse local population was unable to supply. In this respect, the River Plate region was still favoured, in that it constituted the point of entry for slaves for the entire Southern region of the Spanish Indies. There was an abundant supply of slaves from the beginning of the eighteenth century.

Indeed, the proportion of the coloureds within the population of Buenos Aires increased in the course of that century, from 16.5 per cent in 1744 to 25 per cent in 1778 and 30 per cent in 1807. In the rural areas the proportion of the coloured population was smaller. This is an additional proof of the concentration of liquid wealth in urban activities, for there is no doubt that – contrary to what is generally supposed – where it *was* used, slave manpower was efficient for rural work, especially in agriculture. However, the entry of slaves into the expanding Littoral in the eighteenth century still did not result in this region having a black proportion of the population comparable to that of certain zones of the Interior, where the entry of slaves had taken place during the previous century. In Tucumán, in 1776, the black population constituted 44 per cent of the total. In the Interior, however, a high proportion of the coloured inhabitants were emancipated. In Tucumán itself there were four free Negroes for every slave, and in Corrientes the proportion was similar. In Buenos Aires, on the other hand, there was, in 1810, only one free Negro for every ten slaves.

Therefore, although characterisations which are perhaps too rigid suggest that economic activities connected with slavery, both the traffic in slaves, and the large-scale use of slave labour, belonged to the more archaic sectors of the economy, there is no doubt that the impact of slave labour contributed to the weakening of the traditional order of things in the Littoral cities. Although domestic employment did not have any decisive influence in this respect, craft employment was, however, of importance: we have already observed how the free craft sector was ill able to resist competition from slave labour. It was, in the long run, the presence of these slaves – and of their politically influential masters – which was one of the important factors preventing the rise of a system of craft guilds in Buenos Aires and favouring the precocious triumph of industrial freedom.

River Plate society, therefore, reveals itself as being less affected by the renovating currents in the economy than is often supposed. Moreover, the renovating influence was nearly always destructive, and even the outline of a more modern ordering of society was still not apparent. Yet, at the same time, the traditional order was being threatened from all sides. Its trump card was still the maintenance of the Colonial pact. As long as that subsisted, the mercantile hegemony which was its local expression was also destined to survive. But the Revolution was to mean, among other things, the end of that Colonial pact and, in the longer term, the establishment of a new one, in which the relationships with the various metropolises were to take a different form. This essential fact would be sufficient to provoke a crisis in the social order inherited from the Colonial period. But this crisis was to be accelerated by other less predictable contributions made by the Revolution – in the course of forty years which were apparently devoid of major economic developments the mercantile hegemony was to be

The background

replaced by that of the landowners, the import of luxury goods by that of mass-produced consumer goods, and exports dominated by precious metals by other exports even more exclusively composed of livestock products. But this transformation could not take place without social changes, the first evident aspects of which were to be destructive. The first impact of the Revolution was to appear as a mutilation and an impoverishment of the economic and social order of the Colonial period.

2 REVOLUTION AND THE DISLOCATION OF THE ECONOMY

The Revolution was to bring, in the economic sphere too, the blessings of liberty. Even if its benefits had not been accompanied by unexpected drawbacks, and its application had been more continuous and well-intentioned, it is hard to see how the victory of economic liberalism could have sufficed to offset the prejudicial consequences which the same Revolutionary process involved. These consequences were, in the first place, the mutilation and fragmentation of the commercial hinterland of Buenos Aires, and secondly, the profound transformation of overseas trade, which henceforth was to be subject to British hegemony. One could cite as an additional factor the burden placed on a treasury already impoverished and subjected to further strains by the war, and the increasing burden which the financial needs of a state forced by circumstances into aggressive mendicity placed upon the entire economy.

THE MUTILATION AND FRAGMENTATION OF THE VICEREGAL ECONOMIC TERRITORY

The first effect of the Revolution was to mutilate the commercial hinterland which geography and Bourbon policy had created for Buenos Aires; from 1810 it lacked an essential part, Upper Peru, which was in Royalist hands until 1825, except for two brief periods, the first in 1810–11 and the second in 1814–15. This development closed the road to the North, which previously had survived the most varied changes of circumstances. The entire mercantile Interior, which had grown up around this route, immediately suffered the consequences. One eloquent example is that of a merchant of Jujuy, Don José de Rodrigo y Aldea, who set out in 1811 on one of the many trips he made to the Altiplano, taking with him merchandise from Tucumán, and bringing back cheap cloth. He was hit by the storm, and never returned to his native city. The brief notes in his accounts book[1] show him wandering through Upper Peru, fleeing for his life from the Patriot armies, and finally settling in the South of Chile, involved in the chancy business of supplying umbrellas to the Royalist troops. This was, undoubtedly, an exceptional case; but even those who remained on the Argentine side of the line of battle suffered severely as a consequence of the rupture, as is shown, for example, in the continuously decreasing figures for trade in overseas products recorded in the tax registers of Salta. This is one of the reasons why the Revolution and the war were received in the Northern cities with mixed feelings, especially among the well-to-do classes.

The rupture was not, of course, total: the Royalist authorities in Upper Peru – especially when they were represented by General Olañeta, who was related to the old families of Salta and anxious to make a fortune – was prepared to turn a blind eye to many activities. A persistent tradition in Salta asserts that the local resistance, too, derived part of its resources from the according of protection, in return for remuneration, to clandestine trade. As late as 1823 a by no means favourable witness, the future General Paz, gave, in his *Diarios de marcha*, a vivid picture of the merchant class of Tucumán, which was more anxious to gain the goodwill of the Royalist authorities of Upper Peru than to give expression to Patriotic fervour. Men were seen in the street loading a piano destined – there was no secret about it – for the wife of Olañeta. This was the tribute of a Tucumán merchant who hoped to acquire the discreet protection of the lady's powerful husband.[2] Moreover, behind the merchants were all the regional economic forces which hoped to salvage something of the links with Upper Peru: local governors thus tolerated trade with the enemy, and not merely out of venality or lack of patriotic spirit.

This trade reached a level sufficient to give new life to a route which previously had been little used, that of the Despoblados, which crossed Salta to the West of the traditional route. Paz himself was able to observe the increase in the commercial activity of the Catamarca villages in the initial stage of this route.[3] But this was, of course, not sufficient to palliate the consequences of the interruption of legitimate trade. Although it is impossible to measure the extent of clandestine trade, the consequences of that insufficiency are clearly perceptible, and not only in the sector most closely linked to the Upper Peru trade.

The first of these consequences was the scarcity of precious metals. Beyond the actual line of rupture, the crossing of which was hazardous, Potosí in its turn suffered the consequences of the war: in the fifteen years after 1810 the production of silver declined sharply; it recovered after 1825, but never reached the level of the last decades of the Colonial period.[4] The Interior, that zone of transition between the two poles of the late Colonial economy, became a cul-de-sac. Despite the low level of its consumption of overseas products (and, as we shall see shortly, the new style of commercial life tended to increase this consumption), it was enough to cause an outflow of precious metals, which was merely a continuation – with the source cut off – of the flow of precious metals which in late Colonial times had continuously taken place across the Interior. The lack of coinage led to an increased local demand for it, which explains the enthusiasm caused by the attempts at local minting in the Interior. In Mendoza, in 1823–24, a sort of mania overcame the owners of silver objects, who were anxious to send them to the recently founded mint.⁵ But this appreciation at the local level was a consequence of the rise in value of silver money in Buenos Aires; all the more so because, up to 1810, the chief dispatching port of the Spanish economy attracted currency. In the Interior, where currency was in short supply, the monetary adventures of the provincial governments not only raised the hopes of those who trustingly delivered to them their family silver. Even its worst coinage, which was quite obviously debased, circulated beyond the orbit of the political power which sponsored it. From the end of the first Revolutionary decade it was Salta coinage, 'Güemes's money', which invaded the entire North. When these crude discs with too high a copper content were withdrawn by order of the central government, they were to be found circulating from the plains of La Rioja as far as Santiago del Estero.⁶ The example of Güemes was to be followed by his rival in Tucumán, Aráoz; his 'federal pesetas', which had a quite evidently high copper content, also advanced triumphantly across that monetary desert. Everywhere they suffered discrimination – above all, the provincial treasuries were not prepared to accept them at their nominal value. But they were also imitated: Ibarra, the Governor of Santiago del Estero, waged an implacable war against the coinage of Tucumán, but once he had eliminated it from the province, he, too, founded a mint, which because of the scarcity of raw material used the sacred vessels from the Church of the Merced – here again, alloyed with copper. Moreover, the withdrawal of the rival coinage was carried out in a very curious way: the Cabildo of Santiago, when it discovered that it had an excess of Federal money in its treasury, did indeed decline – in accordance with the new prohibitions – to allow it to circulate again in the province, but made arrangements to sell it off *en bloc* to a merchant who was prepared to spend it in areas where it was still accepted.⁷ During the second decade after the Revolution, minting became more frequent. In Mendoza, where the mint produced money with a particularly low silver content, the government soon encountered the rivalry of a group of counterfeiters with solid roots in the local economy. But this mania for coining money gradually died out in the second half of the 1820s, when even the La Rioja mint, despite the fact that it enjoyed the advantages of a reliable source of silver, reduced its activities to a low level. The reason was that, from 1825, the Upper Peru route was again open. In the old Royalist stronghold, the victories of the Northern armies had established the Republic of Bolivia. For the Interior – except for interruptions which, even there, took place – the worst was over. After 1825, however, relations between Upper Peru and the rest of the old Vicegeral territory were not destined to be reconstructed along the lines inherited from the Colonial period: the Altiplano, like Chile, had escaped from the Atlantic orbit in which Bourbon policy had placed it, and while the Panama route was waiting to be revived, that of Cape Horn – the potential dangers of which for the hegemony of Buenos Aires had already been observed in pre-Revolutionary times – was used for overseas trade, and Valparaíso became the centre of British commerce in the South Pacific. The small ports of Southern Peru – especially Arica – became dependent on the economy of Chile, and through them the overseas trade of Bolivia was firmly directed towards the Pacific.

The Interior, then, was to become for Bolivia a supplier of livestock and certain other local products. It was no longer to be the intermediary between the Altiplano mining region and Buenos Aires, the port of entry for Spanish trade. The more perceptive Buenos Aires merchants realised only too well that it would not be possible for them to dominate again, from the Atlantic port, the area which had been a principal part of its zone of influence: in 1829, we find a powerful Buenos Aires commercial firm, that of Lezica, opening branches in Valparaíso and Arica. But this perhaps excessively bold measure meant competing, without the advantages of a firm local base, with the commercial network of Great Britain, which was directly connected with the new exporting centres. Upper Peru was lost for ever to the big merchants of Buenos Aires.

Moreover, the commercial rivalry of Valparaíso even threatened their predominance in less remote regions. At the end of the second decade after the Revolution, a merchant as prosperous as Miguel Burgoa – active from Mendoza and San Juan to Catamarca and Santiago del Estero – sold throughout those provinces British cloth purchased in Chile.[8] During the same period, in an Interior that was now ineluctably relegated to the sidelines by the reorientation of the commercial routes, a military commander on the Córdoba frontier, Manuel López, needing some medicine which he could not find in the chemists' shops of Córdoba, characteristically ordered it from Santiago rather than from Buenos Aires, although the latter was geographically closer. He asked his colleague in Mendoza to buy the article the other side of the Andes.[9] And in 1835 the danger of disintegration of the economic area already mutilated by the Revolutionary crisis was one of the reasons that persuaded Rosas to give some attention to the needs of the Interior provinces in the Customs Law for the 1836 fiscal year.

Finally an equilibrium was established, in the Interior provinces, between the rival influences of Valparaíso and Buenos Aires, until, in 1852, the Atlantic again became completely predominant. Meanwhile, these dangers of an increasing restriction of the commercial hinterland of Buenos Aires were accentuated by the fragmentation of this economic area. This was due not so much to any isolation of the Interior – which could be expected, on account of the fragility of its economy, of which monetary penury was only a symptom. On the contrary, despite all the difficulties, the Interior was unable to resist the pressure of imports accentuated by the renovation of commercial structures as a result of the Revolution. Economic fragmentation was more directly linked to political fragmentation, and only through the latter to other economic innovations. In this respect, too, even though we cannot say that politics altered the direction of economic processes, it at least appears to have determined the rhythm of their progress.

In the Revolutionary area there soon began to appear new centres of political power to rival that of Buenos Aires. The first decade of the Revolution was marked by rivalry between the Viceregal capital and the Littoral ruled by Artigas; the beginning of the second decade was characterised by an even more drastic fragmentation: neither Buenos Aires, conquered and humiliated, nor the Littoral, impoverished and deprived of its most resolute leaders and, moreover, rent by internal strife, could any longer maintain control over the Interior. Only after a complex cycle of civil wars could the hegemony of Buenos Aires be reaffirmed, from 1841 onwards, and even then it had still to encounter armed opposition.

In the meantime, political dissensions were inevitably accompanied by commercial consequences. Even when they were deprived of their alternative outlet of Montevideo, the Artigas-led territories of the Banda Oriental, Santa Fe, Entre Ríos and Corrientes attempted to eliminate Buenos Aires as an intermediary in their overseas trade, and thus the Federal provinces tried to strike at Buenos Aires by diminishing its commerce. Such measures were, of course, only partially effective, firstly because complete rupture with the Revolutionary metropolis was intermittent, and secondly because also the territories dominated by the Protector of the Free Peoples suffered severely as a consequence of the disruption of trade.[10]

In Santa Fe, the dissident movement led by Artigas began to have its effects on trade with the Interior. The weakened defences along the Indian frontier in Revolutionary times were to make dangerous two trade-routes which, in the last days of the Colonial period, had experienced an expansion of traffic: the Southern route which, running along the Southern Indian frontier, linked Buenos Aires directly with Cuyo, and the Porongas route which, passing dangerously close to the Chaco frontier, linked Santa Fe with Santiago del Estero. Almost all commercial traffic, therefore, was again concentrated on the Santa Fe – Córdoba route, which meant that political disturbances in that province or in Santa Fe, as soon as they reached sufficient intensity, completely isolated Buenos Aires from the Interior. Even in the first decade after the Revolution closures of the road would take place, and these would be repeated at regular intervals. A consequence was the accumulation of hundreds of wagons on each side of the Arroyo del Medio, awaiting a return, albeit a temporary one, of peace. This occurred in 1820, to the great alarm of the Governor, Bustos,[11] and it happened again in 1828–9, after Lavalle's rise to power in Buenos Aires. With more prudence, both Rosas and Paz preferred to avoid a commercial breakdown in 1830, and only in its later stages did the civil war between the Federal League and the Interior have this extreme consequence. But it

The background

happened again in 1835–6 (as a result of a rupture with the Reinafés, who held power in Córdoba and were responsible for the death of Quiroga), in 1838 (after a rupture with Cullen, who governed Santa Fe for a brief period), in 1840 and in 1842. These intermittent closures, however, had less effect than did other more lasting characteristics of the post-Revolutionary climate. The civil war was inevitably accompanied by a form of economy that was destructive, and based on rapine and looting. In later chapters we shall observe how this affected the life of the new nation as a whole. As regards the stability of the currents of trade, the consequences were particularly serious: merchants were obliged to cross those convulsed provinces with their tempting cargoes of goods and cash; they had to leave their goods in warehouses which constituted an exceptional concentration of booty for the soldiery; they were, therefore, the inevitable targets for looting. Hostile writers have lent immortality to the activities of Juan Facundo Quiroga during his repeated conquests of Tucumán. Even though, perhaps, such writers are guilty of an injustice in emphasising in such detail what was in a sense merely a professional habit, their allegations were not without foundation. Indeed, the merchants of the great Northern commercial centre, which had become the most important since the decline of the Upper Peru trade had led to the decline of Salta as a commercial centre, were obliged to face, to a greater extent than other local sectors, the harsh taxation imposed by their conqueror. The latter, eventually, was not satisfied with this and, quite uninhibitedly, commandeered the goods stored in the warehouses, and his partner Braulio Costa sold them in Buenos Aires. Even twenty years after the death of Quiroga, British merchants were still trying to claim compensation for goods which they had consigned to Tucumán in those turbulent days.[12] The mass lootings in Tucumán became particularly notorious because the wealth of the city made them especially profitable, but they were far from being exceptional. Quiroga himself, when he marched on San Juan to restore the unity of the faith, did so accompanied by an ominous train of empty wagons. On his return the wagons were full, even though the city had suffered the previous visit of Aldao from Mendoza, who had previously marched on San Juan to restore the hegemony of the enlightened party. The loss of their goods was not the worst that the merchants had to fear. Quiroga himself, in a moment of doubt as to his ability to crush his adversaries, thought it opportune to give some advice to his protégé, the merchant Miguel Burgoa: he would do well to leave Santiago del Estero as quickly as possible, rather than fall into the hands of the enemies of his party, who would probably not spare his life.[13]

But inter-regional commerce was not only affected by the blows directly struck against it: in regions undergoing such hazardous experiences, although it was not usually difficult to find vendors, for example, among landowners who were only too willing to sell their livestock quickly, before armed bands stole and slaughtered it, or even those very bands when, after satisfying their hunger, they found themselves with an unexpected booty of hides, it was not so easy to find purchasers. In Entre Ríos, in the abandoned and terror-stricken Gualeguay of 1816, Isidoro de Urquiza voiced his complaints as a frustrated salesman: 'My bones are aching from so much galloping to and fro'. But the impossibility of doing business was part of a general climate which the visitor readily observed. He too was affected by the uncertainty as to the future expressed by the cautious attitude of the inhabitants of Gualeguay: 'Every day I have the suspicion that something is in the wind', he wrote to his father, whom he supposed to be better informed, 'don't forget to send me some news'.[14]

These sensational incidents – avidly published in the factious versions of the competing parties, each of which visualised its rivals as hordes of bandits – are perhaps less interesting in themselves than as a symptom of an atmosphere which was destined to persist even in times of peace. For even then inter-regional rivalries persisted: in 1825 Catamarca was still at peace with La Rioja, even though its governing group abhorred the strong man of the Plains, Juan Facundo Quiroga. But even in peacetime inhabitants of Catamarca who were caught trying to emigrate clandestinely, attracted by the mining boom in La Rioja, were severely punished. The government did whatever it could to frustrate the economic progress of the neighbouring and rival province. In this dangerous game reprisals were only too easy, and financial measures complemented acts of violence; San Luis, through which passed the traffic destined to enrich Mendoza, considered itself prejudiced and found this an additional incentive to increase transport tariffs.[15]

The Revolution, therefore, multiplied the effects on internal trade provoked by geography and accentuated by the political organisation of the Colonial era. The difficulties of keeping the commercial routes open in that vast unpopulated area constituted by the River Plate region in Viceregal times were, undoubtedly, immense. The habitual activities of the winegrowers of San Juan included, for example, journeys of an almost heroic nature: they had to travel for forty days without water to reach Salta, passing through uninhabited country, and travelling to Potosí took even longer and was no less dangerous.[16] Numerous examples of this could be given; and it has already been pointed out that an unusually high proportion of human and economic resources was totally absorbed by the maintenance of the transport system. From the wagons which were incapable of surviving many journeys across the plains and had to be constantly replaced, to the mule-trains which needed quick replacements of the animals, despite the slowness of the entire rhythm of transport, everything contributed to making the maintenance of this internal traffic more costly. Moreover, the Colonial taxation system placed a heavy burden on transport and internal trade. Even though it is not necessary to take literally the allegations of interested parties, who saw in it the principal cause of their difficulties, its extent still cannot be ignored.

The background

Nevertheless, the situation in the Interior in the last years of the Colonial period was to be remembered with nostalgia in the epoch after Independence. To the difficulties already existing, the Revolution was to add the consequences of insecurity. The picture of a vast country spontaneously peaceable and orderly could be remembered with nostalgia, and contrasted with a situation full of hazards for those who dared to venture into those vast uninhabited territories, crossed by armed bands accustomed to commandeering and looting. This climate did, of course, offer new opportunities for audacity: merchants who, out of sheer boldness or counting on the protection of those holding local power, ventured into the temporarily isolated zones could make exceptional profits in a very short time. But the post-Revolutionary situation, which favoured these exceptional feats, at the same time made more difficult the maintenance of the inherited commercial structure, which was based on the utilisation, with high profit margins, of a system of transportation which was no doubt slow and costly, but was at the same time very reliable.

Behind this tendency towards looting, which took the form of sensational incidents and of others less newsworthy but much more frequent, was the chronic penury of the post-Revolutionary administration. It placed an increasingly heavy burden on the economy as a whole: the diminution of normal resources was influential in this respect, as were the fragmentation of political power between rival centres and the multiplication of the immediate financial requirements provoked by the Revolutionary war and then by the civil wars.

THE INCREASING BURDEN OF THE STATE

Even if other circumstances had remained unchanged, the economic separation of Upper Peru would have been enough to provoke a serious crisis in the finances of the ex-Viceroyalty. There was an anticipation of this event in the last year of the Colonial period: one of the reasons for the adoption of free trade in 1809 was the temporary suspension of shipments of precious metals from Upper Peru, provoked by the insurrections of that year, which caused a direct loss of revenues to the Viceregal treasury.

To this new problem free trade had provided a solution which was, of course, to have many side-effects, not all of them beneficial, but which nevertheless fulfilled its main purpose. From 1810 until 1930 customs duties were to provide the most reliable source of revenue for the new state, but these funds were insufficient, especially because war vastly increased the expenditure of the state. How was the war to be paid for? It was admitted from the first that the system of taxation, even if amplified, would not be enough: from 1810 onwards voluntary contributions began to play their part, at first a limited one. Such contributions were not necessarily in cash. The detailed lists of them show that, on the contrary, they took extremely

varied forms, and included cattle, horses, foodstuffs and slaves. However –
even discounting the gradual loss of their voluntary character – these forms
of contribution were of limited efficacy. Even though they increased in size
when a military campaign was being prepared, and took place chiefly in the
zones directly affected by the organisation of such a campaign, they had to
be supplemented by the monetary resources of the State, and the latter
could not be augmented through the taxation system. Or, rather, there was
no attempt made to augment them by this method. This fact, which was
known from the beginning, was interpreted by Emilio Hansen as a form of
self-defence on the part of that essentially commercial community constituted by Buenos Aires, which was responsible for the general direction of
the war.[17]

This interpretation is not entirely convincing: the burden which fell on
the Buenos Aires mercantile community was very heavy, even though it did
not primarily take the form of taxation. Moreover, there were objective
reasons for the inflexibility of the tax system. In a country where the
control exercised by the central power was becoming increasingly less
effective, the only accessible source of revenue continued to be overseas
trade, which was obligatorily channelled through the capital. There were
also very good reasons for the stability of the system of customs duties. The
very penury of the Treasury made impossible any reform that was too
ambitious and did not guarantee an immediate return. Moreover, it was
extremely dangerous, for both financial and political reasons, to offend the
sector which Revolutionary policy had made dominant in the Buenos Aires
market: the British merchants.

All this contributed to persuading the authorities, even when they were
trying to obtain additional monetary resources, to have recourse to extraordinary contributions rather than undertake any profound change in
the tax system. Indeed, the system of contributions made it possible to
impose the greatest sacrifices on the most vulnerable sectors within the
commercial class. Firstly there were the Spaniards, whom it soon appeared
justified to harass into gradual but inexorable ruin, and then the native-
born merchants. The system offered the same advantages in the rural
sectors: contributions were raised wherever they could be raised, with an
intensity that varied according to the needs of the moment.

These short-term advantages were offset by drawbacks in the longer term
which, though they were realised, were regarded as inevitable. The requirements of the State were met by the merchants; the intermediary was
the Consulado, the principal function of which soon came to be that of
collecting agent for the contributions. These began very early. In November 1811 the Government exacted, at one week's notice, a loan of
150,000 pesos at 5 per cent, promising that its reimbursement would be
effected 'with priority over all other liabilities'. The Consulado passed on
the same exaction to the merchants, giving two days' notice for payment. In

fact, however, the operation took longer, and on 18 December only 136,000 pesos had been collected. Finally the Consulado decided to make up the sum required from its own funds, and on 14 January 1812 paid this into the Treasury.[18] Four months later there was yet another extraordinary contribution, whereby merchants 'owning shops, including foreigners active in business and craftsmen who buy wholesale' had to pay 228,000 pesos per year. This new contribution, although extraordinary, was of a permanent nature.[19]

The Consulado found the task assigned to it embarrassing, and it tried to orientate its activities in such a way as to favour the native-born merchants. Very characteristically, it suggested that, bearing in mind 'the personal service being rendered by the sons of the nation because of the present events, and the merits they have accumulated', they should be dispensed from the extraordinary contribution. It did not succeed in this attempt, but it used to the same end its opportunities of distributing the burden of the new contribution within the merchant sector as a whole. Even though in that stronghold of local merchants formed by the Consulado there was a heartfelt dislike of the British, it was considered more prudent to harass the Spaniards, who were totally defenceless in the new political situation. The zeal to protect the group of native-born merchants was quite understandable. In May 1813 there was yet another extraordinary contribution – also destined to become permanent – of 100,000 pesos, levied on warehouse-owners, store-keepers, soap-manufacturers and makers of blocks of candle-grease.[20] In the same year the total quantity of the retail sales tax was fixed by edict at 20,000 pesos (previously it had been 8,200 pesos, and in the meantime commercial turnover had decreased). This increase in the old tariffs and the creation of new ones was accompanied by lesser contributions, exacted no less imperiously, though always described as loans, whenever the urgent requirements of the Treasury made them inevitable. Thus in December 1815 the Consulado was asked for an extraordinary loan of 10,000 pesos, 'with the object of purchasing the valuable armaments of war which had arrived at La Ensenada'.[21] In January 1816 there was another contribution of 200,000 pesos, from which the British, 'who have made advantageous offers to the State', were exempted.[22] The British mercantile sector, moreover, aspired to gain complete exemption from extraordinary contributions: in June it tried to gain exemption from the monthly dues fixed in 1814, much to the indignation of the Consulado, which foretold the progressive ruin of the native-born merchants.[23]

This resistance on the part of the Consulado was to find, in the early days of the Government of Pueyrredón, a fresh echo. The Supreme Director thought it possible – now that the war in Europe was at an end – to look for new openings which would put an end to the increasingly burdensome hegemony of the British. In October 1816 there was a new loan of 150,000 pesos, to which the British were also called upon to contribute: they were to hand over 40,000 pesos (the Spaniards, by now very impoverished, had to contribute 60,000 pesos, and the American-born 30,000 pesos). What was more important was that the increase in customs duties on imports fixed by the Directory's decree of 29 March appeared to obviate the need to have recourse to new extraordinary contributions: 'by this means', wrote the delighted Consulado, 'the Government has found means to defray the considerable expenditure occasioned by the support of the national cause without using the disagreeable methods which had been inevitable before'.[24] These duties, which were to be based on a merchant's turnover, would do away with the privileged situation enjoyed by the new British masters of the local market. But this happy prophecy proved ill-founded: in 1818 and 1819 the Directory was obliged, to an even greater extent than in previous years, to call for extraordinary contributions and loans, and once again – and more ostentatiously than on previous occasions – the British were to be protected from the impatience of an impoverished Treasury.

The increasing difficulties of the latter caused it to seek still further ways to raise revenue from the mercantile sector. In the first place, this sector was the principal recipient of the paper which, in the payments of the Revolutionary state, was replacing the increasingly scarce coinage.

Treasury bills and customs vouchers came to constitute supplementary media of payment to fulfil obligations to the suppliers of the State. They were only recognised at their face value by the State, and even then not for the payment of all obligations: the customs vouchers were honoured only by the Customs, and treasury bills were occasionally accepted in lieu of money for the payment of the forced loans. These papers, however, also circulated in wider sectors, where they were quoted at considerably below their face-value. Customs vouchers, for example, might be bought up from the unfortunate suppliers of the State, when they were in urgent need of ready cash, by other merchants who would present them to the Customs, which would accept them at their face-value. In this way, too, the rapacious penury of the Revolutionary state acted to the detriment of the traditional commercial sectors which were less well protected against it.

This situation was characteristic of the first decade after the Revolution. After that, the end of the financial effort necessitated by the war of independence and the relief brought about by the dissolution of the national State and the concentration of almost all its revenues in the Treasury of the new province of Buenos Aires liberated the merchants of the city from this intolerably heavy burden. Though of comparatively brief duration, the pressure which this sector had to suffer was particularly decisive because it made its impact in circumstances which made adaptation very difficult. In the Interior, on the other hand, the situation, which at first was perhaps less grave than in Buenos Aires, was destined to persist and become aggravated in the course of the second decade after the Revolution, and to continue, varying in intensity with the recrudescence of civil war, even in later times.

The background

The burden of the war of independence was felt in the Interior in a different way from that in which it affected Buenos Aires. We have observed above how it was above all the cattle-ranchers of the Northern and Andean provinces who constituted the chief and not always voluntary support of the war effort. This support was considerable. If we examine, through the wealth of documents contained in the Archive of Juan Facundo Quiroga, the significance of that continued tribute paid by a region still remote from the principal theatres of operations such as the plains of La Rioja in the first decade after the Revolution, we are able to realise the impact this must have made on the stock-raising economy. Quiroga – still just the son of a landed family, and completing the first stage of his training in the local militia – had as his chief task the rounding up of men and of cattle. The scarcity of the latter grew so serious that in 1819 slaughtering for commercial purposes was reduced by half, and even then the implacable pressure of the Revolutionary state showed no signs of waning; on the contrary, the exactions increased. In 1820, because militia commanders no longer dared to continue devastating their own areas of jurisdiction and made raids into those of their neighbours, conflicts arising out of such raids became ever more frequent.[25] This was not a purely local situation. In the same year (1819) local authorities which the citizens considered only too ready to fulfil the exactions of the central government, such as that of Córdoba, were obliged to inform San Martín that it was impossible to commandeer more horses from the Córdoba countryside: even that rich source seemed to have been exhausted, too.[26]

Yet these exactions, even though they might appear intolerable, were slight compared with those provoked by the civil war. While they were complying with the exactions of a remote central power, the local authorities looked after as best they could the interests of those they governed, and the picture of intolerable penury which they painted is not to be taken as literally true. The exactions of the civil war, on the other hand, were to be fulfilled more strictly, both because the adversary was considered a deserving victim of the extortion (and the change of tone in this respect is clearly perceptible in the documents of the Archive of Quiroga from 1820 onwards), and, above all, because the political disintegration had created provinces incapable of meeting their current requirements from their own fiscal resources, and even less capable of paying for the war with them.

The Littoral, under the leadership of Artigas, had already known this situation, which after the dissolution of the national state in 1820 was to prevail throughout the Interior. The new provinces, which were almost all established on the basis of Cabildos (town councils), inherited from the latter a typically municipal system of taxation, based on tariffs on trade and transport. These were, of course, increased after the Revolution, but their yield was still small. A province such as Córdoba, which had inherited from the Colonial order a relatively complex administrative and judicial organisation, that of the Intendancy of Córdoba, found it increasingly difficult to maintain it with local fiscal resources. Of course, the majority of the new provinces did not present, in this respect, such serious problems. This was the case because they had reduced their political and administrative machinery to the minimum. The greater part of their expenditure, even in peacetime, was military. Partly because peace between the provinces was always insecure, partly because internal order had to be rigorously maintained in order to avoid bankruptcy, partly, also, because the armed bodies inherited from the Revolutionary era, which were in more than one case the support of the local political set-up, though occasionally over-manned, had no intention of being disbanded, but on the contrary considered that they had the right to absorb the lion's share of the provincial revenues.

The consequences of this complex situation may be examined through one example which – precisely because it is an extreme case – is singularly glaring: that of Entre Ríos at the end of the second decade after the Revolution, as described in his correspondence with the Governor of Buenos Aires, Manuel Dorrego, by his capable agent Domingo de Oro. León Sola, the Governor of Entre Ríos, though disposed to follow the policy of Dorrego, needed in order to survive a monthly subsidy of 900 pesos. Without them 'the revolutions here would be endless'.[27] Sola was so desperate that he was prepared, in any case, to sign bills on the Buenos Aires government. He had already done so for 2,000 pesos, against the advice of the Buenos Aires agent. The latter advised Dorrego, anyway, to pay up: 'Unless he signed those bills the supplier of meat to the troops was not going to supply any more', in which case, the troops were threatening to indulge in an orgy of looting, and it would be 'uncontrolled vandalism'. Sola did not, however, survive the discontent of his militia. A revolution replaced him by Zapata, who hurried to satisfy the urgent needs of his armed supporters, by asking for a subsidy of 4,000 pesos from Buenos Aires. He could not raise this money from the merchants of Santa Fe, because the insolvency of the Entre Ríos treasury was too notorious. He had to succour his troops immediately, and was reluctant – as he decorously expressed it – to have recourse 'to a forced contribution which would be equivalent to looting'.[28] Oro left Entre Ríos, after complying with the requests of the new Governor.

The delegate from Buenos Aires understood only too well the vicious circle in which Entre Ríos found itself: it was that of poverty – private poverty in this province crossed and recrossed by the devastating machine of civil war, and public poverty which was a necessary consequence of the private kind. Revenues, which had been as high as 120,000 pesos per year, were now as little as 20,000 pesos – a poverty-stricken provincial state had become the perpetuating and multiplying agency of this very poverty.[29] Perhaps Oro should have been less surprised: even the Government of Buenos Aires, which still enjoyed a monopoly of the only source of revenue which was still giving a good yield, that of the Customs duties,

The background

proposed to reward Oro's efficient work in the Littoral, not with good money derived from those revenues, but with the hypothetical booty from the sack of the Brazilian territory of Misiones, from which Oro was, in anticipation, assigned 'one thousand head of cattle over two years' old'.[30]

This perpetual poverty of the Treasury led to an increasing aggressiveness in the search for the funds which were essential for the survival of the State. There began to appear an ever vaster blurred area between ordinary tax-gathering and plain and simple looting – and this was to remain a feature of provincial life. Forced loans and extraordinary contributions of men and livestock took place repeatedly. When Oro himself – despite his sensitivity to the sufferings of impoverished Entre Ríos – emphasised the violence employed by its government to wring out of the province support for the army that was fighting Brazil, his intention was to praise the serious manner in which that government was fulfilling its obligations.[31] Violence was, indeed, the inevitable accompaniment of this policy of expoliation. Even in peacetime provincial finances were, to judge from their objectives and the methods used to supply them, war finances, and war itself merely intensified these characteristics of an ambiguous peace. Exploitation based on violence was one of its inevitable concomitants. Doubtless years of military life, which in other respects was incredibly monotonous, gave the soldiers and the militia an appreciation of the liberation that looting brought from the servitude of daily life; looting was the dreadful *fiesta* of this way of life. But it would be as well not to exaggerate the importance of this propensity when one tries to understand the perpetuation of the phenomenon. Looting was, in any case, unpopular with its victims, and it did not affect only the few rich people – as might be supposed from an oversimplified picture. The horror of looting which the leaders of the rival factions displayed was sincere to the extent that it reflected a desire to avoid it as long as it was possible to find alternative methods of maintaining themselves. But such alternatives were not so easy to find. In 1829, when General Paz, who knew that his popularity was very shaky, wanted to advance through the Interior without having recourse to extortion to maintain his troops, he soon found it impossible to do so. His resources were, quite simply, insufficient to maintain his troops. From many experiences of this type, both in his own case and in that of others, that shining example of an honourable and disciplined military man derived a moral of disillusionment. We find it applied, in his Memoirs, to a remote incident, the rising of Borges in Santiago del Estero in 1815.

Encouraged to rise against the central authorities by the successes of Artigas and Güemes, Borges 'allowed to pass through without interference some treasure that was on its way to Buenos Aires and, what is more, he did not allow the filching of one sabre or one carbine, even though he was in sore need of both, from a wagon-train which was carrying a considerable shipment of arms for the Army'. The aristocratic colonel from Santiago did not want to be mistaken for a highway robber. The comment of Paz on such 'propriety of behaviour unbecoming to those peculiar circumstances' is unexpectedly contemptuous: even though 'it did credit to his sentiments, it is a classic proof of his incapacity as a military leader and his tendency to get himself into a dangerous situation without calculating how he was to get out of it'.[32]

Thus looting became a normal accompaniment of war, and it took, moreover, the most varied and ingenious forms. In cities that were about to fall, those who had anything to hide took hurried steps to hide it. In the orchards of Tucumán, San Juan and Mendoza, money and silverware were buried when the arrival of Quiroga was announced. Quiroga – a more decisive character than his rival Lamadrid, who in La Rioja wasted valuable time scouring the countryside in search of treasure supposedly buried by Quiroga – did not waste time in fruitless searches, but took hostages, condemned them to death, and fixed a high ransom price for each of them. Even Sarmiento's father, who was notoriously poor, was obliged to purchase his life for two thousand silver pesos during the occupation of San Juan by the men of La Rioja in 1829. Even those who unceasingly reproached Quiroga for his violent expoliations were forced to employ the same methods: in 1840 the Northern League rose against Rosas, chiefly as a belated protest at the anti-Bolivian policy which Rosas had pursued without regard for the immediate interests of the Northern provinces. This rising in favour of peace, prosperity and orderly commerce soon found itself without resources and issued paper-money to pay for the war against the much richer Buenos Aires. The method chosen was, no doubt, less openly brutal than that preferred by Quiroga, but here, too, violence eventually made its appearance. The inhabitants of the Northern provinces stolidly refused to accept this dubious paper-money, and the Tucumán government could find no milder way of imposing it than that of decreeing the death penalty for those who refused to accept it.[33]

Thus the civil war affected urban and liquid fortunes more directly than did the war of independence. But in addition to the lootings in the urban zones, memorable for certain newsworthy incidents which were repeatedly evoked by the victims concerned, the pressure on the livestock of the Interior was maintained and accentuated. The style of war which developed in the second and third decades after the Revolution, which made necessary the mustering of increasingly numerous bodies of armed men, made the problem of supplying rations and remounts to the troops particularly onerous. Even in Buenos Aires, with its exceptionally abundant resources, requisitioning was a normal procedure (according to the expert judgement of Rosas, these methods, even though inadvisable in the case of remounts, because they resulted in very inferior horses, could be employed to get ration beef).[34] The less prosperous provinces of the

Littoral and the Interior used this method more decidedly: the 'enemies of the system', according to a custom which seems to have begun in Salta, where the war of independence was at the same time a civil war, were the first victims, though not the last ones. By simply substituting open confiscation for the giving of receipts, which implied the recognition of a debt where there was no possibility of paying, it was possible to force all the landowners into supplying livestock free. Even in the first decade of the Revolution the cattle of the Littoral region suffered the consequences of civil war: Corrientes was devastated by the followers of Artigas recruited in the neighbouring territory of Misiones, while Entre Ríos suffered, from the Buenos Aires expeditions of 1814 and the Portuguese ones of 1818, damage the consequences of which would be felt throughout the second decade after the Revolution. Santa Fe was more methodically sacked and destroyed by the invaders from Buenos Aires. Local governors were scarcely less burdensome than conquerors from rival zones: for the last of his military exploits, the abortive incursion into Santa Fe, Francisco Ramírez in 1820 extracted from his exhausted province of Entre Ríos no less than 60,000 head of cattle.[35]

From 1820 onwards, the Interior was involved in this process: the invasions of Carrera and local raids in the rural areas of Córdoba in 1820–1, internal conflicts in Tucumán, Salta, La Rioja. The civil war of 1826–7 was to make its impact on a scene already impoverished by previous experiences. In the face of such penury, armies had to have recourse ever more openly to looting. Bustos, the Governor of Córdoba, was forced to admit to his ally Quiroga, who had become transformed, through his unexpected victories, from a protégé into the dominant partner, that he could no longer find in the provincial Treasury the money required of him. This did not matter: he was invited to round up such livestock as he thought necessary 'whoever may be the owner, if he enters this province, for in such cases there must be no respect for persons'.[36] Such an offer of the pillage of private wealth as an alternative to exacting contributions from an impoverished treasury is extremely characteristic. It not only reveals the extent to which such a solution had become customary (only thus can one explain the nonchalance with which the Governor envisages the prospect of the devastation of his province by his allies), but it also provides an opportune reminder that – whatever might have been the satisfaction afforded by this economy based on rapine and destruction to leaders and troops – its perpetuation was linked to the emptiness of the public purse. The civil war – an indirect response to a Revolution which was unwilling or unable to fulfil its promises – accentuated the very penury which was its cause. Fiscal rapacity, which in this period reached a frenzied intensity, was at the same time a means of pressure exercised by the administrative and, above all, by the military apparatus on economic structures which were too weak to offer it spontaneously the means of survival.

Revolution and the dislocation of the economy

The increasing cost of the State was a consequence of the fragmentation of the Viceregal area, which cut off Upper Peru, which had been so important for the public finances and for the economy of the River Plate region, and of political fragmentation, which stemmed from the establishment of civil war as a recurring trait of the post-Revolutionary situation. It was particularly burdensome because of the way in which it made itself felt: in a climate of factional struggles, marked by political tensions which, in moments of crisis, took the form of civil wars, the burden of this more costly state fell at very irregular intervals in time and, moreover, very unequally. These inequalities, however, did not have unfavourable consequences for everybody. It was at least possible to try to adapt oneself to the new climate, and to turn its dominant characteristics to advantage in the economic struggle. The increase in the cost of the State had an effect similar to that of other post-Revolutionary innovations: the process unleashed by them, the destructive aspect of which was from the outset the most obvious one, was nevertheless accompanied by the slow creation of a new equilibrium, whose main tendency was towards the transformation of commercial structures.

THE BREAKDOWN OF THE PRE-REVOLUTIONARY COMMERCIAL STRUCTURES

The Revolution led to both the disappearance of the commercial system that had matured during the Viceroyalty, when the connection with Upper Peru was of decisive importance, and the swift decline of the comparatively autonomous centre of overseas trade which the world crisis had allowed to form in Buenos Aires. From the end of 1809 the provisional commerce regulations recognised the existence of a new metropolis more capable of maintaining its hegemony than the Spanish one. Ten years later that hegemony had led to the establishment of a mercantile system as regular in its procedures, as accustomed to routines which were in the long run more profitable than any speculative adventures, as the old system which had been so harshly condemned by Argentine economists of the Enlightenment. The Liverpool route replaced that of Cádiz and, although the part played by the former in the international trade of the new country never reached the extent of the 'Cádiz monopoly', and was to decline after 1830, it was able to give a decisive bent to the economy of the River Plate. Before the consolidation of a new mercantile order the first decade after the Revolution was chiefly prolific in bankruptcies: those of many of the merchants connected with the Cádiz route, and those of nearly all the 'conquerors of new provinces' who had indulged since 1795 in the most reckless speculations, and even those of not a few of the British merchants to whose disruptive activities were attributed, not altogether without justification, the difficulties encountered by local trade.

The background

From 1806 – the date of the first British invasion – the British presence helped to accelerate the crisis of the commercial system. That abortive attempt at conquest had as a result not only booty in precious metals triumphantly exhibited in London but also a first attempt to open the local economy to a new economic metropolis. The attempt was too brief, and too much compromised by the context in which it took place – that of a military occupation which soon became unpopular and was incapable of working out a policy adequate to gain local support – and its consequences were limited. More serious, though less direct, were those of the second invasion: in Montevideo the British occupiers left behind an abundant booty, consisting of merchandise, chiefly textiles, which they had intended to sell in the territories which they hoped to conquer. The Viceregal authorities tried – all in vain – to prevent this merchandise circulating within the area of its jurisdiction. Even though the penalties decreed for offenders were stringent enough, British cloth provoked, even in remote areas, a fall in prices which the importers of Spanish cloth, which had become scarcer and dearer because of the isolation imposed by the war, considered to be catastrophic.[37] This experience, in the opinion of many, was a demonstration of what would happen if restrictions on overseas trade were abolished.

The abolition of the restrictions was not to be total. The provisional trade regulations tried to maintain those which were absolutely necessary to assure local merchants of their monopoly of the local trade, in which the foreigners were forbidden to participate. As soon as the regulations were put into force, even before the Revolution, it became obvious that in this respect their enforcement would be somewhat difficult. As early as 3 March 1810 the Consulado found cause to complain that 'the British merchants, without seeking a Spanish consignee, sell their goods quite openly, both wholesale and retail, just as they find convenient'.[38] The remedy proposed by this body, as the spokesman of local commerce, was always the same: the strict enforcement of the provisional regulations, without the granting of any new franchises to foreigners. In January of the same year it was the presence of some of these foreigners who 'taking advantage of the tolerance accorded to their residence in the capital had gone so far as to establish public factories for making tallow blocks, storage of hides and similar activities' which alarmed the Consulado: expulsion seemed to be the only adequate solution.[39] A month later it advised that permission should be denied to Patrick MacIntyre to open a general business agency, and in March it opposed the application made by the broker Francisco Díaz Arenas to open a public auction-room to sell goods imported by the British.[40] The Revolution was to have no effect on this attitude of the Consulate: on 5 July it reiterated the same point of view with regard to a similar application by the broker Julián Panelo.[41]

In the face of these demands, the Government was able to reaffirm, on

7 February 1812, the limitations placed on foreigners by the provisional regulations. Though reiterated, the regulations were not any more efficacious, and six months later they were to be repealed.[42] Resistance to the new commercial sector persisted, and in 1813 the Sovereign Assembly reintroduced the limitations established in 1809.[43] It was all in vain: the executive power forced the assembly to retrace its steps, emphasising the financial penury which would result from the elimination of the foreigners from the circuits of internal commerce. The Assembly yielded, and from the moment of that confession of impotence the Revolutionary power would never again attempt to protect the local merchants by placing limitations on the freedom of action of the foreigners (which in the first decade after the Revolution meant mainly the British). It would be wrong to conclude that the angry complaints of the Consulado fell on deaf ears; on the contrary, they reflected an increasingly stronger sentiment of hostility towards the British presence, which certainly extended beyond commercial circles. However, this sentiment was accompanied by the realisation of the weakness of the local financial and commercial structures in the face of the overwhelming impetus of the new overlords of the economy. For this very reason, it appeared to resign itself in advance to the impossibility of taking any active measures.

What were the causes and what were the consequences of this British victory? The first cause is quite obvious: Great Britain constituted, in the first decade after the Revolution, both the chief exporting centre and the chief consumer market for the overseas trade of the River Plate. Such a commercial relationship, where the dominant party was a mature economy such as the British one, inevitably led to a predominance in the transport and financing sectors of that overseas trade. From 1810 onwards, it was the British merchants who controlled access to world trade. The big local merchants were extremely ill prepared to defend themselves against their British competitors. Their superior position had derived, either from their good relations with the now displaced centre of Cádiz, or the swiftness with which they adapted themselves to the new mercantile situation caused by the power vacuum which the affirmation of the British commercial hegemony had brought to an end. As importers, their opportunities consisted of purchasing in Great Britain, or, if their resources were more limited, in Rio de Janeiro. In either case they were up against the competition of British merchants, who had in Britain efficient connections with industrialists searching for new markets, who were prepared to share part of the risk of their mercantile adventures. Similarly, in Rio the Buenos Aires merchants encountered the predominance of their rivals, whose overwhelming hegemony had been affirmed since 1808. Of course, some big businessmen of Buenos Aires took this new road: there is abundant evidence of this in the papers of Anchorena, whose firm established connections during the first and second decades after the Revolution with firms in Rio de Janeiro, and even extended its operations to Liverpool and London. However, despite Anchorena's solid financial basis, which made it possible for him to adapt more effectively than others to the new circumstances, the new mercantile system was less favourable to it than the previous one, and the severe competition from the British left a tenacious and bitter memory in that mercantile family which subsequently took to cattle-ranching.

As far as exports were concerned, the situation of the local merchants was even less favourable. During the Viceregal period the chief export had been precious metals. The most important Buenos Aires business houses were organised principally for that trade, and it is not surprising that their network of agents was spread chiefly across the Interior, Upper Peru and Chile. The Revolution did not, of course, abolish the exports of precious metals, but it was to make the livestock products of the Littoral the principal export. Adaptation to this new situation was not easy for merchants who had attained prosperity under the old system. What made it worse was that their British rivals, new to the market, were from the beginning organised with this predominance of livestock exports in mind.

In such circumstances, no legal prohibition would have been enough to maintain the British newcomers in the purely complementary rôle *vis-à-vis* the local merchants to which the Provisional Regulations assigned them. Legal prohibitions, when they were not systematically ignored, could, under the lax supervision of the authorities, be easily circumvented by the use of consignees who were only nominally independent of their British suppliers. However, when they had managed to entrench themselves in the circuits of local commerce, the transforming and destructive rôle of the British merchants was not concluded, but had, indeed, only begun. The detailed and reiterated complaints of the Consulado reveal the nature of the transformations provoked by them.

Such transformations tended to set up systems of internal commerce parallel to those already existing, and characterised by greater simplicity and lower costs. The mercantile system, as it had grown up in Viceregal times, was based above all on importing, and distribution in Buenos Aires took a different form from in the hinterland. In the capital the importing firms sold their goods for cash to the retailers; the agents in the Interior, however, usually purchased the goods on fixed-term credit.[44]

The innovation introduced by the British into urban commerce was the systematic use of sale by auction. The possibilities of its utilisation were limited by Spanish mercantile law, and still further limited by local practices. The new conquerors of the market took no notice of either: in March 1810 the Consulado was already expressing its alarm not only because the 'auctioneer-brokers assist the foreign supercargoes in retail sales', but above all because of 'the innovation...of opening public auction-houses for the sale of large quantities of goods in small lots', which, besides being prohibited, would be 'greatly harmful to the interests of the Spanish merchants, because...their shops would lose all their custom'.⁴⁵ In other words, the practice of auctioning was dangerous because it would allow the small shopkeepers to bypass their usual suppliers. And it would be to their advantage to do so – the arguments of the Consulado, according to which, in the excitement of the auction, people would pay higher prices than usual, are not convincing. The struggle against the spread of the practice of auctioneering was continued, with more obstinacy than success, by the Consulado. In 1812, in the case of a sale to be carried out by Robert Billinghurst in the house of José Matías Gutiérrez, the Consulado insisted that such sales should only take place in the official auction-rooms, and not in the private houses of merchants.⁴⁶ It is enough, however, to look through the advertisements in the newspapers of the second decade after the Revolution to realise to what extent the auction had become part of the mercantile customs of Buenos Aires. Through its establishment, the British merchants managed to make rapid and direct contact with local businesses, substituting their hegemony for that of the great importing firms of Viceregal times.

Of relatively greater importance were the changes introduced by them into the commerce of Buenos Aires's zone of influence. The latter, in fact, had witnessed the greatest degree of development of that mercantile system based on high marketing costs, which often concealed those of usury, and which had given Buenos Aires its predominance over the Viceregal economic area. That system, however, which presupposed, and at the same time perpetuated, the lack of specie in that zone of influence, and maintained the latter in the position of a perpetual debtor *vis-à-vis* its mercantile metropolis, was particularly vulnerable to the style of commerce introduced by the British. The network of agents, consignees and subsidiaries supported by capital originating from the great commercial houses of Buenos Aires required, in order to maintain its solidity, both tranquillity in the Interior, which was increasingly rare after 1810, and the maintenance of that monetary penury which had been responsible for the establishment and perpetuation of the system.

The post-Revolutionary political situation favoured a less regular style of commerce, based on a less complex marketing apparatus. And there is no doubt that, as soon as they appeared on the River Plate scene, the British proved more capable of adapting themselves to these new demands. As early as 1811–12 their presence was denounced to the Buenos Aires Consulado by its alarmed deputies in Mendoza, Córdoba and Santa Fe.⁴⁷ Such a presence not only implied a violation of the terms of the Provisional Regulations; it also meant an important innovation with regard to traditional mercantile practices. Now the importer was no longer making his presence felt in the Interior through agents closely tied to him, above all by heavy debts; at the head of the wagon-trains, he himself became a transporter and vendor in the secondary centres of the Buenos Aires mercantile area. In the long run, this new style of commerce could not be efficient. When the regular currents of traffic began again, it again became advantageous to administer from Buenos Aires a complicated and costly system of marketing. But in the short term this more dynamic mercantile style tended to multiply the disruptive effects on the pre-Revolutionary commercial structures of the new situation created by the Revolution.

An even greater disruptive effect was caused by another innovation introduced by the British into internal trade: the systematic use of cash in transactions. In producing zones chronically short of specie, payment in cash ensured the possibility of purchasing at very low prices, and above all, it made it possible to make direct contact with local producers and small distributors, evading the obstacles created by the traditional marketing mechanisms; even though, in the monopolistic situation which the latter enjoyed before 1810, their apparent defects – their irrational organisation and consequent high costs – could be turned to advantage by those who dominated them, with the appearance of a rival sector more willing to take risks these strengths were transformed into weaknesses.

This was particularly true in the Littoral stock-raising sector, over which, even in Viceregal times, the predominance of the mercantile sector had been less absolute than in the Interior–Upper Peru complex. In the Littoral even the merchants of Buenos Aires noticed the advantages that could accrue from evasion of the legal courses of trade. It was, above all, the newest cattle-raising zones that showed in many places the traces of this attitude. Big businessmen from Buenos Aires or Montevideo, dispensing with the help of local merchants, took their boats up the rivers, encouraged the shipments of hides that were often stolen, and thus helped to maintain in being an entire economic sphere which was illegal but no less vigorous for that, as, for example, in the South of Corrientes and the North of the Banda Oriental.[48]

Yet these activities were, economically as well as legally, marginal. The British newcomers were to extend them more systematically: both their opportunities and their needs impelled them in this direction.

Firstly, their opportunities: although the commercial conquest of the River Plate basin was an enterprise undertaken by the British with limited resources, they were able to dedicate them totally to this adventure, and they formed, in the first decade after the Revolution, a monetary *masse de manoeuvre* in constant circulation. Secondly, their needs: in the first phase of their activity the British merchants established in the River Plate region had very little autonomy *vis-à-vis* the exporters and shippers of Great Britain. It was the schedule of arrival and departure of the ships which, to a great extent, regulated their transactions: every ship had to leave port having exchanged its cargo for products and cash, without leaving any credits or debits outstanding. Of course, the consignee established in the River Plate region did not have to regulate his own transactions according to such a rigid system, but he could not depart from it too far without imprudently risking his capital and credit. His activity was seen, not so much as an integrated activity within a stable commercial system, and destined therefore to continue indefinitely, but as a speculative enterprise which had to make a profit in a relatively brief space of time.

This new commercial style soon gave the British a particularly solid predominance in the marketing of the Littoral's livestock products. As early as 1815 the Consulado reported that British subjects had warehouses, tallow factories and ranches, and no less than twenty small vessels to bring from the Banda Oriental the livestock products purchased from the *estancias*.[49]

This was the impressive result of a singularly audacious commercial policy. This policy – the side-effects of which, with regard to the trade in produce, have been noted – derived, above all, from the need for expansion of Britain's export trade. It is a well-known fact that, in the face of the commercial isolation of Europe, overseas markets were sought with increasing urgency by a Great Britain deluged by an oversupply of industrial goods of the most varied nature. It is also necessary to remember that the end of Napoleon's Empire did not immediately bring about the end of this situation. Continental Europe, devastated by the war, and in almost its entirety suffering the consequences of the elimination of Napoleonic protectionism, turned out to have an unexpectedly low capacity of consumption: the European crisis of 1817 was, without a doubt, a consequence of this situation. Even after 1815, therefore, the River Plate was still of interest to the new economic metropolis, above all as a market for surplus products of a very varied nature. It is significant that until 1820 the port with which Buenos Aires had most trade was London, which did not serve any industrial zone in particular, but was the most important mercantile centre of Britain. After that date, it was also to be significant that London was replaced by Liverpool, the textile port.[50]

Before 1820 British commerce in the River Plate area was an adventure partly inspired by desperation. The merchants of London and the capitalists who were behind these merchant venturers typical of the first decade after the Revolution were prepared to run great and continual risks. Characteristic of this stage is, for example, the adventure of Samuel Haigh. This young man of twenty-two was invited by a rich relation to go in 1817 to Chile, which had just been liberated by San Martín, with a shipment dispatched by that relation and two other partners in order to take advantage of the 'cream of the market' which had for so long been isolated.[51] Speed and secrecy were essential, for not only were the capitalists anxious to conceal their participation in an enterprise that was not devoid of risk, but they were also anxious that excessive dissemination of the news should not encourage the appearance of competitors. More complex, but basically similar, was the better-known case of the Robertson brothers. Behind them was their protector, Mr Parish, who lived in Bath as a rentier, in lordly style. But there were also businessmen in Liverpool, and Glasgow and Lancashire industrialists, prepared to produce cloth to the specifications of the two enterprising brothers and deliver valuable shipments on consignment. On this complex financial basis, the Robertsons made constant attempts to enlarge the scope of their activities, adopting a very agile commercial policy. In the early years they travelled through the countries in the throes of revolution, taking advantage of the opportunities offered by local situations of abundance or scarcity: from Buenos Aires to Santa Fe, La Bajada, Corrientes and Asunción, using the Paraná route, they made their appearance in the provinces convulsed by war. From Santa Fe, isolated for a long time by the Royalist control of the rivers, they brought a shipment of produce and sold it at a profit in Buenos Aires. With the proceeds they bought textiles, gun-powder and arms which they intended to take to Paraguay. Artigas frustrated that attempt, but they reached a close understanding with the Protector of the Free Peoples. In Corrientes they made incursions into a countryside isolated by fear of Artigas's bands and extracted a rich booty in hides. Even when, later on, they adopted a more sedentary style of life, the firms they founded lasted only for a short time: John, established in Liverpool for three years (1817–20), decided to close down his business after an hour's conversation with his brother, who had just returned from Buenos Aires: he went off to Chile to seek his fortune in the wake of San Martín, who had set off on the conquest of Lima.

This adventurous phase ended around 1820. It left a legacy, the full details of which cannot be found in the prolix lamentations of the Buenos Aires Consulado. The latter was, in fact, the spokesman of the local merchants. For this very reason, whereas it paid great attention to the prejudicial effects on this sector provoked by the activities of its most powerful competitors, it was much less interested in the effects of these on the economy in general. Thus, so important an aspect of the new situation as the rise in imports was relegated to second place. For example, although the Consulado did not fail to emphasise the ill effects of the new system on the craft sector, nevertheless, when they proposed solutions they omitted to establish any causal connection between these events and the influx of products from industrial Britain, preferring to attribute them to certain sharp commercial practices of their rivals. It is not difficult to understand this attitude. Nothing was further from the intentions of these merchants than the diminution of the intensity of the overseas trade of the new nation; their ambition was to obtain a less meagre share of its profits.

This increase in imports was, however, perhaps the most important innovation introduced into the international trade of the River Plate region during the first decade after the Revolution. What made it even more important was the fact that it was accompanied by a change in the nature of those imports. Textile goods for popular consumption began to appear on the market, and these were destined to dominate the import trade of the

River Plate region until the later years of the nineteenth century. Before the Revolution imported textiles were of high quality, mainly woollen cloths and silks. In the fifteen years before 1810 there took place an innovation which was obviously very important: the appearance of medium-quality textile goods, which were imitations of the more costly ones, and together with them millinery products of comparatively low price, but even so not destined for popular consumption. This innovation – sustained above all by the German textile industry – was destined to last but, nevertheless, the innovations brought about by the Revolution relegated it to second place. With the Revolution an increasing influx of calico began to inundate the country, a process that was to be accentuated between 1820 and 1850. This invasion of Lancashire cotton cloth was made possible by the fact that in the first decade after the Revolution the way lay open for it. In 1814 Argentina was already importing from Great Britain three million yards of calico and muslin, even if these imports were to become very much greater; already at that date cheap cloth had won its victory.[52]

It won this victory so easily partly because, contrary to what might be supposed by the facile application of certain theories, it did not need – at least in the Littoral – to incorporate that entire economic sector into the market economy. On the contrary, British textiles did not replace in this area the cloths woven by the women at home, but it replaced the Peruvian cloths, from which, as we have observed, all the poorer sectors of the Littoral made their clothing. And the latter began to become scarce precisely after 1810. The isolation of Upper and Lower Peru cleared the field for the importers of British textiles, at the most opportune moment, of dangerous rivals. But it is obvious that British cotton cloth did more than replace native *tucuyo* and linen: it advanced, both in quantity of sales and in intensity of consumption, at a speed unknown in Colonial times. The three million yards imported from Britain in 1814 grew to over fifteen million in 1824, and to over twenty million in 1834, by which date, in any case, Britain had ceased to be the only supplier of cheap cloth. This progress was facilitated by the commercial style introduced by the British in the first decade after the Revolution. By often selling off surplus stocks at sale prices, they accustomed even the poorest to purchase from them. The introduction of metal coinage into commercial transactions had consequences tending in the same direction, since it created new sectors with purchasing power. The post-Revolutionary situation gave an additional impetus to these changes. Whereas, at first, it prejudiced the sectors which had been most prosperous during the period of the Viceroyalty, the merchants and officials, it appears, however, to have improved the situation of the popular sectors. By withdrawing from the labour market, by military recruitment, an ever increasing proportion of the available labour force, it caused a rise in wages, especially urban wages, which was soon regarded as scandalous.

The background

However, the textile consumption of the middle and upper sectors was also modified during this new phase. Impoverishment brought cheaper textiles into favour, and moreover, after the Revolution, the population of Buenos Aires followed the trend of fashion more closely. The preference for lower quality, but showy, textiles, was bitterly represented by French commercial agents as the basic reason for the lack of success of their country's products, 'too good for a public that judged only by appearances'.[53]

With regard to textiles, therefore, the conquest of the Littoral urban sector was extremely rapid. In the countryside the process was, apparently, slower. Although, for any date from 1807 onwards, we find impressionistic evidence of the area being inundated with British products, the very detailed descriptions of convicts sent from the rural areas of Buenos Aires to the capital in the years 1830–50 are far from suggesting so clear a picture.[54] No doubt British-made ponchos were increasingly abundant despite the protectionist legislation of 1835, but in addition to them one still finds woollen ponchos from the Interior and the Pampas; nor does the predominance of English coarse frieze in the remainder of the clothing worn appear very evident. It is difficult to provide, on the basis of this abundant but incomplete material, a quantified picture of the process. It appears, however, undeniable that in this field the local craft products were better able to defend themselves. The reasons were complex: on the one hand, fashion was less important than in the city, and on the other hand local production was never entirely halted as a result of war.

With regard to the Interior, here even in Colonial times the upper classes used textiles imported from overseas, and only during periods of isolation could local production aspire to replace them briefly. The popular sectors used local or Peruvian textiles, but in any case, a high proportion of local production was outside the market economy. Here the Revolution introduced changes which were less far-reaching and, above all, slower. There is no doubt that British textiles tended to replace Spanish ones completely among the urban upper class. The pictures of them dressed in locally-produced cloth are excessively retrospective. Sarmiento in 1851 placed that lost golden age around the beginning of the nineteenth century,[55] and V. F. López, writing in 1873, thought it was still flourishing around 1840.[56] Among the popular sectors, the adoption of cheap cloth from overseas was a slower process. As late as 1824 British merchants observed that the consumer market for their imports was concentrated in Buenos Aires and the immediately surrounding countryside.[57] Around the middle of the century, the proportion of such imports absorbed by the remaining provinces has been the subject of extremely discrepant estimates, none of which, however, places it at lower than sixty per cent of the total.[58] Even then the growing consumption of imported textiles does not seem to have struck a decisive blow at local craft production, for the 1869

Revolution and the dislocation of the economy

Census was able to demonstrate, in the occupational structure of the Northern and Central provinces, the part which domestic textile production still played in their economy.

The consequences of this influx of overseas textiles were, then, less seriously and immediately ruinous for the local textile craft industry than is commonly supposed. Of course, within the general situations described above, it is necessary to point out significant variations. Thus, cotton production in Catamarca suffered a catastrophic decline after 1810, whereas in the same region, production of woollen cloths maintained a vitality still noticed by a none too optimistic observer in the 1870s.[59] These phenomena, however, were not enough to affect the general picture; a craft industry, no longer very vigorous, survived after 1810, slowly declining for three-quarters of a century, and it was, in fact, the railway that finally killed it. Perhaps it would not be necessary to reiterate these conclusions, were it not for the fact that, at least as regards the rhythm of the process of decline, they differ from an interpretation of the process which tends to be voiced with increasing frequency: that which envisages it as a sudden catastrophe which not only impoverished an enormous craft sector, but also frustrated a potential industrial development which the overwhelming overseas competition suddenly made unthinkable. Presented in this form, such an interpretation is unfounded. Perhaps its principal fault, however, is that it limits the scope of the problem: the most important consequence of the new pressure caused by imports, which manifested itself most significantly in the field of textiles, was, not so much the direct frustration of certain possibilities of internal industrial expansion through inability to compete with increased imports, as the acceleration and aggravation of a lack of equilibrium in the balance of trade which would in any case have been provoked by the disappearance of the principal export item of the Viceregal period.

This very imbalance, however, tended to frustrate any diversification of production. As a result of it, the pressure caused by imports was accompanied by a growing interest in increasing exports of goods to replace those of precious metals, and only livestock products could fulfil this function for any length of time. Thus, the growth of pressure caused by imports was connected with the accentuation of the trend of the local economy towards stock-raising and exporting. This import pressure, the most obvious manifestation of which took place in the field of textiles, also extended to other sectors, not all of them industrial ones.

Indeed, the predominantly British origin of industrial imports was duplicated by a predominance in the commercial structures which made itself felt – at least during the first post-Revolutionary phase – in the imports of mediterranean and tropical agricultural produce. The isolation of the zone served by the route of the River Paraná (due, up to 1814, to Royalist incursions, and then maintained intermittently by the followers of

Artigas) made possible the partial substitution of its imports by rival products from Brazil, for example tobacco and *yerba mate*. To these was added the importation of Brazilian sugar, which had already taken place in the years of the Viceroyalty, and of coffee, which expanded with the consumption of this beverage after the Revolution. This process of substitution was facilitated by the liberalisation of internal trade and production: the most noteworthy event of this process was the suppression of the tobacco monopoly, which seems to have been known beforehand by the British merchants established in Buenos Aires.

A similar process took place in the case of the imports from the Mediterranean zone, wine and oil, and to a lesser extent wheat and flour. Even before the Revolution the isolation from Spain had led to the disappearance of these imports from the River Plate region. This constituted a respite for the agriculture of the Andean zone, which had been so hard hit by the competition from Catalonia and the Levante. After 1810 this situation was maintained for a time. From 1815 onwards, however, the fruits of the agriculture of the old metropolis reappeared in Buenos Aires, and by then they too were incorporated into the commercial apparatus of Great Britain, and were imported via Gibraltar. Only in the following decade, despite the protests of the spokesmen of the agricultural provinces situated at the foot of the Andes,[60] this flow of imports – which acquired increasing importance – was again using Spanish ships. A few years later, the picture of Mediterranean imports became more complex: the Sardinian merchant marine appeared off Buenos Aires, first as a transporter of Spanish goods, then as the carrier of the olive oil of Genoa and the wines of Southern Italy. This was resisted by the French, who did not manage to impose their wines until the middle of the century.[61]

In any case, this diversification – which was to take place in wider sectors of the import trade – was preceded by a phase in which this trade was monopolised by British commerce and shipping. And during that phase, under the impact of those excessively powerful competing influxes, the local mercantile structures suffered a defeat from which they were never to recover. After 1820, both international trade and the production orientated towards it tended to proceed in a more orderly manner, but by then it would be too late for the larger merchants of Buenos Aires to use this new situation to recover the ground they had lost.

The larger merchants of Buenos Aires formed, in the last decades of the Colonial era, the nucleus of the local upper class. This assured them an influence over the political apparatus which they were still able to use to their advantage during the first decade after the Revolution. It would have been surprising if they had not tried to use this influence to defend their threatened position. In fact, such a defence did take place, and took simultaneously two directions: on the one hand, attempts were made to persuade the Revolutionary State to protect the Buenos Aires merchants as a group, and on the other hand, some powerful merchants tried a more individual road to salvation by using their political ascendancy to take part in speculations that promised to be profitable, and which were made necessary by the new requirements which the war of liberation imposed on the State.

As regards the first facet of this defence, the chief agency was the Consulado. We have already observed the indignant attention which it paid to the ruin of the pre-Revolutionary commercial structures and their incredibly swift replacement by others dominated by British merchant-venturers. It has also been observed how this interest was conditioned and orientated by the tutelary function *vis-à-vis* the interests of the local commercial sector which the Consulado had assigned to itself. This orientation was revealed even more clearly in the attempted solutions which that body proposed.

Attempts were made, in the first place, to afford some privileged status to the local merchants. Although, from 1813 onwards, the Consulado had already given up hope of obtaining for them the legal monopoly of any sector of the market, they did, nevertheless, enjoy certain tax concessions which, although they were comparatively modest, it was prepared to defend tenaciously against the foreigners. This stubborn defence of the last vestiges of the old protectionist system was accompanied, every time that a pretext offered itself, by more ambitious proposals. Through them expression was given, not only to the sentiments of hostility to the foreign merchants but also to the desire – not exclusively inspired by the situation which the competition of the latter had created – to place severe limitations on the opportunities of the local small merchants. Both the solutions proposed in the Consulado in 1815[62] and the proposal for a mercantile company made by J. J. C. de Anchorena in 1818[63] evinced the same tendency. The former proposed to prohibit all trade with overseas to merchants who did not possess a comparatively large minimum capital, and the latter proposal envisaged making such trade the privilege of a company which, formed as a corporation by the local merchants, would be dominated by the most powerful among them. Such reforms were an attempt to shut out the foreign competitors from contact with those small local merchants who had been too ready to act as their associates and 'front men'. These proposals, accompanied by the protests recorded above, were not accepted. Although the allegations of the spokesmen of local trade against a commercial free-trade policy which only brought ruin found a public increasingly prepared to accept their validity, it was precisely that gradual ruin which made it increasingly difficult to impose effectively a new commercial policy.

Although this corporate defence of the local mercantile group was deplorably ineffectual, the attempts to escape the common destiny by taking refuge in speculation proved, on the contrary, most promising. Indeed, the

The background

crisis of the State opened up new opportunities for speculative activities, when the appearance of a new predominant commercial route closed those which had existed in the fifteen years before 1810. The Revolutionary State was both poor and inexperienced in the many new tasks which devolved upon it through the war of independence. It was not surprising that it should seek the help of merchants both rich and experienced in the ways of the international markets, in order to remedy its deficiencies. It was the Catalan merchant Juan Larrea, a member of the first Revolutionary Junta, who was the first to dominate the finances of the movement. Around him their began to revolve important figures, both of the Buenos Aires commercial world and of that more adventurous and cosmopolitan sub-world which the world crisis had brought to the River Plate region. This led to the accentuation of characteristics which were not entirely new – even in the last years of the Colonial period, the Viceroy Liniers had surrounded himself with a Court full of shady characters – but, in a way that was also typical of the old régime, that Court was accused of monopolising smuggling. Now the financiers connected with the Revolutionary régime also took part in the provisioning of the Army and Navy which the new régime was improvising, and in funding privateering expeditions. These transactions were made both more risky and more profitable by the increasing insolvency of the State. The purchases of merchant ships for conversion into warships seem to have been particularly profitable. A man very close to Larrea, the Bostonian William Pius White, who had already been involved in shady deals with the occupying forces during the British Invasions, seems to have made extremely lucrative deals in connection with the fitting out of the first Patriot fleet, which Brown was to command in the River Plate region.[64] Similarly, the Buenos Aires merchant Aguirre, on a mission to the United States, does not appear, *pace* the favourable interpretation of his activities perpetuated by his family, to have had much cause to regret his financial transactions. The latter were less welcome to those with whom he had dealings: they found it difficult to obtain payment for the ships and war *matériel* which they sold to this agent.[65] In the same way privateering, which became a normal method of obtaining fresh funds, aggravated the assiduity of that court of speculators which surrounded the Government. The Revolutionary authorities not only granted letters of marque to corsairs based on Buenos Aires, but even sold them in the United States, using as intermediaries the Aguirres, each of whom took with him twenty-five blank letters of marque to sell in America, and the American David de Forest, who devoted himself on a bigger scale to this same traffic.[66]

These activities proved only moderately attractive to the big merchants of Buenos Aires: they were – as we have already observed – extremely risky. The penury of the Treasury tended to impel it towards ever more brazen forms of expoliation, and its associates ran the risk of becoming its first victims. More ingenious – and more typical of that upper sector of commerce – was the way chosen by Don Ambrosio Lezica, who always gave generous help to the Revolutionary Treasury. In return, he only asked for a certain benevolence on the part of the Customs authorities for his importing and exporting activities. Lezica became the 'King of the Customs', and the Government of which he was a considerable creditor felt no inclination to prejudice this predominance.[67]

Though attractive in the short term, this type of speculation was nearly always ruinous in the long run. Of the prosperity of the financiers of the first decade after the Revolution, there was to be very little left in the second decade. Of course, the situation did not exclude other less new-fangled types of speculation, ranging from those available in internal trade to the opportunities offered by the establishment of a State fiduciary issue. Neither of these, however, offered favourable prospects to the big businessmen of Buenos Aires; in both fields they were to encounter competition from more favourably placed foreigners. This unfavourable climate for speculative investment was only one aspect of a diminution of opportunities that became increasingly accentuated. Even the types of investment which in Colonial times had seemed to offer security, though with less spectacular profits, now seemed to lack such guarantees.

These types of investment were, above all, the purchase of shares in Spanish privileged enterprises (in particular those of the Philippines Company were to be found, as a sad reminder of a more prosperous past, in the patrimony of more than one Buenos Aires family that had been wealthy, or was still so) and the construction of buildings for letting. As has been shown by José Torre Revello,[68] in the last two decades of the Colonial period there was intensive building of rooms and small houses for letting, and not infrequently a whole row of these was built against the back wall of the more sizeable family residence of the proprietor-speculator. This kind of investment, quite adequate for Viceregal Buenos Aires, which was undergoing a rapid demographic expansion, became less easy after the Revolution. The latter looked for troops for its armies above all among the poorer classes, and the result was a rise in wages which was considered scandalous. On the other hand, its effects on those middle sectors which provided the tenants of the new houses (which were small but comfortable, and situated conveniently near the main square and had been built for speculative purposes), were unfavourable: an intolerable rise in prices struck them more heavily than other social sectors. This led to the ownership of houses for letting becoming an increasingly troublesome and precarious method of assuring oneself an income. The tenants increasingly failed to pay their rent, the wives of soldiers were legally entitled to suspend payment altogether, and it was not easy to increase rents.

Neither speculation nor the purchase of highly reputed shares in overseas companies, nor investment in property, therefore, offered an outlet any longer to those local merchants under increasing pressure from foreign competitors. This difficulty in finding alternative forms of investment perhaps explains the lack of increase in the rates of current interest during the first decade after the Revolution, even though money was becoming increasingly scarce because it was being exported.

Like the misfortunes suffered by the textile craft industry of the Interior, those suffered by local merchants used to be explained within the broader perspective of the changes introduced into the economy after 1810. Both sectors were the victims of a lack of equilibrium which, in addition, had effects beyond the limits of those sectors. The economy of the Viceregal period, for all its tardiness and distortions, justly emphasised by Argentines of the Enlightenment, was an economy in equilibrium. From year to year, the outflow of precious metals and of hides by far exceeded the imports which the small local demand kept at a comparatively low level.

Now, however, the crisis of metal exports was accompanied by an increase in imports provoked by the pressure of the new masters of the market, which led to a rapid expansion of consumption. This lack of equilibrium was permanent and cumulative; year after year, more was imported than was exported. During the first decade after the Revolution, this lack of equilibrium did not encounter any countervailing mechanism, and its prejudicial effects on the economy of the region were revealed with particular clarity.

These consequences were not, however, seen as aspects of an overall phenomenon. Nor could they be; we have already observed that, among the dominant sectors in the local economy even the most hostile to these innovations maintained an ambiguous position towards them. Rather than a return to an economy more isolated from the world they aspired to the control of the new sources of profit introduced by free trade.

The explanation for the lack of equilibrium, therefore, and of its consequence, the scarcity of specie, was looked for in the monopolistic nature of the new exporting sector, which allowed it to pay excessively low prices for the products of the country, and in certain aspects of monetary policy, which did not take account of the real price-ratio between precious metals.

With regard to the first factor, the members of the Consulado were in no doubt that the British exporters had a common pricing policy, by which they arranged to avoid mutual competition.[69] Thanks to this policy, they managed to pay steadily diminishing prices for hides, and indeed in 1814 that organisation gave an impressive proof of its efficacy by provoking a sharp fall in prices. However, while there is no doubt of the existence of agreements on prices among the British merchants, they do not appear to be the only reason for the price fluctuations denounced by the Consulado. The normalisation of Anglo-Russian trade, and with it the return to the British market of its chief supplier of livestock products, and the European crisis of 1813 were among the factors responsible for the local fall in the price of hides in 1814. Anyway, the explanation offered by the Consulado, which was rather too anxious to blame individual culprits, at least had the merit of being the first attempt to point out the presence of a prejudicial factor which was destined to endure: the vulnerability of the local economy to changes in circumstances in the economically metropolitan countries. There seems to be less justification for the conclusions of the Consulado with regard to the effect of these price-fluctuations on local producers and marketers. Even though it was true – and was to be true in the future – that local situations of scarcity might be accompanied by low prices, the converse could also occur: the years from 1816 to 1820 were a period of both rising prices and rising livestock exports. But it is, above all, far from evident that the consequences of the new situation affected producers in the same way as they did local marketers. On the contrary, all the evidence seems to indicate that the former sector enjoyed at least a part of the advantages derived from the fall in marketing costs. Faced with ruin, the local mercantile interest would have preferred to speak on behalf of the national economy as a whole, and to do this, it was obliged to turn a blind eye to the varied nature of the effects of the commercial policy it was condemning.

Even less lucid was its interpretation of the causes of the scarcity of specie. According to the Consulado, this was due, on the one hand, to a perverse tendency to export precious metals on the part of the British merchants, and, on the other, to a legal gold–silver price ratio which under-valued the former metal. There is no doubt that the foreign merchants did tend to repatriate profits in the form of precious metals. They had many motives for doing this, ranging from the scarcity of precious metals in Europe during that period to the comparatively low value of the products of the River Plate. In order to fill their hulls with merchandise of a value equivalent to that of their imports, they were obliged to supplement the hides, which were too bulky and of too low value, with cash and precious metals. The export of cash was allowed from July 1810 onwards, and shortly afterwards, this permission was extended to virgin silver treated with mercury and to gold bullion for coining. In 1811 the prohibition was again put into force, and then the prohibition was repealed for precious metals, but not for cash. In 1813 exports of cash were again permitted, and in 1815 there was again a total ban on the export of precious metals. These rapid changes in the legal measures in force do not seem to have had much influence on the export of metals: in such cases, smuggling was particularly easy, and was practised avidly.[70]

Nor did the change in the legal gold–silver price ratio stop the outflow of metals. According to the members of the Consulado, the ratio of 1:16 which the law established between the prices of gold and silver had the effect of overvaluing the latter metal, and so the changing of silver money for gold destined for export became an additional source of profit. When the change

The background

in the internal legal value of gold accorded recognition to its increasing value, the motives for exporting it were to disappear.

However, although the proposed solution was basically justified, and the increased local value of the metal in fact could put a brake on exports of it, the proposals of the Consulado were mistaken in supposing that a change in the legal gold–silver ratio from 1:16 to 1:17 would be enough to prevent the export of the former metal. On the contrary, when the new ratio was adopted, exports continued, and only in the following decade, after the establishment of a monetary system based on paper-money, would the local appreciation of gold and also of silver reach such a level that, by making these metals dearer locally than any other exportable product, it would eventually bring the outflow to a halt.

Were uncontrolled exports of specie the only reason why the scarcity of currency made an increasing impact? This does not appear to be the case: one of the consequences of the new mercantile style introduced by the British was the expansion of the part played by the monetary economy in the economic life of the region. The Robertsons have left us a particularly impressive testimony of this process in the case of Corrientes, where they found barter trade going on even in day-to-day transactions in the city. The modest capital brought with them by the entrepreneur brothers began to have revolutionary effects in the economy of Corrientes.[71] This process took place, though in a less extreme form, in regions which had previously been partially incorporated into the money economy. However, although the British merchants now introduced into circulation quantities of money which the former scarcity made appreciable, they tended to withdraw it too quickly, and with interest, from this internal circulation. Moreover, the scarcity of currency was aggravated by them in so far as, by transforming the processes of exchange, they had increased the demand for that currency. The fact that scarcity was also linked to new needs can be seen more clearly if one bears in mind the type of money the lack of which was principally felt. In fact, it was during this period that the lack of small denominations began to have effects, although this was already a characteristic of the Colonial monetary system. If it was now felt with greater intensity, this was only because now lower social sectors and economic activities at a more modest level were more fully incorporated into the money economy. The provisional solutions to the problem are well known: the division of the smallest silver coins (those of four *reales*) into four tiny irregular pieces, to each of which was assigned the value of one *real*,[72] and the issue of disks and vouchers by shopkeepers for use by their customers. Only in the province of Buenos Aires was there a more permanent solution to this problem: firstly, the minting of copper coins, from 1823, and later the inflationary printing of paper-money were to ensure the supply of low-value currency that the new organisation of the market required.

Up to that moment, however, the penury provoked by the outflow of

Revolution and the dislocation of the economy

precious metals had been aggravated by the increase in the local demand for currency. In this respect, too, the first decade after the Revolution was characterised by the vain search for a new equilibrium, the main outlines of which were only to appear around 1820 in Buenos Aires and its surrounding rural areas, and at even later dates in the rest of the new country. Even then, one of the aspects of this new equilibrium was to be a deficit in the balance of trade. In the first decade after the Revolution this deficit was to be even more clearly observable. Imports rose irregularly; exports did not succeed in reaching the level of the most prosperous years of the Viceregal period. Imports from Britain alone reached and surpassed the level of imports of the last decades of the Colonial era: the figure of 2,000,000 pesos per year, the equivalent of £400,000, was surpassed in 1814 (the figure for that year being £476,653), in 1817 (£548,689) and in 1818 (£730,908); in the year of lowest imports, 1816, the figure was £311,658.[73] Exports of hides, however, remained below the level of 800,000–1,000,000 units per year, which seems to be an acceptable average for the Viceregal period. And before 1810, livestock exports amounted to twenty per cent of the total for the Viceregal period, whereas now they were the only exports that counted, and could only be supplemented by precious metals by having recourse to the mass of metal in circulation, which was already insufficient in Colonial times, since Buenos Aires had definitely lost control over the mining centres.

It was this deep-seated cause of all the imbalances which the merchants embodied in the Consulado preferred not to mention. It was this which made commerce, during those troubled years, a sort of game of chance, and not only for those Buenos Aires merchants who in 1810 believed that the way was open to domination of the market, but also for the still insecure victors of the battle.

Of course, the merchants of the Consulado had – as we have observed – good reasons for not wishing to draw attention to the fundamental cause of the imbalances: the last thing they wanted was to eliminate it. But the situation itself furnished excellent excuses for not drawing attention to it. The lack of structural equilibrium was masked by other short-term imbalances of a particularly severe nature.

This was not surprising: even after the establishment of free trade, Buenos Aires was still far from being the market model presupposed by classical theory. Supply and demand were still far from adjusting themselves easily to price movements, and it is easy to understand why. Supply, derived from agricultural and livestock production, which showed only slight sensitivity to the favourable or unfavourable stimuli provided by price fluctuations, underwent rises and falls which, in their turn, had little effect on the world prices of products of which the River Plate region was still only a secondary supplier. Of course, the volume of supply did affect the level of the local price of exportable products, but in this

The background

respect the even more irregular fluctuations of demand were perhaps more influential.

Demand was governed, in a market as small and as divorced from the rest of the world as was Buenos Aires, by the alternating abundance and scarcity of merchant ships, and prohibitively high or excessively low freight rates which followed a desperately irregular pattern. There is no doubt that the succession of these extremes was the result of the expectations of ship-owners and merchants regarding the situation of River Plate exports in the metropolitan market, but it was also the result of expectations regarding the future of metropolitan imports into the River Plate market. It is not surprising that this answer to a complex forecast does not adequately satisfy the requirements of only one of the factors taken into account for this forecast, that is, the availability of products for export. What is even more serious, that response by a commercial and transport system which displayed no tendency towards centralisation often took the form of an over-reaction which, instead of leading to equilibrium, led to a new imbalance in the opposite direction from that which it was trying to correct. Again, it was the small size of the market which aggravated this situation still further. Even though a temporary shortage of shipping might attract ships to the River Plate, thus provoking a brief abundance, the result threatened to be a catastrophic fall in freight-rates. Similarly, a slight excess of imports attracted by the hope, not necessarily ill-founded, of finding an under-supplied market could be enough to fill the warehouses of the import-export firms for months.

These imbalances were aggravated by certain aspects of the commercial style of the new overlords of the market. It has already been observed how, before 1820, the latter, rather than establishing mercantile enterprises of a permanent nature and a more or less constant turnover, tried to take advantage of the possibilities offered by the changing circumstances in order to indulge in short-term speculations. In this way they exposed themselves, and exposed the entire commercial structure which they now dominated, to catastrophic bankruptcies.

However, this somewhat spasmodic rhythm was destined to last. After 1820, when a slow process centred on production rather than on trade began to correct the basic lack of equilibrium that affected the River Plate region's balance of trade, commercial activity was still to be of a hazardous nature.

This happened, no doubt, because the consequences of the reduced dimensions of the market persisted, and also because some of the indirect consequences of the expansion of production provoked commercial instability. In particular, the appearance of alternative forms of investment made scarcer and dearer the money available for the mercantile sector, and this in turn made it too onerous to apply certain correctives to the lack of equilibrium of the market, especially the accumulation of stocks of merchandise until such time as the limitation of supply made it possible to sell at a profit. Above all, however, it happened because the correction of the basic lack of equilibrium was itself slow and gradual. In 1822, when the figures for exports and imports already revealed the existence of a new structure of exchange, the value of imports was still double that of exports. It would be necessary to wait for something over a quarter of a century for this situation to be fully corrected.

This correction was to come, as we have observed above, in the sphere of production, whose growth was what finally made up the deficit in the trade balance. However, expansion of production was to take place much later and very unevenly. Only the rural areas of Buenos Aires, in a process which began to be noticeable around 1816 but which really only got under way after 1820, were completely transformed as a result of the opportunities opened up by the freeing of international trade. This transformation – which arose from essentially economic stimuli – had far-reaching social and political consequences. It created, for the Creole élite of the capital – from whose point of view the Revolution seemed to have failed so badly to fulfil its promises of increasing prosperity – a new base of economic power, which complemented in a most opportune manner the power which the Revolution had conferred on it socially and politically.

As early as 1817, the American Brackenridge noticed that 'the so-called *estancias* or cattle-ranches constitute the principal source of wealth of the rich'.[74]

One sees here the beginning of a far-reaching reorganisation of the internal equilibrium of the economically dominant sectors, as a result of transformations in international trade. Before the Revolution, it would be difficult to describe the cattle-ranchers as the dominant sector even in the rural areas, the social and economic hierarchy of which was of so little importance in comparison with that of the city. This was so partly because – as has been observed above – the Buenos Aires stock-raising industry found it so difficult to compete with that existing beyond the Rivers Paraná and Plate, but also partly because the commercial style described above assured the hegemony of the merchants *vis-à-vis* the cattle-ranchers.

The mercantile revolution introduced by the new British overlords of the local market, though destined above all to favour this dominant sector, had among its other consequences the liberation of the producers from the domination of the old-style marketers, and there were some among those producers who very soon noticed the advantages of encouraging the freeing of overseas trade. Very revealingly the delegate of the British merchants of Buenos Aires in 1809, Alexander Mackinnon, showed a keen interest in the preparation of the *Representación de los hacendados*, the stock-raisers' petition for free trade.[75] Once that liberalisation of trade had been achieved – and despite the heartfelt protests of the Consulado merchants – the producers were not to be prejudiced by the abolition of a style of commerce which burdened them with the costs derived from its own deficiencies. The signs of prosperity in the stock-raising business became evident from 1816 onwards. They are reflected, for example, in the statistics relating to prices of cattle for one *estancia* from 1803 onwards published in the Statistical Register, to which Miron Burgin has justifiably drawn attention.[76]

However, the possibilities opened up by the new commercial régime were to be utilised in a very uneven manner. The Banda Oriental and Entre Ríos, both devastated by the civil war, were to lose their positions as the centres of expansion of the River Plate stock-raising business. In Santa Fe and Corrientes it was only the lesser degree of prosperity of the last years of the Colonial period that made the slump of the Revolutionary and post-Revolutionary years appear less pronounced. Thanks to this vacuum, stock-raising in Córdoba and Santiago del Estero, until then of a marginal nature, was able to make considerable progress, but it was above all the rural areas of Buenos Aires that benefited from the crisis of the Littoral stock-raising business. It had strong advantages compared with the Interior: a shorter distance from the exporting centre, a rural order that was still unstable but was more solidly based than that of the Interior provinces, and its proximity to a centre such as Buenos Aires, where – despite the highly differentiated effects of the economic transformation that took place after 1810 – the small amounts of capital needed for the expansion of stock-raising were less conspicuously absent than in the smaller centres of the Interior.

Even so, the landowners never achieved, in Buenos Aires in the years 1816 to 1820, that economic and social predominance which they were later to enjoy undisputedly, and moreover, the sector itself had not yet begun to be renovated to a significant degree by the entry of the survivors of the catastrophes which urban wealth suffered after 1810. This situation, which was even more ambiguous than the over-precise description of Brackenridge would seem to suggest, was also reflected in the policy followed by the Government of Buenos Aires towards the incipient expansion of stock-raising. The first problem which the latter had to face was the limited extent of the land available, and the obvious solution was the advance of the frontier, which had been stabilised since the 1780s along the line of the River Salado. But the Revolutionary Government had, in fact, neglected the problem of the defence of the Indian frontier, and had withdrawn its veteran troops from that theatre. Although this did not have the extreme consequences provoked by similar measures taken in Santa Fe, it excluded the possibility of any further conquest of Indian lands. Even so, the 1815 Census revealed the existence of a scattered population of nearly 2,000 to the South of the Salado. From 1816 onwards, the Government of Pueyrredón explicitly recognised the need for expansion into Indian territory.

However, invoking (with good reason) the financial burden of the war, it tried to transform that expansion into a financial enterprise privately maintained by the landowners themselves, who were to provide money, rations and men for it, and be recompensed with empty lands opened up by the proposed advance of the frontier.[77] This admission on the part of the State of its inability to face the financial effort required by expansion did not imply any lack of sincerity in its support of that expansion. This was not the only occasion on which Pueyrredón's Government renounced in advance projects which it considered necessary but which were beyond its increasingly slender resources.

A better reflection of the ambiguity of the situation of the landowners, a consequence of the still incomplete transformation of the economic order in the countryside, was the attitude of that same Government of Pueyrredón to the expansion of the meat-salting plants, to which it attributed the scarcity and high cost of meat, which reached alarming proportions in Buenos Aires in 1817. According to the opponents of the salting plants, it was the latter which, by diverting towards processing and export meat previously destined for local consumption, were creating increasing difficulties for the latter. This interpretation of the causes of the acute shortage was, without doubt, mistaken. The lack of livestock for beef is more accurately explained, for that year of 1817, by the fall in the metropolitan demand for hides, which led to the exportation of these to Britain being the lowest for the entire decade – 272,645 as against 719,558 in 1816 and 683,460 in 1818. Since the price level did not justify slaughtering just for the sake of the meat, this had as a consequence a drastic fall in the supply of animals for consumption. Yet this explanation of the shortage was never taken into account in the course of the conflict, which was to attract, at an early date, the attention of Argentine historians. The reason for this was that Juan Manuel de Rosas was at that time, together with his partners, the owner of one of those controversial establishments. This is not, perhaps, the best approach to the not unduly complicated events of 1817. There is little in them that anticipates the political conflicts of twenty years later, and the clue to them is to be found, rather, in the merely incipient transformation of the Buenos Aires stock-raising business and its markets. Within this framework, the expansion of the activities of the salting-plants is a factor that cannot be ignored. Nevertheless, those plants did not absorb – and still did not absorb even after their further expansion in the following decade – a volume of meat as high as that of the city's consumption, and, except for occasions when there was a drastic fall in exports, such as in fact happened in 1817, it was the entire consumption of beef of the province – urban, rural and also meat destined for processing and export – which was insufficient to ensure the full utilisation of all the animals slaughtered for their hides.[78] There was not, therefore (again, not counting exceptional situations), a real shortage of meat for consumption. At the same time the appearance of the salting-plants meant something more than an increase in the demand for beef. It lent new strength to mechanisms of marketing of livestock which increasingly escaped the control of those which had dominated the market in Viceregal times. And the conflict that raged around the salting-plants involved both those traditional overlords of the stock-raising market and their rivals: salting-plant owners and suppliers expressed their points of view before the Government came to a decision. Who were the salting-plant owners, from the point of view of their rivals? They were not, of course, a group entirely lacking a rural basis, since they included 'one or two landowners of great prestige'. Their power was, however, more urban and commercial than truly rural. They were 'powerful personages of great wealth...highly reputed, and connected with the foreign merchants, and also with certain influential people among the authorities, including some lawyers...'[79] Such a characterisation seems accurate enough in the case of Pedro Trápani, a Buenos Aires warehouse owner of Uruguayan origin, until recently a partner with Staples and McNeil in the salting-plant which the latter had opened in 1810, and now the sole legal proprietor of that establishment, the first to be opened on the Buenos Aires side of the River Plate. It was fairly accurate, too, in the case of Juan Manuel de Rosas, who first made his money in the administration of *estancias*, then increased it by the purchase and transport of livestock, and was still far from being the big landed proprietor which he gradually became after the closure of the salting-plant which he had opened in 1816. The rival group preferred to see itself as a sector both more solidly based in the countryside and less opulent. They were 'small farmers, landowners, cattle-owners, suppliers and craftsmen', freely admitting that they were 'less highly educated and of limited abilities' but adding that they were 'generous and well-intentioned'. However, such modesty in self-characterisation was little more than the traditional rhetoric to be found in the submissions of the River Plate landowners. From the point of view of the salting-plant owners, their adversaries were the beneficiaries of a system of marketing which had enriched them and systematically reduced the income of the producers. Writing in 1818,[80] Juan Manuel de Rosas described those mechanisms with admirable clarity. The dominant characteristics of such mechanisms stemmed from the comparatively static nature of the demand which they had to satisfy: high profit-margins, and greater precautions against over-supply than against shortages. With the advent of the salting-plants, this system suffered a severe blow because the salting-plant also opened a less rigid market for beef, which made possible the expansion of production without a catastrophic fall in prices.

Rosas's description – which was also a condemnation – was implicitly based on the acceptance of the opportunities opened by a fuller incorporation into world trade which was one of the most revolutionary aspects of the Revolution. And there is no doubt that Rosas was not deceiving himself, or his readers, when he proclaimed that the producer of livestock had everything to gain from incorporation of the beef market into that wider economy. The expansion of the salting-plants was in keeping with the future that the mercantile revolution had opened up for Buenos Aires. However, the Government of Pueyrredón tried to apply a harsh brake to it by the closure of all the salting plants.

This decision was not inconsistent with the general orientation of that Government. We shall see later how, being sensitive both to the penury of the popular sectors and to the progressive dismantling of the pre-Revolutionary bases of the economic power of the Buenos Aires élite, Pueyrredón's Government sought to find the way to prosperity in a return to the past, rather than in any leap into the future. However, although that Government, which was weak and only too conscious of the limitations which that weakness imposed on its freedom of manoeuvre, was bold enough to ignore the protests of the salting-plant owners and re-impose on the rural producers the harsh domination of the city-based distributors, this was no doubt due to the fact that the salting-plant owners were not those proud overlords of the rural economy described by José Ingenieros, and the fact that the rural producers did not occupy that preeminent position in the economic and social hierarchy of the province attributed to them by Brackenridge.

The year 1820 marks – in this sphere as in the political one – a decisive turning-point. The government of the Directory collapsed. Manuel de Sarratea, who for years had enjoyed the confidence of the British mercantile and political interests in Buenos Aires,[81] and had been at the same time a discreet opponent of the previous *status quo*, authorised, in his capacity as Governor of the province of Buenos Aires, the re-opening of the closed salting-plants. It would, however, be mistaken to interpret this decision from an excessively political standpoint. Sarratea was soon to be removed from power, and his successors and adversaries – several of whom had been identified with the Pueyrredón régime – did not renew the ban on meat-salting. What happened was that Buenos Aires in 1820 marked out both a new political direction and a new direction for its economy. From that year onwards, it accepted without hesitation the possibilities opened up by the freeing of trade in 1809. The change in the economic climate was noticed even by an observer as uninterested in such matters as General Iriarte:

> The desire to employ capital in the most lucrative business encouraged the stock-raising industry, which until then had been neglected, in spite of the fertility of the soil which offered secure and abundant returns on this kind of speculation. And even the British merchants – the most enterprising businessmen – employed large sums in the stocking of new *estancias*, thus increasing the wealth of the country in its most important sector.[82]

The rate of interest – Iriarte continued – rose sharply; cattle-ranchers were able to prosper even when using other people's capital, on which they were paying interest of over one and a half per cent per month. Even though the road to prosperity undertaken with such a heavy burden was less easy than Iriarte supposed, it is true that the expansion of stock-raising caused a sudden rise in the cost of money. The city-based distributors were not, of course, immediately displaced from their previous predominant position. As late as 1823 they were accused of being responsible for yet another meat shortage. The landowners, according to a letter to the *Argos* (16 August 1823) signed by a 'friend of the Fatherland and of humanity', although 'there are more than enough beef-cattle for the city's consumption', were not bringing them in for slaughtering 'because the monopolists of public distribution offer them such a low price'. In the long run, however, it was to be the distributors who were to suffer the consequences of an increase in the price of beef which, for political reasons, they were unable to pass on to the mass of urban consumers. Being a middleman ceased to be lucrative, and supplies had to be organised directly by the very landowners who were supplying the salting-plants. From that time onwards, until the middle of the nineteenth century, the price of beef for consumption was fixed by administrative decree and, in Buenos Aires, it underwent slow and sporadic rises. No doubt the producers lost some potential profits as a result of these measures, although this was partly offset by the political defence of the price-levels during the blockades and the mass slaughter of cattle which followed them. Above all, they benefited from the elimination of those costly intermediaries, the city-based distributors. From now on, however, the plight of the distributors was but a minor aspect of a vaster process. Between 1820 and 1823, the frontier of the province advanced until the area of the latter was doubled. The bringing into exploitation of these new lands was, of course, a slower process, which was to take place over the following two decades. From 1830 onwards, the British market proved incapable of absorbing the increasing exports of hides from the River Plate, but the sellers of hides found on the Continent – through Le Havre, but above all through Antwerp, the port for Germany – an additional market, which by the 1840s was absorbing a greater volume than Great Britain. From 1820 onwards, therefore, the economy of Buenos Aires had again found the road to prosperity. As far as that province was concerned, the promises of Independence seemed to have been fulfilled, while the inland provinces adapted themselves to the new circumstances, which were less systematically unfavourable than is sometimes supposed, but which in any case did not favour any improvement over the levels of production and trade of the last years of the Colonial period, and the Littoral faced a period of adversity which, though it stemmed from political causes, did not for that reason have a less disastrous influence on the economic situation. In 1825, marching at the head of his troops to the battlefields of Brazil, the future General Paz passed through some villages of the rural areas of Buenos Aires, and was amazed at the hitherto unknown prosperity,[83] and a superficial examination of the registers of trading licences for the next two decades is enough for one to notice the multiplication of bakers' shops, clothing-stores, shoe-shops, and coaches for private transport, all demonstrating the growing complexity of the style of life of those rustic corners of the world. But the prosperity of stock-raising affected not only the countryside. Increasingly dependent on it was the prosperity of the city, through the commerce of which the products of that countryside were channelled. And, both in city and the country, a landowning class endowed from the outset with strong urban roots and enriched from 1820 onwards with new recruits from the upper classes of the city was now, without any doubt, predominant in the province. It shared economic power with import-export firms, overwhelmingly foreign, from which it was not separated by any fundamental conflict of interest, and it had an increasing weight in the entire life of the province.

In this way, the economy of Buenos Aires acquired a new centre of gravity. Buenos Aires society had a dominant sector more cohesive than at any time in the past. These changes were, undeniably, the consequences of the success of the economic revolution that began in 1809. It should be pointed out, however, that the social and, in the longer term, political, consequences which this success brought about in Buenos Aires were not very different from the consequences which in other provinces resulted from its failure. This happened, no doubt, because success did not entirely eliminate the consequences of the prejudicial aspects of that revolution. There were sources of urban prosperity which were to dry up until the middle of the nineteenth century. The impoverishment of the lay and ecclesiastical corporations continued and was in more than one case the prelude to their suppression, which actually took place in the 1820s. The administration and even – despite the return of war to the River Plate scene – the Army fulfilled to a much more limited extent than in the first decade after the Revolution their function of providing an income to a considerable sector of the urban population. However, even had this not been the case, and even if the transformation of Buenos Aires had taken place exclusively as a result of rural growth without any partial crisis of urban prosperity as a contributory factor, its consequence would still have been a transfer of economic, social and political power from the city to the countryside: the same consequence which, in less favoured areas, derived exclusively from the crisis of the urban functions of the city.

A quarter of a century after 1820, Sarmiento was to reproach Argentina for having opted for what he called barbarism, for the countryside which still lay outside history, as against the cities which were making efforts to follow the rhythm of the world. He saw both the cause and the consequence of this option in an increasing isolation, and he hoped that the end of that isolation, which events themselves would eventually impose, would mean the end of that inclination towards barbarism. Perhaps the situation was even more serious than it appeared to Sarmiento. The over-confident opening up to the outside world, to those simultaneously transforming and destructive forces of the metropolitan economy, had the same consequences as that isolation in which he saw the necessary accompaniment, and perhaps the cause, of the political and cultural degradation of post-Revolutionary Argentina.

PART TWO: FROM VICEROYALTY TO 'UNITED PROVINCES OF THE RIVER PLATE'

3 THE CRISIS OF THE COLONIAL ORDER

THE WAR AND THE WEAKENING OF IMPERIAL TIES

War on a world-wide scale gradually begins to affect the Spanish Imperial structure in the course of the eighteenth century. The decision of Bourbon Spain to align itself in the struggle against the rising hegemony of Great Britain, even though it could not be explained from an exclusively dynastic standpoint, in any case imposed on the nation an ever-increasing effort, in pursuit of a goal that became increasingly remote. Victories, defeats and near-defeats made very little difference to this general trend. In international politics, too, the resurgent Spain of the second half of the eighteenth century set its sights on objectives too ambitious for the possibilities opened up by a resurgence that was no doubt real enough, but limited in scope.

However, although the Imperial order as a whole soon suffered the consequences of this over-ambitious policy, in the River Plate region the first effect of this policy was to consolidate that order. The Crown, inspired to an important and perhaps decisive extent by considerations of international policy, directed its efforts at administrative, economic and military renovation reaching a particular intensity in this region. Moreover, it was here that the attempts to erect a bulwark against the encroachment of the British bloc – represented in this region by Portugal – were comparatively successful. At the same moment as the establishment of the Viceroyalty, the Spaniards took definitive possession of Colônia do Sacramento, which for a century had been a military threat and a disruptive element in the Spanish mercantile system in this corner of the world. Thus, whereas in Northern Spanish America, in those Caribbean islands which had always been more closely threatened than the less attractive Southern region, the brief British occupation of Havana, which took place in 1762, and the experience of eleven months of free trade with the occupying power offered for the first time the clear prospect of an alternative to the Spanish order, the latter was reaffirmed with more vigour than ever in the River Plate region.

For this reason, the crisis of the Colonial system was to have more abrupt repercussions in the River Plate region than elsewhere. It was, in fact, a power that had been showing signs of increasing strength which began to wither with an unexpected rapidity: indeed the years before 1805 hardly showed any evident sign of the coming catastrophic collapse.

In those years, however, we can see in outline some of the factors which were to become dominant after the dissolution of the Imperial order. In particular, it was the innovations introduced into the mercantile system to adapt it to conditions of war which introduced such factors. We have already observed how, from 1791 onwards, a series of measures taken by the Crown increased the autonomy of Buenos Aires as a commercial centre *vis-à-vis* the metropolis. These measures, which were essential in order to alleviate the consequences of the increasing isolation of Spain from its American colonies, were received with an attitude different to that which had motivated their imposition as transitory palliatives designed for an emergency. For one thing, they were bound to provoke tension between those prepared to take advantage of the measures and the local agents of the Imperial order, who were fearful of the consequences for them of any attenuation of the metropolitan hegemony. Such tensions and conflicts have been the object of close attention by Argentine historians, who are accustomed to detect in them traces of a divergence of interests which was to culminate in the Revolutionary clash after 1810. It seems doubtful that such an interpretation is justified. We have already observed that the post-Revolutionary system hardly found a place for the majority of these supposed precursors, some of whom were even to be found among the supporters of the displaced régime. However, the existence of this hiatus between the increasingly insecure mercantile hegemony of Spain and the introduction of the system that was to displace it was decisive. Not only did it exalt, in the economic life of the country, individuals who owed nothing whatever to the dying 'Colonial Pact', but it also opened up opportunities for progress independent of that system.

These opportunities were soon recognised. We find a reflection of them in the notion that Buenos Aires had become the centre of the commercial world, after having been one of the remoter corners of the Spanish Colonial world. Such a recognition, of course, did not directly prejudice the survival of the political connections with the metropolis, but it was to cause the gradual transformation of the image of those connections prevalent in the Colonial area. There is evidence of this transformation, and of the rise of a new image, both more complex and subject to more rapid changes, in the writings of the 'enlightened' economists who arose in Buenos Aires as an element in the increasing social complexity of the Viceregal capital.

Of course, once the Revolutionary process was unleashed, these men were to express regret for their collaboration with the monarchical and Spanish power, and Manuel Belgrano, who, as Secretary of the Consulado, had lent such collaboration for many years of his life before the Revolution, was to explain it in his *Autobiografía* as the fruit of hallucinations stemming from ignorance as to the inevitably prejudicial nature of the Colonial connection. But the severity with which this revolutionary judged the young who had not yet discovered his way did not, despite his condemnatory tone, conceal the fact that this twenty-three year old Creole, who had graduated in Valladolid and qualified as a lawyer in its Chancery, who, under the influence of the changes in ideas provoked by the French Revolution 'among the men of letters of his acquaintance', had been entirely won over by the ideas of 'liberty, equality, security and property, and considered as mere tyrants those who tried to prevent Man, whatever his origin, from enjoying the rights which God and nature had granted him, and which even human societies had agreed, directly or indirectly, to establish', who both knew and accepted the doctrine of the Revolution in the light of the French Revolutionary experience, also accepted the fact that the Crown, within the framework of 'enlightened' monarchy, could be the appropriate instrument of that revolutionary transformation. A minister who had had some experience of the world proposed that he should be Secretary of the Buenos Aires Consulado, and Belgrano accepted enthusiastically.[1]

This behaviour might appear inconsistent, but Belgrano could hardly be expected to see in the Crown, which furnished the political support for the Colonial order and which provided the force which maintained the domination of the metropolis and its agents over the wealth of the Americas, the necessary enemy of the fundamental transformations which would of necessity threaten that predominance. It would be difficult for him to hold this view of the Crown, when it was the agents of the latter who had created an instrument for economic and social changes and had invited him to occupy a place from which he could decisively influence the direction of those changes.

There is no doubt that, during his tenure of office as Secretary, Belgrano was to discover some unpalatable facts. After entrusting him with the task of struggling against stagnation and hide-bound attitudes, the Royal authority left him on his own to fight an impossible battle against the beneficiaries of that very stagnation whom it had installed in the Consulado. Judging their activities, not by the intentions of remote administrators in Madrid, but by their results, Belgrano could not see in them anything that could not be explained by the application of two fundamental directives: the maintenance, in all essentials, of the Colonial Pact, and its attenuation in certain respects to enable it to withstand better the dangers that threatened it. The Court of Spain 'showed vacillation with regard to the methods it used in extracting all it could from its Colonies, and that is why we have seen legal measures which have been simultaneously liberal and illiberal, and which have betokened the fear of losing those Colonies'. But this policy, vacillating and of dubious sincerity, though it destroyed the deeply felt loyalty of one who was beginning to achieve a clear realisation of its nature, did not necessarily bring to an end the collaboration of the future revolutionary.

In justifying his continued collaboration, Belgrano emphasised, in the first place, a reason that was no doubt decisive: he did not believe in the possibility of a sudden collapse of the power of the Spanish Monarchy, and thought that the River Plate region would have to develop within that framework for another century. This was an important reason, but not the only one. The Colonial system, after three centuries of continued existence, was not a foreign occupation. It had put down strong local roots. The adversaries of the changes that Belgrano thought necessary dominated the local economy even more effectively than the central political apparatus. Even the vicissitudes suffered by Belgrano in the Consulado were a proof of this. Doubtless the Crown had not given him sufficient support against a majority group composed of merchants who had enriched themselves by monopolistic practices; but that majority had not been the result of the arbitrary choice of the Crown; it was only too representative of the groups which effectively dominated the commerce of Buenos Aires and which of necessity dominated that corporation of merchants, the Consulado. On the contrary, it was only thanks to the attenuation of the predominance of those local elements ensured by the counterweight of the Crown which had enabled Belgrano, imbued with reforming fervour, to become secretary of that body. It would certainly not have been the beneficiaries of monopoly who would have chosen such a stubborn adversary.

Political power, therefore, appeared as an instrument of the transformation of an economic order which did not seem capable of producing renovating forces of sufficient strength. Experience showed, no doubt, that this instrument was not very efficient. It was beginning to show that changes in circumstances increasingly weakened it, forcing it into continual compromises which displaced it from its directing rôle. It was also beginning to reveal another factor: the ability of the local economy to transform itself under the stimulus of changes in circumstances which were often due to political causes, but in any case to causes independent of the Crown's decisions. These economic transformations, and the changes to which they led in the relative strength of the sectors involved, became overwhelmingly evident in the last fifteen years of the Colonial period. Could Belgrano have hoped, from these changes, for what he no longer hoped for from the central authority?

This is extremely doubtful. With regard to the importance of those same forces, the Secretary of the Consulado appears to have had less optimistic views than some historians of the origins of the Revolution, and doubtless with good reason, for although the rise and enrichment of merchants doing business independently of the Cádiz route was a very important phenomenon from the political point of view, the economic consequences of this innovation were to be ephemeral, and were not to outlast the simultaneous breakdown of the ties with Spain and with Continental Europe provoked by the naval victories of Britain and still not replaced by the new and unequal relationship with the victor-

The crisis of the Colonial order

ious power, which already appeared destined to inherit the hegemony of Spain.

The noncommittal attitude of Belgrano towards these innovations was, no doubt, a personal trait. In contrast to him, Hipólito Vieytes unceasingly proclaimed the present and future greatness of the Tyre of America.[2] There was, however, another reason of a less personal nature for him to consider as indispensable the arbitrating rôle of political power in relation to the development of economic forces: like almost all Spanish Americans of the Enlightenment, he hesitated to place an unquestioning faith in the spontaneous mechanisms of the economy. There is evidence of this in the roundabout and hesitant way in which he reported on one of those measures, 'simultaneously liberal and illiberal', of the Crown. 'Sometimes', wrote Belgrano, 'it decided to encourage agriculture and, to provide labour, it adopted the dreadful traffic in Negroes, granting privileges to those who undertook it: among these was the export of produce to foreign countries'. At the King's command, the Consulado reported that 'hides were not produce, and therefore were not to be included in export licences granted in return for trafficking in Negroes'.

'I became discouraged', Belgrano continued, 'and realised that nothing would be done for the Provinces by men who habitually put their own particular interests above the common good'.[3] On this occasion, therefore, our reformer was faced with two alternatives, of neither of which he could fully approve. He felt discouraged by the restrictionist policy adopted by the Consulado, but he could not give full approval to the liberalisation of the 'dreadful traffic in Negroes'. This was, no doubt, an extreme example. Not all the supporters of economic liberalism were prepared to extend its principles to the traffic in human beings. But, as an example, it was indicative of a more generalised attitude, and it was to be found again, both in Belgrano and Vieytes, with regard to the sector of the economy which most interested both of them, agriculture.

The subordination of economics to politics which characterised both men, and the entire corpus of Enlightened thought in the River Plate area, are less incompatible than appears at first sight with economic liberalism which, as popular histories tirelessly repeat, was characteristic of the Enlightenment. That liberalism, in fact, took the form of a discovery of a sector of reality – the economic one – governed by laws peculiar to itself and which could not be ignored with impunity. But to recognise such laws did not mean submitting passively to their consequences. On the contrary, it implied the intention of using them for a specific purpose: as with nature, one dominates economics only by obeying it.

Such domination, however, not only presupposed the existence of a political authority capable of arbitrating between the internal forces of the economic process. It implied a presupposition of broader scope, in so far as it envisaged economic science as incapable of determining objectives for the process which it studied. Its rôle was to indicate the methods appropriate to the achievement of objectives which it was not its business to determine. The consequences of this can be observed in the attitude of Vieytes and Belgrano towards the drift towards an economic production exclusively based on stock-raising, the development of which they viewed with apprehension and for which they sought political remedies. However, both realised only too well that, if that trend was taking place, it was doing so because it was determined by the real facts of the situation, and they demonstrated this in reports in which they pointed out how the recently discovered laws of economics were being fulfilled in this process. In the divine judgement of the free market stock-raising achieved – or so it appeared – a legitimate victory. This victory should, however, be prevented, because its consequences would run counter to the ethical and political ideals of the Buenos Aires economists. Those ideals, of course, were not very different from those which lay at the base of contemporary liberal economic thought: the political ideal was one of a society which would freely find its equilibrium thanks to the sum of the individual efforts of its members; the ethical ideal was that of productive work harnessed to the conquest of the material world. However – for these observers from afar of the process unleashed by the Industrial Revolution – there was no certain guarantee that the forces unleashed by that process would spontaneously realise those ideals. This was the reason for the constant recourse to the political authority. But could that authority perform the services required of it? That was extremely doubtful. Tied as it was, in the short run, to the interests of those who were bound to be hostile to the necessary changes, even if it freed itself from those over-powerful supports it would, perhaps, plan a very different future from that which the Argentines of the Enlightenment desired for their region. Of such a future one can, perhaps, detect traces in the *Memoria sobre el estado rural*,[4] written in 1801 from Batoví, the settlement he had founded in the Banda Oriental, by that exceptionally perceptive servant of the Crown, Félix de Azara. This envisages a future based on stock-raising, with all the consequences that this would entail: a low density of population, especially in the rural areas, and family and social instability. He defended the system against predictable objections. How could one describe as poverty-stricken a region which would be capable of exporting millions of pesos' worth of hides and salted meat? It was, indeed, this consideration which should have been dominant in the outlook of a good servant of the Crown. The objective of the latter was not the abolition of the Colonial Pact, the possibilities of which were now exhausted, but its replacement by another pact which would link a commercial and industrial metropolis with colonies orientated towards primary products. This over-ambitious project, which was soon frustrated, was not that which Belgrano and Vieytes would attribute to a monarch really concerned for the welfare of his overseas subjects.

The crisis of the Colonial order

However, despite its weakness and the ambiguity of its outlook, the Crown was to continue to play, in the thought of Argentines of the Enlightenment, a necessary rôle. In recognising this, were these Enlightened thinkers merely yielding to the prestige of traditionalist theories which still exerted a great influence even over innovators? This is far from evident. After years of experience had revealed the Crown's increasing incapability of fulfilling its directing rôle, when the monarchical power itself vanished in the great crisis of 1808, adaptation to the new political climate would cause an increasing rapprochement with the postulates of orthodox economic liberalism. Such a rapprochement was no more than the recognition of the decisive rôle of economic forces, which it was now recognised could not be governed by political measures. Of this process we find traces, for example, in the increasingly vacillating attitude of Belgrano towards the problem of the division of rural property. Although, in an article published in his *Correo de Comercio* on 23 June 1810, he was still proclaiming that the chief cause of the backwardness of agriculture in Buenos Aires Province was the lack of access to land-ownership for small farmers (and he proposed solutions, such as the fixing of rents by administrative measures or the conversion of rented land into emphyteuses which presupposed the existence of a political authority capable of imposing itself on economic forces), on 4 August of the same year he was already denying that the progress of agriculture depended on a redistribution of property or an improvement in the lot of the small farmers. This time the method he was advocating was the imposition of a stricter labour discipline, which would lower wages and increase profits.[5]

From now on, the favourite instruments of transformation were to be those which accorded with the interests of the locally dominant economic and social forces. The adoption of this new criterion of choice was linked, undoubtedly, with the collapse of the monarchical authority, together with the already consummated breakdown of the Imperial connection. But, in an even clearer form than in any of the writings of Belgrano, the nature of this new situation can be seen in the *Representación de los hacendados* of 1809. In this document, the conversion to economic liberalism is total and unreserved. The Crown, to which peremptory entreaties are addressed, is no more than a phantom, and the foreground is occupied by the group represented by Mariano Moreno, those landowners sure of their rights and even surer of their power. The sententious and emphatic prose of this document marked the close of a chapter in the history of thought in the River Plate region. The image of the monarch as a provident and just arbiter who distributes prosperity and welfare among his subjects, that archaic image on which the thought of the Enlightenment had left its renovating traces, had now vanished for ever. But it was also the close of a chapter in the briefer history of economic thought. Together with the confidence, so often shown to be misplaced, in the regulating and directing power of the Crown, it was the confidence in the very possibility of the domination of economic forces by political methods which was progressively being weakened. This new pessimism was not, of course, without foundation. The Revolutionary governments were to have, *vis-à-vis* the locally predominant economic forces, less autonomy of decision than the Colonial Government. In such circumstances, it is not surprising that the attitude of 'enlightened' Argentine economists (who were soon to become revolutionaries) towards the dying Imperial connection should have been, up to the last moment, ambiguous. Increasingly conscious of the limitations – both forced and voluntary – placed on the renovating rôle of the Crown, they also appear to have been conscious of the difficulty of replacing that instrument of transformation, which was insufficient, with another more effective one.

Should these vacillations be interpreted on an exclusively personal plane, as evidence of the complexity which economic thought in the River Plate region precociously achieved, among the few who were interested in such matters? This does not appear to be the case. It is extremely suggestive that the ambiguity of thought of the economists of the Enlightenment *vis-à-vis* the Imperial connection should have coincided with a phase of history in which the weakening of that connection was not accompanied by the equally vigorous rise of the system which was to replace it. The River Plate region, dominated by a mercantile sector, within which effective power was concentrated in the hands of a small number of merchants who were agents of the metropolis, was already facing a crisis. Nevertheless, of that future in which the primary sectors would dominate the economy and the landowners would be the leaders of society, of that future consolidated by the establishment, after the Revolution, of a neo-colonial connection with a new economically dominant power, there were still only a few prefatory signs, although these were observed with alarm by the local observers of the economic and social situation. What was ephemerally guaranteed was the strengthening of speculative mercantile sectors, favoured by the weakening of the Imperial connection owing to the war, but in no way destined to benefit from the complete destruction of that connection and its replacement by another. It would, without a doubt, be unjustified to see in Vieytes and, above all, in Belgrano – who felt nostalgia for the 'old faith in commerce'[6] – the spokesmen of these adventurous merchants. The complexity and also the ambiguity of the solutions they proposed are, however, better understood if one bears in mind that at the moment when they were examining the economic and social situation in the River Plate region, there was still no real sign of the triumph of those new forces which would only achieve decisive importance after the breakdown of the Imperial connection and as a consequence of that very breakdown.

In this way the war weakened the economic connection which in the relations between the metropolis and its colony was superimposed on the political connection, but this weakening did not necessarily herald a more

The crisis of the Colonial order

profound crisis in the colonial relationship. Precisely because it had been weakened, the economic connection became for many people much more acceptable, and when Hipólito Vieytes, a future member of the Revolutionary Junta, described Buenos Aires as being placed in the centre of the commercial world and prophesied for his city a future worthy of that privileged position, he did not think it necessary, even by implication, to establish as a condition for the fulfilment of that prophecy a further weakening of the Imperial connection. Within the framework of that connection, as reformulated first by the Bourbon reforms and then by the semi-isolation imposed by war, he thought that this splendid destiny could be fulfilled.

Both as regards the real situation and the ideological approaches which were formulated in response to it, the economic changes arising out of the new war situation no doubt laid the foundations for a total crisis in the Imperial connection, but did so only slowly. Only two years before the revolutionary breakdown of that connection, Belgrano was still expecting it to last for a century. The political crisis developed more swiftly: from 1806 onwards, its successive stages followed one another with bewildering speed.

Until that date, the Imperial apparatus in the River Plate region had an overwhelming importance in public life. The renewed vigour infused into it by the reforms of Charles III gave no indication – as has been observed above – of its coming collapse. There was, however, even before it led to a public clash, a more hidden crisis in the Imperial political connection, which was also affected by the train of events in the outside world. One aspect of this still inchoate crisis was that which popular histories describe as the new ideological influences. Throughout the second half of the eighteenth century, and with increasing intensity, curiosity with regard to these political and ideological innovations spread to the most unexpected quarters. Was this new trend decisive? One may be permitted to doubt this. Even before the ideological innovations of the Enlightenment contributed to the undermining of the system of ideas on which the prevailing absolute monarchy was based, this system already evinced a certain inconsistency which had done nothing to weaken the institution itself. Even before the Enlightenment, the political thought of the Baroque era had displayed an admiring curiosity *vis-à-vis* political institutions and ideals which were utterly incompatible with those prevailing. Thus, long before they received public homage from the benches of the Convention, Republican virtues had been venerated throughout centuries of absolute monarchy on the benches of the schools, as a part of that semi-rhetorical cult of the Classical legacy which the Counter-Reformation had zealously preserved as part of its cultural baggage. Of course, neither the glorification of the virtuous Lucretia nor that of the last paladins of the dying Roman Republic signified any real danger for the ruling monarchy. Nevertheless, they did constitute a highly unexpected component of the mental furniture of its loyal servants.

It would, of course, be unjust to dismiss the avid curiosity aroused by the renovation of political thought due to the Enlightenment as a mere continuation of that previous curiosity directed towards less relevant matters. It is, however, sufficient to observe the indignant surprise with which many habitual Spanish readers of the *philosophes* viewed the fall of the French Monarchy to realise that they found it amazing that those audacious ideas should actually have been put into practice.

Even so the great Revolution did not put an end to the curiosity. Even the opponents of the revolutionary novelties were grateful to hear news of them. The persistence of an ambiguous attitude which not even the storm of revolution was to terminate was shown by the correspondence maintained with friends at Court from Córdoba by the Dean, Gregorio Funes, who presented, in his funeral oration for King Charles III, a very detailed picture of a system of political thought in which adherence to Enlightened Despotism was only tempered by a continuing attachment to even more archaic ideas.

Funes received from a Spanish cleric who preferred to use the pseudonym of 'Francisco', but whose identity was known to the recipient of his letters, news bulletins inspired by an undisguised enthusiasm for the 'modern Rome' which he supposed Jacobin France to be. 'Francisco' followed with keen interest the development of Spain's policy towards the French Republic, and sympathised with the efforts of that 'noble Spaniard' Aranda to avoid involving Spain in a dynastic war with its Northern neighbour. What is more curious is the fact that 'Francisco' knew very well that Funes did not share his point of view, and he was even more certain that there was absolutely no risk of that defender of the monarchy against revolutionary innovations doing his duty as a loyal subject by denouncing him as a subversive. Furthermore, he knew that he would be pleasing his readers by sending them the score of the Marseillaise, so that the Dean's brother, Ambrosio Funes, who was even more conservative, could exercise his musical talents.[7] This episode is significant. It shows that even after the French Revolution had revealed the fragility of the European monarchical system, loyalty to the Spanish Monarchy survived intact in the mind of several of the future revolutionaries, yet that loyalty did not become more militant when the fragility of the institutional order it supported was revealed. While the Spanish political system fell into a progressively critical state, those who continued to be its faithful servants devoted themselves to learning a political culture to replace it. This activity, inspired by what those who undertook it no doubt judged sincerely to be mere curiosity, nevertheless revealed its full usefulness after 1810. When the new order required a new language of expression and a new political ideology, there was already a widespread capability of adaptation to these new requirements.

In this way the increasing dissemination of ideological innovations, the supposed precursor of the Spanish American Revolution, acquired practical relevance once the Revolution itself had taken place. More significant, perhaps, was the knowledge, necessarily less widespread, of the crisis not only of ideas but also of institutions which the European revolutionary cycle was provoking in the Spanish monarchy. There was an echo of this new situation in the circular letter on the Royal Catechism issued in 1790 by Archbishop San Alberto. This ecclesiastical servant of the Bourbon monarchy, who during his tenure of office as Bishop of Córdoba had enjoyed the collaboration of Funes, showed himself much more willing than his old collaborator to direct, from his position as Archbishop of Charcas, a militant resistance to the Revolutionary ideological innovations. The danger was, in his opinion, very serious: the Indians of Upper Peru, 'simple-minded, gullible and ignorant', ran the risk of being easily duped by this propaganda which was both heretical and subversive, 'with its false science, its seductive persuasiveness and above all with its fictitious promises of independence, freedom of conscience and exemption from tribute'. The pamphlets arriving from overseas which spread the new poison presented a problem more pressing than the most urgent ecclesiastical duties. Parish priests were called upon by their archbishop to leave their churches and seek out clandestine literature wherever they heard that it was circulating. In addition to this task of vigilance, it was the duty of the clergy of the Archdiocese to spread the antidote, in the form of the *Instrucción política* published ten years previously by the Archbishop himself. When, in 1780, he had published this popular exposition of the point of view of the defenders of absolute monarchy, he was careful to emphasise that the opinions expressed did not claim to be dogmas of the faith. Precisely for that reason, he had not wanted to employ the word 'catechism', although the treatise took the form of questions and answers. Indeed, in the opinion of many people, 'the term *catechism* can only be applied, strictly speaking, to a document which treats of no other matter except what is precisely and necessarily relevant to the Faith'. In 1790 he gave orders to his parish priests that 'if anyone, whoever he may be...should proclaim or teach anything contrary to what we have taught in our afore-mentioned *Instrucción*, be it known that such things are not deserving of faith, *but of anathema or a curse*'.[8]

Compared with the lukewarmness of Funes, therefore, San Alberto appears as a militant servant of the old order. But even for him the political crisis brought about by the Revolution had effected a change. If, in 1780, he still retained a firm belief in a system of collaboration between the civil and ecclesiastical powers in which the former played a directing rôle, in 1790, although his devotion to the Crown remained intact, he seemed to have much less confidence in the Crown's ability to react adequately in the face of the emergency. He expected much more from the spontaneous action of prelates and clergy. Even for its loyal though troubled servants, the decline of the monarchy was a factor to be taken into account, and it led them both to defend the institution and to seek a certain degree of emancipation from its past tutelage. In 1791 San Alberto himself was to show a perhaps even more revealing sign of this new attitude. He thought it an opportune moment to give an account of his attempts to prevent the dissemination of novel revolutionary ideas, and he submitted this account, not to his sovereign, but to the Supreme Pontiff.

In 1790 Spain herself was only just beginning to feel the impact of the revolutionary situation, which was to lead to an alliance with Republican, and then Imperial, France, and the growing loss of prestige of that monarchy allied to the regicide Republic. One must not, however, exaggerate the immediate consequences of this development, above all in the remote Colonial areas. It was, rather, the fact that Spain was again the weakest link in the alliance, and the connection with its overseas territories was revealed as particularly vulnerable, that had its effect on the Colonies.

And this lent fresh importance to a fact which in itself had but little: the existence of secret but determined adversaries of the Colonial régime in Spanish America acquired increasing importance as the crisis of the Colonial connection was made more acute by the march of events. What was the source of this disaffection? One may mention, in the first place, the crisis in the equilibrium between the castes constituted by the Peruvian rebellions, which had repercussions, albeit attenuated ones, beyond the actual area where the events took place. In the Littoral, however, dissidence was above all encouraged by overseas contacts. The so-called French conspiracy of 1795, even though it attempted to exploit the discontent of the Negro slaves and counted among its followers at least one victim of caste-discrimination (Díaz, the *mestizo* from Corrientes, who, even before he hoped for an end to his tribulations from a Jacobin triumph, had hoped for it from a victory of the Peruvian rebels),[9] was, nevertheless, led by merchants and, to an even greater extent, by craftsmen of European origin, who were, however, incapable of really arousing the slave population, among which the first informers had arisen. This incident – which was magnified by the fear of the Government – was, perhaps, less important than the maintenance of contacts which served to aggravate a merely potential dissidence among the upper sectors.

The development of the local economy and the disruption of the normal commercial channels in fact lent increasing importance to the presence of foreigners in Buenos Aires. Linked with this presence were the earliest Masonic organisations. The first lodge, founded in 1804 by a Portuguese, included among its members merchants and bureaucrats. One of the former group was Manuel Arroyo y Pinedo, who was to have a long, though not brilliant, political career after Independence. The second group included Gregorio Gómez, an official of the tobacco monopoly, who had learned to 'drink Masonically' and had his own table reserved in the Los Tres Reyes tavern, where he was always being invited by the British merchants. The organisation was discovered, but its members were not prosecuted. According to one story, a bribe paid to the Vicereine, and according to another, the author of which was General Martínez, the presence of a numerous group of highly-placed officials, saved the first Masons of Buenos Aires from official wrath.[10]

The differences between this new group and the earlier one are obvious. Its membership, recruited among higher economic and social sectors, guaranteed its safety, and this difference in origin of its members perhaps also explains the unsubversive character of its activities. This does not make any less significant the existence of these new groupings composed of Spanish-born and Creoles, together with the increasingly numerous foreigners passing through or established in Buenos Aires. This was especially true because the widespread suspicion that these foreigners were real or potential agents of their countries of origin was not without foundation, in some cases. At least, the agents who were to be active in the River Plate region found in these partly institutionalised connections an adequate field for penetration.

Besides the agents, who were to become increasingly assiduous, there were those who lent their services occasionally. The well filled archive of the Quai d'Orsay was to accumulate the reports of the captains of French ships calling at Buenos Aires, and although British activities were more discreet, they undoubtedly went on. Those seafarers and merchants whom a convulsed war situation had driven to Buenos Aires and also to other remote corners of the planet formed a strange and turbulent cosmopolitan society, small in numbers but influential. The friendships and enmities formed showed the traces of this adventurous existence. The differences which separated the *ci-devant* Comte de Liniers and the Bostonian William Pius White were a continuation in Buenos Aires of a conflict that had begun in the Indian Ocean, where the hazards of trade and war had previously taken the two men. In Buenos Aires, however, it took deep root and left a complex heritage. Behind the hostility between Liniers and Álzaga, and the tension between Moreno and Rivadavia, it is still possible to see traces of that distant clash.

Of course, the Colonial authorities had no immediate danger to fear from this sector. It was fully occupied in speculative activities which required the favour of the political authorities and was not going to risk its position by committing itself to subversive adventures. But as soon as the Colonial power began to weaken, this sector was to play a significant part in its dissolution. On the one hand, it was connected with the most influential local sectors, and on the other with the foreign powers, so its scope of manoeuvre was considerable.

Against this influence, little could be achieved by the zeal with which the

Colonial authorities tried to guarantee ideological orthodoxy. Badly served by many of its officials, hampered by their previous activities which linked it too closely to renovating tendencies, the attempt of the authorities was a failure. Although the threats that faced it were insignificant, and although for the moment both the capacity and the serious intention of clashing with that authority were absent, its power was, nevertheless, undermined by the train of both local and world events. This was to become more obvious when it was faced with a crisis as a result of the gradual spread of the world conflict. Then it could be seen to what extent, in the calm years that went before, the loyal vassals of the King of Spain in the Indies had become accustomed to the idea that the King could fail them, and how they had gradually been preparing, by the renovation of their ideological outlook and the formation of new systems of personal relationships, the solutions to that future crisis.

THE BRITISH INVASIONS AND THE INSTITUTIONAL CRISIS

In 1806, therefore, behind an imposing façade, the Spanish Imperial order displayed weaknesses the extent of which it is not easy to measure. This gradual debilitation does not explain its sudden collapse. It can be said of it, as was said of the unity of the Roman Empire, that it did not die of its own accord – it was murdered. The beginning of that onslaught from outside which the Spanish Empire was to be so impotent to resist took place in the River Plate region itself, within the context of that world-wide struggle in the course of which, only the year before, Spain and France had lost, at Trafalgar, even the hope of disputing the rule of the waves with their mighty British enemy. The consequences of this new naval equilibrium were to be felt in a colonial system linked to its metropolis only by the ocean, and the authorities in Madrid did not need a Trafalgar to foresee a British attack on Buenos Aires. Eight years before the defeat which had heightened this probability, detailed plans had been drawn up for the defence of the Viceroyalty in the event – which it was considered difficult to obviate – of the loss of its capital. These plans were based on the factor of isolation, which would cut off the invaders and force their withdrawal.[11]

This prudent plan took into account the increasing deterioration which, from the military point of view, had affected the Vicegeral system, which in 1797, and to an even greater extent in 1806, bore few traces of its martial origins. The shortage of regular troops – who had to be recruited in Spain – was only inadequately compensated by the local militias. The poor quality of the latter, which was due in part to the lack of enthusiasm for the profession of arms on the part of the local population, did not cause much worry to the authorities, which feared an equilibrium of force in which the local forces would be more powerful than the regular ones. Moreover, the most important elements of this increasingly ineffective military force had

The crisis of the Colonial order

been deployed in the rural areas and on the Indian frontier, which even further diminished its ability to resist a British invasion of the Viceregal capital.

This situation, tacitly realised by the authorities in Madrid, did not appear so obvious in Buenos Aires. From the local point of view the loss of the city, captured on the 27 June by the small force commanded by Beresford, was both an unexpected catastrophe and a scandal that required an explanation. It was the very weakness of the Colonial system which was suddenly revealed by this incident. The corporations of the captured city, although they were impelled by the very suddenness of the change to adapt themselves to it immediately (and they did so with more submissiveness than they cared subsequently to remember), gave themselves over – displaying an attitude that was logically contradictory, but explicable from an emotional point of view – to a heated discussion as to who was guilty and responsible. The invaders did nothing to discourage this, for they hoped that it would eliminate every trace of solidarity among those who had shared power in the system which their incursion had overthrown.

The Cabildo, the higher officials and the ecclesiastical dignitaries made haste to express their loyalty to those who were governing them in the name of the King of England. Beresford viewed with delighted surprise this unanimous and unhesitating submission. The Prior of the Dominican Order, speaking in the name of the clergy, was not content with quoting the Pauline text concerning the divine origin of the powers that be, he even went so far as to prophesy – on a more mundane level – a glorious future for Buenos Aires as a consequence of the new system imposed by the conquest. And, speaking in their own name and that of their city as well as in that of their new overlord, the members of the Cabildo wrote to the Viceroy, who had fled to Luján, to ask him to return to Buenos Aires the public treasure which he had managed to save from the invader: the latter was threatening to acquire alternative booty by raiding private coffers. Sobremonte decided to spare the wealthy of Buenos Aires this danger, and returned the Royal treasure, which was triumphantly exhibited in London. This was the culmination of a trend which had been evident ever since the Viceroy, on abandoning the city, had ordered the *oidores* to resist to the last. Neither they nor the Cabildo had wanted to face a destructive battle in the city, and had preferred to surrender to the invaders.

There were, of course, some who were privately indignant at such meekness. Manuel Belgrano spoke for all of them in his *Autobiografía*; the servility displayed by what he still referred to as 'my Consular Corporation' revealed yet again that 'the merchant recognises no country; no King and no religion, other than his own interest'. Belgrano had wanted to leave the city, with the official seals which were in his custody, and join the Viceroy at his headquarters. The Prior and the members of the Consulado, after changing their minds on the subject several times, preferred to remain in Buenos Aires and serve their new overlord.[12] Yet the corporations not only survived the conquest in this manner, but they never suffered any subsequent reproaches for their somewhat craven attitude. On the contrary, some of them were to take part in the chorus of indignant protest that arose, once the invaders had been ejected, against the cowardice and ineptitude of the Viceroy who could neither defend nor reconquer his capital. Perhaps more important than the complex of motivations which determined this conduct – among which the instinct of self-preservation was no doubt the most powerful – was the very fact that such conduct was possible. From June 1806 onwards the colonial institutions acquired a power which they were no longer prepared to cede to the Crown, the crisis of which followed hard upon the regional crisis provoked by the British invasion. The system within which they had grown up and which had established limitations – though not always very strict ones – to their attempts at insubordination, was beginning to disintegrate from above. The British conquest, despite the adversity it brought in its wake, at least showed corporation members and officials a new type of relationship with the supreme authorities, according to which the latter sought – by threats or by promises – a submission which previously had never even been questioned. It taught them then to discover, for the activities of corporations and public institutions, a new dimension, of a more strictly political nature, which in the past had been absent, and nothing that happened between then and 1810 caused them to entertain any doubts as to the essential importance of this discovery.

This new situation did not provoke unmixed enthusiasm among those who found their powers enhanced. It was more welcome to those who maintained less direct links with the central administration, which was, of course, the chief victim of this change. Between 1806 and 1810 the cautious policy followed by the Audiencia of Buenos Aires was principally directed towards arresting the decline – which was, in any case, inexorable – of an institutional system which seemed to be dissolving into warring fragments. It would, no doubt, be mistaken to seek for a similar continuity in the behaviour of the impetuous Bishop of Buenos Aires, but he too – even though his vigilance relaxed occasionally – seems to have detected in this new tendency, above all other considerations, a threat to Spanish power, of which he was a passionate supporter. These misgivings were not shared to anything like the same extent by those who felt the sources of their power to be less closely dependent on the full maintenance of the link with the central administration. In the Church, canons and other dignitaries – and, to an even greater extent, the heads of the regular orders – appeared more prepared to travel in a carefree spirit along the paths which the new situation had opened for them. In the sphere of civil administration, it was, above all, the Cabildo which thought the hour had come for the satisfaction of claims long overdue.

The new situation, therefore, offered opportunities for the solution of conflicts which had been building up for some time. The case of the Cabildo was typical. Whereas the Bourbon administration had made efforts to achieve its gradual subordination to career officials appointed by the Crown, the increasing prosperity transformed the beggarly corporation of the seventeenth century into a body capable of supplying the necessary financial backing for its growing political ambitions.[13] At the moment of the invasion, the discontent of the Cabildo had led to one of those insoluble and protracted conflicts with the Viceregal authorities which Madrid had learned to resolve by a policy of indifference; the invasion and the swift liberation seemed to offer an unexpected opportunity of solving that conflict. It was, above all, the liberation which presented this opportunity. While the Viceroy Sobremonte, from his refuge in Córdoba, was mustering, without any sense of urgency, the armed forces needed to recapture his capital, and his subordinates and collaborators had transferred their allegiance to the invaders, and local attempts at resistance had failed, it was a naval officer exiled in Montevideo who persuaded the local governor to give him command of the troops stationed there, and who defeated the British after two days of fighting. Liniers became immensely popular. In the city which he had liberated all those who had long-standing motives for not desiring the return of the Viceroy to his Fortress, and all those who had ignored his authority when, as a fugitive, he was preparing for a military action for which his past steady bureaucratic career had made him so unsuited, capitalised on this enthusiasm as a most welcome political weapon. After a victory which had only dealt with what was assumed to be merely the first phase of an attack which was to be renewed, there could be no course more dangerous than to re-establish in power someone who had proved so incapable of resisting the initial threat.

This was the basis of the rapprochement between the discontented elements and the man who had defeated the invading forces. At their head was the Cabildo which convened, on 14 August 1806, only two days after the Reconquest, a Council of War which was to limit the Viceroy's authority. The Viceroy entrusted Liniers with the military command of the capital, and devoted himself to the preparation of the Banda Oriental to resist a fresh British attack, a task for which – as events were soon to demonstrate – he was not particularly well equipped. The solution, imposed by popular pressure to which the members of the Council proved particularly amenable, was accepted, though not without hesitation, by the Viceroy, and had the support of the Audiencia, which was anxious to see the Viceregal system survive those turbulent times without a definitive breakdown of the institutional order: a partial delegation of authority appeared preferable to the violent overthrow of the Viceroy.

The winners were the members of the Cabildo and Liniers, who together undertook the enterprise from which there was to arise a force that was to give them solid support, but which was also, as events were to show, to destroy those who had united together to create that force. It was necessary to create a military force in the Vicegeral capital, in order to face the new British threat. When this enterprise, initiated in a spirit of complete agreement, began to be marked by the rivalry between the Cabildo and Liniers, it was to appear increasingly as the beginning of a kind of social revolution deliberately provoked by the victor of the British in order to assert his personal power. This was noticed, amid the universal indifference, by the Viceroy Sobremonte. He found it particularly disturbing that the militiamen armed as part of this immense defensive effort were allowed to keep their weapons in their homes. At the beginning of 1809 it was the Cabildo itself which denounced 'those who had made their fortunes by surrender and capitulation, those who bear arms unnecessarily and live at the public expense, who have exhausted the Treasury...when they could devote themselves to useful occupations, and contribute to the progress of industry'. In April the attorney-general of the city pointed out that if Buenos Aires was contributing so little to the embattled mother country it was because Liniers was already showing a tendency to seize those funds and distribute them 'among gaolbirds and vagabonds, to whom...he has distributed the honours and perquisites of the highest military offices'.[14] In those months, Diego Ponce de León described the followers of Liniers as 'all the lower orders of Buenos Aires, all the corps that he has recruited, eighteen hundred officers whom he has picked from the scum of the earth, ruining the Treasury by their exorbitant pay, and in addition a group of Frenchmen on whom he has conferred the principal commands in this militia which is as strange and outlandish as its creator'.[15] As early as October 1808 the Cabildo had described the officers appointed by Liniers as 'those whom a short time ago we saw as convicts, labouring in fetters on the public works, those against whom proceedings for theft are still pending, prison-warders, corporals, and others of the *canaille*, today we see them wearing the badges of rank of lieutenant-colonels'.[16] Even in 1811, in a context already completely transformed, even such a loyal revolutionary as Juan Manuel Beruti, when describing 'the individuals who under the old Spanish régime were nothing at all, and rose up afterwards',[17] found in the militarisation initiated by Liniers the primary cause of the swift changes which were fortunately limited later on by a government under which 'those who are appointed to high military or political posts are persons of standing' or at least possessed personal merits that made up for lack of it. In other words, according to this untiring chronicler, 'Señor Liniers and the first members of the Junta' used their power to arrange the systematic promotion of persons of humble origin. How much truth is there in this interpretation, which was to be repeated subsequently, and without any pejorative intention, by the historians of those troubled years? It must be noted that the biassed evidence of the adversaries of Liniers was too obviously orientated towards ruining him in the eyes of the central government. The importance attributed to the presence of Frenchmen in this improvised officer corps is in this sense revealing. It must also be pointed out that the more disinterested testimony of Beruti was excessively generalised in nature. He quotes only twenty-four names, in a list headed (clearly with pejorative intent) by that of Cornelio de Saavedra, and although he adds that he is interrupting the list of names 'because there are so many that to give them all one would need another notebook', he goes on to qualify this assertion by saying that, although there are 'a great many who have now been promoted who held high rank under the old Spanish government, yet those named here, had it not been for this metamorphosis, would surely never have risen from the status they formerly occupied, and the same is true of many whose names I have not given. However, there are among them many of illustrious families and good standing, who have held public appointments under the Cabildo as *alcaldes* or councillors, such as Saavedra, Rezával, etc'. In other words, not even those twenty-four men were genuine examples of people who had reached high rank from complete obscurity, and the somewhat confused Beruti now appears to be suggesting that the six years of 'metamorphosis' had provoked surprisingly little change in the previous equilibrium.

It is, however, undeniable that militarisation implied a change, and a far-reaching one, in the social equilibrium of Buenos Aires. In the first place one must emphasise, as did the perceptive enemies of Liniers, the creation of those 'one thousand eight hundred officers'. (They were, in fact, a little over twelve hundred in number, including non-commissioned officers.) In a society in which commerce and the public administration had provided, *par excellence*, the occupations considered to be honourable, the sudden creation of such a large number of salaried appointments in itself signified a radical innovation. Not only did it give rise – as was soon to become apparent – to tension between the old civilian officials and the new militia officers; of even greater importance was its direct effect of increasing the local costs of the administration and thus distributing in Buenos Aires a quantity of money that previously had found its way to Spain, and which was of the order of a million pesos a year, equivalent to 20 per cent of the value of the Viceroyalty's exports in the years of normal traffic across the Atlantic. Thus there began a process of redistribution between the mother country and the colony, and within the colony itself, which was subsequently accentuated by the Revolution. Yet it would still be necessary to determine to what extent this would provoke a replacement, or at least a broadening, of the ruling sectors, and this brings us back to the point emphasised so resentfully by contemporary observers of the process.

Of course, the method by which these officers were appointed – by election from among the militiamen themselves – seemed to offer opportunities for the rapid ascent of previously unknown figures. This possibility, however, did not pass unnoticed, and attempts were made to limit the risks inherent in the system. We find clear evidence of this in the writings of Belgrano. Returning after the Reconquest from his refuge in the Banda Oriental he found the Corps of Patricios in the middle of an election:

> From that moment I began to see the stratagems used by nonentities to rise above men of real merit; and if I had not supervised the counting of the votes myself, two obscure men, more distinguished for their vices than for anything else, would probably have risen to command the corps...Finally, the election was won by two men of some distinction, but even then there were obstacles which I had to overcome: I formed the men up again in the presence of General Liniers, who rode down the ranks with me and heard the general acclamation of the two men, so as a result they were appointed.[18]

Two obscure men, more distinguished for their vices than for anything else: this characterisation, which was both social and moral, but with the latter consideration predominant, should not lead us to forget something that Belgrano did not emphasise because it appeared to him obvious. That is his decision to prevent a popular election, through lack of adequate supervision, resulting in the election of people who had formerly held positions not considered to be honourable. Election by universal suffrage by a militia into which every able-bodied man had been recruited was a thin disguise for the broadening by a process of co-option of the dominant sectors.

Within this context, it is easier to understand the results of this early electoral experiment. Who were, in fact, the high-ranking officers of these newly formed units? The first commanding officer of the Patricios was Cornelio de Saavedra, whom not even the ill will of his enemies could represent as a *homo novus*, for he had occupied appointments in the Cabildo, as had his father before him. Serving with him were Esteban Romero, a prosperous merchant, and José Domingo de Urien, chief accountant of the Consulado and an officer in the somewhat shadowy militia that had existed prior to the invasion. The other officers were from a similar background. Most of those elected were merchants, and the rest held posts in the higher and middle levels of the Viceregal bureaucracy. If we reconsider, in the light of these facts, the invectives against the social levelling provoked by militarisation, we can see that the data recorded are often accurate, but they do not justify the conclusions that these prejudiced witnesses draw from them. Does this mean, therefore, that the creation of a force of eight thousand armed men, and the recruitment of 1,200 officers and non-commissioned officers in a city of under 50,000 inhabitants, of whom thirty per cent were slaves, had no substantial effect on the power equilibrium? This would not be a necessary consequence of the fact, which is not surprising, that those who dominated this new force held a less marginal position than is sometimes supposed in the structure of power and prestige existing before 1806.

On the contrary, their presence, at the moment when the position of the metropolis was becoming more tenuous as a result of geographical isolation, was to have decisive consequences. These improvised military forces were gradually becoming the basis on which the Viceregal power rested. And these forces were locally recruited and locally financed; they were, moreover, overwhelmingly composed of the American-born. Even in the second half of 1806 this latter factor does not seem to have been realised, nor its possible repercussions. The misgivings responsible for limiting the military recruitment of the Creoles seem to have existed only in accounts which are both retrospective and of doubtful validity. On the contrary, after the first spontaneous enrolments there were evident efforts on the part of the entire administrative apparatus to extend this mobilisation to those as yet unaffected by it. What appears less improbable is that the Cabildo should have wanted to reserve for itself control over the new military power through the Corps of Patriots of the Union, in which American-born militiamen were placed under the command of predominantly Spanish-born officers, in whom the Cabildo had a trust which was to prove unfounded. But such precautions did not mean that the mobilisation that followed the reconquest did not take place in an atmosphere of substantial agreement. When did this general agreement begin to break down? Before this happened, there was an end to the enthusiasm that had accompanied the first wave of mobilisation. The exercises in the early mornings gradually began to appear absolutely useless to the militiamen, who eventually agreed with those who derided them for their attendance. In late 1806, when the Banda Oriental was threatened, it was again necessary to dispatch there the regular troops, who until then had been employed in instructing the new militia. The latter had to be subjected to a new system of discipline, with permanent quartering in barracks and pay for officers and soldiers. Only the units recruited from the American-born were affected by this change; those formed from the Spanish-born, whose military instruction took place only once a week and did not interfere with their normal activities, remained unpaid. This shows that, even though among the officers it was difficult to perceive differences between the 'Spanish' and the 'American' units, there was a clear distinction as far as the soldiers were concerned. The 'Spanish' units were only in exceptional cases able to recruit from that semi-employed or poorly paid sector to whose members a monthly remuneration of twelve pesos was sufficient compensation for the abandonment of their peacetime activities.

It was, therefore, those units recruited from the American-born which introduced new elements into the power equilibrium. This was not only because power was now conferred on those who previously had not had it. The situation was also affected by those who, although they had in the past formed part of the upper sectors and had exercised power and influence, now enjoyed an immense increase of both. Even Ignacio Núñez, for all his malevolence, had to admit that Cornelio de Saavedra, 'the offspring of a distinguished family...had enjoyed among the Spaniards a degree of consideration which the native-born rarely attained'.[19] His former enviable position, however, did not give Saavedra anything like the power that he was to enjoy as commanding officer of the Corps of Patricios. However, the consequences of urban militarisation were only to become fully apparent when the institutional crisis became really serious, and above all when that crisis was not faced with the same unanimity that had characterised the thinly disguised elimination of Sobremonte. Meanwhile, the need to ensure the goodwill of the strengthened Creole élite became gradually more apparent, and even before its open break with Liniers, the Cabildo took advantage of the re-election of its members in January 1808 to ensure that its new composition would display an equal balance between the European-born and the American-born. This innovation was all the more impressive because the outgoing Cabildo – unlike many of its predecessors – had been entirely composed of the Spanish-born. Even so, it is doubtful whether this anxiety to appear more broadly representative was primarily occasioned by the new power which militarisation had conferred on Creole merchants, officials and professional men who had become first militia commanders and then officers in regular units. In addition to this factor, one must bear in mind the increasing political ambitions of the Cabildo, which, as it increasingly detached itself from the rest of the administrative apparatus, was impelled to find a broader basis of support outside its own ranks. It appears that, until they were cruelly deceived a year later, the leaders of the Cabildo expected to be able to count on the support, or at least the passive acquiescence, of both the American and the European units. The attempts at establishing a military equilibrium more favourable to the latter, by means of intrigues to which Belgrano refers, and the importance of which it is difficult to measure, and even through the disbandment of American units and their provisional replacement by Spanish ones, whose members agreed to serve without pay until the arrival of reinforcements from Spain, are not incompatible with that confident trust, without which the attempt of January 1809 would have been inconceivable.

It was the second British invasion which inspired in the Cabildo the belief that its rising power could no longer be disputed. The Cabildo was the protagonist of the new victory, and whereas Liniers, after an unsuccessful attempt at resistance, withdrew to the North-West, within the city the resistance of the Spanish and Creole regiments saved the stronghold which was at one time completely surrounded. The Defence, even more than the Reconquest, was a victory for the city, for its regiments – both Creole and Spanish, and for all its inhabitants, even for the slaves, armed in the hour of crisis with steel weapons and displaying a loyalty and courage which surprised those who had hesitated about arming them. It was, above all, a victory for the Cabildo and for its presiding chairman, Don Martín de Álzaga, a wealthy Spanish-born merchant whose ambitions were even more far-reaching than those of the institution with which he identified himself.

Of course, Liniers's modest participation in the victory did not directly affect his situation, which had been consolidated institutionally ever since, in June, news had arrived that the Crown had decreed a change in the arrangements for filling provisional vacancies in the office of Viceroy. Instead of the President of the Audiencia, it was to be the highest ranking military officer who was to take the Viceroy's place. Madrid had in mind Pascual Ruiz Huidobro, a naval officer and governor of Montevideo. His capture and departure for England as a prisoner left the way clear for the hero of the Reconquest, who as early as January, by a debatable decision of the Cabildo which the Audiencia did not dare to contest, had seen the sphere of his military jurisdiction – previously limited to the capital – broadened to include the Banda Oriental, which was threatened by a fresh British attack and which it was proposed to defend with troops the command of which it was considered imprudent to place under the authority of the Viceroy Sobremonte. Sobremonte was, however, the victim of the second British offensive. His participation in the abortive resistance in the Banda Oriental – among other things he was reproached for not having given Liniers the support he promised – was even more ignominious than his behaviour in 1806. After Montevideo had fallen to the British – this happened on 3 February, and the news reached Buenos Aires four days later – his immediate suspension from office was decided by a War Committee which only debated as to which would be the least brusque method of effecting a removal which all judged to be unavoidable.

Thus the popular hero of 1806 became, in 1807, the head of the Royal administration in the River Plate region. His power had not, of course, lessened as a result of this change, but its basis was changed, and the new basis was of necessity an ephemeral one. Liniers knew only too well that he would never occupy permanently the place which a train of fortuitous events had given him on a purely interim basis. This was also known to his old allies and recent adversaries. The Cabildo, which had at first maintained excellent relations with the architect of the Reconquest, became gradually more hostile towards him in the course of 1808, until finally a violent quarrel broke out. Its cause was the increasing rapprochement between the successor of Sobremonte and the latter's collaborators, with whom the Cabildo had long-standing disputes and on whom it had hoped to wreak condign vengeance once their leader was out of the way. To find them again in control of the Viceregal administrative apparatus was an unpleasant surprise. In this way, by increasingly identifying himself with that narrow clique of senior officials whose inadequacy had been so ruthlessly exposed by the events of 1806 and 1807, Liniers was losing the support of those who had supported him in his meteoric rise to power. The dangers this posed seem to have been completely unnoticed by him. The Cabildo, however, was well aware of the risks it would be running if it lost control over the man who had been its champion, but its efforts to recover this control only hastened and aggravated the clash. From the point of view of the Cabildo, Liniers was both the representative (albeit temporary) of legitimacy and a serious rival for the domination of those new forces which militarisation had introduced into the balance of power. For this reason, the Cabildo was especially sensitive to Liniers's attempts to extend military recruitment outside the city boundaries, by the creation of new regiments of soldiers recruited in the rural areas, the Littoral and even the Interior, and whose officers would be appointed not according to the complex system employed by the urban militias, but by the Viceroy's successor directly.

In this case, as elsewhere, Liniers's perceptive adversaries appear to have grasped more clearly than did he himself the line of action that it would be in his interest to take. Behind the creation of these units with French officers and soldiers unaffected by the turbulent political atmosphere of the capital, it is, in fact, difficult to discover any vast plan by which the ephemeral successor of the Viceroy might have been attempting to create a power-base for himself. Had that been his intention, he would no doubt have devoted greater effort to the project. The somewhat intermittent attention which he gave to it seems to show that, hastily adopting the narrow professional stand-point which his new status was wont to induce in those who had reached it, Liniers's main preoccupation was with furthering the careers of his closest associates.

Indeed, the other accusations levelled against him by the Cabildo were less of a novelty in the long and unsavoury history of institutional conflicts in the Spanish Indies: Liniers allegedly protected the commercial interests of those who were his friends. A more serious accusation was that similar favours – apparently not, in this case, bestowed freely – were conferred by his mistress, against whom the indignant enemies of Liniers untiringly penned excessively monotonous attacks. Those who were loyal to him did not attempt to refute these accusations. Ignoring the more scandalous charges, they confined themselves to pointing out that administrative corruption had existed before the appearance of Liniers, and that several of those who denounced it so violently knew only too well, and not only from hearsay, that this was the case. One cannot, of course, act as arbiter of these labyrinthine polemics, in which the most violent accusations were levelled all the more freely because they were addressed to a Court so far away that messages took months to reach it, a Court which could only take cognisance of the facts it was supposed to judge through blatantly partial witnesses. Nor can one find traces, in these alignments of interests which the speed of changes in the commercial situation (deriving partly from local decisions, but to an even greater extent from the course of the world war) necessarily rendered ephemeral, of a continuous pattern of behaviour which would make it possible to speak of the secret existence of a 'Spanish party' and a 'Patriot party', nor even of the growth of these on the basis of rivalries between commercial cliques.

The crisis of the Colonial order

Nevertheless, there is no doubt that, by ignoring the commercial interests of those who controlled the Cabildo and favouring, in a necessarily arbitrary manner, other people with a perhaps less solidly prosperous backing, Liniers was aggravating a conflict which it would have been in his interest to attenuate. Thus, less than a year after the Defence, the Captain-General and the Cabildo were in open conflict. Both sides believed that they could count on the support of that new force created by militarisation, but neither side was prepared for a frontal attack against the adversary which would only prejudice its case, which was subject to arbitration by the Crown. One must not, therefore, exaggerate the immediate consequences of the militarisation provoked by the Invasions. As long as the Crown still carried weight as the source of legitimacy that force, however effective, could not be fully utilised in local conflicts.

Yet it was, precisely, the crisis of Spain itself which would contribute new factors to the changes initiated locally in 1806. There was a foretaste of this when, at the beginning of 1808, the Portuguese Court arrived at Rio de Janeiro, fleeing from the French invading forces which had captured Lisbon. Thus the war again approached the River Plate region. Spain had supported the French action against Portugal, and the Royal refugees had reached their American domains guarded on the journey by warships of the British Navy. The old dispute which the Iberian countries had carried on along their South Atlantic frontier threatened to break out again, this time within the wider context created by the Napoleonic wars. The acting Viceroy, the governor of Montevideo (since the British withdrawal Colonel Elío had filled, on appointment by Liniers, the post vacated by Ruiz Huidobro), took steps to find out what offensive preparations were going on beyond the Rio Grande frontier. The Cabildo of Buenos Aires thought the moment opportune to adopt once again the grand policy which it was from now on to follow consistently. Álzaga travelled to Montevideo to make arrangements with Elío for the defence of the Banda Oriental against a possible Portuguese attack. An indication of this was seen in the mission of Brigadier-General Curado, who was to take to Buenos Aires a message from his sovereign for the Viceregal authorities. The latter suspected him of having the less honourable intention of spying on the military preparations in progress. He was never to reach the Viceregal capital, since Elío had orders to keep him entertained in meaningless conversations, and he was still in the Banda Oriental when the turn of events in Europe transformed him from an enemy into a potential ally. Even before this, open conflict had broken out between the Viceroy and the Cabildo. In May Liniers decided to seek a *modus vivendi* with the Portuguese Court which would open Brazilian ports to River Plate commerce. The Cabildo had many objections to the project. It suspected that such an arrangement would provide further opportunities for profit for those merchants closely associated with the Viceroy who were already finding opportunities in abundance. It also suspected the envoy chosen by Liniers, Lázaro de Rivera, who was both the Viceroy's brother-in-law and a former official of dubious reputation. It was, moreover, alarmed by the new-found capability of initiative of an official who had previously been more circumspect: ever since the Crown had ratified his promotion, Liniers had appeared more self-assured and less ready to submit to the arrogant supervision of the Cabildo.

However, the motive of the quarrel was not well chosen: the Viceroy could ignore with impunity the still courteous observations of the municipal corporation, and suggest that it should mind its own business. The Cabildo could hope for no better support from the Audiencia, which had viewed with alarm the power and ambition of the rival body. In any case, the Cabildo did not cease to cast suspicion on the loyalty to Spain of the Viceroy, and that suspicion was soon to be expressed, in the light of a fresh turn in world events, in a more sensational way. Indeed, owing to the new political alignment, Liniers's French origin became the motive for quite legitimate suspicion. His local enemies, who had already tried to represent him as being too friendly to the Portuguese and the British (and they were to continue in the future to reproach him for those contacts, which even the new alliance was not to make appear totally innocuous), did not let this unexpected opportunity pass, and untiringly accused the acting Viceroy of being a long-standing agent of Napoleon. This accusation had no serious foundation. There is no doubt that, in the days of the alliance that had now been renounced, Liniers had expressed admiration for Napoleon, but he was not the only one to do so. True, he had drawn attention to his French origin in a message to the Emperor, but these demonstrations of zeal, which were, in any case, expressed quite openly, took place against the background of an alliance which made them perfectly compatible with a loyalty to Spain which in Liniers was very deeply felt, and which was to become even stronger when he himself became the highest local representative of the Spanish Imperial system. His attitudes after the anti-French rising show him to have been in substantial agreement with other officials who were only too well aware that their future was identified with the Colonial connection. Although his cautious attitude towards that unwelcome Napoleonic envoy, the Marquis de Sassenay, who arrived in Buenos Aires in August 1808, and his ferocious denunciations of the new enemy of Spain, demonstrate very clearly that Liniers had obvious reasons for speaking with exaggerated fervour, his privately expressed anger at the officials who were prepared to submit to a pedantic examination the titles of legitimacy of the Seville Junta which was making war on France in the name of the captive King was motivated by the same sentiments which he displayed in public. There is no doubt that this adherence to a principle of legitimacy, which he appreciated chiefly for its usefulness in the perpetuation of the Colonial connection, would not have prevented him from accepting a change of dynasty if the metropolitan country had accepted it. Here again, however, his attitude was the same as that of the majority of the Crown's officials in the Americas, from whom there was never any reason to expect any revolutionary initiative.

This quite evident innocence was eventually accepted even by his enemies. In the opinion of Diego Ponce de León (writing on 10 February 1809), the danger of collusion between Liniers and France, though real enough in the past, had disappeared thanks, adds the diarist, to the action of Elío in Montevideo. The archtraitor who governed in Buenos Aires was not for that reason any less dangerous; he was now thinking 'of independence, of joining forces with Carlota, and of giving her sovereignty over this colony'.[20] Although this denunciation is an inaccurate description of the motivations of the hated acting Viceroy, it does, on the other hand, provide a good reflection of the bewildering changes which had already taken place in the worldwide context within which the River Plate crisis was taking place. The independence party, so small in reality but exaggerated in the popular imagination by the precautionary measures taken against it, was mentioned with increasing frequency. Each of the conflicting sectors unhesitatingly accused its adversaries of belonging to it. The friends of Álzaga denounced the supposed pro-independence tendencies of Liniers, while Belgrano and his friends – who still believed independence to be impossible – attributed similar sentiments to a group of ambitious men, without a doubt that led by the arrogant *alcalde*.[20] Belgrano's denunciations were addressed to the Princess Carlota Joaquina, whom he begged to exert her influence before the revolutionaries, by a surprise *coup*, established an independent republic in Buenos Aires.

The Infanta, who had arrived in Rio de Janeiro with her royal husband, did in fact offer a solution to the crisis provoked by the collapse of the central authority. From Rio de Janeiro, protected from the French threat by the ocean and the British Navy, she could with perfect legitimacy invest those who were to govern the Americas in the name of Spain. The advantages which she possessed as a symbol of the vacant throne over the Juntas that had arisen in Spain were not only due to the precarious military situation of the latter, but also to the very debatability of their claim to act in the name of the captive King. In the face of such claims, the thesis that the Spanish realms were only legally united through common submission to the same sovereign was so obvious that it was already beginning to be used to challenge the right of certain European-born Spaniards, who had received their investiture at the hands of the people of the Peninsula, to govern the American realms. None of these objections applied to the Princess. Her Regency – or, as others preferred to call it, her elevation to the rank of provisional Queen – could only, in fact, be based on the support which her cause might enjoy in the Americas, and in law such support would be not the cause, but the consequence of a just title to government based on dynastic reasons and not on any popular investiture.

The Infanta could thus fill the void produced at the summit of the Spanish monarchy, and safeguard the dominant characteristics of the political system based on it. This doubtless explains why many Royal officials were attracted by *carlotismo*. It is not so good an explanation of why it had support from some veterans of the independence party and from some others who, while not being in favour of independence, had no reason to devote themselves to saving absolutism at all costs. For the latter group the determining factor was the specific content which the alternatives to *carlotismo* were beginning to acquire. Of such alternatives, allegiance to the Seville Junta was undoubtedly the least attractive. Although nominally commited to a thorough-going revolution in the Spanish political system, the Junta, and its successor in Cádiz, preferred conservation rather than innovation as far as the Americas were concerned. This not only meant the rejection of any far-reaching transformation of the basic statutes governing Spanish America, but in a more immediate context it created an implicit solidarity between the Junta and the agents which the *ancien régime* maintained in its colonies. The Junta thought that support for this group was the best defence for its own fragile authority. Separation offered an alternative, not perhaps, through the establishment of a republic, but more probably through the formation of a Junta which might or might not acknowledge the supremacy of the Seville Junta (even if it did so, the effective authority of the latter would be drastically curtailed). But this alternative did not attract those who in the past had appeared receptive to the possibility of utilising for their own ends the crisis of the Spanish system, and who were now professing an alarmed legitimism. Why was this? Their denunciations show the reason quite clearly. It was because they did not consider themselves strong enough to undertake such an audacious task and thus seize control of the local government. Belgrano, Vieytes, Nicolás Rodríguez Peña, Castelli could not be 'republicans' because the members of the Cabildo already were. The latter controlled the institutional apparatus which the former needed to create a new locally based power structure. There was another factor in their favour: identified as they were with the European-born Spaniards, who in one way or another depended on the maintenance of the Colonial connection, their innovating tendencies would doubtless find a more benevolent reception in what remained of the mother country than would the views of certain American subjects whose loyalty had always been somewhat suspect.

In fact – as events were to show – those who were attracted to *carlotismo* and later went over to the Revolution could always fall back on their military superiority. But this required the unanimity of all the American units and their leaders, and this was for the moment lacking. Even if they could count on that support, the outcome of a military confrontation was far from certain. What was more important was that the River Plate region, despite the crisis in Spain, was not so isolated that an open breach of

The crisis of the Colonial order

legality could be consolidated by merely local military superiority. Portugal and Britain, those awe-inspiring new allies of Spain, were elements that could not be ignored. It was not surprising that the future Patriots should have taken care to preserve the mantle of legitimacy, and should have supported in the Infanta Carlota a new representative of the latter, hoping that under her sway the local equilibrium could be altered for the benefit of those very Americans among whom they recruited her first supporters, and that – faced with even more immediate choices – they should have supported the acting Viceroy, and thus been in agreement with the hated administrative apparatus which, without allying itself with the Viceroy, also viewed with alarm the manoeuvres of the Cabildo, the consequences of which were unpredictable within the context of Spain's collapse.

In this way – repeating the course followed by other new forces – that which militarisation had introduced into the River Plate region was to begin by consolidating its power and by giving indispensable support to a tottering legitimacy. Thus it saved Liniers from his momentarily triumphant adversaries, and provided an unexpected – and merely temporary – *dénouement* to a conflict which had been increasing in intensity since September 1808. Subsequently, the authority of Buenos Aires and of the acting Viceroy was challenged by the dissident movement of Montevideo and its Junta headed by General Elío, whom Liniers had in vain tried to dismiss from the post to which he himself had appointed him after the British withdrawal from Montevideo. There is no doubt that the decisive manner in which Elío defended his threatened authority was a determining factor in the growth of dissidence in the Banda Oriental, but it is equally true that Elío was able to rely on very firm support because his action expressed regional as well as personal tensions. The rivalry between Montevideo and Buenos Aires had already manifested itself on several occasions. The capital of the Banda Oriental, a garrison city with a hinterland containing the richest cattle-raising lands of the Viceregal territory, was ill disposed to accept the predominance of its older rival, which in any case knew how to extract very tangible commercial advantages from the situation. The invasions represented a fresh opportunity for demonstrating these hostile sentiments. Montevideo affected to feel ignored by a Buenos Aires which was celebrating the Reconquest as its own feat of arms. After the final British withdrawal, it found fresh reasons for discontent in the prohibition against trafficking in the merchandise which the defeated invaders had left behind in the city.

But the popular mood in Montevideo was only one aspect – and not the most important one – of the new situation. The basic characteristic of the latter was a flagrant breach of legality; the chief protagonists began by invoking attenuating circumstances. They took action, according to their own accounts, under irresistible popular pressure, and to avoid greater evils, at a moment when the disappearance of the Viceroy's emissary, provoked by the alarming situation in Montevideo, in any case made it impossible to comply with his instructions. In this way the Montevideo Junta hoped to be recognised by the Viceregal authorities, but that hope was soon frustrated. Magistrates, officials and military commanders supported the Viceroy; the Bishop of Buenos Aires went so far as to forbid the dispatch to the rebellious city of an image which was taken to Montevideo every year to be carried in a procession.

In the face of the united front, provoked by alarm, of the representatives of legitimacy, Montevideo drew its strength not only from the difficulty inherent in any attempt to subdue it by military force, but in the sympathies it evoked in Buenos Aires itself, in that very Cabildo which it had become accustomed to look on as an enemy stronghold. Prudencio Murguiondo, the commanding officer of a unit of Basque troops on detachment in Montevideo with the soldiers which the capital had sent there in expectation of a renewed British attack, was the spokesman of the rebel Junta. Not only he, but also Elío, maintained clandestine contact with Álzaga and the Cabildo. In October the latter thought it advisable to take the offensive, and it took advantage of the marriage of a daughter of Liniers to a citizen of Buenos Aires, which infringed the rules (which were frequently flouted) forbidding the formation of family ties by higher officials in their districts of jurisdiction. This attack was defensive in character. The Cabildo was afraid that, on the occasion of its imminent renewal, which took place by co-option but was subject to the Viceroy's approval, the latter would seize the opportunity of subduing that focus of dissent. When the Cabildo informed the Audiencia of the scruples which prevented it maintaining communication with a Viceroy who, in the opinion of the Cabildo, had ceased to hold office, their intention was to seek support for their decision not to inform him of the list of new Cabildo members and simply proceed with their investiture, dispensing with the Viceroy's approval. The Audiencia was unimpressed by this stratagem. It had already asked Seville for a decision concerning the marriage of the Viceroy's daughter, and until that decision was given it did not intend to accelerate the crisis of the Colonial institutions by again condoning the deposition of a Viceroy by his subordinates. This decision of the Audiencia was, in the view of the Cabildo, yet another proof that the Viceroy had transformed that body into an instrument of his policy. Even though this conclusion was unjustified, since the Audiencia had quite undisguisedly stood apart from the alliance between the Cabildo and Liniers, and now confined itself to opting for the rival which seemed best able to defend institutional stability, it at least proves that the Audiencia's position as the local arbiter of legitimacy could be a decisive weapon in the hands of the Viceroy.

This was the case not only when dealing with the Cabildo members and career officials. In addition, the military apparatus which, as the crisis grew more acute, became the arbiter of the situation, found that the question of legitimacy was of decisive importance. There is no doubt that, as was pointed out by the Cabildo before it was emphasised by those historians who decided to support its cause, the military commanders had a professional interest in maintaining the authority of the Viceroy. Even so, they would perhaps not have defended it so openly had they not known that this attitude could not be held as reprehensible from the point of view of the Colonial judicial and administrative system. The fact that military support was going to be decisive, at least in the early stages, was soon realised by both rivals. On the 10 October 1808, when there were widespread rumours of an imminent rising in support of the secession of Montevideo, a statement signed by the majority of military leaders, including nearly all the commanding officers of those units which had been placed on a paid basis and subjected to military discipline, expressed their willingness to lay down their lives for the Viceroy against the hypothetical insurgents, and requested him to make every effort to seek out and punish them. This reflected the same alignment of forces which was to recur on 1 January 1809, when there was an attempt to overthrow the Viceroy.

In fact, on that day the new Cabildo was designated by the outgoing members, and the list submitted for the Viceroy's approval, which was immediately granted. This unexpectedly peaceful solution to the conflict, which had appeared to be growing more acute during the previous week, was immediately offset by the outbreak of a riot in the main square. Its protagonists were a mass of people, the composition of which it is impossible to define precisely, though they hardly numbered a hundred, and the militiamen from a light infantry unit, who had been previously called to arms by the Cabildo in expectation of a *coup* by the Viceroy. Both groups demanded the establishment of a Junta and the deposition of the Viceroy. While negotiations were going on in the Fortress, the main square threatened to become a battlefield, with a confrontation between the light infantry and the Corps of Patricios and others who had arrived to oppose them. There were some skirmishes, and after the intercession of the Bishop the Patricios withdrew from the square, leaving their rivals believing that they had won a victory. Liniers offered his resignation, but was not prepared to accept the establishment of a Junta. Ruiz Huidobro, who had returned from his brief spell of captivity and had been designated Viceroy by the Junta of Galicia, though this designation was invalidated by the subsequent submission of that Junta to that of Seville, had been rejected by Elío as Governor of Montevideo (an appointment to which Liniers had designated him at the suggestion of the Audiencia), and was now, at this most opportune moment, in Buenos Aires, ready to replace Liniers according to the new rules governing Viceregal vacancies. Whereas Liniers demonstrated that even in these circumstances his primary concern was to save the Spanish system in the service of which he had enjoyed such a brilliant career, his supporters made his proposed sacrifice unnecessary.

The Patricios and the Andalusians again occupied the square. On their behalf, Saavedra declared that he would not tolerate the seditious deposition of the Viceroy, and the latter then retracted his resignation, which had already been formally tendered. The defeat of the Cabildo was complete, and the repression of it began immediately. Some of its members, together with commanders and officers of units that had taken part in the rising, were deported to Patagonia, to be liberated later by the dissidents from Montevideo, where they found refuge. The subversive regiments – the Basques, the light infantry and the Galicians – were disbanded. While the Bishop rejoiced over the defeat of the subversive plot, which had been an imitation of the more successful movement in Montevideo, it was not only the defeated side which thought that the city was now at the mercy of the whims of a Viceroy only too well served by his military followers. Of a particularly scandalous nature was the seizure of the hoard of bullion hidden by the Cabildo's attorney Villanueva, which signified a booty of over 200,000 pesos for the public treasury, which was in financial straits due in large part to the militarisation itself. '...They lay hands on the most sacred things', observed an adversary of Liniers who was also a rich merchant, 'for they searched one house and violently stole 30,000 pesos'; such, observed the legal representatives of the Cabildo members sent away into captivity, were 'the sad, fatal consequences, at all times and in all places, which experience has recorded when the military element usurps functions which are the exclusive preserve of the civil power'.[21]

However, this new military power, the importance of which was revealed by the events of January, was at the same time a revolutionary novelty in the local balance of power and the standard-bearer of legitimacy. It celebrated its victory characteristically, on the 8 January, by swearing allegiance to the Seville Junta, the only repository of sovereignty in the absence of the captive King. The 1st January, then, appears to have witnessed a confrontation between the unexpected defenders of the old order and those in favour of throwing themselves into the turbulent stream of the political crisis which was transforming the Spanish monarchy, with results that were still unforeseeable. But was that, in fact, the essential point of difference between the rivals of that day? They themselves do not seem to have thought so. The defeated side turned, without feeling that this implied any disloyalty to its ideals, to the Seville Junta, from which it expected redress. Several of those who had supported the Viceroy remained, both before and after the 1st January, receptive to possible alternative solutions of the political crisis, and were not limited in their explorations by a strict loyalty to the monarchy. Another interpretation of the clash that had occurred seemed to find an immediate echo among the losers, and to arouse a later echo among those of the winners who were to find themselves, a little more than a year later, leading the Revolution. It was the interpretation which found in the alignments of that January day traces of the antagonism between the Spanish-born and the American-born.

Even this interpretation, however, does not seem to do complete justice to the complexity of the tensions which underlay the clash of that day. Not only was there a mixture of Spaniards and Creoles in both contending parties. There was a similar mixture among those who were to separate when, after 1810, the breakdown of the unity of the Spanish system presented itself as a clear probability. Among the supporters of the Cabildo were some who were to be the most intransigent revolutionaries – these included Mariano Moreno and Hipólito Vieytes, both American-born, and Juan Larrea, a Spaniard – and the Viceroy was supported by some who were to support another Viceroy in 1810. Moreover, until the clash actually occurred, the two rivals preferred to avoid too narrow an identification with 'Peninsulars' or Creoles, which would have prevented them seeking simultaneous support from both groups. The Cabildo – which appears not to have expected the unanimity of the opposition of the military units – enjoyed the support of one of the commanders of the Corps of Patricios, Esteban Romero, and it thought that the moment had come to reap the fruits of their cautious approach to certain American-born figures which, even before the renewal of 1808, had been demonstrated by their appointment of Juan Martín de Pueyrredón, a native son of the country whose uncertain political orthodoxy must have been known to the Cabildo, as their legal representative at the Spanish Court. Liniers, although – as the beneficiary and promoter of military recruitment – he was accused after his victory of having systematically encouraged rivalry between one group and another, would have been unable, for several reasons, to have adopted so unequivocal an attitude. The loyalty of the American-born had for long been an object of suspicion to the Spanish authorities on whom Liniers depended, and an even more pressing reason was that too close an identification with the Creoles would have deprived him of the support of the magistrates and officials, and of the help of those Spanish military units which finally came out in favour of the Viceroy and against the Cabildo.

However, although the rivalry between these two sectors was not the only cause of the conflict of January, the consequences of the latter as regards the equilibrium between the two were immediately perceptible. The disbanded regiments had grouped together the natives of those regions of Spain from which those who dominated the commercial life of the Viceregal era had also come. Together with those regiments, it was that hegemonic sector which had been defeated and humiliated to such a degree that there had to be a Viceregal edict prohibiting the public defamation of the ex-members of the disbanded units. As for the Spanish-born among those on the victorious side, they either came from regions of Spain accustomed to sending less prosperous emigrants to America (such as the Andalusians) or they were connected, not so much with big business, that stronghold of the Spanish-born, as with that other stronghold, the upper bureaucracy, which in the hour of crisis had refused to follow along the road of political adventurism. The members of this group were too bewildered to rejoice unhesitatingly over their own victory, and on the other hand those who did celebrate it attributed to the outcome a connotation both American and plebeian which was to alarm the Seville Junta and be untiringly emphasised by the defeated side.

The outcome of the clash appears, therefore, to have been ambiguous, and this ambiguity was closely related to the fragility of the victory of the Viceroy and his military supporters. In representing themselves as the standard-bearers of legitimacy, they were implicitly submitting to the arbitration of the final arbiter within the Spanish political system – the Seville Junta – and they could not count on its benevolence. If they did so, it was not only because the long-standing habit of loyalty to Spain could not disappear overnight. Loyalism – which was not felt with equal sincerity by all the victors of the conflict – was moreover the only common ground among those who had to be united in order to win the day. But by giving their victory this interpretation, they in fact limited its scope. Within a very short time the victors and their enemies were to agree that the clash of the 1st January had not resolved anything, but that the battle was still on. In these circumstances, the Bourbon Infanta and her agents were able to continue their work of agitation. They were not entirely successful. As the terms of the conflict which was maturing in the River Plate region became clearer, the indecision which Carlota and her emissaries did so much to encourage became increasingly difficult to sustain. By the end of 1808, the prejudicial consequences of that indecision began to be clearly observable. The Infanta found it to be in her interest to denounce to the River Plate authorities her own agent, the Englishman James Paroissien, whom she suspected of playing a double game in favour of a project of republican independence. The suspicion appeared to be without foundation, and Carlota's star seemed momentarily to wane. In the middle of 1809 it was to have a brief resurrection, when the victors of the January conflict, disowned by Seville, dreamed for a moment of making the Infanta the head of a legitimacy to rival the one that had treated them so ungratefully. Letters expressing submissive devotion to the dynasty were again sent from Buenos Aires to Rio de Janeiro. It was a somewhat limited response to the extensive propaganda carried on on behalf of the Infanta, who was tyring to win over all those who, at this moment of evident crisis, might be able to influence the future course of events. A list of the recipients of *carlotista* propaganda provides an accurate picture of the ruling sector at that moment when political struggle, expressed as the rivalry of military forces, was beginning to emerge from a past which had only known the tenacious battles in which the ecclesiastical and administrative institutions had traditionally engaged. This picture – described for us by observers who were no

The crisis of the Colonial order

doubt not infallible, but were certainly sensitive to the changes in the political situation – is not yet the image of a political class, but it is no longer that of a substantially bureaucratic élite. The list drawn up by Felipe Contucci in November 1808,[22] for the information of the Minister Rodrigo de Souza Coutinho, includes elements outside the framework of the Colonial corporations and even outside that of the new nuclei of power created by militarisation. It was a list, with a breakdown by occupation and geographical location, of the 'loyal and respectable persons' in Buenos Aires who could, in the opinion of Contucci, be trusted by the Portuguese Government (see table).

	Buenos Aires	Littoral	Interior	Chile	Upper Peru	Others	Total
Clergy	29	2	2	—	1	1	35
Royal officials	11	4	—	1	1	1	18
Corporation and Cabildo officials	2	—	—	—	—	—	2
Officers of new regiments	23	—	—	—	—	—	23
Officers of militia	7	—	1	—	—	1	9
Officers of regular units	2	2	—	—	—	—	4
Lawyers	13	—	2	—	—	3	18
Landowners	8	—	—	1	—	—	9
Merchants	1	—	—	—	—	—	1
Others	3	—	—	1	—	—	4
Total	99	8	5	3	2	6	123

Of the 123 persons on the list, 59 belong to categories that formed part of a classic Colonial élite (35 clergy, 18 Royal officials, 2 Cabildo officials, 4 officers of regular units). Even among these, the numerical predominance of the clergy indicates that the institutional crisis, which was by now evident, had introduced significant changes in the power equilibrium. Of course, the value of these figures is limited by the fact that it was precisely among the groups which for a long time had held positions at the decision-making level that the definition of political attitudes took place most quickly. It is, therefore, obvious that the fact that only two people connected with the Cabildo appear on Contucci's list does not mean that the Cabildo had taken no part in the struggle for power, but that they had already assumed attitudes which would not permit Rio de Janeiro to expect much from them. Nevertheless, the massive contingent, not only of canons and other Church dignitaries, but also of urban and rural parish priests, is an indication of the uncertainty in the face of a future in which it was supposed that new political options would emerge and call for an active definition of attitudes on the part of much broader sectors of the population than those which participated in the decision-making process under the Colonial system, and of the way in which this situation was already affecting the internal equilibrium of the older and numerically smaller group.

Were the other 64 names on Contucci's list the result, purely and simply, of an expansion of the ruling sector? With regard to the most numerous category – that of officers of new regiments (23 names) – it has already been observed that this was not the case. The criteria governing their appointment, as we have seen, took account of the social origin of the candidates for selection. Even more obviously connected with the upper sectors were the eighteen lawyers (was not the law precisely the profession that the Buenos Aires élite preferred for their sons?), and the landowners and militia officers (the latter group being recruited predominantly from the former) – these categories almost complete Contucci's list. In this second sector too, therefore, the changes affected above all the internal equilibrium of what was before 1806, in the broadest sense, the upper sector of Viceregal society. But such changes were still of great significance. What general trend underlay them? In the first place, as the institutional crisis became increasingly acute, a position in the institutional apparatus became a less important determining factor. Less obvious, but perhaps no less important, is the growth of an influence which has already been observed – that of the ecclesiastical sector. In the face of the possibility of increasingly wider conflicts, which were to affect nuclei of humanity hitherto excluded, this potential influence on considerable groups of the population is an element in the balance of power which counted for more than it did formerly. Similarly, the numerical predominance of the landowners over the merchants is revealing, for it does not reflect in any way the relative economic power of these two groups in the last years of the Colonial period. There is no doubt that the triumph of the landowners within the power equilibrium which was taking shape appears to be magnified by the fact that, among those who figure in other categories in the list, there were several who were also merchants or lived on the commercial wealth of their families. Even so, it is still true that, although the title of 'landowner' appears sufficient to include the person concerned in a census of 'influential' people that of 'merchant' seems less decisive in this respect.

Another element which does not presuppose any innovation – and which the table given above could not indicate – is still of great significance. It is the presence of entire family groups, represented totally or partially in the list. The five Belgranos, excluding the one who was already the most famous of them all, form the most numerous group, but there are also two Funes, two

The crisis of the Colonial order

Pueyrredóns, two García de Zúñigas, two Obligados, and two Molinas in Tucumán, and family ties which the surnames do not reveal also existed between others included in the list; for example the García de Zúñigas were related to the lawyer Anchorena, who was in turn related to Juan Pablo Aguirre, who is listed as an officer in the Corps of Patricios. Family solidarity had, in fact, formed the texture of the Colonial élite, and the fact that it was still so abundantly evident indicated that it would resist the breakdown of the Colonial system better than other institutions.

In this way, the main outlines of a possible new order were beginning to be perceptible. The future evolution of the process which was hinted at on this occasion was to depend both on local forces and on the world situation, the changes in which had already encouraged those which were beginning to take place in the River Plate region. Seville had no need of the flood of tendentious information and outright calumnies directed towards proving the disloyalty of Liniers to establish as its aim the discreet liquidation of that centre of autonomous power which – without any formal breach of legality – the events of 1806 and after had established in the River Plate region. As early as September 1808, Manuel José de Goyeneche, the delegate of the Junta in the River Plate region, after painting an unflattering picture of the Audiencia judges, who were 'undeserving of trust', the members of the Cabildo ('unprincipled men who owe their fortunes to chance circumstances and meddle in the business of government and politics'), and making an essentially favourable assessment of Liniers, nevertheless concluded that what was needed was a new Viceroy, a man 'of character, sagacity, energy and integrity', to reorganise all the branches of the administration which, owing to the circumstances, were in a phenomenal muddle.[23]

Neither prudence nor tact was among the virtues recommended by Goyeneche. But they were to be those judged most necessary by the successor to Liniers appointed by the Seville Junta, the naval officer Baltasar Hidalgo de Cisneros. The latter fully understood the difficulties of the mission to which he had been assigned. Before entering his capital he demanded, from his staging post in the Banda Oriental, the allegiance of the corporations and magistrates and the agreement of his predecessor. This cautious attitude was fully justified. The commanders of the regiments had at first considered the possibility of ignoring his appointment on the grounds that it had been made by an illegitimate authority, and of keeping Liniers in power. When this project failed owing to the refusal of the beneficiary himself to head a conflict with the authority which everyone had recognised, there were still those who toyed with the idea of establishing a Junta, and we have observed above how the arrival of the new Viceroy caused a brief resurrection of that moribund force, *carlotismo*. Yet none of this constituted an immediate danger to Cisneros, who spent a month patiently waiting in Colonia del Sacramento, and received there, on 26 August, the homage of Liniers and of the commanders of the regiments. The new Viceroy, in return for this allegiance, had to desist from his intention of appointing General Elío (who had abandoned his rebellious attitude and acknowledged the new Viceroy) Deputy Inspector of Armaments, as the Seville Junta had ordered.

For the moment, the military commanders were able to give, 'without any feeling of repugnance', their allegiance to the new Viceroy. Belgrano, who – according to his own account – considered such conduct to be excessively servile, preferred to retire once more to the Banda Oriental. This action was also dictated by prudence, for he did not imagine that those involved in the past attempts at political change would be free from threats in the future. In this respect, his pessimism was unfounded, for six months later he was again in Buenos Aires, publishing a newspaper subsidised by the new Viceroy. This was the admirable *Correo de Comercio de Buenos Aires*, which, true to its title, managed to maintain, throughout the turbulent year of 1810, the serene attitude of those newspapers which had been published and had educated their readers in the useful truths of economic and agricultural science during the years of the unquestioned domination of enlightened monarchy. His friends, who were also receptive to new ideas, gradually held their meetings more openly, even though the Viceroy in November had formed a committee of vigilance to counter subversive propaganda and activities. Did this group of friends deceive Cisneros, and persuade him that those who had met in the past to organise audacious political activities were doing so now only to discuss the publication of a newspaper which strictly eschewed political matters? Or was he perhaps – as Belgrano himself suggested – making a cautious attempt to find a power-base for himself between the existing factions? Whereas in the far North of the Viceregal area, in Chuquisaca and La Paz, a revolution which had set up Juntas and had had time to receive the blessing of that of Montevideo, received from the Royal authorities a very different treatment from that meted out to the secessionists of the Banda Oriental, the future revolutionaries of Buenos Aires impassively watched the death-agony and the brutal repression of the revolutionary movement in Upper Peru. Under the orders of Vicente Nieto, who had arrived in Buenos Aires with the new Viceroy and had been given by the latter the appointment which the Seville Junta had intended for Elío, it was the Patricios and other soldiers of the regiments formed in Buenos Aires after 1806 who crushed the revolution in Chuquisaca. Is it surprising that the Viceroy preferred, in return for these practical services, to ignore the limitations of the loyalty which he was sedulously trying to cultivate among the people of Buenos Aires?

In order to conserve this loyalty he was prepared to go further. Departing from his instructions, he allowed Liniers to go off and establish himself, not in Spain, but in the Interior of the country. When he faced the

The crisis of the Colonial order

problem of solving the conflicts which had riven both Buenos Aires and Montevideo since 1808, he showed an evident anxiety to maintain an equilibrium between the rival groups. On the 11 September 1809 the military establishment of Buenos Aires was reorganised. The principal objective was to alleviate the burden which this structure had imposed on the Viceregal treasury. (A year earlier, Goyeneche had proposed a military reform 'so that the Viceroyalty may produce revenue for the metropolis and not absorb it all in its own defence. Things cannot go on like this, because it is consuming all the revenue it produces').[24] There is no doubt that some of the disbanded battalions had taken part in suppressing the January rising, and it is also true that, under the name of the Corps of Commerce, some of the units disbanded after that conflict reappeared. Nevertheless, the essential basis of the military equilibrium reached at the outcome of that conflict was acknowledged. The reluctance to incur increased expenditure, and the unwillingness of most of the Spanish-born to become regular soldiers, caused the disbanded units to be resurrected as militia subject to weekly military training, but not permanently quartered in barracks. Even leaving aside this trend, which again made those defeated in the January clash, now partially rehabilitated, weak military rivals of their former conquerors, the latter had reason to celebrate the conservation of the essential basis of their power and advantages in a situation which had been totally transformed and which for a moment they had believed would be implacably hostile towards them. There was, of course, a price to be paid for this survival, and it was the commanders of the victorious units who pleaded with the new Viceroy for clemency for those on trial for their participation in the defeated rising. In this way Álzaga and his companions in comparative misfortune were enabled to return to Buenos Aires from their refuge in Montevideo and be welcomed by a city filled with rejoicing.

Can it be said, then, that under the rule of an official who applied with prudence the rules of a somewhat obvious art of government, but during his stay in Buenos Aires does not appear to have awakened great enthusiasm in any sector of his subjects, the wounds in the Colonial system caused by a local crisis followed by a global one were being healed painlessly? This would be too extreme a conclusion to draw. However, it appears less debatable that, even when exercised by representatives with dubious credentials, the legitimacy of the monarchy and of the Spanish connection still retained an immense prestige, and that only a new crisis, heralding that loss of the whole of Spain which in the days of past quarrels each group had accused its adversaries of including as a factor in their plans for the future, would bring into question the Colonial connection itself. In the meantime, was it not, perhaps, the widely held view that it was in the Peninsula itself that the fate of Hispanic unity was being decided that explains the unexpected atmosphere of concord that Buenos Aires enjoyed under its last Viceroy? Be that as it may, the official whom many of his subjects, on his arrival, described as 'poor Cisneros' appears not to have been so pitiful. While the Viceroy, apparently without effort, survived the difficulties inherited from the past, the Viceregal area was adapting itself, calmly if unenthusiastically, to the institutional change decided in Spain. The cities began the process of election of the delegates to the Cortes who would at last give the Indies a say in the government of the Spanish dominions. If not everything, then almost everything now depended on what happened the other side of the ocean, but the next time a collapse took place in Spain it would not find the River Plate sectors which since 1806 had been creating the embryo of a political struggle as unprepared as in 1808. Although before the fall of the monarchy the rivals in the struggle for local predominance had merely taken steps to exaggerate their displays of devotion to the metropolitan authority, in the hope of thus obtaining its decisive support, the very experience accumulated as a result of the events during and after 1808 made it less certain that any new political change in the metropolis would evoke the same response among the Crown's discontented vassals in the River Plate region.

THE REVOLUTION

The Viceroy was aware of the extent to which the local situation depended on that in Spain, and for this reason he tried to prevent the dissemination of the news which was beginning to arrive concerning the disastrous course of the war. He failed in this intention, of course. There were too many people who – in tones of the gravest consternation – were spreading from Rio de Janeiro and Montevideo news of the successive stages of the collapse of Spain. Meanwhile, some were beginning to take it for granted. From Upper Peru a zealous servant of the Imperial system, José Vicente Cañete, wrote a prophetic analysis of the predictable effects of a military defeat and the best ways of attenuating these. He proposed that the Viceroys should order a reorganisation of Spanish America which would include the establishment of local representative institutions. Cañete was, however, well aware of the tensions against which he was proposing to build defences which he himself did not consider sufficiently solid. The lack of internal cohesion in the social apparatus of the Indies, which he envisaged as threatened with breakdown because of the rivalry between the Spanish-born and the Creole élite, made any optimism impossible. Even in the eyes of this defender of the established order, the latter had very limited chances of surviving the approaching storm. This fundamental pessimism also seemed to underly the conduct of the last Viceroy, who was prepared to do what he thought to be his duty right to the bitter end, but not to anticipate the predictable crisis by risking a confrontation with those groups which, he knew only too well, had only given him provisional allegiance and were waiting for news from Spain in order to retract it.

The crisis of the Colonial order

It was, therefore, those groups which, not encountering any longer any organised local opposition, were to separate Buenos Aires from the metropolis, where the authority of Seville had succumbed to military defeat and internal dissensions. The Junta which was established in Cádiz to replace it was not recognised in the capital of the Viceroyalty. The official news of its establishment arrived too late to influence the crisis of the Colonial connection, which had been swiftly brought to a head by the decision, now so resolute, of the same people whose caution had made possible the unexpected atmosphere of concord which marked the brief incumbency of Cisneros. This caution was now to be rewarded. Military power remained in the hands of those who had won it in January 1809. Although the support of the Imperial administrative apparatus, which had favoured that first victory, was now replaced by an implacable hostility, the fresh aggravation of the Spanish crisis inevitably weakened that sector. Nor had the brief months of Cisneros's administration been spent in vain by those who in January 1809 had made an excessively rash attempt to seize power. The Cabildo of 1810 was not animated by the same evident ambition to increase its power which had characterised that of 1808. Those who had dominated it before had not succeeded in recapturing what had been their stronghold, and were, moreover, less sure of their ability to maintain such high-flown political ambitions. Some of their followers – like the prosperous Catalan merchant Juan Larrea – and advisors – such as the brilliant Creole lawyer Mariano Moreno – were now to be found, together with the military leaders who had defeated them in January 1809, among those who were preparing to strike a decisive blow against the old order. What was even more remarkable than these defections was the passivity with which those who did not join the victorious movement watched its triumph, which was almost publicly prepared. This passivity was a reflection not only of a more sober realisation of the real power of that sector, but also of its disillusionment with a Colonial system which had shown itself so ill prepared to support its defenders.[25] Cisneros had respected, in all essentials, the equilibrium of power that he found on his arrival. He had also authorised trade with Britain, a thing Liniers had not dared to do (even though the mere proposal to do so had led to his being reproached as if for a crime by his enemies who still controlled the Cabildo), – a measure that inaugurated that commercial revolution so feared by the merchants who had formed the nucleus of the defeated party in January 1809. It is, therefore, not surprising that this sector should have preferred not to run the risks of an active defence of the system which was serving their interests so badly.

This passivity – added to the natural prudence of officials faced with a crisis involving the authority from which their own power derived – did not eliminate all opposition to the approaching change, but channeled that opposition in directions opened for it by the leaders of the revolutionary process, and it took the form, in the last resort, of a legitimisation of the process itself.

In this way, the entire course of the institutional crisis was decided between the advocates and the adversaries of a change in the system, in which the former group exercised constant pressure, but the latter group did not regard this as a good enough reason to abandon a struggle over the outcome of which they had few illusions. On the contrary, this element of coercion was either ignored, or invoked to justify perseverance in the search for agreed solutions, which were poor disguises for the capitulation of one sector to the other. It was precisely the need to avert a greater evil (a violent confrontation) which was offered as an explanation for the gradual concessions made by those who, while opposed to change, really did very little to prevent it.

In opposition to them there was, in the first place, that military force of which Cisneros had not dared to transform the internal equilibrium. On it depended, in the last resort, the outcome of the crisis, and it was only when he was effectively disavowed by that force, when its leaders declared themselves to be incapable of maintaining order, that Cisneros realised that the only course open to him was to yield to the victors. Yet this decorous confession of impotence was not an exact reflection of the attitude of those officers who recognised the leadership of the commanding officer of the first regiment of Patricios, Colonel Saavedra. Rather than being remiss in the defence of the old order, they took an active part in its destruction. This was to happen in one turbulent week, from the 18 to the 25 May, which took place against the same background and with the same characters as the clash of January 1809. The vast spaces of the central squares of Buenos Aires, overlooked by the Fort, were filled only intermittently by a crowd – as to its size and degree of representativity, contemporary witnesses are in no closer agreement than are the historians.[26] In the Fort and the Cabildo building flanking the squares officials, Cabildo members, dignitaries, eminent citizens and officers of the new army, after months of the frozen equilibrium which Cisneros had been able to ensure, were again making, on the reduced local political chessboard, moves that they knew to be decisive.

Of those troubled days the protagonists appear to have preserved only a confused recollection. The first event was the official publication on the 17th of the bad news from Spain. Resistance to the French was only continuing in Cádiz Bay, and the Seville Junta had been tragically suppressed by a mob seeking those responsible for the defeat. This news, deplorable though it was, seemed to be less so in comparison with the rumours with which it was competing for the attention of an incredulous public opinion. Its very publication was universally forgotten by the protagonists of the process, even by the Viceroy who ordered it. As a precautionary measure, the troops of the mobilised regiments, which were still, as we have observed above, the successors of those which in January 1809 had supported Liniers, were confined to barracks, and in the name of their officers the Viceroy was induced to resign his appointment, deemed to have lapsed as a result of the suppression of the supreme authority from which it was derived. In the name of the same officers, the Cabildo was requested to take action in the emergency. On the 21st pressure was brought to bear in a less discreet manner. A small crowd of probably under a thousand in number, recruited from the lower classes by three efficient agitators, gathered in the square. The Viceroy and the Cabildo decided to deal with the situation by summoning a General Junta of citizens, which included the most distinguished ones of the city, and on his part, Colonel Saavedra offered the assistance of the troops under his command to ensure order during the meeting.

This Open Cabildo thus created an entirely new situation, and offered the defenders of the existing order an opportunity to reassert themselves against the pressures being brought to bear on them. In contrast to the version of events perpetuated in a persistent myth, the selection of those invited to the Junta was controlled by the Cabildo, which was ill disposed towards the new movement, and the roll-call system of voting employed at the meeting, excluded even the possibility of intervention by participants not included among those invited. But of these, nearly half (two hundred out of four hundred and fifty) preferred to stay away. Among those who did appear, those prepared to defend the existing order found themselves, from the beginning, to be in a minority.

We shall not make another attempt to reconstruct – on the basis of an account of the proceedings that is hopelessly condensed[27] and a mass of subsequent testimony that is excessively verbose – the arguments expounded at this meeting, which was opened by an appeal by the Cabildo for moderation and prudence in the meeting's deliberations. It is enough to point out that the actual truth of the institutional crisis was never laid open to doubt, nor does there appear to have been any disagreement as to the legal bases of any solution. The possibility of a popular decision to fill, on a provisional basis, the vacant appointments in the sovereign authority was solidly based on legal texts, and, perhaps more to the point, the crisis of dissolution of the Spanish absolute monarchy had again conferred on such texts an unexpected relevance. The debate of 22 May was not, therefore, an ideological one, but a legal dispute between rival groups which were trying to utilise a normative system whose legitimacy they did not question in order to inherit the vacant power. At this stage, there was no longer any fundamental discussion as to whether the authority of the Viceroy had or had not lapsed according to the law. There was even less discussion as to whether the appeal to the popular will proposed as a means of creating a new authority was inspired by the principles of the Seven *Partidas* of King Alfonso the Wise or by the opinions of certain seventeenth-century jurists.

What was of much greater interest was the question of who was going to fill the vacant posts.

To this question the reactions of the meeting were varied. The prudent absence of many people guaranteed a majority for the innovators, but it did not provide them with the cohesion they needed. Those who had been responsible for both pressure and agitation seem to have been ill prepared for the confrontation in the Open Cabildo. The very fact that voting took place in an order which took no account of the leadership structure already established within the innovating group would have made necessary an extremely strict voting discipline. The result was a decision which no doubt signified a break with the old order, but left to the Cabildo the task of establishing a new government. This solution had, in any case, been quite openly suggested in the Cabildo's address at the beginning of the meeting.

Thus the Cabildo was left as master of the field or, to be more precise, as master of the next move. It had only limited freedom of manoeuvre, and its ambitions had already been curtailed by the experience of 1809. The solution which emerged from its deliberations was obviously inspired by prudence. The Viceroy was transformed into the President of a Junta. Of its four members, two (Colonel Saavedra and Dr Juan José Castelli) were the visible heads of the movement which was pressing for institutional change, while the other two – Canon Sola and the Spaniard, Incháurregui – had on the 22nd supported that centre party which had simply wanted to leave power in the hands of the Cabildo. The Governing Junta was, therefore, a faithful enough reflection, in its very incoherence, of the equilibrium of forces revealed at the Open Cabildo. The revolutionary leaders appointed do not seem to have hesitated to join the Junta. But on the very day (the 24th) that the Cabildo handed over power to the Junta it had created, the conflict broke out anew. The officers were ill disposed to leave the supreme military command in the hands of Cisneros, and those who represented them in the Junta resigned from it. The Cabildo tried to defend its creation, but again received the solemn disavowal of the military leaders. The members of the Junta established on the 24th, faced with the resignation of their President, do not appear to have thought that their own investiture was invalidated. On the morning of 25 May they requested the Cabildo to designate a successor to Cisneros. Another day of disturbances led to a different outcome. The main square was once again the scene of popular agitation, and the crowd presented a petition which the Cabildo hastened to accept: a more broadly-based Junta than that appointed on the 24th was to replace the authority of the Viceroy. Its President was Saavedra, who thus at last received the supreme military power. Its members were Juan José Castelli and Manuel Belgrano, both lawyers and both veterans of the political discussion circles which had played such a big part in the preparation of these events, and the cleric Manuel Alberti, the landowner and militia officer Miguel de Azcuénaga, and the Spanish-born merchants Juan Larrea and Domingo Matheu. The secretaries – who still had no voting rights – were the Doctors Juan José Paso (who on the 22 May had drawn attention to himself by making an effective, though not very solidly based, defence of the right of Buenos Aires to take decisions on behalf of the entire Viceregal area) and Mariano Moreno, who enjoyed the confidence of the Cabildo and in 1809 had been one of the supporters of Álzaga's *coup*.

It is not easy to ascertain the origin of the idea behind the establishment of this body. A later testimony attributes it to a sudden inspiration on the part of one of the agitators who came to the fore on the 21st. This excessively simple version may be hard to believe, but it is difficult to replace it with another and more satisfactory one. It is, moreover, significant that, from Saavedra – whose behaviour between the 22nd and the 25th followed a less direct course than in the immediately preceding period – to Moreno, who was surprised at his own appointment, Belgrano, who declared that he 'did not know how or from where'[28] the new Junta had arisen, and Azcuénaga, who before joining the Junta decided to express his legalistic scruples about the matter – most of the members of the Junta who have left us comments on their appointments agree as to their lack of any connection with the process which gave rise to the Junta's establishment. One is, then, forced to admit that a movement firmly controlled in its early stages by a leadership which had a strong hold over it was superseded by a new and spontaneous movement, which was, moreover, destined to last only a short time. The establishment of the Junta and the concentration of political and military power ensured the institutionalisation of the same leadership whose efficacy was demonstrated in the clashes that occurred before the 22nd.

However, although there may be some doubt as to the precise origin of the solution imposed on the 25th, there can be none as to the mechanisms by which that solution was imposed. It was, once again, the military leaders who delivered the city to those discontented with the Junta created by the Cabildo. The petitions presented to the latter body also bear the marks of having been elaborated within the context of the urban military organisation. Can it be said, then, that the events which put an end to the Colonial system were the result of the action of a small élite of professional military officers, who were boldly prepared to take advantage of the passivity resulting from the disenchantment not only of the representatives of the *ancien régime* but also of the mass of the urban population? This is the conclusion which some historians have thought fit to draw from facts which are well known in their essential outlines and have been analysed in detail by those same scholars, the most insistent representative of this school of thought being Dr Marfany. But this conclusion does not necessarily follow from the facts expounded, and such writers perhaps over-simplify their task by postulating as the only alternative to a military revolution a popular one, which, to be worthy of that name would have had to enjoy the support of the majority of the population, expressed by behaviour which would enable present-day scholars to reach satisfactory conclusions, based on statistics, as to the real existence of that majority support. Is it necessary to point out that so exacting a definition makes the notion of a popular revolution completely untenable? One would, however, search the works of such writers in vain for an examination of the specific function of the military organisation in the political and social context of pre-Revolutionary Buenos Aires. In 1810 Buenos Aires had about forty thousand inhabitants living within the city limits, and perhaps fifty thousand including the suburbs. There were three thousand soldiers and non-commissioned officers in the urban military units on 24 March 1810. This number, which was undoubtedly the lowest since urban militarisation began in 1806, includes only soldiers and non-commissioned officers quartered – more or less effectively – in barracks, and it shows that an unusually high proportion of the active population was still subject to military discipline. Their leaders were those who had arisen from the frantic organisation of urban units which took place from 1806 onwards. Few among them were living on the remuneration – which was very low, but still represented a heavy burden on the hard-pressed Treasury – assured them by their military activities. Many of them still continued, despite their military duties, the activities which had occupied them in more peaceful times. And even among those who had found in the career of arms a new profession, in which they were to continue after 1810, this change of activity was relatively recent, and certainly did not separate them from the social sectors from which they had been so recently recruited.

But to suggest, as mutually exclusive hypotheses, a 'military' and a 'civilian' origin of the Revolution, is even more absurd if one remembers that it was only through militarisation that the sectors of the Creole élite had assured themselves both an institutional organisation and also institutionalised channels of communication with the urban masses. The simple fact is that there did not then exist, for the sectors desirous of ending the Colonial connection, any other organisational framework than that provided by militarisation. But this militarisation, so broad in scope, within the framework of which the organisation of the sector that was to become revolutionary necessarily took place, only permits one to define the revolution as 'military' in a sense which makes this definition, if not inaccurate, only barely enlightening. The military revolution was at the same time the revolution of the entire Creole élite. The two terms, which might appear to be mutually exclusive, simply designate, in this context, two aspects of the same phenomenon.

It had been the solid support of the urban regiments which had ensured a transition without violence or flagrant scandal. The Viceroy had signed the successive documents which bore witness to the gradual abdication of

The crisis of the Colonial order

the old régime, but the Revolution still had to ensure the obedience of the entire territory which it aspired to govern. On 25 May, it was decided to send missions with military support into the Interior, to spread the good news and crush any possible dissent *vis-à-vis* the new order.[29] Neither the Revolution nor the war had dared to pronounce their own name, yet both were now established in the River Plate region, and were not to abandon the scene until they had thoroughly transformed it.

This transformation was felt, above all, in the sphere of politics and administration, not only because it put an end to the predominance of a Spanish-based bureaucracy, but also to the extent to which it affected the very group which replaced that bureaucracy. That Creole élite which the events of 1806 and after had endowed with local power had to create from within its own ranks a political class and a professional military apparatus which it still lacked; its new rôle as the protagonist of events therefore imposed on it profound changes, which could not take place without some upheavals. From it were to come men who were to follow what was called, most significantly, the 'career of the Revolution', but as misfortunes accumulated it was to find it increasingly difficult to recognise itself in those men (whose audacity had somewhat perturbed it, and whose necessarily arbitrary power was eventually to alarm it even more), who had identified themselves with an enterprise that at first had appeared easy and revealed itself as almost desperate – the Revolution.

4 THE REVOLUTION IN BUENOS AIRES

THE BIRTH OF POLITICAL LIFE

The events of the 25th had created a new focus of power, which was both the adversary and the heir of the one which had fallen. This new power intended to use the principle of legitimacy as its trump card. It not only used this as a legal argument to demand the obedience of the entire jurisdictional area subject to Buenos Aires, from the Atlantic to the plateau of Upper Peru, but from the very beginning it used this extreme legitimism as a somewhat unexpected but nevertheless vital element in its own revolutionary ideology. The adversaries of the new order were 'rebels', and the authorities used this term in just as pejorative a sense as their predecessors had done. Even in late 1810, the poet of the new glories of Buenos Aires, Vicente López y Planes, celebrating the first Revolutionary victories in the North, proclaimed:

> Glory to the great Balcarce; eternal glory
> to his warrior legion
> which reddened its butcher's sword
> with rebel gore![1]

Like the poet, the Revolution suffered no qualms over the condign punishment of the rebels, and did not hesitate to publicise it as a legitimate instrument of intimidation. Moreover, this legitimism also represented an attempt to halt the slide of the Revolution into civil war. As the heir to the old régime, the Revolutionary government also inherited from it the sense of identification with the whole of Colonial society, rather than with a particular sector of it, and the new power wanted to deal, not with whole groups, but with isolated individuals. Although the drift into war could not in the long run be avoided, and the entire group of the Spanish-born eventually became suspect and therefore subject to discriminatory legislation, at first this deliberate reluctance to be associated with a specific social base contributed to making the new political authority isolated. By preferring to base itself on a legitimacy which was in any case debatable rather than on an unambiguous identification with those sectors discontented with the old order it did not encourage the unreserved support of those sectors, whose members were, moreover, restrained by prudence.

The Revolution thus began as a strictly personal adventure on the part of some citizens of Buenos Aires, and they found the hesitations which they encountered on the part of others somewhat alarming. As late as January 1811, the *Gaceta* founded by the Revolutionary government and intended to be its spokesman was to deplore 'the silence of many educated men of our city (one cannot see for what reason) on the affairs of the day'.[2] Of course, the new order did have at its disposal the means of threatening people into obedience. The oath of loyalty, which at first was only demanded of the higher officials, was eventually made compulsory for all heads of families. Yet it was precisely the readiness of the adversaries of the Revolution to give it this obligatory allegiance which made the latter less significant. Neither friends nor enemies were deceived as to the value of such forced declarations; the Revolution appeared to find a surer method of calculating its sincere supporters by means of the monetary collections it sponsored. Of course, the voluntary character of the donations received does not seem to have been above all suspicion. It is, at least, suggestive that on the 5 July, a report of the donation of his only slave by the European-born friar José Zambrana emphasised that the donor had 'a staunch character, and could not be swayed by adversity or by flattery'.[3] However, the clearest indication of the voluntary nature of the donations was their very scarcity. A week after reporting the news of Fray José's donation, the *Gaceta* observed, still without openly expressed alarm, that it was the poor who were most disposed to behave with generosity:

> The middle classes and the very poorest members of society are the first contributors, and hasten eagerly to consecrate to the Fatherland a part of their modest resources; the rich will begin to make contributions appropriate to their fortune and their zeal; but although a rich merchant may excite one's admiration over the large amount of his donation, he can no longer deny the poor man the merit of having been so prompt with his contributions.[4]

But the rich showed no eagerness to engage in this onerous competition, and the flood of donations appears to have dried up. The reaction of the *Gaceta* shows how the holding of a census of adherents was not the least important of the aims of the collections of donations: 'Knowing as we do that a high proportion of the most well-disposed people', we read in the number of 2 August, 'decline to make a donation because their scarce resources do not permit them to give adequate expression to their noble ideas, we must point out that they should not feel the slightest embarrassment, for the smallest donations are accepted, and it is realised that these reflect the most sincere conviction and adherence to the just cause of unity, which is based on the sacred rights of our legitimate and august Sovereign Don Fernando VII'. However, without acquiring excessively numerous testimonies of allegiance, the collection campaign soon lost its original connotations. On the one hand, the increasing financial requirements of the new state led to the primary emphasis being placed on the revenue-collection aspect of this activity, and on the other hand, donations seem to have become the most obvious way of ingratiating themselves with the régime on the part of its internal adversaries. When we read the over-obsequious message that accompanied the donation of the Spaniard Francisco Antonio Molina, a native of Málaga, who offered 500 pesos 'with an expression of his allegiance to the present system, and without words to express the gratitude which he quite justly feels towards these countries, where he had acquired the wealth he possessed as a result of his fortunate migration to them',[5] and we remember that this eloquent testimony was offered at the moment when the discussion of fresh discriminatory measures against the European-born occupied such a large part of the political activity of Buenos Aires, we may allow ourselves certain doubts. When we read the less effusive note sent by Archbishop Moxó of Charcas with six thousand pesos collected among the clergy of his archdiocese 'for the army defending these provinces and for the Public Library', and we compare with his subsequent behaviour the proclamation of his 'fervent patriotism, and unvarying love and gratitude...towards a country from which he has received so many favours',[6] no doubt whatever is possible: the Archbishop was not speaking sincerely, and preferred to follow the dictates of prudence when giving this onerous proof of an allegiance which he was very far from feeling.

Thus, this more forceful manifestation of allegiance to the new order was not necessarily more sincere than the solemn oath. The fact was that the situation necessarily cast suspicion on the sincerity of any statement of allegiance which could not be refused without danger. It was to be the existence of an alternative danger – derived from the possibility of a return of the old order – which lent, if not a more sincere, at least a more definite, character to certain expressions of allegiance to the new system. Yet even this regulating element was of only relative efficacy. Reconciliation with Spain, by way of submission, still seemed in 1815 to be a viable solution, and not only to secondary figures but to prominent revolutionary leaders, and – as the studies of José María Mariluz Urquijo have shown[7] – Spain itself had not abandoned the hope of regaining the allegiance of some who had explicitly sworn it to the Revolution in the River Plate region. Even so, the fear of the reprisals that would follow any restoration was a valuable element in encouraging the cohesion of the Revolutionary sector. The very notion of 'commitment to the Revolution', that is to say of an unequivocal allegiance that would make impossible any reconciliation with the old order, is a clear demonstration of the emphasis which, very early on, was placed on this element in the creation of Revolutionary solidarity.

This element was made even more necessary by the fact that this solidarity was marked by hesitations, even among the leaders of the movement themselves. Even if there is no truth in the report that the very secretary of the Junta, Mariano Moreno, approached the Audiencia in order to allay his scruples before accepting the appointment, it is true that Miguel de Azcuénaga, a member who was later to distinguish himself by the zeal with which he persecuted the disaffected Spanish-born, did just that, and, on a more private level, another member, Domingo Mateu, was able to write to his relations in Cádiz and express a remarkably detached attitude towards the political movement he was supposed to be leading. It is not necessary to move very far from the centre of power to find hesitations – and even discreet opposition – which were both ready to increase as soon as the first hardships were felt. This isolation, against the background of a public opinion which was either hostile or felt a sympathy tinged with scepticism, has been emphasised in his memoirs by Saavedra, and makes it easier to understand the efforts made to identify the new order with complete legality and the representation of the whole of society – efforts which, as we have seen, the Revolutionary leaders made at an early stage. Unsure of support from any particular sector, those leaders only expected to save themselves by avoiding direct confrontations and taking advantage for this purpose of the similar incoherence of the opposition which was beginning to rise up in its path.

Was the Revolutionary power-base really so isolated? Even though its leaders may have felt this, the evidence of those to whom their victory was repugnant tells a different story. The Revolutionaries were masters of the streets, and their enemies prudently refrained from disputing this mastery. Behind closed doors, these angry witnesses hoped for the ruin of the victors, but they do not seem to have foreseen any concrete course of action capable of turning the tables. As masters of the urban army and of the entire administrative machinery, and of the Viceregal capital, where hostility abounded but did not dare to express itself openly, the Revolutionary leaders did not have much to fear from Buenos Aires in the immediate future. Nevertheless, they had to consolidate their new-found power. The group which had stormed the stronghold of political power had been transformed by its very success into the title-holders of power, and this made it necessary for it to establish new ties with the entire subject population, which had only been partly affected by the military and political processes which had led to the rise of a Revolutionary faction supported by a popular following. In establishing such ties, the authoritarian style of the old order was not to be abandoned. The prestige and the means of coercion derived from the traditional use of power proved to be definite advantages when dealing with those marginal sectors. In its dealings with them, the new government tried to use the Church as a somewhat unwilling intermediary. An order to preach sermons on the political changes and the blessings deriving from them was given to all parish priests, in an atmosphere of increasing intimidation of those ecclesiastics who disagreed with the new order of things.[8] Of even more importance as an instrument for controlling and disciplining the population was the police system inherited from the Colonial régime: that of *Alcaldes* and Assistant *Alcaldes*, who were part of the municipal organisation. The new régime, which, from its commencement, enjoyed the wholehearted support of these people, as was shown by the voting of those of them who were present at the Open Cabildo of 22 May, used them as its agents for the application of the increasingly complex legislation of surveillance and repression. In August 1810 the *alcaldes* were ordered to keep records of people's residence and changes of residence, and also

> to make sure, in the blocks under their supervision, that no suspect meetings were held...If anyone were apprehended committing this crime they were to be taken immediately, without consideration of rank or privilege, to the Prison in the case of men, or to the House of Correction in the case of women.[9]

The need for greater political vigilance was the explanation given for the stricter control of people's movements. A law passed in July decreed the confiscation of the property of those who abandoned the city without authorisation, and all sorts of punishments, 'including the death penalty', were decreed for those still hiding arms. The *alcaldes* were immediately made responsible for registering and licensing these. The same sanctions were threatened for those caught corresponding 'with persons in other cities, causing political divisions, lack of confidence, or conspiracies against the present government'. Of course, such fearful penalties were meted out only after careful consideration, and in any case the edicts providing for surveillance were often no more than the resurrection of other laws which had in theory been in force for a long time, but had not been applied in practice. Nevertheless, it is undeniable that the Revolution made the authoritarian presence of the state felt among that marginal urban population which the Colonial administrators had found it more prudent to ignore, and that the new mechanisms of control would make themselves felt with increasing intensity among the sectors more closely integrated into urban society. But it was not only a case of seeking out and neutralising dissent, what was also sought was to bring allegiance under disciplinary control. Here too, without showing any trace of originality, the new régime followed in the steps of the old one. It found it perfectly natural to control in an authoritarian manner expressions of public rejoicing, just as in Colonial times religious and Royal festivals had been closely regulated. Street illuminations arranged by enthusiastic citizens were subject to regulations laid down by the supreme power, which also decided how many days they were to continue. Here too, the *alcaldes* in each quarter played a decisive part, as organisers of the collective celebrations and controllers of the enthusiasm of those under their jurisdiction. It is easy to understand how in this atmosphere the external signs of allegiance to the new order were supported even by those who had strong private reservations about it. The logical consequence of this process was the situation described by the

American, Brackenridge, in 1816. At that time, the European-born Spaniards who had not managed to obtain citizenship were immediately recognisable, because they were the only people in the streets not wearing the Revolutionary cockade.[10]

By this time, however, the Revolution had become part of customary habits, and allegiance to it, though still universally attested, was accompanied by less external manifestations of fervour than in the past, when 'this enthusiasm, like that of the French Revolution',[11] had suffused the life of Buenos Aires. However, during those years of fervour, through the collaboration of an authority anxious to affirm itself and the sector of the population which supported it, a new Revolutionary liturgy had been created. Although some of its manifestations were ephemeral – such as the adoption of the Phrygian Cap of Liberty, which was imposed for a few months in 1813, with arbitrary punishments for those who failed to incorporate it into their daily attire, but later fell into desuetude – most of them were destined to last. The festivals of 25 May – which at first developed in conjunction with the traditional religious festivities – eventually rivalled and displaced the latter. Thirty years after the Revolution, when the exiled Juan María Gutiérrez wished to explain to his sister, who was living in Buenos Aires under the rule of Rosas, the part played by patronal festivals in the life of a Northern Italian village, he said by way of comparison 'It is these villages' 25th May'. Although the Revolution had now been firmly relegated to past history, this shows the extent to which this civic festival, the culminating moment of the new Revolutionary liturgy, was still the most important collective experience recognised in Buenos Aires.

These festivals were a mixture – elaborated over a period of time – of the old and the new. In 1811 there were four nights of illuminations, 'salvoes of artillery, ringing of bells, fireworks, music, triumphal arches and countless other amusements, such as masquerades and dancing...The people were beside themselves with joy, and thought of nothing but diverting themselves in a spirit of brotherhood'.[12] Behind all this spontaneous enjoyment was the discreet preparation and supervision exercised by the police: 'The Junta gave orders', wrote María Guadalupe Cuenca de Moreno, filled with rancour against those who had brought about the political ruin of her husband, 'that the *alcaldes* in each quarter should tell the citizens to erect triumphal arches and other things, to show their patriotism, and to put up double illuminations besides their usual contribution. I haven't given anything'.[13] 'So as to keep order', Beruti pointed out in his turn, 'all the taverns were closed...and there were many patrols going the rounds of the city, with the *alcaldes* in charge of each district'. Dances and masquerades were nothing new, nor were illuminations. Though not totally new, what was more important than in the past was the part played by the armed forces in the celebrations. In May 1811, on the pyramid which the Revolution had commanded to be built to its own glory, and which was still unfinished, 'on each of its four sides there was inscribed a ten-line verse celebrating the achievements and victories gained by the valiant troops of this immortal city...Their flags and standards adorned the pyramid during the four days of the festival'. Yet, here again, these innovations of style and content took place within the context of traditional rituals adapted to the new circumstances. The celebration of the 25th May opened with the carrying past of the Royal standard, borne, as always, by the Royal standard-bearer of the Cabildo. The ceremony had formed part of the ritual of the vigil of the patron-saint of Buenos Aires, Saint Martin of Tours, and had been incorporated into the new civic festival.

What notions and what beliefs was this celebration expressing and trying to disseminate? From very early on, the prevailing political instability made it impossible for the celebration to be an expression of support for a particular ruler or faction, although no doubt popular enthusiasm displayed at the festival might be interpreted as a sign of satisfaction with the prevailing political situation. Obviously, the importance attributed to the first anniversary of the Revolution was connected with the desire of the faction which had managed to displace its rivals among the revolutionary groups to see itself supported by popular fervour, and when María Guadalupe Cuenca – in contrast to other less biassed witnesses – recorded that 'the festival has been a poor thing, and the crowds have been small', she concluded with satisfaction: 'It seems to me that the people are not contented'. She too, therefore, was disposed to measure the political attitude of the city towards its government by the degree of enthusiasm displayed by the crowds during the celebration. Yet, although it is possible that extreme discontent might cast a cloud over the festivities, the latter were held in honour of the Revolution itself and not of its temporary leaders, who everybody knew were ephemeral. What precisely, in the Revolution, was being celebrated? In the first place, the city was celebrating itself. Intoxicated with its own glory, 'immortal' Buenos Aires represented itself as the liberator of a whole new world. The second aspect was the celebration of the liberty of America, after centuries of Spanish oppression. In a spirit of opposition to the old metropolis, with which, however, the political connection had not been broken, the Indian past was reasserted as the common heritage of all Americans. In 1812, during the festivities with which the parish of Saint Nicholas, in Buenos Aires, celebrated the failure of the counter-revolutionary conspiracy led by Álzaga, the four children who 'sang from time to time various songs in harmony' were dressed as Indians, and in the same year the first trench-mortars cast in Buenos Aires were christened 'Tupac Amaru' and 'Mangoré'.[14] There is no doubt that this exaltation of collective pride in the political and military achievements of the emancipated city implied a new image of the political and social order, but in both aspects of this order the Revolutionary creed contained an element of discretion. As regards the first aspect, the political transformation initiated in 1810 had certainly been very far-reaching, but it cannot be said that it had been too successful in solving the problems which the change itself had created. As regards the second aspect, the idea of equality, which was voiced in loud tones against the privileges – which had, in any case, lacked legal sanction even within the Colonial system – of the European-born Spaniards, and also evoked to proclaim the end of the servitude of the Indians – who were conspicuous by their absence in Buenos Aires – was employed with very much more caution when criticising the social hierarchy that actually existed and which, in any case, appeared to be explicitly confirmed by the Revolutionary ritual. Thus, the alms distributed to celebrate the second anniversary of the Revolution appear to have been clearly directed towards different social categories. Three thousand out of the eight thousand pesos distributed were earmarked for giving dowries to 'six girls, honourable, poor and of good family', in other words to guarantee suitable husbands for the offspring of the least affluent sector of the upper class (this, as we have observed above, followed a traditional practice), whereas only 1,600 pesos were assigned for 'assistance to families known to be honourable but impoverished', 1,000 pesos to war widows, and 1,200 pesos to those wounded in action. In the same way, the largesse distributed by Beruti during his memorable celebration of the repression of Álzaga's mutiny took three different forms, a splendid dinner for the clergy and 'various distinguished citizens', a 'big meal' of chocolate, biscuits and spirits for more guests, and a distribution of money, thrown from the balcony to the crowd in the street below. On the same occasion, 'money was thrown to the common people'[15] by some enthusiastic patriots in the main square. (The custom of throwing money to curious onlookers was traditional. It had taken place, for example, on the occasion of the oath of loyalty to Ferdinand VII decreed by Liniers.)

Thus, the Revolution not only refrained from introducing innovations which might affect the most significant of the social differences inherited from the past. It still, in a manner analogous to that of the *ancien régime*, incorporated them into the image it projected of the body politic. In the decree abolishing titles, promulgated on 6 December 1810, which was animated throughout by a violent rejection of all forms of political privilege, were included the words 'since our national militia should not be confused with the mercenary militia of the tyrants, it is forbidden for any sentry to prevent the free entrance to any public function or meeting to *decente* citizens'.[16] In this way the notion of 'decent people', which reflected in all the complexity of its nuances the delicate social equilibrium characteristic of the old order, was incorporated – as though it possessed a validity so evident that there was no need to emphasise it – into the most categorical of the Revolutionary declarations. It is not surprising, therefore, that, in September 1811, the authorities responsible for supervising the admittance into the main square of those who were to elect the deputies and representatives of the city should have thought it perfectly legitimate to deny admittance, not only to 'women and people on horseback', but also to 'Negroes, boys and other common people'.[17] As another witness, Juan José Echevarría, put it, admittance was only granted to the *gente decente* and the *gente de medio pelo* were excluded.[18]

This attitude marks the limits of the political mobilisation that the Revolution was sponsoring. It is true that since May 1810 the presence of the lower classes had made itself felt to a greater extent than at any time in the past, and at certain times the desires of this new political clientèle did affect the course of the internal crises of the Revolutionary régime. Furthermore, as the Revolution came to appear to those popular sectors not merely as a faction in conflict with other factions, but as the State itself, and more disposed than its predecessor to make its presence felt, the mobilisation of those popular sectors became easier and more broadly based. In early April 1811 it was the influence of the mob from the outlying suburbs, mobilised and controlled by their *alcaldes*, which saved the dominant faction from what seemed certain ruin. Yet that very experience provoked a fresh spirit of prudence among all the Revolutionary leaders, even those who had directly benefited from this popular intervention, and perhaps the caution which was displayed in September in controlling the admittance of voters stemmed from the fearful possibilities revealed by the events of April. The threat of a permanent broadening of the sector fully incorporated into political activity was thwarted with surprising ease. This happened because the mobilisation of the popular sectors, though impressive because of its massive character, was at the same time very incomplete. It was characteristic that the leaders of the events of April were not figures who had arisen from the mob itself but people appointed by the Revolutionary authorities to control it.

Though limited, the politicisation of the masses was a very real fact. The Revolutionary government, which had no desire whatever to transform plebeian public opinion into an important element in the new political system (in particular, in the complex interplay of factions within the movement), did not, however, scruple to evoke it in its own favour. This happened for several reasons, of which the most evident one was that, since the Revolutionary leaders occupied an unimportant place within the group that traditionally dominated society and administration, they had to seek support outside that group. It was the proclamation of the rights of all Americans that transformed those who had been in a disadvantageous position in the internal rivalries of the Colonial élite into the leaders of what were to become new nations. However, as long as that new-found superiority did not encompass the destruction of their adversaries within the élite, and while, therefore, the war went on, the community of interest of all Americans was to have definable effects on the political equilibrium of the Revolutionary party. There was a further reason: the war was to make necessary an increasing mobilization of the popular sectors and – as we shall see later, chiefly for economic reasons – principally of those which in the Colonial era had remained rigidly excluded. It is true that in the case of these groups compulsion was used frequently, but some persuasion was necessary, since the enthusiasm of the members of these marginal sectors recruited into the Army does not appear to have been universal. Their aggressive responses found an increasingly wider scope after the Revolution, in the shape of the spread of banditry, which had to be harshly suppressed from 1812 onwards.

The content of the Revolutionary credo which it was intended to disseminate among the popular sectors was related to the function of controlled and unspontaneous support assigned to those sectors, and with the aggravation of the military burden which the Revolution imposed on their marginal fringes. For both these reasons, patriotic and military motives received the principal emphasis. As for the political aspects of the revolutionary changes, it was preferable to leave these in the hands of a more restricted sector, which was thus not limited in its freedom of decision in this sphere by the demands of that broader public opinion which the Revolution was, however, making efforts to mobilise.

Even if one recognises its limitations, however, it would be unwise to ignore the extent of popular mobilisation, above all in the city, which did not wait for the events of May 1810 to find a new dimension, increasingly political in nature, to its collective life. The Utopian character of the campaign of ideological clarification launched in 1810 by the more staunch revolutionaries, the most extreme manifestation of which was the attempt to make Rousseau's *Social Contract* a primary school textbook, has been emphasised by many writers. The meticulous care with which the more moderate sector, once it had rid itself of its embarrassing allies, put an end to those efforts, gives one reason to suppose that some danger existed. Several witnesses have recorded the fact that in Buenos Aires the printed word was a means for the dissemination of ideas which was by no means restricted to a small minority. Printing-presses multiplied after the Revolution, and were kept busy, and indeed in 1818 it was difficult to find a ten-year-old boy who could not read.[19] The progress of egalitarian sentiments is equally well attested, though not always with approval. If the 'most eminent citizens' were not able to walk the streets of Buenos Aires without running the risk of being splashed with mud by a cart-driver or jostled by a horseman, the reason for it – according to *La Prensa Argentina* in its number of 11 June 1816[20] – was that 'that was one of the rights supposedly derived from equality' in the view of that 'insolent rabble' which now felt itself to be 'raised to the level of a common equality'.

Popular mobilisation, however limited, could not, therefore fail to have political consequences. This was recognised, in terms demonstrating substantial agreement, by the Supreme Director, Pueyrredón, and an unsympathetic observer, the United States agent Thomas Bland. Summarising the lessons derived from his experience of government, Pueyrredón observed that

> since the natural talents of the people are almost in contact with the knowledge of the educated class, the people has followed closely in the steps of those who have led it; however, one can count on their docility only up to a certain point; they express their opinion by signs that admit of no ambiguity, and which no one has been able to oppose with impunity.[21]

Similarly, Bland observed that, even though the Revolutionary régime could not be considered as representative, 'the sentiments and wishes of the people, as in all similar circumstances, have had considerable sway over this newly-created Government. There is a point beyond which it does not go; and a limit, as the numerous changes that have taken place clearly show, beyond which the forebearance of the people cannot be stretched'.[22] This limitation of their own freedom of action encountered by the Revolutionary leaders became increasingly serious as their policies diverged from those which the Revolution had originally adopted. In fact, whereas the most favoured tactics were direct confrontation, and war was the instrument *par excellence* of this, the massive propaganda designed to imbue all the inhabitants of Buenos Aires with a proud consciousness of the political, economic and military might of their city served the purpose of gaining support for the leaders among the plebeian opinion thus roused. However, when those leaders discovered, as a result of very painful experiences, the limitations of that power, and adopted tactics more in accord with the really rather modest resources at their disposal, they despaired of their chances of diminishing the more extreme aspects of that somewhat blind optimism which they had been encouraging among their supporters for years. That did not mean, however, that they could ignore the existence of a body of public opinion which still believed with the same passionate faith in the invincibility of their city and their revolutionary enterprise. Thus the gulf increased between a political leadership which was privately perplexed, and a mass of humanity which was advancing with blind assurance along the path opened for it by that very leadership. Although that hiatus did not make itself felt in the course of the war of independence, this was principally due to the fact that the intransigence of the enemy made the prosecution of the war the only possible course. But the wavering – and sometimes rather undignified – policy pursued by Buenos Aires towards Brazil and the Banda Oriental displayed for over ten years an oscillation between the cautious attitude of the leaders – which at times approached complete passivity – and the people's faith in a revolutionary war as a sure instrument of victory. When, in 1827, Lord Ponsonby reproached the ephemeral President, Rivadavia, for his concessions to the 'wild spirit of the mob', his accusations, though exaggerated, were less absurd than they appeared if one bears in mind the essentially oligarchical nature of the political system then in force. Although it would be unjustified to maintain that plebeian faith in the invincibility of Buenos Aires ever determined the policies directed from that city, it is, nevertheless, undeniable that no government there could with impunity entirely ignore that factor.

Was this unflagging faith in the Fatherland, which was at the same time the city and the Revolution, the only sentiment that underlay the limited political mobilisation of the popular sectors? If one were to assert this, one would run the risk of ignoring the progress of egalitarian ideas. The very efforts to limit, even on a theoretical plane, the scope of the revolutionary notion of equality show that the possible consequences of its dissemination did not pass unnoticed. What made this even more evident was the very fact that, from the summit of authority, the allegiance of the popular sectors was now eagerly sought. This was perhaps a sign more indicative than any doctrinal pronouncement of the increasing weight which those sectors were recognised as possessing. In a less direct manner, the effects of the Revolution on the internal equilibrium of the Buenos Aires élite, where it provoked sudden collapses and declines and no less surpring rises to power, were bound to diffuse a less rigid image of the social order.

In any case, it is undeniable that it was principally the internal equilibrium of the élite which was affected by the Revolution. Its indirect effects on the image of the new order adopted by those who had not belonged and still did not belong to that élite were, no doubt, less immediately decisive than the gradual displacement of those who had formed the nucleus of that élite in Colonial times by those who had occupied a subordinate place in it.

This process began in the shape of a political struggle between the Revolution and those opposing it. As has been observed above, the movement at first was not prepared to admit that entire sectors were hostile to it, but preferred – as long as this was possible – to maintain the fiction that it was only confronted by the dissent of certain individuals. It did, however, explicitly admit from the very beginning that there was one sector where examples of such dissent were abundant: that of the high-ranking Spanish-born career officials. Also from the beginning, through its very efforts to postpone the conflict, it seemed to admit that there was another and much broader sector on whose goodwill it could not rely: that of the Spanish-born in general.

As regards the first sector, the Revolutionary government was openly hostile to it from the beginning. It chose it as its main adversary not only because in fact its opposition was inevitable but also because, being small in number and intensely unpopular, it offered an admirable target for collective hostility. Individual and collective insults were hurled in abundance at the once proud servants of the Crown, those 'bosses' whose 'crazed thirst for dominance' led them to resist the change of government. Attacks on individuals were just as violent. In describing Marshal Nieto, on

6 September 1810, the revolutionary *Gaceta* uttered a string of pejorative adjectives: 'that vile, coarse, disreputable old man Nieto...a loathsome man who has left in every city on the route [to Upper Perí] deep impressions of his baseness'. The transformation of the high-ranking career officials into the appointed victims of the Revolution had the advantage of emphasising the booty which the Revolution offered to its adherents, identified by the generic term of 'Americans'. In liberated Córdoba, according to the *Gaceta* of 17 September 1810, there again reigned an order as perfect as that existing before the counter-revolutionary attempt. 'There is no noticeable difference', it added, 'except that the sons of Córdoba itself now occupy those appointments which the previous incumbents had profaned'. And it immediately pointed out the moral of this exemplary tale: 'You, generous patriots, who suffer the yoke of oppressive overlords, do not lose hope, for your courage will in the long run place you in those posts which they abuse in order to oppress you'. The character of an internal mutation within the élite which the Revolution was beginning to have is emphasised in this passage. The patriots were identified as the personnel to replace the office-holders in a bureaucratic apparatus which was in any case small. However, besides the immediate beneficiaries, the entire American-born population could feel itself identified with them and share vicariously in their rise. Vast crowds – if we are to believe the *Gaceta* of 15 November – welcomed the Revolutionary expedition which marched into Salta with a ditty which ambitiously proclaimed: 'To us belongs the domination of all things in the Indian nation'.

This, without a doubt, was the Revolution as its initiators would have desired it. When they replaced the old overlords, they both took political power into their own hands and symbolically satisfied the demands of all those American-born individuals who at one time or another had felt themselves discriminated against in favour of the Spanish-born. Once the officials appointed from Spain, who were, after all, not very numerous, were removed, the Revolution had no more enemies. However, things did not work out that way. The hostility of the Spanish-born did not wane, even though the Revolutionary government had tried to allay it. A decree of 26 May ordered severe punishments for those who 'sowed discord between European-born and American-born Spaniards, which is so prejudicial to the tranquillity of citizens and the general good of the State'.[23] And on 13 August 1810, during his brief spell as Intendant-Governor of Córdoba, Juan Martín de Pueyrredón called upon the clergy to intercede between the American- and the European-born. 'Cause to disappear' Pueyrredón eloquently requested them, 'with your wise counsels the tragic seed of discord which ignorance has spread among the native-born and the Europeans. This precious part of ourselves, industrious, virtuous and so necessary for our future greatness deserves our urgent care'.[24] Three days before it had been the Buenos Aires Junta which appeared to be disputing with the dissident Royalist movement in Montevideo for the privilege of receiving the refugees from the Peninsula, at the very moment when it was breaking off all relations with the rival city: 'Since it is probable that there will arrive many families from Spain, which have fled from the provinces occupied by the enemy, they are invited with sincerity and warmheartedness to proceed to the territory of the Capital'. The Junta offered these prospective immigrants not only its guarantee of 'close union and friendship with our brothers, the Europeans', but also 'fertile lands for cultivation, assistance in the provision of housing, advance payments for their first work, and the well remunerated exercise of their respective careers, arts and professions'.[25] By that time, however, the real existence of tension between Europeans and Americans, though deplored, could no longer be denied. In speaking of it, the newspaper which was the spokesman of the Revolution thought fit to distribute the blame equally. There were Americans – wrote a correspondent from Córdoba in the *Gaceta* of 16 July 1810 – 'who seem to desire the defeat of Spain; they are possessed with that old, though unfounded sentiment that their merits have not received recognition...and they imagine that their good fortune depends on the defeat of Spain'. All too often, the Europeans feared 'that in the future they will not have in these parts that influence and esteem which they have enjoyed hitherto'. Both groups would do well to remember 'that the public and private interests of Americans and Europeans are closely connected, indeed they are one and the same, and that the distinction made between one group and the other is only nominal, for an American is none other than a man born in America but the son of Spanish parents (I am speaking of the upper class of society); whereas the European was born in Spain, but has settled in these parts'.

The exhortations of clerics, journalists and anonymous correspondents were not sufficient to prevent the growing division between the Spanish- and the American-born. The *Gaceta* of 15 October 1810 appeared surprised that the hostility of the former towards the new system was not relaxing: 'For the overlords to behave thus would not be so surprising... What is astonishing is that the merchant, the craftsman, the landowner and the workman show an implacable hatred of the Fatherland's cause'. This opposition should not cause undue alarm, for the Fatherland needed only the support of the Americans, to whom it owed 'that abundance of resources, which are multiplied in a thousand ways' and who maintained the war effort. Thus, the Revolution finally recognised that Europeans and Americans were in fact two hostile sectors, and that it could no longer avoid choosing between them. The consequences were soon to be felt. In a circular of 3 December 1810, the Junta reserved new appointments for Americans, although at the same time it was 'making efforts...to behave with moderation and long-suffering, to an extent further than any other government has gone, and has resolved to reconcile the welfare of foreigners with the rights of the native sons of the country' by retaining in their appointments Spaniards prepared to display 'good conduct, love of the nation and allegiance to the government'.

The resolution described the Spanish-born as 'foreign persons'. They had ceased, therefore, to be 'a precious part of ourselves'. But was this really the case? A few days later, the measure was repealed. With an engaging frankness, the Junta declared it to be too unpopular to enforce: 'The general disagreement has led the Junta to modify its previous view...It has felt obliged to satisfy the justified complaints of the European-born Spaniards who, being the heads and the noble originators of patrician families, receive offence as a result of their universal dismissal from all appointments'. The ambivalence of the relationships between the Spanish-born and the Creole sectors of the Buenos Aires élite is here clearly revealed. It was to show itself even more evidently in March 1811, when the Junta decreed the banishment of unmarried Spaniards. According to the Government's calculations, between three and four thousand people would be affected by this measure. On this occasion opposition to the measure was expressed more openly, and was used to effect a rapprochement between the revolutionary faction formerly led by Mariano Moreno, which in December of the preceding year had lost control of the Junta, and the Cabildo, reorganised in October with members indubitably loyal to the new order yet feeling a sense of rivalry towards the Junta. The followers of Moreno had founded a political club, where Julián Álvarez spoke eloquently against the harshness of the measure. 'Americans', said this orator from a rostrum erected in a café in the city centre in imitation of those of Revolutionary Paris,

> turn your eyes on those who surround you, look with care into those faces, which you have seen so many times in the squares, in the avenues, in the churches, at your family reunions, in your own homes; look at them well, and you will recognise men who not long ago were your friends, your companions, united with you by business relations, personal friendship or blood.

The Cabildo, on its part, proposed to grant exemption to those who swore before that municipal corporation their allegiance to the new system, with a guarantee of their persons and property and the sponsorship of a 'native son of the country of known patriotic sentiments'.

The entire ambivalence of the relationship between the American-born and European-born sectors of the élite is revealed in this instance. From the end of the eighteenth century the rivalry between the two groups was recorded by alarmed observers as a drama taking place within the context of the family. The proposal to co-opt some of the Spaniards into the new Revolutionary élite (since to remain in it a personal commitment was not enough, and a Creole of some prominence had to provide a guarantee) shows that, even for the politically more radical sectors of that élite, the elimination of the political danger represented by the disaffected Spaniards, although it was designed to facilitate the control of local power by the Creole group, was not supposed to involve the plain and simple liquidation of their intimate rivals. The Junta was prepared to go further in its generosity than its supplicants requested. Although it expressed a reminder that in the past no attention had been paid to the pleas addressed to the Spaniards by friends and relations who 'tried to persuade them to take the interest they should in the great cause of the Fatherland, the comfortable life they had achieved there, the trade they were carrying on, their children, their wives', it had only praise for the generosity with which the Creoles were protecting their mortal enemies from a harsh, but just measure: 'All hastened to give the Government, by word or in writing, the fullest possible guarantee for their respective protégés'. This moving display of sentiment achieved the miracle of ending the resistance of the Spaniards: 'The odious distinction between Americans and Europeans has from today been replaced by a general harmony between compatriots and fellow-countrymen',[26] and as a result, the Junta was able to repeal the measure which it had only decided to impose by running counter to its humanitarian sentiments.

It is not necessary to postulate that the Junta believed everything it said. It was only too evidently guided by prudence in the face of the concerted offensive of its enemies. But it is, nevertheless, of some significance that the latter should have found in the defence of the Spaniards a cause calculated to win them broader popularity, and that the Junta should have preferred to avoid battle on that ground. However, the events of March 1811 did not put an end to the increasing discrimination against the Spaniards. This continued for two different reasons: the first was that the limited democratisation had given expression to a sector of plebeian opinion whose anti-Spanish sentiments do not appear to have been subject to any ambivalence, and it was precisely to that sector that the Junta had recourse in order to overcome its domestic rivals. After the events of 5 and 6 April, reconciliation was no longer the objective of the Revolutionary authorities in their dealings with the Spaniards. It is true that – even though it figured in the popular petition – the expulsion of the unmarried Europeans never took place, but the lack of physical measures was offset by a verbal offensive which became increasingly ruthless. From now on the *Gaceta*, adopting an attitude which a year earlier it had condemned in certain Creoles, emphasised the reverses suffered by the anti-French forces in Spain, and although one correspondent, a Spaniard and a patriot, complained that the newspaper seemed to take a delight in these reverses and attacked all Europeans indiscriminately, this merely provoked a violent attack on the correspondent himself. Only if his patriotism was feigned, replied the *Gaceta*, could he find anything to object to in the impassioned articles which had appeared. The *Gaceta*, after emphasising the lack of contributions from

Spaniards for the campaign against Montevideo, declared that such obstinacy would be punished, if the Spaniards did not make swift amends: 'It is in your power', it concluded, 'to avoid the blow which is becoming inevitable: do not complain afterwards of our conduct'.[27] No amends were made: in February 1812 'a villainous old European Spaniard of seventy' dared to interrupt the patriotic sermon of the Mercedarian friar Manuel Aparicio, in the church of Saint Nicholas in Buenos Aires, to cast doubt on his assertion that the loss of Spain was irreparable (this, apparently, being the doctrinal point expounded in the sermon), and although the offender 'was arrested, and taken from his house to the prison, where he awaits his just punishment', on the following Sunday it was 'over sixteen Europeans in the congregation, and some three or four native sons favourable to them, prejudiced and hostile to their country' who interrupted the sacred orator, who had them arrested by 'a passing patrol'. They were, apparently, condemned to imprisonment.[28] Of more significance than the incident itself was the tone adopted by the chronicler Beruti, whose lack of stable opinions made him particularly sensitive to climates of opinion: the Europeans appear in his account as *ipso facto* enemies of the new order.

The conspiracy of Álzaga was to confirm this point of view, and to mark a complete rupture between the two sectors of the élite. Until it was discovered, in fact, the links between the two groups did not fail to have political consequences, and the first rumours of the conspiracy were disbelieved because, since the plot involved Spaniards very close to Pueyrredón, it appeared to be an intrigue designed to diminish his influence in the Revolutionary government. The conspiracy, with its plans for a bloody repression of the American and patriot sector, was followed by an immediate intensification of the anti-Spanish measures. Over a thousand invalids were deported in July to the Luján frontier. At the end of that year, after the discovery of a fresh conspiracy, hundreds of Spaniards, 'particularly the unmarried ones, who are those who can cause most harm,' were also banished. Even within the city discriminatory measures affected the Spaniards, who were forbidden to ride on horseback, or to go out in the streets at night. In response to plebeian demands, the Spaniards were eliminated from the retail trade, and were forbidden to own stores. They were given three days in which to find someone to replace them. All this took place in an atmosphere of harsh repression, which for some days took the form of fresh executions carried out in the Main Square. Even at this stage, however, the most seriously affected among the Spaniards seem to have been the more humbly situated ones. No discriminatory measure was applied in the case of wholesale trade, and the most eminent did not even suffer confiscation. In this way, the considerable fortune of Álzaga was saved for his children, who were Creoles (one of them, Félix de Álzaga, was destined to have a successful career in the Army and the Buenos Aires Legislature). The following year, the creation of the status of citizenship of the United Provinces at last provided a legal instrument to distinguish between Spaniards favourable and hostile to the new order. The certificate of citizenship was necessary for continuance in public appointments and the practice of commerce, and it could only be obtained by Spaniards who could give positive proof of their services to the patriot cause. Again, as in 1811, the Creole élite was not interested in protecting the interests of the Spaniards as a group, but of 'saving their respective protégés' by offering in their favour a guarantee which was enhanced in value by the prestige and influence of the person granting it. Thus the new élite, essentially Creole, reserved to itself the right to co-opt certain Spaniards. For the others, the situation became increasingly difficult, as the legal restrictions were intensified, until by 1817 the Spaniards could only marry Creole women with the authorisation of the Secretary of Government.[29] At that time Spaniards who had not managed to obtain citizenship were pathetic figures. Brackenridge described them wandering along the Poplar-walk beside the river, 'passing like ghosts of the Styx, with a look in their eyes that words cannot describe'. A few pages later, in a less sentimental tone, the same observer offers a more precise picture of this numerous group of pariahs of the new order 'the studied raggedness of their clothes and the rough and coarse expression on their faces are due to the fact that they are treated like a new kind of Jew by those whom they were accustomed to consider as vastly inferior to them'.[30]

In this way, the Revolution had confronted an entire sector and had excluded it from the society which was beginning to take shape under its aegis, and only accepted the recruitment of individuals from that sector. The Spaniards, who under the old order had no separate place in the system of caste-differentiation, were particularly numerous at certain levels and in connection with certain social functions: the higher administration and trade. Could this give rise to a process of levelling down through which those levels and functions, in which Spaniards predominated, would appear as committed to the old order and therefore destined to have a less honoured place in the new order? Not necessarily: the higher administration constituted the principal booty sought by the Revolutionary leadership, which therefore had no interest in devaluing it. With regard to trade, the ambiguity of the relationship between Spaniards and Creoles, who were rivals but nevertheless 'united by business relations', in the sphere of big business, protected the big Spanish merchants more effectively than those of lesser degree, who were calmly abandoned to the vengeance of the populace. Nevertheless, it was precisely the sectors in which Spaniards predominated which were most adversely affected by the changes introduced by the Revolution. With regard to the merchants, we have already observed the reason why this was so. The commercial revolution that accompanied the political one left them defenceless in the face of their new rivals, the agents of those economies which free trade had placed in closer contact with the River Plate region. As regards the upper bureaucracy, motives were closely connected with the political transformation provoked by the Revolution. The decline of the corporations and civil and ecclesiastical institutions was not only a consequence of the new economic and financial climate, although, as happened with local big business, they were to provide the chief victims of the urgent financial exactions of the State. It was the fruit of a deliberate policy, now no longer connected with the presence of anti-revolutionaries – who, earlier on, had in fact been very numerous – in the administrative structure, but arising from the ambitions and style of behaviour of the new-born Revolutionary state. The action of the Revolutionary authorities did not take the form in this case, as it had in that of the Spaniards, of the exclusion of an entire sector of Colonial society, but of the readjustment of the equilibrium between sectors which were all destined to survive the Revolutionary changes. Notwithstanding the improbable forecast of the liberators of Córdoba, the Revolutionary River Plate region began to become different from that of Viceregal times. Nowhere was that differentiation more evident than in the fate suffered by the higher civil and ecclesiastical bureaucracy.

THE CRISIS OF THE BUREAUCRACY

Although it did not want to have enemies within the body politic, the Revolution proposed a new image of corporations and other civic offices which in fact deprived them of that pre-eminence which had been recognised within the Colonial system. The transformation was justified in a sweeping and emphatic manner in the decree suppressing titles promulgated by the President of the Junta in December 1810. The political essence of the decree was the transfer of the supreme military command, previously invested in Saavedra, to the Junta as a whole, but the remaining paragraphs constituted a short treatise on republican virtue for the use of higher officials. The decree condemned 'those privileges which to the detriment of humanity were invented by tyrants, to suffocate natural sentiments'. From olden times, 'the usurper, the despot, the assassin of his country bears through the public streets the veneration and respect of an immense crowd, but earns for himself the execration of philosophers and the curses of good citizens'. Under 'the sweet dogma of equality' everything was to be different. Straightforward dealing would be the primary characteristic of the official's conduct. Until that time the Junta, running counter to its intimate convictions, had consented to receive, in the person of its President, the traditional honours accorded to the Viceroy, 'presenting to the people the traditional pomp of the old masquerade, until repeated lessons made it disposed to receive the precious gift of its liberty' without fear of making a mistake. This brief period of apprenticeship was now at an end. No one any longer believed 'that the popular leaders do not possess the noble character of those who used to come to us from Spain'. In future the official was 'to observe religiously the sacred dogma of equality', and he would not have, outside his functions, the right to 'other considerations than those merited by his own virtues'.[31]

This severe discipline, which the Junta imposed on itself, was to be applied with even greater rigour to the other officials. When the irreconcilable dissidents of the Audiencia were replaced by new judges, chosen from among lawyers prominent in the legal life of Buenos Aires, these not only received lower salaries than their predecessors, but were deprived of all external marks of rank. The very simplicity of the ceremony of their installation in their posts was emphasised with satisfaction by the *Gaceta*. It appears that the repeated lessons in the dogma of equality were rapidly assimilated by their recipients among the populace. In his *Memorias* Gervasio Antonio de Posadas, a member of the governing Triumvirate and later Supreme Director, mentioned, among other reasons for the concentration of power in the hands of one person, the fact that the triumvirs 'whether walking separately, or all together in the street, received numerous insults'.[32] And the unpopularity of the higher officials of the old order, which was untiringly evoked by Revolutionary propaganda, affected those who replaced them, who were closely watched so that they did not make any attempt to repeat their predecessors' arrogance and tyrannical behaviour. The dogma of equality, literally interpreted, also alerted public opinion to an additional danger: that of the officials discovering, beneath the political rivalries created among them, an essential solidarity of interests, in opposition to those under their administrative jurisdiction. When, in one of its first decrees, the Revolutionary government decided to finance the military expedition into the Interior 'with the salaries of His Excellency Don Baltasar Hidalgo de Cisneros, those of the tribunals of the Royal Praetorian Audiencia and that of Accounts, and the revenue from tobacco, with others that the Junta may see fit to curtail', and hastened to add that this measure was taken 'in the full knowledge that individuals drawing salaries were not to be completely deprived of their income, because this is the manifest will of the people',[33] the new governing sector seemed to reveal in this limitation more its own scruples than those of the governed. Less than a year later, among the demands of the mob which took part in the clash of 6 April 1811 was the demand that no pension or severance pay be granted to officials dismissed for political disaffection. This was only provisionally accepted by the governing faction that owed its power to that clash. On the 1 September 1811, it decided to pay, retroactively, a pension to the officers under arrest and to issue rations to the civilians suffering the same sanctions.[34] But it is still significant that this limited measure of solidarity with colleagues who had fallen on hard times had to wait for the relaxation of pressure on the part of a public opinion which the Revolution had alerted to the dangers inherent in a new caste of officials.

In any case, even in Colonial times, solidarity between bureaucrats had not eliminated internal tensions, and the Revolution was to increase the latter to a greater degree than the former. Even leaving aside the purge of dissidents initiated by the Revolution, the latter created a supreme authority which felt with very much greater urgency the need to affirm its supremacy over its bureaucratic instruments and could, moreover, keep them under closer surveillance than could the remote Court. In this way, what Revolutionary ideology represented as the supremacy of the people over its corps of civil servants was really that of a centre of political power which was not prepared to allow the growth of possible rivals. The magistrates formerly appointed by the Crown were, after the Revolution, subject to the whims of the holders of Revolutionary power. An element of instability was introduced, both in fact and in law. When, in 1812, the Audiencia was replaced by a Court of Appeal which was never to attain the power or the prestige of its predecessor, the new judges were appointed for two years only, instead of for life. This instability not only undermined the will to resist of the career officials. It was a consequence of the introduction into their ranks of somewhat improvised recruits, who were expected above all to display an appropriate Revolutionary fervour, and who only partially managed to identify themselves with the bureaucratic positions in which fortune had placed them. It is enough to compare, in the extremely suggestive text of the *Memorias autobiográficas* of Posadas, the constant and affectionate mention he makes of the appointment of curial notary which he had held from Colonial times with the detachment with which he refers to the much more exalted posts he attained after the Revolution, to note how the latter had succeeded in breaking down the strong bureaucratic structures which in Colonial times had been both refuges and strongholds engaged in perpetual internecine conflict.

The Revolutionary authorities only hesitated in the face of one institution, that of the Cabildo, which in the May clashes had managed to conserve a hold over the government established under its aegis. Although in October 1810 the Buenos Aires Cabildo was purged, its new members, whose tenure of office was prolonged until the end of 1811, retained the right to elect their successors. When in 1815, this system of renewal was abolished in favour of that of popular election, the reform merely confirmed the Cabildo in its situation as the only corporation whose power did not derive from the supreme Revolutionary authority, and which, moreover, in addition to its municipal functions, fulfilled that of filling the vacancies – which the hazardous politics of the Revolution were to provoke repeatedly – in the government itself.

This vitality on the part of the Cabildo – due partly to the fact that the new authority was, from the beginning, formally subject to it, and that the Cabildo perhaps offered the most solid of the links of legal continuity between the Revolutionary régime and the Colonial system whose legitimacy it claimed to inherit – was, however, the one exception among the institutions, and it presented an even greater contrast to the abjectly obedient attitude of the officials who were directly dependent on the central power.

The affirmation of the new supreme authorities' power over a bureaucracy and judicial institutions accustomed to the looser control of a remote Court was given further encouragement by the reorientation of the finances of the River Plate region towards military purposes. Because of this, both corporation members and officials were to have, in the new State, a less unquestioned right than in Colonial times to dispose of public revenues. As early as 7 June 1810, the Revolutionary Junta found it necessary to clarify certain aspects of the order prohibiting the Treasury from making any disbursement without its express authority. 'It is necessary to correct the mistaken impression that some have, that the salaries of civil servants have been suspended or delayed'. What was being taken was a precautionary measure 'so that priority in dealing with applications for funds should never depend on the whim of junior officials, because in the event of unexpected insolvency, the Junta must deal with the deficit according to the amount and urgency of the outstanding amounts'. Although it promised that 'the official who works will never be denied his salary', the Junta accompanied this promise, which might appear to be categorical, with a description of the mechanism adopted to ensure this payment 'unless urgent financial demands make it impossible'. A future characterised by financial penury, in which the punctual payment of the salaries of civil servants might not be given the highest priority was thus anticipated by this alarming declaration.[35] In fact, delays in payment of salaries were to become frequent. At the end of 1811 there was, in addition, a general reduction in salaries of civil servants and the pay of officers not on the active list. The sum subtracted was, indeed, described as a loan, but that made little difference to the situation.[36] And throughout the first decade after the Revolution the only change in the situation of public officials and employees was for the worse. 1819 marked the last stage of that incessant deterioration, when an administration on the brink of collapse got rid of numerous civil servants whom it could not afford to pay. Even the chronicler Beruti, who had lost much of his revolutionary enthusiasm with the years and with the misfortunes he suffered, though considering the measure 'harsh and cruel', admitted that it was necessary...[37]

Like the employees directly subject to their authority, the corporations which in the past had enjoyed their own patrimony were to see it sacrificed to the needs of the Revolutionary war. The first sign of this was seen in the attempts of the Royal Treasury to collect its debts – some of them long-standing ones – from the Cabildo or the Consulado. The flow of credits very soon changed direction, and both Cabildo and Consulado were repeatedly called upon to make patriotic sacrifices. Ecclesiastical corporations did not escape the same fate. Donations of slaves and money were made, and in 1815 the entire patrimony of churches and religious brotherhoods was handed over to the State, to be returned 'when the causes that have motivated this measure shall have ceased'.[38]

This loss of wealth, power and prestige placed officials and corporations in increasing subjection to the supreme authority, which – after jealously reserving to itself the essence of power from the very beginning – eventually reassumed the external signs of supremacy. The concentration of government in the hands of one person, the Supreme Director, was accompanied by the now definitive abandonment of the austere egalitarian ideal which the Junta had set itself in December 1811. The Viceregal band and escort again accompanied the person of the holder of the highest office, and his ministers were, like him, addressed as *señoría*.

The instability of Revolutionary politics did, indeed, make these restored marks of respect less impressive. Those who were granted them could soon be deprived of them, and – rather than any political lesson – Beruti deduced from the continuous succession of rises and falls, which provided a spectacular confirmation of the mutability of human fortunes, a lesson of Christian resignation. On a more mundane level, the former Supreme Director Pueyrredón observed with some perception that, despite the heartfelt desire to establish an authority as respected as the pre-Revolutionary one, 'one missed that strength which the seal of antiquity gives to human institutions', and that the scandal which all too often accompanied changes in the leadership aggravated even further this decline in the prestige of authority.[39] Even so, a bureaucracy even more seriously affected by instability was in no position to take advantage of this weakening of the supreme power to emancipate itself from its tutelage, which became increasingly strict.

The Church was in a special situation. The new government could not employ with this institution the methods it had used to reduce the civil administration to obedience. Open enemies and lukewarm supporters of the new order abounded in the Church, and the Revolutionary government had to learn to live with them. The purge was therefore incomplete and above all gradual. True, the three bishops whose dioceses were in Revolutionary territory – those of Buenos Aires, Córdoba and Salta – were the object of measures openly or indirectly connected with their sentiments towards the Revolution. The Bishop of Buenos Aires was forbidden access to his own Cathedral during ceremonies involving the Chapter with which he had a dispute, and this situation continued until his sudden death in 1812, whilst the Bishop of Córdoba, involved in the counter-revolutionary conspiracy of Liniers, remained in Buenos Aires, subject to confinement of varying rigour, from 1810 to 1816, and the Bishop of Salta was deported to Buenos Aires in 1812 on the orders of General Belgrano, and stayed there until his death in 1819, even though in 1817 he took a solemn oath of allegiance to the independent nation. It is also true that the bishops, thanks to their status, were accorded treatment more considerate than that meted out to less illustrious dissidents, but nevertheless the government showed towards them a new-found arrogance. 'The only legitimate religion', declared the first Triumvirate to the Bishop of Córdoba, Orellana, when informing him that it had decided to end his confinement in Luján and authorise him to reside in the capital, 'is definitely that which does most to consolidate a government based on the sole principle of legitimacy. Consequently, its ministers have a right to the respect of this government in accordance with their elevated character...Your Grace has been a worthy successor to the great Augustine, in following his example by reforming your opinion in accordance with the principles of the interests of society'. This beneficiary of the Government's generosity answered with his 'thanks to God for His mercy, for He has given us a just and pious government, which, breaking once for all the fetters and chains that bind bodies and turn away the hearts of men, has been able to enslave those hearts by its sweet ties of love and brotherhood'. This answer, despite its enthusiastic tone, glosses over many questions. It made no comment on the triumvirate's claim to be based on the principle of legitimacy, and still less did it mention the assertion that the Bishop had abjured his own previous principles, and the sense of the concluding sentences was deliberately left vague. Was it the entire country, or just the Bishop, who had previously been confined by the Revolutionaries, who had been liberated by these? Nevertheless, anyone reading the correspondence columns of the *Gaceta* might have concluded that a year of imprisonment had overcome the misgivings of the Bishop,[40] and his subsequent behaviour was to lend force to this interpretation. Orellana and his companion in misfortune, Videla del Pino, were to be found among those present at the ceremonies which the Revolution held to celebrate its victories; and both the Bishop of Córdoba and that of Buenos Aires were to attend the inauguration of the Patriotic Society in January 1812.[41]

Thus, whatever their private sentiments, the Bishops were only accepted in the new order (and, even then, as slightly suspect characters) if they lent it the prestige of their ecclesiastical rank.

The very acute awareness that ecclesiastical policy had more complex effects on those subject to it than the policy followed with regard to the civil servants thus lent it an increased ambiguity. It was a simultaneous attempt to neutralise the hostility of the clergy, a thorough purge of whom would be impossible, and to use the Church to help in the affirmation of the Revolutionary authority. Thus, in its message of 21 November 1810 to the Bishop of Buenos Aires, the Junta not only imposed, as has been observed above, the reading of the *Gaceta* from the pulpit, but it also demanded a complete list of parish priests and other clergy.[42] A stricter control was soon to be exercised. In November Bishop Lue, acting on the orders of the Junta, was obliged to dismiss the abbess of the Capuchin nuns, who had been keeping up a correspondence with the dissidents in Montevideo. Her successor hastened to offer 'her complete allegiance to the public good and the fortune of the government'.[43] The government went on to act even less circumspectly towards the congregations than it had when dealing with the bishops. After communicating to the Visitor of the Franciscan Order, on the 9 June 1810, the order of expulsion of two friars, 'for important reasons connected with the Royal service', it gave orders for this to take effect immediately, and 'in case you should encounter any difficulty in the carrying out of this order, you are to report them to this Junta, which will resolve them by the considerable means in its power'. The threat to have recourse to physical force recurred constantly, as in the case where the Warden of the Recollect was ordered to reprimand Father Lacunza for not having preceded his sermon on Saint Clare's day with greetings to the civil authorities present. The message continued that if such offences were committed again they would not be overlooked.[44] And again, when issuing a reprimand for the disorders that had taken place among some monks of the same Recollect: 'if the Government is devoting all its vigilance and care to maintaining order in secular society...it would be strange indeed to expect indulgence on the part of that same authority' towards incidents that 'would result, within the cloister, in a scandal difficult to suppress and outside it in a public scandal among the people'.[45] In short, the Revolutionary government was punctually carrying out the programme anticipated in its bittersweet letter to the Bishop of Buenos Aires, of 23 June 1810, in which it stated itself to be prepared 'to teach every man in the territory under its jurisdiction that its precepts should be obeyed not only *propter conscientiam sed etiam propter timorem*'.[46]

There was one factor which both complicated and facilitated the work of the Junta. Since its action had to be, despite everything, more prudent than in the case of the civil administration, it would never be able to eliminate the tension between adherents and opponents of the new order by the simple elimination of the latter group. The Revolution led to an immediate intensification of the internal conflicts among the secular clergy (with an open rupture between the Bishop and his ecclesiastical chapter) and the regular clergy, particularly in the Franciscan Order where the political conflict, which was a continuation of another internal one, led to a fight with fists and knives. In the face of these conflicts, the Revolutionary government often declined to define its attitude. This conserved the allegiance of those ecclesiastics who had given it from the beginning, and disciplined their internal enemies through the double fear of the political authorities and their close patriot rivals. In this way the very internal conflicts among the clergy, in the face of which the political authority postponed its arbitration, ensured the submission of both friendly and hostile clergy, and made possible the imperious style adopted by the political power in its dealings with the ecclesiastical power.

From the beginning, this took the form of an unbridled use of church property, increasingly ill guarded by the intimidated clergy. In the former College of Saint Charles, now converted into a barracks, one room contained the library left to the institution by the late Bishop Azamor. On the 7 August the Junta curtly informed the Bishop that 'since the room which is filled with the remains of the library of Sr. Azamor is needed for the troops...Your Grace is to take immediate steps to clear out the room for the use of the barracks'. This order, which gave no room for prevarication, was the response to the Bishop's complaints as to the danger to the books represented by the soldiery. A month later, the incident was concluded with the demand that the books be handed over to the public library. In the same imperious manner, the lime destined for repair work on the Cathedral was assigned by the Junta for military purposes. Another order commandeered for military use the building next to the Caleza Chapel, belonging to the Franciscan Order, by means of an order to the custodian that he was to vacate it 'at his earliest convenience'.[47]

No less impressive than the arrogance of the civil power was the submission of the ecclesiastical power, which – in language perhaps more significant than its authors realised – was defined in a declaration of the Ecclesiastical Chapter as another class within the State, and obliged therefore 'to share in the conservation of the whole, on the existence and increase of which the welfare of each part depends'. It is not surprising, therefore, that the action of the State should have been restrained only by its own discretion. Only after 1816 was one to hear less submissive language from the spokesmen of the clergy. The state, which in many respects was governing the Church, possessed, in order to affirm its supremacy, a less brusque but perhaps more effective method than intimidation. This was favourable treatment for its adherents, by exercising privileges inherited from the Colonial power, and those which it had to assume *vis-à-vis* a Church isolated from Rome firstly by the captivity of the Supreme Pontiff and then by the decision of the Vatican not to maintain official relations with Revolutionary Spanish America, and isolated from Spain by the war of independence itself.

As a result of this isolation Buenos Aires was to remain without a Bishop for a quarter of a century, and the regular orders, even before the reform to which they were subjected in the 1820s, began to be governed in more than one respect by resolutions emanating from the civil power. The institution of a *Comisario General* with authority over the regular clergy, to supervise all the convents in the Revolutionary territory, is an indication of the creative impulse of the Revolutionary government in a sphere which in less abnormal circumstances would have been forbidden territory. The isolation (and the fact that when it began the Pope was not in a position to define what the attitude of the clergy should be) also explains the lack of reaction to the intrusive spirit of the civil power. The resistance which the latter encountered among the clergy, which was considerable, had a political basis. Those who recognised it as the legitimate power also tended to accept its decisions on points of ecclesiastical discipline, and its perfect right to take such decisions. In this way, the civil authorities even went so far as to reform canons of the Council of Trent. This constant advance of the political authority did not directly affect the prestige of religion in the life of society. After some initial passivity, which was harshly judged by public opinion, the Revolutionary government took its rôle as defender of the Faith perfectly seriously. Nevertheless, a Church which in the past had proudly held its own throughout labyrinthine disputes with the local agents of the Crown could not fail to lose prestige when it showed itself in its new rôle as the submissive follower of a power which was dispensing its protection from above.

This was even more true because this closer subordination to the civil power threatened to contaminate the ecclesiastical power with the instability which afflicted the former. In the absence of a Bishop, Buenos Aires was governed by vicars-general who did not remain long in their posts. They were proposed by the ecclesiastical Chapter, but their appointment was subject to government approval, despite the initial efforts of canons and other dignitaries to shake off this restriction. That meant that not only was there, on that level, vigilance against the adversaries of the Revolution (a vigilance that at less exalted levels led in 1816 to a numerous group of parish priests being forbidden to hear confessions, and in 1818 to the deportation of Spanish-born clergy who had not obtained citizenship),[48] but the factions in the internal conflict among the Revolutionary groups had repercussions in the government of the Church in Buenos Aires. To give one example of this: in January 1814 the Government decided to increase from ten to thirteen the number of prebendaries in Buenos Aires Cathedral. Among those appointed with a haste that did not fail to cause comment was Dr. José León Planchón,[49] apparently then considered to entertain irreproachable Revolutionary sentiments. In 1815, when the post of vicar-general of the see fell vacant, the government rejected Planchón, who had been proposed by the Chapter (and attacked by the ecclesiastical prosecutor Antonio Sáenz, who was very close to those momentarily in power), and preferred to appoint Dr Achega, declaring that it had taken into account, in addition to his specific qualifications for the appointment, 'one particular quality, his staunch and renowned patriotism'.[50] It is not surprising that even such patriotism might suffer vacillations. Thus, an anonymous Royalist observer recorded that Fray Hipólito Soler, although involved in the Revolution, would gladly serve the Spanish cause, because his close contacts with the party defeated in 1815 had made him disillusioned with the Revolution[51] (although

The Revolution in Buenos Aires

he did not figure among the ecclesiastics banished after the fall of Alvear).

A Church thus invaded by political turbulence was ill placed to defend that position which Church and religion had held in the River Plate region in more tranquil times. That position was not, of course, threatened by any frontal attack. However, it suffered an inevitable erosion, provoked both by the closer contact with adherents of other religious faiths which resulted from free trade, and by the development of the new civic liturgy, which implicitly competed with the predominance of religious festivals as an expression of the collective life of the city. It would, of course, be over-hasty to deduce from the more limited rôle of the Church and the Orders an equally rapid decline in allegiance to the received Faith. The reaction to the ecclesiastical reforms of the 1820s indicates that the systematic modification of the position of the Church in society could, even then, encounter widespread opposition. The progressive secularisation of collective life, when imposed by circumstances and not by deliberate policy, provoked, on the other hand, only limited reactions. Of this we again find evidence in Beruti, who was to be hostile to the subsequent ecclesiastical reforms and to look on freedom of worship as a threat to morality. Although, as late as 1813, he noted the 'scandal among the timorous' provoked by a bullfight, and a theatrical performance to celebrate the victory of Salta 'in this holy time of Lent', in 1815, when a man was executed on Easter Sunday, he attributed the 'extraordinary and universal repugnance' caused by this incident, firstly, to the fact that the victim was a *patricio* (that is, not a Spaniard) and a man of singular merit, and only secondly to 'domestic etiquette and the fact that it was a holy day'. When, in 1818, a festival was held to celebrate the declaration of the independence of Chile, the chronicler no longer even mentioned that this took place during Lent (the celebrations went on from the 5th to the 8th March, and the 22nd of that month was Easter Sunday).[52]

This secularisation of collective social life was the counterpart to Revolutionary politicisation. Both reflected, in the sphere of social behaviour, the increasing subordination of the ecclesiastical to the civil power. Despite the limitations imposed by circumstances, the policy of the supreme Revolutionary authority towards the Church was on the whole successful. This policy might be summarised as being a process of absorption of the resources, power and prestige of legal institutions and corporations which in Colonial times had enjoyed a varying, but in all cases considerable autonomy, for the benefit of the new supreme power which the Revolution had installed in Buenos Aires. However, effective though it was in crushing its potential rivals, this power was less successful in inheriting the power and prestige of its victims. Its attachment to coercive methods to impose allegiance arose not so much from desire as from necessity, and was a constant indication of the limits of the consensus on which the Revolutionary power rested, not only among the opponents but also among the supporters of the new order.

But did not this use of coercion, which was only one aspect of its desire to exercise a much closer control over the entirety of its subjects, oblige the new régime to create an apparatus for administering that coercion more complex and powerful than that existing in the past? And did not this apparatus, the indispensable adjunct to the new power, constitute a danger to it? This was certainly the case, and in the Interior, where the Revolutionary government exercised little control over these subordinate executive authorities, the latter became the beneficiaries of a gradual transfer of power, the extent of which would only be noticeable after 1820. In the capital, on the other hand, where these minor authorities were very rapidly invested with new attributes, the effects which this had on the political equilibrium were discernible from a very early date, and from then the successive Revolutionary governments maintained a remarkably effective vigilance against this potentially dangerous dilution of their authority.

In Buenos Aires these authorities were those which formed the police and lower-level municipal justice, inherited from the *ancien régime*. It has been observed above how the Junta invested these officials with increasing attributions. Surveillance of residences and of the political mood in their respective districts were their responsibility, as were functions as varied as the control of arms and the apprehension of vagrants and unemployed men for recruitment into the Army. It has also been pointed out that this accumulation of new functions – or functions made more important by the circumstances of the Revolution – transformed the *alcaldes* and assistant *alcaldes*, from the point of view of the popular and marginal groups of the urban and suburban population, into the representatives of the new authority, and at the same time into an effective cushion against it. The consequences of this were brutally revealed on 5 and 6 April 1811, when the incursion of the plebeian mass from the suburbs saved the faction in power from the violent attack of its rival. Leading this mass were the *alcaldes* and assistant *alcaldes*, who in its name presented imperiously-worded petitions. This rustic and plebeian invasion, which Beruti, a follower of Moreno, immediately distinguished from the 'true people' whose intervention had been a feature of Buenos Aires life between 1806 and 1810, caused widespread alarm – even among those whom it saved from political ruin – to those whom the Revolution had granted the direct exercise of power. What was even more perturbing to the latter was that this development was leading to the emergence of what could become a rival élite, formed by leaders whose fame was confined to an outlying quarter or a suburban district, and whose ignorance of the polite ways of the big city might make them appear comic, but whose power, after the events of April, could no longer be doubted. The emergence of Dr Campana, a lawyer of dubious reputation who became the intellectual influence behind the now influential *alcalde* of Las Quintas, Tomás Grigera, boosted by the events of the day into the post of secretary of the Supreme Junta, was a development both scandalous and alarming.

This tendency was to be watched carefully and, finally, curbed. Political authority, threatened with breakdown by the events of April 1811, gradually returned to its normal channels of development. This was partly due to the fact that the political and military course of the Revolution, which was taking an increasingly unsatisfactory direction, could not be ignored by the dominant faction and favoured those within it who supported a change of course. But it was also, no doubt, due to a sort of tacit agreement between the Revolutionary factions, by the terms of which they would in future refrain from calling on the support which had been decisive in April in order to modify the equilibrium in their favour. This tacit agreement also seems to have applied to the political police machinery which the Revolution had contributed to establishing in the city, and to the advisability of putting an end to its growing strength. This explains why there was a continuous succession of measures directed towards this end, even though in other spheres Revolutionary policy was far from displaying the same continuity. At the end of 1811, the appointment of *alcalde* in charge of a district – which until then had been for life, except in cases affected by the Revolutionary purge of August 1811, which had replaced by executive fiat certain disaffected *alcaldes* – was put on a year-to-year basis. Although this measure was only an anticipation of the general suppression of appointments with life tenure in the municipal sphere, the consequences in the case of the *alcaldes* were more significant than in that of other officials with more limited attributions. From January 1812, therefore, these appointments were filled by candidates designated by the outgoing Cabildo, subject to approval by the supreme power. The reform which, from 1815 onwards, provided for the renewal of Cabildo appointments by popular election did not affect the district *alcaldes*.[53]

This solution, of course, obliged the supreme power to share control over the recruitment of *alcaldes* with a Cabildo which it only partially dominated, and with which it had intermittent conflicts. But, on the one hand, the Cabildo, which might not be in full agreement with the political orientation of the supreme power, was as alert as the latter to the dangers inherent in a subordinate apparatus which might become too powerful (the Cabildo, for example, led the agitation which resulted in the alarming Dr Campana being removed from the post of Secretary to the Junta and banished to Areco). Moreover, although the supreme power recognised the Cabildo's share in the appointment of *alcaldes*, it reserved to itself, through a widespread reform of the police organisation, a much closer control over the activities of the latter.

These measures, in any case, enjoyed the full support of the Cabildo, which in some instances actually initiated them, in total contrast to the tenacious opposition which it had shown towards similar measures during the *ancien régime*. On the initiative of the Government, the post of Intendant of Police was created, in December 1811, and to it was appointed one of the candidates which the Cabildo, at the suggestion of the Government itself, had submitted to the latter. Although the Cabildo thus associated itself with the appointment of this new official, it had no jurisdiction over him, and it had, of course, even less jurisdiction over the Intendant-Governor of Buenos Aires, a post restored in January 1812 by the Government at the request of the Cabildo to take over the administrative functions which in the jurisdiction of the Buenos Aires Intendancy had been retained by the Viceroys, after a brief and unsuccessful attempt to share power with an Intendant in the same city. These functions had of course been inherited by the Revolutionary governments. In April 1812 the Cabildo again took the initiative, proposing the establishment of a *Comisión de justicia* to be responsible for dealing with cases of theft (robbery with violence had become increasingly frequent). This Committee was empowered to mete out severer punishments than those provided for in ordinary legislation, yet even this body, which left a memorial to itself in the shape of a considerable number of bandits executed, was subject to the Government and not to the Cabildo.[54]

The attitude of the Cabildo can only partly be explained by feelings of prudence towards a supreme authority exercising a closer control than had the Crown of Castile. It was, above all, a response to the intensification of the problems of public order which accompanied the Revolution, and which was connected both with the Revolutionary agitation itself and with reactions to the growing pressure of the political authority on the popular and marginal sectors. In this effort to control a trend which had created permanent strongholds of banditry in the outlying suburbs of the city, the autonomy of the district *alcaldes* was to be drastically curtailed. The police regulations, drawn up in December 1812, placed the rural justices and district *alcaldes* under the orders of the Intendant of Police and his subordinates. They were to submit to him the register of residents for which they had been responsible since 1810, and the Chief Intendant of Police, who had under him a body of salaried officials (the *comisarios*) and a small body of armed constables, was in future to be responsible for the control of vagrants and the unemployed, and also for compiling the register of the 'genuinely poor', with the object of eliminating the 'idlers and good-for-nothings'. All these tasks had acquired a new significance since the State, as has been observed above, preferred to recruit its soldiers among the marginal sectors of the population. The unemployed and the 'sham poor', while waiting for the accommodation that government welfare plans intended for them, could count on the hospitality of the Army.

In this way the relationship between the new State and the popular and marginal sectors, which from the first had been ambiguous, intensified its authoritarian and repressive aspects. At the same time, the importance of the district *alcaldes* in the apparatus for controlling those sectors was sharply curtailed. In this sphere the Revolutionary government not only modified what had been its previous attitude towards those sectors, but also changed the procedures current under the *ancien régime*. The district *alcaldes*, citizens enjoying local prestige who put that prestige at the service of an order of which they were considered as the representatives, were by no means anomalous figures in the Colonial administrative system. They had one advantage which the Crown – desirous of making the administration of the Indies a profitable business – gratefully appreciated: they cost the Treasury nothing. The counterpart of this advantage was that the position of these benevolent servants of Spanish authority was ambiguous. They represented that authority *vis-à-vis* those under their jurisdiction, but perhaps felt more closely identified with the latter than with the governmental apparatus in which they occupied the lowest rung. The Crown could afford to ignore this danger. It aspired to only a loose control over its subjects; even as late as the end of 1809, in a climate of growing political unrest, when issuing more detailed instructions to the district *alcaldes* in order to deal with that unrest, the last Viceroy displayed for that 'just and rational liberty which is permitted to each individual' and which might be threatened by excessive zeal on the part of the *alcaldes* a care which one was to seek in vain in his Revolutionary successors.[55] The Revolution was more ambitious: not only did it intend to impose new beliefs and a new style of behaviour on the governed, but also, in order to survive, it had to obtain from them a more active support than the *ancien régime* had enjoyed. To leave these important tasks in the hands of officials over whose appointment it had little control and, even if that had not been the case, which had a power-base independent of the government which appointed them and who therefore, whatever norms might regulate their relationship with it, were in a position to seek independence of and even control over their hierarchical superiors – such an attitude would have been extremely dangerous. The gradual replacement of the apparatus formed by the *alcaldes* and their deputies by a police force both centralised and paid by the central Treasury was, within this context, a perfectly understandable decision. Thanks to it, the Revolutionary authorities were able to prevent the rise, within their own capital, of a nucleus of potential rivals.

This solution, however, though actually feasible in Buenos Aires, was much less practicable in the Interior, and this was so for a variety of reasons. In the first place, the Revolution had been born in Buenos Aires, and from the beginning could, within the city, count on at least the support of the group which had initiated it. In the Interior, the search for local support was even more urgent, and the subordination of bases of local support to leaders appointed from the capital might prejudice such bases. Moreover, the Interior was, from the point of view of the Revolutionary authorities, a source of manpower and resources for the war. Like the Crown of Castile, they proposed to make its administration a profitable business. This placed financial limitations on the apparatus of government and control established from Buenos Aires – an apparatus which had already encountered the political limitations observed above.

Moreover, even in Buenos Aires the affirmation of the authority of the supreme power over its local agents was not primarily based on the small professional police force created to support it. Even at the moment of their greatest power, during the clashes of April 1811 which were later to be remembered with unanimous horror by the Revolutionary political élite, the *alcaldes* and their suburban followers were not acting alone. At their side were the military leaders, who had taken part in the previous *jornadas*: the Army was still the arbiter of political decisions. But, when it led to war, the Revolution completely changed the army's military organisation and its position in the city where it had arisen four years before. Such changes could not fail to have a political dimension. They were introduced in such a decisive manner by the Revolutionary authorities not only because they were essential in the circumstances of war, but also because they led to the armed forces being better equipped to bear their full weight in the internal political equilibrium, playing the part which the authorities considered to be appropriate.

THE REVOLUTIONARY LEADERS, THE ARMY AND THE URBAN SOCIO-ECONOMIC ÉLITE

To hostile observers, the process of militarisation initiated in 1806 – the need for which, after the change of alliances in 1808, was far from being evident – had gradually become a pretext for the organisation and financing of one of the local factions which the crisis of the Imperial order was placing in confrontation in Buenos Aires. The very legitimacy of that urban army, which was only partially subject to regular military discipline, continually had doubts cast upon it. The Revolution, by unleashing war, put an end to this situation, and immediately increased the prestige of the military. The militarisation of the daily life of the city was again intensified, after showing evident signs of relaxation in the immediate pre-Revolutionary phase, and the consequences did not fail to cause alarm to the new authorities: 'The peoples pay a very high price for the glory of arms', to quote the decree establishing the Buenos Aires Public Library, 'if the government does not deploy its authority and its zeal to obviate the tragic outcome to which so dangerous a situation gradually leads, polite customs are replaced by the ferocity of a barbarous race...Buenos Aires is threatened with this terrible fate; and four years of military glory have silently undermined the enlightenment and the virtues that made this glory possible. Necessity led to the provisional requisition of the College

The Revolution in Buenos Aires

of Saint Charles for use as a military barracks; young men began to enjoy a licence as dangerous as it was agreeable and, attracted by the brilliance of the arms which had won our glory, they wanted to be soldiers, before educating themselves to be men'.[56]

Yet the lamentations expressed in this soberly cadenced prose were of little avail in attenuating the process to which the new authorities were forced to lend their support. In a proclamation of 29 May 1810,[57] it was stated bluntly that 'it is necessary to recognise a soldier in each inhabitant', and the defeats were to make this need even more evident. After the disaster of Huaqui, which put an end to the Revolution in Upper Peru, the programme of thoroughgoing militarisation was applied to the fullest possible extent. 'The Fatherland is in danger', proclaimed the Junta on 6 September 1811,

> and the war must be the principal object of the Government's attention. Military virtues will be the path to distinctions, honours and dignities...All citizens will be born as soldiers and will receive from their infancy an education appropriate to their destiny...The cities will offer no other image than that of war. In short, every citizen will look on...war as his natural condition.[58]

The life of Buenos Aires did not, of course, change as radically as this ambitious proclamation might lead one to suppose; indeed, the actual legal provisions accompanying it had surprisingly modest objectives. Even so, the tendency to make the Army the most important pillar of the new State was unmistakable. The profound change effected in its situation, compared with that of the career officials of the civilian bureaucracy, can be observed for example in the resolution of 31 December 1811,[59] which has already been mentioned, imposing a general cut in salaries on all civil servants and on officers not on the active list. There was, of course, nothing new in officials of the administration having to suffer (in the shape of delays in the payment of their salaries) the consequences of an expansion of the Army. But whereas in the past the indignation provoked by these postponements could be openly expressed, and take the form of derogatory attitudes towards the new military units, on this occasion self-sacrifice on behalf of these was pointed out as a duty:

> To maintain, with a small part of the fruits of our industry and at the cost of a few privations, these illustrious men who, facing all the perils and fatigue of war, risk their lives in the defence of our rights, is a duty imposed by gratitude, in addition to being an essential obligation of society.

This increase in the prestige of the military was also accelerated by the style of popular political mobilisation preferred by the Revolutionary leaders, which, as has been observed above, emphasised patriotic and military motivations. The elevation of the military as the first pillar of the State found in that image a valuable support, and in that climate of opinion, partly spontaneous and partly organised from above, the military leaders enjoyed a popularity which few civilian leaders could rival. We have already observed how in the new Revolutionary liturgy the image of the armed forces had acquired an importance unknown in the past. This image was, quite legitimately, even more dominant in the festivities which took place only on particular occasions, and were therefore more impressive, after Revolutionary victories. On such occasions it was military glory that received the principal emphasis, even when the objective of the celebration was the consolidation of the advantageous position of a particular faction within the context of internal politics. To give one example of this, there is no doubt that the triumphal reception accorded to Alvear after the capture of Montevideo, 'with a retinue and a pomp never before seen, like that of a monarch', was the prologue to a further exaltation of the leader of the then dominant Revolutionary group. Nevertheless, it was the fact that 'the Fatherland had triumphed with its arms over proud Montevideo' which had caused such a great crowd to acclaim his arrival.[60] The use for political purposes of military prestige presupposes the existence of a consensus of opinion recognising that prestige as more important than administrative and political talents. Of this there is another example, less spectacular but perhaps more revealing because of its very spontaneity, in the incident remembered with nostalgia in his old age by Colonel Manuel A. Pueyrredón. After deploring the severity with which his parents forbade him to take part in the rowdy street manifestations of patriotism to which the youth of Buenos Aires was so addicted in the first decade after the Revolution, the old warrior evoked the golden memory of the only day when, escaping from his parents' vigilance, he 'went out with one of those bands, singing of Chiclana', about whom they sang the following song:

> The sharp sword of our Chiclana...
> When he girds it on, all Spain trembles[61]

Born in 1761, Chiclana was a militia captain from 1806, when he was aged forty-five, and an officer in the regular army from 1809, and was never known for excessively brilliant military actions during his brief time at the front in the Revolutionary war. From 1783, however, he was one of the most famous lawyers of Buenos Aires, and after 1810 he became an impetuous Revolutionary politician, whom successive régimes could not ignore. However, when his fame was celebrated, it was the very improbable image of the fearsome warrior which received the principal emphasis.

This military supremacy had repercussions which caused increasing alarm among the burseaucratic élite. Having suffered a diminution of its income and its prestige, it also had to suffer patiently the direct attack of its more fortunate military rivals. 1815 marked the limit of this tendency, which took the form of offences recorded by the plaintive pen of Beruti: the case of Major Carranza, who insulted, struck and arrested a member of the highest court of law because he was not wearing a Revolutionary cockade; the case of Major Ramón Larrea, who had arrested and insulted the priest Erescano because he had spoken ill of the regiment commanded by Larrea; the case of Brigadier-General Soler, who had struck and knocked down the priest Martínez, because the latter had addressed him without first taking his hat off. 'These events and many others that have happened', concluded Beruti, 'have caused scandal among all the people, and no citizen has been spared similar insults and outrages...because every colonel imagines himself to be the Supreme Director'.[62] But even if intense alarm was caused by such arrogant behaviour, it is not certain that it was as universally felt as Beruti supposed, for the popularity of the Army did not appear to be affected by it. What these scandalous episodes emphasised, in a brutal manner, was a change in the internal equilibrium of the ruling group which plebeian public opinion had already taken for granted, and which anyway affected it to a lesser extent, and not always unfavourably.

Of course, the adaptation of the Army inherited from the experience of Buenos Aires after 1806 to its newer and broader responsibilities was to be marked by the same characteristics that could be observed in the Revolutionary action as a whole. The advances of egalitarianism, which was part of the credo of the movement, were, in this sphere too, to be kept under strict control. However, the Army, with its constant need for new recruits, was the least appropriate sphere for the emphasising of such misgivings. As was stated in the order giving the status of a regular corps to the regiment formed by Mulattoes and Negroes, the Revolutionary government had to express its tenacious opposition to those anti-egalitarian prejudices 'which diminish the mass of people effectively aiding the great cause of our liberty'.[63] This did not, of course, imply the abandonment of all misgivings. Although that sector which was 'so numerous, and so capable of any great enterprise on the part of our population' was now no longer impeded by the 'accidental difference of colour' from acquiring the status of regular troops, they were still not allowed to become officers, for even in the Negro regiments these were always white.

However, the search for new recruits, which in the Interior was to create tensions, sometimes extreme ones, between the Army and the local population, had less drastic consequences in Buenos Aires. As soon as they realised that they would have to prepare for a long war, the Revolutionary authorities limited the obligation to bear arms to the marginal population. On 29 May 1810 the Junta ordered the return to active service of all discharged soldiers, but immediately granted exemption to those engaged in 'some mechanical craft or public service'. In the same way, when it simultaneously ordered 'a rigorous levy' it declared that this only applied to 'vagrants and men without known occupation, between the ages of 18 and 40'.[64] The strictness with which it meant these limitations to be applied (above all by the recruiting parties, whose chief objective was to fill their quota of new soldiers with any men they found available) is shown in the resolution of 21 August 1810,[65] in which, after pointing out that 'some wagon-trains have been brought to a complete standstill because all the peons have been recruited', forbade 'parties detailed to recruit vagrants and idlers from taking men engaged in some occupation of public benefit'.

This shows that, even though the hunting down of these unemployed individuals was not always an easy task (on the contrary, the pressure to increase recruitment seems to have been connected with the spread of banditry which followed the Revolution), the Government was resolved not to have recourse to the free and economically active population. Reasons both political (the part of the population that would have accepted without excessive hesitation incorporation into the Army had already been enlisted between 1806 and 1809) and economic, which are easily comprehensible in an area characterised by a chronic labour shortage, explain the tenacity with which this decision was maintained. Moreover, the slaves appeared to offer a less difficult alternative than the vagrant population. Ever since the Revolution, the donation of slaves to the nation had become a sign of allegiance to the cause, and both individuals and corporations continued the practice. Later, in early 1815, the slaves of European-born Spaniards were confiscated and formed into a new military unit, and even before that date the State had begun to buy or requisition slaves for the same purpose. In 1816 only the stubborn resistance of certain powerful slave-owners prevented the Director, Pueyrredón, from carrying out an almost universal recruitment of those still held in slavery.[66] In this way, even without taking into account the rural sources of recruiting which were now being tapped, the composition of the military units had changed greatly. They had arisen from a movement in which the voluntary element had been predominant, but were now inundated by vagrants, petty criminals and slaves incorporated into them by executive decree. Making the military units thus formed the principal support of the Revolutionary authority, against its internal as well as its external enemies, contained elements of danger which could only be guarded against by careful precautions.

Yet it was precisely the professionalisation of the Army which, by reducing the politically significant sector of it to the officer corps, countered the dangers involved in the recruitment of soldiers drawn to an excessive extent from the lowest and marginal sectors of society. It was not, therefore, only the war which encouraged this professionalisation, which had, in any case, begun before the Revolutionary government was completely aware of the extent to which armed struggle was inevitable. On the 29 May, after paying tribute to the political merits of the urban militia ('you have given a firm authority to your country...you have known how to reconcile all the fury of a fervent enthusiasm with the serenity proper to a citizen...the peoples of antiquity never witnessed so moving a spectacle'), it hastened to conclude that the new order needed armies and not militias: 'Although for the just glory of the nation it is necessary to recognise a soldier in each citizen, public order and the security of the State require...a properly organised force appropriate to the dignity of these provinces'.[67]

In this way, the transformation of the militia into a regular army was carried a stage further. This was accompanied by a tightening up of discipline, which appears to have gradually relaxed during the last months of Colonial rule. It is significant, for example, that it should have been necessary to prohibit soldiers from going to their homes for the night without authorisation. However, the process of professionalisation and the imposition of stricter discipline was at first slow. Internal conflicts among the Revolutionary leadership made the support of the militias commanded by Saavedra, leader of the moderate faction, too valuable to be endangered by too far-reaching reforms. Even so, there were some reforms of the regulations. In October 1810,[68] the Junta ordered officer-cadets to attend courses in the School of Mathematics, for a period of two months, at the end of which the principal was to testify whether the candidate possessed 'capacity for military science'. This modest attempt to create an educated officer corps was accompanied by a reform which was potentially more significant, but destined to have almost no practical consequences: 'the Junta has resolved', we read in a resolution of 19 October, 'that sergeants and soldiers of merit and good conduct should be given special consideration for appointment to commissions'. It is enough to read the *Tomas de razón de despachos militares*[69] to notice the caution with which this new provision was applied. It was not in the interests of the new order to diminish the distance between officers and men.

The political crises of 1811 gave the moderate faction an ephemeral victory, gained by an appeal to the suburban mob, which alienated the sympathy of the entire Revolutionary political class, but put the triumphant moderates in situations which cruelly revealed the inadequacy of the political solutions which they favoured. It was this that deprived that group of its control of the political situation and thus eliminated the principal obstacle to the professionalisation of the Army. In December 1811 there was open resistance by the first regiment of Patricios, where the non-commissioned officers and men mutinied, appointed new officers and submitted to the Government 'a heap of ridiculous demands, which could not possibly be met'. Among those that most shocked Beruti was the proposal that officers should be elected by the soldiers, a practice that was certainly nothing new in Buenos Aires. After various attempts to obtain the peaceful surrender of the rebels, and an exchange of shots that lasted for fifteen minutes, the resistence of the Patricios ceased and the repression began. Six non-commissioned officers and four soldiers were executed and their bodies were exhibited in the Main Square, a further twenty were condemned to imprisonment, entire companies were disbanded, and the purged regiment was demoted from first to fifth place among the units of the Patriot Army. This episode appears at first sight to reflect an already traditional pattern, with parleys between the mutineers and the Government, and the mediation of prelates (in this case the Bishops of Buenos Aires and Córdoba) who were trying to prevent bloodshed. But certain new elements are observable, among them the fact that the movement involved only non-commissioned officers and enlisted men. Although public opinion connected it with the influence of some officers and, above all, ex-officers of the regiment, these preferred not to participate openly in the mutiny. A new division, which had not existed in the militia created after 1806, was thus revealed in all its significance. From now on, a stricter discipline was imposed, to restrain these dangerous spontaneous movements among the troops. In March 1814 a very limited attempt at mutiny among the infantry grenadiers ordered to go on board a warship unleashed an unusually harsh repression:

> They were put ashore, and...some were sentenced to punishment by running the gauntlet...and the three ring-leaders to be shot by firing-squad...They had only two hours to make their confessions and prepare themselves for death...It was something never before witnessed in this city, that they should have been tried, sentenced and executed, all in so short a time; but in the present circumstances it was urgently necessary, so that the troops should be restrained by this example.[70]

As was to be expected, the severity was even greater in the operational theatres of the war than in the case of troops stationed in the capital. In any case, the process led within a few years to a marked separation between officers and men, and even at times when military discipline became extremely relaxed, this was only true in the case of the officer corps. The Swedish envoy J. A. Graaner, who visited the Army of the North at a time when, under the command of Rondeau, discipline had completely broken down, was able to give a shocked testimony of the 'truly Oriental manner' in which the commander-in-chief was living, 'with all the comforts of a seraglio, among a multitude of women of every colour'. He judged with equal severity the officers, 'who are, the majority of them, mere fops, of disorderly habits, without habits of discipline, lacking in military talents and displaying an insulting lack of concern for the welfare of their soldiers'. For the other ranks, on the other hand, he had only praise. But what most amazed him in them was their spirit of resigned obedience:

> One could not find in Europe a more easily contented soldier than the Creole of these provinces. It has now been three years since the soldiers of the auxiliary regiments from Peru and Chile received two pesos of pay, although the State is supposed to pay them three or four *reales* a day. Despite all this, and the fact that they go half-naked and without boots...both on the icy summits of the mountains and the burning sands of the valleys, one never hears from them any complaint, nor disobedience to their officers to whom they show complete submission.[71]

The Revolution in Buenos Aires

Thus the Revolution had transformed the urban militia, subject to only a partial military discipline and forming the nucleus of a political agitation which had little respect for either the traditional hierarchies or the newer ones established by the militia organisation itself, into a regular army in which the cardinal virtue of the soldiers was obedience to their officers. This transformation, encouraged by the war, had a concrete political result. The corps of officers did not owe its political power to its ascendancy, which had to be perpetually reaffirmed, over militia troops who were to a great extent volunteers and were very alert to crises of political power. Now the corps of officers exercised its political influence in its own right. It no longer constituted the link between an élite and the broader sectors which the crisis had momentarily mobilised, but became instead the direct controller of the means of coercion which had among other objectives that of maintaining power firmly in the hands of that élite, thus limiting the scope of that process of democratisation to which the Revolution owed its origin.

For the professionalisation of the Army did not abolish its political functions. In October 1812, although – in deference to the tradition of the earlier Revolutionary clashes – the change of leadership was requested by petitioners who defined themselves as 'the people', the action of the commanding officers of the regiments reorganised for war was even more overt than that of the militia leaders in the crises of 1809, 1810 and 1811. The petition, according to the Cabildo's report, was 'made to this Most Excellent Cabildo by a great mass of people, supported by the entire armed forces of the capital'. The names of those who were to head the new Government were discussed by the Cabildo with 'the military commanders of the force occupying the city' and only later submitted for the approval of the 'immense crowd which filled the corridors and galleries of government offices'.[72] Ultimate guarantor of the political stability of the Revolutionary régime, promoted to the status of first pillar of the new State organised for war and victory, was the officer corps to form the nucleus of the new governing sector? It would be going too far to say this. Even though the professionalisation of the Army signified for the Revolutionary régime, anxious to limit the changes from which it had arisen, the political advantages which have already been pointed out, it was primarily a necessity imposed by the war, the outcome of which appeared uncertain. However limited its success, professionalisation transformed the officer corps into a specialised sector, both with regard to the tasks entrusted to it and the technical preparation needed to deal with them. This entailed the danger of a progressive separation from the non-military leaders of the Revolution. Most characteristically, in the first mention of the dangers of militarism to appear in an article in the *Gaceta* (the authorship of which the editors preferred to attribute to an anonymous 'patriot worthy of that name'), although it was emphasised that among the officers there had arisen an unfounded sentiment of superiority 'over their fellow-countrymen', which led to quarrels with them, the most alarming prospect was not that of a growing political hegemony of the Army, but rather that of an increasing depoliticisation of the officer corps, entrenched in a proud isolation.[73]

This danger appears to have been more remote than was feared by the anonymous correspondent: as late as 1818, the United States envoy Brackenridge found that the relationship 'between the citizen and the soldier' could be based on a mutual friendship and confidence which was entirely lacking in Brazil, 'where the military constitute a distinct order, as if they were of a different race of men'. Although he certainly admitted that some of the officers 'were somewhat presumptuous', this did not affect 'the straightforwardness and simplicity of republicanism', measured by the exacting standards of a Yankee of the time.[74] Yet perhaps the influence of the expanded officer corps could not be fully measured by an examination of the attitude of its members as they walked the streets and exchanged cordial greetings with their childhood friends. The complex readjustments which their presence made necessary in Revolutionary Buenos Aires were, in any case, partly unnoticed even by the protagonists of the process. It is not surprising that outside, or retrospective, observers should have had even greater difficulty in analysing them.

As has already been observed, professionalisation both gave a new pre-eminence to the officer corps, since on its competence depended the fate of the Revolution, which was to be decided by war, and differentiated it in many respects from the other Revolutionary political groups. The first of these differences was that as professional requirements came to the fore the criteria governing recruitment and promotion changed. The first to feel the consequences of this were the career officers, surviving from the military structure existing before 1806, who had been relegated to a secondary rôle with the rise of the officers of the urban militias, very few of whom were recruited from the former group. Although the catastrophe of 1806 had dealt a blow to the prestige of the older officers, that of the militia leaders also suffered as a result of the years of military inactivity and intense political activity which followed the operations of 1806 and 1807. When the Revolution led to a war that was more exacting from the point of view of military organisation than the operations of urban resistance to the British invasions, it seemed only natural to have recourse to those people whose excellence in the art of war might sometimes be questionable, but whose experience of the administrative and organisational problems involved in the maintenance of a permanent army – which now had to engage in continuous operations – was unrivalled in the limited milieu of the River Plate region.

In this way, the Revolution increased the importance of a most peculiar group of people. Between 1776 and 1806 Buenos Aires possessed a military organisation, the growing deterioration of which was harshly exposed in the last of those years, but which in the meantime had made

The Revolution in Buenos Aires

career officers a well defined sector within Buenos Aires society. Their appearance was only a secondary aspect of the changes in power and prestige within urban society provoked by the Bourbon administrative reforms and the expansion of trade within the Empire. Among the groups that emerged as a result of this process, the officers seem to have had a secondary and relatively isolated place, as was proved by the large number of marriages between families of officers (a pattern of behaviour characteristic of a group which attributed to itself a social position higher than others were prepared to accord it) and even perhaps the quasi-hereditary nature of military ranks, denounced after the Revolution as an intolerable privilege, but which in any case served to guarantee the recruitment of new officers, since the sons of distinguished families did not find the military career attractive.

There were exceptions to this state of semi-exclusion. In the rural areas officers appear to have achieved, through matrimonial alliances and the purchase of land, a solider place among the local élites, but the entire rural sector was secondary in importance in the River Plate region in pre-Revolutionary days. There were also certain corps d'élite – such as the Guards and the Royal Navy – in which places were sought for their sons by the most distinguished families. In such cases, however, officers were very often posted away from the River Plate region and found the way open to the highest ranks in the administration in Spain. These exceptions, therefore, did not diminish the secondary status of the officer corps of the River Plate garrison. This became intensified between 1806 and 1810, when even their control over the armed forces was successfully disputed by the leaders of the urban mobilisation provoked by the Invasions.

This same status relegated the officers of the regular army to a secondary place in the process which eventually led to the Revolution. It is, therefore, all the more remarkable to observe them, after that event, enjoying a rise which was to be unchecked. As a result, military dynasties founded by some associates of the Viceroy Cevallos were still to be found in the Argentine or Uruguayan Armies at the end of the nineteenth century. There was no sector of the Spanish administration where the Revolution left so few marks. Jaime Viamonte, a Catalan, an infantry lieutenant, appointed as an officer-cadet in 1786 his son who had been born in 1784. This son was promoted colonel in November 1810, then he became a general, and Governor of Buenos Aires. Francisco González de Balcarce, a Castilian and a Colonel in the Royal Army, married his two sons, also officers, to two daughters of José Martínez de Fontes, a Valencian and also a Colonel in the Royal Army. This gave rise to a numerous clan of officers who during the first quarter of a century of independent life were to have increasing influence in Buenos Aires. There was also Joaquín Pablo de Vedia, a Spanish officer, the father of Nicolás de Vedia, who was an officer from 1803 and became the grandfather of three colonels and a general. If the career officers passed almost unscathed through the trials of the Revolution, this was not because of any influence they might have acquired over the new government. Thus, when the brothers Agustín and Ambrosio de Pinedo, sons of the ex-Governor of Paraguay and President of Charcas, retired with the rank of colonel in November 1810, making no attempt to disguise their lack of support for the Revolution, which led Agustín to seek refuge in Montevideo, his son of the same name continued in Buenos Aires a military career which he had begun as a cadet in 1806, reaching in 1819 the rank of colonel, and finally that of general. In this case the more direct family influences could not have favoured a career that was no doubt unspectacular but was reasonably successful. The decisive element was, rather, the limited military knowledge inherited and acquired by the grandson of Brigadier-General Pinedo.[75] The recognition that certain technical skills were required, and the shortage of officers (and also the reluctance to use the other ranks as sources of officer-candidates) explains why the Revolutionary government was less stringent as regards the political past of its military servants than when it was selecting its administrative ones. As time went by, increasingly frequent recourse was had to the incorporation of Royalist prisoners into the Patriot Army, not only as men but also as officers, provided they took an oath of allegiance to the new nation.[76] The Director Pueyrredón, after he left power, boasted of having systematised this practice.[77]

In 1812 there appeared in the River Plate region military skills less superficial and routine than those inherited from Colonial times. Their exemplars were career officers who had fought in the Royal Army against France and now joined the Patriot cause. José de San Martín, incorporated into the Revolutionary army with the rank of colonel, adapted systems of organisation and tactics of French inspiration, while Carlos María de Alvear edited an infantry instruction manual based on ideas from the same source. In the case of such men, the superiority of the military man was not primarily that of the warrior in a community which had made the prosecution of war its most urgent task, but rather that of the technician able to carry out that task with a skill that he alone possessed. As we read in the ode addressed to Alvear after the capture of Montevideo in 1814,

> Oh Buenos Aires! So splendid a triumph
> is due to the best of thy sons.
> Of them all was the valour and the hardihood,
> of them all the perseverance,
> but of him alone the tactics and the talent.[78]

Courage and skill, the professional virtues of the military man, were the attributes not only of the career officers, but also of those whom the Revolution had to create. In contrast to what happened with the ephemeral civilian appointments, identification with the prospects opened up by a military career was extremely rapid. Everything worked in its favour. It was society as a whole that recognised for the military man the place which he assigned to himself within that society, and which made the military virtues the supreme virtues of the citizen. In this peculiar atmosphere the outlook of the career officer could be formed in a matter of months. The case of the future General Paz is particularly impressive. When, in his *Memorias*, he describes with affectionate condescension his commander-in-chief in the Army of the North, General Belgrano, whose character as an improvised military commander Paz never lets us forget for a moment, he does not seem to remember that he himself, until he enlisted in that army a few months earlier, was a law student at the University of Córdoba.

This form of training hastened by circumstances did not prevent Paz from being the model – unattainable and for that reason irritating – of the professional officer, who believes in discipline, in the slow administrative preparation of armies, in calm calculation rather than heroic improvisation on the battlefield. Such attitudes were certainly not dominant in the armies created by the Revolution, and it is understandable that Paz should have considered as unmilitary those of his brother-officers who classed insolence towards their superiors as an additional proof of the rather wild courage they displayed on the battlefields. But such officers, who were doubtless more abundant than the adherents of the exacting professional ideal adopted by Paz, were trying to give expression to a different image of military life. Some characteristics of it might be considered negative, but they were no less specifically military than the qualities preferred by Paz. The positive virtue in this context was courage carried to the point of rashness. The basic ingredient of the military life is risking one's life, and that risk gives a right to all the compensations offered. For the young men joining the corps of officers it was an article of faith that 'the illustrious men who, facing all the perils and fatigue of war, expose their lives in the defence of our rights' had, in fact, the right to live on the industry and the privations of the civilians. A common dedication to heroism not only united these officers, it separated them from those who had chosen a less exalted calling and endowed them with a superiority which they did not trouble to disguise. The welfare of the civil population was not their objective. It was right that it should suffer, and, although there was danger, too, in rendering its privations too extreme, this fact would not lead them to change their attitude. Valour overcame all, and heroes were born to overcome greater dangers than the illwill of a population motivated by a somewhat ignominious love of peace. This attitude, which was to result in abundant examples of heroism dutifully recorded in school textbooks, might have been dangerous to the military destiny of the Revolution. For example, not the least significant of the victories of San Martín was the one he gained over these dangerous tendencies among his officers, which he did not tolerate either in camp or in battle. Nevertheless, it was difficult to eradicate such attitudes in a corps of officers whose members had only in exceptional cases embarked on their military careers after methodical professional training, anticipated by family tradition, and had more often turned to the career of arms as a result of a sudden conversion. They were influenced, moreover, by the example of that other corps of officers which legend was already portraying as having conquered Europe by improvised audacity. The cycle of wars of Revolutionary and Napoleonic France attained an exemplary force all the more effective because it had to remain in semi-clandestinity. Napoleon was, after all, the arch-enemy of a revolution which was attempting both to establish its claim to be the heir of Spanish legitimacy and to secure the benevolence of Great Britain.

This image of war as a luxury activity, as a festival of consumption and destruction, which underlay the image that most of the new military officers formed of themselves, also owed its strength to the fact that in certain aspects it corresponded only too well to the real situation in the River Plate region which the Revolution had transformed into a theatre of war. The holocaust of war destroyed not only the wealth of the State and the corporations, but also the hierarchical bonds on which the established order had been based – an order in which the promoters of the Revolutionary movement had been far from occupying a completely marginal place. But, accepting this undeniable fact, and often emphasising it with unnecessarily brutal attitudes, the officers who in such a natural manner assumed the first place in the new State created tensions, which were most evident in the Interior, where the officers sometimes acted like conquerors, but which were also present in Buenos Aires, despite the climate of enthusiasm for the war which, even though attenuated with the passing of time, reigned in the Revolutionary capital.

Tensions arose, in the first place, with those local sectors which had dominated the economy and now saw themselves threatened by the double pressure of the war and of foreign commercial competition. These witnesses of the revolutionary process, whose prosperity was being dissipated, were disposed to pronounce harsh judgments on the carefree way in which the glittering officers of the Revolutionary army marched forward towards victory and penury.

But there were also tensions with those who were directly responsible for the management of political affairs, and the officers experienced a decline in the benevolence of those groups from which they had arisen, as long as the excessively costly Revolution stubbornly refused to provide the fruits expected of it. For those sectors, too, the unthinking identification of the officer corps with a policy which gave absolute priority to the war – a policy which, despite everything, could not be modified – was somewhat irritating: they tended to see those officers as the only beneficiaries of the sacrifices imposed by the war. And these sacrifices, even though they did not necessarily affect economically the direct leaders of the Revolution, were nevertheless extremely costly politically.

A slight broadening of the basis of recruitment of officers, and their very elevation to the position of chief pillar of the State which – especially *vis-à-vis* the sectors of public opinion recently incorporated into political life – gave them an undeniable advantage, were, then, the causes of a growing separation between the Revolutionary leaders and the corps of officers as such. Though the source of an indispensable political support, this corps could also become a serious political rival. This danger was all the more real because its identification with all-out war, which differentiated it from the Creole élite of Buenos Aires, coincided with the feelings and – to a certain extent – with the interests of the popular sectors.

But this danger was attenuated by other factors. In the first place, however swiftly *esprit de corps* was consolidated, it encountered a very serious rival in the spirit of faction. The complaints of the *Gaceta* at the lack of participation of the officers in the internal struggles of the Revolutionary group is, therefore, less absurd than would appear at first sight. By taking part in them, the corps of officers would be divided along the same lines as those separating the civilian factions. Such a division was further facilitated by the lack of solidly-based professional criteria governing the promotion of officers, which made it easier for those close to the politically dominant group to gain promotion, and this was observed with resentful impatience by their rivals. But even without taking account of the repercussions which these political dissensions had in the Army, the ill-defined character of the criteria governing promotion, together with the discretion on this point left to the senior officers, created rival cliques within the officer corps and thus diminished its coherence as a professional group. In this respect, the undeniable limitations of professionalisation (which can be measured, for example, by the fact recorded above, that two months of academic education seemed sufficient for a professional officer) had effects similar to those of certain characteristics of the process of professionalisation, which was an aggregate of pioneering efforts undertaken separately rather than a unified transformation of the Army as an institution. To a perceptive observer such as General Paz, an officer trained by Belgrano, by San Martín or by Alvear could be recognised by the way in which he handled any limited task which was part of his duties. The consequence of this was that the rivalry between cliques found an additional source in the opposition between schools of military thought. Thus, when the officers of the Army of the North, in 1814, rejected with a rare unanimity the replacement of their commander-in-chief by Alvear, they were not only defending their right to live under the indulgent rule of the former, but also their professional future, threatened by the probable massive incursion of rivals identified with the military outlook of the new commander-in-chief.

In this way, not even professionalisation always led to an increase in the *esprit de corps* of the Revolutionary officers. Moreover, in accounting for its limited development, it is necessary to bear in mind the continuous impact of other factors equally inimical to the formation of an officer corps endowed with firmly based corporate characteristics. The most obvious of these was the fact that, despite the new insistence on professionalisation, military duties were not the only activity expected of the most prominent senior officers. Even a man with so little inclination to active politics as Belgrano was obliged to abandon the command of armies for years and devote himself to diplomacy. Nearly all the senior officers were, in addition to being soldiers, actual or potential political leaders. Their careers, which abounded in unexpected setbacks, were divided between the Army and the political arena. Juan Manuel de Pueyrredón figures in Udaondo's Biographical Dictionary as a military leader, and he did in fact first attract public attention by leading a bold but unsuccessful attempt to counter the first British invasion. During that episode he had raised a regiment of hussars. But, sent by the Cabildo of Buenos Aires as its representative to the Court of Spain, his activity for three years was to be politics, accompanied by intrigues, imprisonment and successful escapes. This precursor of the Revolution was created an administrative official by it. He was Intendant first of Córdoba and later of Charcas, and then returned for a few months to his military vocation, as commander-in-chief of the Army of the North. From then on, he was to experience abrupt falls and rises: he was a member of the Triumvirate, which exercised the supreme power, was dismissed and imprisoned in October 1812, and Supreme Director of the State from 1815 to 1819, but he never returned to a military command. Similarly, in the more decidedly military careers of Rondeau or Álvarez Thomas there were civilian interludes which were, it is true, briefer. Carlos de Alvear, whom we have seen represented as the supreme military man, the possessor of the secrets of the art of war, was able in that context to envisage his entire military career as a chapter in a more complex and essentially political career, which was to culminate in the attainment of supreme power. But in conquering this for himself, Alvear was not conquering it for the Army, which, nevertheless, he tried to make his most secure power-base, but for a faction, which was even more powerful in the Revolutionary assemblies or in the Chapter of Buenos Aires Cathedral than in the Army itself.

Thus, although the Revolution had destroyed the traditional identification with corporations or legal institutions which the bureaucrats of Colonial times had exaggerated to an almost pathological degree, it was not able to endow with an equally intensive cohesion the only institution which emerged from the Revolutionary crisis strengthened rather than weakened, and one of the basic reasons was that, viewed as an individual adventure, the career of arms culminated, in the context of the River Plate Revolution, in a political career in which the military leader did not act exclusively as the representative of the points of view and the corporate interests of the Army, but as a politician whose military status might at times give him means of action lacked by his other colleagues, but who owed simultaneous loyalties to family alliances, the solidarity of a secret lodge or agreements between factions. In this context it is easy to understand the attitude of General Iriarte, whose *Memorias* are a lengthy meditation on his own professional failure. It was not failure in his military career, but in what the general called the career of the Revolution, and which was in his eyes unmistakably a profession, one of public service, which had come to include all the professions which the Colonial régime had kept separate. Iriarte's efforts to transfer from the military sphere, where he eventually obtained reasonable promotion, to that of general politics, although they invariably ended in failure, which he attributed to the perversity of the times, demonstrate very clearly that for this career soldier, who had spent the first part of the war of independence in the Royalist camp, the military career no longer existed. The professional success of a military man now consisted in his political success.

'The career of the Revolution': the expression itself is a good indication of the dual loyalty maintained by its protagonists: to the Revolution, to that movement initiated in 1810, the direction and objectives of which were still far from clear, but the abandonment of which was the only thing that, in the eyes of Buenos Aires opinion, constituted pure and simple treason, and parallel to that, to the *career*, that is to say, to the promotion of the individual. Between them, little place is left for the old loyalty to an institutional structure which in some way had in the past integrated individual and group ambitions. Because of this, and the vagueness of content of loyalty to the Revolution, the motivation of personal ambition now came to the fore with a crudity which had been absent in the past. The monotonous criticisms, couched in a moralistic tone, of the corruption of Revolutionary times are an inadequate explanation of the process, but in their way they are a good reflection of it. The breakdown of an entire system of institutions and collective values was not the only cause of the rise of an ambitious self-interest that appeared to be unbounded. The Revolution, from the very first, made an explicit appeal to personal ambition, which underlay to a great extent its denunciations of the *overlords* of the *ancien régime*, whose legitimate heritage was to be acquired as a result of Revolutionary merits. Moreover, the actual course of the Revolution, which very soon showed the ephemeral nature of the promotions to which it gave rise, impelled men to seek, in a political and economic context characterised by constant insecurity, a security derived, either from the use of political influence for the purposes of self-enrichment, or the abandonment of one's own political loyalties and close attachment to those factions which became successively dominant. Both methods were, in general, less successful than was thought by a public opinion which was increasingly sceptical. Of course, spectacular *coups* were still possible, but in the long run – as has already been observed –

excessive contact with a political authority aggressive in its methods of collecting funds was dangerous to private fortunes. Every factional fight led to the rise of replacement personnel who were not always prepared to share the booty with those who had enjoyed it in the past. A high proportion of the Revolutionary leaders came to be considered by public opinion as corrupt, but their real or alleged corruption made them less prosperous than some who untiringly denounced them and deplored their own situation as victims of an insatiably greedy Treasury. Financial corruption, like the lack of clear political orientation, appears to have been not so much a symptom of overweaning ambition as a pathetic defence mechanism *vis-à-vis* a destiny more abundant in risks than in promises.

This leads us back, albeit indirectly, to the problem of the breakdown of an entire context of institutions, of collective beliefs, of values, which the Revolution destroyed without providing any replacement. Insecurity resided not only in the train of events itself but – perhaps more – in the manner of judging it, and is all the more impressive when we observe it underlying the conduct of so many Revolutionary leaders. The Revolution emerged from the collapse of the Spanish Imperial system, and accelerated and terminated that process. As a replacement for the complex system of loyalties inherent in that system it offered only loyalty to itself. And the sense of discipline inspired by that loyalty was so defective that the chief disciplinary mechanism continued to be, quite simply, fear of the reprisals of the adversary. After years of triumph of the Revolutionary movement, the notion mentioned above of commitment to the Revolution, in other words of Revolutionary identification so intensive as to make impossible any return to loyalty to the monarchy and to Spain, was still in full force. It is true that events had demonstrated to what extent a position of ambiguity could be maintained by those who wished to keep open the possibility of a reconciliation with the old order, yet there was an increasingly intensive search for new forms of definitive allegiance which would give no ground for equivocation. According to the Swedish envoy Graaner, who was doubtless echoing opinions he had heard in Buenos Aires, the declaration of independence had, among other advantages, that of making obligatory a choice for those who hitherto had eluded it. Anyone swearing allegiance to the independent nation would find it difficult subsequently to claim that he was actuated only by the uninformed zeal of a loyal subject of the King of Spain, whose only fault had been to put his trust in those who claimed to be the legitimate representatives of that monarch.

Yet the declaration of independence was, in a very explicit form, both the culmination and the end of the Revolutionary phase, and there was only one unfulfilled task left: war. Independence meant the identification of the Revolutionary cause with that of the nation, which had been born out of a course of events which might be celebrated or deplored (more often the latter than the former) but which was, nevertheless, irreversible. The

The Revolution in Buenos Aires

Revolutionary leadership had already found out that it could not found its fundamental justification on a system of ideas (which, in any case, the events taking place in Europe were making obsolete and dangerous), but in its ability to satisfy the desires and interests of the country which it was governing and which – as was to become increasingly clear – the Revolution, which had destroyed so much of the old order, was incapable of re-creating according to a new and coherent plan.

Until that moment, however, the Revolutionary Government had taken upon itself a more ambitious mission: that of creating a nation, and creating an order in accordance with its own ideas. This had provided a kind of implicit theoretical justification for an undeniable fact, the practical consequences of which that same Government at times found alarming. These were, firstly, the distance separating the Government from what was still not a nation, but merely the territory dominated by the Government, and, secondly the identification of that Government with a faction, the ill-defined nature of whose members and objectives had the effect of diminishing the authority deriving from it. The difficulty implicit in the problems connected with the study of the new Revolutionary political class is anticipated by the practical problems posed by this situation. It is not surprising that the relationship between that political class and certain social and professional sectors is not always clear, when one considers that even contemporaries found it difficult to determine who exactly belonged to that class. Nor is it easy to determine what mechanisms furnished that class with the cohesion needed to act with the efficiency (albeit limited) which it in fact displayed, if one bears in mind that this problem – which today is of only theoretical interest – was perhaps the greatest practical problem faced by the Revolutionary leadership, which at certain times seemed to be more afraid of itself than of anything else, in view of its infinite capacity for indulging in quarrels on subjects that were sometimes of no consequence.

What first became the unifying characteristic of the Revolutionary sector was the consciousness of common participation in an adventure in which most of them were reluctant to become fully involved. In order to embark on that adventure, the officers of those regiments which at a decisive moment had refused to support the authority of the Viceroy joined forces with other individuals who had perhaps realised beforehand the dilemmas and opportunities provoked by the crisis of the Imperial system. Although several of them, from Pueyrredón to Belgrano, took part in the militarisation which began in 1806, their prestige was not based on the position which they held in the militia regiments, but on their experience in the attempts at organising, when they foresaw the crisis of the Imperial system, sectors of opinion capable of facing it without flinching and with ideas, already thought out, as to what should be done. Although these people – following the example of other more famous precursors of Independence – did not hesitate to claim to represent the whole of Spanish America, they did not always find it easy to convince others of a representative character less broadly based geographically, but with a solider basis in fact. On the other hand, those who acted as purely military leaders – such as the President of the Junta – had behind them a perfectly identifiable group to which they owed their strength. The Revolution, from the very beginning, introduced some modifications into this simple situation. The most important, perhaps, was not the encouragement of popular agitation outside the structure of the militias, an agitation which culminated in the *jornadas* of May (although one of the leaders concerned, Domingo French, had himself been an officer since 1810). The rise of large political clientèles established outside the militia structure does not appear to have been one of the objectives of the Revolutionary government. Of more importance for the future was the inclusion in the ruling group of individuals incorporated into it as the representatives of certain social sectors. Thus, Father Alberdi obviously owed his place in the Junta to his status as a clergyman, and the inclusion of Larrea and Mateu was connected with their status as merchants. The inclusion of such people is a proof that, from the very beginning, the Revolutionary authorities were sensitive to the problem of opening up channels of communication with society as a whole. The solution decided upon was, however, too facile: the ecclesiastics and merchants, not elected by their peers, were less representative of those sectors than were recruits from the group identified with the Revolution, which they no doubt endowed with a broader basis but did not save from isolation.

Thus, the composition of the sector which had paved the way for the Revolution (the corps of officers of certain urban militia regiments, and certain loosely organised sectors of opinion) underwent no fundamental variation in the early stages of the process. This duality – which could lead to rivalry – was still reflected in the division of the Revolutionary ruling group symbolised by the figures of the President of the Junta, Cornelio de Saavedra, and one of the secretaries, Mariano Moreno. This lawyer, whose brilliant career had carried him a long way from his comparatively humble origin (his father had been a career official of very modest means), was to display not only an intellectual clarity which the President lacked, but a revolutionary enthusiasm which his rivals thought inappropriate to an undertaking which they preferred to view from a calmer standpoint. Moreno was to prove no more reluctant than his adversaries to take on the mantle of legitimacy, but despite this he proposed, with a frankness which some found irritating and others found dangerous, a programme of which he took no pains to deny the revolutionary nature. A similarity of outlook created an increasing solidarity between Moreno – who, although an enthusiast, was only a recent recruit to the Revolutionary ranks – and the majority of those who, for many years, had approached the problems arising out of the crisis of the Imperial order with a full understanding of the possibilities and problems which it posed for those who wished to take advantage of it. These were more numerous, of course, among those who had discovered their ideal *milieu* in the discussion-circles than among those who, by reaching high rank in the militias, had achieved a power which, without feeling the need to think about more complex problems, they had used chiefly to achieve yet more power. Thus the opposition between Saavedra and Moreno was reflected in the creation of different currents of thought within the Revolutionary sector and, although these did not correspond exactly to the differentiation based on origin which had always existed within that sector, they did reflect it to some degree.

Thus the Revolutionary group, formed from the beginning from two distinct sectors, tended to divide into two opposing factions. However, the power relationship existing in May 1810 appeared to guarantee an unchallenged hegemony to that sector based on the militias which recognised Saavedra as its leader. Its slow erosion, only temporarily halted by such *coups de main* as that of December 1810 (the incorporation into the Junta of delegates from the Interior, and the resignation of Moreno) and April 1811 (the *jornada*, mentioned several times above, which again gave the followers of Saavedra complete control of power), was essentially due to two closely inter-connected reasons. The first was that the Revolution was to destroy – as has been observed above – the urban militias which had unleashed it; the second was that a fuller understanding of the needs of the Revolutionary movement was to lead to a gradual move of the more far-sighted militia leaders towards the points of view, if not the leaders, of the rival sector.

At the same time, the slighted followers of Moreno only became a faction when their leader had already left for a diplomatic appointment in London which death was to prevent him from taking up. This posthumous party, which never found a replacement for its leader, was soon to find more motives for solidarity in its common sufferings at the hands of the rival faction (these were considerable: in particular, after the April *jornada*, many followers of Moreno suffered exile or imprisonment) than in continuing a political line which the very fluidity of the revolutionary situation tended to make untenable. Thus the division between factions was less rigid than the conflict between trends of opinion. But, at the same time as it created a division, difficult to judge rationally, but not for that reason any less acute, within the Revolutionary bloc, the experience of the first year of the Revolution taught both factions an essentially identical lesson as regards the dangers of democratisation. The war, which transferred attention to remote fronts and was making it necessary for the Army to return to a more traditional structure, made possible, on this point, a change both very radical and very discreet. But was not this very change dangerous? A revolutionary authority which felt itself to be disturbingly alone in the context of the social sectors from which it had arisen was now making efforts to find its main base of power in the professional army, which enabled it to dispense with the militant support of any social group. This would allow it not only to halt the process of democratisation, but also to obtain greater independence from the propertied groups, which it could not exempt from the financial burdens of war. This decision appears less hazardous if one bears in mind the socio-economic context in which it was taken. The war, coming so soon after the change in the pattern of trade of the River Plate region, at first chiefly affected the higher urban sectors, both Spanish and Creole. Its effects on the popular sectors were more mixed (and probably, if one weighed up advantages and disadvantages, might even be considered favourable). This – together with other and perhaps more immediate reasons – makes it easier to understand why limitations could be placed on the process of democratisation without provoking serious conflicts with those popular sectors, but it held out no hope for an increase in support for the Revolutionary authority within the more limited context of élite opinion to which it was increasingly confining itself.

The situation was, however, even here less desperate than it might appear. In the unusually favourable situation of the years between 1806 and 1810, politicisation had made very rapid progress. At that time the opportunities it opened were more evident than its dangers. Those who ventured into that unknown territory were able to feel protected by the presence in it of legal institutions and corporations which had invited them to undertake that adventure. Besides, the scope of this endeavour – if one leaves aside the potential development which only the future was to reveal – was very limited and so, therefore, were the risks involved. After 1810 the situation changed radically. Despite the efforts made by the Revolutionary authority to lay claim to monarchical legitimacy, it was well known that such claims did not convince its rivals. The increasingly frequent recourse to the death penalty for those who resisted its advance (a measure inaugurated at the instigation of Moreno, but continued by his successors) was a certain guarantee of the fulfilment of the gloomy Revolutionary prophecies of the bloodbath that would follow any restoration of the old order. In such circumstances, it is understandable that those who had not been attracted to political activity when the latter offered obvious advantages and concealed risks were even less attracted when such risks became graver and more obvious.

In this climate of opinion, the crisis of confidence in the Revolutionary leadership – an attitude which became permanent in the public opinion of Buenos Aires – led not to militant opposition, but to a posture of cautious detachment. The lack of total identification on the part of any sector of Buenos Aires society with the Revolutionary leadership, which in 1810 had appeared as a weakness to be corrected, was still evident nine years later. During this time the Revolution had learned to live with it, and its political leaders were able to reflect calmly on this curious characteristic of Revolutionary political life. When the ex-Director Pueyrredón referred in 1819 to the 'strange contrast between the few of us who, presiding over the destinies of the people, have sometimes subordinated the public interest to our personal interest, and the staunch resignation of the rest of the citizens in lending themselves continually to experiments that have always been carried out at their expense and risk; yet claiming on their side the right to call a halt to those who carried them out unsuccessfully',[79] he was in fact alluding, not to the existence of a new plebeian public opinion created by the Revolution, but to that of a sector of opinion doubtless more accustomed to passing judgement on the Government, but which had been taught by the Revolution the need for resignation. Only in the face of an authority already weakened by excessively outrageous failures would that sector of opinion ever inspire effective action.

But such an attitude of reserve, which avoided both whole-hearted allegiance and effective opposition, was not the only attitude existing among what remained of the urban upper sectors *vis-à-vis* the Revolutionary government. Through its two bases of prestige and wealth – commerce and the higher bureaucracy – those upper sectors were too dependent on the benevolence of the new authority to ignore it completely. It has already been observed how – albeit in a tardy and lukewarm manner – the external signs of allegiance were eventually given by everybody, and how, in order to eliminate that excessively numerous sector which was trying to avoid a definitive commitment to the Revolution, those external formulae became increasingly specific, until they included an oath of loyalty to the independent nation. However, in addition to these signs of allegiance which were a condition of survival in Revolutionary Buenos Aires, and which might be partly limited in their consequences (for example, by systematic benevolence towards Spaniards, Royalists and prisoners-of-war, which – whether inspired by humanitarian motives, political solidarity or mere opportunism – could be easily attested in case the Revolution lost the war), the mere passage of time created new bonds of solidarity – not necessarily political ones – between the members of the upper sectors and the Revolutionary régime. An obvious source of these was the economic activity of the Revolutionary State. Though more voracious than the Viceregal administration, in contrast to the latter the Revolutionary Treasury spent most of its revenue within the country. It has already been observed how business relationships with a State that was both mendicant and prodigal, though dangerous, were for some very tempting. Wartime commercial regulations, which were full of prohibitions against trading and also of not always obviously justified exemptions from such prohibitions, also offered opportunities to those who had the contacts that enabled them to use them.

Such contacts were not always based on pure and simple corruption. An idea of the complex form they could take can be gathered, for example, from the autobiography of Francisco Saguí. Saguí, born in Buenos Aires in

1794 'of pure Spanish stock', and the 'nephew and godson of a millionaire' established in Montevideo, Don Juan José Seco, was until the Revolution the captain of one of his uncle's ships, engaged in the transport of Negro slaves and salted meat. He sympathised with the Revolution, and took advantage of his trips to Montevideo to take news and instructions to the revolutionaries of that city, who included a son-in-law of Seco, Francisco Joaquín Muñoz, and the latter's brother-in-law. Seco died, Muñoz took refuge in Buenos Aires, but Saguí stayed on in Royalist Montevideo, looking after the business and Seco's widow. Only after the 1812 armistice was he able to go back to Buenos Aires. When the battle against Montevideo began again, 'the sons of Seco's widow undertook the complete provisioning of the besieging army', and Saguí took command of the ship transporting those provisions, running the blockade several times. In December 1813 he proposed to engage in privateering in addition to his other activities. Together with his cousin Muñoz, he purchased a pilot's boat, but he was refused a licence because the government was assigning top priority to the creation of a navy. In the latter Saguí was to find a place, when Martín Thompson proposed that he enter it: 'I accepted the offer with enthusiasm; I was then nineteen years and three months old'.[80] In this way Francisco Saguí – among many others – formed increasingly close ties with the Revolutionary régime. From his first intervention as a courier between Buenos Aires and Montevideo to his joining the Navy as a regular officer, his career not only followed along lines appropriate to his political militancy, but reflected the new economic importance which the war had given to the State. Even before officially joining the Navy he had, as the captain of a ship supplying the troops, begun to derive his livelihood from the war. But perhaps more significant than the individual example of Saguí was that of his entire clan, which – with the closing of the African and Cuban routes – found ways to insert itself into the war economy, using to that effect affinities with the Revolutionary leadership which were apparently close enough to secure them the exclusive provisioning of the expeditionary force in the Banda Oriental.

It has already been observed that the advantages offered by this solution were sometimes illusory, but nevertheless necessity sometimes decreed its adoption. Moreover, even the representatives of the most solid local commercial wealth, such as Lezica who, chiefly because of the desertions of his old rivals, headed the biggest of the Creole business firms until his resounding bankruptcy in 1836, or Llavallol, who followed a more modest but also less hazardous course, did not disdain the business of supplying provisions or credit to the State. Nevertheless, despite the extent of these contacts based on self-interest, they were not enough to identify the upper sectors as a group with the Revolutionary ruling élite. In the first place, these activities were carried on in an atmosphere of arbitrary favouritism which created, outside the small circle of the favoured, a wider circle of hostility, and the ambivalence of these relationships should not be forgotten: a political change or a sharp increase in the penury of the State might transform a beneficiary into an aggrieved victim.

This complex web of interests created therefore between the holders of Revolutionary power and the economically influential sectors (both Creoles and foreigners: the latter were becoming increasingly powerful, and benefited from the political influence of their countries of origin) relationships both more intimate and more ambiguous than the mutual detachment observed above might lead one to suppose. There was hardly any political measure that did not affect economic interests, and those affected tried, by using friendly contacts or the means of pressure at their disposal, to modify such measures to their own advantage. In 1816 the agents of the United States Government soon discovered that several of the United States citizens who were defending the cause of Artigas with such enthusiasm were above all defending the privateering licences which the Uruguayan leader had so liberally distributed among them. But these causes of rapprochement or hostility between the political authority and economic interests did not alter the fact that, for most of the holders of economic power, the increasing influence of the Revolutionary State in the economy was – as that State itself recognised – intrinsically prejudicial, and only circumstantial advantages could be derived from it. This was an additional reason why the bonds formed as a result of the utilisation of such advantages could not be consolidated in the form of an identification of that entire sector of interests with the Revolutionary leadership.

There was thus a barrier, almost imperceptible but extremely solid, separating the Revolutionary ruling group and the urban upper sectors from which it had emerged and which refused to recognise its own fortunes as being committed to the venture of those of its members who decided to risk the hazards of political life. This being the case, the position which despite everything the Revolutionary leaders maintained within the local upper sectors did not entirely contribute to lending vigour to the movement. It is true that the Revolutionary régime benefited from the process by which, through the sheer passing of time, Revolutionary Buenos Aires – despite the lamentations of Beruti over the continual mutability of fortune – again acquired a clearly stratified society, in which the place formerly held by the great Spanish families was now occupied by certain Creole ones. Distinguished families appear to have recovered, in Revolutionary society, a position which higher officials and corporation members did not reconquer so easily. Between them and the new authority there were established relationships similar to the ones which they or their rivals had maintained with the Spanish administration, and this circumspect interchange of courtesies with those who now occupied the summit of Buenos Aires society increased the prestige of an authority often accused of being upstart.

However, these illustrious political outsiders, although they sometimes went further than according, with their measured courtesy, implicit recognition to the legitimacy of the new authority, were not possessed of sufficient militancy to overcome their preference for staying in the background among less politically prominent people. In 1816 the United States envoy Brackenridge received from one who knew Buenos Aires better than he some excellent advice: to visit Señor Escalada. It was true that Escalada 'is a plain citizen, and has never taken any other part than that of a private individual, but he has been enabled, from the possession of considerable wealth, to render service to the cause'.[81] His wealth, added to his long-standing prestige (his father before him had been a man of great fortune in Buenos Aires, and a member of the Cabildo in 1757) gave him an influence which many had learned not to disdain. Before Brackenridge, a Creole officer who had left the Royal armies to join the Patriot cause, and had no personal or family connections in Buenos Aires, José de San Martín, found in Escalada's house, besides valuable contacts, his future wife. His marriage to Remedios de Escalada y de la Quintana, whether or not it was inspired by political motives, had undoubted political effects. It gave him – even though his in-laws, if we are to believe persistent reports, never really considered him as their equal – that position in Revolutionary Buenos Aires which his dedication and his talents were apparently unable to attain for him. Of course, this advantage was to be repaid, especially after San Martín came to be recognised as the most brilliant military leader of the Revolution. The two sons of Escalada, Brackenridge records, 'one of eighteen and the other of twenty years of age...are serving under the very eyes of San Martín'. But the Revolutionary militancy, staunch yet discreet, of the Escaladas, was far from being predominant in the upper strata of society which, despite everything, enjoyed unquestioned preeminence. A comrade of San Martín, Carlos María de Alvear, had no need to seek new family alliances in order to embark on a career which was at first brilliant but was soon to be interrupted. His mother's family (the Balbastros) offered a sufficiently solid base, and the rest was achieved by his extraordinary talent for playing the rôle of young military prodigy which public opinion had assigned to him. That influential family, which had been represented in the Cabildos of Colonial times and had been able to send one of its sons to the Vergara Nobles' College, did not waste much time in mourning the passing of the *ancien régime*, but neither did it reveal any precocious Revolutionary fervour. This did not prevent it from retaining an influence capable of helping the ambitious Alvear.

By thus allying themselves to a local upper class which was unenthusiastic towards the Revolution, were not the leaders of that enterprise being imprudent? It is unlikely that they thought of the problem in these terms. That group to which they remained united had always been, for many of them, their own group, while for others of them it was the group by which

The Revolution in Buenos Aires

they had always aspired to be accepted. Furthermore, it was for that group that the Revolution had been launched. It was the appointed beneficiary of the elimination of those cliques of the Spanish-born which, using their commercial and bureaucratic contacts with Spain, had successfully contended with it for the first place in Buenos Aires. As such, only its inborn prudence, intensified by the growing difficulties that arose out of the course of the Revolution and the war, had placed limitations on its identification with the movement. And this detached attitude towards political commitment had its advantages: as Pueyrredón had already observed, it prevented the formation of too violent *frondeur* movements, except at moments of crisis, when that Fronde fulfilled a useful function by accelerating a change in political orientation which was in any case dictated by the march of events.

The danger, rather, appeared to arise from the lack of coherence of that group with which the Revolutionary leadership established ties without expecting fully reciprocal treatment. Although the adoption of a more European life-style gave the life of Buenos Aires a more glittering tone than it had possessed in the past, the Revolutionary storm had broken down the basic structure of Colonial society (which was, in any case, of too recent creation to be really solidly established) and had not been able – despite a few deceptive appearances – to replace it entirely. This upper class, deprived of its Spanish-born sector, the close integration of which into that class only became noticeable when it became possible to get rid of that sector altogether, struck by economic setbacks which had a very unequal effect on its members, torn between cruel political options which, despite the efforts made to elude a choice, eventually broke down commercial and even family ties of solidarity, that upper class did not incorporate itself as a group into the Revolutionary movement because, among other reasons, it was no longer capable of acting as a group. And by remaining too closely tied to that class, were not the Revolutionary leaders running the risk of being affected, not by its coherence, which was vanishing, but by its capacity – exacerbated by the difficulties of the times – for dividing itself into rival bands and factions? Here, then, was another reason why, from the point of view of a revolutionary ruling group not too subject to external pressures, the principal problem was that of its own internal discipline.

This problem slowly came to the fore in the leadership of Revolutionary politics. Seen retrospectively, the struggle between the followers of Saavedra and those of Moreno – that conflict between two different images of the Revolution, which, as we have seen, soon became a blind rivalry between factions divided above all by persistent personal hostility – appeared to be the first example of the dangers of a division within the Revolutionary leadership, but already in the context of that struggle the foundation in March 1811 of a political club by Moreno's followers marked the beginning of a new style of political action no longer aimed at making an addition to the numbers of politically active citizens of Buenos Aires, but to organise those among them who were already opposed, or could be persuaded to be opposed, to the moderate tendency within the leadership. A proof of this were the signatures on its first public proclamation, which requested clemency for the unmarried Spaniards, then threatened with imprisonment, a request which did indeed represent a curious inauguration of political activities reinitiated in the name of the supposedly extremist tradition of Moreno. Of the eighty-three who signed, forty-four had been or were to become military men, all of them officers, and fourteen had been or were to become civil servants. Perhaps the most remarkable aspect of this new attitude, which introduced to the public the leadership of a faction, without the slightest indication as to whether this enjoyed the support of a numerous popular following, was that so important a part in it was played by Domingo French, who in May 1810 had organised the popular demonstrations of support for the Revolution. (The importance of French is revealed by the fact that, of the eighteen signatories who were officers before 1810, seven had served in the Hussars, as had French, and of the twenty-six who joined the Army after 1810, ten entered the America Regiment, which French raised and commanded.) After a brief persecution at the hands of its adversaries, the club recovered even before its members achieved power. On 13 January 1812 it was refounded as the Patriotic Society, with a 'solemn and majestic' ceremony presided over by civil, military and ecclesiastical dignitaries. This solemn recognition of its place in the Revolutionary order did not soften its attitude towards a government which it did not control. In October 1812 it finally achieved victory, when a movement from within the now highly professionalised Army swept away the indirect and dubiously loyal heirs of Saavedra's faction, then led by Bernardino Rivadavia, a Creole, the son of a wealthy Galician merchant, who, as a follower first of Liniers and later of Saavedra, had maintained towards Moreno a hostility which reflected on the political plane what was also professional rivalry, and by Juan Martín de Pueyrredón. These leaders, who, after the almost undisguised search for a *modus vivendi* with the Royalists, had confronted with vigour (and with a prodigal use of the gallows which made the memory of the Jacobin furies of Moreno pale into insignificance) a Royalist conspiracy, led by Álzaga in Buenos Aires itself, were now the victims of, above all, their ability to control the complex electoral apparatus created alongside the Triumvirate which in September 1811 replaced the Junta. Despairing of removing them by legal means, the Army leaders simply drove them from power. But this vindication of the Patriotic Society marked both the high tide of its power and the rise of a rival that was soon to be successful, the Lodge. The Lodge was not differentiated from the Patriotic Society either by its tendencies or, to any marked degree, by the persons of its leaders. It was, however, its function within the Revolutionary political system which was utterly different. It was no longer a question of giving increased firmness to the convictions of the entire politically active sector of the city. The objective was, rather, to achieve a tactical unity which previously had been lacking among the leaders of that sector. By submitting them to the strict discipline of the Lodge, both the unity and the continuity of the Revolutionary régime were guaranteed.

Although these hopes at first appeared to be without foundation, the very constitution of the Lodge and the recognition of its rôle as the source and supervisor of political power were an accurate reflection both of the progressive limitation of the sector endowed with the power of political decision-making in Revolutionary Buenos Aires – the militia regiments having made way for the Patriotic Society, and the latter for the Lodge – and also of the acceptance by the Revolutionary leaders of the fact that, since their power was less and less effectively limited, the greatest dangers for the course of the Revolution lay in themselves. In this way, although the Lodge was in origin an import from overseas (it did, in fact derive from the secret societies organised on Masonic lines in the garrisons of Spain and the circles of exiles in London), its success was above all due to the perfect appropriateness of its functions within the context of River Plate politics. About its internal organisation really very little is known. Its members, bound by a vow of secrecy, displayed extreme discretion in this respect, and those who have studied the institution have usually been more interested in the problem of whether the Lodge was authentically Masonic, a possibility which would throw some doubt on the Catholic piety of its members, several of whom – particularly San Martín, who has proved resistant to the attempts of many authors to convert him posthumously to orthodox religious beliefs – were also members of undoubtedly Masonic organisations. The inferences as to the existence of an Assembly and a Council of the Lodge, based by Juan Canter on the list of members supplied in his old age by General Zapiola to General Mitre,[82] which in effect divided them into members of one or the other body, are unfounded. Even a quick glance at the Biographical Dictionary of Udaondo is sufficient to establish that the 'Assembly' was the General Constituent Assembly and the 'Council' was the Council of State. What is revealed, however, by the list of Zapiola, who, like San Martín and Alvear, had been a member of secret societies in Cádiz and London and was one of the organisers of the one in Buenos Aires, is the extent to which the objective of the Lodge was control over the various branches of the Government. After the military *coup* of October 1812 the Constituent Assembly was to be carefully organised, using the positions already secured in the central administration and in the provincial cities, and was transformed into the basis of the dominance of the Lodge over the Revolutionary State. Moreover, of the members of the Assembly who were also members of the Lodge (who totalled, according to Zapiola's list, twenty-five out of thirty-four members of that body), only ten took part in the secret decisions of the Lodge. The other fifteen 'are not let into the secret, because they merely follow the most powerful faction and act purely according to their own convenience'. This is a clear demonstration of the manipulative character of the Lodge.

But to what ends was this manipulation directed? There seems to be no doubt as to the primary objective of the Lodge: to ensure the complete integration of the River Plate Revolution into a greater revolution, Spanish American, republican and orientated towards independence. In this respect, the Lodge was decisively embracing the tradition of Moreno and – in a situation in which alternatives were already more clear – expressing it even more decisively. There is no doubt that the Assembly of 1813 marks the apogee of this newly reinitiated revolutionary line. Its members addressed one another as 'citizen' and cultivated republican virtues unhesitatingly. But this general orientation in no way reduced the complexity of the situations which the Revolutionary authority was obliged to face. These were of such a nature that general principles frequently shed very little light on the options open to the Government. In particular, two types of problem were now beginning to reveal their true magnitude. One was that of dissidence in the Littoral, encouraged by the use of local support in the struggle against the Royalist stronghold of Montevideo, which had led to this support acquiring sufficient strength of its own to resist attempts to subordinate it to the central authority. The other – which appeared, though perhaps wrongly, to be more serious – was the unexpected flood-tide of the Restoration which was beginning to cover Europe. If this continued to advance, the Buenos Aires leaders might find themselves faced with a restoration of the Spanish Bourbons, in whose name they were still governing. As regards the first problem, Republican faith had little to contribute. What expressed itself more obviously was the feeling of superiority of an authority which, even though it claimed to be revolutionary, knew that it was the heir to Viceregal power, and the pride of Buenos Aires, which in comparison with the recently settled Littoral appeared as a society characterised by a hierarchy solidly based on tradition, and which tended to look on its adversaries, the leaders of those new lands, as dangerous and ridiculous upstarts.

But although revolutionary and republican faith had very little to say in the face of the problem of dissidence in the Littoral, it was directly challenged by the anti-Napoleonic advances in Europe. To survive in such difficult circumstances, it again had to take on a new guise. After the audacity that characterised the early stages of the constituent assembly, a return to prudence (and consequently to ambiguity) soon became evident. This constituent assembly was never to draw up any constitution, nor to proclaim independence. Its meetings became less and less frequent, as it became the instrument of political manoeuverings over which it had lost control. The growing inappropriateness of the more radical ideology adopted at the inspiration of the Patriotic Society and the Lodge to the hostility which the Buenos Aires Revolution was encountering both in the Littoral and overseas strengthened still further the tendency, already implicit in the creation of the Lodge, to concentrate attention on short-term tactical problems, pushing further and further into the background the ultimate objectives of the Revolutionary process. The transition from the Patriotic Society to the Lodge had not only meant, as we have seen above, a further narrowing of the ruling group, but also a change of emphasis, from the ideological enlightenment which was still the declared objective of the former body to the manipulation of influence for political ends which was the main purpose of the latter.

This growing attention to immediate problems, fully understandable in a movement, the very survival of which was threatened, facilitated another change of objectives, the new tendency being to identify the survival of the Revolution with the conquest and retention of power in the hands of a specific political group. The Lodge thus became a machine for political domination totally controlled by Alvear's faction. This new revolutionary group was profoundly different from those which had previously emerged out of very real disagreements as to the policy which the Revolution should follow. What Saavedra's and Moreno's factions had eventually become (groups with a solidarity based mainly on shared ambitions and resentments), Alvear's movement was from the very beginning. It certainly accepted fully the ideological presuppositions of the Lodge, but it was not this that differentiated it from its rivals within the Lodge, but rather its utter devotion to the immediate objective of the conquest of power. In order to achieve and retain the latter, the new faction relied above all on its astuteness, a quality which came to be considered as a fundamental revolutionary virtue. In one of the songs composed in honour of the principal hero, Alvear, after his conquest of Montevideo, this rearrangement in the Revolutionary value-system is revealed even in the changed connotations of the word *viveza* (*astuteness* in the colloquial speech of Buenos Aires) and in the glorification of an episode which the admirers of Alvear would later prefer to forget: the repudiation, after the fall of Montevideo, of the terms of surrender which had allowed him to march into the city unopposed. This perhaps somewhat dishonourable behaviour had had highly beneficial results:

> the picture is well drawn
> by your *astuteness* and talent...
> The vanquished admits it
> and all this people *en masse*...
> and the clever American
> now holds the entire city.
>
> If in such manner you have won it,
> without yielding to entreaties,

> these are glories of your triumph
> which you have given to the Nation
> and which redound on us all.
> The State grows in strength,
> and is given such increase
> by your astute and valiant hand
> that without losing one fellow-countryman
> you leave the Nation wealthy.[83]

The display of such pride in somewhat dubious feats, in circumstances that in more simple times would have inspired instead a profession of faith in the miracles wrought by revolutionary heroism, is a clear revelation of one of the innovations introduced by Alvear's followers. As was only natural, the sagacity of which the group boasted was not placed only at the service of the Nation. It was primarily employed by the group itself in its conquest of the State, and was severely criticised by their momentarily unfortunate rivals. This did not mean that shared ambitions were the only basis of the unity of the new group. An all-important element, though one not always easy to understand, was unquestioning admiration of the leader, despite the fact that his political talents soon revealed themselves to be limited. The men associated with Alvear, in several cases, retained that admiring loyalty even after his fall from power. Even so clear-sighted a politician, so obviously superior in this sphere to his idol, as Canon Valentín Gómez, in the middle of a brilliant career recommenced independently of the fallen Alvear, no sooner saw the latter reappear on the political horizon, ten years after his fall, than he immediately placed himself at the service of Alvear's undiminished ambitions. And this rather blind devotion was passed down from father to son. It was the son of an Alvear supporter of the 1813–15 period, Vicente Fidel López, who after the fall of Rosas wrote to Alvear. In López's view, in an Argentina dominated by the figure of Urquiza and in which Mitre and Sarmiento were playing prominent rôles, there was a lack of men...would the general, generously forgiving the ingratitude of the country towards his past services, not deign to return and provide the leadership that was absent? Though anti-*unitario* and anti-Rosas, López overlooked the fact that Alvear had lent his sword to the *unitario* cause and had later been a diplomat under Rosas. He overlooked all the twists and turns of a career which misfortune had made even more tortuous, and remembered only a hope that for him was still not dead, a hope that in 1812 so many had placed on the brilliant twenty-three-year-old officer who had just returned from Spain.

Such an ascendancy, however, could only be exercised within a limited circle. The formation of the Alvear faction was made possible thanks to the previous narrowing of the Revolutionary power-base, which in effect enabled a faction to achieve power by accumulating and utilising the adherence of people with the power to make decisions, but who lacked a popular following which was no longer necessary. What, for such people (discounting the already mentioned powers of persuasion of their leader), was the attraction of Alvear's movement? The fact that it accepted as fundamental the objective to which they were already devoted: the conquest of power, and its retention in the hands of a specific group. San Martín, who was more faithful to the original objectives of the secret society, and more prepared to accept the priority of military victory as a Revolutionary objective, and, above all, to accept from a personal point of view the consequences of such a priority, could be swiftly excluded from the group, first by being given command of the Army of the North which was on the point of breaking up, and then by being appointed governor of the Intendancy of Cuyo, which had been detached from that of Córdoba. Alvear, who did not shirk military activity, but considered it only as an aspect of his political career, and had ensured for himself an unavoidable victory at Montevideo by assuming command of the besieging army shortly before the fall of the city, responded better to the almost undisguised aspirations of the leaders who, though recruited from previously opposed factions (mostly from among Moreno's followers), identified themselves with his leadership.

The political machine thus constructed served the interests of a necessarily small group, and provoked predictable reactions from those who felt themselves to be victims of an unjust exclusion. The complaints of Beruti, which became louder in the course of 1815, are good evidence of this – although partial evidence, of course. Beruti, a follower of Moreno, was discovering that his faction had failed completely to regain power and influence as a result of the rise of Alvear.

The dominant sector was the circle of friends and relations of the Director, which controlled the Assembly and in January 1814 appointed as Supreme Director of the State Gervasio Antonio de Posadas, an ecclesiastical notary who eluded all commitment to the Revolution, who had been subsequently persecuted as a Moreno supporter (although, as he assures us in his autobiography, this motive was mistaken, for he was in fact a Royalist) and whose most obvious merits were his family relationship with Alvear and his own insignificance, which was a guarantee of his future docility. But Alvear's faction was too faithful a reflection of that Buenos Aires which had undergone years of revolutionary upheavals to coincide exactly with a clan or even with an alliance of clans. Even though Posadas might owe his rise to his family ties, and, thanks to similar ties, Major Fernández might avoid all punishment after killing a sergeant in a fit of temper, in the presence of the entire regiment he commanded, nevertheless French, who was also a blood-relation of Posadas and Alvear, was still condemned to imprisonment under heavy guard, a measure decided for mysterious reasons by the Supreme Director, his cousin and brother-in-law.[84]

Better organised than ever for the fulfilment of its primary task – the retention of power – the Revolutionary group, under its new leadership, was no more fully integrated into urban society. On the contrary, in the ranks of Alvear's movement there were numerous adherents who were not natives of Buenos Aires and had no more influence there than that conferred on them by their appointments and corporation membership, or their progress in the 'career of the Revolution'. These included, among others, the Uruguayan priest Fr Figueredo, transferred to Buenos Aires in 1812 as an army chaplain, Fr Valentín Gómez, who was certainly a native of Buenos Aires, but who could only leave his post as parish priest in Canelones, in Uruguay, thanks to his revolutionary merits, the Uruguayan priest Fr Pedro Pablo Vidal, the military officers (also Uruguayan) Ventura Vázquez and Javier de Viana, Nicolás Herrera (also Uruguayan), a professional politician unhampered by any excessive consistency of ideas, who had begun his public career in the Napoleonic Cortes of Bayonne and, before it ended, was to enter the service of the Brazilian Empire. These figures constituted another indication of the extent to which, for the reasons given above, the political authority had gradually become isolated from any firm base of social support in the capital.

Was improved internal discipline enough to avoid the dangers involved in such isolation? It is true that in the beginning the Alvear faction had little reason to fear adverse reactions within the capital. Nevertheless, its initial failure to organise the support of sectors outside the small nucleus formed by those who took the decisions did not exonerate it from the need to find some support for that State apparatus which it so completely dominated. Such support could only come from the Army. Characteristically, the Alvear faction moved the entire garrison out of the capital and concentrated it in a camp outside the city limits. From there those six thousand men, isolated from any agitation on the part of the citizenry and commanded by officers of unquestioned loyalty, could guarantee the Government against any surprise. This garrison, however, was not the entire Army, nor was the capital the entire Revolutionary territory. In addition to the dissident movement in the Littoral, which they had not been able to suppress, Alvear's followers had to take account of that less systematised dissent which its sharp methods of political domination were encountering in many sectors. In 1814, when Posadas was still Director, Alvear, after his triumphal return from Montevideo, was sent to the Army of the North to replace its commander-in-chief, Rondeau, whom he had previously replaced during the siege of the Uruguayan capital. The officers calmly refused to receive him, and the hero of Montevideo was forced to beat an inglorious retreat. In Cuyo, San Martín, who was refusing to submit to the mechanism of control dominant in Buenos Aires, had become dangerous. Here again, a replacement was sent, and the Cabildo of Mendoza rejected him. Again, the supreme government yielded to a resistance which it did not dare to meet with violence.

In these circumstances the promotion of Alvear to the appointment of Supreme Director, handed over unhesitatingly by his less illustrious uncle, was an emergency measure in a situation recognised to be critical. Although the abundant proofs of lack of control over the Revolutionary territory were ominous enough, it was the more active resistance in the Littoral which led to the final crisis of the ephemeral hegemony of Alvear's party. Throughout 1814 and 1815 the Artigas dissidence spread from the Banda Oriental to Entre Ríos, Corrientes and Santa Fe. Attempts to suppress it by force of arms were unsuccessful. Alvear, the unhappy Supreme Director since January 1815, after ordering the evacuation of the Buenos Aires troops, which handed Montevideo over to the dissidents, decided to use part of the garrison of the capital to stop the advance of the Federalists, who had again captured Santa Fe. The vanguard of that expedition staged an uprising on the road to the North, in Fontezuela. The Director spent his last days in his post in an acrimonious conflict with the Cabildo, from which he obtained, not without having recourse to threats, an explicit condemnation of the dissident movement and of its leader, Artigas. However, twelve days after the *pronunciamiento* of Fontezuela he embarked in a British ship, leaving his adherents to the mercy of their worst enemies, who slowly savoured the delights of the vengeance they were to wreak.

Why did Alvear and his followers fall from power? The most obvious reason was that the corps of officers, which the faction had made the arbiter of its authority, eventually pronounced an adverse judgement. But that judgement, in turn, requires explanation. It was partly a consequence of the very concentration of power. In order to be effective, the Lodge had of necessity to be an organisation restricted to those at the top of the hierarchy, but for that very reason it was also necessary for that hierarchical structure to be accepted, and its orders obeyed, by those who knew themselves to be excluded from the decision-making process, and also often deprived of the best opportunities for promotion offered by the career of the Revolution. By brutally reserving to itself all real power, the Lodge had guaranteed the establishment of instruments to which betrayal was a constant temptation. In such circumstances, the mechanism schematically presented by Pueyrredón had to function with complete efficiency. The secret society could only maintain its hegemony as long as its policy was unmistakably successful. As soon as there were reverses, the ascendancy of the governing group began to suffer erosion, and this immediately affected its internal solidarity. The leader of the Fontezuela rising, Álvarez Thomas, a native of Arequipa, a career officer since Colonial times and a Revolutionary from the very beginning, did not belong to the small group which under Alvear shared effective power, but had been favoured by

Alvear and appeared to give unquestioning loyalty in return. But this loyalty was not sufficient for him to risk active opposition from his subordinates, who had little inclination to prosecute a civil war against the Littoral's insurrection, which appeared invincible. He preferred, therefore, to lead them. In the capital it was Miguel Estanislao Soler, also a career officer since Colonial times (the offspring of a military family, he had been a cadet at the age of twelve), and also a Revolutionary from the beginning, who gave the *coup de grâce* to Alvear's party, which had made him a senior colonel and Intendant-Governor of Buenos Aires. This was, perhaps, betrayal, but Soler only acted when the Cabildo, encouraged by the *pronunciamiento* of Fontezuela, had begun its offensive against Alvear, and urban public opinion had begun to look on the Cabildo members as champions against what was already being called the tyranny of the Supreme Director. He, too, appears to have had to choose between disloyalty and ruin. His decision becomes even less surprising if one bears in mind that the narrow circle of advisers of the Director were now agreed on securing his immediate resignation: it was necessary to offer this propitiatory victim to an impatient public opinion. Alvear refused to accept this verdict, and it is possible that his prevarication, which wasted decisive days, made the ruin of his faction more certain.

However, the fall of Alvear and his party, accelerated by that very concentration of power which had been the cause of their original strength, was essentially due – as we have observed above – to the reverses it suffered. These reverses, in their turn, were blows directed at a policy which antedated the triumph of Alvear's party and even its original rise. To Alvear and his adherents, the failure of that policy was above all the consequence of the world-wide advance of the Counter-Revolution, rather than of certain errors in their appreciation of the local situation on which the Buenos Aires Revolution impinged. As a result, the dominant faction was prepared to make a progressive abjuration of its Revolutionary credo, and to seek – by way of a British protectorate or even a reconciliation with Spain – a way to liquidate with a minimum of loss the entire Revolutionary enterprise, which now appeared as an adventure doomed to failure. In this pessimistic diagnosis of the failure and these attempts to avoid its consequences, the Alvear faction was not alone. Although not all were prepared to go so far in their abandonment of Revolutionary expectations, the view became increasingly widespread that the political process initiated in 1810 could only be brought to a successful conclusion if it found a way of adapting itself to a world climate hostile to revolution of any kind.

In addition to this external problem, however, the internal one had now been revealed in all its gravity. In order to survive, the Buenos Aires Revolution had to adapt itself simultaneously to a hostile outside world and to the country it aspired to govern. As the undertaking of a minority, prepared to impose by any means its policy on a population not inclined to sacrifice itself for objectives the need for which had not been convincingly demonstrated, the Revolution had exhausted its possibilities in five years. Using force as its principal argument both in domestic and foreign politics, the Revolutionary authority had gradually made the Army its political instrument *par excellence*. It had managed to cut the ties between that Army and the urban political mobilisation from which it had emerged in the last years of Colonial rule, but it had not been able to isolate the officer corps, to which the Revolutionary process had restored complete control over the armed forces, from the pressures of the *milieu* within which those officers acted. The weariness of the élite sectors of the capital, and the more widespread discontent prevailing over such a large part of the territory ruled by the Revolutionary régime, thus found a means to express themselves, indirectly but no less effectively. The Army, to the needs of which the welfare of both urban élites and vast sectors of the rural population were sacrificed, did not always resist the temptation to avenge those very grievances for which it was responsible. This attitude was less absurd than might at first sight appear. Underlying it was the conviction that the prevailing system could not last, and that the enterprise undertaken in 1810 could only be saved from ruin if it succeeded in identifying itself with sectors of the population which until then it had been content to dominate and utilise. The negative consequences of this initial attitude were, perhaps, more clearly visible in Buenos Aires, but it was more relevant in the territories which the Revolution had claimed to dominate from the capital. In the case of those territories, the Revolution had faced a problem both more serious and apparently less urgent than in the capital: the need to create new means of political articulation which would in some way reflect in those areas the radical change which the Revolution claimed to represent. There was a strong temptation, however, to use for its own benefit the ties of subordination inherited from the *ancien régime*, making those ties even stronger so that they could effectively serve a Revolutionary régime which needed to extract from the dominated areas more abundant resources than those required by its weary predecessor. Between these two alternatives the Revolutionary authority followed a middle course, which at times oscillated wildly, but which nevertheless almost always inclined towards the second of these solutions. The reactions it provoked (the detached attitude in the Interior, and the growing opposition in the Littoral) posed an increasingly urgent problem for the Revolutionary leaders, who, in seeking British protection or hoping for the improbable benevolence of a restored King of Spain, appeared to be taking refuge, not so much from the reactionary mood of the era which was beginning in the history of the world, as from the long-postponed wrath of their subjects. The fall of Alvear under the blows of an army that was supposed to suppress the dissident movement in the Littoral only emphasised the degree to which it was in the territories subject to its control, rather than in its turbulent capital, that the fate of the Revolutionary régime was being decided.

THE END OF THE REVOLUTION AND THE BEGINNINGS OF ORDER

The collapse of 1815 seemed to impose on the Revolutionary régime a dual reconciliation, with an increasingly conservative world and with the country whose frontiers were being established by the Revolution's military victories and defeats. Both processes, however, seemed to necessitate essentially similar changes. In the country, and especially in the Interior, where there had not been any movement of resistance such as that in the Littoral (where it was directed as much against the hegemony of the capital as against the policies imposed therefrom) resistance appeared to be provoked, above all, by attempts to effect too radical changes in the pre-Revolutionary order. Not only the attacks – deliberate and otherwise – on organised religion, but also the attempts to break down the equilibrium between the castes in the areas where that differentiation was a significant element in the social order, were among the mistakes which – in the opinion of Saavedra's followers – had led to the catastrophe which ended the first advance into Upper Peru. It is true that the Revolutionary authorities did not wait until 1816 before making strenuous denials of any lukewarmness in religious matters and, as far as the second aspect was concerned, the condemnation of the policies pursued by its earlier emissaries was perhaps unfounded. Although it took longer to mature than the discontent of the aggrieved parties, the support of those favoured by the policy of Indian emancipation was already beginning to make itself felt around 1815, and as a result, despite the advances of political conservatism, that policy was to be maintained. In general, the administration in the Interior was no more prepared to sacrifice immediate advantages out of loyalty to the new dominant moderate ideology than it had been in the past to sacrifice them to the radicalism currently fashionable. This lent an element of speciousness to the interpretation of the rapprochement with the country as merely the encouragement of a conservative reorientation; but even so a careful assessment of the changes of policy towards the Interior allows one to draw the conclusion that almost everywhere respect for the locally powerful sectors led to an increased respect for the *status quo*. And despite the growing seriousness of the problems posed by the Interior, the most immediate political influences still came from the capital, from that Buenos Aires where the élite sectors, tired of the arrogance of the military and of the dominant political cliques, had demonstrated in the crisis of 1815 that, despite their lack of militancy, their opinions could not be ignored with impunity. The rift between the governing groups and that social élite suddenly revealed its inherent dangers, and to close the gulf the new conservatism seemed a singularly appropriate instrument. When the restored national government promised to put an end to the Revolution and establish order it was expecting to gratify a public that was less remote from it than were the chanceries of Europe. From Europe, the Buenos Aires envoy Manuel José García wrote at that time of the dangers of a political power not controlled by those who had also economic power. Rather than the almost universal suffrage established in 1815 (in fact, not many electors troubled to take advantage of the right to vote), it was the recruitment of those elected which alarmed him. Even though – as has been pointed out by J. M. Mariluz Urquijo[85] – García's thoughts were so closely inspired by Benjamin Constant that his writings verged on plagiarism, what moved him to seek that inspiration was his experience of Revolutionary Buenos Aires. To convince himself that it was necessary to place political power in the hands of the holders of economic power (or, as he preferred to call them, the 'inhabitants settled in the country...who depend absolutely on this land'), it was enough for García to remember what had been said 'in the last Constituent Assembly, without taking into account aspects of the private lives of individuals'. It is true that the programme outlined by García would not have been easy to carry out, if only because of the persistent caution evinced by most of the economically prosperous sectors towards temptations to political militancy. Yet, although there was no increase in their direct intervention in the conduct of the Revolution's affairs, they undoubtedly exercised more influence than before 1815.

This political reorientation was all the more impressive because it was not accompanied by any sweeping replacements within the Revolutionary political leadership. True, the fall of Alvear was followed by a seemingly unavoidable succession of courts of enquiry, which condemned many to exile or imprisonment, and even the death penalty was discreetly restored. But the immediate inheritors of power were to enjoy it only for a brief spell. From the outset there was tension between the Cabildo, which was the stronghold of the eminent citizens of Buenos Aires and had been encouraged by the crisis to broaden its political ambitions, and the military leaders who had collaborated in the overthrow of Alvear's party, and now found it difficult to find a ground of agreement among themselves. As political instability returned to Buenos Aires, the concord which had followed the fall of Alvear (celebrated by the Armies of the North and of the Andes, whose commanders-in-chief – Rondeau and San Martín – had no reason to be grateful to the fallen party, and also celebrated by Artigas, the leader of the dissidents in the Littoral), was destined to be short-lived. Artigas in particular, after the fall of his enemy, to which his victories in the Littoral had contributed so greatly, found no reason to limit his ambitions, and soon began to lend his influence to the process of political reorganisation initiated by the fall of Alvear. In August 1815, in answer to the persistent dissidence of Artigas, Buenos Aires troops occupied Santa Fe, but this ephemeral victory was to lead to a lasting rupture.

For the moment, however, the secession of the Littoral – in so far as open conflict could be avoided – did not add any fresh problems. In the new conservative mood, Artigas would perhaps have sounded a discordant note, yet in that mood Buenos Aires and the Interior were beginning to find a common ground of understanding which had been lacking in the past. The political instability was reflected by the fall of the interim Director Álvarez Thomas (the titular Director, Rondeau, made no haste whatever to abandon his command in the North), the victim of a train of events characterised by a certain poetic justice. It was now Díaz Vélez, sent to fight Artigas, who was again triumphant in Santa Fe, who joined forces with Artigas to overthrow the 'arbitrary and tyrannical' successor of Alvear. Meanwhile, the slow electoral process from which a new Constituent General Congress would emerge continued. This Congress, the convocation of which had been decided by the Cabildo, would meet in Tucumán, thus offering a proof of the new attitude of the Revolutionary government towards that Interior which had been loyal to it. It did, in fact, meet in Tucumán in March 1816, and at the beginning of May elected as Supreme Director of the State Juan Martín de Pueyrredón, who had been banned to San Luis in 1812 by the triumphant military uprising, and had been elected deputy for that remote district.

Once appointed, the Director embarked on the slow journey to the capital, which he found to be on the brink of a new political crisis. His presence obviated it. The rival factions in Buenos Aires, which were on the point of engaging in open conflict, preferred to yield to a man who had not taken part in their recent quarrels and could, moreover, invoke a higher authority than that of any of the local leaders. Yet Pueyrredón was never to forget that originally fragile basis of his power during those early days of his rule in 1816, when disaster was only avoided by 'the forbearance of the people, which has never taken part in events which it has been unable to escape' in contrast with 'the inexperience and impetuosity of the less numerous class', when it was the decision of that people which, '...observing the fluctuating counsels of those who had directed its steps, preferred to stand firm on the brink of a precipice, while their leaders became reconciled', which saved the country from 'turning aside from the illustrious path of its glories'.[86] These incidents provided the only arresting images in an autobiographical record abundant in reflections which are often perceptive but surprisingly abstract.

Was it only popular passivity that made it possible to avert the crisis? One must also take into account the emergence of new bases of political power. The frontier armies, which Alvear's party had made no haste to dominate or win over to its side, were now more influential than at any time in the past. The new Congress, meeting in Tucumán, protected by distance from any *coup de main* by the factions in the capital, was able to confer on the strength of those armies the mantle of legitimacy. Moreover, despite the exclusivist tendencies with which it had been reproached, Alvear's party had succeeded in recruiting the most expert among the politicians formed in the career of the Revolution. Among those who emerged after its fall were some figures whom only the serious nature of the crisis persuaded to renounce their withdrawal from the most prominent positions, among whom were several members of the Cabildo, while others were leaders whose prestige was certainly not above question, even among the adversaries of the defeated party. (An example of these was Juan José Passo who, justly or unjustly, enjoyed a resounding reputation as an unsuccessful intriguer.) All of them, although they had too little in common to impress a coherent political line on the new situation, were too aware of the dangers involved in such incoherence to allow themselves excessively violent confrontations. Another factor making for discipline was the increasingly powerful dissident movement in the Littoral. Above all, that part of the Army stationed in Buenos Aires, which knew that it was destined to be the first line of resistance to any fresh advance of that movement, was for that reason less prepared to weaken the solidity of its future rearguard by supporting the political ambitions, which were not always modest in scope, of some of its leaders.

Thanks to all these factors, the arrival of Pueyrredón in Buenos Aires heralded the peaceful establishment of a new order. The degree to which the new order had broken with the Revolutionary past was untiringly emphasised by its spokesmen. On 9 July 1817 the deputy Castro Barros, from the pulpit of Buenos Aires Cathedral, used the first anniversary of the declaration of independence to describe that event, not as the culmination, but as the rectification of the Revolutionary process initiated in 1810: 'The indiscreet enthusiasm [of that process] has been replaced by judgement and circumspection...One has, indeed, seen in the course of our struggle certain exotic publications which attacked the fundamental bases of many respectable governments in Europe'.[87] But now this pernicious attitude has been renounced, and 'our complaints have nothing in common with the vague and exaggerated declamations of those who give the Rights of Man an elasticity without rule or measure'. After suggesting that the rights of the Indies were based on sound historical fact, the orator went on to say that, despite this, the question had ceased to be a legal one. For incomprehensible reasons the King of Spain had taken it into his head to execute subjects whose only fault had been to maintain an unswerving loyalty to him: 'We are not speaking of our rights, it is now a question of our lives. Is it just that we should allow ourselves to be murdered with impunity?' At this point the ideal debating-opponent to whom Castro Barros is addressing himself has changed. Rather than the sovereigns of Europe, it is the population of the new country, which wants neither to be revolutionary nor to return to the old order, which is now being exhorted to carry on a struggle which has abandoned its original justification. Revolutions often bring in their train major disasters, of which the most serious, and the one that makes revolutions less frequent, is 'the difficulty of returning matters to their previous state'. Thus reflected the *Gaceta* of 7 June 1817, but it concluded that, despite the difficulties, the government was not renouncing this enterprise of restoration. It was, however, a restoration limited in its possibilities because, although Buenos Aires might decree the end of the Revolution, it could not decide the end of the war, which had become a struggle for survival.

In this way the new régime was proclaiming itself to be the heir to an unwanted heritage. Whereas up to 1815 the government had been identified with the group which had imposed the Revolution on the country, now it wished to represent itself as the first victim of that Revolution. Fortunately, the end was already in sight: one last effort would bring victory and peace. Thus, in a very different ideological context, the war maintained the highest priority, and this had consequences perhaps more serious than those of the past because, on the one hand, the 'calamitous years' that had gone before had exhausted the Treasury's reserves completely, and, on the other, the political influence of the frontier armies, in particular that of the Andes and its commander-in-chief, San Martín, ensured a zealous control over the efforts of the government to finance the war.

Even so, and within the narrow limits imposed by the continuing war, the Directory sought ways to 'put back in their place all the elements of public happiness', displaying a new sensitivity to the poverty of the masses and, especially, to the uneasiness of the local economic élite, which had been prejudiced by the revolutionary changes. The Directory declared itself to be inspired by a warmhearted care for the urban masses, and did in fact give priority to the problems arising from the shortage of food. A ban on the export of wheat, flour and salted meat (May and June 1817) invoked that shortage as a justification, and there is no doubt that the ban on the export of salted meat had a serious effect on the profits of a certain part of the upper sectors, which was sacrificed – according to the arguments used in support of the measure – to the welfare of the consumer masses. Although, as has been observed above, the measure had perhaps more important consequences on the internal equilibrium of certain upper sectors undergoing a process of accelerated change, there is no doubt that popular discontent over the scarcity of food contributed decisively to its adoption. This attitude of sensitivity towards popular discontent had really very little in common with the Revolutionary notion of equality, which, severely limited from the beginning in its practical application, was now increasingly openly renounced. This was noticeable both in its methods and its language: the latter expressed the paternal concern of the ruler, his sensitivity to the sufferings of the masses which, through lack of direct contact, he cannot know but can imagine. 'The clamour of the poorest families, though it does not reach my ears, is present in my imagination. My feelings are distraught at the thought of their privations'.[88] Rather than the sentimental reasons invoked, it was fear of turbulence among the desperate masses that inspired these emergency measures against scarcity. In its genuine fears, as in its rhetoric, the Directorial phase, coming after the Revolutionary cycle, was a continuation of the *ancien régime*.

The beneficiaries of this somewhat disdainful benevolence seem to have noticed this only too well, and the popularity of the new régime among the urban lower classes seems to have been always limited. Awakened after 1806 and 1810 by a rise of consciousness in which, as has been observed above, patriotic and military motives had eventually displaced political ones, the growing departure from the Revolutionary tradition was not likely to excite their sympathy. This new orientation was, moreover, justified by increasingly harsh criticisms of the myths – of the invincibility of Buenos Aires, of the inevitable victory of a popular revolution – which still formed the essential core of the awakening political faith of the urban plebs. What was more serious, the criticisms levelled by the new régime against Revolutionary optimism were reflected in the Littoral by a policy of resignation in the face of the reappearance of the Portuguese on the other bank of the River Plate, a resignation which only thinly disguised a more active complicity in that disturbing encroachment. It is not a question of deciding to what extent an anti-Portuguese policy lay within the possibilities open to the régime established in 1816. It should be sufficient to point out that the very duplicity displayed by the Pueyrredón administration throughout the episode is a proof of the extent to which it recognised the impossibility of publicly justifying a policy which, nevertheless, it judged to be most appropriate to its objectives and resources.

Yet by presenting this policy to the public in a necessarily insincere manner, it merely weakened the confidence, which was slight enough to begin with, deposited by the revolutionary masses in a ruling group openly dedicated to eliminating the Revolutionary heritage. In February 1817, Pueyrredón announced that, although Portugal did not want war, Buenos Aires would fight unless Portugal evacuated the Banda Oriental, and then regretted that he could not prepare to deal with future Portuguese actions because he did not know what they would be, and his ignorance was caused by the fact that public opinion, astutely manipulated by his adversaries, had refused to tolerate the sending of a diplomatic mission with purely informative objectives ('the Government...has not been free to do even that, because of the insolence of the demagogues'). When he made these statements, he probably did not have very high hopes of being believed. Did that plebeian opinion, deprived even before 1816 of any possibility of directly influencing the course of the Revolution, which was now declared to be a heritage from the past that it was better to forget, still possess a means of making its discontent felt? Only a slight one, certainly. The reason that it was not even smaller was that this discontent was beginning to be shared by members of another and more influential sector.

In fact, the new régime was also to redefine its relationship with the Army. The frontier armies had, of course, been decisive influences in its rise to power, and with them the régime was to maintain even closer relations than had existed in the past. But the frontier armies had suffered great changes. Under the indulgent command of Rondeau, the Army of the North had suffered the worst of its defeats in Upper Peru at Sipe Sipe, and the defence against the Peruvian Royalists was left increasingly in the hands of the provincial forces of Salta. The Army of the North, withdrawn to Tucumán, and busy for some months in suppressing ephemeral Federalist uprisings in the Interior, was then reorganised under the command of Belgrano and no longer had, either in size or in function, the importance it had had in the past. Now the most important of the frontier armies was that of the Andes: organised along austerely professional lines by San Martín, it was not to know that proliferation of officers which the Army of the North had known in its better (or worse) days. In the Littoral the crisis of 1815 had already demonstrated the dangers involved in a total war against a dissident movement pursued with excessive vigour. Political action was, therefore, preferable to military action. Could not the Portuguese invasion induce Artigas to accept a reconciliation on terms less unfavourable to the central government, and – if he continued to refuse it – would not this bring about the downfall of that redoubtable rival? Meanwhile, the Army was deprived of a function which had absorbed a considerable part of its energies. Both in Buenos Aires and in the rural areas the regular Army, which Alvear had intended to make an instrument of his supremacy, was partially relieved of its functions as custodian of internal order. New militias – the 'civic battalions' – were recruited after the downfall of Alvear's party, and the Cabildo, which was on the winning side, reserved to itself command of them.[89]

This reduced the career opportunities of several officers commissioned during the process of militarisation. For lack of other employment, they were attached to the General Staff. In a decree of 22 July 1817, published on the 26th by the *Gaceta*, the Government addressed that 'large number of officers...who cannot be posted...to the regiments of the line or other active appointments owing to the lack of vacancies, nor be given the pay owing to them on time because of the shortage of funds in the public treasury'. It invited them 'to settle on properties along the line of the new frontiers which are to be extended', where they would be 'given preferential treatment in the distribution of free land, and helped with a sum of money to get started, provided from the State treasury'. It is understandable that the offer of lands which had still not been conquered from the Indians was received with indifference, and that there was no lack of unemployed military men among the agitators of those masses whose activity the Government viewed with growing concern.

In the face of this discontent, the Government tried a policy of repression which represented another innovation *vis-à-vis* the brief Revolutionary tradition. In contrast to the intransigence more usual in the past, Pueyrredón preferred to accuse himself of excessive indulgence, 'in these wretched times so much delicacy is dangerous, and private hatred finds pleasure in depriving its object even of the opportunity to exercise virtue'. Acting against his inclinations, he had to suppress in good time a revolution which was obviously being plotted against the Government, because 'one more revolution would bring the State to barbarism'. The repression, however, he announced as both limited and moderate, and not only for humanitarian reasons, but rather out of prudence. The fragile existing order was ill able to withstand excessive upheavals. For this reason it exiled 'the most spiteful and dangerous intriguers' who, although too weak to strike a decisive blow at the existing order, 'lost no opportunity of tempting, seducing and corrupting senior and junior officers of the militia'. Pueyrredón preferred an arbitrary but very moderate repression to the more lengthy alternative of judicial prosecutions. This was because the latter would mean punishing 'men who on other occasions have rendered distinguished services to the Nation', and also, perhaps, that 'half of the people' which according to the disillusioned governor got mixed up in all revolutions. There was a further consideration: the need to keep secret the network of agents which had enabled the Government to prevent the revolution. 'it would be necessary to leave society without friends and the Government without zealous citizens capable of warning it of danger, if we were to publish the means by which we have had daily knowledge of all the plans' of the revolutionaries. This perhaps deliberately tangled text nevertheless makes it perfectly clear that the Government had already renounced any attempt at popularity. The coldly rational tone of its declaration makes it clear that it was addressed to that necessarily small circle of sensible people, free of passions and fanaticism, which constituted the ideal public in the eyes of the Supreme Director. The lack (admitted as inevitable) of a broader basis of support was also recognised in the care taken to keep secret the network of government agents. In the first years of the Revolution informing had been publicly praised and rewarded, although, of course, excessive publicity made it difficult for the informer to continue his activities. Nevertheless, the example itself would ensure that a replacement was forthcoming, and the example would anyway find imitators, thanks to the support of a sector, perhaps forming a majority, of public opinion whose revolutionary fervour bordered on fanaticism. Now, however, the intelligence network patiently built up by the minister Tagle (appointed with Álvarez Thomas and retained by his successors, who considered him indispensable) had been consolidated by the recognition of mutual interests and the clever management of official favour, which had nothing to do with any fervent political sentiment. One can understand that it would have been difficult to replace, had an excess of publicity rendered it ineffective.

Although it renounced attempts at a broader-based popularity, the Pueyrredón régime still desired the considered support of more limited sectors, to which it represented itself as the least bad alternative for administering the catastrophic legacy of the Revolution. In its dealings with the Creole élite, which had suffered so many blows since 1810, it could invoke the financial prudence which it was trying to maintain in spite of the war, and its new-found care in measuring the prejudicial consequences of a voracity on the part of the Treasury which it was, in any case, impossible to reduce radically. But – as has already been observed – this new financial policy was not destined to be very successful. The reform of the Customs duties led to an intensification of contraband, and a fall in Customs revenues. As had been malevolently predicted by the Government's adversaries, 'the public spirit of our compatriots' was not sufficient to enable them to resist the temptations of smuggling, and only through the suppression of smuggling would 'our contributions give the Government the means to conclude a struggle which we ourselves have prolonged by misbehaviour of every kind'. Contraband – concluded the *Gaceta* of 1 April 1818 – was the cause of all the disorders: 'without contraband all would be well in our country'. However, although the *Gaceta* was right to point out that 'a State such as ours is not maintained by arguments against the Customs duties', it was not maintained any better by arguments against contraband. The financial imbalance, which in the past had inspired that arbitrary fiscal rapacity which was retrospectively condemned by the customs reform of 1817, still subsisted, and its consequences threatened to repeat themselves. In 1819 Beruti might complain again not only about the misfortune of the civil servants dismissed from their posts because there was no money to pay them, but also about the return of heavy-handed methods of revenue-collection: Colonel Díaz Vélez, to extract money from the really impoverished European-born Spaniards, organised what was, to put it bluntly, a system of hostages. Even before this undisguised return to the usages of a past supposedly buried, the attempt to overcome it by the issue of State promissory notes to pay overdue debts caused more irritation than gratitude among the supposed beneficiaries. The Ministry of Finance tried hard to prove that these amortisable notes were not being issued too abundantly. Those remaining in circulation would hardly suffice to pay half the Customs duties, at the new tariff rate of 33%, on the foreign merchandise that had accumulated in the warehouses. These far-fetched arguments did nothing to alter the fact that the State's creditors were obliged to sell at well below their par value notes which for payment of the State's debts were reckoned at par. It was also true, as the same Ministry pointed out, that if the creditor did not want to lose forty per cent of the sum due to him he could return those dubious notes. He could not expect to be paid in cash. It would be absurd that 'simply to pay off overdue debts...attention should be distracted from enormous expenditures made necessary' by 'the great task which Providence has entrusted to the present generation'. However – excluding this absurd supposition – 'the State would again recognise the debt outstanding, and pay it in full on a more favourable occasion'.

This argument was not by any means nonsensical, but when we observe the government of Pueyrredón entangled in an increasingly bitter polemic with those very interest groups whose adherence it had intended to secure through an attention more solicitous than that given by previous Revolutionary régimes, we can begin to measure the magnitude of its failure. The penury of the Treasury, which imposed a return to the heavy-handed style of the past, prevented the State from assuming that rôle of benevolent arbiter between economic and social groups from which it hoped to obtain their solid support.

There was yet another circumstance which made this task more difficult. The society on which Pueyrredón's government was trying to make an impact was undergoing a rapid transformation. We have already seen how, as early as 1816, Brackenridge had observed that 'what are called the *estancias*, or grazing farms,...constitute the principal fortunes of the rich'.[90] It is true that the Pueyrredón administration did not ignore rural problems, and appointed Juan R. Balcarce as commandant-general of the rural areas. The advance of the frontier, stabilised since 1780, was given attention, which took the shape of a plan of expansion based on private investment. Balcarce, according to a decree of 22 July 1817, was preparing to organise expeditions to the Indian territories, and was authorised to effect a free distribution of the lands conquered: 'Those who assist this expedition with their own persons or with donations will receive preferential treatment in the concessions granted...it is hoped that the big landowners...will show their generosity in the effective help they give; for without it the project will be impracticable and unable to sustain itself during the first four years of the new settlements'. However, leaving aside this invitation to the landowners to resolve their own problems, the point of view of the Pueyrredón Government towards its relationship with the economy and society of Buenos Aires was most decidedly more urban than rural. The economic reconstruction which it was anxious to initiate was seen above all as a restoration of the pre-Revolutionary systems of economic and social hegemony, and it will be remembered that during the Viceregal era the landowning group was inferior in wealth and influence to the big merchants. Yet in thus defining its objective it made it even more unattainable. It was not only the weakness of the State, it was the irreversibility of the change in the economic structures initiated by free trade and accelerated by the Revolution which doomed the attempt to failure.

Even though it had discovered the importance of the urban economic and social élite, and the need to adopt a policy calculated to obtain from that sector a less hesitant adherence, the Pueyrredón government was no more capable than its predecessors of achieving this objective. Rather than a new orientation, its preoccupation with this sector of public opinion was destined to provide it with a more acute consciousness of the limitation imposed on its freedom of action by the not always totally passive resistance of that group. This explains, for example, the reluctance of Pueyrredón and his minister Tagle to impose the additional sacrifices which would have allowed Buenos Aires to share in the financing of San Martín's expeditionary campaign in Peru. Although, as San Martín suspected, there was an element of exaggeration in the pretext that the city no longer possessed the volume of money required (the project under discussion was to raise a forced loan of half a million pesos), there was some foundation for the fear of the reactions which the collection of this loan might provoke.

The war, by perpetuating financial commitments greater than could be met from the normal resources of the new State, therefore made impossible that return to a stable order which had become the new Revolutionary objective. But it was not only through its drain on the treasury that the war frustrated this attempt, although Pueyrredón was no doubt perfectly right in seeing it as the fundamental reason for the distant attitude of the upper sectors, if not towards the Revolution itself, then at least towards those governments that burdened them with part of the cost of the war. A struggle for survival does not need to be based on a revolutionary ideology to maintain a factious outlook, in revealing contrast to the moderation which animated the new political style. One may compare the carefully worded proclamation in which Pueyrredón ordered the banishment of certain dissidents with the laconic report of the execution of a Spaniard found with arms in his possession ('yesterday there was put on public display the body of an obstinate Spaniard...these wild beasts who feel no compassion for their own children forget the dictates of Nature, when they are moved only by feelings of resentment in the presence of our generosity'),[91] to observe how extremism, which was being excluded from the realm of ideas, characterised actual occurrences. This background of brutal violence contrasted with the peaceable style preferred by the writers of the *Gaceta*, which had turned its back on its former vehemence. On 7 February 1817 it lent the admiring hospitality of its columns to the report of the Salta commander-in-chief Juan Antonio Rojas, who boasted of having had 'the glory of having cut the throats, in San Pedrito, of a whole squadron of the Extremadura Regiment' and described with rapture the fruits of this bloodthirsty feat ('many boots, epaulettes and coats...some very pretty carbines'), adding a note that is perhaps more sinister than his open boasts ('by an extraordinary miracle, seven prisoners were taken'). On 22 May of that year, the *Gaceta* reproduced the ultimatum of La Madrid to the Royalist commander in Tarija, which informed him that if he did not surrender in half an hour, 'both you and it [the division he commanded] will be put to the sword. May God keep you many years'. Thus the war made impossible a return to order. Only when the war had ended could the Revolutionary phase really be said to be terminated. Meanwhile, the Pueyrredón régime had been trying to gain new strength from the nostalgia for order which inspired so many 'judicious patriots'.[92] However, by raising hopes destined to be soon dashed, this attitude failed to obtain more solid support for the régime.

Therefore, the relationship between the Revolutionary leadership and the social élite continued to be, as it had been before 1816, problematic, and the support of the popular sectors had waned considerably. The discontent in both sectors was indicated by the banishments ordered in February 1817 and the imprisonments of August 1818. The first measure, which affected opposition military leaders, such as French, Chiclana and Pagola, an opposition journalist, Pazos Kanki, and some officials, the most prominent of whom was Manuel Moreno, was a clear revelation of the desire to deprive of spokesmen a sector of opinion whose loyalty to the original orientation of the Revolution coincided with the sentiments dominant among the urban masses, and which found in the Portuguese policy of Pueyrredón the most powerful argument to use against him. The later sentences of imprisonment struck at a sector of less open but perhaps more dangerous opposition, which was based on the same upper sectors that Pueyrredón had tried to win over. The most prominent victim was Manuel de Sarratea, that turbulent politician whose capacity for intrigue made him particularly redoubtable. He was the dominant personality of an aristocratic salon enlivened by the caustic wit of his sister Doña Melchora, and which was the centre of what the Robertsons called the Whig faction in a Buenos Aires governed by the Tory Pueyrredón.[93] Among those imprisoned at the same time were Juan Pedro Aguirre, a financier involved in privateering and connected with the financial activities of the Revolutionary governments, and Miguel Yrigoyen, who – like Aguirre – would regain prominence in the agitation of 1820, as the repository of the confidence of the economically dominant sectors, who resolutely countered a direct threat to their predominance. This new opposition, though partly inspired by certain decisions which were an accurate reflection of the moderate orientation of Pueyrredón – particularly the restrictions imposed on privateering, which seemed to have earned him intense unpopularity among those who financed that activity – became dangerous because it gained support among those who had not been affected by the measures but who feared the return of arbitrary exactions which the failure of the financial reforms made inevitable. Having dissipated the goodwill of the masses by systematically departing from the Revolutionary tradition, the Pueyrredón government had no more success with the upper sectors. The marriage of convenience which it had proposed to these sectors, to put a swift end to the war by means of a supreme sacrifice, and then to lay the foundations of a more stable order, had been calmly rejected.

Though lacking solid support, the régime could count on the timidity of the opposition, especially the timidity of those who enjoyed sympathy within the upper sectors. The lukewarm militancy of the opposition lent effectiveness to an apparatus of repression characterised by widespread espionage but not by severe punishments, and at the end of 1817, commenting on the increase in the number of voters in the election of the Cabildo of Buenos Aires (for the first time, the voters numbered over a thousand, and they voted unanimously for the same names), the *Gaceta* was able to conclude triumphantly: 'The party which supports the cause of order has become so large that there is no opposition left. Concord has produced uniformity'.[94] Rather than being extinguished, the opposition had been successfully excluded, without it showing any decided resistance, but its flexible tactics, although they made it ineffectual, also made it indestructible.

The problems posed by this divorce between the régime and urban opinion were not, in essence, new. They no doubt appeared aggravated by the detachment of plebeian opinion, the impact of which on the actual political process had already been severely restricted, and by the fact that for the first time this problem had been considered urgent and an attempt had been made – albeit unsuccessfully – to resolve it instead of ignoring it. Nevertheless, Pueyrredón had good reason to be confident that his unpopularity in the capital, although it might aggravate a crisis arising in another sector, could not by itself provoke such a crisis.

This problem, which was both insoluble and of little urgency, was therefore relegated to the background. The problems posed by the Interior were, however, of more immediate importance. The most urgent were those connected with the dissident movement in the Littoral, which, as it had before 1816, perhaps constituted the most direct threat to the Buenos Aires government. But now there were also problems – and this was a new aspect of the situation – posed by Tucumán and Cuyo, to which the Pueyrredón régime had tried to give a more active rôle in revolutionary politics.

5 THE REVOLUTION IN THE COUNTRY AS A WHOLE

THE INTERIOR

However complex the problems posed by the Revolution in Buenos Aires — both as an urban centre which had achieved a high degree of politicisation and as the administrative headquarters of the Viceregal area which the Revolutionaries aspired to dominate — the problems posed by the Interior were of necessity to be even greater. The first thing demanded of the territory by the Revolution which had triumphed in Buenos Aires was an explicit allegiance to the new government on the part of the authorities subordinate to the old one. This first intention led almost everywhere to a repetition of the process undergone by Buenos Aires. The delegates of the latter and the local officials who wished to elude responsibility nearly always agreed to submit to the arbitration of an Open Cabildo, without, of course, refraining from applying to that body all the pressure at their command.

From the very beginning, however, the ascendancy of the local authorities and of the new authority established in Buenos Aires were supplemented by a new source of pressure: that of force. In part, of course, this had its origin in the new Revolutionary headquarters. It will be remembered that the first decision of the new régime was the dispatch of military expeditions to the North and to Paraguay. But the force sent from Buenos Aires had to be complemented or anticipated by other forces with a stronger local basis. Only in Córdoba was the Revolution affirmed as the victory of a Buenos Aires expeditionary force over local resistance. In the remainder of the territory which the new régime was able to win from the old one the support of the militias was decisive in the early stages. In Mendoza, to choose an example in which that force was exerted most openly, the victory of the new régime over the old was also that of the urban militias in their confrontation with those of the Indian frontier (even if here the prudence of both sides stopped this developing into an open battle). Only exceptionally were the regular forces the final arbiter. This was the case in the Misiones frontier region, which these forces won for the new order, and in Montevideo which, at the instigation of its naval garrison, opposed that order. However, open cabildos, militias and, for the most part, even corporations and judicial institutions, in those minor centres where the number of career officials was necessarily small and the links between them and the locally powerful sectors were very close, were all under the control of a very small group, sometimes divided against itself but more homogeneous than one might be led to suppose from those clamorous quarrels indulged in between family clans, each supported by large clientèles. It is true that, as in Buenos Aires, the Revolution signified in the long run the exclusion of those among the European-born who did not demonstrate, in good time, unequivocal allegiance to the new system. But the influence of this group, except in Salta, where anyway it had established solid family ties with the oldest local dynasties, was less than in the capital. Did the Revolution have no other path open to it than that of gaining the support of those recognised as the leading sectors by the *ancien régime*? It might have taken an entirely opposite direction, that of encouraging a decisive change in the social equilibrium, which in the Interior was above all an equilibrium between castes. Both alternatives offered advantages. The first resulted in the swift conquest of an entire territory for the Revolution, whereas the second, although it threatened to unleash violent conflicts – thus accentuating the potential hostility towards the Revolution of those who for the moment controlled the local situation – could in the long run ensure for the Revolution a more solid basis than the support of the ruling sectors. Moreover, the choice between these options was governed by other considerations. The preoccupation with social stability, which characterised the action of the Revolutionary authority in Buenos Aires, was also evident in the Interior, with an intensity that decreased in direct proportion to the remoteness of the area to be won for the Revolution. Conversely, the least conservative solution might be unavoidable in places where the support of the dominant sectors was from the outset lukewarm or hesitant. For both reasons the Revolution was to be more audacious in Upper Peru, where it took little hold and eventually lost the battle, than in Tucumán and Cuyo, where it acquired a more solid predominance, or in the Littoral, where, on the contrary, the extreme hostility to the changes threatening the pre-Revolutionary equilibrium was one of the reasons for the local reaction which gave prominence to a model of revolution different from that proposed by Buenos Aires.

There were, therefore, three solutions: a deliberate attack on the preexisting equilibrium (Upper Peru); the conservation of that equilibrium, which was not for the moment opposed by considerable local forces (the Interior); and the defence of that equilibrium, threatened by the very advances of the Revolutionary processes that Buenos Aires had at first tried to extend (the Littoral). These three solutions, and the divergent destinies of the territories where they were applied, will be considered separately.

The Revolution as a social revolution: Upper Peru

The Northern frontier of the Intendancy of Salta, which was to become that of the nation created by the Revolution, was at first easily crossed by the Army of the North. Upper Peru, which in 1809 had been shaken by revolutions and repressions, welcomed the advance of the Buenos Aires troops, who marched into towns which had already declared in favour of the invaders. Not even the execution by the Patriots of those responsible for the repression of 1809 had the effect of destroying the apparent unity of the adherences to the new order. Behind this unanimity, however, there was much hesitation and, above all, misgiving as to the future. Would the Revolution affect the delicate equilibrium between the castes in Upper Peru? The leader of the expedition, Antonio González Balcarce, on 29 November 1810 reported from Potosí the complete pacification of Upper Peru, which was giving obedience 'with the greatest pleasure on the part of all the inhabitants' to the new government. But he hastened to add that this unanimous obedience stemmed from the respect inspired by the armed forces of Buenos Aires.[1] A few days later he received from the Intendant of La Paz a letter full of verbose protestations of loyalty to and zeal for the cause of Buenos Aires, but also sufficiently explicit to indicate the causes of alarm felt by that conscientious official. The urban masses in La Paz wanted to be issued with arms. Nothing could be further from the intentions of the Intendant, who distrusted the 'intrinsic disorder of that numerous plebs which always needs restraint when it does not recognise the duties of man...especially at this time full of novelties'. But it was not only the city that caused him alarm; in the jurisdictional district of La Paz, 'the Indians are now saying that until the arrival of the men of Buenos Aires' they did not intend to pay the *tributo*. It would be necessary for the emissaries of the capital to order its immediate collection. Meanwhile, the diligent Tristán was doing his best in this direction, 'for this treasury is the best in the Viceroyalty'.[2]

It is not surprising that relations between the armed heralds of the Revolution and their nervous collaborators in Upper Peru should have been tense from the outset. When the occupation of Upper Peru ended in failure, after the military disaster of Huaqui in June 1811, which gave control over the entire region to the army organised by the counter-revolutionaries of Peru, this tension took the form of a swift change of attitude on the part of many adherents of the liberators from the South. It was the moment for attributing blame and responsibility, and, in a Revolutionary ruling group already deeply divided, the still dominant Saavedra faction chose as scapegoat Juan José Castelli, who had accompanied the expedition as representative of the Junta, and was now accused of imprudent behaviour stemming from an excess of Revolutionary zeal. It is true that, on 25 May 1811, Castelli, at a ceremony held against the background of the ruins of Tiahuanaco, had proclaimed the end of the centuries-long servitude of the Indians. Although the proclamation had no immediate legal effects, since less than a month later the entire zone was lost to the enemy, it certainly served to aggravate the alarm of those whose main preoccupation was with the future of the social and racial equilibrium in that zone.

This pro-Indian policy, however, did not stem from the personal initiative of the delegate, but was indicated in the instructions given to him by the Junta.[3] It was, moreover, necessitated by the war itself. The army which reached Upper Peru, and had acquired on the road to the North more men than resources, needed numerous auxiliaries, whom only the Indians could provide. Guns and equipment had to be carried by Indian labour, and in the case of a counter-attack by the Royalists the support of the Indian masses, which had the advantage of numbers, although they were very insufficiently armed, might make the difference between defeat and victory for the emissaries of the Buenos Aires Revolution. This audacious innovation in the legal status of the Indians was certainly calculated to cause disaffection in other sectors, but there were few illusions as to the sincerity of the allegiance of those sectors. In the case of the upper classes, Upper Peru required 'a harsher policy' than that applied in Tucumán. At certain critical moments, there were plans for the mass deportation of Spaniards, and even during less critical periods a systematic purge of the administrative apparatus and the local judiciary appeared unavoidable. This complex process would, of course, make impossible any reconciliation with the enemies, so harshly punished, of the new order, but it would gain for that order solid support among the leading Creoles, who would be entrusted with local power. The Revolutionaries were, in other words, trying to utilise the tensions existing between Spaniards, half-castes and Indians, and those existing within the first category between the European-born and the Creoles. This project was certainly not easy to carry out. The growing restlessness among the Indian masses served to restore and strengthen the solidarity which, despite everything, still existed in the other sectors. In a system based for centuries on keeping the Indians at the bottom of the scale, it was in fact all the privileged sectors, officials, mine-owners, landowners, clergy, and even that half-caste urban mass which lived by serving those sectors, which would suffer the immediate consequences of Indian emancipation. They would be affected as regards their standard of living, their sense of security (it was only twenty years since Upper Peru had experienced a racial war, which had left a considerable legacy of potential violence), and their prestige, which they conceived as being dependent on the existence of groups condemned on ethnic grounds to remain at the lowest level.

Indian emancipation therefore appeared as a threat to the status of the other castes in Upper Peru, but it was not the only threat implied by the

The Revolution in the country as a whole

Revolutionary policy. The Revolution needed soldiers (on the road from Buenos Aires to Potosí the thousand who set off had become nine thousand), but it also needed to obtain material resources: cattle and horses from a region less well endowed with these animals than the lower-lying provinces, and also rations and money. Forced contributions were an inevitable consequence. In a context in which many of the rich were aware that they faced the threat of deportation, these could be both successful and highly resented. Police measures against the disaffected were equally inevitable, and were to be applied in a society in the upper sectors of which Spaniards and Creoles, and the supporters of the old and the new order, were often united by very intimate ties. It is not surprising that the hatred provoked by repression was not confined to the group which was the direct victim of it. Among all the causes of tension, the basic one at last became obvious. Upper Peru did not know whether it had been liberated or conquered. Its men felt themselves to be different to the newcomers from the South. Moreover, the Revolutionary leaders could hardly fail to look on the future of their cause in this territory as uncertain, and act accordingly. The ambiguity of intentions arising from this uncertainty regarding the future demonstrated itself in a variety of ways. A remote but undeniable consequence of it was the attitude of the new régime in Buenos Aires to the greatest item of booty provided by control of Upper Peru: the mining complex of Potosí. The government certainly tried to maintain production, and for easily understandable reasons. But at the same time it was interested in developing the mines of the Famatina region, in La Rioja, which was better protected and closer. It suggested the deportation to that area of the greatest possible number of capitalists, technicians and workers from the mines of Upper Peru whose loyalty was in any way suspect, 'to put them to work in Famatina if they are workmen or to live in the township of La Rioja...if they are wealthy and of good class'.[4] It was not surprising that the loyalty of the whole population of Potosí became increasingly lukewarm. Its inhabitants who, under whatever régime they were to live, wished to maintain their prosperity based on mining, considered the liberators from the South to be capable, in the case of defeat, of effecting irreparable damage to the mines in order to prevent the silver of Potosí from enriching the enemy.

With regard to the pro-Indian policy, there was the same legitimate suspicion. It was above all a weapon of war, used without too much thought about its consequences for the future of upper Peru. Castelli certainly felt more identified than other leaders of the movement with the egalitarian ideology which the Revolution had adopted. But when it was a question of applying this policy in a less remote context than that of Upper Peru he was much more circumspect. He never, for example went so far as to confer the honour of 'distinguished soldier' on members of the half-caste regiments which in fact had distinguished themselves in battle without having received the explicit authorisation of the Junta. This caution on the part of the most audacious of the Buenos Aires Jacobins shows that it was the hope of political advantages, rather than sincere conviction, which inspired the pro-Indian policy. It was precisely for this reason that it survived the supremacy of the moderate faction in Buenos Aires and was to assert itself with more vigour after the defeat and the loss of Upper Peru. After the battle of Huaqui, in fact, the cities of Upper Peru became a solid bloc of hostility towards the Revolutionary troops, who were attacked and driven out of almost all of them. The indignation of the liberators at being expelled by the liberated populations rather than by the enemy's counter-attack was understandably very great. Those 'peoples...without virtues, and born and bred to be obscure slaves...only fully understand the terror or the lash to which they have been subject since they first saw the light of day', wrote the Buenos Aires Intendant of Charcas, Juan Martín de Pueyrredón, in a passage of his report to the Junta which the latter preferred to omit when it published it in the *Gaceta*.[5] After the defeat, and the anti-Revolutionary explosion which followed it, the Revolutionary leaders felt even less responsibility than in the past for the future destiny of Upper Peru. The sole objective, unchecked by any other, now became the pursuit, in that society characterised throughout by the degrading heritage of age-old servitude, of advantages that it might offer to the Revolutionary cause. It was Pueyrredón himself who, when informing the Indians of Upper and Lower Peru of the decree of the Junta which finally (on 1 September 1811) abolished Indian tribute, declared his admiration for the Indians of fifteen villages of Upper Peru who had decided to continue the struggle, in 'a sort of war akin to their military constitution'. It was the weakest part of Peru – as Pueyrredón was making clear – that maintained the rights of man and of peoples. The measure which he thus announced to its beneficiaries not only abolished the tribute but also personal service, and declared to be free of charge the services of parish priests and the officials of justice and the administration. It can readily be seen that Indian emancipation would act to the detriment of an apparatus of domination and exploitation by no means exclusively controlled by the Spaniards.[6]

This policy was never to be abandoned. True, although identification with the Indian inheritors of the pre-Hispanic past became a commonplace of Revolutionary rhetoric, the old attitudes based on a feeling of caste superiority survived. The Swedish envoy Graaner maliciously observed, in 1815, the efforts of Colonel Díaz Vélez to ignore the presence of an Indian chief who was visiting the camp of the Army of the North, whom he thought it demeaning to greet.[7] Moreover, in the zone for which it had direct responsibility the Revolutionary régime tried to limit the progress of Indian emancipation. When, on 10 January 1811, the Junta decreed that in each Intendancy a representative of the Indians should be elected, so that the latter could 'realise the advantages of their new situation', it explicitly excluded the Intendancies of Córdoba and Salta. The representatives of the cities and towns in those jurisdictional areas were certainly in no mind to receive as their equals deputies from an inferior caste.[8]

However, the pro-Indian policy, reserved for the insecure areas of the extreme North, became a method of causing perturbation of much wider scope to the enemy. It was the entire Andean massif, from which the resistance offered by the Viceroy of Peru was extracting most of its resources, which this policy was attempting to convulse. And not without some success. In 1814 a rising led by Pumacahua affected the Cuzco area. After the third advance into Upper Peru ended in 1815 with a third military disaster, the revolutionary presence survived in the *republiquetas*, those pockets of resistance which rendered insecure the rearguard of the triumphant Royalists, and in those places the Indian contribution was decisive. It is easy to understand why this policy was supported by the moderate as well as by the more radical revolutionaries. This was due, not to a blind adherence to ideologies utterly irrelevant to the realities of the situation in Upper Peru, as has been suggested by certain Bolivian historians still affected by the resentment of the Creoles who felt themselves betrayed by their liberators, but to a fairly accurate diagnosis of the social and racial forces in conflict in the area, and of the use which could be made of them as external supports for a Revolution which, almost from the beginning, seemed to look on Upper Peru as foreign territory.

Revolution in stability: Tucumán and Cuyo

In those less remote areas, where the domination of Buenos Aires was only challenged for brief periods by the Royalists who ruled Peru, the attitude of the Revolutionary régime was different from the outset. Of course, actual differences in the characteristics of the regions concerned were at the source of this variety of attitudes. The Indian population integrated into the Spanish areas was everywhere in a minority. Its utilisation as a massive human bloc whose adherence to the Revolutionary cause could strengthen the latter decisively was, furthermore, made difficult by the heterogeneity and mutual isolation of those Indian groups, several of which were completely Hispanicised. At least equally decisive was the well-founded hope of keeping those lands of the Interior within the area controlled by Buenos Aires. This not only lent its entire weight to the conservative tendency which had characterised the social policy of the Revolution from the outset, but lent it an additional justification in the need to avoid disturbing the economic life of regions destined to lie in the rear of the Revolutionary armies, which would depend on them for their rations, their mounts, and, to a lesser extent, their supplies of war matériel.

The prospect of any change that would threaten the hegemony of the *gente decente* over the masses was, therefore, absent from the outset.

However, if one takes into account the capacity of the ruling group to divide against itself, it would be only natural to expect an event like the breakdown of the Colonial system to encourage fresh quarrels. The trump card in such disputes had traditionally been the support of those arbiters, the high-ranking career officials, who by allying themselves with a particular local clique threw the whole weight of the Colonial administration in its favour. The replacement *en masse* of the officials appointed by that administration, and the appearance of emissaries of the new authority, some of whom had themselves been originally natives of the Interior (Colonel Ortiz de Ocampo, for example, the first military leader of the Revolutionary expeditionary force, in whose ability to recruit fresh allegiances the Revolutionary government had placed hopes which were to prove unfounded) or had strong contacts with the region, no doubt provided a very definite encouragement to new local alignments, based on rivalry for the favour of the new arbiters. At the same time uncertainty regarding the future of the Revolutionary movement and the fear of possible reprisals against its adherents placed a restraint on this tendency. It gave grounds for the fear that support would be forthcoming principally from those who had least to lose and most to gain, because they occupied a marginal position within the upper sectors. And such support could be self-defeating, especially if the emissaries of the new authority rewarded the people concerned too generously. By so doing, they ran the risk of changing into hostility the prudent caution of the locally powerful groups, who could not view without alarm the rise of those who in the past had not even dared to challenge them.

In the face of these dangers, the attitude of the emissaries of the Revolution became increasingly circumspect. At first, the alignments seemed to be sufficiently clear. In the open cabildos, at the private meetings of eminent citizens, in the less frequent confrontations between armed forces (which only in Córdoba resulted in a pitched battle, which soon ended in the victory of the expeditionary force from Buenos Aires over local forces ready to flee at the first opportunity), the distinction between supporters and opponents of the movement seemed easy to make. But it was not as easy as that: the Funes brothers, who in Córdoba had done so much to destroy the unanimity of the resistance to the new order, as soon as the latter had triumphed locally used their influence to protect their previous enemies from persecution. Later they were to boast that the counter-revolutionary Bishop Orellana owed them his life. In this activity they were not only guided by humanitarian motives. As has been pointed out by Ceferino Garzón Maceda, Dean Gregorio Funes, appointed by reason of his revolutionary merits to membership of the Supreme Junta of the movement, continued nevertheless to advise his brother to show the greatest possible caution in his demonstrations of adherence to that movement. In a less personal context, Garzón Maceda has also observed

The Revolution in the country as a whole

how the University of Córdoba maintained, towards the change of régime, a silence which contrasts suggestively with its previous willingness to make pronouncements on less important problems.[9] These hesitant attitudes made the situation in the Interior gradually less clear. As a result, the attitude of the delegates of the central authority also became gradually more cautious. It was a question of gaining the maximum advantages that could be obtained from support that was sometimes timid, or even completely insincere, and therefore the most appropriate method was to avoid submitting that support to too severe a test. The instructions left by Feliciano Antonio de Chiclana to his successor in the post of Intendant-Governor of Salta,[10] in December 1810, show an acute consciousness of the complexity of the problem. Chiclana certainly continued to propose solutions which were, from the outset, those adopted by the Revolution: favouring the American-born for appointment to public office, and giving special attention to the Indians, who had to cease being 'considered as slaves'. In both respects, however, he had already learned to take into account other considerations. With regard to public appointments, 'well reputed merit' (a notion which comprised not only technical competence, but also an acceptable social origin) was mentioned before the status of native sons of the country among the qualities candidates were supposed to possess. With regard to the Indians, the first consequence of their liberation was to be their deportation to the mining zones, taking them away from the frontier *reducciones*. Moreover, the need for a more balanced attitude was categorically emphasised: 'The most important thing is for the bands and parties to disappear altogether...As long as the Government refrains from supporting any of the Parties, I am certain that they will fail to gain strength. Impartiality...will keep the People in peace and tranquility, for the jealousies and piques derived from the bestowing of special favours by the leaders are what displease the less well protected...'

These instructions were, of course, difficult to reconcile with the need to reward the Government's friends, which was particularly felt by a Government that needed their solid support in the war against the Counter-Revolution. Chiclana did not forget that 'there are...many good patriots who deserve attention', and urged his successor to continue to show them favour. The Government should, however, as far as possible ignore the existence of opposition to the Revolution, which for the moment was 'restrained, because the majority of citizens, and the success of our arms, does not allow it to act in accordance with its intentions'. With such people, 'great care must be taken, although they must be treated in a politic and courteous manner'. The same treatment should be accorded to the European-born, who formed the nucleus of that potential opposition:

Although not all of them are patriots, all may eventually be of good use: and to this end you must place trust in them, taking due precautions, but in such a way that they do not notice these, for in any case they must be accorded attention even if only in a formal manner, by visiting their houses and families, etc. For the point is that even if one cannot make friends out of enemies, they should at least be put in a position where they are not discontented, nor cause us trouble, as would happen if they were treated with the contempt which they generally deserve.

This passage of labyrinthine prose is an accurate reflection, in its very complexity, of the policy which the Revolution was obliged to follow in the Interior, even towards its enemies. But, with this enclave of implacable hostility only partly neutralised, the emissary of the Revolution must above all take care not to increase its strength by paying attention to 'gossip and stories', against which it was necessary to guard in Salta more than in other provinces. He will also be doing useful work if he makes efforts to reconcile the Bishop – that prelate richly endowed with 'prudence and patriotism' with whom it was necessary to preserve complete harmony – with the Cathedral Chapter.

This programme of action was eminently sensible, but difficult to put into practice. How, in fact, could the emissary of a power both superior to Salta and external to it avoid aligning himself with one of the factions of the small local upper sectors? Once again, the solution proposed by Chiclana was unobjectionable but somewhat vague. The emissary should entrust the investigation of any denunciation to 'honourable men, of whom there certainly are some in this town'. In short, he should choose among his possible local allies those least deserving of distrust. Since such people could not be entirely detached from the conflicts which rent the group to which they belonged, the emissary of the supreme authority was in danger of being trapped with them in the labyrinth he had tried so hard to avoid. With regard to the advice of Chiclana, therefore, one should bear in mind not so much the practical rules to which it gave rise as the general principles underlying it: that of reducing to the minimum the disturbances which, whatever it did, the Revolution was bound to provoke in the internal equilibrium of the upper sectors in the Interior.

This equilibrium was based, not on individuals, but on families. Of course, even in Buenos Aires the importance of family ties was not to be disdained. However, this was true to a lesser extent than in the Interior, for a variety of reasons. An immediate reason was that the Revolution had developed in the capital as a result of a lengthy process, and did not therefore provoke the sudden shock which its impact on the Interior was to cause. Families divided in their political loyalties were particularly numerous in the capital, and the solidarity of such families, without vanishing completely, was affected by such divisions. Another and less immediate reason was the intensity of the changes undergone by Buenos Aires society in the second half of the eighteenth century, which resulted in it having a comparatively unconsolidated structure when the Revolution came.

However, the strength of the family structure in the Interior was immediately increased by the explicit recognition which it received from the Revolutionary authorities. The same ties that in Buenos Aires almost concealed their political effects (it was, for example above all their enemies who pointed out that Posadas was Alvear's uncle, and owed his promotion to that fact), in the Interior they were invoked as an adequate justification of such effects. Thus, in Córdoba a Royalist was granted protection, with the political virtues of his brother-in-law offered as justification. In Salta, too, in carrying out the census of supporters ('the Saravia gentlemen' and 'the Figueroa gentlemen') or opponents ('the Isasmendi family'), Chiclana took almost as much account of families as of individuals. But perhaps the best example of this care to maintain a certain equilibrium among the dominant lineages was to be found in the measures that followed the execution of Colonel Allende, implicated in the armed resistance to the Junta which had taken place in Córdoba. Not only did the Junta address a message to the victim's nephew, Tomás de Allende, expressing respect for 'the illustrious house of the Allendes', which – the Junta had no doubt – 'would not remember the death of your uncle with such horror as the intolerable aberration with which, betraying his blood and his country, he bent all his efforts in favour of the conspirators'. So that that distinguished family 'should not miss...an individual who shamed it for the last third of his life', the patriot Tomás de Allende was granted the rank of Colonel, of which his uncle had been deprived together with his life.[11]

Thus, the execution of the most eminent member of the Allende clan did not prevent its retention in the family patrimony of the victim's colonel's commission, together with other appointments in Church and State. Tomás de Allende declared himself satisfied with this outcome, through which 'Your Excellency has saved the house of my name from the prejudices of the lowly'. Their collective honour having thus been saved, the entire Allende clan now 'ignore the languid voice of blood-relationship and listen to the imperious echoes of the tutelary genius of the Nation'. By disowning that withered branch, which the Junta's decision had rightly cut off, the family-tree was saved from damage. It is true that both the Junta's declaration and Allende's reply may have been echoes of the protests of the Enlightenment against the traditional notion of family solidarity prevailing in cases of dishonour as in those of honour, but the whole episode is a confirmation of the strength of that solidarity. Thoughout it, Tomás de Allende spoke on behalf of the entire family group.

This care to preserve the equilibrium within the ruling sector, the limits of which were in any case not significantly extended, lent the awakening political life of the cities of the Interior a monotony that was able to survive apparently more radical changes. We can see, in the archive of Dean Funes, the political horizons of one of those dominant lineages, which in this case had very early on identified itself with the Revolution. The Funes, until

1810, had had a career marked by ambition and disappointments. After a promising start, the Dean's career apparently came to a complete halt. Bishop San Alberto, who had favoured him, went off to higher things in Upper Peru, and the Dean never occupied the episcopal throne of Córdoba which he coveted. He and his immediate family faced the hostility of the family groups which enjoyed the favour of the Intendant-Governor Sobremonte, whose energetic government seemed to offer excellent opportunities for his protégés. In 1804 Sobremonte left Córdoba, but the circle which had enjoyed his confidence still dominated the scene there. In 1810 the Funes saw the Revolution as, among other things, an unexpected opportunity to escape from their long exclusion. Despite their hesitations, in ever-cautious Córdoba they played the part of decided Revolutionaries, and indeed the Revolution did initiate for the most illustrious Funes a career which, though full of abrupt triumphs and setbacks and never assuring him economic solvency, made the ambitious priest from Córdoba one of the most celebrated, though not the most influential, figures in the new State.

This career took the Dean to Buenos Aires. There remained in Córdoba, as the most eminent member of the family, his brother Don Ambrosio Funes, who was to be for a short time, between 1815 and 1816, Intendant-Governor of Córdoba. Don Ambrosio wrote many letters to his brother to warn him of the storms which he continually saw on the horizon. Although he also worried about more important things (in particular, he was constantly alarmed over the growth of impiety), the brother who remained in Córdoba followed especially, with anguished care, the fluctuations in the power of the family within a context which remained essentially unaltered. In March 1811 Don Ambrosio, after expressing his fears that his previous letters had been intercepted by the Revolutionary authorities of Córdoba, drew up for his brother's benefit a list of enemies and future traitors. He mentioned 'the mad actions and wicked gossip of Lucho Aguirre and his followers', the mischief wrought by Cabrerita, the outrages committed by Saráchaga towards the University, the continuing influence of 'the old gang of the Conchas, Rodríguez, followers of Sobremonte', and he told the Dean not to trust 'Díaz or Baigorri or anybody'.[12] On 5 May he was complaining again: the Pueyrredóns (one of whom was to command the frontier militia in Córdoba, and through him that Buenos Aires family would preserve its influence in the province) were trying to found a party, recruiting for it 'even Mulattoes and women'. Don Ambrosio, to justify his condemnation of that attempt, had only to name its supporters: Díaz, Cabrerita 'and other good-for-nothings',[13] and Baigorri. There was a simple remedy: 'Rid this province of tricksters and ridiculous figures'. Some measures had already been taken. Now it would be necessary to complete the good work by purging the local Junta, created by a dangerous decree of that of Buenos Aires. It would be a good idea to appoint as Intendant-Governor Ortiz de Ocampo or Juan Bautista Bustos. Since both men were needed in Buenos

Aires, the post should be given to José Norberto de Allende, and Díaz, Cabrera and the newly appointed adviser to the Provincial Junta, the staunch Royalist Ortiz del Valle, should all be driven into outer darkness. Eleven days later he was less optimistic: the terrible prospect of a local government dominated by Cabrera or Díaz seemed very close.[14] There was silence until November 1815. In those four years there had been several political revolutions. Córdoba had joined the dissident movement in the Littoral headed by Artigas. The threat of a return of the *ancien régime* had been replaced by that of Revolutionary extremism. But Don Ambrosio's diagnosis was unchanging: 'This people has given itself over to wickedness'. But the wickedness bore the same names as ever: Cabrera, Isasa, 'who is governing today' and who as early as 1811 had been mentioned without enthusiasm, that ignorant man Bulnes, who without being a 'doctor' had had the audacity to succeed in being elected deputy to the next Constituent Congress, the other deputies, whose too loudly exhibited doctors' hoods transformed them, in the eyes of Don Ambrosio into 'untutored pedants, without virtue or repute'.[15] We do, however, begin to observe that between Don Ambrosio and those contemptible adversaries the hostility was not total. Although Funes expected little of that 'great trickster of a son-in-law', the brother of the insolent deputy Bulnes, he thinks it possible to gain, in a lawsuit against these men arising out of a complicated inheritance, the favour of his 'nephew and co-godfather Cabrera'.

In spite of this unexpected ground of understanding, the expressions used by Don Ambrosio remained as emphatic as ever. The offences against honest administration continually committed by that gang of ignorant and corrupt men were bitterly criticised. Isasa was collecting the best of the loot offered by an administrative apparatus gradually slipping towards penury. Although his avarice even caused trouble with his supporters, the latter were imitating him to the best of their ability, and were cheerfully accumulating remunerated deputies' posts and administrative appointments which were also remunerated. Five years later the dissident movement in the Littoral had collapsed, Artigas had begun his thirty years of exile in remote Paraguay, the central authority no longer existed, and Córdoba was – as it was said at the time – independent, that is to say that, even though it did not aspire to the status of a nation, it did not recognise any national authority superior to its own local ones. This great number of changes did not transform the outlook of Don Ambrosio Funes. For the vanished national authority, he had no reason to feel very much nostalgia. Its representative in Córdoba, in the view of this exacting critic, had been too outrageous. He certainly was alarmed at the rise of José Javier Díaz, the same man whom in 1811 he had suspected of Royalism, the follower of Artigas in 1815, the same detestable rival as ever. Even though, adapting himself to the mood of the time, Don Ambrosio composed an ode in honour of Díaz which was not greeted with much applause when recited at the festival which followed the establishment of the latter in power, he celebrated with greater sincerity the swift fall from power of the champion of Federalism. His enthusiasm was all the greater because that fall was provoked by the rising influence of Juan Bautista Bustos, who had already figured in 1811 in Don Ambrosio's brief list of respectable characters: he was, moreover, a relative.

The victory of Bustos, it is true, did not put an end to the worries of Don Ambrosio. How could it be otherwise when he could see the reappearance, displaying their usual mimetic virtues, of his insolent rivals of ever among the followers of the victor? In October 1823 the detestable Ortiz del Valle was still an adviser. Don Ambrosio found it difficult to secure the repeal of judgements he had made in alliance with the equally detestable Doctor Saráchaga.[16] In January 1824 a son of Don Ambrosio could also join in the lamentations: the Dean had been made Minister of Colombia in Buenos Aires, and Córdoba, enviously, watched his triumph with consternation. 'But what can these miserable creatures do if merit and virtue are invincible?' In any case, they would let the Dean feel the consequences of their increased rage. Even Baigorri, who was listed as untrustworthy in 1811, was one of those who 'give the orders in this government'.[17]

In 1824 the national State was again being organised, and Bustos made sure that the Dean was a member of the Córdoba deputation. The Dean, in the opinion of Don Ambrosio, would do well to be wary. Behind this decision Don Ambrosio noted the intrigues of 'that man Saráchaga, the accountant Lozano and Baigorri', who were certainly not trying to do him any favours. Moreover, the electors had first elected Baigorri. Only by the resignation of that obscure canon could the illustrious Dean, the man of letters whose fame had spread throughout both worlds, replace him in the deputation, only to find himself in the humiliating company of that same Eduardo Bulnes who in 1815 had created such a scandal as deputy for Tucumán, and who was still 'both arrogant and ignorant'. In short, in Córdoba all was still subject to the intrigues 'of Saráchaga, Baigorri, his friend Canon Rodríguez, and other Goths'. So things had come full circle: one could still see the followers of Sobremonte, who for over a quarter of a century had conducted against the Funes an untiring guerrilla warfare in the Cabildo and in the Cathedral Chapter, who had been their rivals for the favours of the Royalist Intendant, the Revolutionary delegate and the autonomous Governor, who had employed against them the weapons of intrigue and corruption rather than of forensic science in the law-courts. One could see those execrable men still in possession of all their resources and all their vigour, after a long period of catastrophes.

Even if we discount, in this excessively gloomy picture, attitudes stemming from Don Ambrosio's progressive hypochondria (which eventually made insufferable to him even the presence of his closest relations), the image of stability amid change which his evidence suggests was not,

The Revolution in the country as a whole

however, the fruit of excessive suspicion. The names recorded at both times by his pen were, in fact, those of the men who, in 1810 as in 1825, were very close to those who made the decisions in Córdoba. Moreover, it would be wrong to reject completely the outlook from which Don Ambrosio Funes saw the political process taking place in his province and in the nation. In the political conflict which he followed with alarmed attention, he was interested above all in the rivalries between groups within the urban élite, which were often, though not always, connected by family alliances. (This factor does not of itself, however, explain their rise, among other reasons because in a group as small as that it would not have been easy to find two people not connected in some way by family ties, and also because the family, which might be the basis of a community of interests, also offered admirable opportunities for the growth of fresh rivalries.) That attention was the individual expression of a collective attitude. Within a framework which the Revolution was ceaselessly transforming, what the eminent citizens of Córdoba expected from their political activity was essentially the same as in Colonial times. In the words of Manuel Serapio Funes, the most soberminded of Don Ambrosio's sons, 'they live in a state of continual restlessness', yet even though the news of the Dean's diplomatic career had driven them to 'inconsolable lamentations', 'they quietened down a lot with the establishment of a new post in the University with a salary of six hundred pesos'.[18] In the dispute over this new portion of a booty which had not increased for a long time, they appeared to have forgotten the outrageous successes of the Dean.

In this little world formed by urban élites locked in perpetual conflict with each other, the neutrality so categorically urged by Chiclana might be the most prudent solution, but it was impossible to achieve. The very first of its decisions committed in some way the new agent of the central authority, and assigned him a place in the system of affinities and hostilities in which the locally dominant sector was organised. Yet, although by so doing he ran the risk of becoming entangled in conflicts which were not always easy to control, this did not seriously threaten the equilibrium which the Revolution encountered. On the contrary, by occupying within it the place left by the officials who had served the Crown in that territory, it served to confirm one of the essential characteristics of the system. That equilibrium, however, was characterised by perpetual instability. The alliances and conflicts between rival groups within the élite did not need too many external stimuli to break down and be re-formed. The psychological and moral interpretation of these conflicts given by those who participated in them is a fairly accurate reflection of certain essential elements of that political life, the continual disturbances of which had no effect on its basic characteristics.

However, this continual agitation round a fixed central point, which in

Viceregal times would not have amounted to a serious threat to the existing order, had much more serious consequences in a context transformed by the Revolutionary crisis. To interpret the conflicts in Córdoba simply as an external crusade of certain family clans against others is extremely tempting, especially when some of the protagonists seem to have been incapable of seeing any other aspect of it. But now there was a very important difference, namely the fact that these almost intimate disputes easily became connected with the conflicts between the Buenos Aires Revolution and Artigas's movement, thus amplifying those internal conflicts and eventually unleashing a crisis which would immediately surpass the limits in which the more stable Colonial order had always been able to contain such struggles. It is, therefore, understandable that the agents of the new Revolutionary authority should have given such high priority to attenuating the internal tensions of the élite sectors of the urban centres of the Interior, and that, for example, the success of San Martín as Intendant of Cuyo should be measured by his ability to reconcile the local factions, which had found in the conflicts unleashed in the capital an incentive to divide along the same lines as in Buenos Aires. But the cohesion of the Saavedra and Moreno factions in Mendoza seems to have stemmed, not so much from their common allegiance to their respective models of Revolution, as to the former behaviour of both groups, the rivalry between which actually antedated the Revolution.

Is this to say that in the Interior the activity of the Revolutionary authority was limited to assuaging the differences and alleviating the internal conflicts of an élite which it proposed to recruit *en bloc* for the new order? This was not the case, for several reasons. The Revolution was, however many efforts were made to limit its scope, a break with the past. Because of it, the old system of hierarchies at least had to be justified in a new manner. And, above all, the Revolution had unleashed war. In the Interior, too, the latter was to show itself perhaps as revolutionary in its consequences as the political movement from which it had arisen. The Interior had to contribute to the war effort: from 1810 onwards, little news from the area was as widely disseminated as that which referred to donations for the Army. These accompanied the advance of the Revolutionary armed expedition of 1810, and as late as 1816 and 1817 they survived the affirmation of Revolutionary power throughout the country, after the most serious of the crises it had faced so far.

Those lists of donations reflected the direction of the changes which the war was introducing into the Interior. The earliest lists still show traces of the image of society which existed before the Revolution: explicitly, as in that sent by the Cabildo of Santiago del Estero on 1 February 1810, characteristically entitled 'report on contributions from the Cabildo, the Clergy, the Eminent Citizens and those of lower estate', or implicitly, like other lists of donations headed by the names of corporation members or ecclesiastics.[19] What was even more important was that, except in Corrientes – where the money economy had still scarcely penetrated – the lists are almost always of donations in money, the amounts concerned often being proportionate to the position occupied by the donor in the local hierarchy. It was, therefore, the modest monetary savings accumulated by the urban élites which offered the first tribute to the Revolutionary cause, and the tribute itself was also of modest proportions. Six or seven years later the situation had completely changed. Firstly, the donations were no longer accompanied by the names of the donors, and the voluntary element had almost entirely disappeared. Secondly, donations of money had been largely replaced by those of livestock, grain, and even local cloth.[20] This change of emphasis is understandable: it was precisely by the supply of those articles – and, one might add, by the recruitment of soldiers – that the Interior was able to offer the most abundant resources. Before this happened, however, there had been serious inroads on urban wealth, which in this territory was more limited than in Buenos Aires.

The Funes archive indeed reflects, in addition to the elements of continuity to which an almost obsessive attention was paid, these elements of change which, although less categorically emphasised by the Dean and his correspondents, were still extremely significant. In 1810, although the Dean was not optimistic with regard to his future ecclesiastical career, his post in the Cathedral Chapter of Córdoba guaranteed a satisfactory standard of living, the tithes of Cuyo were the source of his decanal stipend, and the collection of these took place without tiresome delays. Moreover, his family was engaged – for the moment successfully – in commercial transactions in the pursuit of which Sixto Funes, a son of Don Ambrosio, visited both Lima and Buenos Aires. These trading activities were the first to suffer the consequences of the Revolutionary crisis. Sixto Funes was obliged to leave Lima, where the adherence of his family to the Buenos Aires Revolution had compromised him. He brought with him a huge shipment of cocoa hulls, and was unable to find a purchaser either in Chile or in the River Plate region. More serious than the failure of this speculation was the fact that it was no longer possible for him to return to Peru. The family fortunes never recovered from the blow dealt by the end of the commercial connections with the North, a territory now lost to the Revolution. It is true that Don Ambrosio showed some initiative in the face of this adversity. Why not industrialise *jume* – that plant rich in sodium carbonate which grew in the arid and nitrate-rich lands of North-Western Córdoba province – for the manufacture of soap? At the same time, he aspired to supply nitrate and sulphur to the gunpowder factory which was established in Córdoba, and even to sell these products in Buenos Aires. The nitrate was produced in a 'factory' under the supervision of Don Ambrosio himself, following the methods described in books he had found in the Dean's library. He bought the sulphur in La Rioja. 'By ensuring the supply of nitrate and sulphur

I believe that I will soon offset our losses', asserted Don Ambrosio confidently, 'in future we must extend our business into other fields which will be both profitable and compatible with the public good'.[21] On 16 March he had already invested nearly three thousand pesos in the undertaking. He had only produced fifteen *arrobas* of nitrate, but his plans 'look forward to producing two or three *quintales* a day'. On 20 August he admitted that the sulphur business had been disastrous, and he was obliged to sell the produce at a loss, thus transforming a commercial operation into an unforeseen patriotic contribution. As for the manufacture of nitrate, others with more capital had gone into that business, and 'there is so much of it that we shall not harm one another's business'.[22] Four years later he still remembered that unfortunate enterprise, which had left a net loss of six thousand pesos. He was then completely ruined and was under pressure from his creditors. Nevertheless, he raised further loans and opened a calfskin factory, and employed a craftsman who was a refugee from the Banda Oriental, whose skills were much envied by the Fragueiros, who were already engaged in this business. Prosperity once again seemed attainable, if only his creditors would grant him a stay of execution of one year. His new career as an industrial innovator applying the techniques described in the incomplete encyclopaedias in the Dean's library, filled him with enthusiasm: 'I want to die among books and factories. In our old age we hit upon the true fountain of wealth'.[23]

This, however, was not to be. While he went ahead with his plans, Don Ambrosio, in order to survive, had to find a purchaser for his books, although he knew that no one would pay the price that they were worth. Neither as a supplier to the Army nor as an industrialist had he succeeded in recovering his vanished prosperity. While Don Ambrosio Funes was gradually being ruined despite his ambitious hopes, he arrived at a more sober appreciation of the prospects of his illustrious brother. The latter had two principal sources of income: some mills, out of the profits of which – in a moment of enthusiasm which he was to regret for a long time – he had endowed the Chair of Mathematics in the University of Córdoba, and his ecclesiastical stipend, together with the salaries from his civil appointments. The mills ran at a loss throughout the first decade after the Revolution. On several occasions the nephew who was managing them on the Dean's behalf considered the possibility of donating them to the city. This situation was caused by natural catastrophes, recovery from which only became impossible because of the complete absence of monetary reserves in the hands of the Funes brothers. Even the disbursement of a sum of just over one hundred pesos was the subject of lengthy correspondence among the members of the family.[24] The ecclesiastical stipend, which up to 1810 was the most important item of the Dean's income, and the civil salaries added as a result of the Revolution, became increasingly difficult to collect. This was so because the local authorities responsible for collecting them for the Córdoba Cathedral Chapter became progressively more independent of the supremacy of the Governor of Córdoba. From 1814 Cuyo was detached from the Intendancy of Córdoba. Although La Rioja was to remain part of it until 1820, the authority of the provincial capital in that area became increasingly weaker. Moreover, the war imposed new priorities. It was significant that when, in 1821, the Dean managed to persuade the Mendoza authorities to send him his arrears of stipend, those authorities insisted that the operation should remain a secret: their creditors in Mendoza itself would be indignant if they learned of the privileged position accorded to the Dean. This position was not to secure for him immediate tangible advantages. As was pointed out by the Dean's correspondent in Mendoza, Manuel Ignacio Molina, although the Government had recognised in principle its obligations to those who were owed arrears of tithes, 'the actual payment of these will be liable to long delays'.[25]

This was not the only way in which the war and the internal instability had a detrimental effect on ecclesiastical incomes. In answer to the Dean's expression of surprise at the small amount of the tithe-payments, his correspondent became somewhat indignant: 'It is surprising that you, knowing that the men of Santa Fe, on the pretext of their conflict with Buenos Aires, are making it their business to rob the muleteers and cart-drivers of Mendoza, should be ignorant of the reason for these reductions'. Since the exports of produce had declined and the collection of tithes had become increasingly difficult, there was a drop in the number of people ready to bid for the farmed tax, and their offers were ridiculously small. Was this, in fact, the only reason, or must one take into account the attitude of local authorities more prepared to favour local and often influential bidders than the remote beneficiaries of tithes? Be that as it may, the penury of the Mendoza government was by no means feigned, and from that quarter, as from San Juan, the Dean received only lengthy excuses.

In addition to external and civil war, it was the transformation of the commercial structures which adversely affected the Dean's income. Molina considered that prosperity would rapidly return to Mendoza – and in consequence to Mendoza's eternal creditor, the Dean of Córdoba – if the city recovered its place in the Peruvian and Chilean trade. In gratitude for the city's services to the Revolutionary cause, San Martín should use his influence in Lima 'to deprive the British of some of the trade that they carry on by sea, and which they have usurped from us'.[26] If this was a hint that the Dean should use that influence which the naïve provincials still imagined he had on the course of the Revolution, no attention was paid to it. The Dean preferred to use that influence to persuade the Liberator of Peru to defend his own right to the tithes payable by the governments of the Cuyo region, which, he had no doubt, would find a way to pay them if they really looked for one,[27] and meanwhile his relations in Córdoba wanted San Martín to help in collecting debts owing to Sixto Funes in Lima when he left so hurriedly in 1810.[28]

It was not only in Mendoza that economic setbacks were having their effects. Throughout the Bishopric of Córdoba, the farmers were demanding to pay their tithes in produce instead of in money, which was growing increasingly scarce. The Chapter refused: to convert into cash tithes received in this form would be both onerous and complicated.[29] After 1820, the consequences of growing political fragmentation were felt even more severely. The government of Mendoza abolished tithes on livestock, that of San Luis abolished all tithe payments to the see of Córdoba, and that of La Rioja simply allowed its debt to accumulate.[30] The Canons had lost even the desire to continue negotiations with 'the sovereign authorities of those *Insulae*', and preferred to share out among themselves the tithes of Córdoba province, leaving to the absent Dean the rights to the tithes of those provinces that refused to pay them. Ambrosio Funes, on his brother's behalf, accepted the payment in flour proposed by La Rioja. The fact that his brother Mariano had, in conjunction with the mills he was managing, established a bakery, facilitated the immediate utilisation of the tribute from La Rioja. Moreover, Don Ambrosio had previously had experience of collecting tithes in money minted in La Rioja, which had a precious metal content of only 30 per cent and had to be melted down to extract the silver, so he preferred to collect the tithes in produce.

Difficulties, therefore, continued. Don Ambrosio unceasingly deplored the perversity of the times. What was needed was 'an authority and a force capable of stamping out these crimes committed by the usurpers of the property of the Church'.[31] But for the moment there was no such authority and Don Ambrosio tried, without much success, to make up for its absence by brandishing over La Rioja the threat of 'the canonical sanctions incurred by those who interfere with or usurp ecclesiastical income destined for the upkeep of religion and the sustenance of its ministers, whatever may be said by immoral people and freethinkers'.[32]

The civil salaries which were supposed to complement the Dean's ecclesiastical income were not always easy to collect. As a deputy on various occasions between 1810 and 1827, the Dean did not receive his salary from the Treasury of Buenos Aires, but from that of Córdoba, and again there were unceasing lamentations from Don Ambrosio over the delays in payment of the latter body. Thus the illustrious citizen of the Republic was poorer than he had been as Dean before 1810, and it was this penury which drove him to accept positions not always free from danger. From 1821 onwards he wrote articles in the *Argos*, and thus – as Ambrosio did not cease to remind him – committed himself, despite all his caution, to the ecclesiastical polemics and those arising from the rivalry between his province of birth and that of his residence. It was to be his close connection with Bolívar which freed him from that perilous position as a journalist. To it he owed his appointment as Minister of Colombia in Buenos Aires and his deanery in La Paz Cathedral. However, this entry of Funes into the orbit of Bolívar was viewed with misgivings in Buenos Aires, especially because the Dean considered these appointments quite compatible with his continued membership of the Constituent Congress. Don Ambrosio expressed the wish that he would resign his post as deputy, which was particularly dangerous because a new total crisis of the political order was approaching. Again, however, the Dean was not in a position to comply. His Colombian and Bolivian incomes were not always any more regular than that derived from his corner of the provinces. Thus, both the Dean and Don Ambrosio approached death's door without freeing themselves of penury, and it was that penury which filled their letters with innumerable allusions to small sums of money, the collection of which could, however, change everything, and which endowed the Dean with an over-cautious attitude which eventually finished his political career, and led to Don Ambrosio's ending up as a vendor of relics of doubtful authenticity.

Whereas both Church and State showed themselves increasingly incapable of ensuring the decorous sustenance of that proud family, the mills, after 1820, enjoyed a period of prosperity. Mariano Serapio Funes seemed to be an efficient manager. He had also established a bakery, to ensure an outlet for the flour ground in the mills. He also received grain from Mendoza, where his purchasing agent was José Albino Gutiérrez, a landowner who was later to become Governor of his province. But the limited resurgence of these mills was not sufficient to save the Funes family from decline: 'It seems like a jest', observed Mariano Serapio Funes, 'that this busy factory should be the only source destined by Providence for the maintenance of such a large family. All eat and clothe themselves from these profits'.[33] This did not happen, however, without a painful adaptation. 'Four years ago', wrote Mariano Serapio in 1821, referring to his sister Ignacia,

> I had the painful experience of finding her one day crying on account of her poverty – she did not have half a loaf of bread to give her pretty little daughter. When I learned the cause of her sorrow, I lent her a few pesos to buy grain, grind it in our mills and maintain herself on the profits. In fact, this business turned out very well, and she has lived on it for four years and, moreover, has been able to save a tidy little capital sum of six or seven hundred pesos, with which she has been able to buy a bakery.[34]

Thus was Ignacia Funes enabled to escape from poverty. It is true that her humble activity in the retail trade was less socially humiliating in a zone where that activity enjoyed a long-standing prestige. Almost contemporary with Mariano Serapio's letter was the proclamation of that Governor of Tucumán who, when setting off to take part in the civil war, declared that he had abandoned the shop-counter to gird on his sword. Even so, however, the Funes family carried on their lives – when the worst of the crisis had passed – at a standard of living so depressed that a sum of under a thousand pesos could be looked on as a 'tidy little capital sum' capable of ensuring the future.

This collapse was not just that of one family: it was that of the most obvious sources of urban wealth that had existed in late Colonial times. Certainly, not all who had belonged to the urban élite during that period suffered so severe a setback from the Revolutionary crisis as did the Funes. In Córdoba itself there were some who resisted the setback more successfully, because they had a more solid basis in commerce and depended to a lesser extent than the Funes on administrative and ecclesiastical incomes, and, above all, because they had something that the Funes lacked: extensive rural properties. While Don Ambrosio was untiringly lamenting his own ruin, he found occasion to deplore that which, unexpectedly and for only a short time, seemed to threaten his friend, the Mendoza correspondent and business agent José Albino Gutiérrez, who after being Governor of Mendoza was thrown out of office and ran the risk of losing a fortune 'of perhaps over three hundred thousand pesos'.[35] This incident was all the more serious because, with the co-operation of Gutiérrez, Don Ambrosio not only hoped to obtain the payment of the tithes owed to his brother, but to recover his own fortune by offering his protector from Mendoza opportunities for speculation in Córdoba, which Don Ambrosio was unable to exploit more directly through lack of the necessary capital. These are examples of the way in which the Revolution meant ruin for some sectors of the urban élite, but protected others from that fate.

The career of José Albino Gutiérrez was, in its way, as typical as the gradual ruin of the Funes family. Born in Mendoza in 1773 of a Spanish father and a Creole mother, he inherited extensive properties and a fleet of wagons – employed on the trade with Buenos Aires. These he managed efficiently and made more prosperous. Simultaneously he pursued an inactive career as an officer in the Mendoza militia cavalry. He was a lieutenant and then a captain in 1808, a squadron commander in 1816, and in the same year was given command of the entire militia cavalry of Mendoza. While the officers of the Regular Army whom San Martín had recruited in Cuyo followed him to Chile, Gutiérrez, commanding a militia recruited to a large extent from among his own peons, took a decisive part in the maintenance of internal order.[36] This did not interrupt the process of self-enrichment. Nevertheless, that wealth and the number of men employed by him in his rural and transport enterprises ceased to be a purely private matter. His public career and his political influence, which seems not to have been sought deliberately, were derived from those very factors. This happened, no doubt, because the Revolution had weakened the political power bases that might have counterbalanced those at the disposal of Gutiérrez, and which even before his rise had been less important in

Mendoza than in a place like Córdoba, which was the seat of a Bishopric and an Intendancy, but also because the increased commitments imposed by the Revolution obliged the political authority to effect an increasing delegation of functions and attributions to figures who occupied positions like that of Gutiérrez in the economic and social system.

The effects of this progressive delegation of power are revealed even more clearly in the rise of a figure who, like Gutiérrez, only came into the foreground of public life after the dissolution of the national authority in 1820, but was to occupy there a far more important place than the prosperous landowner and reluctant public man from Mendoza: the leader from La Rioja, Juan Facundo Quiroga.

It has been observed previously that Quiroga's origin closely reflected the history of those Rioja plains which had evinced a marked economic rise during the Viceregal period. His father, José Prudencio Quiroga, was a native of Jáchal, in San Juan, and had brought capital and livestock from his home, bought and settled *estancias* and married an heiress from the Plains. In the last years of the Colonial period his name figured as the holder of police and militia appointments in the Plains region. In such functions, he appears to have been completely obedient to the authorities which delegated their powers to him, for he was, at least, quoted as an example to his turbulent son.[37] At first the Revolution changed very little of this. La Rioja was still subject to the Governor of Córdoba, and the rich man from San Juan continued to fill his usual appointments, alternating in them with members of other dominant families of the Plains region: the Villafañes, the Brizuelas, the Ocampos.

Although, however, just as in Córdoba, the Revolution provoked little change in the composition of the dominant sector in the Plains, in other respects the innovations brought by it were considerable. From the point of view of the Revolutionary authority, La Rioja, remote from the areas where the fighting was going on, was above all a supplier of men, horses, mules and cattle. While in the minute capital city the families connected with the Cabildo continued to indulge in their habitual rivalries, this new function which the zone had acquired lent increasing importance to those who could in fact supply the resources which the new authority required.

This transformation had more obvious effects in the Plains than in the Andean foothills of La Rioja. In the Plains there was a relative abundance of men prepared to leave their homes and ride as soldiers over the roads which they had got to know on their peacetime journeys with their droves of mules and herds of cattle, and there those mules and cattle, which were needed by the Revolutionary armies, could also be found. This reservoir of resources located in a secure but close rearguard area had to be governed energetically. The local authorities, which in Colonial times had been subject to only a lax control in their police and minor judicial functions, acquired new powers as a result of their satisfying these new requirements. It was in this context where innovations were beginning to take place that Juan Facundo Quiroga began his public career, which we can follow in his Archive. In 1816 he replaced his father as a militia captain in San Antonio de los Llanos, and in January 1818 he replaced Juan F. Peñaloza as military commander of Malanzán. In both appointments his principal task was the rounding up of cattle for the army fighting in the North, and also for the factions which successively dominated the complex political scene in La Rioja. In a province where the slaughter of cattle had led to a shortage of beef for consumption, and where, therefore, commercial exports to other areas were reduced to half by executive decree,[38] the pressures applied to obtain cattle naturally became increasingly intense. And it was the military commander who could despoil those under his jurisdiction of their principal wealth, but who could also – if he chose to be merciful – spare them by looking for other victims. For those who did not have too much to lose the authority of the captain and his superior the military commandant conveyed a more direct threat: they were the first to suffer the effects of the levies (only as a last resort had the 'well born'[39] been called to the Colours in La Rioja). Even more unprotected was the itinerant population and those without fixed employment, who in Western La Rioja were numerous. Here, as in the other provinces of the River Plate region, the work-certificate system for the peons was again put into force. The vagrants were the first candidates for the extraordinary levies and, even without counting them, enlistment was the usual punishment for recidivist criminals.[40]

The circumstances of war therefore conferred wider powers on these local executive authorities, military, police and judicial, which in Colonial times had occupied a decidedly secondary position in the administrative system. Moreover, the new functions and the reactions which they provoked obliged those officials to arrange adequate armed protection for themselves. Militarisation, which at first had affected only the areas directly touched by the war, was extended to the entire Revolutionary territory.

There was thus formed, in the first decade after the Revolution, a network of subordinate and executive authorities which were to display more solidity than those from which they took their orders. In this first phase – which was decisive for their subsequent consolidation – this rise took place under the aegis of the central authority, rather than in conflict with it. Even if Juan Facundo Quiroga still occupied, in the hierarchy of political power, a place so low that the supreme authority was still unaware of his existence, the intermediate authorities congratulated him, no doubt sincerely, on the efficiency with which he carried out his orders. As a captain and later as a commander, he always managed to supply at the right time the men and resources which the authorities demanded. Why was the Revolutionary Government, which was so sensitive to the dangers of too great a transference of power to the subordinate authorities in its capital, so indifferent to similar dangers in the territory which it governed from that

The Revolution in the country as a whole

capital? There is, perhaps, a partial explanation in the Spanish and European political tradition, which saw in the unruly urban masses the source *par excellence* of potential political disturbances, a tradition confirmed by the experience of the years preceding the Revolution, when it was in fact growing urban agitation which eventually unleashed that movement. But there is another and even more decisive reason: even if it had been aware of the danger, the Revolutionary régime would have been able to do very little to prevent it. In the Interior it was looking for men and resources and had to extract them from the territory by imposing a strong authority. The increasing cost of the war which obliged it to embark ever more resolutely on the path of forced contributions also forced it to grant increasing freedom of initiative to its agents, whom it had had to recruit among those who already possessed local bases of power and prestige.

In order to follow any other path, the Revolutionary régime would have had to have precisely those resources which it lacked. To create a body of officials paid by the Treasury for each rural district, and supply them with the armed support needed to secure obedience, were both undertakings too costly for the new state. For this reason, its only possible course was to delegate local authority to those who, even without it, were already the most powerful figures on the local scene.

Around 1820, the political consequences of this process were still far from evident. It is true that in the Interior, even before that date, there were confrontations with the central authority, but these had as their basis the regular armies, as in the case of the passive rebellion of the Army of the North against Alvear in 1814, or the local Cabildos, as in Córdoba and La Rioja at the time of the brief adventures of Federalist secession in 1815, or a combination of both (for example the refusal of Mendoza to accept the replacement of San Martín as Intendant-Governor ordered by Alvear). In all those conflicts the new type of local political authority, which war was strengthening, still had a secondary rôle, if it played any part at all. However, although its impact on the political equilibrium of the entire country was still not evident, the displacement of power was already taking place. The new relationship revealed in the commercial transactions between the Funes family and José Albino Gutiérrez was to have its political counterpart some years later in the relationship between the Governor of Córdoba, Bustos, and the Plains chieftain Quiroga, on whose protection he depended to preserve his power.

In this way the Revolution, which impoverished the cities of the Interior and gave new political power to its local agents, who on its behalf had to requisition the human and economic resources of the rural zones, opened up new opportunities for the local leaders, whom the Revolution had recognised and consolidated in a position of authority, the local roots of which antedated the Revolution itself. The dissolution of the central authority in 1820 swiftly revealed some of the consequences of this unforeseen innovation, which was certainly the most important introduced by the Revolution into the equilibrium of power in the Interior. Its full scope, however, only became evident gradually, in the course of the complex process initiated by the collapse of 1820.

An unforeseen innovation... There was, however, one corner of the Interior where that innovation was introduced quite deliberately and on a greater scale than anywhere else. In Salta, after three unsuccessful attempts to achieve the definitive conquest of Upper Peru, the River Plate Revolution resigned itself to fighting a defensive war, and preferred to do so with local resources. This obliged the central authority to delegate to the local executive authorities much wider functions than those which in more sheltered areas were sufficient to ensure an adequate flow of men and resources for the war. But not only was the extent of the attributions delegated much greater, the actual area over which these new powers were to be exercised was much more extensive. It was not a militia captain's or major's jurisdictional district, but an entire province which broke off from the direct political control of the central authority with the complete approval of the latter. 'Güemes's system' seemed to run counter to the most profound tendencies of that régime of the Directory, which was not really revolutionary in content, and which – far from disputing his control over Salta – accorded him decisive protection. Here the political revolution stressed, rather than hid, the simultaneous social revolution. It is true that this attitude did not result in any radical and systematic transformation of the social order, but nevertheless the very suggestion ran counter to the posture of increasing respect towards the inherited order which the River Plate Revolution had adopted after 1815.

It is true that this original character of the course of events in Salta was due to Salta itself, to its pre-Revolutionary past and the outbreak there of an interminable war. These peculiar features are, however, more understandable if one bears in mind that – even outside Salta – the action of the Revolution in the Interior was necessarily less respectful towards the established order than the Revolutionary leaders had actually intended. By submitting the Interior to the dual impact of a transformation in the pattern of trade and of a war effort which could not fail to affect the social and political equilibrium of the region, the Revolution was to impose on that area changes which were destined to last. In this context, Salta under the rule of Güemes was an extreme case rather than an exception in the Interior.

Salta and 'Güemes's system'

Up to 1815, Salta had certainly been more intensely affected by the war than other areas of the Interior, but this difference was reflected to only a limited extent in the vicissitudes of Revolutionary policy there. As the seat of an Intendancy, Salta had experienced in 1814 the detachment from its jurisdiction of the new province of Tucumán, which included Tucumán, Catamarca and Santiago del Estero. It had been governed – except during the intervals of occupation by Royalist troops – by Intendant-Governors appointed from Buenos Aires and often alien in origin to the province to which they were assigned. Within this formal continuity, however, changes had already begun to take place. In no other place had the Revolution created more profound divisions than in Salta. Although at first they were not more serious than those experienced by other more sheltered areas, the prospect of a swift return of the city to Royalist control gave the supporters of the old order a tenacity which was generally lacking in places where they could see no other future than one of persecution at the hands of their ardent enemies. This explains the continued existence of a Royalist sector of opinion which found support among some of the most influential families, and the harshness of Revolutionary policy in this theatre of war provoked fresh antipathy to the movement.[41] Furthermore, support for the Revolutionary cause was no more unanimous among the rest of the population. It was the Royalist occupations, especially the second one, when Pezuela systematically sacked the city, which consolidated the Revolutionary party in Salta, still with the leaders it had had since 1810. Resistance began in the South of the province, its principal leader being Apolinar Figueroa, the head of the family which in 1810 had donated twenty-two of the twenty-eight thousand pesos collected in Salta for the expedition to Upper Peru. It was then that Güemes reappeared in Salta, whence he had been banished in 1812 by a resolution of Belgrano.

His presence was to have an immediate effect on the course of events in Salta, which until then had followed along lines roughly similar to those of the other districts of the River Plate region. The war had, of course, led to militarisation, which also followed conventional lines. There were two urban military units, divided by a rigid caste barrier, and numerous corps of rural militia organised and equipped by the big landowners who commanded them.[42] The Invasions had constituted the acid test for this system of militia units. Some had ceased to exist effectively, whilst others became the nuclei of a resistance which took the form of stubborn guerrilla warfare. What contribution did Güemes make to this movement of resistance which had begun in his absence? Martín de Güemes was the son of a Crown official who failed to make his fortune in the Indies, in spite of his marriage to a descendant of the founder of Jujuy, which gave him some landed property. This origin gave him a place in the upper class of Salta. Marriages between Spanish-born officials or merchants and heiresses from families well endowed with coats-of-arms and land but not with money, had given rise, in the second half of the eighteenth century, to a group which for two centuries was to occupy a dominant position in the province. The modest nature of his family fortunes placed him, equally unmistakably,

From Viceroyalty to 'United Provinces of the River Plate'

outside that smaller nucleus whose leadership was recognised by the upper class as a whole. His career – a military one, in a distinguished regiment – was also typical of that sector to which he belonged. Between 1805 and 1810 it was to take him to Buenos Aires, and in 1810, the Revolution took him back to Salta for two years. In 1814 it was a decision of San Martín that took him back to his province for a second time. On the Frontier, the parts of Salta bordering on Tucumán, this career officer organised militias which had greater success in battle than those raised by the big local landowners. In this activity, however, he was able to count on the support of one of those families of big landowners, the Gorritis, who were powerful both on the Frontier and in Jujuy. He was promoted lieutenant-colonel in May 1814, and full colonel in September of that year. His successes against the Royalists occupying the city of Salta obliged them to abandon it. The national Army advanced across this territory which had been cleared of the enemy, and Güemes found it difficult to find in it a post worthy of his ability. While tension mounted between him and the commander-in-chief, Rondeau, in the city the Cabildo received without enthusiasm the new Intendant appointed from Buenos Aires, General Hilarión de la Quintana, whose efficiency in collecting further contributions for the army certainly did not increase his popularity. When Güemes, in April 1815, resigned from the national army, Quintana had already left his post, and the Cabildo of Salta was exercising those functions on an interim basis. In May, when the news reached Salta of the fall of the Director Alvear, that same Cabildo convoked an assembly of distinguished citizens which appointed Güemes Governor, after the submission of a popular petition and plea by Doctor Pedro Arias Velázquez, the city's legal representative and related through his wife to the leader who was to be elected.

This outcome of the dual crisis – administrative and military – of Salta is easily understandable. Güemes was able to offer the Cabildo, which by getting rid of Quintana had won only a battle, not a decisive victory, a guarantee against the interference of the emissaries of the factions successively dominant in Buenos Aires. With the central authority itself facing a serious crisis, the acceptance of the *fait accompli*, in exchange for Salta's loyalty to the new holders of the central power, became much easier. In achieving this solution, Güemes's contribution was decisive. It was not only a question of the prestige he had won as a successful military leader; the following of men and the booty of small arms which he had brought with him in his withdrawal were perhaps even more immediately useful. With them and with new deserters from the regular army, whom he welcomed with systematic hospitality, Güemes managed to create, in addition to the locally recruited militias, units recruited from the whole province and made up of soldiers with a longer, though not necessarily more brilliant, combat record, who could also offer the Governor an undivided political loyalty, because the officer commanding was no longer merely the landowner who had raised the unit in the area of his influence, and he felt entitled to political (and not merely military) leadership over his men.

The rise of Güemes, accepted from 1815 onwards as leader by his peers of the Salta upper class, to an increasingly undivided authority, coincided with the permanent presence of the war in Salta. Reconciliation with the central authority posed no difficulties. Rondeau, who had outlawed Güemes, was obliged – on his return from Upper Peru, where he had suffered a catastrophic defeat – to be reconciled to him. Although, under the Directory of Pueyrredón, the reconstitution of the political centre of the Revolution in Buenos Aires took place more quickly and successfully than might have been expected in May 1815, it contained no element of opposition to the political system which had been established in Salta. In return for the services which Güemes was giving in the North against the Royalist threat, his local pre-eminence would no longer be disputed.

These services, however, imposed on the entire province a heavy burden. Repeated Royalist invasions and the maintenance of military forces numbering several thousand, in a province where the total population did not exceed 50,000, was a severe blow to a regional economy already affected by the closure of the Northern route, on the traffic of which the greater part of its productive activities had depended. All this could only be carried on on the basis of contributions, the voluntary nature of which became increasingly dubious, and which were the cause of increasing tension between the Governor and that upper class whose domination of the corporate institutions (the Cabildo and the deliberative and electoral assemblies convoked at various times by the Governor) was never even questioned by the new system. That upper class, however, found itself in a situation of enforced collaboration with the Governor whom it had helped to instal, and who possessed outside that sector solid power-bases among the plebeian classes of Salta, which seemed to have abandoned their passivity, especially in the Eastern and Southern parts of the province, and which considered themselves to be the protagonists and principal beneficiaries of Güemes's 'system'; nor could it count on the support of the central government, to which it was essential that Salta should continue to play its rôle as the Northernmost bulwark of the movement, even at the cost of the ruin of local fortunes.

Plebeian adherence to Güemes's 'system' was in fact wholehearted, and for easily understandable reasons. In that area where the distance between the plebs and the upper class was very great, the mobilisation unleashed by Güemes made of the plebeians the first class in the State. In contrast to an élite which was far from being unanimous in its support for the Revolutionary cause, the Patriot plebs identified itself with the revolution in Salta. And that unexpected recognition granted by the new political power was accompanied by other advances that were perhaps no less significant. The government had freed tenant farmers from the obligation to pay tribute in money, labour or produce to the proprietors. One would, of course, need to have fuller information as to how far this law was given practical effect, but even so, it is difficult to credit the assertion of Dámaso de Uriburu, who in his highly biassed *Memorias*[43] asserted that the peasants had too much respect for their landlords to take advantage of this measure, and with a moving unanimity continued to pay their dues. The government had also undertaken the responsibility of ensuring the upkeep of those overnumerous armed forces, only to transfer that responsibility to those who possessed the resources to meet it. It was the owners of livestock and alfalfa plantations who, in the last resort, paid the costs of keeping that cavalry in the saddle. The worst conflicts seem to have arisen out of the distribution of that excessively heavy burden. In the resentful recollection of the Salta landowners Güemes's system was summarised in the recurring image of the Patriot gauchos riding into the carefully irrigated alfalfa-fields, undoing in hours the labour of years, and carrying off the cattle to sate their hunger with beef. In such episodes it was the sources of both their wealth and their hegemony which appeared threatened. The destruction was all the more alarming because those who inflicted it had for centuries accepted the harsh discipline of the landowners.

The Governor was, of course, aware of the extent to which this method of financing the war was alienating those who had established him in local power, but he had no alternative. It was, very characteristically, one of those assemblies in which the Creole élite had complete control which rejected the Governor's proposals for establishing a system of taxation which would no doubt be more onerous but would be based on objective criteria, and would affect commerce and transport. It preferred to keep the system of extraordinary contributions, imposed by the authorities on various groups and persons, which left a greater margin for arbitrary decisions. For the time being, in fact, those members of the élite who were to continue to lend Güemes their increasingly unenthusiastic collaboration do not seem to have considered such arbitrary methods to be reprehensible, and it is easy to understand that they should have preferred them in so far as they allowed them to pass a disproportionate share of the burden onto those who were less well protected politically, principally the Spanish-born, who in 1818 and 1819 were still being subjected to extraordinary exactions.[44] Despite these expedients, which might offer a certain immediate relief, sympathy for a régime which seemed prepared to destroy by warfare the entire wealth of the province naturally began to wane. Güemes did try – at first with some success – to avoid exasperating this latent opposition. He treated even the most open forms of it with a moderation exceptional in Revolutionary Argentina. Although, after his death, some of his enemies tried to picture him as a monster from Hell, they found it less easy to point to a single victim who had lost his life as a punishment for opposing that tyrant. Such magnanimity was possible thanks to the broad nature of the support which

Güemes enjoyed outside the élite. The latter ran the risk of being destroyed if it confronted the Governor openly, when he was the idol of the Salta masses.

The solidity of this political order did not alter the fact that it had in its very foundations a cause of progressive debilitation: the war. The method of distributing the burden of the war was, no doubt, the reason for Güemes's popularity with the masses. In the long run, however, that burden, first thrown onto the shoulders of the upper sectors (and, above all, its less well protected individuals and groups) was to fall on the entire population of Salta. This happened with ever-increasing intensity and, although the resistance against the Royalists from Peru was successful, the success only seemed to make possible an indefinite continuation of that resistance, which was exhausting the province. This consideration carried little weight with the Buenos Aires Government, which offered Güemes its unconditional support. However, the progressive dissolution of that central authority made its support an increasingly less important factor, and a similar development within the Royalist camp (which eventually came to be represented in Upper Peru by the almost independent authority of General Olañeta) deprived the struggle of much of its urgency after 1817, at least from the point of view of Salta. From then on, the days of 'Güemes's system' were numbered. While it lasted, however – and it lasted for the lifetime of its founder, killed by a Royalist invading force in 1821, so that it outlasted the régime of the Directory in Buenos Aires – it constituted a somewhat unexpected component of that political system which boasted of having emptied the Revolutionary régime of all revolutionary content.

It was the constant presence of war which determined the originality of the course of political events in Salta. It was war, too, which underlay the dissident movement in the Littoral. Both in Salta and in the Banda Oriental the Revolutionary régime tried to utilise local support which it later found difficult to contain. The Banda Oriental, however, and to an even greater extent the territories to which the Littoral dissident movement spread, formed part of the area over which Buenos Aires had exercised a direct and unquestioned control. This was one of the reasons why the revolutionary experience in the Littoral, which had so much in common with that of Salta, took place not in harmony with the central authority, but in constant antagonism to it.

THE OTHER REVOLUTION: ARTIGAS AND THE LITTORAL

After 1811, in fact, a revolutionary process which Buenos Aires had encouraged, but over which it soon lost control, took place first in the Banda Oriental and then in the rest of the Littoral. In 1815 it advanced beyond the frontiers of what was already being considered as its own territory, towards Córdoba and La Rioja, and for a moment it seemed as if its influence was to be imposed on the Northern territories of the Revolutionary nation. Although these advances were ephemeral, even in 1820 the Littoral dissident movement was able to overthrow for a second time the Revolutionary authority established in Buenos Aires, thus giving the decisive blow to that central authority, which was not to be reconstituted in the River Plate region for another forty years.

This process, however, which soon surpassed the local and regional context, terminated – as did the more limited experiment in Salta – in a total collapse, and – again as in Salta – without leaving any heirs to a system of political ascendancy which nevertheless survived in the memory of the popular following which had taken part in those experiences. This retrospective loyalty was not shared by the leaders who managed to retain their influence in the very different political climate after 1820. In Salta, the old allies of Güemes unceasingly denounced his tyrannical and rapacious government. In the Banda Oriental it was the former followers of Artigas – Rivera and Lavalleja – who joined in the chorus of condemnation and solemnly promised never to imitate the behaviour of the man under whose leadership they had entered the lists. The dissident movement in the Littoral and Güemes's system were, therefore, the fruit of war: they were born with it, and they died from it. But if this makes understandable their disappearance as feasible political options after 1820, it does not explain the universal condemnation to which they were retrospectively subjected, which was usually justified in terms of opposition to the socially revolutionary orientation of those movements. Even when Federalism in the Littoral was almost at an end, the Buenos Aires *Gaceta* was still able to represent it as an insurrection of those who had nothing to lose and therefore took a delight in destroying other people's wealth. We may observe in this hostile picture two distinct elements: on the one hand, the dissident movement was denounced as a faction led by those who were not resigned to continue in a state of social, economic and political inferiority; and, on the other hand, it was represented as an orgy of destruction of laboriously accumulated wealth.

Neither of these reproaches was the product of sheer fantasy. Neither, however, exactly describes the original characteristics of the Littoral experience. The social bases of the process were, from the very beginning, complex, and, moreover, the impact of the movement on the social equilibrium was far from being identical in all the areas affected. It was certainly much greater in the Banda Oriental than in the provinces to the West of the River Uruguay, and even in the former area it was particularly intense in those localities along the banks of the river where Artigas's movement established its first base. It was there that figures of comparatively humble origin rose to positions of leadership. This phenomenon, however, which was in part due to the more direct influence exercised by Artigas himself on the movement in that district, may also be explained by the characteristics of the region. There was a large number of absentee landowners, who lived in Buenos Aires and wished to see their properties remaining in territories controlled by their city; and, especially in the North of the district along the river bank, there was an even greater number of squatters without title to their property, not all of whom were necessarily poor. In this context a farm overseer, a squatter or a cattle-dealer of modest means did not have to overcome the rivalry of socially superior or economically more powerful figures in order to emerge as a political leader. The innovation – a scandalous one in the eyes of those who saw with increasing alarm the deterioration of the pre-Revolutionary social order – consisted, not so much in the emergence within the district of leaders who in the past had occupied humble positions in local society, as in the very emergence of those marginal districts as the centres of a new power.

For this reason, the revulsion provoked by Artigas's movement was not qualified by the reflection that in other zones of the Banda Oriental it found local leaders who belonged more unmistakably to the élite than did those of the riparian district: the Rivera brothers, whose lands extended from San José to the North of the Río Negro, Lavalleja in Minas, Otorgués in El Pantanoso, quite close to Montevideo. Even under those leaders with a socially more acceptable background, it was a region accustomed to keeping quiet and obeying orders which was now claiming a share of power. For this reason, the accusation of 'upstart' was levelled even at Artigas, who was the grandson of one of the founders of Montevideo and had been born into one of the most highly regarded families of the city's élite. Even though it gives us a systematically deformed picture of the origin of the future leaders of Artigas's movement, this hostile description of the character of the movement was then by no means a mere fantasy. The establishment of a centre of political power in the rural areas of Uruguay was not a mere geographical displacement. It was, at the same time, a displacement of the social bases of political power. Benavides, a farm overseer, and Lavalleja, the son of a small landowner, and even Fructuoso Rivera were able to occupy, in that corner of the territory which they conquered for the Revolution, a place of eminence which antedated the beginning of the Revolutionary process. But there is no doubt that even in the context of the Banda Oriental, let alone in that of the River Plate region as a whole, their position in the pre-Revolutionary period did not offer them any opportunity of dominating the political scene.

The revolution of Artigas was, therefore, essentially a rural insurrection. In the course of it, the displacement of the bases of power from the city to the countryside, which took place as a gradual and almost unnoticed process in the entire River Plate region in the first decade of the Revolution, was exceptionally rapid, and led to open conflicts which in other places were averted. The reasons for this were, among others, the peculiar characteristics of the pre-Revolutionary situation in that zone, which in economic terms was one of the expanding frontiers of the Viceregal territory, which resulted in the lack of stability and hierarchy in society which have already been indicated, and it was also disputed as a hinterland between Buenos Aires and Montevideo. Both circumstances combined to make more complex and problematical the relationship between the Uruguayan rural areas and the urban centres which exercised influence over them, and therefore to facilitate the emergence of a predominantly rural political movement. It was, however, the course of the revolution and its expansion into the Littoral which made this, to a certain extent, inevitable.

The *pronunciamiento* in Buenos Aires placed Montevideo on the side of the dissidents, but – in contrast to what had happened in 1808 – it was, above all, the naval garrison which imposed this decision. The Cabildo was for a moment inclined to follow the Viceregal capital. The land forces, which had failed to confront the naval ones in time, were partially disarmed before they could launch their intended counter-attack. The new dissident movement, therefore, had a much weaker local basis than in 1808, but it compensated for this weakness by a more aggressive attitude, making maximum use of its military superiority in the Banda Oriental and on the rivers. The whole of Uruguay, including the part of it not subject to the jurisdiction of Montevideo, thus acknowledged the new secession, despite the previous declarations of support for the Buenos Aires movement made by the smaller localities.

Even so the dissident authorities – based on the superior power of the naval garrison – had only limited military support in the rural areas. Moreover, those who, from the city, exercised influence over those rural areas were distinctly hesitant, their attitude varying from lukewarm support, mingled with a desire to avoid risks, to equally cautious and passive opposition. Before the rural rebellion, therefore, the presence of the city in the rural areas was already increasingly limited to its purely military aspects. The urban sectors whose position gave them influence in the countryside hesitated to use it to full effect. This was not to be the last time – in the Littoral part of the River Plate region – that the audacity of the rural leaders was encouraged by the caution of the urban ones. There is no doubt, however, that the latter occupied, in the system in force before the Revolution, a higher position than the former. It was only the biggest landowners who could afford to live in the city and it was the most powerful merchants who had their stores there. From the beginning, therefore, the leadership of the rural movement was recruited from the countryside itself, and its emergence was to take place, if not in conflict with, then at least outside the hierarchical system which was based on the countryside, but nevertheless had its summit in the city. Furthermore, even in the countryside the emergence of certain leaders did not depend directly on their position in the social scale before the Revolution, but on their ability to recruit a following. This ability was, no doubt, connected with the social status of the potential revolutionary leader, but the relationship was too complex for eminence within the pre-Revolutionary social order – even in the rural sectors – to be a sufficient reason for the emergence of leaders within the rural movement into which the Revolutionary impetus was to be channelled. The fact that this movement expressed itself through war – a war in which the abundance of men thrown into the battle was to be systematically used as a compensation for the impossibility of arming them adequately – meant that the positions which before the Revolution had conferred powers of command over other men (whatever the social status conferred by such positions) were a better basis for a Revolutionary career than were other socially equivalent or superior positions incapable of offering the future movement a nucleus of men organised around the authority of one leader.

The rural movement did not, however, take place in isolation from all urban influences. Those influences – both that of Montevideo and that of Buenos Aires – were now to be felt essentially in the military sphere. Montevideo tried to collect in the rural areas resources for the unequal struggle which its leaders had imposed on it, and thus created fresh motives for rural hostility. Buenos Aires, which looked on Montevideo's dissidence as the most immediate of the threats which faced it, was prepared, in the case of those who were resisting Montevideo's action from the rural areas of Uruguay, to abandon the reservations which it felt, as a regional metropolis confronted with spontaneous movements in areas where it preferred passive obedience to a more active cooperation, which might be a first and disturbing symptom of independence. It was not only the immediate danger posed by Montevideo which explains this initial favourable attitude towards the Uruguayan insurrection, which the Buenos Aires leaders would never cease to regret. In addition, it was felt that the necessary victim of that insurrectionary spirit in the countryside was to be Montevideo, and throughout this whole phase the feeling of rivalry with the other River Plate port was an important element in the policy of Buenos Aires. It was most characteristic that, in the face of the dissidence of Montevideo, the Buenos Aires authorities felt little inclination to explain it as the decision of a small group of officials oppressing a population anxious to free itself from their rapacious tyranny. Thus, in February 1811, when prohibiting all trade with the Uruguayan capital, the Junta did not direct its diatribes against those who had imposed that dissident movement on Montevideo by force, but against the city itself, against the 'illegal, imprudent and rash conduct of...that population deprived of judgement and good sense...[which] has offended our dignity on more than one occasion, to the extent that we have needed all our moderation to tolerate its insults, born of its stubbornness and coarse ignorance'.[45]

In this way, by initially offering assistance to the rural movement in the

Banda Oriental, the Buenos Aires Government not only felt that it was countering the threat represented by the dissident movement established in Montevideo, but that it was guaranteeing for itself a more permanent advantage by weakening the city which it reproached for not resigning itself to occupying the humble position for which, in the opinion of Buenos Aires, it was clearly destined. This assistance – granted to Artigas, who had been a refugee since the end of 1810 – not only endowed him with an established position on the basis of which he could subsequently erect a power independent of Buenos Aires. It endowed the entire rural revolution with a legitimacy which was, of course, dubious, but certainly no more so than that of the authorities which, from Buenos Aires, were claiming to govern the Viceregal territory on behalf of the captive King.

Thus, it was the conflict between Buenos Aires and Montevideo which made the rural insurrection possible, and which, at least in the early stages, decisively affected its course. In a few months, from February 1811 onwards, the rural areas of Uruguay were made unsafe for Montevideo's troops. In April Elío, who had returned to govern the city with the title of Viceroy, was obliged to bring in troops from the city in order to defend the surrounding country from which he was receiving his supplies. The result was the victory of Artigas in the pitched battle of Las Piedras and the beginning of the siege of Montevideo, the only walled city in the entire River Plate region. The walls of Montevideo now seemed to hallow and consolidate the divorce between city and countryside, which was to be one of the elements in the delicate equilibrium of Uruguay even in times of peace. However, the magnitude of the victory of the dissidents in the countryside increased their strength within the city as well. The urban elements which had enjoyed a dominant position in the rural areas were preparing to come to an understanding with the authority which governed there. Several of the big land-owners, and the owners of meat-salting plants (whose establishments were, in any case, outside the city and in the hands of Artigas's followers), abandoned the besieged city, and, furthermore, the Royalists knew very well that they could not count on the unswerving loyalty of those who remained behind.

The erosion of the city's authority by a successful rural insurrection, which was destined to happen again in the history of Uruguay, was, however, interrupted by the Portuguese intervention, which was requested by the Royalists – who at first had tried hard to avoid it – when they realised that their defeat was now inevitable. After many tergiversations, Buenos Aires made peace with Montevideo in October 1811. The entire rural areas of Uruguay and even the Eastern half of Entre Ríos were again made subject to Montevideo. It was hoped in this way to drive out the Portuguese invaders, whose intervention had been represented as a defence of the threatened authority of the King of Spain.

The result of the armistice was the *Exodo*: the withdrawal of the entire military force which recognised Artigas as its leader, and of eighty per cent of the population of rural Uruguay to the interior of Entre Ríos. The exodus of the Uruguayan people definitely consolidated the leadership of Artigas, and signified a new advance in the creation of a rural revolutionary movement. This movement was not, of course, supported only by the rural lower classes. Those taking part in the exodus included landowners who abandoned their properties not only with whole wagon-trains, but even with coaches and slaves, who were a symbol of wealth by no means confined to those possessing vast properties. Moreover, some of the big landowners who thought that they could remain in rural Uruguay under Portuguese protection were soon cruelly disillusioned by the rapacity of occupation forces. But amid the universal penury of the Ayuí encampment that wealth which in the past had made them powerful in the countryside now meant little more than the possibility of escaping to some extent the rigours of the common misery. It is true that the return to Uruguay (made possible by the negotiated withdrawal of the Portuguese, reluctantly undertaken by Rio de Janeiro under pressure from Britain) limited the effects of the exodus. Nevertheless, the character of Artigas's movement was profoundly influenced by the exodus, and was confirmed by the massive utilisation of scarce human resources to offset inferiority in weapons. This lent increased importance to the rural marginal sectors, which included not only the itinerant 'vagrants' still numerous there but even the Indians, whom Artigas had systematically tried to incorporate into his following. In an area where the population probably did not exceed ten thousand, Artigas raised four thousand troops in 1811, and over six thousand in 1816. Among the latter, however, the proportion of elements from outside the Banda Oriental – especially Indians from Misiones – was considerable. This vast mobilisation made impossible any return to economic normality in the countryside as long as the war lasted, even though Artigas, who was far from being insensitive to the problem, tried to attenuate the detrimental effects of militarisation on the economy.

Was the power of Artigas, then, based only on his control of a military organisation? The war had destroyed, in rural Uruguay, the economic bases of the hegemony of certain powerful landowners and merchants from the city, and, by doing serious damage to the productive process, necessarily also weakened other forms of hegemony based on the authoritarian organisation of rural labour, except where these had served as the basis for the emergence of a new leadership of a decidedly political and military character. This being the case, did the victory of the rural movement mean a break with that past in which the rural and urban bases of power had been inter-connected in such a complex way as in the Banda Oriental? It is not, of course, impossible to find evidence which suggests that this process took place. The title of *Jefe del Pueblo Oriental* (leader of the Uruguayan people) which his position as head of the exodus had definitely conferred on

Artigas, did not prevent the growth of tensions within the Revolutionary movement. After the complex experience of 1811, Artigas seemed to draw the conclusion that it would be impossible simply to hand over the direction of the Revolution and the war to Buenos Aires. The capital was only too capable of distinguishing between its own interests and those of the areas beyond the River Plate, where it had encouraged insurrection only to abandon the inhabitants to their fate as soon as the Revolution there ran into more resistance than had been expected.

Of course, the eminent citizens of Montevideo who now came to Artigas's support did not need anybody to teach them to distrust the hated rival city. Nevertheless, the intransigence of the Uruguayan leader began to lose him the sympathy of that group. The incipient dissent was provoked not so much by the political objectives of Artigas as by his preparedness to impose sacrifices, which the leading citizens considered to be too prolonged, in the pursuit of those objectives. After the experience of war on land and on the rivers, of the blockades and of Portuguese rapacity, the return of peace seemed more urgent than the conquest of objectives only attainable – if at all – after a struggle of uncertain outcome. Only the experience of the occupation of Montevideo by the Buenos Aires forces in 1814, when the new administration seemed less interested in economic reconstruction than in favouring its scanty supporters, and was incapable of establishing peace in the countryside in the face of the continued dissidence of Artigas, against whom unsuccessful but extremely destructive expeditions were launched, persuaded most of the leading citizens to return their resigned, rather than enthusiastic, support to Artigas. It is true that the new experience which was to begin with the evacuation of Montevideo by the Buenos Aires troops offered almost no reasons to revive that almost forgotten enthusiasm. Even leaving aside the abundant legendary accounts of the humiliations imposed by the first of Artigas's delegates, Otorgués, on the citizens of the city finally conquered in its backlands, very real motives of discontent still existed even when Artigas replaced the brusque Otorgués by the more flexible Miguel Barreiro. Now more than ever the leading citizens of Montevideo were unable to see advantages which justified the extremely high cost of the proud attitude of Artigas towards both Buenos Aires and the Portuguese. It is not surprising, therefore, that when the latter invaded the Banda Oriental in 1816, confronting the hegemony of Artigas with a threat which Buenos Aires had never been able to pose effectively, it was the leading citizens of Montevideo who led in the path of defecting to the enemy.

This background of disagreements, which expressed a conflict only occasionally explicit but always present, was, however, only one aspect of the complex relationship between Artigas and that predominantly urban élite which the Revolution appeared to have deprived of its power-base. For although Artigas stubbornly refused to renounce, as an act of conciliation to the hesitations of that group, his extreme political aspirations, it is also true that he reserved for that same group, within the political system of the zone under his control, a rôle which the real relationship of forces certainly did not oblige him to grant it. Thus he made possible the continued existence of that incipient dissidence, the detrimental consequences of which were only to be intensified by the decline of the political fortunes of Artigas's movement. Why did Artigas insist on an attitude which did not appear to stem from urgent need and the dangers of which were only too evident? There were, of course, many reasons for this, but underlying them we can distinguish two basic elements. One was Artigas himself and his previous career which, while it encouraged an attitude of independence towards the aspirations of the Montevideo élite, did not drive him towards an open confrontation with them. Another factor, connected with the foregoing one, was the recognition that although, in the climate created by the war, the importance of those leading citizens was necessarily reduced, any attempt at economic reconstruction after, or even before, the return of peace was impossible without their cooperation.

In fact, the entire career of Artigas before his rise as the Leader of the Uruguayans reflected the complex inter-connection between the Uruguayan rural areas and the capital. It has already been pointed out that Artigas, grandson of one of the founders of Montevideo, belonged by origin to that élite with which his relations were always to be ambivalent. His immediate family had even improved upon the position guaranteed by the founder-grandfather: new lands were added to those inherited. The Artigas family – according to the accurate characterisation of John Street[46] – formed part of that 'aristocracy of service' which was more important in Spanish America in colonial times than after independence. They had thus combined big rural land-holdings with a military and administrative authority, in the militia cavalry and in the Cabildo of Montevideo, which made itself felt beyond the boundaries of their actual properties. José Artigas, born in 1764, studied in the Franciscan school frequented by the sons of the best families of Montevideo, then began his working life as a cattle-dealer. There seems to be no doubt that he complemented this activity with some smuggling. At this time rural order in the Banda Oriental was by no means firmly established. In the North of the territory the cattle-ranch had still not displaced the destructive hunting of wild cattle, and even in the South the illegal outlet represented by the Brazilian market was an attractive complement to the legal, but irregular, market of Spain. As posthumous defenders of Artigas were to point out, the illegality of some of these transactions in which he was involved implied no stigma whatsoever. It would, nevertheless, be worthwhile to examine to what extent the concentration of Artigas's activities in the most remote corners of the savage rural areas may have begun to establish some separation between him and the sector from which he originated. Even so, the subsequent evolution of that sector did not fail to affect the destiny of Artigas. In the last decade of the eighteenth century the crisis of destructive cattle-hunting, which was resulting in the extinction of the herds, gave those who from Montevideo and Buenos Aires dominated the rural economy of the Banda Oriental a more unanimous interest in the maintenance of order in the countryside. Cattle-hunting and smuggling, the activities of the relatively numerous itinerant population, led with dangerous ease to sheer banditry. The raising of the *Blandengues de la Frontera* (Frontier Cavalry Regiment) in 1797 was an attempt to restrain this disturbing process, and was all the more effective because, by recruiting the soldiers from that section of the population, it offered them an alternative preferable to a progressive slide into totally illegal activities.

In this context, and with the support of some of the most influential Uruguayan landowners, Artigas began his career in the King's service. At first promotion was rapid, then it was made more difficult by his past which, although it gave him a marked ascendancy over the new soldiers and fitted him to command them, at the same time made somewhat disturbing, from the point of view of the Royal authorities, the prospect of his promotion to positions which would give him too wide powers of decision. His possibilities of advancement within the Colonial administration had encountered – as Artigas was slowly to discover – limitations difficult to overcome. At the same time, his service in it was to add new experiences to those already accumulated from the very different perspective of a cattle-dealer and smuggler.

Among these experiences, those provided by his contacts with Félix de Azara seem to have been particularly important. This official, to whom we owe some of the most penetrating studies of the River Plate region in the Viceregal era, was from early 1800 responsible for the establishment of settlements in the immediate rearguard area along the Brazilian frontier. As his assistant, Artigas became acquainted with a set of problems, in the solution of which the perspicacity of Azara had no doubt been decisive, but which was a more faithful continuation than is usually supposed of the traditional approach of the Royal administration. The need to populate the frontier arose from an essentially military objective, that of halting Portuguese expansion, and from a more strictly political one – populations concentrated in villages were more easily governable. The interest of the Crown in both objectives is easily understandable, as is the impatience of conscientious officials at the obstacles to the new organisation of the frontier lands erected by all who had a vested interest in the maintenance of the order (or rather disorder) prevailing there. These included those who claimed exceedingly dubious rights over vast tracts of land, and those who were able to take advantage of the prevailing lack of order to engage in smuggling. Thus, the political interest of the Crown favoured the establishment of centres of relatively dense population, which could only main-

The Revolution in the country as a whole

tain themselves by an economy not exclusively based on livestock, and, concomitantly with this, a relatively wide distribution of ownership of land among the settlers. It has already been pointed out by many authors that this administrative tradition, which had nothing whatever to do with any concern for social equality, was, nevertheless, the basis of the series of solutions which Artigas was to try to give, in the name of the Revolutionary principle of equality, to the rural problems of the Banda Oriental. Less notice has been taken of the extent to which the problems encountered by the Royal official in the application of his less ambitious plans anticipated those which were to face the Leader of the Uruguayans.

For it was not just the intrigues of a few unscrupulous men prepared to defend by any methods the advantages accruing to them from rural disorder, which placed obstacles in the path of this plan of reforms. Other and perhaps more serious obstacles were provided by the prevailing circumstances themselves. The shortage of men, which immigration from Spain was not enough to alleviate, made necessary a concentration of the available labour force in cattle-raising activities which Azara eventually declared to be inevitable, in what was chronologically perhaps the first defence of monoproduction based on economic arguments, his *Memoria sobre el estado rural del Río de la Plata* (Report on the rural situation in the River Plate region), published in 1801 and written in the settlement of Batoví which he had just founded with the help of Artigas. Yet the actual course of the foundation of settlements directed by Azara showed an even greater variation from that model of settlement of frontier areas gradually evolved by the Colonial administration. The distribution of vast tracts of land to candidates who were probably destined to become absentee landowners, a practice which had been so eloquently condemned, nevertheless took place in Batoví. The motives were not necessarily disreputable, but for that very reason they make more questionable the correctness of those programmes of relatively dense settlement which, after enjoying the constant approval of the Crown and of its lay and ecclesiastical servants, have more recently gained the support of several Latin American historians of Leftist inclinations. The alternative to the creation of a new class of absentee landowners seems to have been to renounce settlement altogether. Either because the latter measure seemed to him particularly undesirable, or because – from a more personal point of view – he preferred a dubious success to a resounding failure of the enterprise in which he was engaged, Azara seemed ready to admit in practice a state of affairs which he did not cease to condemn in his writings.

This complex experience did not fail to leave its mark on the attitudes of Artigas. Through it, he no doubt learned to discover the connection between the glaringly obvious problems of the rural economy of the Banda Oriental and the characteristics of land distribution in the region. Thanks to it, it was perhaps easier for him to extract from the Revolutionary principle of equality conclusions which imposed a wider – though not necessarily less unequal – distribution of rural land ownership. It was, however, only the Revolution itself which was to allow these problems to be discussed on a much larger scale and with greater urgency. Until that moment, the reflections which his activities as assistant to Azara may have inspired in Artigas did not alter the fact that his principal task was the maintenance of a rural order which did little to satisfy any ideals of equality. In this task, he continued to enjoy the confidence of all those who had an economic interest in the maintenance of peace in the rural areas. During his periods of retirement from the Army, ostensibly on the grounds of health but perhaps connected with his growing lack of interest in a career which, after a brilliant start, seemed to be leading nowhere, Artigas, who did not enjoy the complete confidence of his superiors, still enjoyed that of those substantial men who, when they became pillars of rural order in the last decade of the eighteenth century, loudly proclaimed to the Royal authorities that that order could not be safer than in the care of the man who had served them so well in that still recent past when they had found in disorder a source of rapid prosperity. Between 1797 and 1811 the implicit agreement between Artigas and the big Uruguayan landowners suffered no interruptions. This circumstance is perhaps as important for the understanding of the emergence of Artigas as a Revolutionary leader as was the continuing loyalty he was able to inspire in his followers, who were at first organised outside the framework of the legal order (those 'starry-eyed youths' who were surrounding him when the future General Vedia met him in 1793), and later organised on a military basis; and also the loyalty which, through that following, he inspired among the unruly rural masses.

Thus, the limitations surrounding the political adherence to Artigas of the urban sectors which wielded influence in the countryside arose, not so much from any distrust of his person or his objectives, as from a prudence which manifested itself above all in the absence of any attitude of militancy, and only much later would lead to a systematic dissent from Artigas's movement and all it signified. This affinity of origin is not, however, the only reason why Artigas – without being forced to do so by any military consideration – transformed the régime established in the Banda Oriental under his auspices into a sort of diarchy, in which his supreme authority, although unquestioned, was not always strictly obeyed. The brief period of a little over a year which followed the evacuation of Montevideo by the Buenos Aires forces, during which the Banda Oriental was at last politically united and the war was taking place outside its territory, is in this respect particularly instructive. After replacing Otorgués, Artigas entrusted the government of Montevideo and its territory to the Cabildo, and thenceforth scrupulously accorded it the necessary marks of formal respect for the authority which he had vested in it. Thus, he requested the

Cabildo's approval for sending Rivera to Montevideo as military commander of the city ('I ask Your Excellencies to be good enough to recognise him, and he will obey the orders of Your Excellencies and keep order among his troops and maintain the individual security of each citizen'.[47]) It is true that this formal courtesy did not disguise where the real supremacy lay. It is interesting to note that the possibility of Rivera's appointment being disallowed was not discussed, even hypothetically. Furthermore, the fact that the members of the Cabildo were replaced as a result of every change in the military control of Montevideo established yet another tie between the Leader of the Uruguayans and those installed in the Cabildo under his influence. Nevertheless, this division of political and administrative tasks was not just for the sake of appearances. The very remoteness of Artigas – who during this period was devoting himself to organising, in Purificación on the River Uruguay, his headquarters and that of a large proportion of his military forces – gave the authorities in Montevideo a greater margin of decision. The absorption of Artigas in the struggle that was continuing to the West of the River Uruguay was an additional reason for leaving in the hands of Montevideo unexpectedly extensive governmental functions. Those functions were subject to strict limitations only in matters relating to the struggle. For example, total ban was imposed on trade with the territory dominated by Buenos Aires, a measure no doubt unpopular with the Cabildo, but nevertheless imposed by Artigas's fiat, and a ban was also placed on the movement of people to those territories or to Portuguese-held areas, which meant that the freedom of movement of the inhabitants of Montevideo was confined to the Banda Oriental and Entre Ríos. A further measure even provided for the expulsion from Montevideo of the Spanish-born and the politically suspect, who were all to be interned in Purificación. Yet, even on these points, although the Cabildo never expressed its disagreement by overt opposition, it was able to give expression to its reluctance when carrying out the orders of the Leader, with consequences which were perhaps more serious than those of an explicit dissent. Thus, the deportation of the Spaniards, both in quantitative and qualitative terms, took an entirely different form from that intended by Artigas. Not only were those deported less numerous than Artigas had ordered, even if it had only been his intention to deport a minority among the numerous Spanish-born population of Montevideo, but, what was more important, the victims of the measure were not, as Artigas had intended, 'those who through their influence and power still hold a certain sway over the People', and who apparently still retained a certain influence over the Cabildo itself, but were 'mostly wretched people'.[48] Despite the different political context, both in Montevideo and Buenos Aires the more prosperous among the Spanish-born found it easier to evade discriminatory legislation. As in Buenos Aires, it was that same Creole urban élite which in the past had resented the pre-eminence of the

Spaniards which now placed obstacles in the path of any thoroughgoing measure directed against that sector. Again, despite the differences in the political context, that élite seems to have been just as successful in this sphere in Montevideo as in Buenos Aires, where its political predominance was unquestioned.

Although the application of measures arising out of the war provided occasions for disagreements – admittedly only partial ones – between Artigas and the Cabildo of Montevideo, these disagreements did not emerge in the area of economic reconstruction, for which Artigas thought that the appropriate moment had arrived. The theatre of war had moved away from the Banda Oriental and for a moment, in that year of 1815, full of expectations and early disappointments, it seemed that the entire River Plate region was prepared to be reorganised according to the principles maintained by Artigas's movement. In this field, it appeared that there would be a greater measure of agreement. The Cabildo, which was dominated by the upper sectors of Montevideo, and which wished to protect the persons belonging to those sectors who had suffered the consequences of supporting factions other than that of Artigas, was of course interested in a speedy reconstruction of the regional economy. Artigas, who was no less convinced of the urgency of this objective, admitted that in order to attain it there had to be a progressive limitation of the military authority which was, in the last resort, the foundation of his political power, and a strengthening of the administrative system headed by the Cabildo. Thus, on 2 October 1815, he ordered the troops who, under the command of Otorgués, appear to have been guilty of further depredations, to be concentrated in Otorgués's encampment or sent to guard the Portuguese frontier, leaving the '*alcaldes* to carry out the orders of Your Excellencies'. This – in the midst of war – amounted to the restoration of the authority of the civil authority over the rural areas. It was also an attempt to reorganise the entire administration with a view to future peace and economic reconstruction. It was more necessary than ever, in the view of Artigas, not to attract people away from economically productive activities and into the administration or the militia. 'There should be no multiplication of authorities or administrators...labour, industry and commerce are the channels through which felicity comes to Peoples, and the latter breathe more air of liberty the less they shelter in their bosom those mercenary men. A few men, well paid and aware of their responsibilities, are quite sufficient'.[49] In the same categorical manner he proclaimed the urgency of resolving once for all the situation of uncertainty regarding the ownership of cattle which were the heritage of the past disorders. Artigas showed equal anxiety over public revenue. He preferred not to return to the imposition of extraordinary contributions (the very term, he said, made him tremble). Although at first he approved the one imposed by Otorgués, at the suggestion of the Cabildo, on the merchants of Montevideo, he very soon abolished it and returned to the enforced contributors the sums already collected.[50] This extreme orthodoxy which in general characterised the economic and financial policy of Artigas did not, however, gain for it the wholehearted support of the Cabildo members recruited from the economically dominant sector of Montevideo.

This is less surprising than would appear at first sight. After all, the discovery on the part of the Montevideo élite of the advantages of a more orderly productive economy was fairly recent (it dated from the last decade of the eighteenth century), and had by no means provoked a total change in the attitudes of the group. Moreover, the war favoured a reversion to practices which had been partly abandoned. It was again possible to make profits, which were no doubt ephemeral but were still considerable, by taking part in destructive cattle-hunting in rural Uruguay, a practice which the war, and the high proportion of the rural population recruited into the Army, made inevitable. The war also offered other opportunities for making profits – by supplying the Army, for example – which made several of the members of the urban élite feel no urgent need to return to a peacetime economy. Similar considerations prevailed with regard to the contributions. In Montevideo, as in Salta, it was the military leader who was interested in returning to a less arbitrary system of taxation, and it was the Cabildo which served as the political stronghold of a sector of the pre-Revolutionary élite which, on the contrary, preferred to retain those arbitrary fiscal procedures. The reason for this has already been pointed out: it allowed that sector of the élite identified with the dominant political faction to transfer to others the principal share of a burden which the impact of the war made it impossible to reduce.

The consequences of this were that – in contrast to what the Cabildo of Montevideo, retrospectively, would have us believe – the Cabildo appeared to be on better terms with the arbitrary Otorgués than with the more orderly Artigas. The disagreement between the latter and the Cabildo was shown particularly clearly in their approach to the problem which, in the view of Artigas, was fundamental in a region to which, he thought, peace was returning: the *fomento de la campaña*, the restoration of a properly organised cattle-raising economy in those lands which had been thoroughly devastated. For the *Jefe* of the Uruguayans this task could not be postponed. The alternative was to abandon the countryside to a permanent deterioration, which would condemn the province to everlasting poverty, and leave 'completely dissipated the most precious treasure of our country'.[51]

Rural reconstruction was to take place along the general lines laid down, after laborious negotiations, in the *Reglamento provisorio de la Provincia Oriental para el fomento de su campaña y seguridad de sus hacendados* [Provisional regulations of the Province of Uruguay for the development of its countryside and the security of its landowners].[52] The promulgation of these Regulations took place at the instance of the Cabildo. In the early stages of its preparation the opinion of the landowners, who were growing impatient at the continuing arbitrary seizures of cattle by Artigas's military forces in the countryside, played a dominant part. Even Fructuoso Rivera, the military commander of Montevideo, voiced this discontent in the face of a situation, which in any case the regulations were designed to correct. The final stage of discussion of the regulations took place, not in Montevideo, but in Artigas's encampment. There the provincial *alcalde* Juan de León and León Pérez, a big landowner and a brother of Manuel Pérez, who on behalf of the landowners had submitted to the Cabildo proposals in connection with the projected regulations, obtained from the *Jefe* of the Uruguayans his approval of a set of guiding principles which in their final form clearly showed the traces of the outlook on rural problems of Artigas himself.

The objectives of social reform which inspired the regulations have often been emphasised, and are undeniable. The sixth article, in fact, contained one of the clearest expressions of socially egalitarian tendencies ever bequeathed to us by the River Plate Revolution ('the most unfortunate shall be the most privileged'), and it drew equally clear conclusions from this principle. In the distribution of lands to be settled, 'the free Negroes, the *zambos* of that class, the Indians and the poor Creoles can all be given a plot of land, if by their work and virtues they contribute to the felicity of the province'. It is true that, as has also been pointed out with increasing insistence by the more conservative Uruguayan historians, alarmed at the idea of the national hero being transformed into the precursor of future revolutions, the regulations were entirely provisional, as was the distribution of lands to be settled. For this reason, Article 16 prohibited the alienation or mortgaging of lands received, 'until the formal organisation of the province, when the latter will decide on the most convenient arrangement'. This provision, however, which again reveals Artigas as prepared to maintain as a formal principle the supremacy of the popular will, as expressed by its duly chosen representatives, does not justify the conclusion that in the view of Artigas the principles governing the redistribution of land were of a merely provisional nature. What was perhaps more important was that this redistribution, the social effects of which were deemed to be beneficial, was considered as particularly urgent because it was expected to lead to the rehabilitation of the rural economy. In fact, the result of the distribution of land might well be an improvement in the lot of the unfortunate, but its principal purpose was to entrust those lands to people who could exploit them effectively. What were, in fact, the lands that were distributed? Those of the 'émigrés, bad Europeans and worse Americans who up to the present date have not been authorised by the leader of the Province to retain possession of their old properties' (Article 12). In other words, the lands of those who had abandoned both their residence in the province and the exploitation of their lands, and the lands of those who

The Revolution in the country as a whole

were politically too dangerous for it to be prudent to retain them in positions of influence in the countryside. Their replacement by new settlers seemed to be the quickest way to bring those properties back into production. In the same way, the strict limitation of the maximum holding which could be granted to any single beneficiary (an area of a league and a half by two leagues, that is, 7,500 hectares), although it did have an egalitarian intention and also reflected a principle respected in theory, though not necessarily applied in practice, in colonisation experiments in Colonial times, nevertheless had a more immediate purpose – that of guaranteeing that the holdings concerned were swiftly brought into exploitation. Since war had dissipated the greater part of the scarce stock of capital, this could only be achieved by replacing the investment of capital with that of labour. Such replacement was perfectly possible if one bears in mind that to make possible the exploitation of a cattle-ranch it was enough to build 'a hut and two corrals' (the livestock was to come from 'the ranches of the Europeans or bad Americans'), and this being the case, a distribution into smaller units seemed in fact to be a more effective method than the creation of big properties, the new owners of which would lack the resources to begin the immediate exploitation of them.

To what extent did the reorganisation of the countryside affect the rural history of Uruguay? The resurgence of cattle-raising which it tried to encourage was harshly interrupted, almost before it had begun, by the new Portuguese invasion, which was launched in 1816. With regard to the redistribution itself, the monumental work of Sala de Touron, Rodríguez and De la Torre abundantly proves that this was much wider than is frequently supposed, but that its effects were short-lived.[53] The governments which successively dominated the rural areas of Uruguay systematically destroyed what had been created, to the extent that a completely illegal occupation of land might be preferable, from a legal point of view, to an occupation which had its origin in a grant from Artigas. Was it, then, a social revolution, which reflected in the distribution of land the principles of Artigas's movement in the political sphere, and which was then discreetly liquidated both by the adversaries and by the disloyal heirs of Artigas? Not even the authors mentioned above, who combine admirably sound scholarship with open sympathy for Revolutionary ideals, would go so far as to assert this without reservation. The failure of the experiment was due, according to them (and it is hard to disagree), to the absence of a coherent social sector benefited by it and prepared to defend its new advantages. The military leaders who followed Artigas appear to have been more interested in continuing that economy based on rapine, the effects of which had already become intolerable, rather than encouraging the formation of a sector of medium-scale rural proprietors. It was even more significant that none among their followers was disposed to exert systematic pressure to oblige them to fulfil that second role, towards which they felt no spontaneous inclination. It seems that a less unequal distribution of land was not a very widely shared aspiration during that period of the history of Uruguay. It was, perhaps, for this reason, that the application of the regulations had to be entrusted to the *Alcalde* of the Province, with appeal from his decisions to the Cabildo. Even though the latter, and the social sector with which it was identified, showed little sympathy for some of the solutions adopted, it was, at least, interested in that restoration of rural prosperity towards which the military leaders, who were to offer the only alternative solution to that adopted by Artigas, had shown such indifference.

In the application of the principles governing the redistribution of land the Cabildo showed that it, too, did not see in the process a very serious threat to the social equilibrium of the province. In applying them it certainly followed the same tactics of selective obedience which it had already used with other directives of Artigas. In this way, it managed to carry out only a slow and partial redistribution of the lands in fact available. Yet its objective appears to have been not so much the avoidance of radical changes in the system of land tenure, as the protection of the interests of some of those 'bad Europeans and worse Americans' with whom the members of the Cabildo still felt a certain solidarity. In cases where the old proprietor had neglected to maintain those contacts, the destiny of his lands seems to have been a matter of indifference to the members of the Cabildo.

In this context, the insistence of Artigas on securing the cooperation of the Cabildo seems to be more understandable. They were united by a common interest in the re-establishment of a peacetime economy. It is true that in that process of economic restoration the Cabildo did not always display the same vigour as the *Jefe* of the Uruguayans, because it was too strongly influenced by the temptation to preserve some of the advantages gained during the disturbed period of its participation in political power. Nevertheless its members were, in these specific circumstances, those who were closest to sharing the general principles, if not all the detailed corollaries, of the aspirations and views of Artigas with regard to the economic problems of the province.

From this partial agreement there emerged a partial collaboration, with which Artigas would have to be content, and which extended to spheres other than the ones described above. The Cabildo was, of course, ready to give full support to that other aspect of the reconstruction of cattle-raising: the imposition of obligatory labour on those not owning land ('the landowners will issue work certificates to their peons, and anyone found without one of these and without other gainful employment is to be taken' to Montevideo or to the headquarters of Artigas to be enlisted in the Army – Article 27). Nor, even though they perhaps did not obey it to the letter, did the Cabildo members object in principle to the ban on landowners slaughtering cattle not of their brand, and cows, and exporting cattle to Portuguese territory. This, as they well knew, was the unpleasant price it was necessary to pay for the replenishment of the threatened herds.

In this way, the displacement of the basis of political power from the city to the country, and within the latter from those rich in land, livestock and money to those who could mobilise a relatively numerous following of men – who were sometimes, but not always, those same rich men – a process further aggravated by the impoverishment of the urban élite and its increasing dependence on political influence to save the remains of its prosperity, was not sufficient to effect a decisive change in the social bases of political power in the Banda Oriental. The new authority sought – and in fact paid a high price for – the collaboration of the institution which that urban élite continued to dominate, and governed the province in conjunction with it. This experiment in diarchy did not fail, of course, to produce tensions. These were, however, not enough to explain the eventual repudiation of Artigas's movement by that sector of the Montevideo élite which had supported it. Here again, it was the war and its return to the Banda Oriental which explain this rupture. In the Banda Oriental, as in Salta, a military and political movement which arose out of the war was brought to an end by that same war. It does not matter that, contrary to the agreed myth disseminated by those who in 1816 abandoned Artigas and went over to the Portuguese conqueror, the leader had felt, with more urgency than had those collaborators who now abandoned him, the need to return to a peacetime economy. It was his obstinate resistance which prevented the return of the only peace that was still possible – a peace the price of which was defeat. For that reason his allies in the urban élite, after calmly leaving him to his fate, wished him, no doubt sincerely, swift and utter ruin. And they began to fabricate, on the basis of the tensions which had undeniably existed throughout their previous collaboration with the *Jefe* of the Uruguayans, a new image of that collaboration, which they now represented as having been enforced by fear of his tyrannical rule. Behind the excessively numerous, and often imaginary, crimes for which Artigas was reproached was the real one, his refusal to abandon his political schemes as soon as his collaborators from the traditional élite began to feel that the price to be paid for their fulfilment was excessively high.

Of course, to deduce from these impassioned retrospective accusations the existence of intolerable political tensions with the bloc that supported Artigas, and to see behind those political tensions social conflicts liable to lead to violent confrontations, are temptations not always easy to avoid. Yet, even though this retrospective version is exaggerated, it is true that in Uruguay Artigas's movement represented the creation of a political authority based on groups partially distinct from, if not necessarily hostile to, those which had been dominant in the pre-Revolutionary situation, and thus initiated a radically new experience. The consequences of the latter as far as a change in the social equilibrium was concerned were no doubt limited, but its repercussions in other respects were undeniable. For nearly a century the existence of a rural political leadership insufficiently controlled by, and sometimes in conflict with, that of Montevideo was to be the most pressing problem in the political history of Uruguay. In those lands to the West of the River Uruguay, into which Artigas's movement spread after 1814, the displacement of the social bases of political power took place to a lesser degree. Except perhaps in the North of the Mesopotamia area, in Corrientes and, above all, in Misiones, adherence to Artigas's movement did not have the implications which had characterised it in the province where it originated.

In that Littoral which was to be the theatre of its rapid expansion, Artigas's movement appears from the very beginning as a pre-existing political force, the support of which it was possible to utilise in the conflicts which the actual course of that war was to create between Buenos Aires and the territory it administered. Although this is not the most important reason for the success of Artigas's movement in the area, it was no coincidence that the latter had belonged since Colonial times to the Intendancy of Buenos Aires. Dependence on the capital therefore affected lower levels of the administration than was the case in the Interior. Only in 1814 did the central government seem prepared to recognise the influence of Artigas in the Banda Oriental and grant Mesopotamia administrative existence as the seat of an Intendant-Governor, though it was still to be ruled by officials subordinate to the capital. This attempt came too late to alter the situation fundamentally. As regards Santa Fe, precisely because the central government thought it possible to maintain it in complete obedience it was even less prepared to grant it any administrative autonomy.

Why did the central government react with such hostility to the expansion of Artigas's movement in the Littoral? The question may well seem otiose: there is nothing surprising in a government's wishing to be obeyed. Nevertheless, the existence of other dangers – those deriving from the war against the Royalists, and that of internal disintegration, which was aggravated by the increased intensity of the sacrifices required – might have led one to expect an attitude of more tolerance. Apart, however, from the fact that the latter might merely serve to increase intransigence (if the expansion of Artigas's movement were tolerated, would not this serve as a dangerous encouragement to further advances of the internal disintegration which already threatened?), it was not only the need to maintain the unity of the threatened Revolution which drove Buenos Aires along that road. It was also the defence of lands which it had always considered its own, and which were expected to provide in the future a high proportion of the exports which would permit it partially to recover its mercantile prosperity. Artigas's movement made possible a reorientation of the Littoral's

The Revolution in the country as a whole

trade, which could use Montevideo – and even the smaller ports on the other bank of the River Plate – to ship goods overseas. Was this danger pressing? Even if one cannot assert this, it is at least certain that – between 1810 and the triumph of the railway over river transport, which was also the definitive triumph of Buenos Aires over her rival less strategically situated in the continental mass – the governments established in the former Viceregal capital thought it a very real danger, and acted accordingly.

However, for that Littoral still subjected to Buenos Aires's harsh rule the very existence of Artigas's movement created an alternative, which was all the more tempting because the struggle first against the Royalists and then against Artigas caused more severe consequences of the predominance of Buenos Aires. The Littoral was being increasingly drained of men and cattle. Moreover, it was Buenos Aires itself which had introduced Artigas into the lands West of the River Uruguay. After the 1811 armistice, which handed over the Entre Ríos shore of the River Uruguay to the Royalists, it not only admitted Artigas, with his army of four thousand soldiers and a numerous following of refugees from the rural areas of Uruguay, right into the heart of Mesopotamia. It gave him, in addition, the governorship of Yapeyú in Misiones, thus offering him an opportunity to apply, West of the River Uruguay, tactics he had learned in the Banda Oriental: the utilisation of a marginal population as a political and military power-base. The Guaraní Indians of Misiones offered Artigas the first and also the strongest of the supports he was to find in Mesopotamia. But did not such support in fact exclude that of other groups in Mesopotamia, which wanted nothing less than to be confused with the Guaranís of the old *reducciones*? It did not turn out that way; it was, perhaps, the loose structure of human settlement in those lands which allowed Artigas to elude options which might appear to have been unavoidable. It is true that his partiality towards the Indian province did provoke tensions among his adherents in Corrientes, but such tensions arose chiefly out of certain secondary consequences of that policy, for example his tolerance of Indian raids into the parts of Corrientes bordering on Misiones. The members of the Cabildo of Corrientes and those of that of Santa Fe, therefore, agreed to place themselves under the protection of a man who was also protecting the most rustic local leaders of Entre Ríos and the Guaranís from Misiones. But it was not only the comparative mutual isolation of the territories formally under his protectorate that allowed Artigas to be all things to all men, adapting his policy to the equilibrium existing in each place. An even more immediate influence was the common aversion to Buenos Aires and its dual economic and political domination.

It was that hostility, accentuated by the increasing burden of the war, which from 1811 offered Artigas a potential support, towards which the *Jefe* of the Uruguayans at first showed extreme caution. Only after the definitive rupture with Buenos Aires in 1814 did he decide to use for political ends adherences and contacts formed during the confused struggle against Royalist and Portuguese raids in Mesopotamia, in the period between the 1811 armistice and the Portuguese evacuation negotiated in Buenos Aires in 1812.

Then the whole of Mesopotamia fell into his hands in a few months. The offensive of the central government against Entre Ríos only confirmed the regional victory of Artigas, who had succeeded in overcoming the dissident insurrection in Corrientes and at the beginning of 1815 wielded unquestioned authority in the Banda Oriental. Within a few months Santa Fe, too, was to fall to Artigas's movement, not without some external military action – from neighbouring Entre Ríos – but thanks, above all, to local pressure in favour of this solution. This led to the establishment of the Union of Free Peoples, which recognised Artigas as its Protector. The Free Peoples were, in fact, not one but several political units, in dealing with which, as has been pointed out, Artigas faced problems which were different in each particular case and which he also resolved in ways which he tried to adapt to the varying context concerned.

There was, therefore, one form of *artiguismo* in Entre Ríos, another in Corrientes and yet another in Santa Fe. Furthermore, in the three provinces adherence to the federalism introduced from beyond the River Uruguay was limited, not so much by the presence of groups which consistently opposed it (these, although they existed, were rapidly made powerless) as by the defections of the federalists themselves. The way in which these internal crises in the federalist movement arose reveals fairly clearly the reasons for its previous success in the region. In Entre Ríos it was the experience of *artiguismo* which really gave the province unity. That new birth was to aggravate, rather than alleviate, the consequences of the lack of cohesion among the lands settled between the two tributaries of the River Plate. The local leaders of the little villages of Entre Ríos, none of which had a population of over a thousand inhabitants, most of whom had already achieved more than local celebrity by bringing the region into the conflict on the side of the movement of 1810, were to be the protagonists of the swing towards federalism. The first to achieve renewed celebrity were the leaders of the Paraná bank district, because it was against them that the military offensive of Buenos Aires, which soon failed, was directed. Nevertheless, Entre Ríos, made a province in 1814 by a central government which had little control over it, and integrated into Artigas's system by the action of a group of leaders none of whom clearly predominated over the others, was judged by Artigas useful as a token of exchange for greater political projects. The uncertain loyalty of Mariano Vera, the *artiguista* Governor of Santa Fe, was cultivated by appointing his brother José Ignacio as Governor of Entre Ríos. It is true that the Veras – and behind them Santa Fe – had close connections with that half of Entre Ríos comprising the bank of the Paraná, where the biggest ranches were owned by citizens of Santa Fe, and which supplied, year after year, a high proportion of the beef consumed by that city. It was precisely this relationship, intimate but not necessarily devoid of tensions, which precipitated the conflict. While Santa Fe continued in obedience to Buenos Aires, Hereñú, the *artiguista* leader who ruled in the Bajada and who, thanks to his victories over Baron Holmberg, an aristocratic Austrian ex-officer who was the unsuccessful champion of the central government in the inhospitable lands of Entre Ríos, had reached a position of *primus inter pares* among the *artiguista* leaders, devoted himself to sacking estates in his territory owned by citizens of Santa Fe. This development, together with the political hegemony of Hereñú in the Bajada, was brought to an end by the appointment of Vera as *artiguista* Governor of Entre Ríos. Hereñú was not prepared to accept his fall from power; he took refuge in Buenos Aires, and was to return to his province at the head of troops armed by the central government. Not even the more direct intervention of the latter was enough to save the enterprise. Hereñú had, of course, counted on the support of other leaders of the region who also disapproved of the rise of Vera. Samaniego, the chieftain of Gualeguaychú, and Correa, the chieftain of Gualeguay, joined forces with him. All three were defeated by Francisco Ramírez, the basis of whose power was in Concepción del Uruguay, and whose action saved Entre Ríos for the Union of the Free Peoples. As a result of this Ramírez became Governor of the province. Somewhat unexpectedly, his old rivals continued to hold power in their respective districts, now completely reconciled to the new provincial authorities. The career of Ramírez was, then, the most successful of any undertaken in Entre Ríos under the aegis of Artigas. It has already been observed that, from the point of view of his rivals in Buenos Aires, that career represented a rise from the lowest social level. It has also been observed that this judgment is far from accurate. Francisco Ramírez was the grandson of one of the founders of Concepción del Uruguay, the Maltese Tadeo Jordán. His father had been a Paraguayan who, after engaging in trade and navigation on the River Uruguay, had settled on his own lands in the Arroyo Grande. His mother, after being left a widow, married an Andalusian, a warehouse-owner and merchant in Concepción, and the influence of the children and grandchildren of that second marriage was to be felt in the political history of Entre Ríos until the last quarter of the nineteenth century. Even before 1810 Francisco Ramírez was a law-enforcement officer in Arroyo Grande, and from that date, he was a valued collaborator with the Patriot authorities. His career, commenced under the aegis of the King, continued to make solid progress under the auspices of the Buenos Aires Revolution and later that of Artigas's movement. Only after 1818 did he surpass the confines of his homeland, rule his province, take part in the conquest of Buenos Aires, become a successful rival of Artigas, unify the whole of Mesopotamia as the Republic of Entre Ríos (after his victory over the much-diminished Protector of the Free

Peoples), and finally return to the lands to the East of the Paraná and die a tragic death there without being able to overcome the new hostile alliance in which Santa Fe and Córdoba had united with Buenos Aires. Even in those final three years of forlorn hopes, Ramírez by no means fulfilled the role of a leader of the masses devoted to the carefree looting of other people's wealth. This rural landed proprietor shared to the full the prevailing anxiety over the economic future of Mesopotamia. Although he exacted great sacrifices, even that malevolent posthumous enemy, Ferré from Corrientes, had to admit that for his province the brief rule of Ramírez had been preferable to that of Buenos Aires, which had been represented there by 'a public company of thieves', and to that of Artigas, who had handed over 'the entire province to the mercy of the Indians from Misiones'. Ramírez, on the other hand, albeit at the cost of the 'liberty and independence' of Corrientes, and of 'the blood of the flower of its sons, taken away from their homeland', 're-established order'.[54] This dual preoccupation with administrative efficiency and social stability – the former, in the view of Ferré, being neglected by Buenos Aires and the latter by Artigas – was evident in the regulations which the leader from Concepción laid down for his Republic of Entre Ríos.[55] These made provision for an essentially military régime: military commanders, appointed by the *Jefe Supremo* of the Republic, were to govern the departments, and they were to appoint the judges, who would cooperate with them. Public finance attracted a more sustained interest than political organisation (51 articles, as compared with the 41 dealing with the latter), and the regulations governing the use of official stamped paper were even more minutely detailed (33 articles). A decree published in an appendix laid down emergency rules to deal with the crisis of rural production. This entire document was more administrative than political in character. The only holder of strictly political power was that *Jefe Supremo* who appointed all officials, and could revoke their appointments, and could modify or repeal those regulations which, in any case, had been promulgated on no other authority than his. The document was, however, animated by a very acute awareness of the seriousness of the crisis provoked by the long war and of the need to impose strict order on those excessively turbulent lands. In the first place, there were measures governing the movement of people. No-one could take up residence in a department without the express authorisation of the military commander there, and no one could remain there, even as a transient, without a passport, which was subject to inspection by the departmental judge. Any resident giving accommodation to strangers without informing the authorities would be subject to criminal proceedings. The political reasons for this interest in the surveillance of people's residence are evident. There were also, however, economic reasons, and it was not mere chance that these regulations were closely connected with others banning the sale of stolen hides or cattle, and which differed only in detail from measures introduced

The Revolution in the country as a whole

in Buenos Aires and elsewhere. The most urgent task was that of replenishing the herds of cattle, and the slaughter of animals – in those excessively depopulated lands – was not only drastically curtailed by direct prohibitions, but also by certain indirect ones such as those affecting the tanners' purchases. Although a distribution of new lands to those without property might have been considered as an encouragement of the swift productive rehabilitation of the rural areas (Artigas had already considered it from this angle), the Regulations contained no reference to solutions of this kind. They confined themselves to offering the support of a state apparatus which they wished to be vigorous and efficient to those who already dominated the rural scene.

To adopt this socially conservative solution, Ramírez does not appear to have had to resist any pressure in favour of more innovatory alternatives. There is nothing surprising in this. In the neighbouring Banda Oriental, after episodes which had shaken the fragile social stability of the rural areas much more profoundly than anything that had happened in Entre Ríos, the cancellation of the land distribution undertaken by Artigas was to be so easy because there was no coherent opposition to counter the tenacious activity of those who governed Uruguay after 1820. It was not that there was no opposition between the rural masses and the upper rural and urban sectors interested in the restoration of a very peculiar kind of rural order. But the former group displayed against this proposed restoration, not a militant defiance based on adherence to a different rural order, but indifference towards a change in the advantages of which it was to have no share. When Artigas's military commanders supported a rural disorder which was enriching them, they could count on the implicit support of their armed followers. In order to prepare the transition to a peacetime economy, Artigas had no other path open to him than that of collaboration with the previously dominant sectors which had managed to survive the crisis, with which he had in common little more than an interest in ending the disorder brought about by the war.

In Entre Ríos the disagreements were considerably less marked. Its political system, based on an almost universal military mobilisation which nevertheless reserved the dominant positions for those who had previously held them at the local level, was possible precisely because of the absence of social antagonisms in that province, which had only suffered from interregional ones. The efficacy of this political formula survived the fall of Ramírez. As late as 1826, in those rural areas of Entre Ríos which still bore traces of the war, Colonel Paz was to discover, in the co-existence of an authoritarian political system accepted without question and a universal attachment to the notion of equality, the still vigorous heritage of the experience which had created Entre Ríos as a political unit.

It was this climate of social concord which made it possible for Ramírez to organise an army with a discipline greatly superior to that of the armies led by other *artiguista* leaders, and to that of the mediocre detachments of the National Army which suffered defeat at his hands. This concord was, however, partly explained by the past history of Entre Ríos. That frontier territory undergoing a rapid economic expansion had not yet created internal antagonisms. A history that was too brief and marked by too constant a prosperity had prevented the consolidation of an upper sector as closed to outsiders as was the case in areas of longer settlement. In Concepción del Uruguay, Ramírez played the part of a descendant of an old-established lineage because his grandfather had settled there. Instead, as has already been observed, there was antagonism between Entre Ríos and the small urban centres which had made it a frontier for settlement: Buenos Aires with respect to the bank of the River Uruguay, and Santa Fe with respect to that of the Paraná. Yet it was precisely this antagonism which served to consolidate the social and political cohesion of Entre Ríos.

It was the simplicity of the structure of this new land which gave it its political cohesion and made its adherence to Artigas's movement so firm and monolithic. But there were other reasons why the militancy of Entre Ríos in that cause was more intense than that of Corrientes or Santa Fe. Even before embracing the cause of Artigas, Entre Ríos had taken a more active part than the other areas of the Littoral in the struggle against Royalist Montevideo and the Portuguese invasion. Half its territory had been ceded, by the armistice of 1811, to the Royalists, and it was to experience further Portuguese incursions. As a military enterprise independent of Buenos Aires, Artigas's movement had already put down strong local roots. In the case of Corrientes and Santa Fe it was, rather, an external support to be utilised (though not without some misgivings) against the excessive domination of Buenos Aires. At the same time – at least in the East of Entre Ríos – the commercial rupture with Buenos Aires, which was the consequence of the province's joining the alliance of the Free Peoples, was less costly than was the case in Corrientes or Santa Fe, whose only outlet to the outside world was by way of the Paraná, the mouth of which was under the control of the central government.

The relationship between those areas of longer settlement and Artigas's movement was to be, from the outset, more ambiguous. In Corrientes the federalist victory was ensured by the advance from Misiones of the *artiguista* leader Blas Basualdo, who had begun his military career in the North of the Banda Oriental, as a militia captain, in the last years of the Colonial period. But that advance was so easy precisely because Artigas's movement was received without hostility in the province. The domination of Buenos Aires was associated with sacrifices for the war effort which were beginning to be considered excessive. Furthermore, the central government still did not refrain from manipulating, from a distance, the political equilibrium of Corrientes, imposing on it a Lieutenant-Governor from outside the province and partially modifying the composition of the

The Revolution in the country as a whole

Cabildo elected by co-optation by the outgoing members at the end of 1813. The entry of Corrientes into the orbit of Artigas was reflected in the election of Juan Bautista Méndez, the commander of the regular troops in the city, as Governor, but the composition of the Cabildo remained unchanged. This development, although it changed the relationship of Corrientes with the other River Plate provinces, apparently had only minor effects on the internal political and social equilibrium. By changing the pattern of its external alliances, the locally dominant group seemed to have ensured for itself greater freedom of action. Also very characteristic of this restricted interpretation of the change signified by the province's incorporation into the Free Peoples, and of the autonomy which was retained within that system by the Cabildo of Corrientes, was the decisive manner in which the latter countered those measures of Artigas which seemed to it dangerous. Thus, the idea of granting, within Corrientes, a refuge for Indians from the other bank of the Paraná was rejected out of hand. The passionate appeals of Artigas to the egalitarian sentiments of the Cabildo members ('it is not justifiable to maintain our rights and exclude others who also have rights...can we call ourselves patriots if we are indifferent to this evil?')[56] did not persuade the Cabildo any more than the hint that for Artigas benevolence towards the Indians was a question not only of principle, but of political tactics.

However, incorporation into the Free Peoples could not fail to introduce more far-reaching changes. In contrast to the decisive attitude of the Cabildo, which wanted to limit such changes as far as possible, Artigas was trying, discreetly but tenaciously, to change the internal political equilibrium. His instrument for this purpose was the Provincial Congress, which he convoked as soon as he knew that Corrientes had declared in his favour.[57] After some tergiversations, which it justified by attributing them to a misinterpretation of Artigas's verbal orders, the Cabildo only convoked the Congress under pressure from certain rural militia commanders. The latter, in fact, became a sort of electoral college, and came to dominate, either directly or through nominees, the Provincial Congress, in which the provincial capital had only one representative. However, this broadening of the political base constituted by the establishment of a predominantly rural Congress as a parallel organisation to the predominantly urban Cabildo by no means succeeded in giving Artigas that solid basis of local support which he needed. The first event to break the solidity of this new political order was the defection of Artigas's personal agent and President of the Congress, Genaro Perugorría, who came to an understanding with some members of the Cabildo and led a pro-Buenos Aires movement simultaneous with that of Hereñú in Entre Ríos. Thereafter, it was the political manoeuvres and rivalries of those same commanders which were to determine – after the defeat and execution of Perugorría – the turbulent course of events in Corrientes under the rule of Artigas.

The Protector appeared to resign himself to being unable to count on unwavering support in that province, and preferred not to contribute to the accentuation of the political antagonisms there. He did insist on the deportation of the Spanish-born, but here, as in the Banda Oriental, he had to face the only partially passive resistance of his local allies, and was obliged to yield to it, sadly concluding, in a message to the Governor of Corrientes, Silva, 'you tell me that the bad ones have gone, and may God grant that you have found the good ones'.[58] Although the Protector did not consider the incident closed, and did not refrain from uttering vague threats and more detailed prophecies of future misfortunes, attributed to the lack of zeal of Silva, he was careful not to insist on orders which ran the risk of being disobeyed. Moreover, when confronting dissidence among the American-born, Artigas was nearly always more prepared to overlook it than were his associates in Corrientes. Thus, when sending back from his headquarters Ángel Escobar and Francisco Araujo 'because the accusations levelled against them by this government did not provide any motive for greater misgivings as regards the system',[59] he concluded with an exhortation not to 'encourage rivalries, which extinguish the Patriotic fire and love for the public cause'. It is true that occasionally Artigas showed greater severity, as in the case of the Cabildo member Ángel Fernández Blanco, implicated in the movement led by Perugorría, whom he refused to send back from his headquarters, where he was holding him prisoner. He accompanied his refusal with the usual threats – this time somewhat less vague – concerning any possible relaxation of zeal on the part of the Governor, Silva.[60] However, he soon revoked this decision: on 27 June he sent word to Silva himself that Fernández Blanco, who 'after all is an American' and who appeared to have recovered during his captivity his enthusiasm for 'the system', was being sent back to Corrientes. It would be up to Silva, who had interceded on his behalf, to decide on his definitive release. Artigas, on his part, spoke of his 'mistaken opinions' as not proven beyond reasonable doubt, and concluded that he had not 'seen any documentary evidence of his misbehaviour'. The imprisonment of Fernández Blanco, and the banishment of the most important figures implicated in Perugorría's rising, were from the outset merely temporary measures, designed to neutralise the influence of that group of uncertain loyalty during the imminent election of a new Provincial Congress.[61]

This comparative leniency was not only the expression of humanitarian sentiments which Artigas was proud to acknowledge;[62] it stemmed also from a certain pessimism regarding the quality of the support which he had received in Corrientes. To his first partisans there, Artigas was merely an external support, which it was prudent to keep at a distance. Artigas, after realising that he could not expect from Corrientes any more enthusiastic adherence than this, concentrated his efforts on obtaining from it the maximum benefit for his overall policy. He did not, it is true, cease to give excellent advice to the authorities under his protection: he called on them to 'wipe out the excesses of despotism' and the 'accursed custom of a man's high social standing being decided in the cradle', to take sincere steps to protect 'the unfortunate, and not leave them defenceless when their only crime has been poverty'.[63] He also refused to countenance disorder and looting among the armed forces – 'Your Excellency will, in the case of the slightest disorder among the troops, hold their commanders responsible, so that the innocent citizen may breathe freely'.[64] However, the first of these golden counsels was of too general a nature to be expressed in the form of practical proposals, and as for the second, nothing would have pleased the Cabildo more than to follow it, but a well-founded fear prevented it from doing so, and the support offered by Artigas, who said that he was prepared to 'reprimand military commanders' against whom well-founded charges were brought was only too obviously limited. Artigas was, however, both more precise and less circumspect when it was a question of defining the contribution of Corrientes to the political and military action of the League of Free Peoples.

It was necessary, in the first place, for Corrientes to follow his directives regarding military organisation, and on this subject Artigas issued detailed and lengthy instructions. Corrientes was spending too much on its militias. The Uruguayan militias had a far lower rate of pay (and, for that reason, as Hernán Gómez maliciously observed, they also had considerably less respect for other people's property).[65] At the same time, Corrientes should pay more attention to the organisation of its regular troops. In the same way, it was necessary for Corrientes to regulate its commerce according to the directives of Artigas, who thus hoped to possess a means, albeit of limited effectiveness, of pressure on Buenos Aires. It has already been observed that the cost of these frequent bans on trade was, for Corrientes, excessively high. Nevertheless, Artigas was prepared to impose the ban. He found it surprising that the Cabildo of Corrientes should request authorisation to carry on trade with the city which had declared itself the enemy of all the Free Peoples. The impoverishment which the ban would signify for Corrientes was, in his view, a mere pretext. 'Poverty is no crime', he declared sententiously, and concluded by observing that the Banda Oriental had renounced peaceable trade five years before, and had been reduced to poverty, but that 'that had not sufficed to suffocate its sentiments of honour, but had spurred it on to give fulfilment to them...If this example does not serve as a lesson to the other peoples, then we must conclude that all virtue is dead among them'. Artigas found it impossible to believe such a thing of Corrientes, to favour which he had already made considerable sacrifices (apparently, those connected with the establishment of a Government loyal to himself). He was sure that these considerations would induce the Cabildo members to desist from making a 'request which discredited them'.⁶⁶ They did, indeed, abandon their insistence, since they had discovered that their Protector, so tolerant in other respects, would allow no vacillation on this point. The entire episode, however, shows the equivocal nature of the relationship between Artigas and his allies in Corrientes. The latter felt no Revolutionary enthusiasm whatever, and exhortations to make constant sacrifices provoked little response among those who had decided to support the cause of Artigas principally out of motives of prudence. This rapprochement marked by profound misgivings was not to survive the change in the fortunes of the movement provoked by the Portuguese invasion of the Banda Oriental. This was not only because the people of Corrientes had no desire to continue supporting a cause which they had never really regarded as their own. The reason was that, as that cause encountered difficulties, the sacrifices that were demanded on its behalf became increasingly onerous. Just as in the time of the domination of Buenos Aires, Corrientes had to send an increasing number of troops to fight outside its boundaries, and a train of supplies had to follow the troops. It was the moment for a reconciliation with Buenos Aires, which had already showed in Salta and, more discreetly, in other parts of the Interior, a greater willingness to reach an understanding with the locally dominant sectors. On 24 May 1818 a *pronunciamiento* by the small regular force that remained in Corrientes deposed Méndez (who had been reinstated as Governor) and initiated a cautious movement of dissidence, which was terminated by the swift success of an invasion by Guaraní Indians from Misiones led by Andrés Artigas. The hour of Guaraní rule in Corrientes had arrived. Despite the restoration of Méndez, and the establishment of a Cabildo and of rural military commanders mostly recruited from among those who had held those offices before, the province was to experience a humiliation which it would be hard to forget. Like the rule of Otorgués in Montevideo, that of Andresito in Corrientes was to give rise to a vast number of semi-legendary accounts of the sufferings inflicted by the conquerors on the proud population. As late as 1929 Hernán Gómez was to mention among the first measures of that 'régime of terror and shame' the decree obliging the citizens of Corrientes to return the Misiones Indians carried off as booty in a frontier skirmish by Colonel Vedoya, and who 'were shared out to work as domestic servants'.⁶⁷ In addition to these affronts, which were, of course, not all imaginary, the subjection of the entire economy of Corrientes to the service of the last resistance of Artigas's movement was another, and no less deplored, consequence of the conquest by the Misiones Indians. Even after this episode, Artigas tried to re-establish an understanding with the Cabildo of Corrientes. In September 1819 he promised to withdraw the Misiones Indians from the territory of Corrientes. He had failed to do so before then only because the provincial authorities had omitted to inform him of 'the excesses which they say have been committed'.⁶⁸ After so much disillusionment, however, *artiguismo* in Corrientes had lost much of its vigour, and was never to recover it.

Artiguismo in Corrientes had, from the beginning, been a political attitude adopted by men accustomed to managing the affairs of the province, rather than the emergence of a new political group. It is true that pressure from Artigas accelerated the process which was to give participation in decision-making to the military commanders in the rural areas. This development was, however, similar in nature and scope to that which was taking place in the territories governed by Buenos Aires. It is, moreover, difficult to conceive of a militarisation process of the kind that happened in the River Plate region taking place without those who organised the countryside for the war effort acquiring, in one way or another, greater political power. Moreover, the process was no more radical in its scope or its political consequences than it was in those territories governed according to the dictates of social conservatism. As a force from outside, imported into the province with the support of a substantial group drawn from the social elements which already participated in its government, Artigas's revolution was neither willing nor able to identify itself with a political counter-élite in rivalry to the one it found already established. Any innovating tendencies were, in any case, counterbalanced, because the new elements which from time to time they tried to introduce into the balance of forces were alien to Corrientes and traditionally considered as hostile, not only by the élite, but by the population as a whole. Thus, the Indians from Misiones might serve as an instrument of external domination over Corrientes, yet the first condition of the re-establishment of any understanding with elements representative of the local forces had to be the promise of their withdrawal. Corrientes did, indeed, have its own Indian population, confined to reservations, but it was too small in numbers and too isolated from the remaining population of the rural areas, to serve as a decisive support for any new distribution of political power. There was a more fundamental reason: the inhabitants of the Corrientes reservations, accustomed to accepting their fate with resignation, seemed unwilling to abandon their age-old passivity and respond to the stimuli offered by Artigas's movement, which were necessarily limited by the fear of losing other supports which might be more lukewarm but were much more powerful. Although the identification of the reservation Indians with those from outside the province seems to have been above all a stratagem designed to increase the unpopularity of the former group, the dangers which a real emancipation would pose for some members of the governing sector in Corrientes can be seen in the first petition submitted by the Indians of the village of Santa Lucía to the first Provincial Congress. This document was full of denunciations of usurpation of communal lands by landowners from the provincial capital.[69]

Would this new equilibrium within the dominant sector, which gave an increased influence to the rural elements, not have effects on the future course of political events in Corrientes? After all, the city of Corrientes was something both more than and less than the capital of a vast rural district devoted to cattle-raising over which, in any case, as has been observed already, the city did not exercise full control. It was also the capital of a much smaller agricultural district, the products of which found a market in Buenos Aires, and the centre of craft industries more highly developed than in other urban centres of the Littoral. Can one speak, then, of a policy of the city, of that city which was an anomaly within the structure of the Littoral, because its economic activities were directed towards the River Plate market, and a conflicting policy of the countryside, which was a fragment of the vast Littoral cattle-raising area, which sought prosperity in an outlet to overseas markets? The possibility of such a divergence was, in the long run, undeniable, although it was to be conditioned by the fact that the markets for the small livestock production of Corrientes were to be found in the neighbouring lands across the River Uruguay more frequently than in Europe. For the moment, that divergence did not become evident, and for a very good reason: the policy of Artigas was equally prejudicial to city and countryside, since it progressively isolated Corrientes from its potential markets (of which only the Paraguayan one was lost for reasons unconnected with that policy), increased rural disorder, and imposed on the economy of the province an increasing burden in order to sustain the war. The process of gradual detachment from *artiguismo* does not appear to have created more profound divisions than had adherence to it. When Artigas, after his first defeats at the hands of the Portuguese, ordered that 'the zeal of the magistrates must make an example of those indolent citizens who cannot be persuaded by moderation or loving treatment or convincing reasoning to offer themselves in the service of their country',[70] he was reacting to the dissatisfaction of ever wider social groups with a war which required the constant dispatch of men to remote lands. When he proposed to liberate the slaves and incorporate them into the regular military units,[71] he was running the risk of accentuating that same disaffection among the upper sectors which were directly experiencing the consequences of commercial isolation.

Thus the stability of the politically dominant groups was reflected in the continuing influence of certain leaders, at the local and the provincial level. Elías Galván, the very popular Lieutenant-Governor sent in 1810 to govern Corrientes on behalf of the Buenos Aires Revolution (and whose dismissal and replacement by another official less popular with the Cabildo of Corrientes was a factor influencing the adherence of the latter to Artigas) was able to return in 1818 to his native city, and find intact his following among the local leading citizens, who were to support him in the secessionist adventure drastically suppressed by the Guaraní invasion.

Corrientes had joined Artigas's camp because its leaders had accumulated grievances against the capital which they considered extremely serious. But there was another and more immediate reason: any other solution would have been both more dangerous and more costly. The geographical situation of the province, close to the centre of Artigas's power in the Banda Oriental, Misiones and Entre Ríos, and its less efficient communications with Buenos Aires (from which, in any case, it could only expect limited support), left it with no alternative. This perhaps explains why Santa Fe, which was suffering from Buenos Aires more serious grievances than was Corrientes, delayed longer in taking the same step and thereafter displayed so much vacillation. In Santa Fe, the risks were less unevenly distributed between the political options open, and the choice was, therefore, more difficult.

For several reasons, control over Santa Fe, or at least a reasonable certainty that it would not adopt a hostile attitude, was vital for Buenos Aires. That small province was not only – despite its poor and small population – an essential piece on the Littoral chessboard. What was even more important was that its territory constituted an essential link between Buenos Aires and the Interior. Buenos Aires could not, therefore, resign itself to seeing the province decisively integrated into a hostile political system. Nor did Santa Fe feel entirely well situated as a member of the union of the Free Peoples. Apart from the dubious privilege of suffering the first blows in any offensive of Buenos Aires against the *artiguista* bloc, and the equally dubious one of offering Artigas the most effective instrument of pressure on Buenos Aires, a factor which impelled the Leader of the Uruguayans to encourage constant tension between Santa Fe and its former overlords, the egalitarian union with the peoples beyond the Paraná represented a profound innovation as compared with the previous situation, in which Santa Fe had transformed the Western half of Entre Ríos into its sphere of influence and had maintained with the rest of the lands now dominated by Artigas less significant relations than it had had with Paraguay and, above all, with the Interior and with Peru, where it had found a market for its principal livestock product – mules.

These vacillations were ended again and again by the brutality of Buenos Aires's policy, which from the outset eliminated even the possibility of a viable agreement with the locally dominant elements in Santa Fe. This possibility was, however, a very real one. After 1820, Santa Fe was to demonstrate – with only short-lived exceptions – an exemplary loyalty to any political power which achieved stable control of Buenos Aires. The history of Artigas's movement in Santa Fe was, however, to be marked by repeated outbreaks of resistance to the military presence of Buenos Aires, followed, as soon as that presence was removed, and to the considerable alarm of Artigas, by an increasingly undisguised search for a *modus vivendi* with that overpowering neighbour.

The arrival of *artiguismo* in Santa Fe was comparable in some respects to its advance in Corrientes. There was, in the first place, potential discontent with the Buenos Aires Revolution, which hesitated to give the Lieutenant-Governorship to a local figure, and there had also been incidents reminiscent of the best traditions of the *ancien régime*, in which the Cabildo attempted to attract the wandering attention of the supreme power with profuse – and also confused – accusations regarding the tyrannical rapacity of that power's local agents. Finally, there were more serious causes of this discontent. The Revolution first deprived Santa Fe of the income of the Cabildo, which was diverted to the Treasury of Buenos Aires, and eventually took away the majority of its regular troops for the disastrous campaign against Artigas which took place in Entre Ríos in 1814. The Indian frontier was left dangerously unguarded, and after the alarms of 1811 and 1812 the events of 1813 seemed to announce its total collapse. The Indians were drawing increasingly nearer to the city itself, even reaching the orchards in the suburbs. The result, for the owners of lands which had been secure, was ruinous. For the mass of the population of Santa Fe, brought up to feel hostility and fear towards the Indians, the risk of an even greater catastrophe appeared imminent. Meanwhile, the loss of the supplies which had come from the Northern rural areas and the increasing isolation from the Entre Ríos bank of the Paraná, which had been used by Santa Fe for raising cattle, caused an increasing shortage of beef.[72] The chroniclers of Santa Fe invite us to commiserate with the fate of a population thus condemned to eating fish – those yellowish and oily fish from the slow and muddy Paraná, which were henceforth to be the most favoured dishes of Santa Fe's cuisine.

Buenos Aires was insensitive to the laments of the Santa Fe élite, which had not decided to embark on the path of dissidence, the risks of which were only too obvious. The decision finally made was only partly spontaneous. When Santa Fe joined Artigas's movement, there were already in its territory troops of the Free Peoples from beyond the Paraná. Under the aegis of Artigas, the new governor was to be the elderly Francisco Antonio Candioti, the richest of the Santa Fe mule-dealers, whose character as a country gentleman, endowed with an exotic nobility, has been felicitously described by the Robertson brothers. But it was Candioti himself who had just written to his friend the acting Supreme Director Álvarez Thomas, asking him to send to the province the military assistance which would have made the dissident movement unnecessary.

The vacillations of the visible head of *artiguismo* in Santa Fe are easily explicable. In the association of the Free Peoples Santa Fe was not destined to find the peace which it needed above all. The pro-Indian policy of Artigas was to provoke even more misgivings in this province than in Corrientes, although the weakening of the military defences against the Indians had already obliged the citizens of Santa Fe to make compromises, without, however, renouncing that hostility which had its roots in age-old struggles, and which in 1815 had led to the massacre by an infuriated crowd of an entire settlement of Indians pacified by Candioti and settled in Guadalupe. At last, when the Governor lay dying, the longed-for help from Buenos Aires arrived. It was not the arms that had been asked for, but a military force commanded by General Viamonte and prepared to make its weight felt in the politics of Santa Fe. It was this army which imposed as Candioti's successor Tarragona, a prosperous manufacturer of soap and candles who since 1810 had entertained political ambitions looked on with disfavour by the Cabildo. The unpopular Lieutenant-Governor (Tarragona had accepted this demotion, which was symbolic of the renewed obedience of Santa Fe to Buenos Aires) and his even more unpopular armed protectors were to be driven out in April 1816, in an incident in which the still inexperienced men of Santa Fe showed but little of that deadly efficiency in war which was to characterise them in the future. The insurrection against Viamonte was sparked off by the frontier troops, whom the Buenos Aires general had only just reorganised. It was led by Ensign Estanislao López, who even before 1810 had begun his military career on the frontier under the discreet protection of his father, a Royal official. The frontier troops, however, although they occupied the countryside without difficulty, were not capable of wresting the city from its garrison of Buenos Aires troops. It was to be reinforcements from beyond the Paraná which, at the invitation of the urban leaders of the insurrection, were to defeat Viamonte and capture the city after a few days of fighting and looting. In August, after a deceptive interlude of peace during which a pact was signed between the delegates of the central government and those of rebellious Santa Fe, Buenos Aires troops again occupied the city. They remained there for nearly a month, subjecting the place to a methodical sack, and fighting off the harrassing local forces. The final outcome was no more successful than in April, although the Buenos Aires commander – this time it was Eustoquio Díaz Vélez – managed to avoid capture by a timely flight across the river, followed by most of his troops and the voluminous booty accumulated in four weeks of looting.

The immediate dangers, therefore, seemed to have been overcome, but the future did not appear promising. The relations between Santa Fe and the most typical *artiguista* leader the other side of the river, Eusebio Hereñú, were almost as acrimonious as before the incorporation into the alliance of the Free Peoples. After their first liberation, the people of Santa Fe were hard put to get rid of their grasping saviours from Entre Ríos. For their second liberation, they could no longer count on any help from their nominal allies. The only course left, therefore, was a policy of equilibrium between the claims of Buenos Aires and those of Artigas's movement, although even this policy involved considerable dangers. In November 1816[73] Artigas had thought fit to strike at Buenos Aires through Santa Fe's territory, and there seemed to be no way of ignoring his will without risking his indifference in the face of any renewed offensive on the part of Buenos Aires. What made the situation even more complicated was that Santa Fe had by no means achieved solid internal unity. The events of April 1816 had resulted in Mariano Vera's becoming Governor. He was the scion of an old family, being a descendant of the founder of Corrientes through a branch which included a general, his uncle, and a Royal standard-bearer of the Santa Fe Cabildo, his father, and he possessed a reasonably large fortune which had made it possible for him to organise private, though not notably successful, campaigns against the Indians. He came, therefore, from that élite with a predominantly rural basis which, as has already been observed, also dominated the city of Santa Fe, without suffering any serious rivalry from the excessively small nucleus of not very prosperous merchants. The appointment of Vera as Governor seemed, therefore, to favour the consolidation of this group. This was not to be the case, however, and the relations between the Governor and the Cabildo which had ensured his triumph soon became tense. In the view of the Cabildo, the Governor was exceeding his attributions, which the Cabildo appeared to consider as consisting merely of the fulfilment of the directives emanating from that body. The resignations submitted in protest by various members of the Cabildo were rejected without any argument directed towards flattering their sensibilities: they were simply ordered peremptorily to continue with their functions.

Vera thus triumphed over those who had considered themselves his peers, and was able to assume the unquestioned leadership of the political life of Santa Fe. In 1817, Artigas, already influenced by the unsuccessful course of the Uruguayan resistance to the Portuguese invasion, resolved to gain the full support of the cautious Governor. We have already mentioned how, with this purpose in view, he had appointed the Governor's brother as Governor of Entre Ríos. Meanwhile, the advantages of this policy were not immediately evident from the point of view of Santa Fe. The Indian menace was still present, and the Governor was accused of not doing enough to combat it. Above all, the Cabildo did not abandon its hostile stance. The signs of a new threat from Buenos Aires (and the Cabildo, after having shared the fear of the excessive influence of Artigas, declared that it was even more afraid of a discreet compromise between the Governor and Buenos Aires) seemed to make necessary a firmer leadership than Vera, in the opinion of his enemies, was capable of imposing. In July 1818 a revolution which began in the Cabildo and concluded with the intervention of the frontier troops made Estanislao López Governor. In pursuance of the arguments invoked in the Cabildo against Vera, work began simultaneously on the drafting of a provincial constitution, which was to be promulgated in 1819.

Although López did not belong to the circle of Cabildo members, the latter were the first to recognise him as the leader whom the province needed. One member of that circle was Don Domingo Crespo, who interrupted the monotonous account of catastrophes in his *Memorias* to praise that 'political leader famous in the Revolution of America...the fortunate hero throughout his career, in short, a naturally great man'.[74] López made a contribution to his alliance with this group which Vera had lacked: that of his prestige as a professional officer in his dealings with a military force which the constant Indian menace had made it necessary to enlarge. Indeed, that menace, both from the North and the South, had eventually affected the whole territory of the province and had made necessary the systematic reorganisation of the militias. It is true that the ascendancy of López over these armed bodies of men was not unquestioned from the outset. Militia troops from Coronda figured among the inhabitants of that locality who after 1818 sought refuge in Buenos Aires, and whole regiments of mulattoes from the city marched off to Paraná with the fugitive Mariano Vera. But after López's victories over Buenos Aires in 1819 – achieved by tactics inspired by much rustic astuteness, with false retreats of cavalry which were transformed into ferocious counter-attacks as soon as the enemy broke formation, and the capture of enemy horses under cover of mist – his hold over Santa Fe was never again to be seriously challenged during his twenty years of rule. This was, no doubt, partly due to the extreme prudence which the old frontier leader employed in managing the affairs of the province. Ruined by invasions and wars, Santa Fe was grateful to its Governor, not so much, perhaps, for the victories which it achieved under his leadership, as for the way in which his firm guiding hand made it possible for the province to avoid fresh conflicts.

However, this fortunate policy does not provide a complete explanation. The consensus which characterised the long government of López was also made possible by the social structure of Santa Fe, which was never threatened or even questioned throughout the process. Vera had carried on the struggle against the lawless semi-employed sectors in the countryside and against rural indiscipline which had been initiated by the delegates of Buenos Aires. In the more solidly-based order imposed by López the protection of peace and security in the rural areas, through a rearrangement of the system of productive activities which reaffirmed the predominance of the landowners, occupied an essential place. It was, therefore, the simplicity of the cattle-raising society in the Littoral which was reflected in the political solidity of the solution imposed in 1818. This simplicity was, of course, less evident in Santa Fe – which had had a long and complex history in which its rôle as the port of the middle reaches of the Paraná had been of some importance – than, for example, in neighbouring Entre Ríos. But in Santa Fe, too, the commercial decline had initiated a process of simplification finally completed by the war, which systematically destroyed urban wealth and, by cutting the route to Upper Peru, had put an end to even the possibility of the dual economic activity, based on cattle-raising and trade in conjunction, which had created the prosperity of Candioti and other citizens of Santa Fe. Now the most urgent task – in Santa Fe as in the rest of the Littoral – was to gain a stake in the overseas export economy and, with this end in view, to replenish and increase the herds of cattle. This undertaking, in which the collective interests of the province and those of its upper class coincided so exactly, was the economic corollary of the consensus assured under the aegis of López.

All this was true, but not all the members of the Santa Fe élite were landowners, nor was the identification of the landowners with the enterprise of economic reconstruction sufficiently complete to stifle in all of them political ambitions incompatible with the stability of López's rule. Doctor José Elías Galisteo and Father Amenábar, who placed their political and administrative experience at the service of the leader of Santa Fe, might well have used their talents more independently. The unruly and alarming Doctor Juan Francisco Seguí, a man possessing very little besides his talent for stratagems which were not always morally commendable, the Cabildo members who had promoted López because they were tired of the arrogance of Vera, and the militia commanders who had followed the latter, all constituted a redoubtable potential opposition. Despite his successes, in 1822 López had to deal with a conspiracy organised by disaffected militia commanders, held as prisoners in the city after a prolonged exile, and by members of one of the most illustrious families represented in the Cabildo. The conspiracy was, however, easily suppressed, thanks to information provided by a prison warder, and López took swift and selective punitive action. The militia commanders were executed, and the most compromised man among the instigators of the conspiracy among the Cabildo élite was banished after refusing to flee at the Governor's suggestion. The enquiry was interrupted before it could reveal evidence of more widespread disaffection in that group of families connected with the Cabildo. Thenceforth, the loyalty of that group was confirmed by the conviction that the overthrow of López was too risky an enterprise.

This was the case because López had a power-base independent of that élite: a military organisation financed by the province but bound to its leader by a loyalty that was more personal than institutional. He enjoyed, moreover, a popularity which surpassed the bounds of that élite and was the fruit of the successes already achieved in the search for a stable peace for that province which for too long had been devastated by war. In this way, the fulfilment of a programme which in essence combined economic rehabilitation with social stability was accompanied by a very real broadening of the political power-base, which was no longer controlled by the élite associated with the Cabildo. Moreover, that broadening appears to have been one of the reasons for the success of the substantially conservative policy followed by López, in so far as, by disciplining the traditional élite, it counteracted its

The Revolution in the country as a whole

tendency to divide internally into rival lineages and clans, which was a serious potential threat to the stability achieved. In this respect, the solution reached in the only half-heartedly *artiguista* Santa Fe of 1818 was an anticipation of future developments. After 1820 it was to take place in more than one province of the Interior and, after 1830, certain of its characteristics were to be evident in Buenos Aires under the régime of Rosas.

6   THE DISSOLUTION OF THE REVOLUTIONARY ORDER

POLITICAL FRAGMENTATION (1819-21)

During the first decade after the Revolution two rival political systems had made it their first task to achieve victory on the field of battle. Around 1816 the war ceased to be popular, and weariness began to weaken the solidity of both rivals. On 30 November 1816 Artigas could write in a resigned tone to Miguel Barreiro[1] that 'our fellow-countrymen are now less energetic than [they were] in other circumstances; it is necessary to oblige them, and if the conviction of their own interest is not enough to move them, then it will be necessary to use severity'. At about the same time, the Pueyrredón Government in Buenos Aires was ceasing to think of the war as a glorious collective enterprise, and thought of it merely as an evil which could only be ended through victory. But, in the first case, the idea of endowing again with fighting spirit a peasantry which was fighting at a disadvantage was quite impracticable; and in the second, the government's admission that the war was in fact a calamity did not make it any easier to extract from the country the resources needed to prosecute the war. In each camp – in that of Artigas, owing to the harsh anticlimax that followed the *annus mirabilis* of 1815, when it had seemed that his movement was going to acquire control of the entire River Plate region, and in that of the Directory through a slower but equally inexorable process – the wear-and-tear suffered by the Revolutionary political system was aggravated. In both camps the decline of the supreme authority coincided with the increasing vigour of the regional authorities. The process was evident in the Federal League, where the loss of Artigas's immediate power-base in the Banda Oriental diminished his prestige among his former subordinates in the Littoral. In 1819, Santa Fe under the rule of López was an uncertain and hesitant ally, while Entre Ríos under Ramírez was showing a new independence. Only Corrientes, under the surveillance of the Guaraní troops from Misiones, was still completely obedient to the Protector of the Free Peoples. However, albeit in a more discreet manner, an analogous process was taking place in the territory controlled by Buenos Aires. Here the first symptom was the growing inefficiency of the governmental apparatus, which by 1819 was almost paralysed. Further disintegration of the system ruled by the Directory was only prevented by that institution of more than local scope, to which the Revolutionary Government had devoted most of its resources – the Army.

The dissolution of the Revolutionary order

Nevertheless, not even the presence of the National Army was enough to call a halt to the disintegration of political authority in the territory controlled by Buenos Aires. As had been made clear in 1815, the Army itself could not avoid being affected by this process, and from 1816 onwards the Directory tried to limit the use of the Army as a weapon in internal politics, partly because the shift of the theatre of war to the Pacific Coast and the reduction of the State's revenue obliged it to reduce the size of the national armed forces operating within the country. For this reason, it entrusted the defence of the frontier with Upper Peru to a provincial force, and left the Portuguese free to destroy the power of Artigas in the Banda Oriental, which in early 1815 had shown itself to be invulnerable to the attacks of Buenos Aires. Pueyrredón had, therefore, made efforts to frame a policy which, by taking a more moderate stance and combining this with the search for local support in the Interior, would offer an alternative to the military-based authoritarianism dominant until 1815. The return in 1819 to the policy which had led to the collapse of 1815 was only the prologue to an even greater political collapse, made inevitable by the diminished power of the military apparatus at the Government's disposal and also by the increased strength, achieved in agreement with or in opposition to the central government, by regional forces which it was now too late to confront.

There was no general confrontation, however, because the instrument on which the government of the Directory counted fell to pieces in its hands. That part of the Army which was still within the national territory gradually began to disintegrate, along with the political system in the territories which it was supposed to be guarding. This disintegration was encouraged by the increasingly unmistakable atmosphere of decay that surrounded the Buenos Aires régime after 1819. At the beginning of that year, claiming that he was suffering from the results of a household accident which had affected his 'most noble parts', Pueyrredón had requested leave of absence, and left General Rondeau in charge of the government. This man, who was appreciated for his inclination to live and let live, seemed to be the appropriate figure to attenuate the tensions which the steadily increasing severity of the régime of the Directory had provoked. Half way through the year, after a brief return to office, Pueyrredón submitted his definitive resignation. He thought fit to see, in the constitution which Congress had just promulgated, the crowning event of that phase of history which he had been called on to direct. The situation was, in fact, very different, and the constitution was to be the cause – or the pretext – of fresh conflicts. It was decidedly centralist, and its adversaries also attributed to it an aristocratic spirit which was reflected in the composition of the senate and the arrangements for elections, which not only limited the right to vote but sought to achieve an even greater control of the vote by the use of indirect suffrage. Underlying these aristocratic tendencies, the enemies of the Directory were alarmed at the constitution's barely disguised monarchical orientation, a trend which had, in fact, characterised the régime of the Directory and was merely one aspect of its attempts to find in Continental Europe a force to counterbalance the hegemony of Great Britain. But, whatever justifications might be advanced for this flirtation with monarchism, it allowed the very diverse factions opposed to the predominance of the Directory to unite under the banner of a republican crusade. This opportunity could no longer be turned to advantage by Artigas, who in early 1820 was failing in his last attempts to save at least some part of the territory of Uruguay from the Portuguese invaders. Instead of the irresistible advance of the dissident movement in the Littoral, which in 1815 had threatened to overwhelm the entire Revolutionary territory, what was emerging in 1819 was a new and much looser combination of the various forces which, for very varied motives, had finally decided to confront the central government. A change in the current political vocabulary reflected this transformation of the nature of the opposition to the central government. The term 'federalist', being too closely identified with the *artiguista* past, was gradually abandoned in the Littoral, and remained practically unknown in the Interior. The enemies of the central power preferred to call themselves 'liberals'. This term had the advantage of being less precise in meaning and also of marking a new political beginning, and it attracted the allegiance both of those who were turning against the central government and those who were prepared to shake off their allegiance to the Protector of the Free Peoples.

The disintegration of the system ruled by the Directory began in Tucumán. Ever since, in the middle of 1819, the best troops of the Army of the North had been sent off to combat the dissident movement in the Littoral, the city had been garrisoned by a force of about two thousand troops, recruited from the province itself. It was this garrison which, on 11 November 1819, overthrew the Intendant-Governor Mota Botello, who had held the post since October 1817. Mota Botello, who had previously been Lieutenant-Governor of Catamarca and had no following of his own in Tucumán, had been sent to replace the over-powerful Colonel Bernabé Aráoz. The latter not only belonged to a family with numerous ramifications, solidly established in the Cabildo of Tucumán. As a landowner and the possessor of a considerable commercial fortune, he had contributed to the cause of the Revolution an entire clientèle bound to him by personal loyalty. In 1812 his action had been decisive in the recruitment of those rustic militias which had fought alongside the regular troops in the battle of Tucumán. In addition to this loyal following of men, Aráoz increased his influence by his sheer wealth. As Intendant-Governor he paid out of his own pocket for the canal which ensured for the city a permanent supply of water,[2] of which the inhabitants had suffered a scarcity for a century and a half. The government of Tucumán was, therefore, merely confirming and consolidating a previously existing situation. Aráoz did, indeed, obey the

The dissolution of the Revolutionary order

decision of the central government and, in a disciplined manner, handed over his post to Mota Botello, yet two years later he was to be something more than the passive beneficiary of the military rising, in the preparation of which he had a part. The movement had two results: it restored Aráoz to the Governorship, to which he was elected by the Cabildo at the suggestion of the leaders of the military movement,[3] and it handed over the military command of Tucumán to those same leaders, among whom a decisive part had been played by Major Abraham González, an officer of Uruguayan origin whose career until that moment had not been especially brilliant. It was true that, in formal terms, the breakdown in legality was by no means total. The Cabildo, for example, appointed Aráoz interim Intendant-Governor 'until such time as the Supreme Government of the Nation, using its exalted and exclusive prerogatives, shall appoint another Governor or shall approve the election made by this Municipality'. Even so, the deposition of Mota Botello created a local authority based on decisions which were also local. For its creation, however, the influence of Aráoz was combined with the support of a garrison which until then had formed part of the National Army, had been partly maintained by the resources of the central government, and was only in part locally recruited.

It was this important part played by the fragments of the National Army which survived the collapse of the central authority which constituted the original characteristic of the political experience which was beginning in several regions of the Interior. These garrison troops, in fact, recognised leaders who were not always the same as those holding sway in the region the destiny of which those troops were helping to decide. As regards Abraham González, we have only a conventional, and not very favourable, portrait. Nevertheless, this second-rate officer had gathered a sufficiently large following to play the part of leader of the 'corps of officers' on whose behalf he was directing the movement, and it was this that led to his promotion to General and his appointment as Governor of Tucumán, although it is true that he held the latter appointment for only a few months, marked by upheavals, until his definitive eclipse in January 1822. In this way the military garrisons, being forces partly alien to the milieu in which they were acting, threatened to constitute within that milieu an element in the new political system only loosely controlled by the local leading citizens, who, since they controlled municipal appointments and the organisation of the militias, seemed destined to fill in each regional centre the vacuum left by the moribund central authority. Moreover, the crisis of the central authority was accompanied by a crisis in the internal equilibrium of those garrisons, which dramatically overturned the existing system of leadership for the benefit of secondary figures within the officer corps. There was a scandalous manifestation of this process in Tucumán in the shape of the imprisonment of Belgrano, who had, indeed, already retired from command, by the hitherto unknown González. The influence of the garrison troops seems to have made possible the promotion to leading positions of figures which had been excluded not merely from the local ruling sector, but from the dominant sectors elsewhere in the United Provinces.

The dangers which this situation posed for social stability did not pass unnoticed in Tucumán. It is suggestive that in January 1820 the Cabildo, after examining an analogous problem, decided to purge the civic force – that was the name given to the urban militia – of 'that mixture of servants, wage-earners and European prisoners who had been incorporated into that force'.[4] Yet one must not exaggerate these dangers: the subsequent promotion of González was due, not only to the support he enjoyed in the garrison, but also to the help of Aráoz, who put him in command of the military forces of his Republic of Tucumán, and his rapid fall from power would seem to indicate that the forces supporting him were not strong enough to dominate the situation in Tucumán. Moreover, while González was preparing the ground for his ephemeral triumph, Aráoz was unmistakably the dominant figure in Tucumán, a province which he was to convert into a Republic. Did the return to power of the man who had occupied it on behalf of the central government from 1814 to 1817 ensure any continuity of political style between the Intendancy and the new Republic? This was partly true, but in the second period certain traits which were present in the first period were accentuated. Thus, the wealthy President found it increasingly difficult to distinguish between his private fortune and the official funds of the province. Although the continuity between the first and the second period was manifested in acts of generosity of which an example has already been described, these were offset by even more generous countermeasures. In return for having financed the canal which finally ensured the water-supply of Tucumán, Aráoz in 1817 requested that from that water he should be supplied with 'as much as is necessary for the use of his household and rural properties, without cost'. In 1820, after referring to the 'sacrifice, both personal and of his fortune' made by the Supreme President, and not forgetting the unforgettable canal, the Cabildo, now transformed under the republican constitution into the First Court of Justice, made him a donation of 'all the public lands in the district of orchards to the North and West which formed part of the communal lands of this city'.[5]

Thus, despite the complex institutional apparatus with which Aráoz attempted to surround his rule, the personalist nature of that rule soon became obvious. Continuity within the hegemonic group did not, therefore, ensure continuity of political and administrative style. This was true, above all, because that continuity did not exclude the presence of new elements, which were not confined to the garrison left behind by the central authority. The influence of that garrison was, of necessity, to decline. After the dissolution of the national authority it had to rely for its upkeep on the resources of the region which it had helped to separate from that authority. And, apart from the use of intolerably violent coercion, which could not serve as a basis for a stable solution, those resources could only be obtained through agreement with the locally dominant sectors, and this inevitably led to a transfer of power to the latter.

Although the influence of the garrison troops was only a passing phenomenon, the solutions subsequently decided upon were to enjoy military support more firmly based in the local system. Those supports, although they were organised in militias which, if they were paid at all, were paid from State funds, lent a new strength to the rural followings of the political leaders which were to dispute the domination of Tucumán. Thus Don Bernabé Aráoz, related to members of the Cabildo and ecclesiastical dignitaries, and the possessor of a fortune which – like all the large ones in Tucumán – was based on commerce rather than on land-ownership, appears in the history of Tucumán surrounded by those militiamen the description of whose 'semi-barbarous' aspect lends, for a moment, a more colourful tone to the usually austere prose of General Mitre. In the same way his most serious rival, Javier López, who was to have him shot in 1824, even though he was so proud of his status as a prosperous shopkeeper that, when he went into battle, he declared that he had left the counter to gird on his sword, found his followers among the inhabitants of the rural area where his property was situated rather than in the city. The renovation of the bases of political power did not necessarily imply a change in the politically dominant persons, but it did mean a change in their style of behaviour.

Nevertheless, this change in the political style consolidated rather than threatened social stability. Though assuring itself more rural and popular bases of support, the Tucumán government showed no lack of zeal in the defence of rural labour discipline. On 21 November 1823[6] the Cabildo re-enacted its legislation regarding vagrants, which provided that 'they should be collected together in the gaol and distributed among the employers...They should each be issued with a work-certificate, and a vagrant found in any place without this certificate is to be arrested and assigned to an employer'. The appearance of this rural sector in political life, so long as it confined itself to acting as the clientèle of leaders who had been active for a long time in that political life, transformed the latter less than might be supposed. The problems in Tucumán arose, not so much from this source, as from the rivalries which divided the traditional élite. After the interlude created when González overthrew Aráoz, the overthrow of the former by Javier López signified the rise of a rival who could only confront the old President with any prospect of success thanks to his alliance with another branch of that vast family, solemnised by the marriage of the middle-aged pretender to the daughter of Diego Aráoz, the chief rival of Bernabé. Despite this consolidation of a family and political alliance, and the execution of Bernabé Aráoz by his successful rivals, the province was not to find solid stability. The feelings of hostility which that story of blood and treachery provoked in the Tucumán élite could only be kept in check by a style of government which was both authoritarian and fiercely partisan.

In Tucumán it was, in short, the local élite which showed itself incapable of resolving its internal rivalries, and involved the entire province in them. The military garrison, which for a time had shared power with that élite, had now ceased to exist, and not merely as an actor in the political process. In San Juan the garrison appeared for a moment to be seeking undivided power. The alarm this provoked spread to places far from that corner of Cuyo – it was social, as well as political, stability which appeared threatened. On 9 January 1820 there was an insurrection of the first battalion of the Regular Army in San Juan, directed not only against the authority of the Lieutenant-Governor De la Rosa, but also against its own senior officers. A sergeant, who was, moreover, a 'coloured man',[7] emerged as the most active leader of this rising, which easily overcame the resistance of a part of the urban militias of San Juan. After this easy victory, Captain Mariano Mendizábal emerged as the most presentable leader of the victorious troops, and had no difficulty in getting himself elected Lieutenant-Governor by the Cabildo, the membership of which had just been renewed after the 'voluntary resignation' of the old Cabildo.[8] However, despite all the passionate retrospective accusations, it seems undeniable that there was support for the rising outside the ranks of the garrison troops. This is demonstrated not only by the accusations levelled by Mendizábal and the new Cabildo against the supposed tyranny of De la Rosa (which take into account the existence, since at least 1818, of a faction hostile to him and which managed to achieve a majority in the Cabildo to request his replacement as Lieutenant-Governor), but by the very names of the new Cabildo members. These men, although they later thought fit to represent themselves as obliged to support Mendizábal by the terror unleashed by the mutinous soldiery, were quite obviously motivated by objectives of their own. These were, for example, the abolition of extraordinary contributions, the victims of which were by definition members of the well-to-do classes, and the revision of the land grants made to the Governor and his friends in the Pocito area, where the Government of De la Rosa had built irrigation works. These members of the new Cabildo belonged to the San Juan élite, and several of those who had entered the corporation as a result of Mendizábal's mutiny were to be prominent in political activity for a long time, in situations which were not always any calmer.

There was nothing surprising in their grievances against the deposed Governor: in San Juan, too, the war had increased the occasions of arbitrary behaviour. Furthermore, the new Cabildo members managed to represent the movement which they were following as characterised by a scrupulous loyalty to the supreme power. They expressed distrust of the authority of De la Rosa and of his superior the Governor of Cuyo, Don

The dissolution of the Revolutionary order

Toribio de Luzuriaga, a career officer of Peruvian origin, who owed his position to the favour of San Martín. The protestations of loyalty to Buenos Aires of the leaders of the insurrection were perhaps connected with San Martín's increasing coldness regarding the Government of Buenos Aires, which he thought was displaying insufficient urgency in the preparation of the Peruvian campaign, and which he had refused to support in its struggle against the dissident movement in the Littoral. Be that as it may, these protests were rewarded by the Director Rondeau's recognition of the new situation in San Juan. Presented as a purely local change, among the beneficiaries of which were some of the most respected members of the San Juan élite, the only alarming aspect of the San Juan movement was the kind of military support it enjoyed. But even in this respect, if it was true that Mendizábal himself was a man of obscure social origin and was, moreover, a native of Buenos Aires, his marriage to Doña Juana de la Rosa, the sister of his future victim, had already, before the insurrection, given him influence which was to put him in his brother-in-law's place. However, very few of the officers of the garrison had supported the movement. In his proclamation of 16 January, Governor Luzuriaga strongly emphasised the consequences:

> The objective and purpose of the insurrection of the 29th is to put all parties in equal danger; to threaten the lives and properties of peaceful citizens and even of the rebels themselves; to place authority under the arbitrary power of a mutinous soldiery which, once accustomed to insubordination, will tolerate only a precarious influence on the part of the very officers who have led the insurrection. The behaviour up to now of the mutinous battalion fully justifies this warning; it has appointed new officers by election, and the successful candidates have been sergeants and corporals; Captain Mendizábal had distributed among them a sum of money which perhaps may ensure their obedience as long as there are funds to satisfy the vices of an unbridled soldiery; but the moment it runs short of money, it will find it for itself, by any means available, because the limits of its authority are only those of its power'.[9]

In the face of the risk thus created, the solution adopted by Luzuriaga was also characteristic. His first step was to try to prevent the news reaching the Mendoza garrison, which he feared might mutiny. The definitive solution, however, could only come from 'the concentration of the moral force of the province in order to neutralise the physical force' dominant in San Juan: in short, to hand over the local government in Mendoza to those who enjoyed enough local support to maintain themselves in power. The National Government, which Luzuriaga, like his enemies in San Juan, still recognised as supreme, had in fact ceased to count. It was imperative that its heir should have the support of 'the zeal of the magistrates...the honesty of the citizens...the interest of the proprietors in the conservation of their fortunes'. It was, in short, imperative to prevent the political crisis developing into a social crisis.

In order to avoid this fearful outcome, Luzuriaga resigned his authority over the Cabildo of Mendoza and went to Chile. He thus left the 'moral force' – the coalition of local elements which he had enthusiastically described in his proclamation – with the task of overcoming the 'physical force' of the mutinous garrison. The former was to throw itself into the struggle with greater decision because it realised that it would not have to share the fruits of its victory with elements alien to the region.

This was less difficult than the alarmed report of Luzuriaga might lead one to expect. It was true that the first advance on San Juan – led by Major Alvarado, the commander of the regular troops stationed in Mendoza, in whose loyalty not much trust could be placed – was followed by a swift withdrawal as soon as the mutineers threatened to execute the officers whom they were holding prisoner if they advanced any further. Yet, less than five months after the San Juan rebellion, a new force from Mendoza not only beat off the attack of the mutineers but captured the city of San Juan, where it was received with rejoicing by the Cabildo which had supported Mendizábal (and later Corro, who had replaced him in authority at the insistence of the troops). The remainder of the first battalion fled in disorder and disintegrated completely in the neighbouring provinces. A wealthy Chilean resident in San Juan was elected Governor of the province, and thus the complete triumph of the moral force over the physical force could be celebrated.

The influence of the remains of the dissolving National Army was, therefore, less decisive than might be supposed from its initial military superiority in the Interior. In Tucumán it was defeated by its allies within the local élite. In San Juan, where the seizure of power by the garrison signified at the same time a profound upheaval within that body, its military predominance was unable to withstand a frontal attack by forces which, moreover, had less combat experience. Only in Córdoba was the author of a military *pronunciamiento* able, with the support of the regiments which he had weaned from their loyalty to the National Government, to lay the foundations of a local hegemony to which he was immediately able to give strong roots.

The difference between the course of events in Córdoba and those in Tucumán and San Juan was demonstrated even by the *pronunciamiento* which sparked off those events. Since late 1818 the main body of the Army of the North had abandoned Tucumán, after some years of inactive rearguard duty, and was stationed in the lowlands of Córdoba, guarding the frontier with Santa Fe. In June 1819 General Belgrano had handed over command to General Cruz. In December war broke out again, although Estanislao López had shown little desire to recommence it. A force of six thousand men was to converge on Santa Fe from Buenos Aires and Córdoba. The Army of the North was the most effective part of this invading force, which was imposing only on paper, but even it was

The dissolution of the Revolutionary order

weakened by its lack of any active rôle in the recent past, and by the delays of an exhausted treasury in supplying its needs. In practice, all attempts to keep the soldiers' pay up-to-date had been abandoned, and even advances of pay had become increasingly infrequent. The need to avoid exhausting the patience of the populations among whom the Army had to live, and whose loyalty was most uncertain, made it impossible to pass on to them the penury which afflicted the troops. Another factor was the somewhat forced optimism with which Buenos Aires approached the struggle. Before retiring, Belgrano had declared that victory was impossible: the enemy was avoiding a pitched battle, and the vast size of the uninhabited Pampa made it impossible to make contact with him. He suggested a peaceful agreement or, failing that, protection of essential strategic points to keep communications with the Interior open. This pessimism was shared by the corps of officers, and was one of the reasons for the *pronunciamiento* by which they withdrew from the civil war in the Littoral. The scene of this event was Arequito, a place in Santa Fe's territory already occupied by the reluctant army, and was led by Colonel Bustos. It did not, it is true, enjoy the unanimous support of the corps of officers. Especially among the senior ones, there were several who refused to join the movement. Nevertheless, the protagonists were officers, and the rôle of the non-commissioned officers and soldiers was confined to obeying the orders they received through the normal channels of command, which had been broken less completely and, above all, at a much higher level than had been the case in San Juan. At the same time, the officers who declined to join the movement do not appear to have been threatened at any time. At first, it seemed that the outcome was going to be a friendly parting between the units which had joined the movement, and were marching Northwards, and those which had not, and were continuing their march to Buenos Aires. However, the prospect of continuing the war in the service of a moribund government was not very attractive, and the sector refusing to join the mutiny was reduced after a few days to a handful of officers, without any non-commissioned officers or men to follow them. It was the entire Army which marched North, under the command of Bustos, who had been its Chief of Staff. Nevertheless, those officers were not only not handed over to the Santa Fe government, which wanted to hold them prisoner, but they were not even arrested. Each of them was given a passport and a sum of money, albeit a small one, and invited to leave Córdoba as soon as possible. One man who left us a record of this, General Lamadrid, was in any case to return to Córdoba five months later, and celebrate at Bustos's side the 25 May.[10] There was not, then, in the movement which began in Arequito anything to 'alarm the interest of proprietors in the preservation of their fortunes'. But not only was Bustos emphatically not the leader of a movement which threatened the social equilibrium. Even in the political sphere, his emergence signified a more limited innovation than might be supposed. Bustos was, in fact, a veteran in the 'career of the Revolution', and not only in Córdoba, where, as has been observed above, Ambrosio Funes even in 1811 recognised his place among the dominant figures. In the broader national context, he had taken part in political factions since 1810, as an enthusiastic follower of Saavedra. The leader of the army which had mutinied in Arequito was, therefore, in a position to enter the field of politics in Córdoba, certainly as a more powerful element than in the past, but by no means as an alien one. To this end, he was able to utilise the political tensions which were already so acute in that region. The entire Pampa area was attracted towards the dissident movement in the Littoral. Within the city, the group which had called itself 'federalist' and now also called itself 'liberal' had by no means disintegrated in its five years of exclusion from the local government. On 19 January an Open Cabildo, convoked by the Cabildo members who certainly did not belong to that group but who knew the rules of the game, appointed as provisional Governor José Javier Díaz, who had already held this appointment during the brief *artiguista* period in 1815. Díaz considered himself as the legitimate local beneficiary of the fall of the government of the Directory which the Arequito rising was shortly to provoke. He appeared to be unaware of the quite understandable ambitions entertained by Bustos. The latter had accepted and disseminated a justification of the *pronunciamiento* which, without any doubt, excluded the possibility of the recently risen army and its leader establishing themselves in Córdoba. According to this version, it was to throw its weight into the war of independence which was still going on in the North, and deny support to the factions which aimed at civil war.

These high-sounding promises not only ensured for the movement a seal of respectability which Bustos, who had had a long career in the service of the central government, still esteemed highly, but had the additional advantage of not making an alliance with the leaders of the Littoral dissidents, which offered more dangers than advantages, the logical outcome of the Arequito movement. They were, however, destined to remain unfulfilled. This failure was attributed by more than one follower to Bustos himself (in particular, the testimony of the future General Paz has contributed to perpetuating this notion). There were, however, very serious difficulties in the way of a return to the war in the North. The death-agony of the central government meant the disappearance of the source of financial support which, with all its shortcomings, had made possible the upkeep of that military force. The resources of the North were certainly insufficient to replace those of the central government, and there would have been an even more limited willingness to give aid to a force which was not obedient to those who had just seized local power. A symptom of this was the reception which met a small detachment of the army under the command of Colonel Heredia to Tucumán and Salta. The lack of enthusiasm of Aráoz at the arrival of Heredia, who came from the same province and was a potential rival, had a clearly political motivation. But the equal lack of enthusiasm of Güemes, who had to face the hostility of both Aráoz and the Royalists in Upper Peru, was certainly due to the reasons he invoked. Salta was exhausted, and the arrival of auxiliary troops would be prejudicial unless they brought supplies from other parts.

This meant that the return to the North was only possible with assistance, which for the moment was impossible, from Buenos Aires. Bustos was no less aware of these circumstances than were his immediate followers, and it was, moreover, significant that Paz, who reproached him for abandoning the war of independence, left the city of Córdoba first to organise an irregular rebel force in the surrounding countryside, and then took refuge in Santiago del Estero, where he expected to find fresh support for the fight against Bustos.

Anyway, Bustos was in Córdoba to stay. The provisioning of the army which accompanied him meant renewed penury for Córdoba, and – as a necessary consequence – this was to be a certain motive for the unpopularity of the acting Governor, who had to have resort to new contributions.[11] Meanwhile, power was slipping from his hands. The most outstanding supporters of the Directory had resolved to organise a party to support Bustos. When, through a complicated system of indirect election, which made the establishment of universal suffrage completely irrelevant, a Constituent and Legislative Assembly was convoked, three of its sixteen members were to be accused of having held office in the fallen régime. The accusation was rejected, after repeated *impasses* in that body, which proved that the liberal or, as its enemies called it, the *Montonero* [guerrilla] party did not have a majority in it. This was only a first skirmish. The decisive test was the election of the Governor, in which those already committed to Bustos were joined by others who had noticed which way the wind was blowing.

The new Governor could count on the support of those who had supported the last Intendant-Governor appointed by Buenos Aires. This alliance was firmly cemented by the numerous tests to which it was subjected in 1820 and 1821, in the *Montonero* risings in the North of the province, organised by the families of federalist leading citizens who had properties in the area, and more dangerous movements in the Pampa area, where Felipe Álvarez emerged as a leader of purely local ascendancy but remarkable effectiveness. Finally, the province was invaded from Santa Fe, in the last combined adventure of Ramírez and the Chilean émigré José Miguel Carrera, at the head of a fearful host of Chileans, mostly former Royalist prisoners-of-war, and Indians. The Northern guerrilla menace did not appear too serious. Its first leaders were reluctant to risk tarnishing their political respectability by condoning acts bordering on banditry. Later, when other leaders emerged who were more prepared to carry on the war of resources in the only possible manner, and at the same time to increase their own popularity by showing 'the numerous population of the rural areas of Córdoba...the attractions of licence',[12] it was not only Paz, who in narrating the episode seems still filled with retrospective alarm, who decided to abandon the movement to its fate. Its leaders preferred to confine participation in the political struggle within the limits which seemed necessary for the guaranteeing of the social order. Moreover, it was not difficult for them to find, among their complicated network of family relationships, those who could serve as intermediaries for their reconciliation with the new authority.

This authority was affirmed even more solidly thanks to its victories over the Littoral menace, but what was revealed throughout the complex crisis was not so much the mettle of Bustos as that of his Lieutenant-Governor, Colonel Francisco de Bedoya, who had distinguished himself in the repression of the *artiguista* movement in Córdoba in 1816, and who now faced, with a firmness which did not hesitate to use the death penalty lavishly, both the internal and the Littoral threats.[13] In those first years of his government, Bustos appeared, therefore, to be little more than the instrument of an internal faction of the Córdoba élite which, although its composition had varied in accordance with the disconcerting way in which that élite made and unmade alliances between groups and families, was in essence a continuation of the group which had supported the régime of the Directory. However, the gradual affirmation of an authority both more personal and less dependent on the loyalty of those influential supports belonging to the élite was to be demonstrated to the full in the crisis of 1824, when – encouraged by what they thought was the imminent establishment of a central government, which they expected to support them – some members of that élite, who in the past had shown unswerving loyalty to Bustos, conspired to deprive him of the Governorship at the conclusion of his first period in office. They received sufficient support in the legislature to carry out their proposal (although it is true that there was a tied vote, and the matter was resolved by drawing lots, the result being unfavourable to the outgoing Governor). Their triumph was, however, short-lived: petitions organised by the militia commanders began to come in from the rural areas, and in the city there was growing agitation, in which the garrison troops took part. When the legislature met again, those most compromised in the plot which had deprived Bustos of a re-election which many considered to be automatic preferred to stay away, except for the President of the body, who promptly declared it dissolved. To what was this outcome due? As Bustos pointed out in a circular letter to the rural authorities, he had throughout the crisis been in control of the armed forces.[14] Yet the loyalty accorded to him by those same authorities was no less significant. It was, of course, more explicit in the Southern and Eastern areas than in the North, which was still affected by the activities of the liberal leading citizens in 1820. Even there, however, there was no active dissident movement to contest the triumphal return of the Governor. Resistance had been confined to the urban élite and the corporations which it directly controlled. Its unsuccessful outcome was a proof that this political base was no longer sufficient. Why was this? Because in the course of four years Bustos had succeeded in establishing a new power-base, parallel to the military one which he still controlled. He found it in the rural militias, where all appointments down to the rank of colonel were made by the Governor, and he also found it among the civil authorities of those rural districts, which, despite the fact that they were appointed by the Cabildo rather than by the Governor, lent their support to the latter.

This new power-base had been constituted thanks to the judicious use of the immense powers conferred on the Governor by the provisional statute of 1821, not only in military but also in financial matters. The Governor was responsible for appointments in the civil administration, the Church and the University. The functions of the Provincial Congress, or Legislature, were in any case confined to the sphere of general legislation. The predominance of the Governor in the administrative sphere was further emphasised by his supervision of the resolutions passed at Cabildo meetings, which explicitly continued the powers granted by the Regulations for Intendants to those Crown officials.[15] All this was true, but what made the situation of Córdoba original as compared with the other provinces was not the concentration of power in the hands of the Governor, but the more complex institutional apparatus on which this was based, and which reflected the traditions of Córdoba as an administrative, episcopal and academic centre. Furthermore, in other cases such a concentration had not sufficed to ensure a solid political power-base for the Governor. Even in Córdoba, what allowed Bustos to be the arbiter rather than the instrument of the disputes of the urban élite was not the magnitude of his legal attributions, but the support of the regiments of the regular army, which gave him real independence *vis-à-vis* that élite. Thanks to those remnants of the National Army, Bustos could be in fact – and not merely constitutionally – the successor of the Royal Intendants. Yet continuity did not preclude changes: those troops had to be maintained out of local resources, and – in order to be the basis of a lasting political solution – that military predominance had to be utilised, as it was by Bustos, to create other supports which would both be less onerous and have stronger roots in the political life of Córdoba. These supports were not to be found within the élite, which showed itself to be permanently incapable of constituting a solid base for any political solution, because it simply lacked the necessary cohesion. Bustos certainly showed remarkable skill in his dealings with the élite, to which, in any case, he belonged in his own right, but he used that skill chiefly to avoid the dangers to his predominance which might emerge from within that sector. He judiciously declined to assign it a more positive rôle in the organisation of his political backing. This backing was to come above all from the countryside, where the decade which began with the rise to power of Bustos marked the beginning of the decline of the political power of those leading citizens whose power-base was both rural and urban. The network of authority based on the militias, although it did not entirely exclude those figures, promoted other and more rural figures enjoying a purely local influence.

Thus, although Bustos and the members of the urban élite on whose obedient collaboration he could rely preserved, in the political life of Córdoba, a style decisively influenced both by the Colonial and the Revolutionary past, beneath that formal continuity there was a steady accumulation of changes. After the fall of Bustos (which was not, in any case, due to the internal forces of the province, but to the invasion of the latter led by General Paz, in 1829, at the head of forces which had broken off from a new National Army that was again dissolving), what emerged after the restoration of peace was a much more rural pattern of domination. The first provincial rulers were the Reynafé brothers, who had, indeed, been veterans of the liberal risings in the North, but whose influence was more decidedly limited to their little locality of Tulumba than was that of the leading families of the neighbouring districts, who were solidly implanted in the University, the Cathedral Chapter and the law-courts of the provincial capital. After another disturbance, originating from outside Córdoba, overthrew the Reynafés, the inheritor of power was to be, for over fifteen years (1835–1852), Manuel López, a native of the Pampa zone of Córdoba and commander of the Río Tercero militias, who had little influence apart from that deriving from his position in the militia organisation and his personality, which anyway was not very strong. He demonstrated to the full the existence of a new political power-base, which Bustos had taken pains to create and which he had succeeded in keeping firmly under his control.

This discreet strengthening of the rural power-base during the decade of Bustos's rule was, moreover, assured by the progressive reduction of the regiments of the line. This process began during the struggles of 1820–21, in which those units showed a tendency to disintegrate, and it was continued for financial reasons once peace had returned.[16] The military decline of Córdoba was to be revealed to the full during Paz's invasion in 1829, when Bustos could only organise a limited resistance, although he could count on considerable resources. In those ten years his armed force had become an instrument of internal politics, which acted merely by making its presence felt, and for this purpose its low level of professional skill was perfectly adequate. However, when put to the test, its capacity for resistance was shown to be inferior to that of the irregular forces later improvised by Paz's enemies in the hill region of Córdoba.

In the rest of the Interior this rise of a new leadership with a rural base, supported by a militia structure, was affirmed even more rapidly and overtly. That militia organisation had everywhere a predominantly rural basis, and not only because the distribution of the population throughout

The dissolution of the Revolutionary order

the Interior meant that the rural sector was in the majority, but also because the régimes which emerged from the crises of 1819–21 were particularly sensitive to the dangers to the political and social order inherent in a too broadly-based urban militarisation. It has already been observed that the Cabildo of Tucumán insisted on eliminating from the civic force 'servants and wage-earners'. The same anxiety was evident in the provisional statute of Córdoba promulgated in 1821, which limited enlistment in the civic militia to 'citizens possessing a farm or property of a value of at least four hundred pesos; and also owners of shops, or anyone exercising a craft or liberal profession'.[17] However, these limitations on recruitment considerably diminished the military effectiveness of the urban militia except in times of emergency when the regulations were, in any case, ignored. They marked the beginning of its transformation into a purely ceremonial corps.

Whereas the restraints placed on urban militarisation prove that the new political organisations did not want rivals in the capital, they still needed outside it agents to administer the rural areas on their behalf. The problem was not essentially different to that faced by the central government before its collapse. Whereas the end of the war of independence appeared to reduce the burden of the tribute in men and resources exacted from the rural areas, at the same time the fact that what had been the national treasury was now in the hands of the Province of Buenos Aires made it necessary to find alternative sources of supplies within the territory of each of the provinces detached from the central State. Although the provinces tried – with varying success – to restrict as much as possible the size (and therefore the cost) of their central administration, the lesser authorities were still responsible for the collection of revenue which the local economies found excessively burdensome. Even without taking into account the variations of this same basic situation provoked by the frequent power-struggles within each province, this ensured the perpetuation of an essentially military style of government at the lower levels of the administration of those new provinces. This style was military, not in the sense that administration was carried on by professional armed bodies, but because the use of force became a normal administrative practice, and for this very reason each authority had to be able to rely on an armed support which would not play an intimidatory role by its mere presence, but would be actively used as part of the normal exercise of authority.

Nevertheless – and again there is an evident analogy with the situation that had faced the central government – that local authority relying on sufficient armed support could not be financed entirely by the provincial administration; it had arisen, above all, to ensure for that administration the resources which would allow it to survive. The need to rely on those who already possessed a strong local power-base (despite the risks involved in this) was still unavoidable. This did not mean – as will be seen later – that the local agents of the new provincial authority were obliged to make great economic sacrifices to impose their authority. The militia structure in the new provinces was public both in its origin and its sources of finance. But the use of pre-existing hierarchical relationships, derived from the social and economic organisation of the region, made this financing much less costly. This was the simplest form of organisation in the provinces, whereby force was essentially an instrument of the fiscal needs of the provincial governments. There were, of course, variations of this solution, depending on the actual structure of the provinces where it was applied. Thus, in Catamarca it gave rise to sub-regional leaders, who reflected on the political plane the lack of geographical and economic unity of the new province. In La Rioja, it led to the hegemony of the Plains over the provincial capital and the sub-Andean zone, first personified in the emergence of Juan Facundo Quiroga as the supreme military authority and the great elector of the provincial authorities to which he was, nominally, subordinate. In Tucumán, where the capital had from Viceregal times had firm control over its entire jurisdictional area, it took the form of rivalry between leaders belonging to the urban élite but possessing a rural following.

This solution, which allowed of so many local variations, was the simplest, but it was far from being the only one. In none of the new provinces were the armed forces reduced to the level necessary to ensure revenue-collection. The very existence of armed bodies inherited from the preceding era prevented this from happening. Although, if one looks at the long-term process, the progressive weakening of those forces is evident, this could only take place gradually, and meanwhile provinces such as Córdoba and Tucumán were obliged to maintain a bigger military apparatus than they really needed.

However, this inflated military apparatus was not only a costly relic left over from the past. In some provinces it fulfilled an indispensable function: that of guarding the frontier against the Indians. Even before the dissolution of the State, in 1819–21, the influence which the frontier troops could wield in the local sphere could be observed in Santa Fe. The solidity of the political solutions based on them could be measured, in the same province, by the twenty-year government of Estanislao López. In the Interior a similar solidity was to be evident in Santiago del Estero, which Felipe Ibarra was to govern – with brief intervals – from 1820 until his death in 1851.

As Ibarra's government demonstrated, the influence of the frontier troops had complex political consequences. In Santiago del Estero it was a new factor in a process which really began with the Revolution itself, in which the internal rivalries of the region were inter-connected with the rivalry existing between Santiago and the more prosperous Tucumán. It was above all the merchants of the provincial capital and the families also resident there which dominated the scarce irrigated land, which fostered the latter rivalry. Their domination of the Cabildo of Santiago, a legacy from the Colonial past, was preserved apparently without effort during the first decade after the Revolution. This sector, however, was the most severely hit by the consequences of the Revolution itself. The destruction of the Upper Peru trade and the growing shortage of labour (in this province rich only in manpower, on which the Revolutionary governments had preferred to draw to swell the ranks of their armies) were the causes of a decline expressed in the complaints which filled the proceedings of the Cabildo and was demonstrated even more impressively by the landscape of ruins left in the city by the earthquake of 1817 and perpetuated owing to the lack of the necessary funds for rebuilding.

The cattle-raising sector, concentrated in the hills of the South-West and, to a greater extent, in the still narrow belt of settled land stretching towards the Chaco, was less adversely affected. It did, of course, have to contribute to the remount and supply of the Patriot armies, but economic circumstances were more favourable to it than they had been in Colonial times. The inauguration of free trade and the destruction of livestock in the Littoral ensured a more sustained demand for the hides of Santiago. This change in the economic equilibrium was accompanied by another in the political and military sphere. Here, as in Buenos Aires, the veteran troops were withdrawn from the frontier and thrown into the war, and were replaced by troops taken from the local militias, mostly from the immediate rearguard area devoted to cattle-raising. The conditions seemed to exist, therefore, for a change in the local political equilibrium: the hegemony of the capital and of the proprietors of irrigated land, whose stronghold was the Cabildo, appeared to be threatened. This development, which would have been difficult to avoid, was hastened by the crisis of the national government. Since 1814 the latter had placed Santiago in direct subordination to Tucumán, which was now the seat of an Intendancy detached from Salta. Nevertheless, the Cabildo of Santiago had not refrained from organising a somewhat hesitant Fronde, hoping to gain the support of the central authority against the provincial one, which it rightly felt to be hostile. The creation of the Republic of Tucumán aggravated this situation, for now Santiago appeared to be helplessly subjected to the domination of its rival. The opposition of the city and the surrounding lands found expression in the election of electors for the two deputies whom Santiago was to send to the capital of the new republic. 'The citizens with most following' abstained from voting, and most of those who were elected hastened to denounce the irregularity of the entire process. Only the elector from Matará protested that everything had been perfectly normal.[18] The elector from Matará...Matará was the principal township on the Indian frontier, and from 1818 Juan Felipe Ibarra, a captain in the National Army, had been stationed there as commander of the frontier region. Ibarra was, moreover, a native of Matará and belonged to a leading family of that small frontier-town. Felipe Ibarra had been the judge there in 1808, and again from 1823 until his death in 1827; Francisco Ibarra was law enforcement officer in the same place in 1814; Román Ibarra held that office in 1817. In the provincial capital their position was not so securely based. It is true that in 1811 Cayetano Ibarra was an *alcalde de hermandad* there, but no member of the family held office in the Cabildo.[19]

The attitude of the representative of Matará was not, in any case, at all surprising, for the cattle-raising zone had no reason to feel rivalry towards Tucumán. Its apparatus for the defence of the frontier required the support of a political system, the effectiveness of which would be in proportion to the territory and resources which it managed to maintain in obedience to it. Yet, though based on reasonable motives, the support given by the cattle-raising frontier zone to the domination of Tucumán did not prevent its overthrow. The Republic of Tucumán was dissolved, and its authority was replaced by that of three separate provinces. In Santiago del Estero Ibarra's position became particularly delicate, for he faced the hostility of the families which dominated the Cabildo and were now triumphant. He adopted a simple and brutal solution: he advanced with his frontier troops and captured the capital, from which he governed the province for nearly a third of a century.

This solution was imperative, and not only to save the political future of the cautious military commander of Matará. Now Santiago del Estero had to finance, without any external assistance, the defence of its excessively long Indian frontier, and only an undivided hegemony could assure the necessary resources for the 'brave militiamen' guarding the frontier, who were to be, throughout the government of Ibarra, the basis of his power. This power was, therefore, based on a permanent armed force, unlike that of Quiroga in La Rioja, based on militias which were only fully mobilisible in moments of crisis. His power, was therefore, more independent of the social equilibrium in the zones dominated by him, and less shared with leaders enjoying sub-regional influence. The political unification of Santiago del Estero under the rule of Ibarra was more complete than that of La Rioja under that of Quiroga. The latter had managed to crush opposition emerging in other areas of La Rioja, but never exercised full and direct authority over those areas, and the subsequent history of La Rioja is marked by the consequences of this situation.

This independence, however, did not presuppose any revolutionary change in the social equilibrium itself. In the first place, although Ibarra did not belong to any of the families connected with the Cabildo which had dominated Santiago during the Viceregal and Revolutionary years, he was related to them. Furthermore, his rise to supreme power, which, in view of his comparatively high social origin (which had made it possible for him to begin university studies in Córdoba), signified only a limited change in the recruitment of Santiago's political leadership, had been prepared by more

The dissolution of the Revolutionary order

discreet promotions in a less dramatic context. It had been the Pueyrredón Government – which was so sensitive to the need to find support from those who already possessed local power – which had appointed Ibarra commander of the Abipone frontier region. It had been the Cabildo of Santiago which in 1818 had proposed his name, among others, to fill the vacancy of Lieutenant-Governor, which would have given him the administration of the entire jurisdictional district of Santiago. Nevertheless, the stability of Ibarra's government stemmed from the support of the military force from which it had emerged, and from that of a region within the province. If Ibarra was able to entrench himself so solidly it was because the militarisation of that region fulfilled functions, such as the defence against the Indians, which were necessary for the whole province of Santiago.

The existence of a frontier force which included the greater part of the military resources of a province did not always ensure solutions as simple and stable as those of Santiago del Estero or, in the Littoral, Santa Fe. Both in Santiago and in Santa Fe the emergence of the frontier force as a political power-base was due, not only to the military predominance of that force, but also to the crisis of what might have become rival power-bases, principally those of the city. Where there was no such crisis, or where defence against the Indians was not such an urgent task, the frontier forces achieved a less exclusive predominance. The clearest example of this was, perhaps, to be found in Mendoza.

Here the defence of the frontiers had already given rise, in Colonial times, to the establishment of a permanent military organisation, which was to play its part in winning Mendoza for the Revolutionary cause. Although during the first decade after the Revolution – especially after Cuyo came to be administered by San Martín – the policy of peace and alliance with the Indians made the frontier problem less urgent, it came to the fore again, and in a more acute form, after 1820. As a reflection of the symbiosis which, beyond the Andes, was taking place between the Araucanian resistance and that of the last defenders of the Royal cause, in Mendoza too, the presence in Indian lands of numerous fugitives from the new order lent a fresh aggressiveness to Indian activity and again made the frontier problem one of the highest priority. At the same time, the Revolutionary experience in Mendoza had laid the foundations of a military tradition of a new type: San Martín had trained his Army of the Andes there, and the participation of the citizens of Cuyo in its formation had been decisive. Finally, the dispatch of that Army to the Chilean and later the Peruvian theatres of war, and the progressive demoralisation of the fragments of it which remained in Western Argentina, in the atmosphere of political disintegration of 1819 and 1820, brought back into the foreground, as a decisive factor in the maintenance of internal order, the local militias, which had had only rudimentary military training and whose officers were by no means professionals in the art of war.

It is not surprising, then, that when Mendoza began its history as a separate province and the need for military support for the political order again became evident, this multiplicity of military traditions again made its effects felt. Mendoza emerged as a province separated *de facto* from the national government as a result of the already mentioned decision of its Governor, Toribio de Luzuriaga. The military support for this new authority was sought, in a much less innovatory fashion, among the regular troops of the garrison, formerly part of the National Army, commanded by Alvarado. We have already seen how these troops soon revealed their ineffectiveness. The victory over the rebellion of San Juan was achieved by a wider mobilisation, in which the militias, which until then had been an essentially passive guarantee of internal order, were numerically predominant. That victory did not require any great effort: it was due, above all, to the deterioration of the political situation in San Juan. Anyway, the command of the force advancing on San Juan had been given to Colonel Morón, a veteran of the Army of the North who had left it after Arequito. In the face of a new and more serious threat, that of the motley dissident army led by the Chilean José Miguel Carrera, Morón's leadership was inadequate.[20] The victory over Carrera was won by the local militias, under the command of José Albino Gutiérrez, a wealthy landowner and merchant who had no previous real military experience. The victory of the 'moral force' prophesied by Luzuriaga appeared complete, although it had encountered adversaries even within Mendoza. Two officers from Mendoza, veterans of the Army of the Andes, the brothers Francisco and José Félix Aldao, had been responsible for the recruitment of soldiers for a new regular cavalry regiment. Once this was formed, they employed it in the internal conflict, taking the name of 'liberals' which was then fashionable, and so they became the military support of a fragile political situation marked by a desire for an understanding with the San Juan movement and with the dissidents in the Littoral. Although this solution had considerable support in the Cabildo of Mendoza, its adherents were driven from power by the action of the commanders of the urban and rural militias, who thus increased their influence in the political context of Mendoza before obtaining their decisive victory over Carrera. The Aldao brothers, it is true, did not indulge in a tenacious resistance, but preferred to sign a pact providing for the incorporation of their forces – with payment of arrears of pay due to them – into those of the province, and a full amnesty for the leaders who had supported the Governor whom the urban militias had just overthrown.[21] This judicious prudence saved their future. The Aldaos were soon unreservedly incorporated into the order established by the victory of the 'moral force' of which they had been accidental adversaries. And they were to occupy a very special place within it. Their regular troops were used in the sphere where combat experience was still necessary – the defence of the frontier. In the course of the 1820s, the emergence of the Aldao brothers as supreme commanders of the frontier forces seemed to have no immediate consequences in the political sphere. Although conflicts persisted, a wave of prosperity progressively enveloped Mendoza and gradually reduced their asperity, so that direct participation by the frontier force in the political struggle seemed unnecessary. Nevertheless, this phase of consolidation of their military power was decisive in the future rise to political power of the Aldaos. Their ascent during the following decade reflected the full recognition of the predominance of the frontier forces in the political and military equilibrium of Mendoza.

The progress of the leaders of these forces towards supreme power was not only slower in Mendoza than in the cases of San Juan or Santa Fe – for indeed its rhythm reminds one, rather, of the parallel progress of a leader emerging from the countryside of the Province of Buenos Aires – but also the earlier career of those leaders established an additional difference. The Aldaos were veterans of the Army of the Andes, and it was this experience in the context of a professional army operating far from its province of origin which gave them, in conjunction with their origin which placed them very close to those who controlled the Cabildo and through it the institutions of the province, a directing rôle in the military organisation of the frontier, which they were then able to use for political ends.

However, although the political consequences of the military hegemony of the frontier took time to develop, the hegemony itself was very soon affirmed. Here the reason was the same as in Santa Fe or Santiago: the defence of the frontier was essential for the maintenance of the productive economy of the province, and so, therefore, was the expenditure involved in maintaining that defence, and this meant that attention to the needs of the units entrusted with that defence had priority over those of the militias, from which comparable military efforts were only occasionally required. Once initiated, the process developed its own momentum. Having become the military support of the political system of the entire province, the frontier force had little to fear from organisations which could only contest its mastery if they could rely on financial support from provincial authorities which from the outset had decided to refuse such support, and which – becoming increasingly subordinate to the military apparatus dedicated to the struggle against the Indians – also became increasingly incapable of reversing the process.

The rise of the frontier forces to military – and, in the long run, to political – supremacy over entire provinces was only a single aspect of that emancipation of the authorities with a regional basis which had begun before 1820, under the shadow of the central government, and culminated with the dissolution of the latter. A substantially similar course followed the parallel collapse of that rival of the central government, the Federal League. Not only do we also find here – and it is not at all surprising – the rise of authorities with a strong regional base to replace that authority which failed to survive the storms of 1820. It is more significant, and also at first sight more surprising, that those new authorities should have had so much in common with those which in the Interior filled the void left by the fall of the national government.

Here, too, we find, as a support for these new political authorities, a locally-based military power, which in the case of Santa Fe was the frontier troops and in Corrientes the rural militias. One of the most important leaders of the latter, a man already influential and feared during the protectorate of Artigas, Esquivel, was to give decisive support to the political system which emerged in Corrientes after the successive collapse of the hegemony of Artigas and that of Entre Ríos. Only in Entre Ríos, thanks to the survival of that more professionalised military organisation which Ramírez had been able to create, the power left behind by the disappearance of the *Supremo Entrerriano* could be left in the hands of a professional officer without any following outside the Army, Lucio Mansilla, a native of Buenos Aires, the master of an art of manoeuvre of which he was to boast without measure in his unedifying *Memoria*.[22] It is true that Mansilla only maintained himself in power thanks to the interested benevolence of the governments of the neighbouring provinces, which were satisfied to see Entre Ríos in the hands of a Governor who was thoroughly unpopular and therefore had very little freedom of initiative. But the influence of those military units, which was to continue after the replacement of Mansilla by a Governor who was a native of Entre Ríos and could rely on a sufficient following in the Bajada del Paraná, his birthplace, was a decisive element in the political equilibrium of Entre Ríos, with the detrimental financial – and not only financial – consequences which have already been observed.

In separating, therefore, from the loose political system of Artigas, Santa Fe, Entre Ríos and Corrientes adopted divergent solutions. Each of them had its parallel in the Interior. The divergence of destinies between this region and the Littoral, which during the first decade of the Revolution had seemed so obvious, now seems to have disappeared, and the political landscape emerging from the collapses of 1820 appears more marked by extreme variety than by the presence of intense opposition between well-organised regional blocs.

One of these differences seemed to have preserved and even increased its intensity: it was that which set Buenos Aires, the province which was the heir to the defeated central government, in opposition to the provinces which had arisen in the Littoral and the Interior from the ruins of that government. In the era now beginning, Buenos Aires was not only the most prosperous of the River Plate provinces, but also politically that Athens of the Plate became, like its ancient model, the school of the whole nation. It offered the remaining provinces a model which some of them tried desperately to emulate. This was the 'fortunate experience of Buenos

Aires', that brief miracle which, in recollection, was to be embellished until it was unrecognisable. Yet, looked at more carefully, the experience which was beginning in Buenos Aires had certain elements in common with that of the other provinces. Despite the greater magnitude of the scene of events, despite the resolution with which the economy of Buenos Aires, having found the way to recover its lost prosperity, was to follow that way through the years (in marked contrast to the less linear and more fluctuating process in the provinces of the Interior), the political consequences of ten years of revolution, war and exposure to the world economy were not so different in Buenos Aires from those in the rest of the country as might appear in the years immediately after 1820.

BUENOS AIRES IN 1820: POLITICAL RUIN AND RECONSTRUCTION

The rule of the Directory in Buenos Aires had been a period of increasing lack of direction. This was evident at the political level, under a régime which felt increasingly undisguised nostalgia for the times when the very existence of politics as an activity distinct from administration was unknown. But it was even more evident and widespread in a society where the urban élite could see the sources of its wealth and prestige drying up, and was only just beginning to envisage for itself a future based on rural activities. At the same time the popular sectors could see the increasingly evident resurgence, as part of the official ideology of the Revolutionary régime, of that hierarchical image of society with which the *ancien régime* had been associated, and the increasingly explicit sacrifice to it of the revolutionary principle of equality, the practical effects of which were now considered to be the fruit of a revolutionary extremism which merited only condemnation.

This confusion was not necessarily a cause of weakness for the régime of the Directory. It was true that it had had to have recourse to emergency measures to deal with the opposition in the capital, but such measures, which were anyway very limited, had shown themselves to be completely sufficient. And throughout 1819, not even the progressive debilitation of the entire apparatus of government gave new vigour to any visible opposition. Nevertheless, the existence of a strong current of opposition in the capital, though constantly denied by the official press, was implicitly admitted even by the latter in so far as it devoted itself to tenacious polemics against the very opinions which it proclaimed were not shared by anybody. Thus, in speaking of the Colegio de la Unión, the *Gaceta*[23] did not fail to contrast the splendour of the new institution with the wretchedness of that 'other college and...those other pupils who, under the influence of Don José Artigas, are being educated in Santa Fe'. And there is no doubt that fear of internal dissidence in part explained the decision to subdue Santa Fe by force which, taken at the end of 1818, was to be the beginning of the end for the Directorial régime. We have already seen how the troops of the Army of the North who were to complete the circle of men and rifles destined to strangle Santa Fe preferred to abandon their obedience to the central government. The latter thereafter had to face the struggle against the dissident movement in the Littoral with only the resources of the capital and its surrounding countryside.

It was true that the offensive capabilities of the dissidents were now much diminished. In the Banda Oriental, those followers of Artigas who had not yet changed sides were offering an increasingly weak resistance to the Portuguese offensive, and Buenos Aires was now freed from the threat of those redoubtable Uruguayan troops. Even the *Jefe* of the Uruguayans had tried to dissuade his subordinates from the proposed advance on Buenos Aires, which, for this reason too, appeared from the outset as an enterprise undertaken principally by Santa Fe and Entre Ríos. Ramírez and López managed to raise a force of 1,600 men for the invasion of Buenos Aires. In view of the military practices of the Littoral dissident movement – which compensated for the shortage of weapons with an abundance of men – this number seemed too small to overcome the resistance of the remainder of the National Army, which was still capable of raising 2,000 men to block the enemy's path. Nevertheless, a Federalist cavalry charge was enough (on the field of Cepeda, on 1 February 1820) to put to flight the cavalry of Buenos Aires and open the road to the capital for the dissidents. It is true that the still intact Buenos Aires infantry and artillery could take the San Nicolás road without suffering serious harassment, but several decisive days would pass before the consequences of this were noticed. Faced with the advance of the dissidents, whose weaknesses had been emphasised, maliciously but not without foundation, by the *Gaceta*, the government of the Directory spontaneously dissolved. The fact that it was the Supreme Director himself, Rondeau, who had led the cavalry defeated at Cepeda facilitated the transition. This had been, anyway, anticipated on the eve of the battle by the decision of the deputy director and senior *alcalde*, Juan Pedro Aguirre, to banish Pueyrredón's hated minister Tagle. The terror of those who considered themselves compromised with the fallen régime, and that of all who had anything to lose in the prospective conquest of their city by those who had been represented as desirous of imposing 'on a large scale what the Jacobin democrats had done on a small scale...a perfect equality', was reflected in the swift and almost universal acceptance of the consequences of Cepeda. However, in this vertiginously rapid adaptation to a political game which had changed profoundly there was a duplicity sufficiently widely shared to be proclaimed without hesitation. In a forceful proclamation of 1 March 1820, Balcarce began by emphasising that, in order to arrive with his troops, who had taken refuge in San Nicolás, as far as the outskirts of the capital, it had been necessary for him 'to disguise [his] sentiments and use a language alien to [his] character'. This candid invocation of the need for

The dissolution of the Revolutionary order

collective political hypocrisy, of course, somewhat limited the significance of the now unanimous condemnation of the despotic régime which had been overthrown. What was even more significant was that this condemnation was not followed, even under the immediate impact of defeat, when it was still not known that not all the Army had been destroyed, by a plain and simple acceptance of the points of view of the victorious adversary. On 7 February the *Gaceta*, after severely condemning that 'party of oppression' under whose 'despotic administration the word *federation* was a crime', confined itself to announcing that 'this is henceforth to be a subject of peaceful and fraternal discussion between the Southern Provinces'.

The necessary political transformation of Buenos Aires thus began in an atmosphere of ambiguity. The sometimes disconcerting vicissitudes of this transformation have mainly been interpreted by historians from a markedly political–partisan angle. According to this version, it was the party of the Directory, which was co-terminous with the dominant groups in the society and economy of Buenos Aires, which, amid all the confusion, managed, thanks to its superior experience, to turn defeat into victory. In October, after recovering the hegemony of Buenos Aires we see it substantially intact, and displaying again its old arrogance. However, the identification of the party of the Directory with the socio-economic élite – which is more often affirmed than demonstrated, and even more often is implicitly postulated in the use of the word *oligarchy* to describe both groups – is perhaps an oversimplification.

An attempt has already been made to demonstrate how the group which directed Revolutionary politics, although drawn from the Creole élite, was not identical with it, and how the very course of the struggle was to increase the distance between the two groups. It is true that the Directory was aware of the dangers involved in this separation, and sought to eliminate them, but its success in this sphere was limited, and the increasing isolation of the governing group was clearly evident as early as 1819. This questionable identification of the Directory party with the socio-economic élite has, as an additional consequence, an interpretation of the 1820 struggle according to which they were the political manifestation of an open conflict between opposing social groups. There are, indeed, contemporary accounts which support such an interpretation, and it is undeniable that for some interminable months in 1820 the propertied classes in Buenos Aires lived in fear of a plebeian rebellion. What is no less certain is that, although the opportunities for such a rebellion were not lacking, it simply never happened. When we read the observations of Beruti, who was inconsolable over the new breakdown in order, we find, at the culminating moment of that detested disorder, lamentations over that 'fatherland... filled with parties and destined to be the victim of the low-born mob, which is armed, insolent and desirous of striking down the *gente decente*, ruining them and making them equal to their own vileness and misery'.[24] But in April the situation had been even more serious. Then all the arms were taken out of the Fort and 'handed over to the mob',[25] the regular troops were disbanded, while the civic militia amused itself by firing shots in the air, with purely festive intent, but not without some casualties. The regular soldiers 'wander at will through the streets, without shelter or food, and therefore there are no troops; from what one can see this capital is in a state of complete anarchy, and everyone does what he feels like, and the mob is full of insolence'. The power-vacuum became so serious that the deputies of the dissolved Congress were obliged to signal from their prison that the warders had gone off with the rebels of the day. They were told 'to retire to their homes and keep themselves under arrest'.[26] One can observe, then, how the absence of any open social conflict, when the habitual restraints on plebeian behaviour were missing, thus facilitating an uprising, seems sufficient proof that social tensions were less marked than the upper sectors feared. The latter, despite the lack of any armed protection, had nothing worse to suffer than the (unspecified) 'insolence' of the 'low-born mob'.

Does this mean that the conflicts which filled that turbulent year had no social dimension? This was not a necessary consequence of the lack of open social strife. Even though the social revolution feared in October by Beruti was a fantasy born of fear, there were less dramatic political options towards which the attitude of the different social groups was, understandably, different. Although the masses were not as anxious to carry out a frontal attack on those who lorded it over them as the latter feared, nevertheless their enthusiasm to defend a system which did not favour them was very limited. Their readiness to take part in political adventures that might cause lasting damage to the economic rehabilitation of the province could not be confidently excluded beforehand. Rather than the mythical social war, therefore, the most obvious threat to the established order was a counter-attack by the opposition to the Directory. Yet why was such a return considered dangerous? Not necessarily because those opposed to it thought it necessary to preserve continuity with the ruling personnel and the political tendencies of the régime overthrown in February. It was, rather, because among the political solutions which the anti-Directory opposition had proposed and was continuing to propose there were several, the adoption of which would make impossible the swift return of a peace which Buenos Aires needed to rebuild its prosperity.

What, indeed, had been the opposition's complaints against the Directory? Betrayal of the Revolutionary ideology, and, to an even greater degree, loss of faith in the inevitable victory of the movement, and the hesitant policy which resulted. In the face of the Portuguese advance in the Banda Oriental, the opposition would have liked to see Buenos Aires directing an overt struggle. This audacity, which did not flinch at the high cost of the policy it was proposing – a policy which even if successful would have involved further economic sacrifices on the part of the Creole élite which already found its present ones intolerable – was the motive for the principal reproach levelled by that élite against the opposition, in which it saw, carried to their least attractive extremes, the defects of a group which had separated from that élite to embark on the career of the Revolution. It is true that the Directory had failed in its attempt to prosecute the war of independence to the point of victory and at the same time respect the immediate interests of that élite. But it had, at least, emphasised the need to do so and had made considerable sacrifices with regard to the financing of the war (which, for example, moved San Martín to protest), all to soften the impact of that burden on the precarious prosperity of the wealthy classes of Buenos Aires.

True, when – by 1819 – this attempt at economic and social normalisation in the middle of a war had ended in failure, the Directory had had recourse to methods of collecting funds characterised by a brutality which it had condemned in its predecessors. However, even though, for that reason, nostalgia for the régime overthrown in 1820 – of which a retrospective image of extreme financial corruption was beginning to be constructed – could not be very pronounced among the élite, this did not allay its suspicions of those who had openly opposed that régime, and their possible rise to power was considered a sufficiently serious threat for it to be necessary to prevent it even at a very high cost. The old opposition does not seem to have taken this hostility into account, and in assessing its own possibilities it emphasised other elements, which (so it felt) justified a decided optimism. Did not the defeat of Cepeda at the hands of the Littoral dissident movement which had adopted – in contrast to the Directory's flirtations with monarchism – the banner of republican intransigence, prove the validity of the criticisms levelled by that opposition against the lukewarmness towards the Revolution and mistaken Littoral policy of the régime? Who was more capable than that perceptive opposition of guiding Buenos Aires in the search for a place in the new republican and federal order heralded by Cepeda?

Of course, this retrospective justification of some of the arguments used against Pueyrredón by the opposition did not necessarily have the consequences which the latter imagined. As the champion of audacity as against prudence, and the supporter in the past of active resistance to the Portuguese advance on Montevideo, though not necessarily of an understanding with the Littoral dissident movement, the old opposition found that the solutions which it had defended had ceased to be feasible in a context profoundly transformed by the collapse of the régime which it had fought, and that the spirit of audacity which had inspired those solutions was perhaps not the most appropriate for a province which was emerging as a separate entity under the shadow of defeat.

This old opposition had inherited the arrogance of the Revolutionary officer corps, whose ambitions the Directory had been discreetly trying to restrain since 1816, and had also inherited that plebeian faith in the invincibility of a Buenos Aires resolved to rely on popular heroism to defend unhesitatingly its own cause, a cause which was both that of the city and of the republican Revolution. This opposition could not sincerely accept an understanding with the victors of Cepeda, a battle which the officers of the old Revolutionary army had looked on as a scandalous accident to be rectified, while plebeian opinion in Buenos Aires saw it as a humiliation for the city that had launched and led the Revolution – a humiliation to be wiped out. Even had the leaders wished to ignore these sentiments they could not have done so without the risk of losing the loyalty of their supporters, which was their main political asset. It was, of course, possible in principle to imagine a policy capable of satisfying both the pride of Buenos Aires and the declared objectives of the victors: the launching of a republican crusade against the Portuguese in the Banda Oriental. This policy, however, would not only have aroused the hostility of everyone in Buenos Aires who had anything to lose; it was also very unattractive even for the victors.

The reason for this was that the Portuguese conquest had advanced too far for it to be resisted with ease. A week before Cepeda, the battle of Tacuarembó had ended the last attempt to maintain an *artiguista* presence in the Banda Oriental. In March, Fructuoso Rivera, the most influential of the rural leaders who had followed Artigas, joined the Portuguese army. Moreover the Littoral leaders did not seem too distressed by this turn of events. Even in Entre Ríos – and to an even greater extent in Santa Fe – adherence to the movement of the Free Peoples had been qualified by hesitations which came to the fore after the defeat of the central government, the hostility of which had strengthened the solidarity of the dissidents. The complex crisis of 1820 liberated López and Ramírez both from the threat of Buenos Aires and the predominance of their imperious protector, and they were not anxious to annul this second welcome effect through a costly and dangerous campaign against the Portuguese.

One can, therefore, see how difficult it was for the victors of Cepeda and the anti-Directory opposition in Buenos Aires to find a common ground of agreement. Would the victors find it any more easily with the economic and social élite of Buenos Aires, which – after the dissolution of the Revolutionary political élite – was acquiring a more direct influence in the politics of the new province? Agreement would not be easy here, either: the dissident movement had been regarded as a threat to the socio-economic order, as well as to the political predominance of Buenos Aires, although in less precise terms the stern rule of the central government had been identified by the dissidents with the hegemony of Buenos Aires, defended for the benefit of those who ran its economy. Nevertheless, the possibility of an agreement was less remote than might be supposed at first sight. López and Ramírez, even though they might be barbarians or Jacobins, had been the victors of Cepeda, and those in Buenos Aires who were above all interested in a swift return of peace which would make prosperity possible, as soon as they were convinced that the outcome of the battle was irreversible, would accept their influence as a factor in the new political system in which they would have to live. This devotion to their own interests, rather than to any ideological or political tradition – whether the warlike and Revolutionary one of the old anti-Directory opposition, or the conservative and centralist one of the overthrown Directory group – was reflected in the particularly understanding attitude shown by those in Buenos Aires who reluctantly entered the political arena because they had a patrimony to lose in their negotiations with the victors. At the same time, the latter's interest in finding allies in Buenos Aires was necessarily very great. The privileged situation of the new province was not merely a result of Viceregal or Revolutionary policy, but it had more permanent causes, which were still to be operative when Buenos Aires admitted its legal equality with the other provinces of the River Plate region. An understanding with the political forces now dominant in the old capital was necessary, in order that the Littoral, which had for so long suffered the havoc of war, could finally enjoy a stable peace. A more immediate consideration was the fact that Buenos Aires, even after its defeat, still possessed a patrimony of arms and money. This was, no doubt, much diminished by the upheavals accompanying the final crisis of the central government, but it was still found impressive by the leaders of the even more impoverished Littoral. Access to this patrimony could be more easily achieved through an agreement reached in the advantageous situation resulting from the victory than through pure and simple plunder, especially if one took into account the fact that, although the military forces of the victors had been able to defeat the sorry remnants of the National Army which had tried to bar their way, they were not sufficient to maintain a prolonged occupation of the conquered province.

Agreement between the victors and the socio-economic élite of Buenos Aires, which was for the first time prepared to participate openly in the political struggle, was finally reached. If this did not happen sooner, it was because the anti-Directory opposition and the socio-economic élite were not the only elements with which the victors had to deal in Buenos Aires. The career of the Revolution had created, both in the ranks of the Army and among civil servants, a legion of veterans who had learned from their past experience to display a certain political tractability. They were considered unreliable by the interests now dominant in Buenos Aires, and were not necessarily regarded with more confidence by the old anti-Directory opposition. But, if supported by the force of the victors, they were eventually to be, perhaps, accepted by both sectors. It was true that the political solutions ensured by the predominance of these figures of debatable popularity, or of a popularity counterbalanced by the categorical hostility of other political sectors in Buenos Aires, were of necessity weakly based. However, this weakness, in the eyes of the victors, was not necessarily a defect, for it ensured them the loyalty, based on self-interest, of their Buenos Aires allies. It is understandable that the victors should first have sought, among that vast number of people prepared to continue in the career of the Revolution, potential allies more prepared than others to accept the alliance without any discussion of its terms. It was only when these artificial political resurrections had failed that López and Ramírez decided to deal with those in Buenos Aires who possessed strength in their own right, and therefore, even after defeat, did not by any means consider themselves obliged to accept the enemy's terms without any discussion. In order to accelerate this process, the socio-economic élite did not confine itself to the clandestine use of a power that was not necessarily dependent on political fluctuations. It adopted political tactics which changed rapidly according to the circumstances, without refraining – until they reached a final agreement with the victors of Cepeda – from evoking the still potentially active local patriotism of Buenos Aires. This sentiment was capable of uniting the entire province against its conquerors, but it might also, in the course of the struggle, create a new political and military élite which the socio-economic one would find it difficult to control. When the victors realised that the dominant interests in Buenos Aires, although they might find this course unattractive, had no hesitation in encouraging it as a last resort, they finally decided to seek a compromise. By that time Ramírez had left the province of Buenos Aires, returning to Entre Ríos to face the threat of Artigas and filled with great ambitions, both for himself and for his province. Although, in the short term, Estanislao López's keener interest in the outcome of the Buenos Aires crisis meant that he was a tougher negotiator, his long-term objectives were more limited than those of the leader from Entre Ríos: what he wanted above all was peace for Santa Fe, which had suffered so much from the war. In view of the impracticability of the solution most conducive to this end – the imposition of a government subject to the hegemony of Santa Fe – he was obliged to accept without hesitation a less one-sided arrangement.

With this multiplicity of players, the game of political negotiation became desperately complicated, and the complications grew still further because among those players alliances were necessarily fragile, and the very frequent political *coups de théâtre* resulted in rapid revisions not only of those alliances but also of the long-term political solutions with which each group appeared identified. These bewilderingly rapid realignments presupposed frequent personal stances based on insincerity (which, as has been observed, were in some cases retrospectively proclaimed after new shifts of alliances). This makes it even less easy to understand the true meaning of each of the events of that turbulent era.

The dissolution of the Revolutionary order

Cepeda had struck only a temporary blow at the régime of the Directory. The escape of Balcarce with the main body of the infantry was a miraculous surprise which gave back to the defeated side something of its old arrogance. Aguirre handed over the office of Supreme Director to Rondeau, and the man who had been defeated at Cepeda again appeared as the personification of a legitimacy displaying an unexpected capacity for resistance to that defeat. This was only a momentary situation: Ramírez and López did not accept this outcome. Nor was it accepted by General Soler, who had been entrusted by the moribund régime with the organisation of the urban militias for battle. After taking part in the overthrow of Alvear, and then pursuing in Chile a military career interrupted by a disagreement with O'Higgins, Soler had since 1819 held a post on the General Staff in Buenos Aires. Now he discovered both a political vocation and the possibility of fulfilling it. The defeated authority yielded, and handed over the government of the Province to the Cabildo. The national government no longer existed. Ramírez was still not satisfied, and demanded the creation of a government unconnected with the fallen régime. (The Cabildo had, in fact, been elected under its auspices before the battle of Cepeda.) As a result, there was formed, after an Open Cabildo, the first Junta of Representatives of the province. At the instance of the victors, three of its members were dismissed from their posts because of their connections with the régime of the Directory, and the same fate befell the entire Cabildo. After this purge, the Junta elected as Governor Manuel de Sarratea, who had figured among those in opposition to the government of Pueyrredón, and was one of the political figures who had shown the greatest capacity for survival in the hazardous career of the Revolution, in the course of which he had won for himself, by his duplicity, the abiding hatred of Artigas, and had later taken part in the attempts at monarchical restoration. The appointment of Sarratea satisfied the victors, and both parties signed the Pact of Pilar, which made provision for a future federal organisation for the provinces of the River Plate region, but deliberately omitted any specific commitment to action against the Portuguese in the Banda Oriental. In mentioning Artigas, it merely gave him the title of Captain-General of that province which he had already lost – the League of the Free Peoples, therefore, did not last much longer than the national government which it had fought so tenaciously. A secret clause promised Ramírez arms from Buenos Aires for a military action against the Portuguese, which by that time took second place to that leader's intention of settling his quarrel with Artigas.

Here, therefore, were the protagonists of the protracted political drama of 1820, now definitely occupying the foreground. Of these, the least significant appeared to be the Junta of Representatives. This body, which the victors had proclaimed as the legitimate expression of the will of the sovereign people, had, of course, been elected by an extremely small number of voters, and those who had demanded the formation of that institution doubtless expected from it a disciplined obedience to their orders. However, the Junta, or rather the successive Juntas elected after each crisis in the course of that convulsed year, came to be the institutional expression of that group within the socio-economic élite which the pressure of the victorious *caudillos* had obliged to cut its ties with the fallen régime of the Directory, which anyway had lost prestige in the eyes of that group because of its military defeat. From its base in the Junta, this group now began to play a part in a game, the rules of which it was only gradually to discover, after numerous reverses. The first steps, however, were not taken by the representatives: it was Soler who, after discovering that he had been swindled out of the government of the province, denounced Sarratea for handing over Buenos Aires arms to the victors. Before he could reap the fruits of this perilous manoeuvre, he found himself totally displaced by the arrival of Juan Ramón Balcarce, who, by trickery, had obtained from López, Ramírez and Soler free access to the capital. On 6 March the Cabildo appointed him Governor. Sarratea and the fretful Soler had fled to the country, and henceforth the federalists were to be their only support.

However, at the prospect of a renewal of the fighting, Balcarce's forces underwent a sort of spontaneous dissolution. Their leader had to take refuge in Montevideo, and Sarratea was again able to enjoy a dubious triumph. In order to consolidate it, and at the same time satisfy his protectors, he ordered the initiation of criminal proceedings against the accomplices of the very varied crimes now attributed to the fallen régime. At the same time, he ordered the delivery of more arms to Ramírez, not before having obtained the explicit approval of his ally and rival Soler, of the Cabildo and even of the dissolved Junta of Representatives. The reason this approval was granted unanimously was that refusal of it would have led to a conflict for which both Sarratea's public adversaries and his scarcely secret rivals were unprepared. A more pressing reason was that Ramírez was only waiting for those arms to depart for Entre Ríos, where Artigas was disputing his rule.

The Supreme *Entrerriano* did, in fact, leave Buenos Aires, and his influence was thenceforth exercised through José Miguel Carrera. The restless Chilean émigré was training, in the rural areas of Buenos Aires Province, the small army with which he hoped to recover supremacy in his own country, and the Buenos Aires Government, despite protests from Chile, thought it best to tolerate this activity on the part of the protégé of Ramírez, whose goodwill it still needed. The appearance of Carrera was followed by that of Alvear, who in the middle of March sought – and for a moment appeared to obtain – the support of the Buenos Aires military forces, which now consisted of the militia and the few regular troops who had survived the collapse of the National Army, in his attempt to take over command of these in the place of Soler. He failed, and the attempt

The dissolution of the Revolutionary order

compromised Sarratea, suspected, apparently unjustly, of having encouraged it, and also Carrera, who – although he did not approve of the attempt – had felt obliged to leave the road open for Alvear. With his stature thus diminished, Sarratea ordered elections for a new Junta of Representatives. The result was unfavourable to him, and when he tried to reverse it by eliminating from among the elected members those whom he declared to be compromised with the régime of the Directory, he was obliged to resign his post as Governor because he found himself to be incapable of imposing this decision on the representatives. The stubbornness of the latter is more easily understood if one takes into account that relations between Sarratea and Ramírez, and Ramírez and Soler, had deteriorated beyond repair. The representatives thought that their hour had struck, and they appointed as Governor their President, Ildefonso Ramos Mejía. But Soler, from his military encampment in Luján, refused to recognise the authority which had deprived him of the coveted supreme military command, and meanwhile Estanislao López began a new advance on Buenos Aires, with Carrera and Alvear, who joined forces with him. In the face of this danger from outside, Soler again imposed his supremacy on Buenos Aires. The Junta was dissolved, but was convoked again for the sole purpose of confirming Soler in the post of provisional Governor. Soler could not, however, stop the advance of López. In the rural areas a rival legislature was established under the auspices of the latter, and appointed Alvear Governor. Within the city the Cabildo, which, after the disappearance of the Junta, offered the only alternative to the military power-base of the Governor, was in favour of a compromise. On the other hand Soler, Colonel Dorrego, who had returned from the exile imposed by Pueyrredón, and the Uruguayan Colonel Pagola were in favour of all-out resistance to López and Alvear (the latter being perhaps more feared than his protector from Santa Fe). Soler and Dorrego handed over the reins to the Cabildo, which took over the government on an interim basis and convoked an Electoral Junta entrusted with appointing a titular Governor, and meanwhile Pagola became dictator for a very brief period. He was overthrown by the Cabildo, which had the support of Dorrego and of Colonel Rodríguez, who had been organising the frontier troops since the last years of the Directory and had finally brought them with him to Buenos Aires. Rodríguez rejected the Governorship, and it was conferred on an interim basis on Dorrego. Moreover, the absence of any decisive attack from Santa Fe decided the Cabildo to abandon its search for a compromise with that province. With the solid support of the whole of urban opinion, Dorrego was able to carry the war into Santa Fe's territory, but not to achieve a decisive victory over López.

In August a new election created a third Junta of Representatives dominated by those who had also controlled the first and second ones. Dorrego's position became uncomfortable: his policy of all-out war, once the danger of total defeat had passed, became unpopular among those in Buenos Aires who were anxious above all for peace. He was also well aware that those sectors had begun to find in Rodríguez and his frontier troops an alternative military support to that which Dorrego could offer them. His attempt to prevent the expansion of the military forces commanded by Rodríguez only exacerbated the conflict, and in September the Junta of Representatives appointed Rodríguez interim Governor. Throughout this process Dorrego had meticulously respected the legal limitations on his power, and this attitude had made of him the only former leader of the revolutionary opposition to the Directory not totally unacceptable to the now dominant groups. Even so, he was by no means their favourite choice, and he bowed to their decision to replace him, and also renounced the military command – from which, anyway, the new Governor dismissed him. The outcome was another revolution in the city, which involved almost the entire urban militia and also the remnants of the Fijo Regiment; it was commanded by Colonel Pagola and Brigadier-General Hilarión de le Quintana. The movement was crushed, after a fight, by the frontier forces. Marching on Buenos Aires at the side of Rodríguez was Juan Manuel de Rosas, at the head of the militia regiment raised in his own district of San Miguel del Monte. Thus the long internal crisis of Buenos Aires was ended, and repression could begin. The inter-provincial crisis was to be ended soon afterwards by the Peace of Benegas signed with Santa Fe.

Students of this confused process have emphasised the emergence of two new elements. One of these was the Junta of Representatives, which repeatedly and miraculously rose again from its own ashes, and the other was the frontier force, through which the countryside became an arbiter in the dispute between urban political groups. The first element was, for several reasons, more of an enigma: there is no doubt that the Junta was, from the very beginning, the stronghold of what those students usually call, correctly but perhaps somewhat imprecisely, the Buenos Aires oligarchy. However, it did emerge from elections for which the potential electorate was very large, since it was formed by all those who were both citizens and *vecinos*. It is true that the number of those who actually cast their vote was always very small indeed (the representative with most support had received slightly over 200 votes in his favour), but this limited electoral participation seems to have been the result, not of pressures designed to keep away from the polls a part of the potential electors, but of the notorious indifference of the latter. This in itself was not surprising, for it was merely a continuation of the attitudes characteristic of the first decade of the Revolution. It is less easy to understand why these few voters almost unanimously gave their support to candidates who were not identified with those who held power in the city at the time of the election.

Yet this is precisely what happened on three occasions. The second Junta of Representatives was elected when Sarratea was Governor, the Electoral

The dissolution of the Revolutionary order

Junta while Pagola was in control of the city, and the third Junta of Representatives was elected at Dorrego's behest. Through the District *Alcaldes* or by more direct methods those momentarily powerful figures or, for that matter, the Cabildo (whose opposition to the dominant group in the successive Juntas has perhaps been exaggerated, but which anyway was not identified with that group) might have been able to impose a different electoral result, or at least attempt to, but they do not appear to have done so on any occasion. In other words, the electoral victory which again and again ensured for the group represented as oligarchical the control of the body which formally was the most direct expression of the popular will had all the characteristics of a victory based on consensus. In the new political equilibrium which Buenos Aires was seeking an elected institution controlled by this group now seemed to be an unchallenged element.

But was there anything unusual about this? When he gained control of the Banda Oriental, Artigas hastened to delegate to the Cabildo of Montevideo functions which went beyond the purely administrative sphere. He had, indeed, purged that body of his more open adversaries, but its members represented not only a political faction, but above all the system of economic and social interests, the collaboration of which Artigas considered to be essential for the governing of his country. In Buenos Aires, leaders momentarily placed in power by the favour of the victors or by a military superiority always lacking a firm base must have considered such cooperation even more imperative.

The Junta of Representatives in Buenos Aires was, then, the expression of a group of interests and an urban social élite, rather than of a political faction. Some of its members, of course, had in one way or another been associated with the fallen government of the Directory. But even these had not been among the most eminent leaders of that era. People like Tomás Manuel de Anchorena or Vicente López y Planes had in fact had very little power or influence during that period, and this does not appear to have worried them unduly, because their appetite for the risks and attractions of militant politics was also limited. At their side, with unbroken solidarity, were those who had remained carefully apart from the group which supported Pueyrredón, and had even suffered his hostility, and others again who had led an entirely private life during the decade of the Revolution. What united them was their identification with a certain sector, that of the urban élite which had preserved a solid financial position despite the past turbulences, and to which the majority of the members of the successively elected juntas personally belonged.

The Junta was – let us repeat – the expression of a social sector rather than of a political faction. It is understandable that the leaders who thought it imperative to secure the collaboration of that sector should have thought fit to grant it a place in the institutional system of the new Province. But, even if this were the case, it is still not so easy to understand why the Junta did not confine itself to the role which the political leaders who repeatedly sponsored its resurrection obviously expected it to play. Those elected institutions in which a cautious urban élite established its stronghold were not usually characterised by a spirit of ardent political militancy. With their minds concentrated on guarding interests which they considered to be more durable than the successively triumphant political solutions, they became accustomed to adopting without any sacrifice, but also with prudently muted enthusiasm, the vocabulary associated with each of those solutions. This attitude, which meant that they were over-fragile supports of any situation, also seemed to make it difficult for them to constitute any open opposition to such a situation.

Yet this is precisely what the Junta of Buenos Aires did on numerous occasions. The reason for this audacity is to be found, no doubt, in the limited strength of the adversaries which the Junta confronted. It was faced, on the one hand, with victorious invaders who from the outset had only limited military support and displayed an increasingly marked desire to leave Buenos Aires, and, on the other hand, with a corps of officers whose only support was a military organisation thoroughly unhinged by the defeat, and urban militias whose allegiance had to be continually regained by those same leaders through the display of political attitudes bound to make more difficult any agreement with the conquerors from the Littoral. Another factor still was that vast number of discredited political figures who saw in the reigning confusion an opportunity for profitable adventures and who could, by contributing to the confusion by their actions, very soon modify the balance of forces. Finally, there was that body of plebeian public opinion in the capital which had been hostile to Pueyrredón, was equally hostile to the victors, and which had no outlets for its feelings – and apparently sought none – in the institutional apparatus which the province was improvising, and only manifested its attitude through the support (which was anyway inconstant) which some restless military leaders found in the militias.

This multiplicity of comparatively weak adversaries, all of whom might also be occasional allies, made possible the attitude of firmness combined with tactical versatility characteristic of the group which dominated the Junta until the eve of its victory. Sarratea, Soler and Dorrego were its allies in succession, and eventually it eliminated them all from the field. The final victory took place, however, in a different context: Rodríguez and his frontier troops were not looked on as an external support, but as the armed wing of the very group that dominated the Junta. That army had been created to defend the productive economy of the province against the Indian menace, had been partly financed by the landowners, and was led by men who were certainly professional officers, but who were sufficiently far away from the centres of political and military power to have been appointed to those somewhat secondary rôles. That army was the appro-

The dissolution of the Revolutionary order

priate instrument for the Buenos Aires élite which in October 1820 was able to celebrate not only the end of the threats which had been levelled at the entire social order (threats which in retrospect were decidedly exaggerated), but also the end of the Revolutionary decade, so abundant in promises and in disappointments. It was the moment for striking a balance and making a fresh start. Out of the ruins of that political enterprise, both municipal and continental, with which Buenos Aires had been identified since 1810, there emerged a city of which the political collapse could not deprive it of its dominant rôle in the economy of the River Plate region. Behind it, in the reduced rural area of influence inherited from the Spanish system, the new wealth of the Province was being born. A new political order, appropriate to the city which had renounced its political supremacy in order to defend more effectively the economic bases of that supremacy, and also to the rural areas which had demonstrated their increased power in the dramatic finale of the 1820 crisis, was beginning to emerge in Buenos Aires. It was different in objectives and also in style to the order created by ten years of Revolution.

THE 'FORTUNATE EXPERIENCE' OF BUENOS AIRES

October 1820 saw an end to the long test of strength which for months had kept the Province of Buenos Aires on the brink of chaos. The military and plebeian faction, so strong in the city, had been finally overcome by the action of the rural forces. Governor Rodríguez, with his frontier troops and the militias from the South, had provided the force necessary to sustain the new political order of the Province, which seemed to emerge as the continuation of the national authority which had fallen under the blows of the leaders from the Littoral.

This continuity was not, however, so evident as was thought by the more militant adversaries of the régime of the Directory, who were enraged to discover that they were not to be the heirs of the power which the ruin of the Directory had left vacant. The profoundly novel character of the political experience which was beginning in Buenos Aires was soon to be generally realised. The felicity of those brief years of peace and progress was to become, in the turbulent years that followed them, a golden memory, shared, amid the ruthless struggle of the factions, by both the *unitario* party, which represented itself (by a gross over-simplification) as the legitimate heir of that experience, and by the *federal* party, which was to accord its leader the title of Restorer of the Laws, that is to say, of the institutional apparatus which governed the Province in that happy era and had been twice destroyed by the *unitarios*. This dispute over the inheritance demonstrates the extent to which the whole Province had become identified with an experience which at first had been imposed upon it in the face of a stubborn resistance.

A new political order, so appropriate to the needs of the Province that eventually it obtained near-unanimous support, thus emerged from the ruins left by the crisis of 1820. Was this new order the result of a detailed plan of political and economic reconstruction, the fruit of the talents of a man or a political team? This is what is often suggested: the 'fortunate experience' of Buenos Aires, according to this view, was due to the prophetic vision and rare political genius of Bernardino Rivadavia, who was Minister of Government under Rodríguez from late 1821 until 1824. Historians unsympathetic towards that figure make substantially the same judgment, attributing similar merits to his colleague Manuel José García, Minister of Finance under the same Governor. This explanation, however, has to take account of the fact that Rivadavia's 'vision' operated only intermittently. It showed signs of prophetic genius between 1821 and 1824, but became disastrously obtuse between 1825 and 1827. There were similar fluctuations in the effectiveness of the actions of García, to whom his admirers attribute a talent superior to that of his colleague and rival. Neither in diplomacy nor in the management of public finance was he to display, after 1824, such a sure touch as during his tenure of office in the Rodríguez government.

There are further reasons for doubting that the experience which was beginning owed so much to the actions of either of these two men. Its fundamental guidelines had been marked out before either of them reached ministerial office: one has only to re-read the *Argos*, the new newspaper which was to be published throughout the experience now commencing, to realise this. Furthermore, when one tries to determine what it was that ensured such a broad basis of support for this political experiment, one can see that, rather than the reforms which the retrospective admirers of the Rodríguez Government untiringly emphasise, it was a more fundamental change in the objectives and in the very nature of the government which was the decisive factor. What lent an original character to the experiment which was beginning was that it took place in an atmosphere no longer overshadowed by war. The use to be made of the opportunities offered by a return of peace had not merely been a matter for reflection by a few solitary prophets – when peace finally came, it could be seen that there was a relatively broad consensus on this matter. There is nothing surprising in this: during the Directory of Pueyrredón, the Government had already clearly marked out the basic guidelines of a task of reconstruction which it confessed itself incapable of carrying out, but the need for which it wanted to be the first to proclaim. In this task the State was to play its part, chiefly a negative one. It had to dismantle the military machine, intolerably burdensome and not always very effective, which the Revolutionary era had obliged it to improvise. This would make it possible to abandon the system of arbitrary extortion which the penury of the Treasury had made unavoidable, and at the same time to free itself from the pressure exerted by the few really wealthy people, who with a generosity that was always carefully measured had brought a precarious salvation to the Government during its more critical moments.

The action of the public authorities was not, however, limited to this: Pueyrredón had already assigned those authorities the rôle of director of a policy designed to satisfy in the most harmonious possible manner the interests of the various production and consumption sectors. This second objective had also been shown to be incapable of fulfilment. Not only had financial stringency deprived the Directory of the independence necessary for the authoritative assumption of the rôle of arbiter which it had assigned itself. In addition, the difficult economic and social transition provoked by the Revolution had created antagonisms which were so acute that any arbitration would mean the sacrifice of one sector to another. In this confused context, the Directory had embarked on the fickle course of a restoration of the pre-Revolutionary economic order, for the benefit of, above all, that fraction of the commercial sectors composed of the American-born. This project would have been too ambitious even for a government with a less restricted freedom of manoeuvre. It was in this sphere that the crisis of 1820 signified a more profound transformation. Although, even before that event (as has been observed previously), a foreign observer was able to describe the landowning class as having climbed to that first place in society which it by no means occupied in Colonial times, the full consequences of this change only became evident after the fall of the Directory. The political influence of the rural areas, which had ensured the defeat of the urban popular faction, now made its full weight felt, in so far as (as has also been observed) the privileged function of the expansion of cattle-raising within the context of the economy of Buenos Aires became increasingly unquestioned.

It was the discovery of a new and more assured direction for the economy of Buenos Aires, with its promise of a prosperity more general than that induced among the urban popular sectors by the carefree financial measures of the Revolutionary era, which gave the propertied classes the cohesion and solidity necessary to exert a more decisive influence on the actions of the provincial administration. Finally, the expansion of cattle-raising offered an alternative which was more secure, more profitable and also more honourable than those business deals with the State which – although always condemned in theory – had been a temptation difficult to resist in the first decade after the Revolution. The dismantling of the administrative apparatus created in the Revolutionary era and inherited from the dissolved central government by the new Province of Buenos Aires, and its replacement by an administrative system smaller in scope and directed above all at encouraging the economic progress of the province, therefore found almost unanimous support among the upper sectors. Furthermore, it was those upper sectors which – in a less oppressive climate than that of the first decade after the Revolution, and despite the persistence of an urban popular opposition – preserved for themselves more successfully than in the past control over the basic orientation of the provincial administration. Their support, therefore, was due, not so much to what that administration did, as to what it undid; to the consistency with which it destroyed the military and financial apparatus inherited from the Revolutionary era.

This is not to suggest that the political enterprise undertaken in October 1820 did not encounter any difficulties. The support of sectors and interests accustomed to confine their militancy to moments of extreme crisis had as its counterpart the militant hostility of those adversely affected by the destruction of the apparatus inherited from the Revolutionary era. A vast number of people, composed of military officers and the members of two formerly rival political groups (that of the opposition to the Directory and its collaborators), was prepared to exploit ruthlessly any weakness in the new political order, with the objective of reconquering power and thereafter imposing once again a style of administration which they had every reason to remember with nostalgia.

From Montevideo, where he had sought the protection of the flag of Portugal, Pueyrredón had observed with satisfaction the triumph of Rodríguez. That excellent man, who though not learned was certainly shrewd, would hand over power to him in good time. The ex-Director was in no anxiety or haste to recover it: a severe repression of political and social indiscipline was necessary, and Rodríguez had undertaken this with praiseworthy firmness. It would be as well for him to conclude the process and reap the unpopularity attendant upon such salutary severity. 'I want to wait for a little while', declared Pueyrredón to his close friend, Rear-Admiral Jurieu, 'until it is all over'.[27] It was to be a long wait, and the hope was not to be fulfilled. Pueyrredón resigned himself without difficulty to the ending of his political career, but his adherents were less easily consoled. Doctor Tagle, his hated and feared Secretary, was not resigned to the loss of power and influence, and his intrigues were to continue indefinitely. The Directory faction had, indeed, lost its most influential adherents, but Tagle had a personal following which he had carefully cultivated, composed of 'the common people, with whom he keeps in touch through his agents. From the barber and the hairdresser, and from his numerous gossips, he receives information', and he used it, according to the malicious portrait of his character drawn by Iriarte, to facilitate his intrigues.[28] What was more important was that this same capacity for intrigue could serve to create new alliances between formerly enemy factions.

Moreover, the personnel for recruitment into these new factions was soon provided by the new policy itself. Here, however, difficulties abounded: neither the Alvear supporters not subsequently incorporated into the Directory party, nor the outspoken opponents of the latter, felt very much confidence in Doctor Tagle. His blandishments were not always enthusiastically received. Moreover, the increasing attenuation of the repression of political dissidence began to bear fruit. Rivadavia was not boasting in vain when – after being warned by General Iriarte of the intrigues of Tagle – he said that if the new political system became solidly affirmed 'within a short time Doctor Tagle will be an utter nonentity'. 'I was bold enough to be so frank', adds Iriarte, who seemed to realise the dubious nature of his confidential conversations with a Governor from whom he wished to keep his distance, 'because I knew that no harm would come to Tagle: the security of the individual was effective and inviolable'. This liberal treatment, which softened the asperity of political conflicts, made it easier for individuals to come to terms with the new order, and this process was also favoured by two additional factors. The first was the initial scarcity, among the adherents of the new régime, of leaders prepared to make politics their predominant activity. The crisis of 1820 had been sufficiently serious to persuade those who, because of their position in the economy and in society, had much to lose, to abandon their usual reserved attitude. Once less agitated times returned, this attitude was gradually to return to the fore. For this reason, experience in the management of public affairs was still limited, and those who possessed it were able – at least in the earlier phase of the events which followed the collapse of 1820 – to acquire political positions without having to take them by storm. The second, and perhaps more important, reason was that the crisis of 1820 had had an outcome which left no doubt as to who were the victors and who were the vanquished. Among the vanquished was the urban popular opposition, and this perhaps explains why, for example, so extremist a member of that sector as Manuel Moreno should have waited so long before openly opposing the new régime, with which, in the meantime, he collaborated in more ways than one. Also vanquished was the Army inherited from the ten years of Revolutionary war, defeated first in a pitched battle by the dissident movement from the Littoral and then in the internal political struggle, in which the most brilliant of its leaders had thrown in their lot with the urban popular resistance movement, which was finally crushed in October.

In this way, the new authority derived from the circumstances from which it had emerged considerable freedom of manoeuvre, particularly when dealing with the Army, the reform of which was essential for the financial retrenchment which was one of the Government's principal objectives. This military reform was only possible because the corps of officers was handicapped by its own loss of prestige and the rise within its ranks of those whose service had been on the Indian frontier, who had assured the victory of the moderates in late 1820 and whose functions, in any case, made them invulnerable to the increasingly frequent criticisms levelled at a costly military apparatus which served no purpose within the new provincial context.

In these circumstances, it was possible to promulgate the law of November 1821,[29] which granted those retiring after from four to twenty years service a pension equivalent to one-third of their pay, those with more than twenty years' one half of their salary and those with over forty years' service retirement on full pay. All those incorporated into the militarisation process initiated in 1806 could only look forward to a pension equivalent to one-third of their pay. This situation was eased by an advance of twenty-two years' pay, but the advantages of this were dubious, because payment was made in State bonds, which at the time were regarded with distrust. The lot of the officers thus retired (252 as a result of a decree of 28 February 1822[30]) was in general hard: although the bonds they received were eventually to rise to very nearly their par value, for the moment their value was low, and the vast increase in the supply of them as a result of these military indemnity payments certainly did not help to raise it. This was perhaps the reason for the law which forbade the wearing of uniform and placed under police surveillance all who had alienated these bonds received in indemnity, instead of making use of them to join 'the industrious and working class of the country'.[31] Military reform was followed by administrative reform: a law of 7 September 1821[32] granted retiring civil servants pensions even more modest than the military ones. The pension for those with from four to ten years' service was equivalent to only one-quarter of the salary – this, of course, applied to most of those who had entered the civil service since the Revolution. Even before this law was passed, the simplification of the bureaucratic apparatus had begun in the treasury branch. Its objective was not merely 'to obtain, as a result, a saving in this financial year', but to nullify 'that force with which the government offices have attracted a considerable part of our precious youth, which has soon become incapable of any other work, and which is forming a race of men who, accustomed to a fixed salary, tremble to see themselves alone on the road of life and obliged to rely on their own industry. Thus this mania for place-seeking has grown and proliferated'.[33] This was how Doctor García explained to the provincial legislature the ultimate objective of the reform. Both this objective, and the more immediate one of lightening the burden on the public finances, are an accurate reflection of the profound change in political orientation resulting from the events of 1820. The State as leader of a collective enterprise of revolutionary transformation which, though destined to affect all aspects of the life of society, nevertheless had a fundamentally political basis, had been transformed into the *gendarme*-State, with the more modest objective of offering at the minimum possible cost a framework of order and security for the aggregate of individual enterprises, which were also no doubt destined to affect all spheres of social life, but had an essentially economic basis.

Placing itself at the service of private economic enterprise, the State was assigning to itself a more formidable task than might appear at first sight.

The return of peace did not mean that the marginal sectors returned to the position of isolation which they had occupied in Colonial times. Although they were no longer required for war, they were needed for the tasks of peace, and the State was prepared to force them into collaboration in those tasks. On the same day that it decided to place under police surveillance those Army officers who had carelessly squandered their indemnity payments, it promulgated another decree aimed at other and less exalted deserters from the new battle for economic progress: the vagrants, that

> class of vagabonds...unproductive, vexatious, injurious to public morality and conducive to turbulence in the social order. Considered in this true light, the vagabonds appear as a real obstacle to the progress of the country and another motive for the prevention or delay of the fulfilment of the general reform which has been initiated and whose benefits are beginning to make themselves felt.[34]

Although the justifications put forward were couched in new terms, the decree went on to establish the traditional sanctions: vagrants were to be called up for military service or, if they were medically unfit for that, they were to be conscripted as manual labourers for public works. A year later, the attention of the Government was drawn to the beggars, the abundance of whom was particularly scandalous in a country 'which displays the singular advantage of great abundance and low cost of food and even of clothing, and where the lightest and least skilled work earns good wages'. This decree established a register of beggars, who – after authorisation from the police – were to wear 'a visible distinguishing badge, a model of which would be delivered to the Chief of Police by the Ministry of Government', and who were not to beg in public places nor among those attending ceremonies 'such as funerals, the conferment of honours, christenings and weddings'. Those infringing this law and lacking funds were to be confined in the public prison: 'Delinquents addicted to mendicancy' (that is those who had either good health or financial resources) were to be conscripted for public works and, if convicted a second time, were to be banished to the rural areas.[35]

Not only the marginal sectors but also the labour force had to be disciplined. A law of 17 November 1821 punished apprentices who abandoned their work by leaving their factory or workshop, obliging them to serve 'longer than their agreed period of apprenticeship, one month for every week they have been absent'. There were more severe measures in the decree of 17 July 1823, which increased the obligations contained in the written contracts of rural peons.[36] The progress of the country, according to the introductory clauses of this decree, was offering the labouring classes ever

> more tasks...in which to exercise their industry, and as many more means to escape, by their own efforts, from their dependence on daily labour. This is even more true in the case of a country like ours, where wages are so high that, after satisfying more than the bare necessities of those who live on them, they leave a surplus with which to accumulate a personal fortune, which will one day make them independent.

If this happy outcome was not very frequent, the fault lay in 'the immorality of those same classes, which should seek those benefits from their own industry'. On a less exalted plane, the Minister Rivadavia pointed out that 'this immorality reaches such extremes among the peons in the country that, in general, they not only do not aspire to improve their fortune, but they even fail to do for their employers the work they owe them, according to the agreements entered into'. Here again, the sanctions stipulated were less novel than the introductory clauses: they reasserted the requirement for the peons to have a work-certificate, and – when the peon left an employer – to obtain from him 'a certificate recording his good conduct and fulfilment of the contract, or that the contract had been terminated freely and by mutual consent'. The penalties were, in the first case, two years with the Colours and in the second case the annulment of any subsequent labour-contract.

This policy, which brought into force regulations often inherited from the Colonial past, departed from it, and from the more recent Revolutionary tradition, in at least one essential aspect: concern for the interests of the popular sectors, whether as the object of the paternal attention of the government, or as the beneficiaries of the Revolutionary principle of equality, had disappeared completely. It was those sectors themselves which had to improve their lot, using to that end the instruments which the economy provided. In giving new force to a system which in fact was one of forced labour, the State did not feel that it had sacrificed those sectors to the interests of the propertied classes. However, never had it been announced with such emphasis that poverty was by definition the consequence of vice, and never had it been stated so frankly that high wages – in fact a consequence of the shortage of labour – were a prejudicial phenomenon, the progress of which had to be checked. In the labour sector, apparently, economic liberalism did not apply. Not only was official coercion used against peons whose scarcity gave them, in their relations with their employers, advantages considered harmful to the economy in general, but coercion was also used to impose a more severe discipline on the employers themselves, in cases where the shortage of labour might tempt them to infringe the regulations (for example, by giving asylum and work to peons whom another employer had found unsatisfactory). This lack of theoretical consistency was, perhaps, less significant than the extremely negative image of the popular sectors implicit in this entire apparatus of legislation.

It is true that these measures only accentuated – and justified in terms of a more modern economic and social theory – attitudes which were much older. The novelty lay not only in the more systematic nature of these measures, but also in the disappearance of that counterbalancing factor which, even in the most conservative phases of the Revolution, had been provided by the existence of a political enterprise common to the whole of society in the River Plate region, an enterprise in which the popular sectors

The dissolution of the Revolutionary order

had a place which was certainly subordinate, but was never eliminated altogether. Underlying the adoption of a new image of the State and its functions there was a deliberate alliance between that State and the representatives of the economic interests which it protected.

Both measures required a thoroughgoing reform of the structure of the State, which was also made necessary by the fall of the national government, whose power the Province inherited in 1820. This reform had two aspects: on the one hand, the new province-state renounced the political ambitions – which now seemed absurdly exaggerated – of its predecessor; on the other hand, it jealously reserved to itself administrative functions which had previously been distributed among minor corporations. A consequence of this attitude was the abolition of the Consulado of Commerce, and an even more important one was the abolition of the Cabildos, first that of Luján and then that of Buenos Aires. The survival of the Cabildo had certainly created additional tensions in the Revolutionary political system. Nevertheless, despite the progressive diminution of the power of the Cabildo relative to that of the central government, a demarcation of the spheres of activity of the two bodies had still seemed possible. After 1820 this was no longer the case: the Government of the Province not only took over the police functions which its national predecessor had already partly taken over, but also the functions of local justice and economic promotion and control for which the Cabildo had still been responsible. In addition to the elimination of a political rival which was potentially more dangerous now that its territorial jurisdiction was almost co-extensive with that of the new Provincial Government, and the rationalisation of an administrative and judicial apparatus of dubious efficiency, the objective of the Government in abolishing the Cabildo was, without a doubt, that of reserving for itself a new sphere of collaboration with the economically dominant interests.

The process of administrative centralisation and reform did not fail to affect the Army and the Church. The object of the military reform had not only been to end expenditure which placed an impossible burden on the Treasury, but also to orientate the Army towards new objectives. The law of July 1822 created a regular army 2,500 strong, with 113 officers in direct command of troops. The law of 5 December 1823 appointed a further 22 officers to the General Staff, thus limiting the number of officers in the new army to 135. The troops were to be of two kinds: volunteers and conscripts. The latter were recruited on a territorial basis from all over the Province, being selected in each district by a committee composed of a justice of the peace and 'twelve citizens of that jurisdiction, who are householders, married and over thirty years of age', to be selected by lot from among those fulfilling those conditions. Volunteers signed on for a term of from two to four years; the conscripts served for six years if they were between the ages of eighteen and thirty, and for four years if they were between the ages of thirty and forty. Exempted categories were more limited than had been the case before 1820; they still included merchants, proprietors and civil servants, but not wage-earners and craftsmen.

Conscription soon became unpopular. Attempts to effect recruitment in the city gave rise to so many disturbances that the Government abandoned them. By the end of 1823 it had resigned itself to having an Army exclusively composed of mercenaries and men from the marginal sectors. A law of 17 December repealed the articles of the former law providing for conscription, and replaced them by a general authorisation to recruit by force vagrants, 'sons under parental tutelage who refuse to obey their parents', those who 'for fighting with knives and other sharp weapons, or for causing bodily harm, have been sentenced to imprisonment' and 'those who on working days and with frequency are found in gambling-dens and taverns, and at horse-races and similar pastimes'.[37]

However, the Government encountered chronic difficulties in keeping the Army up to strength without having recourse to conscription. The hiring of mercenaries from other provinces, which for a time seemed to offer a solution, thanks to the well-remunerated collaboration of the local governments, was only successful – and even there only relatively so – in impoverished Entre Ríos. The Regular Army had, therefore, to be supplemented by militias. These already existed: the rural ones had played an important part in the early expansion of the frontier and in the political crisis of 1820, and the latter event had resulted in an expansion of the urban militia. The law of 1823 only put these forces on a more firm organisational basis. The militia infantry, organised in the city, were divided into active troops and reservists (consisting of the 18–45 and 45–60 age-groups, respectively). Each category was to have a strength of 1,590, and the first was to have a permanent staff of five officers and 45 non-commissioned officers, all regulars, while the second category would only have regular officers assigned to it during exercises, and would have no paid permanent staff.

In the rural areas the militia cavalry was organised, being recruited from men of between twenty and forty-five years of age. It had a strength of 2,240 and was commanded by three officers and twenty non-commissioned officers, all regulars.

The militia infantry and cavalry were only called to arms in times of emergency, and for a period not exceeding six months. The categories recruited were the same as those previously liable to conscription. The entire militia system was geared to compensating for the insufficiency of the Army. The burden imposed on the population of the province was much more unevenly distributed than the letter of the law would lead one to suppose. The figures for the city and the country in fact fixed an upper limit on the number of men who could be called to the Colours, and whether that figure was reached depended on the current military requirements and the ability of the Regular Army to meet them. With military activities orientated towards the advance of the frontier, it is not surprising that rural recruitment was more intensive than urban recruitment.

Thus the succession of military reforms had created a new army, with a corps of officers reduced by two-thirds and a decided orientation towards the frontier and the rural areas. The whole operation – the political risks of which, despite the favourable circumstances, have already been pointed out – was obviously imperative, if the Provincial Government were to meet its new commitments economically and efficiently. Can the same be said of the ecclesiastical reform? What benefits, proportionate to its high political cost, was the Government expecting from it? It is difficult to discover any. It is true that the suppression of the Regular Orders meant that their patrimony was inherited by the State, but that very patrimony – which had never been very considerable, except for rural and urban properties which were unprofitable and not easily marketable – had been hard hit by the Revolutionary storm. It is also true that the steadily increasing laxity of monastic life, to which Revolutionary politics had certainly contributed, had given freedom of action to figures whose popular ascendancy might be somewhat alarming. The most notorious of these was the Franciscan, Father Castañeda, who had first achieved fame for a Revolutionary fervour carried to almost delirious extremes. (One of the consequences of the Revolution had been, in his view, a more generous distribution of 'grace and Divine charisma' among the fortunate inhabitants of the River Plate region.) He then became so violent an anti-Federalist that, although born in Santa Fe, he won further fame in the turbulent year of 1820 as the intransigent spokesman of the most rabid Buenos Aires chauvinism, and his ferocious preaching was eventually rewarded by deportation to the frontier. It is, however, difficult to see in what way the reform could undermine the position of these friars who had thrown themselves into politics. One is, therefore, forced to admit that the Government embarked on this process without being fully aware of the tensions that it would unleash. And there were good reasons for its lack of awareness: the crisis of the Regular Orders was universally recognised as a problem, and after three centuries of the pre-eminence of the Crown in the government of the Church in Spanish America, and ten years of even more despotic control of it by the Revolutionary authorities, it was hard to see in the measures taken by the civil power to deal with this crisis any unprecedented inroads on ecclesiastical freedom. In insisting that it was only doing what the Spanish Crown and the Revolutionary Government had done whenever they thought fit, the Provincial Government was merely stating the truth. There were, however, abundant reasons why this policy – which was by no means new – provoked more decided reactions than had been expected.

The first reason was the growing centralisation of the Church, that unexpected but perfectly logical heritage of the French Revolution, which had demonstrated the fragility of the legal and patrimonial bases of the

Church's position in the various countries of Europe. This centralisation was not merely an administrative and political process. It was reflected in changes in the image of the Church itself, and of the rôle of the Vatican and of the Supreme Pontiff within it. The unruffled manner in which monarchs and bishops, though devout believers, had defended their own prerogatives against what they considered to be unjustified inroads by the Papacy became increasingly impossible, in so far as the jurisdictional conflict had now acquired a truly religious dimension which the Papacy, despite tenacious efforts, had been unable to impose on it in the past.

But, if Rome was now more successful in changing a jurisdictional dispute into a religious one, this was because this jurisdictional conflict had been employed in the service of a process of secularisation of public life openly supported by the civil power. Without it being necessary to suppose that the latter would utilise its rights in the government of the Church in order to further that process, experience of situations in which precisely this had occurred explains why not only the ecclesiastical dignitaries directly affected but, even more, the mass of the faithful felt alarm at any attempt to limit the clergy's attributions and enlarge those of the civil power. It was even more understandable that those dignitaries should utilise – and even exacerbate – the alarm of their flock and use it as an instrument of pressure against the inroads of the State's jurisdiction.

This was not, indeed, the origin of the resistance which the ecclesiastical reform was to encounter. The reform, in fact, consisted of the suppression of all the monastic houses of Buenos Aires except four, and in the imposition of rigid rules governing entry of novices into the Orders and the fixing of maximum and minimum numbers of inmates of each institution. Indeed, some of the clergy of the local Curia supported the reform from the beginning, and even those who found the measure excessively tyrannical, accustomed as they were by the Colonial and Revolutionary experience to bow to the civil power, confined themselves to expressing their dissent in a manner sufficiently explicit to salve their consciences, but refrained from offering any effective resistance. The source of opposition was, rather, certain political figures who saw in the reactions provoked by the reform an opportunity to rebuild an opposition front in the city. The possibility was immediately noticed by Doctor Tagle, who enlisted in his crusade for the unity of the faith a somewhat heterogeneous collection of retired officers, who had not always been famed for excessive piety. Among the economic and social élite of Buenos Aires, although there were many who were not gratified by the progress of what they considered to be excessive liberalism, the reasons for continuing to support the Rodríguez Government prevailed. Between the restorers of administrative and financial order and the crowd of indigent ex-military men captained by the unscrupulous Doctor Tagle, whose anxiety to return to close association with the centres of power was often explained by his

The dissolution of the Revolutionary order

need to escape financial penury, the choice of all those who had anything to lose was automatic.

Nevertheless, the ecclesiastical reform was to bring back to the political scene an element which had been absent since the plebeian agitation of 1820 had been crushed. By provoking agitation among levels of society which had until then been quiescent, it reintroduced a dimension which seemed to have vanished from the political arena. It was true that those who had been leaders of the popular opposition during the rule of the Directory had had very little to do with this unexpected resurgence. Manuel Moreno appeared to be completely reconciled to the new order, which had given him posts in the legislature, in the directorship of the Public Library and in the University. Manuel Dorrego made himself 'worthy of special remembrance' by leaving his military retirement to command the column 'entrusted with purging the immediately surrounding country' of the adherents of the movement begun by Tagle in March 1823.[38] Those who had created the agitation utilised by Tagle were, in the opinion of the Ministry, the parish priests, especially those in the rural areas, who were guilty, by their preaching and 'going into silent mourning', of having allowed the notion to be disseminated that the ecclesiastical reform was the work of impiety and heresy. After naming four priests as actively involved, the Minister Rivadavia told the vicar-general of the Buenos Aires see to put to the test 'the behaviour of the rural parish priests', distributing copies of the Government's manifesto so that they could expound it 'with all the moral considerations with which the Gospel supports a just government'.[39] The recipient of this imperious invitation expressed his 'unutterable satisfaction' at receiving it. The ecclesiastical sanctions imposed by the Minister of Government on the rebels had already begun to be put into effect, and the text of the government manifesto had been distributed among the parish priests, together with a demand from the vicar-general himself that they should better serve the Government against its enemies.

In this way – using once again an arsenal of governmental weapons that was entirely traditional – the Government reimposed discipline on a Church, some of whose members had been guilty of not condemning with sufficient severity the defenders of its traditional privileges.

Moreover, the threat to the cause of order had served to make explicit the sentiments of allegiance which surrounded it. In the hour of greatest danger, Manuel Arroyo y Pinedo, the cousin and close collaborator of Pueyrredón, appointed by the new régime President of the Legislature, had called to arms the urban militias of the Corps of Order, which he commanded, to combat subversion; and Brigadier-General Alvear, who had turned his back on his guerrilla activities in 1820, had offered the Government a support which the latter – with understandable caution – had preferred not to utilise. As soon as the moment of danger was past, expressions of adherence multiplied. The adherence was not so much to a régime, as to the kind of peace which that régime had succeeded in achieving. From Mendoza, San Martín, who had good reasons for disliking Rivadavia, also expressed his adherence privately, in a letter to his old friend Tomás Guido: 'You know that Rivadavia is no friend of mine, but only an out-and-out scoundrel could fail to be satisfied with his administration, which is the best there has ever been in America'. In contrast to this impressive list of adherences, that of those involved in the plot makes sorry reading: mediocre junior officers, drawn into the plot by Tagle, and the half-forgotten figure of Cornelio de Saavedra, supposed to lend his worn prestige to the government which would be installed if the movement were successful. The Government preferred to believe that it went no further than that. It refused to follow the trail pointed out by one of the conspirators, who insisted on compromising Juan Manuel de Rosas, then on a visit to Santa Fe to see his friend Governor López, and López himself. The Government declared that such accusations were the fruit of madness or perversity, and hastily had the author of them executed.

The Government was certainly not acting thus merely out of prudence: it had ample reason for distrusting the confidences of an already exposed conspirator, who was in turn only repeating those of the devious Doctor Tagle. But although in fact the dissident movement had not managed to gain significant support it was still true that the existing order had been shaken, and the challenge had affected deeper levels than the Government was willing to recognise. It had been demonstrated that it was not invulnerable to a recrudescence of political agitation, and it was to take note of that lesson in the future.

In a less sensational manner, the end of the exclusion of all those sectors alien to the élite had already become evident in the elections for the renewal of the Legislature in January 1823, which were preceded by agitation of an extent that far exceeded the limits within which political life had been confined since 1820. These events demonstrated the weak point, hitherto ill disguised, of the very basis of the political order inaugurated in 1820–21. The new régime had carried out, in addition to a thoroughgoing reform of the objectives and organisation of the State, a decided concentration of power, which by law was entirely invested in the House of Representatives of the Province, which appointed the Governor. This institution, which had emerged as a purely provisional electoral body in the course of 1820, had thus become an essential piece of an institutional mechanism which was gradually constructed by a series of fundamental laws: that of general elections, that of the election of the Governor, that which reserved to the Legislature the right to raise taxes, and several others. This provincial legislature was to recruit its members, to a much greater extent than the assembles of the Revolutionary era, from figures drawn from the economically dominant sectors. These emerged largely from the representatives of the rural areas: out of the nine surnames of the biggest cattle-ranchers in 1824,[40] four appeared in the legislature of 1821, one in that of 1824 and one among those elected to the national congress in the same year.

But it was not only the influence of the countryside – that pointer of the new balance of political power – which eventually ensured a closer relationship between the people who could now be considered as professional politicians and those who appeared as the representatives of the dominant interests. Among the representatives of the city, too (from 1821 onwards the legislature was composed of twelve of the latter and ten from the country), the predominance of the politicians was less complete than in the past. It is true that after 1821 the return of stability led the members of the socio-economic élite to adopt once again their usual reticence towards any very active participation in public life (this was manifested, for example, in the frequent resignations of representatives who had just been elected). Even so, such desertions did not prevent their presence being felt in successive legislatures. What is more, that presence was considered both necessary and useful. In an extremely biassed summary of the vicissitudes of the electoral contest of January 1823 which had resulted in the overwhelming victory of the Government, the winning list was called that of the proprietors and the losing one that of the doctors. The victorious list was composed of 'citizens with a solid fortune', and therefore there was not among them 'even one who could aspire to be a canon, administrator, secretary, government official or a founder of secret political associations' (these, apparently, being the motivations of those who formed the opposing list, whom the *Centinela* seemed to accuse primarily of lacking wealth – a rather strange accusation, considering that the list was headed by Tomás Manuel de Anchorena).[41] There could not be a more explicit repudiation of those whose lack of personal wealth had obliged them to embark on the career of the Revolution.

Furthermore, the correspondence columns of that newspaper at election time were animated by the same spirit, and this similarity is only partly explicable by the dubious authenticity of at least a part of that correspondence. On 22 December 1822[42] it published a list of candidates presented by a group of anonymous market-gardeners as the best guarantee against the return of those times when security was outraged, tranquillity endangered and property violated, when 'the public fortune was the patrimony of a small circle', as was desired by those 'who aspired to feed off the fruits of the sweat and industry' of the citizenry. In that list each name was proudly accompanied by the occupation of its owner: of the twelve signatories, ten were merchants. Another list, of 25 December 1822, was published, and it was pointed out that in it 'there is not one doctor, except for Doctor Agüero', and even he 'has little or nothing of the character of a Doctor; there is not one man who has to carve out his career by intrigues and revolutions; all have sufficient means to be independent, and to realise the care that must be taken to safeguard the public interest; not one of them needs a salary'.[43] On 12 January 1823, the publication in *El Centinela* of two lists obviously designed to split the vote of the opposition, was accompanied by a description, in this case a hostile one, of the professional past of those figuring on the list. In one of them we find six retired army officers, two ex-congressmen and only one proprietor; in the other, six ecclesiastics, three ex-officers, and a doctor.

It might be asked whether this increasingly agitated electoral climate, in the course of which the popular mobilisation which had accompanied the Revolution and which the latter had managed to suppress gradually seemed to be rising again from its own ashes, did not in itself constitute a danger for the solidity of a régime which appealed above all to those who had something to lose, and therefore instinctively shunned political adventurers. For, paradoxically, the new order which identified the interests of the province with those of its economically dominant groups was based on universal suffrage. The law of 14 August 1821, which established the procedure for elections to the legislature, gave an active vote to 'every free man, born in the country or resident therein, from the age of twenty, or before then in the case of freed slaves', and a passive vote to 'every citizen over the age of 25, who possesses some freehold or industrial property', for which no minimum value was fixed.[44] As was to be said in its disfavour by one of its severest posthumous critics, Esteban Echeverría, the system had granted 'the suffrage and the lance to the proletarian', this imprudent generosity being the cause of its downfall. It must, however, be observed, if we are to decide whether this reproach is justified, that the freedom of action of those who laid the institutional foundations of the new order was limited. That order had, in fact, been established thanks to the victory over the urban popular agitation and its allies in the regular army. That victory had been due precisely to what Echeverría called the proletariat of the lance – the rural militias which had reimposed on the city the political and social discipline which for a moment had been shaken. Furthermore, that proletariat of the lance, incorporated into the electorate as a result of the law, assured a solid basis for the régime, as long as it continued to follow the policy of the dominant rural interests. The support of the eleven representatives from the rural areas, who had won elections which were not contested and were quite blatantly rigged by the authorities of the district concerned, allowed it to survive, if not a defeat, then at least a not totally satisfactory electoral result in the city, which elected twelve representatives.

Even within the city, universal suffrage could not be regarded merely as a risk. It is by no means certain that the new order would have been able to make better use of the opportunities offered by a restricted suffrage, which in any case could not possibly have been so restricted as to be limited to the narrow social circle to the service of whose interests the Government was

The dissolution of the Revolutionary order

dedicated. Furthermore, universal suffrage was far from being an innovation. In 1812 the right to vote had been accorded to all free and patriotic citizens, though only in assemblies convoked in the Cabildos' halls. From 1815, however, elections for deputies and for Cabildo members in Buenos Aires had been held in a separate voting place in each district, in a manner similar to that laid down by the law of 1821. All this process not only constituted a legal precedent for the electoral system established in 1821; it also offered an experience, in the light of which it seemed possible to measure the specific incidence of the universality of the suffrage. And this experience apparently showed that the apathy of the electorate was a sufficient guarantee against the effective universalisation of the suffrage. On the other hand, in its dealings with the always limited number of spontaneous voters universal suffrage allowed the Government to deploy its big battalions (and in the most literal sense of that expression: the regular troops always contributed decisively to increasing the number of voters). Of course, the broadening of the suffrage facilitated, at least in theory, the broadening of the ruling circle: in the elections of 1823, when the 'doctors' seemed condemned to universal execration, the victorious ministerial list conceded 'a place to the honourable class of craftsmen',[45] and indeed Mariano Víctor Martínez figured on the list, described as an 'artist'. However, his presence in the legislature in no way essentially modified the basis of recruitment of the representatives. This was considered a sufficient tribute to his honourable class, and Martínez was not to find at his side any other man of the people during his undistinguished legislative career.

However, although it did not signify any real broadening of the politically dominant sector, universal suffrage was to signify an important modification of political practices. In 1821 the voters in the whole city had not numbered more than three hundred, and in by-elections they had been less than one hundred. In the climate of tension created by the ecclesiastical reform, the Government thought it necessary to avert the dangers of a massive vote by the opposition by carefully preparing its adherents. The result was an overwhelming victory. As the *Centinela* observed with satisfaction, for each vote on the opposition's list there were nearly ten on the ministerial one. This result would appear to guarantee the Government against any electoral surprises, but there was one other equally important aspect: the number of voters, mobilised by both the Government and the opposition, had risen in one year from three hundred to two thousand three hundred. In this broadening of the suffrage the most important contribution was that of the Government. Even the staunchly pro-Government *Centinela* admitted that of the two thousand pro-Government voters seven hundred, perhaps, were soldiers and civil servants. Moreover, in 1824, when a complex internal crisis eliminated official intervention, the total number of voters dropped to around one thousand seven hundred, of whom only slightly over seven hundred were Government supporters. In

1825, when the Government reassumed control of the electoral process, the number of voters again rose, to slightly over three thousand, of whom the opposition could count on only a hundred supporters.

The direct risks involved in universal suffrage appear, therefore, to have been minimal. It was enough for the Government to throw its weight into the election for the latter to have a result favourable to the authorities, which could win an overwhelming majority. The mobilisation of the big battalions, in fact, not only guaranteed for the ministerial party a bloc of voters which it would be difficult for the opposition to overcome (one has only to remember that the highest number of voters achieved by the opposition list was still less than a thousand). It had the additional effect of keeping away from the polls the cautious elements, which abounded in the ranks of an opposition whose militancy had been diminished by the absence of an atmosphere of real repression. In this way the Government's victories, even though they had not been achieved by absolutely irreproachable methods, were not accompanied by excessive scandal. It is true that the opposition continually denounced the sometimes brutal pressures exerted by that 'electoral army', but – since it never defied that force openly on the day of the election – this meant that the brutality was to a great extent muted.

It is also true, as has been observed above, that in order to obtain those scandalously overwhelming victories the Government had to adapt itself to a political atmosphere transformed by the broadening of the suffrage. Although the opening of the ranks of the ruling sector to recruits from the lower classes was of insignificant proportions, the great mass of electors, who now numbered thousands, could not be dragooned to the polls by simple executive fiat; the action of the authorities had to be more underhand. Even the troops – by definition the most disciplined sector of that electorate – could only be won over by the benevolence, not just of their officers, but also of more junior leaders. General Iriarte has described the methods employed to bring in the pro-Government vote in the much more excited political atmosphere of 1828. A Federalist, and commander of the artillery park, Iriarte's responsibility was to secure for his party the votes of the civilian labour force of the park,

> over a hundred and fifty in number, to ensure victory for the Government list in the Parish of San Nicolás where, in accordance with the law, they were to vote. The employee in the best position to win them over was the storekeeper Munita, a Chilean by birth, but he was a *unitario*; however, being unable to resist the prestige of my authority, he yielded, and worked hard for the defeat of the list he had previously supported.[46]

It was, of course, the formal authority of Iriarte which ensured those one hundred and fifty votes. Nevertheless, to achieve this end he was obliged to gain the support, which was not spontaneous, but was still absolutely necessary, of some one who possessed not authority but influence among

The dissolution of the Revolutionary order

the electors. Thus, even in the sector subjected to military discipline, or among civil servants disciplined by fear of unemployment, the broadening of the suffrage created new leaders, or lent political relevance to pre-existing patterns of leadership. This aspect of the transformation of the political atmosphere is even more remarkable in the case of that part of the electorate which did not depend, in so direct a manner as the soldiers or civil servants, on the Government's goodwill.

From the elections of 1823 onwards, in fact, political agitation spread out from the circles where traditionally the decisions had been taken to broader circles. Both the sober accounts of the *Argos* and the more detailed (and more partisan) ones of the *Centinela* give a picture of a thoroughly agitated city. In it, patterns of political solidarity were beginning to emerge which also surpassed the bounds of the ruling circle, and these patterns did not appear to be totally ephemeral. As usually happens, there were some who saw in this first manifestation of what could become disciplined political alignments a threat to the liberty of the elector, who ideally should decide for himself, in the light of his personal judgment, for whom to cast his vote. Such alarm, of course, appears exaggerated: none of the factions in dispute had a formal structure of its own. The lists which were competing for the favour of the voters were announced in advertisements in the newspapers signed by pseudonyms. This did not prevent the discipline of the electorate being reflected in its vote for lists which, although not formally legalised, in fact had a monopoly of support (and these lists only exceptionally exceeded two in number). Although it is not easy to measure the cohesion of the informal political apparatus which ensured this discipline, it undeniably existed, and its bases were not to be found only in the Government: leading figures in the city districts were able to bring in recruits who were somewhat more spontaneous than the soldiery in signifying their adherence to the official list. In 1825 this process was alluded to in the presentation of that list by a letter in the *Argos* – the probable author being Ignacio Núñez, who in the usual fashion signed himself 'a proprietor': it was maintained in the letter that 'one hundred men from each parish would vote for the list'.[47] The existence of nuclei of electors in the districts was doubtless the factor which explained the presentation of the electoral support for the list being broken down in this manner.

However, the very fact that the details of this electoral organisation remain unknown proves that its influence was not very great. Despite the broadening of the suffrage, political decisions were still monopolised by a very small group, and the modifications of political style which this group found itself obliged to adopt were rather superficial. What changes, then, did universal suffrage provoke in the political order of the city? On the one hand, by causing the practice of bidding for electoral support and thus provoking agitation among increasingly wider sectors of the population, it created once again that sounding-board among the populace as a whole which in the early stages of the Revolution had given a new dimension to the equilibrium of power within the élite. In this respect, its most important effect was the consolidation of the political influence of the landowners, without whose support those solid electoral fiefs on which the Government relied in the rural areas would have been much weaker. Moreover, by transforming elections which in the past had been a mere formality into battles in which the fate of the Government was at stake, and with it the fate of the 'fortunate experience of Buenos Aires', it subjected the régime to a series of tests, and stamped it, in its own eyes and those of its adversaries, with a provisional character – from which not even its most unquestioned successes could free it. It may seem at first sight paradoxical that this should have been the effect of electoral conflicts which the Government had no difficulty in transforming into overwhelming victories as soon as it set its mind to the task. Such victories, however, were not always as easy to achieve as might have been expected: indeed, the Government list lost in the city in the elections of 1824. The will to fight the electoral battle with all its might depended, in the last resort, on the determination and the internal cohesion of the governing group. A political system based on universal suffrage demanded from it a degree of internal discipline which had been absent in the past.

The image of itself which that group displayed certainly postulates such cohesion. A team of representatives of the interests which dominated the economy of the province, which accepted the leadership of a few extremely capable administrators, but which at the same time exercised overall supervision of the policy which they were following in the province, would not have any other motive for discord than that arising out of a divergence of interests. But in the wave of expansion provoked by the growth of cattle-raising the dominant interests had found the possibilities of a consensus which constituted the most secure basis of the order reconstructed after 1820. Because that image was not entirely accurate, the concord of economic interests did not automatically guarantee political consensus. True, the political leadership could not with impunity modify the policy which systematically favoured the economically dominant interests, by reducing State expenditure, keeping up the payments on the public debt, renouncing all military operations beyond the frontiers of the Province, and putting the forces of order at the service of the development and pacification of the cattle-raising zones. Within this framework, however, the Government enjoyed comparative freedom of manoeuvre. A measure such as the ecclesiastical reform, which found little favour either with the popular sectors or with the economic élite, nevertheless did not undermine the support of the latter for the régime, a support based on the very real services which that Government had rendered the élite. Even less frequently, there sometimes emerged from the economically dominant interests an

The dissolution of the Revolutionary order

individual instance of opposition to the policies enacted in their favour by the Rodríguez Government. In 1822 and 1823 Juan Manuel de Rosas (the cousin of the Anchorenas, who was already a big landowner in the South and had in 1820 played, at the head of his rural militias, the rôle of saviour of the social order threatened by plebeian insurrection), agreed with his friend the Governor of Santa Fe on the need to take advantage of the momentary weakness of the Portuguese occupying forces in the Banda Oriental – due to the crisis of the independence of Brazil – to liberate Uruguay by force, which he supposed would be an easy task. However, although this disagreement resulted in Rosas's consolidating contacts in Santa Fe which in his future career were to be extremely useful, for the moment it did not lead to the breakdown of a political solidarity which, despite all his hesitations, was to last until at least 1825, and which was reflected, for example, in the solidity of the Government's electoral base in those South-Western lands where Rosas's influence was dominant.

It was not, therefore, the breakdown of the implicit pact with the dominant interests which was the source of the most immediate dangers for the ruling political group. That source was to be found in the governing group itself, the transformation of which had been less far-reaching than was suggested by the *Centinela* and its none too authentic correspondents. It is true that the House of Representatives had, to a greater extent than the institutions of the first decade after the Revolution, members who made up for their lack of political vocation by their social and economic power, and who preferred to remain in the background. Echeverría was, perhaps, over-harsh in describing them as a 'crowd of nonentities',[48] but he felt legitimate astonishment at seeing them rise again after all the political storms, with their 'stupid marble faces which seem to have been incrusted on the seats of the House ever since its foundation'. However, although their representative character, which was not affected by political changes because it had very little to do with politics, was their strength, their fundamental political apathy, which they disguised by adopting the colours of the successively dominant political factions, meant that they could exercise no real overall directing rôle. Within a legislature of twenty-three members, it was an even smaller group which in fact established, after reaching an always provisional agreement with the Government, the general orientation of the decisions. It remains to be considered whether this group was accurately characterised by the description of 'merchants' which the *Centinela* applied to almost all the names of the candidates who were subsequently victorious in the the 1823 elections. Among those merchants we find some veterans of the career of the Revolution, such as Manuel de Arroyo y Pinedo, who began that career before the Revolution itself, in 1806, and was never to abandon it. And we find others – like Juan Pedro Aguirre, an outfitter of privateers, and a financial agent of the Government, and Félix Castro – who in the past had come to realise that commercial success and political influence were by no means mutually exclusive. And that list, which hardly displayed innovation in its recruitment, marks the extreme of the process of renewal of the political leaders undertaken after 1820.

Among the members of the provincial legislature there was – from 1821 to 1827 – Manuel Moreno, who lived on his income from his official appointments. Colonel Dorrego figured, albeit intermittently, and so did Vicente López y Planes, who also, as Director of the Statistical Register, received an income from the State. None of these three gave his unreserved adherence to the new order. The three of them resembled, not so much the new type of politician, devoted to the defence of collective interests which his considerable private fortune led him to identify exactly with his own, as to the type which arose during the first decade after the Revolution, and had been obliged to develop professional expertise in the service of the State because the inadequacy of their personal wealth or their neglect of their private interests had excluded all other courses of action. Nevertheless, the Government used its influence to bring them into the Legislature. Its reasons for doing this, in the case of Moreno and, to an even greater extent, that of Dorrego, was that the popularity of those figures, resulting from the persecution they had suffered under the Pueyrredón Government, perhaps served to limit the opposition encountered by the Government's electoral lists; but in the case of López even this explanation is inadequate.

A better reason was that the exclusion of the former ruling group – even of those of its members who least resembled the ideal of the public man now universally accepted – was necessarily less drastic than some would like to believe. The most prominent leaders of the Buenos Aires experience – Rodríguez, Rivadavia and García – were themselves also veterans of the career of the Revolution, and they did not hesitate to remind people of this through the official press when their enemies accused them of lack of patriotism or even of pro-Spanish sympathies. The exclusion of figures because of a too intensive political career in the past could not, therefore, be absolute. Furthermore, it was probably more prudent to give a place in the new system to those who were potential adversaries, rather than drive them into a more active opposition. The reform of the State could not be sacrificed to the convenience of reserving places of refuge for these dubious supporters, who threatened to become decided enemies. But even the new structure of the State preserved positions with prospects and reasonably well remunerated, which could be used as inducements to buy peace. There was nobody who represented better than General Alvear – the protégé of the Revolutionary cliques of 1813–14, the military dictator of 1815, the guerrilla leader closely allied with the Province's enemies of 1820 – the characteristics which the partisans of the new style of politics found reprehensible in the old one. However, there was nothing illogical in the

Rodríguez Government's preferring to make Alvear its diplomatic representative abroad, rather than having to put up with his hostile intrigues in the city. Prudence was not the only explanation of this decision: among the men who directed the political life of Buenos Aires there were some true and faithful friends of General Alvear, who had not forgotten the loyalty which they had given him in the past.

Thus, the service of the dominant economic interests, although it established the general orientation of the political course of the Province, did not prevent those who were directing that process from enjoying a considerable measure of freedom. The use which they made of it demonstrates that, in that profound transformation of political life of which they claimed to be the champions, perhaps the least changed elements were those leaders themselves. The result was that, despite the agreement existing as to the main objectives of economic reconstruction, there was only limited consensus among the members of the Government, and the internal discipline of the group was extremely elastic. When the official press rejected even the term 'ministerial list' given by the opposition to the list which the Government supported, it had good reasons for doing so: the deputies thus elected were far from giving systematic support to the policies of the Ministry. When it reckoned up its friends, the Government preferred to believe that all who were not openly opposed to it were supporters. A stricter discipline was neither necessary nor possible. Underlying the general agreement as to overall policy, a relationship marked by ambiguity was established between the members of a ruling group which made no effort to define exactly who belonged to it. Mariano Moreno, as has already been observed, received from the new provincial government a permanent post in the Legislature, appointments in the University and a position in the official press – in the journals published by the Literary Society, that field for debate which the new régime had prepared for the intellectual élite of Buenos Aires. He repeatedly used these positions to express his disagreements with the Government: writing in the *Abeja Argentina*, the scientific journal of the Society, he condemned the perhaps unnecessarily brutal manner in which the ecclesiastical reform had been applied; and in the *Argos*, the fortnightly also published by the Society, which in 1822 was edited by Moreno and in 1823 by that other dubious participant in the new order and veteran of the career of the Revolution, Dean Funes,[49] were often to be read reservations as to the course of political events, which the more decidedly pro-Government *Centinela* unceasingly denounced as insidious.

But such hesitations and fluctuations were not only to be found on the fringe of that ruling group. The United States envoy, Forbes, followed the gradual evolution of Julián Segundo de Agüero, a Doctor, parish priest of San Ignacio, then a Representative, who was to become one of the pillars of the Government party during the discussion of the ecclesiastical reform law.

The tergiversations of Agüero were due less to his scruples as a priest than to his desire to obtain certain favours for Manuel Arroyo y Pinedo, with whom he had a long-standing friendship which was reflected in a political alliance, and also, perhaps, in a coincidence of interests in other spheres. This was only one example of a more generalised attitude. Despite the introduction of universal suffrage, which superficially modernised the style of political life, and despite the need to serve the dominant economic interests, which established approximate guidelines which were universally accepted, the lines on which the politically ruling group divided were determined by the conflicts and loyalties of minor factions within that same group. Those conflicts were essentially connected with the distribution of favours which the State, despite the reduction of its functions, was still in a position to bestow. One of the causes of the relative concord which had emerged after 1820 had been the reduction of those functions. If these were to be enlarged again, then the grounds for discord, never entirely abolished, would also be amplified to a dangerous extent. However, this passivity on the part of the State was due, not so much to the generalised acceptance of a new definition of its functions, as to the combination of that acceptance and a fiscal penury inherited from the past, which was an even more effective barrier to any ambition of reconquering for the State spheres from which it had withdrawn. That penury was, in fact, brought to an end by the exercise of prudence in government expenditure, which also contributed – together with the prosperity of the livestock industry – to create a more widely felt confidence in the future. Such measures as the granting of special privileges to the Discount Bank, and arranging a loan in Europe, marked the re-entry of the State into the field of financial activities which, although very different from those characteristic of the first decade after the Revolution, did resemble them in that they allowed the State to distribute more considerable economic favours than in the immediate past. The interest of the economically powerful sectors in public affairs was no longer only the interest of a group in guaranteeing the continued existence of a State which could efficiently fulfil its rôle as a *gendarme* keeping internal order. It was the individual interest of some members of that group to reserve for themselves, to the exclusion of other members of the same group, the benefits of official favour. If one remembers the very large sums which the Robertson brothers and Félix Castro pocketed as intermediaries in the arrangement of the Baring Loan, it is easy to understand why this change of attitude took place so quickly. A result of it was that now renewed economic progress was the cause of division, and not merely of union, in the economically dominant group. This division and the consequences of its spreading into the political field can be seen, for example, in the complex vicissitudes of the Discount Bank and its successor and rival the National Bank. For over a year the press bristled with statements in which the rivals, making a generous use of pseudonyms,

The dissolution of the Revolutionary order

levelled at each other the most violent accusations and often incomprehensible innuendos. The culmination was reached in 1825 when, in the expert opinion of Ignacio Núñez, who was representing in Buenos Aires the interests of the absent Rivadavia, the result of the election depended on the outcome of the conflict between the banks: 'The opposition is already celebrating its triumph, but even though its stock of weapons has been increased by the conflict between the banks, I believe that if these problems ...are solved speedily, it will lose the election'.[50] Núñez was not the only man to recognise the political connotations of the conflict, which drove into opposition more than one lukewarm supporter of the existing order. Among these was Colonel Dorrego, who defended the cause of the Discount Bank, which the *Argos*, now in the safe hands of Núñez, was accusing of illegal transactions. The incident also brought back into the lists that redoubtable intriguer Manuel de Sarratea, who 'has involved the country in still greater difficulties with the arms he has brought in to turn the problem of the Banks into an open battle'.

In this way, the increasing divisions within the economically dominant sector rendered even more serious the tensions (which had never entirely disappeared) among the leaders of the Government party. It should be observed that these divisions did not correspond exactly to those between different functions of the process of production. The dispute, for example, between landowner-producers and merchants, which according to many retrospective interpretations was the key to the growing division among the dominant sectors of the economy, appears not to correspond to the facts. It was the financial, rather than the economic, policy of the State which provoked the conflicts, and as regards that financial policy itself, it was not its general orientation that was in dispute, but the distribution of its benefits among rival speculators.

In this way economic rivalries reflected the essential characteristics of political ones. In the latter, too, what was in fact in dispute was not the overall orientation of the State's actions, but the distribution of power and its benefits between strictly personal alliances. Politics based on self-interest, which replaced those based on Revolutionary solidarity, eventually reflected, therefore, in all their confused multiplicity, the world of complicities and rivalries of a small urban oligarchy. This intricate political system could survive, despite its insufficiencies, as long as a fundamental agreement regarding the objectives of the State's activity diminished the importance of the internal conflicts which the loose character of the internal discipline of the governing group necessarily provoked.

However, it was only necessary for that fundamental agreement to be weakened for the disruptive tendencies, which had been present from the outset in that political system, to acquire greater strength. And it was not only the increasing financial activity of the State that threatened that agreement: the return of the province to its hegemonic position in the country as a whole, which was also in part a consequence of the return of prosperity, again gave urgency to problems which at an earlier stage it had been possible to evade. By recognising that the struggle for independence was over, Buenos Aires had won for itself a truce as far as any action outside its frontiers was concerned. *Vis-à-vis* the provinces, it had adopted a policy perfectly appropriate to fulfilling its objective – a modest and essentially negative one – of eliminating Córdoba as a rival aspirant to hegemony. As the years passed, the need for a less passive policy in both fields became evident. This was to make necessary, in one way or another, the modification of the decisions implicitly or explicitly accepted since 1820. Economic and social reconstruction, in a context of peace, could no longer be the universally accepted objective.

In this way, the 'fortunate experience of Buenos Aires' was moving towards a crisis which it was not to survive. But already before it reached that crisis, its ability to resist the temptations of discord was seriously weakened in a context which demonstrated yet again the debility of the entire institutional apparatus, even in the historical climate in which it emerged. This event was the election of a new Governor of the Province, in 1824.

The Legislature was responsible for organising this election; it was, therefore, that firm stronghold of the Government party which was to decide on the successor to General Rodríguez. Nothing, except confusion within that party, could pose any danger to that process of renewal of the authorities. Nevertheless, its preparation was marked from the outset by a curious atmosphere of general uncertainty. From the end of 1823 the pro-Government *Centinela*, without accepting in so many words the proposal for a peaceful revolution, which, by replacing the governing group through elections, would consolidate the institutions of the Province by preventing their permanent identification with that group, nevertheless accepted it in substance. Its only objection was to the use of the term 'revolution' rather than 'change'.[51] What had happened was that the Governor's unpopularity had apparently increased in the course of the year 1823, due both to the unimpressive results of the campaign against the Indians, whose defeats seem to have been systematically exaggerated, and to certain arbitrary acts, and also to the consequences of a drought and an epidemic which led to a shortage of bread and beef to which the newspapers devoted much attention.[52] Furthermore, in June Forbes was able to report two parallel intrigues, one to replace General Rodríguez by his War Minister Cruz, who would continue to have the collaboration of Rivadavia, and another favouring Las Heras (behind whom Forbes feared the rising influence of Agüero, whom he considered to be suffering from nostalgia for the *ancien régime*). Months later, instead of General Cruz, Juan Manuel de Rosas, as a candidate, prepared to ensure the collaboration of the Rivadavia – García cabinet.[53]

What was wearing down the hegemony of the Government party was not, therefore, the existence of an opposition which, although less passive than in the immediate past, could never hope to win an open fight. It was the actual structure of that party, which had obstinately refused to provide itself with the image and the discipline of a political party, but which had, on the contrary, sought to use to its advantage the network of ambiguous rivalries and alliances among that small circle of people whose political influence was dominant in Buenos Aires. Its destiny was decided within that circle. The trends of public opinion affecting wider sectors, ranging from the desperation of those unable to buy bread and meat to the growing impatience provoked by the Government's passivity in the face of the Portuguese intrusion, only made themselves felt in the political game in so far as they awakened an echo within that smaller circle where the decisions were taken, whether by encouraging the fringe supporters to return to an attitude of open opposition, or by offering pretexts for potential dissident activities within the ruling group itself, and thus hastening the breakdown of the fragile solidarity which had always characterised it.

In 1824, therefore, the lack of cohesion of the political group which governed the Province of Buenos Aires became evident. Although, by preserving the decorum which had characterised them from the outset, the Buenos Aires leaders managed to avert a scandal, the breakdown of the never very stable solidarity which had united them in the period which was ending was irremediable. That breakdown was to have far-reaching consequences: it was to result in a civil war involving the whole nation, and was only to be resolved by the deliberate accentuation of the tensions between the winning and the losing faction. It is, therefore, understandable that historians have sought to identify motivations as broad in scope as those consequences, and to suggest that behind the rivalry of the politicians who were trying to dominate the Governor through their advice (the Governor being an old soldier overcome with admiration for his learned advisors), there were the rivalries of entire social groups, economic interests and even regions. This search, however, which has given rise to interpretations of the crisis more notable for their internal coherence than for their fidelity to the facts, ignores one fact which is, nevertheless, quite obvious: the persistence of an essentially oligarchical political framework, made possible – and at the same time relatively innocuous – by the continuing agreement as to the general objectives of political action. Once this disappeared, then the negative consequences of a political system which was too faithful a reflection of the complex interplay of internal solidarities and repulsions of an élite torn to pieces and then rebuilt by ten years of political and economic revolution made themselves felt in the most catastrophic manner. The Athens of the River Plate was better able than its rustic disciples in the Interior to disguise behind a complex institutional framework the essential characteristics of the political order which dominated the province. These characteristics were not, however, as different from those prevailing in the rest of the country as might be supposed at first sight.

What the political order presiding over the admirable experience of Buenos Aires lacked was, in short, coherence. It has already been observed how the coherence that it appeared to display was really the coherence recovered by the whole of Buenos Aires society, once the new road to prosperity had been discovered. However, the progress of the new economic formula which was becoming triumphant in the Province caused a displacement of economic – and even, indirectly, political – power within the élite, and the origin and attitudes of the ruling group failed to reflect this process accurately. Those who represented themselves as having risen as a result of the productive activities now in full expansion were more often veterans of the career of the Revolution, while others were men for whom the Revolution had frustrated promising careers in the urban corporations and judicial structure, and who were again embarking on those careers in a political climate which had become less hostile to them. This differentiation between the political ruling group and the economically dominant group was not viewed with alarm by the latter, which was happy to find somebody to do the work of government for it. Nevertheless, this was one of the reasons for that internal incoherence which in the hour of trial was to be revealed by the political order established in Buenos Aires in 1820–21. There was, however, something in common between this situation and those prevailing in the Interior. In Córdoba under the rule of Bustos, in Santa Fe under that of López, and in Mendoza which in the 1820s was one of the most successful disciples of Buenos Aires and in the following decade fell under the domination of the commander of its frontier force, political leaders had to take account of the internal equilibrium of an élite, the power-base of whose members had been very unequally affected by the tempest of Revolution. In Buenos Aires, as in the Interior, the crisis of 1820 had revealed the rural basis on which from henceforth all political power had to rest, but that ruralisation of the bases of power was only one aspect of a process of ruralisation which affected wider areas of the national life, and which seemed to consolidate that 'barbarisation' which even in 1810 had been seen as one of the consequences of the changes which the Revolution would necessarily introduce.

'Barbarisation', however – to apply an excessively simple term to a more complex and ambiguous process of change – was not the only consequence of that progressive affirmation of a political power with a rural base. This was the result of a process in which life appeared to have been drained out of the higher levels of the political apparatus. What remained of it was an aggregate of separate nuclei of power, the vitality of which had been diminished by the harsh experiences of the preceding decade, and which were not necessarily in rivalry with each other but found it difficult to achieve stable integration into any system, whether institutionalised or not.

The dissolution of the Revolutionary order

The disappearance, without any replacement, of the central government was both the culmination and the outward manifestation of this process. But the voids in the political order resulting from the collapses of 1820 were not only apparent in the relations between the provinces. Within each province, the fragility and inherent instability of the current political situations were painfully obvious. The problem of how to correct this, and of how to create a political order different to this one which was almost as vulnerable to its own weaknesses as to external threats, was the greatest of the problems bequeathed by the Revolution to the nation which it had created. The process of institutionalisation appeared to be, in the opinion of most people, the way to overcome that lack of internal cohesion which afflicted the Argentine political system once the Revolutionary phase was over. Institutionalisation, however, was not possible without a prior network of affinities and alliances on which the new institutional system could be based. Although less explicitly formulated, the need to construct this network of ties of solidarity was generally recognised. There was, of course, in this aspiration, which was never entirely abandoned, both the remembrance and the presentiment of the unity of the State becoming the unity of the nation. It was this aspect of it which occupied the attention of Argentine historians of the second half of the nineteenth century, who were especially interested in the rise of national sentiment and of nationality. There were, however, other and more immediate stimuli. The rise of the rural sector and the fragmentation of the political system did not take place only where the Revolutionary crisis was reflected in economic decline, and in the impoverishment of the pre-Revolutionary élite sectors without their replacement by other sectors of equivalent economic potential. They also happened in places where the replacement of the Colonial economic order had not had such catastrophic consequences: in Buenos Aires, which was achieving a prosperity greater than any it had enjoyed in the past, and in certain provinces of the Interior where the new economic order registered more modest successes, for example Córdoba, Santiago del Estero and Mendoza. And the prosperity recovered in those places depended on the maintenance of international and inter-regional traffic, and this in turn depended on the maintenance of stable and relatively untrammeled relations between the new political units. Political isolation, therefore, could never reach extremes incompatible with the maintenance of an inter-regional network, which might be different in character to that existing in the last years of the Colonial period, but which was still indispensable for the very survival of the regional economies. The areas politically separated were thus obliged to maintain an intimate contact, which made even more dangerous the extreme incoherence of the political order, based as it was on ephemeral partial agreements between some of the regional powers and equally ephemeral tensions between those same powers. In the period before the final solution which the reconstruction of the central government would one day provide, a new political style developed as a result of the dual stimulus of ruralisation and the absence of an institutional framework, and even of any substitute for the latter in the form of a tolerably stable system of alliances of groups and regions on which could be based an order sufficiently defined as regards its essential characteristics. This new style was an attempt to adapt to that hostile context and to avert the danger of fresh crises which its deficiencies perpetually threatened to provoke.

In the final part of this book an attempt will be made to describe, firstly, the consequences for the group of leaders that rose to prominence after 1820 of the experience of the Revolutionary period through which they had all lived, not only to the extent that their own prospects had been affected by it, but above all in the transformations provoked in the lands which they tried their best to govern; and, secondly, the characteristics of that ruling sector, which were partly connected with its place in the society of the River Plate region, and partly with the nature of the political problems which it had to face.

PART THREE: CONCLUSION

7 THE LEGACY OF THE REVOLUTION AND THE WAR, AND THE POLITICAL ORDER OF INDEPENDENT ARGENTINA

THE 'BARBARISATION' OF POLITICS: THE MILITARISATION AND RURALISATION OF THE BASES OF POLITICAL POWER

In 1820 the territory over which the war had assured the political hegemony of the heirs to the power created by the Revolution of 1810 in Buenos Aires had none of the distinguishing marks of a nation, let alone a state. The different regional authorities which shared that dominion were nearly all of an openly admitted provisional character. The institutional framework within which political life developed was non-existent at the national level, and existed only in outline – to differing degrees, but everywhere incompletely – in the various provinces. In some of them, for example in all those of the Littoral – as the Buenos Aires-born Ignacio Núñez, the follower of Moreno and then of Rivadavia, informed the British Consul, Parish[1] – there was no separation between the three powers, 'owing to lack of ideas'. In Córdoba the Governor only convoked the Junta when he felt like it, and exercised the judicial power; in La Rioja, Santiago del Estero and Catamarca there were provincial Juntas, 'but the Governors appear to have no more limits to their duration of tenure than does the establishment of the general government'. In San Luis, the House of Representatives never met, and the Governor remained in his post indefinitely. Tucumán and Salta won Núñez's laconic approval. He accorded more effusive praise to San Juan, where the provincial chambers, elected by direct suffrage, 'occupy themselves during the more pleasant seasons of the year with the reform of public institutions', where there was freedom of the press and security of the individual, and the judiciary was 'as independent as it could possibly be'. Even in these fortunate provinces, however, 'much remained to be done' to achieve a satisfactory institutional development.

It is true that this report of Núñez is not always accurate: in Córdoba the Legislature had created a permanent committee to function when it was in recess; and whatever the criterion selected, it is hard to see how the situation in Tucumán could be described as satisfactory. However, this inventory of local situations is a good illustration of the universally incomplete nature of the institutional reconstruction initiated in 1820. Even in Buenos Aires – which was not mentioned in Núñez's description – the absence of a constitution, although this was effectively substituted, for practical purposes, by the fundamental laws promulgated in 1821, was felt by many to be a weakness in the institutional apparatus of the province.

These institutional insufficiencies and inconsistencies were partly connected with the difficult transition – which was all the more difficult because it had never been envisaged as a problem in its entirety – between the Spanish administrative structure and that of the period of independence. To give an extreme example, the 1819 Constitution of Santa Fe maintained almost intact the public institutions inherited from the Colonial period. The legislature was above all an electoral body, and had been created as a result of the replacement of the sovereignty of the monarch by that of the people, delegated to that assembly. The actual tasks of government were carried out by the Governor and the Cabildo. Even in Córdoba the 1822 Statute, which followed more closely the precepts of European liberal constitutionalism, reserved to the Governor the attributes established by the Bourbon Ordinance for Intendants, and it has already been observed how, although – again in accordance with the most accepted models – the legislature was in this province actually a legislative power, its real influence was limited by the sweeping powers reserved to the Governor and the Cabildo.

Were these survivals the result of the cultural archaism of those areas previously relegated to a secondary rôle and subordinated to the central authority? If one compares what was happening in the provinces with the intransigent liberal-constitutional orthodoxy dominant in Buenos Aires one might conclude that this was the case. Such orthodoxy, however, was in Buenos Aires itself an innovation: up to 1820 the central government had made maximum use of the institutional apparatus inherited from the Viceroyalty, and attempts to reform it had not gone very far. Furthermore, it fulfilled very obvious functions in the context of the local political conflicts, which explains its success after 1820. The abolition of the Cabildo, an essentially urban institution which had regulated the administration of the rural areas, and the consequent enlargement of the attributions of a Governor whose basis of support was those rural areas, and of those of a legislature half of whose members were elected by those areas, do not appear to have had as their principal objective the reform of the organisation of the province in accordance with any renowned overseas model.

It should be added that this cultural archaism – which was less exclusive to the provinces of the Interior than is sometimes supposed – was not in any way militant. Adherence in principle to the most modern institutional solutions would not, in any case, be surprising in entities which had emerged from a movement which everywhere called itself *liberal*. The novelty of the term itself (coined, of course, in anti-Napoleonic Spain), in addition to the innovatory orientation of the tendency with which it was identified, make it easier to understand the criteria applied by the Government of Santa Fe when signifying its approval of British policy (as Estanislao López assured the Consul, Parish,[2] Santa Fe was gratified to discover 'in the Government of His Britannic Majesty an enlightened policy and a liberal conduct worthy of the spirit and knowledge of this century'). This adherence to the political novelties contributed by liberalism did not imply ignorance of its specific content. There were liberal theses which were explicitly excluded from this general approbation, and thus religious liberty, in most provinces of Argentina, was not considered as a legitimate corollary of political liberty. However, even that political liberty, though accepted as a valid objective, existed to only a limited extent in the provinces of Argentina, and the same was true of liberal principles regarding the separation of powers in the State.

Rather than the weight of a pre-Revolutionary administrative tradition, which in any case was more tenuous in the recently created provinces than in the old Viceregal capital or the former seats of Intendants, it was the specific context in which the institutions had to develop which differentiated them from a model, the theoretical validity of which was unquestioned. As Núñez observed, the perpetuation in office of governors and legislators was difficult to avoid: 'In these towns it is absolutely necessary that this should be so, because the state of absolute independence in which they have existed has obliged them to put into the government individuals born or resident in the particular place; but since the educated population is very small in each place, they naturally cannot vary the persons concerned, and they make a law out of necessity'. Núñez concluded that this problem could only be solved by reconstituting the old provinces (that is the Intendancies divided up into smaller units after 1814) 'because in the provincial capitals there is always a greater number of well educated people with whom to staff those governments'. Bustos, too, considered that most of the provinces were too poor and underpopulated to maintain a complex institutional apparatus,[3] and a solution analogous to that of Núñez was to be suggested in the 1824 Congress by the Federalist Dorrego. All these analyses and solutions presupposed a radical difference between the centres which possessed a local administrative tradition and those which did not.

These differences, however, were also reflected on other levels. From the first decade after the Revolution Buenos Aires had been accustomed to seeing its enemies as the representatives of a rustic savagery which had to be checked by any methods. After 1820 the tendency to explain in the same terms the often brutal and direct manner in which authority was exercised in the provinces is easily understandable. However, the facts do not seem entirely to confirm this. Some of the more ferocious acts which accompanied the return of peace after the turbulent year of 1820 were committed by those who had received their education in the military and administrative school of the central Revolutionary government. Although it was the former dissident Estanislao López who exhibited, in a cage, the head of his ally and subsequent rival Ramírez, the man who 'sends it to him as a present' was the Córdoba colonel Francisco de Bedoya, who in 1815 had been a pillar of the resistance to Artigas. At the same time the Bustos-Bedoya government in Córdoba received another equally macabre present, the head of the Federalist leader Felipe Álvarez. The man who sent it to be exhibited 'in Frayle Muerto, the principal place of his district, so that the event of which this shall remind them may serve as a warning to those who have been led astray by his example' was Tomás Godoy Cruz, who had been a leading collaborator of San Martín in his native Mendoza.[4] And even in Buenos Aires, although the *Gaceta* announced that it hoped that rapid burial would be given to the remains of the Supreme *Entrerriano*, thus bringing to an end a spectacle 'both horrific and repugnant', this did not prevent it from publishing, on 19 July 1821, a letter in which 'a respectable citizen of Córdoba' expressed, without any such squeamishness, his gratification over the elimination of those two villains Güemes and Ramírez. It should be added that the exposition of parts of the bodies of executed rebels was a normal practice of the Royal administration, inspired by the intimidatory purpose assigned to it by Godoy Cruz.

It would, therefore, be unjustified to see in this increase of deliberately cruel practices the abandonment of the more refined legacy of the cultural tradition which the political breakdown had made more fragile. It has already been observed how this tradition was more ambiguous in character than is sometimes supposed. Moreover, the experience of Revolution and war had made it even more complex. Before encouraging the political rise of groups with a rural base, the Revolution and the war had changed the attitudes of the groups already dominant. The growth of brutality in political relations (and not merely political ones) was one of the most significant aspects of this change. We have already seen how militarisation played its part in this process. The leaders of the Revolutionary army sometimes appear to have considered ferocity as a professional virtue of which they were proud. In consequence, in the civil war in the Littoral, although Artigas's troops – particularly those from the Banda Oriental, who were systematically underpaid by their leader – might be fearful when it came to looting, those of the central government were even more addicted to ferocity and rapine. This behaviour was sporadically encouraged by the Government itself, with rousing proclamations such as that which invoked terror to produce the effects 'which reason and the interest of society have not been able to produce',[5] and, more continuously, by the troops' own officers. In the Banda Oriental Dorrego, whose undisciplined behaviour had exhausted the patience of San Martín and Belgrano, conducted himself in such a manner that he provoked an impassioned protest from the *artiguista* leader Otorgués, whose daughter – as far as can be judged from a text where detail has been sacrificed to decorum – had been raped by a soldier under his command.[6] In Santa Fe, as has been noted above, Dorrego actually quarrelled with other officers, over the body of a leading citizen of Santa Fe, for the possession of a religious medal of little value. Even far away from the battle area, the supremacy of the military also made itself felt in incidents that were both brutal and humiliating. The physical punishment of leading citizens of Buenos Aires, in public places, by officers bent on avenging real or supposed offences, appears to have been an established custom by 1815.

However, this new style of behaviour was apparent not only among the officers of the Revolutionary army, but it also made unexpectedly rapid progress among the entire élite. In Salta, as B. Frías records, the most elegant ladies went so far as to 'seize each other by the hair in the public street', and one of them, the fanatically patriotic Doña Manuela Arias, had another lady flogged, by a manservant and in the street, 'for being a Goth [that is, a Royalist]'. On this occasion it was Manuel Dorrego who, on hearing the cries of the victim, 'rushed out into the street, drew his sword and covered it with honour by drubbing the rump of that manservant, in defence of that Royalist lady who was the victim of that public outrage'.[7] Frías did not, of course, approve of the brutal conduct of Doña Manuela, but it is characteristic of that writer, usually so reticent about revealing the political failings of the Salta élite, that he should have given the name of the over-fervent patriotic lady, and omitted to mention that of the victim of her fervour. As late as the beginning of the twentieth century the misconduct of the former appeared less serious than the political heterodoxy of the latter.

This deterioration of peaceable social intercourse among the élite was not confined to the strictly political sphere, where the over-excitement produced by the prevailing tensions makes it more easily understandable. Even though it was political conflict which resulted in daggers being drawn in disputes between friars, it was 'disagreements arising out of their respective employments' that led to the murder of a Bethlehemite friar, a male nurse in the mental hospital, by Fray Mariano de Belén, another nurse, who then managed to escape.[8] And the growth of violence was not the only consequence of this deterioration. One does not, of course, have to accept literally the excessively sombre picture presented by General Iriarte of the habits of the social, political and military élite of the Revolutionary nation. He records that drunkenness was almost an occupational vice among the Army officers, while rapacity had led certain distinguished gentlemen of Buenos Aires to organise a gambling-den where people played with dice loaded by the organisers themselves, and the same rapacity led generals and colonels to take part in the looting which followed every advance in the war against the Brazilians with as much enthusiasm as those sinister women who joined the Army as camp-followers.[9] This process led not only to the abandonment of all moral scruples, but also, as can be seen from the examples mentioned above, of that preoccupation with decorum which one might expect from an élite which regarded that virtue as the justification for its superiority. Some of these characteristics are, however, confirmed by less prejudiced observers, and one might add yet more testimonies to demonstrate the increasing crudity of collective life after 1810. Here again, however, the pre-Revolutionary situation had characteristics which foreshadowed a style of social life in which it would be a mistake to discern only factious tendencies: a corps of officials who were often mediocre, and frequently felt themselves to be exiled in the not very agreeable River Plate region, and a local élite which established with these officials complex relationships based on interest, which often produced conflicts and rivalries that were not always tacit – these two sectors were to be the protagonists, all too frequently, of incidents in which the element of violence was often less marked than in the atmosphere which had prevailed in 1810, but in which effrontery and gross rudeness were remarkable features. In the civil and ecclesiastical *Cabildos* verbal disputes, carried on in coarse language which at times is merely suggested to the reader by excessively concise minutes, but at other times is reproduced faithfully, were by no means rare; amid the modest splendours of the ceremonies, disputes arising from precedence between Governors and Bishops were on some occasions carried on in the same style.

Would it be true, then, to say that the political and cultural superiority of this élite formed in Colonial times and exercising a directing role in Revolutionary politics from 1810 onwards was nothing but a fantasy derived from its resentment at the challenge of excessively rustic rivals? Before embarking on the discussion of this complex problem, it would be advisable to establish the limitations within which the supposed superiority of the veterans of Revolutionary politics (and of the sectors that emerged from them) really made sense: the notion that there existed a body of political and administrative skills which few in the River Plate region possessed, and that it was necessary to have recourse to those few when the exercise of such skills was needed, are notions accepted more unreservedly by those who acquired power after 1820 than by those who, a century and a half later, have taken it upon themselves to defend that élite zealously against a tradition of historiography which has represented them as the champions of a dangerous political barbarity. Without it being necessary to give this process an apocalyptic interpretation, seeing it as a manifestation of the eternally recurrent struggle between civilisation and barbarism, one must still recognise that a new duality had appeared in the provinces of the River Plate region: those who held power and those who administered it were now no longer always the same people.

THE HOLDERS AND THE ADMINISTRATORS OF POWER

Even within that more limited scope, this duality was not equally pronounced in all the regions of Argentina, nor did it have the same character in all of them. In Buenos Aires it was the heir to another duality, inaugurated with the Revolution itself, between the men who had thrown themselves into the 'career of the Revolution' and that Creole urban élite to which they belonged, but which declined to follow them along that road, not because it doubted its own ability, but because it was intimidated by the problematical aspects of the Revolutionary venture. The emergence of the rural areas after 1820 substantially signified a new power-base for that same élite, which supported from outside and not without occasional misgivings the political experiment initiated in 1821.

However, even in Buenos Aires the contempt felt by those who considered themselves to be solidly rooted in the economy and society of the province for those who had made Revolutionary politics a profession failed to conceal a certain ambiguity. Emerging from the sector of that élite which had become rural in order to take advantage of the new economic circumstances, and also endowed with political talents which undoubtedly outshone those of any man in Buenos Aires of his generation, Juan Manuel de Rosas was to wait almost ten years, after his decisive intervention in 1820, before participating directly and openly in politics, and a further decade before he discovered that he could manage them by himself. There is no doubt that his hesitation before embarking on a public career was influenced by considerations such as those pointed out to him by his cousins, the Anchorenas, who warned him against the risks involved in an activity more suitable for those who had little to lose. However, he was also influenced by his respect for that specifically political form of wisdom which in the beginning of his public career he thought was reserved for those who had made politics their professional activity. Although the persona which Rosas constantly displayed, that of a rather obtuse rustic who understood little and appreciated less of the refinements of an essentially urban political art, eventually became to a great extent a mannerism, at least in the early stages of his public life it seems to have corresponded fairly closely to the image he had of himself.

Nevertheless, in Buenos Aires that duality manifested itself in a comparatively attenuated form. The distance between the political élite and the partially ruralised socio-economic élite was less pronounced than elsewhere, and although some pessimistic observers deplored the low calibre of many members of the politically ruling group, that calibre was at least higher than in the other provinces. In the latter, on the other hand, the relationship between the holders and the administrators of power was from the outset more problematical. That relationship, full of ambiguities, was one of the causes of the fragility of the political order which emerged from the collapses of 1820.

Who were the administrators of power? It is possible to distinguish among them two types. On the one hand there were the pure professionals, who had embarked on a strictly personal adventure, often far from their place of origin and without social supports of their own in the context in which they were acting. Their careers, which continued in their own way those which had been typical of the career of the Revolution, often surpassed the boundaries of a single province. And on the other hand there were, in each of the provinces, whole groups of people who, whatever justification they might give for their political ambitions, owed their place in public life above all to a certain technical competence in the performance of administrative tasks, based not so much on any systematic training as on long experience. Their place was secondary, and gave them – after the changes of 1820 – only a limited influence. Inherited pride and the memory of a recent past in which their situation had been more favourable resulted in this group of essential collaborators with the political power which the crisis of 1820 had reshaped on new bases being at the same time a group of potential malcontents, who, although they did not have sufficient strength to provoke a crisis, certainly had enough to aggravate and amplify those that arose from other sectors.

It is, therefore, understandable that preference should have been shown for collaborators who were isolated and not properly integrated into local society. Their assistance was both less demanding and less dangerous. Also understandable is the universal unpopularity which they suffered in the province where they worked, an unpopularity which had also surrounded those who from 1810 onwards had anticipated this new human type, the 'secretaries' who accompanied the military leaders or secessionist *caudillos*. In so far as those professional officers and chieftains were supposed to suffer from a complete political innocence – which, somewhat contradictorily, was considered among the first group to be a legitimate excuse for their mistakes, and in the case of the second group an aggravating circumstance – their secretaries and advisors were held responsible for their mistakes, which in the case of the secessionists were classed as crimes. Thus the ex-friar Monterroso was, according to his enemies in Buenos Aires, the inspiration behind the most sinister projects of Artigas, and of those of Ramírez (taken prisoner by the latter in the fight against Artigas, he soon found out how to make himself indispensable to his captor). In the same way the Peruvian half-caste Mejía, secretary to the Indian chieftain from Misiones, Andrés Artigas, was held responsible for the harshness with which that 'good-hearted man' treated the proud citizens of Corrientes, when he was occupying the city.[10]

After 1820 the growing political instability launched on similar careers some people who found it difficult to continue to exercise influence in their place of origin. Perhaps the most illustrious among the leaders who had become aware of the changed circumstances was General Alvear, who tried to re-enter Buenos Aires politics as a follower of the leaders from the Littoral. Others with more modest ambitions found it easier to forget that they had once been influential in their place of origin, and tried to subsist in other places by the exercise of a political and administrative skill which had become their principal capital. Thus Domingo Cullen, a native of the Canaries and a merchant in Montevideo, who was a member of the mission sent by the Cabildo of that city to seek assistance against the Portuguese occupying forces, was never to return from that mission (which was anyway unsuccessful), which had made him suspect to the new Brazilian authorities. He stayed on in Santa Fe, in association with the Governor, Estanislao López, into whose family he married and whom he served as minister for fifteen years. Similarly, Domingo de Oro, compromised in his native San Juan by the defeat of the movement against freedom of worship introduced by the Governor, Del Carril, in which he had taken part, became a highly skilled agent in the Littoral provinces of Governor Dorrego of Buenos Aires. Even twenty years later Adeodato de Gondra, who had fallen out of favour in his native province of Santiago del Estero with Governor Ibarra, whom he had served as minister for a long time, became a minister of the Governor of Tucumán, Celedonio Gutiérrez. There was also the case of Doctor Santiago Derqui, who until 1841 was one of the most active figures in the tortuous politics of Córdoba, and who found a new lease of life in Corrientes, where he had gone with General Paz. There he married and settled down, and became a valued counsellor to the successively dominant political factions. One could give many more examples of this sort of occurrence, and in addition to these definitive or at least very prolonged changes of residence there were even more frequent short-lived ones. Returning from a mission to the North Colonel Manuel Dorrego, a native of Buenos Aires, stayed at the house of the Governor of Santiago del Estero, with whom he apparently got on very well, and as a result, Dorrego represented Santiago at the national constituent congress which met in Buenos Aires. At the same congress the deputy for La Rioja was the Uruguayan officer Ventura Vázquez, who owed his appointment to his association with the strong man of the province, the military commander Juan Facundo Quiroga, who had been his partner in business enterprises. However, his association with Quiroga did not prevent him also serving the latter's new enemies, who had created in Buenos Aires a new central government. As its agent, Vázquez went off to Chile to purchase arms, and died in a shipwreck on the voyage. The choice of Vázquez was no doubt due to the notorious shortage of educated people that afflicted La Rioja. That of Dorrego was influenced by Ibarra's dissatisfaction over the conduct of the deputies whom he had previously sent to Buenos Aires – those members of the small educated class of Santiago, once they arrived at the congress

Conclusion: the legacy of the Revolution and the war

displayed very little of that docility which had characterised them in their native province.

By using Dorrego, Ibarra was able to dispense with the collaboration of those assistants who had suddenly become unreliable. Deprived as they were of any independent base of political power, these men could not fail to be indignant at the unexpected appearance of an external factor which robbed them of that monopoly of political and administrative wisdom which had made them the indispensable collaborators of the victors of 1820. This, without a doubt, was the principal cause of the unpopularity of such outside collaborators, who had often occupied in their places of origin positions similar to those held by those who could not forgive them for acquiring excessive influence in their places of refuge.

However, this picture of the relationship between the holders of power and those who helped to administer it runs the risk of over-emphasising both the tensions between one group and the other and also the internal cohesion of each group. The image of the administrators as identified with a lofty ideal of government, in the service of which they acquired unity and the same time confronted the rustic holders of power, although it can be explained in the political climate of Argentina in the second half of the nineteenth century, when there were specific benefits for those who identified with that ideal, is, at the very least, a deliberate simplification of the facts. The relationship between the surviving urban political élites and the holders of power was marked by a collaboration no doubt enforced by the circumstances and liable to break down when these became less difficult, but nevertheless more long-lasting than the open conflicts between one sector and the other.

It was not, however, only the weakness of the political élites shaken by the collapse of 1820 which impelled them towards an unenthusiastic collaboration. The distance between those élites and the new holders of power was less than some excessively simplified interpretations suppose. To give an extreme example: in Salta Juan Ignacio de Gorriti, a canon of the Cathedral, the son of a wealthy family, deputy to Juntas and Congresses in Buenos Aires in 1811 and again in 1824, possessing a doctorate from the University of Córdoba, Governor of Salta in 1829, appears to be almost the perfect ideal of a member of the urban élite, formed by the Colonial years and liberated from its Spanish rivals by the Revolution. His brother José Ignacio de Gorriti, an officer in the Revolutionary armies, a deputy to the Constituent Congress in 1816, Governor of Salta on two occasions in the following decade, with a doctorate from the University of Chuquisaca, but also a follower of Güemes, from whom he only dissociated himself when the latter's career was nearing its end, was a less accurate reflection of the same type. As for the third brother, Francisco de Gorriti, who had not been anywhere near a university, and spent his time on the frontier managing both the rural properties and the plebeian clientèle of his powerful family, he more closely resembled the new type of leader who came to the fore after 1820. Such differences did not prevent the solidarity existing between the three brothers in the hazardous politics of Salta, and were, in any case, less important than might be deduced from the above deliberately schematic description. The tough and violent polemical style of Canon Gorriti and the mania for litigation of his brother, the general, were perhaps both manifestations of deep-seated tendencies which in the rustic brother, Francisco, were less surprising.

The above is, no doubt, an extreme example, but the situation which it reveals with particular clarity was by no means exceptional. The change in the political equilibrium produced not so much by the Revolution as by the war was, as has already been observed, internal rather than external to the ruling group. Its internal ties were not dissolved as a result of a previously secondary sector acquiring hegemony. It is worth examining from this point of view the processes in Córdoba, Santiago del Estero and Mendoza, despite the differences between them. Bustos, the Aldao brothers and Ibarra were all of sufficiently high social origin for their rise to supreme power to take place without causing scandal. Their political success no doubt intensified rivalries and created new sources of resentment, but it did not separate them irremediably from an élite to which they had previously belonged.

It is true that in consolidating new power-bases they opened the way for successors less fully integrated into the provincial élite. Especially after 1835, when Juan Manuel de Rosas was trying to rebuild on tougher and more solid foundations the hegemony of Buenos Aires, his ascendancy over the Interior was to favour the rise of figures who, even in the new political hierarchy born of the dual process of militarisation and ruralisation, occupied a secondary place. Examples of this were Manuel López in Córdoba, Nazario Benavides in San Juan, and Celedonio Gutiérrez in Tucumán. All three had won slow promotion in the provincial militias and seemed condemned to mediocre careers until the influence of the Governor of Buenos Aires enabled them to rise to a more exalted position. By that time, however, a long history of defeats of their attempts to return to power had demonstrated more clearly to the learned assistants of the new power the limits to their ambitions established by the circumstances. For this reason, the temptation to oppose the new governing figures now emerging, except when there was a crisis of external origin, was no greater than when those figures were their peers.

There was another reason why that 'learned' sector only intermittently confronted the new wielders of power. In the places where it was most numerous and could rely on additional sources of economic power, in commerce or on the land, it was also too frequently divided by internal rivalries. This was the case in Córdoba, where Bustos utilised those rivalries with consummate skill in order to consolidate his own power, and

Conclusion: the legacy of the Revolution and the war

the same thing happened in Mendoza and Salta. An over-sharp differentiation between the holders and the administrators of political power, therefore, errs in ignoring the more complex interplay of intermittent affinities and rivalries. Each sector represented, not so much a group welded together by the solidarity of its members, as a type of political leadership to which – as usually happens – the real figures corresponded only approximately. Although a similarity of experience might create within each of those sectors a coincidence of viewpoints which might lead to adherence to a specific political line, in following which they would become consolidated as real political groups, the complementary nature of the functions of the members of both sectors facilitated the establishment of ties of solidarity which united members of both sectors.

The rivalry of the learned sector which the political collapse of 1820 had relegated to an auxiliary function did not, therefore, in itself imply a serious threat to the order which emerged from that collapse. It was only when a crisis which that sector by itself was incapable of provoking caused an upheaval in the prevailing political situation that it dared to return to the fore. There was, however, no shortage of such crises. Rather than the rivalry of its predecessors, whom it had, on the whole, successfully managed to transform into collaborators, the new order had to be on guard against its own weaknesses, which prevented its consolidation.

Those weaknesses are easily understandable: that new order, which had emerged from a progressive delegation of local executive functions, taking place in an intensely militarised context, was a poor substitute for the now defunct central authority under the aegis of which it had made its first advances, because the latter were due, not so much to the strength of the future victors as to the growing insufficiencies of the central authority in the face of tasks which were beyond its capacity. But the new holders of power often did not possess the resources or the ambition needed to replace the vanished central authority in the fulfilment of functions with which the latter was already coping so inadequately. One revealing example was the performance of the new rural or ruralised political leaders as armed custodians of internal order. It was precisely their ability to fulfil that function which was the key to their rise to power in the first decade after the Revolution. They had performed this task within the framework of a state structure which had delegated those tasks because in that way the cost was reduced, in so far as the economic and social position of the holders of local authority allowed them to demand and receive the free assistance of those who anyway formed part of their clientèles. Nevertheless, to the limited degree that financial support was necessary, this had been the responsibility of the central government.

This was the case even in places where the establishment of order benefited chiefly and immediately precisely the people to whom the central government had delegated the task of imposing that order. This occurred in a very characteristic manner in the reorganisation of the system of rural militias in the province of Buenos Aires, where, although the decree of 1819 laid down that this force was to be paid for by the landowners, the State continued to make its contribution by transferring to the new units career officers who were still paid by the Buenos Aires Treasury. An example of this was the Colorados regiment of San Miguel del Monte, that militia unit which had won fame during the struggles of 1820. Its commanding officer was the landowner Juan Manuel de Rosas, but his second-in-command was José Ambrosio Carranza, from Córdoba, who had been a career officer continuously since 1795, first in the Royal and then in the Revolutionary army. And, as it has already been observed, the military reform of 1821 provided that the State was to be responsible for paying the entire officer corps of these militias. This did not mean that the rural leaders whose power had been demonstrated in Buenos Aires in October 1820 lost control over those military forces. They had simply managed to transfer the entire financial burden onto the provincial treasury.

In this way, the hope of passing onto the treasury – even the penurious treasuries of the new provinces – the cost of what was really their own political power-base partially explains the tendency to remain on the fringe of the new political structure which characterised many of those who from 1820 onwards had a clearly predominant position in that structure. The penury of the political authority, in contrast to the comparative wealth of several of the new holders of real power, tended to create a bond of financial dependence which complemented the political and military connection. Between the holders of real power and the weak apparatus of state which they propped up there emerged, therefore, a complex relationship, which the former element sometimes represented as the cause of its future and unavoidable ruin, but which were often very far from having such fateful consequences. A destitute treasury could not, in fact, defend itself effectively against the exactions of those who, in addition to offering anticipatory payments which that treasury was in no position to refuse, wielded a political influence which at times amounted to absolute control. Thus Juan Facundo Quiroga, that Commander-in-chief of La Rioja who throughout his public career unceasingly complained of the damage it was doing to his private interests, left at his death a very considerable fortune – certainly greater than that which he had inherited from his father. However, his decision to consider as merely temporary the sacrifices imposed on his private purse, and his tenacity in securing reimbursement, were by no means exceptional attitudes. Even in the more prosperous centre of Buenos Aires, they were characteristic of more than one incident in the relationship between Juan Manuel de Rosas and a state organisation destined to fall subsequently under his complete control.

A typical incident occurred in 1820–21, when Rosas agreed to deliver to Santa Fe 25,000 head of cattle, which would make it possible for the victorious but ruined province to reconstruct its economy and would consolidate its reconciliation with Buenos Aires. This tribute – as was clear to everybody from the outset – was eventually to be paid for by the provincial treasury. What Rosas did was to accelerate the rounding-up of cattle and supplement with his own cattle or those acquired privately what he could obtain from other landowners. The rounding-up – of which Rosas himself took charge – could only be done with State support, and Rosas did not hesitate to use the pressure from normal local authorities against, for example, the proprietors of certain lands in the North of the Province who showed reluctance to deliver the cattle owed by way of tithes.[11] In this manner, by fulfilling a commitment which 'has no public, positive character', Rosas acquired in zones outside his direct influence a power which did not derive only from his wealth and the considerable size of the clientèle which maintained its loyalty to him in the South-West of the Province. The State, which was too weak to fulfil the commitment directly, put its limited strength at the disposal of the man who replaced it in that task. Moreover, the extreme penury of the Treasury did not necessarily signify a very prolonged wait for reimbursement for Rosas, who untiringly complained of his sacrifices. In March 1821 he was granted the freehold of the old *estancia* of the King, an estate of six square leagues in the district of Magdalena.[12] This was the beginning of the compensation for the disbursements made by Rosas in the service of the province, among which the future Restorer had not forgotten to make provision for the profits he had lost by devoting less time to his private business. This process was to be repeated in 1833: the expedition into the Indian territory – which promised undeniable advantages for the Province, and equally undeniable political advantages for Rosas – had to be paid for by a destitute government, subject to overwhelming political pressure.[13]

It does not appear that the most useful lesson to be learned from all this was that of political morality so avidly seized upon by the enemies of Rosas. Although the complaints regarding the ruin of his patrimony, with which the Restorer was not sparing, did not have much basis in fact, nevertheless one cannot see why this man who at first conceived of himself as a businessman and who only later and gradually allowed himself to be absorbed by political activity should sacrifice to it a patrimony which it had cost him some effort to accumulate. It is, perhaps, more interesting to observe how even in Buenos Aires the delegation of public functions to private individuals led to a new blurring of the boundaries between the two spheres, a process which benefited the latter element. Rosas appropriated a part of the patrimony of the State and used the coercive power of the latter to fulfil a task which no doubt was destined to benefit the province, but which he had undertaken on his own account.

However, in so far as this solution sacrificed the vigour of the State's organisation to that of its demanding external supporters, and in so far as it concentrated more effective power in their hands, the lax institutional organisation which emerged after 1820 was an even more inadequate medium than a purely formal examination of that organisation might lead one to suppose for ensuring that minimum of cohesion which the provinces of the River Plate region required; for ensuring, in short, reasonably stable internal peace and the continuity of the economic links between the various provinces. Indeed, the downfall of the political apparatus erected during the decade of the Revolution affected not only the central authority. Even some of the provincial ones, from the outset, inherited much of the weakness of the authority which they replaced. Within that loose institutional framework, order depended on the unstable equilibrium between the forces at the disposal of those holders of real power, whose zone of direct influence never in any case extended beyond the boundaries of a province, and sometimes did not even cover that province entirely. The instability which was the price of that redistribution of political power alarmed even its beneficiaries. The search for elements of cohesion to replace those which had disappeared with the collapse of the central authority went on untiringly, although for the moment unsuccessfully.

THE SEARCH FOR A NEW COHESION

There was, of course, no lack of factors which might make for cohesion: inherited from the Colonial past, they survived the tempest of revolution more successfully than the apparatus of state which they were now trying partly to replace. At the lowest level, family solidarity appears to have been – to an even greater extent than in Colonial times – the basis of alliances and rivalries interwoven with the day to day course of political events in several provinces. From Salta to Mendoza, observers recording adherences to the Revolutionary or the Royalist cause do not name individuals, but entire families, which sided *en bloc* with one cause or the other.[14] And a century and a half after the Revolution, historians still apply the same criterion.[15]

Of course, the validity of this criterion is attenuated by the fact that not infrequently families were politically divided. More important, however, than examining the exceptions to a pattern of family solidarity which was still dominant is the search for the origins and the limitations of that solidarity.

It appears to have had a dual origin. In the first place, that solidarity was consolidated by the existence of a patrimony of land, wealth and influence which could only be preserved as long as the family retained its coherence. In this case the family was merely the centre of a much larger grouping, which included collateral relatives and a rustic and urban clientèle whose links with that centre might have an extremely varied legal basis. In Salta, Catamarca, La Rioja and Northern Córdoba there were examples of families which enjoyed an unchallenged domination over an entire zone, in which they held appointments in the militia and municipal posts in the police and the lower judicial hierarchy. However, these large family groups were not by any means stable. They were insufficiently institutionalised (the privilege of *Mayorazgo* – inheritance by the eldest son – which would have ensured the undivided continuity of the patrimony of a family, was not common in the River Plate region), and the number of men which they incorporated appears to have been a function of the economic and political power at their disposal. The case of collateral relations is revealing. In thinly populated districts, where the small class of *gente decente* proudly refused to intermarry with families of baser lineage, there were few members of that class who could not claim relationship with more than one of the really powerful families. Their inclusion in the clientèle of one of them was the often provisional result of the patronage which that family was able to dispense. The degree to which family solidarity survived the lack of such continuity of the central patrimony can be measured with some accuracy in the example, already examined in this work, of the Funes family. There is no doubt as to the solidity of the family ties, and yet that undiminished solidarity within the nucleus of the family – which manifested itself in new ways in times of poverty – served above all to attenuate the consequences of their financial and political penury. It was not sufficient to make the Funes family the core of a larger clientèle, capable of making its influence felt in Revolutionary Córdoba.

However, some of the consequences of that solidarity which survived the disappearance of the family fortune were of considerable political importance. In addition to their much-diminished wealth, what the Funes brothers shared was, in fact, their political influence. For example, that which the Dean possessed in Buenos Aires was to help his nephew to recover outstanding debts in Lima, while the influence acquired by Ambrosio thanks to his private business deals in Mendoza helped to ensure the collection of the Dean's tithes. Such aspects of family solidarity were by no means innovations introduced by the Revolution. That internal solidarity could be the means which each family possessed for defending its place in that constellation of powerful families which constituted the prevailing political order in several parts of the River Plate region, but this defence was only on exceptional occasions made necessary by the occurrence of violent conflicts between family units, unregulated by any superior authority. More often it served to strengthen each family against the rivalry of other families, in a complex process in which the administrative authority reserved for itself the rôle of arbiter. In the fulfilment of that rôle, however, it took care not to ignore the equilibrium of forces between the rivals. The fact that the officials of the Crown, in their dealings with the most influential of those subject to their jurisdiction, envisaged them as being grouped in families, a practice which, as has been observed, the Revolution preserved, merely had the effect of consolidating the internal solidarity of those families, and encouraging the solidarity, not only of those whose patrimony and prestige placed them in the first rank, but also of those which were less powerful but just as anxious to gain the attention of those officials. Even before 1810, therefore, family solidarity existed even where there was a lack of that wealth and abundance of followers which defined and guaranteed the domination of some families over whole districts. It was the existence of this further encouragement to the consolidation of the family as a unit which extended the phenomenon to places where the absence of a system of land-ownership dominated by large properties – or where this system was recently established and still not consolidated – made unthinkable the occurrence of situations such as were found in Salta, La Rioja and some parts of Catamarca and Córdoba. However, by making the family into an organisation orientated towards winning the favour of the authorities, it lent it an element of the instability which characterised the behaviour of those authorities, even in Colonial times, when the replacement of an official could have, in this respect, consequences comparable to the most sensational changes of direction in Revolutionary politics.

With regard to the degree to which the Revolution affected the vigour of the family as an institution, it has already been observed that it accorded to the influence of families a more explicit recognition than the Royal administration had done. The need to find more active support within the country itself in fact impelled it to come to an understanding with a force which it would have been imprudent to ignore. At the same time the Revolution was accused of breaking family ties, and of setting people against each other within those formerly harmonious units. Intergenerational conflicts and conflicts between different branches of the same family were indeed frequent. Moreover, by respecting the patrimony of each family and at the same time depriving disaffected individuals of their share in it, the Revolutionary authorities gave fresh encouragement to those conflicts, in which it acted as a blatantly partial arbiter. Thus, one consequence of the repression of Álzaga's mutiny in 1812 was the transfer of the family fortune of the executed conspirator to his Patriot heirs, and there were similar occurrences elsewhere. In Salta, if one is to believe the impassioned accusations of Tomás de Archondo, it was a denunciation made by his own sons which had impelled Belgrano to deprive him of the possession of his fortune, the administration of which was entrusted to those same sons as a reward for their Revolutionary zeal.[16] Arbitration of this nature did not always involve a transfer of the patrimony. In the case of the Allende family of Córdoba, the Revolutionary Government, by shooting the colonel who was the recognised head of the family and giving his nephew the same rank, was merely giving the family a new head. Thus it was the internal equilibrium of each family which was affected by the new political authority in a more direct and brutal manner than it ever had been by the *ancien régime*, which, however, did also influence that equilibrium. One has only to remember, for example, the large number of civil servants of Spanish origin who married into the founding families of Salta and became their heads. One might expect this growing intrusion to have led to a decline in the power of the most prominent families, but this was not the case. The new régime needed them too much to exercise too zealous and systematic a supervision over them. The progressive delegation of its functions to local authorities which owed their power, whatever its formal origin, to their local strength in the districts under their administration, very soon counteracted the very limited progress of the Revolutionary power, and obliged it to re-adopt the more traditional rôle of arbiter in inter-family rivalries, a field in which its freedom of manoeuvre was even more limited than that of the officials of the Crown.

In this way, the dissolution of the central authority in 1820 restored a large measure of power to the great families which had managed to survive the storm of Revolution and save their patrimony of lands and clients accumulated in Colonial times. The Revolutionary experience had, however, left its mark on them. The delegation of functions itself had caused the rise of more powerful local leaders, and those figures now stood out as individuals within those family units to a greater extent than in Colonial times. True, Juan Facundo Quiroga received as an informal family heritage the appointments which gave him police and minor judicial powers, and the new circumstances had broadened the scope of those appointments and endowed their incumbents with powers which were also new and which were capable of transforming an office held on behalf of a collectively influential family into a position of intensely personalised leadership. Precisely because of this transformation, however, the sphere of influence of that leadership did not coincide with the zone in which the leader's family had enjoyed a direct ascendancy. Juan Facundo Quiroga did, indeed, owe his first chance of embarking on a public career to his position as the son of José Prudencio Quiroga, who was a powerful land-owner in the Plains area of La Rioja and at the same time a militia officer, but that initial advantage was not by itself responsible for his rise to military domination over the whole of the Interior. This extreme example shows with particular clarity the consequences of the appearance of an open political struggle in the local context, which gave a new dimension to the rivalry between family groups. From now on the patrimony and the power of a family were the capital which its leader was continually risking in that struggle. Fluctuations of fortune became, therefore, more intense and more rapid than in the past. Instead of the patrimony and other elements which had determined the continuity of a lineage, it was now the political personality of its head which occupied the foreground.

This process was to take place with even greater intensity in families which, though not possessing any considerable patrimony, had continuously utilised their solidarity to achieve administrative advantages and promotions in the civil service. Even in Colonial times they had suffered from greater instability, and had been subject to a more marked dependence on the ability of the head of the family group. In such cases, the family connection was the basis of a kind of political clientèle centered on the head. Such a clientèle was often constituted as such thanks to his successes in public life, and such successes provided the basis of the solidarity of the family group, formed to defend and take collective advantage of the political capital created by the personal talents of that individual. This happened in Santa Fe with the family of Estanislao López, and in Santiago del Estero with that of Ibarra. In the first case the family group identified with the leader of the province was completely new, because López had been born out of wedlock, and in the second case more than one distinguished family in the provincial capital accepted the leadership of a man who at first had been a comparatively obscure collateral relative. This did not mean that the network of the great families had ceased to count for anything. There were districts where development had been more gradual and political life still revolved around their conflicts and alliances. Even in the areas most thoroughly transformed by the Revolution and its consequences, this desperately complex interplay of forces was one of the basic ingredients of any political grouping.

In short, despite the decline of the authorities with wider spheres of influence, the power of the 'first families' in each district still varied greatly in extent. Only in regions where the rural sector was completely predominant, or where the rural and urban élites were completely fused, with extensive properties which had been consolidated for a long time and had also been relatively unaffected by the Revolutionary crisis, could that power continue to be a determining factor, but there were not, of course, many districts where all these conditions prevailed. The lack of any significant increase in the power possessed by the great families as such accentuated the instability of the political solutions which emerged, but it by no means prejudiced the prospects of a harmonious relationship between political solutions which emerged simultaneously in different provinces or in different districts in each province. The family could, in fact, ensure a very tight cohesion among its members, but that cohesion was above all necessary in order to ensure success in conflicts with rival families. Although, in the provinces of Argentina, there were not many of the bloody feuds such as took place in Brazil or Mexico, in Argentina, too, families were essentially war-machines. Of course, struggles for regional influence or administrative favour did not exclude the possibility of alliances, but these did have an element of antagonism, in that they were contracted in order to join forces against excessively powerful adversaries. It can readily be observed that the great families, with their alliances and feuds, could not serve as the basis for firmly-established political groupings capable of ensuring regional or national order. The partial and relative decline of the power of those families, and the rise of regional leaders who, although they were supported by groups of families and did not fail to favour their interests, became something more than the representatives of such groups, did not hamper the possibility of establishing some measure of cohesion between the different regional powers.

This was, however, basically a negative advantage, and there remained the problem of how to establish such cohesion effectively. It was, moreover, aggravated by the reluctance of the holders of real power to identify themselves with that minimal institutional apparatus which survived the collapse of 1820, and by their desire to control it from outside, which was a continuation in a different context of the attitude of the locally entrenched forces towards the Royal administration. This reluctance to assume the direct management of the government not only resulted – as has already been observed – in the further weakening of the institutional apparatus in more than one province. Another result was that, in the search for a new political cohesion capable of overriding the boundaries between one province and another, that apparatus was an inadequate instrument. In addition to inter-provincial pacts, recorded in ceremonious documents, what was needed was an understanding between the holders of real power in order to lend those texts some substance. However, those holders of power had in fact emerged from the affirmation of the local bases of that power. Firmly entrenched in those bases, they did not always find it easy to make their own influence coalesce with that of those who had emerged outside its sphere.

In fact, a network of personal relations between the politically influential figures was beginning to be constructed across that immense country. In examining the methods and the bases of this process, one must bear in mind the fact that the new leaders had often had a long career of activity within the framework of the Revolutionary state, and thereafter preserved connections which surpassed the boundaries of their home districts, and also that, even more frequently, they had economic interests which ensured the continuity of contacts outside their territories of operation. What the new leaders were patiently trying to erect, therefore, on the basis of that tenuous yet complex network of continually changing personal relationships, was a system of mutual understandings between locally influential figures which would at least partially fill the void left by the ruin of the national state and its replacement by provincial states of only limited political vitality.

This new style of intercourse prevailed throughout the country. Even in Buenos Aires the episode described above, the delivery of cattle to Santa Fe – a simultaneously public and private undertaking – gained for Rosas the extremely useful friendship of Estanislao López. Between 1824 and 1827 Pedro Trápani became the centre of a network of contacts between the two banks of the River Plate which utilised for political purposes the connections established by him in his capacity as a warehouse-owner, cattle-dealer and partner of British merchants. From the Paraná to the Bolivian frontier the list of political associates of the Governor of Santa Fe included many of the names of those who were engaged in trade on that route. It has already been observed how, between Mendoza and Córdoba, Ambrosio Funes and José Albino Gutiérrez had established connections which were essentially based on private interest, but in which the public positions held by both men were still significant. In addition to such coincidences of private interests, connections established in the course of the 'career of the Revolution' were utilised by, for example, Felipe Ibarra in Santiago del Estero and José María Paz in Córdoba, this connection being based on a friendship formed first in the Seminary of Loreto, in Córdoba, and then in the Army of the North. The complexity which such connections could attain was demonstrated by the rise of Juan Facundo Quiroga to a position of national dimensions. Throughout the process, he never held any political appointment, although he did hold several military ones. A study of his Archive shows how his circle of relationships became wider, and how these relationships, though still based on ties of friendship or – even more frequently – private and commercial interests, acquired a growing political dimension. The earliest of those relationships had been formed in his early youth, when he travelled with the herds of cattle and droves of mules which his father was delivering to places outside his province. In the course of such journeys he got to know, for example, influential figures in San Luis, and he kept up his contacts with them, later utilising them for political ends. The entry of such relationships into the public sphere and their transformation into political alliances did not, however, destroy their original character. It is revealing to notice the flood of correspondence on political matters between Quiroga and José Albino Gutiérrez, in Mendoza, being momentarily interrupted by a letter in which Gutiérrez informed Quiroga that he was sending to San Juan – which Quiroga had just captured – ninety head of cattle, 'so that you or your agents can sell them in that place'.[17] A similar intermingling of public and private, political and commercial matters is found in the relationship between Quiroga and his correspondents in Buenos Aires. Ventura Vázquez, the native of Montevideo who owed to the influence of Quiroga over the Government of La Rioja his post as deputy for that Province at the General Constituent Congress of 1824, was the intermediary not only between Quiroga and the National Government which was enjoying a brief resurgence in Buenos Aires (from which he promised to obtain for Quiroga a commission as a general in the National Army), but he also acted as intermediary with the Buenos Aires merchants with whom Quiroga was forming a connection, based on mutual interests, which became increasingly close. The most important of these merchants, Braulio Costa, employed Vázquez as an intermediary to submit to Quiroga his proposals for mining operations in La Rioja.

Conclusion: the legacy of the Revolution and the war

The complex character of the relationships formed by Quiroga during that stage of his career was also evident when he was dealing with the Governor of La Rioja. In this case, too, the person concerned, who owed his appointment exclusively to the influence of Quiroga, was more interested in his private activities than in the apparently light administrative duties which his post involved, and in the course of which he had granted the privilege of coining money to a firm which his family controlled. Swept off his feet by one of those short-lived and frantic waves of entrepreneurial enthusiasm which the hope (soon dispelled) of finding a new way to prosperity occasionally awakened in the somnolent economic climate of the Interior, the Governor, Baltasar Agüero, did not disdain to take part personally in the work of minting, to the permanent detriment of his health as a result of lead poisoning. At the time, apparently, not many people in La Rioja shared the Governor's high hopes. He then sought support for his business enterprises among those who – as everybody knew – had more influence in La Rioja than he had himself. The shareholders of the mint – Agüero wrote to Quiroga[18] – had authorised all the military commanders to purchase a share each. Although Quiroga did not want to do this, his friend the Governor urged him to pretend to do it, paying the necessary one thousand pesos, on which the Governor himself would pay interest at one peso per day. It was necessary for the name of Quiroga to be associated with the business 'in order to make the mint more respectable'.

In this way the political relationship between Agüero and Quiroga was accompanied by an economic relationship, and became one of the manifold connections between the overlord of the Plains region and the immense world surrounding it. Its support from a political and institutional system in which both Agüero and Quiroga had formally defined rôles did not make that relationship more important than those connections established as a result of a chance journey or a more prolonged commercial relationship. Thus, as soon as his new friends in Buenos Aires convinced Quiroga of the advantages of a large-scale mint, the fate of Agüero was sealed, and the Governor not only surrendered control of the minting business to the financiers of Buenos Aires, but also was replaced in his post by a new Governor who had won the confidence of Quiroga. This still did not mean a break with his powerful protector: as treasurer of the province and a member of its minute legislative assembly, his name recurs in Quiroga's correspondence.[19]

Thus the network of individuals and private interests centering on Quiroga grew increasingly wider, and this process – encouraged by his increasing political influence – had immediate political consequences. Many of those who were to follow Quiroga after he had become a national figure were merely transferring to the political sphere a solidarity which had been formed in other and less public spheres. If one wishes to draw a more general conclusion from this example so rich in anecdotal elements, one must emphasise the fact that the dispersal of political power in the River Plate region was not accompanied by economic fragmentation, and the fact that several of the leaders emerging from the crisis of 1820, precisely because they were firmly entrenched in the economy of their own region, possessed economic and personal contacts outside it. This provided for each one of them a network of relationships outside his immediate zone of influence, which could serve as the basis of a system of political alliances. However, the opportunities provided in this way, precisely because they were so wide-ranging, could not serve as a basis for a stable political system. What was still needed was some general principle of organisation to limit those areas of conflict created by that multiplicity of private relationships which all tended to become transformed into political alliances. Such a principle could not be provided by the institutional structure, weak and incoherent enough on paper, and even more so in practice; we have already seen how Quiroga was more decisively influenced by Braulio Costa, a rich merchant of Buenos Aires, than by the legal order in force in La Rioja, as personified by its submissive Governor.

It is not, therefore, surprising that this network made up of coincidences of interests and of private affinities should sometimes have, as a political consequence, the break-down rather than the consolidation of the system of equilibrium between the different regional powers on which an always insecure peace depended. Thus, the hopes awakened by mining operations in La Rioja not only did away with the Governor of that province, it encouraged a *rapprochement* between La Rioja and Córdoba, which possessed considerable financial and human resources, without which the exploitation of the mines would have been much more difficult. However, the alignment of La Rioja with Córdoba marked the end of the solidarity of the Andean provinces – from Mendoza to Catamarca – which since 1821 had determined the equilibrium of the Interior. It would be unjustified to describe this as the only, or even the principal, cause of the civil war which was soon to break out there (among other reasons, because, when war did break out, hardly anybody believed any longer in the prospects of mining in the region), but there is no doubt that, by destroying a system of alliances and rivalries which had guaranteed the peace of the region, it ushered in a period of increasing tensions in which the emergence of fresh conflicts became more probable.

In short, and unsurprisingly, the rich multiplicity of contacts, solidarities and hostilities which was to be found in the economic and social spheres could not, by itself, serve as the basis for a stable political order. This could only be based on specifically political ties of solidarity, within a system able to reduce to the minimum the possibility of conflicts of loyalties. The new incumbents of local power certainly made efforts to create an order of this nature. To this end they affirmed, with varying degrees of success, their own predominance in their zones of influence and sought outside them as solid and widespread a support as possible. An entire political ethic, which posited as the cardinal virtues loyalty to one's pledged word and loyalty to one's leader, was brought into play as the fundamental ideal of that reconstruction of a political system. But, though universally respected, those virtues were not always practised. Nor could they be: as long as that order which it was being attempted to reconstruct had not in fact emerged, the price of survival was constant attention to the factors of an equilibrium in almost constant flux. There had, therefore, to be constant changes in the alliances with external forces which, even though they had appeared as saviours in the past, could become ruinous if too literal a loyalty to one's word resulted in the continuation of such alliances in a changed context. The uncertainties which tormented anyone who was obliged to play this exhausting game unceasingly are admirably reflected, for example, in the correspondence which the Governor of Santiago, Ibarra, carried on with General Paz, from the day that that old schoolfriend and comrade-in-arms took power in Córdoba. Paz was waging a war against Quiroga. Ibarra did not want to be involved in it, but neither did he want Paz, in despair of gaining his adherence, to seek that of Ibarra's enemies in Santiago. In tones of perplexed sincerity, which was largely feigned, he outlined to his friend the alternatives presented by the situation in which he found himself, expressing himself in unexpectedly sentimental terms. How could Paz ever doubt the firm friendship of Ibarra? But at the same time he owed some consideration to Quiroga, who 'during four years of close friendship has not once betrayed my confidence'.[20] Ibarra's problems, of course, were not those of a heart irremediably divided in its affections, but were those of a desperately poor province three of whose four neighbours were more powerful than it. Both the effusive correspondents were well aware of this, and Ibarra did not appear excessively surprised or indignant when his faithful friend Paz supported the rising which obliged him to flee to Santa Fe.

Thus the promises of both private and political friendship were a poor defence for the stability of the connections based on such promises. The use of the language of private affection may invite moral judgements on this ambiguous style of behaviour; its roots were, however, political. The complexity and instability of the equilibrium which emerged from the collapse of 1820 resulted in the attempts to consolidate it on the basis of stable ties between the different regional powers having similarly fragile results, and in it becoming excessively imprudent for any of those regional powers to commit themselves irrevocably in support of these ephemeral groupings.

This situation, however, which made unconditional political loyalty a virtue both highly esteemed and impossible to practise, had further consequences. Since no regional power could rely on the unwavering friendship of any other, it had to undermine the internal cohesion of all of them. From this situation there emerged a corollary which was essential to the craft of politics as it was beginning to be practised in the disunited provinces. Dissidents from neighbouring areas were nearly always deserving of protection, and when those areas were dominated by hostile leaders, then that protection had to develop into active support. Again, the example of Ibarra is relevant: few Governors were as certain as was that of Santiago of his predominance in his own province. Yet he still had reasons for disquiet. Beyond the frontiers of Tucumán, Catamarca and Salta, his enemies were preparing their revenge, meanwhile enjoying the toleration and sometimes the encouragement of governments with which Ibarra, who could not always afford an open rupture, maintained relations marked by the same tone of sentimental perplexity which characterised his correspondence with Paz. It was not necessary for those enemies to have very solid support in Santiago. In Ibarra's view there would always be, for example, men from Tucumán prepared to follow them in any venture. Their purpose was to 'cause extortions...because it appears that the inclination to evil was born with them'.[21] The fear provoked by interprovincial frontiers which could suddenly become permeable to the passage of small bodies of armed men led by dissidents was by no means a fantasy. In 1835 a Governor of Tucumán who had become too powerful in the eyes of his neighbours was to see his province invaded by a force of dissidents organised in Bolivia, which had marched with arms and cattle across the territory of Salta and Catamarca without the Governments of those provinces, which were allies of that of Tucumán, doing anything to stop it. Within each province, as between different provinces, hostility and tension were ineradicable elements in the equilibrium which emerged after 1820. Anyone who wanted to survive in that atmosphere had to be able to utilise those factors to his advantage, but by doing so he was merely accentuating the fragility and instability which obliged him to include such dubious weapons in his political arsenal.

Within that equilibrium, therefore, stability was impossible. This meant that not even those who benefited from the establishment of that system found it satisfactory. But the problem was how to modify it without intensifying the very conflicts whose elimination was being attempted. The most obvious solution, which in theory was universally accepted, was the reconstruction of the institutional framework destroyed in 1820, that is to say, the reconstruction of the central government. That solution, however, would only be possible when the complex equilibrium which it was intended to simplify had already in fact been simplied. Only in a completely transformed context could a new national authority expect to secure effective obedience. Failing such a solution, there remained open the almost desperate one of accepting the fundamental factors of the existing order and trying to maintain a necessarily precarious peace by playing a complicated political game on too many chessboards at the same time. This is what Buenos Aires did, with some success, between 1821 and 1824, but even the economic, financial and political stability of that province was not sufficient to guarantee both a solid hegemony over the rest of the country and a reasonable level of political stability within it. There was a third possible course of action, which emerged slowly from the successive failure of the two previous ones. This was the creation, first in the dominant province and then in the country as a whole, of a truly political solidarity which – without systematically opposing pre-existing ties of solidarity (alliances between families and between inter-regional interests), and even utilising them – nevertheless had sufficient strength to assert its superiority over them and overcome their resistance whenever necessary. This was the solution slowly being prepared by the crises of the 1820s. It matured in the following decade thanks to the tenacity of Juan Manuel de Rosas. From it, in fact, there finally emerged that political order which the Revolution, the war, the breakdown of the economic order of Viceregal times, and the crisis of the pre-Revolutionary élites which resulted from those three processes, had all been preparing. As Sarmiento imperfectly realised, the Argentina of Rosas, its brutal political simplifications reflecting the brutal simplification which independence, war and involvement in the world market had imposed on society in the River Plate region, was the legitimate heir of the Revolution of 1810.

NOTES TO THE TEXT

Chapter 1   The river Plate at the beginning of the nineteenth century
1 General Tomás de Iriarte, *Memorias* (2nd ed., Buenos Aires, 1944), vol. II, p. 70.
2 Salvador de Alberdi to the Consulado de Buenos Aires, 10 September 1805, 'Comercio activo y pasivo de Tucumán', A.G.N., IX, 4-6-4, fos. 69-71.
3 Inventory of the property of Don Nicolás Severo de Isasmendi, 1802, quoted in Atilio Cornejo, *Introducción a la historia de la propiedad inmobiliaria de Salta en la época colonial* (Buenos Aires, 1945), pp. 415 ff.
4 Concolorcovo, *El Lazarillo de ciegos caminantes desde Buenos Aires hasta Lima* (Buenos Aires, 1946), p. 82.
5 Reports to the Consulado of Buenos Aires, by Francisco Manuel Costas, 6 October 1800, A.G.N., IX, 4-6-7, fo. 47; by the same, 5 June 1801, *ibid.* fo. 49; by Pedro de Ugarteche, 30 July 1803, *ibid.* fo. 76. However, the figures quoted, especially the retrospective ones, show significant discrepancies with those given in the registers kept for revenue purposes of commercial transactions in connection with the mule trade. See also Nicolás Sánchez-Albornoz, *La extracción de mulas de Jujuy al Perú. Fuentes, volumen y negociantes* (*Estudios de Historia Social*, vol. I, Buenos Aires, 1965), and 'La saca de mulas de Salta al Perú, 1778-1808', *Anuario del Instituto de Investigaciones Históricas* (Universidad Nacional del Litoral, Rosario), vol. VIII (1965), and in the same vol., pp. 313-24. Graciela Ibarra de Roncoroni, 'Un aspecto del comercio salteño, 1778-1811'.
6 A.G.N., IX, 4-6-7, fos. 86-7.
7 See Enrique Udaondo, *Diccionario biográfico colonial argentino* (Buenos Aires, 1945).
8 Régulo Martínez to President Mitre, Salta, 27 March 1863. in *Archivo del General Mitre*, vol. XII (Buenos Aires, 1911), p. 279. For Salta in the 1850s, see 'Víctor Gálvez' [Vicente G. Quesada], *Memorias de un viejo* (Buenos Aires, 1942), pp. 357 ff.
9 José Álvarez Condarco to the Consulado de Buenos Aires, Tucumán, 9 February 1796, A.G.N., IX, 4-6-6, fos. 6 ff.
10 'Víctor Gálvez', p. 346, n. 8.
11 Iriarte, vol. II, p. 96.
12 A.G.N., IX, 4-6-6, fos, 44 ff.
13 For the imports of Cochabamba shirting material into Tucumán, see the letter of Salvador de Alberdi referred to in Note 2 above. For current prices in Córdoba in 1804, see Bernabé Gregorio de las Heras to the Consulado de Buenos Aires, 27 June 1804, A.G.N., IX, 4-6-6, fo. 128. For current prices in Mendoza in 1809, see A.G.N., IX, 4-6-5, fo. 210. For exports of Tucumán wool to Peru, see Alberdi's letter. It is worth remembering the observation of Hipólito Vieytes: 'even today, if you observe carefully, you will see that our poor people dress with linen from Cochabamba and baize from Cuzco' (*Semanario de Agricultura*, 8 September 1802, reprinted in Hipólito Vieytes, *Antecedentes econónomicos de la Revolución de Mayo*, Buenos Aires, 1956, p. 153).
14 In 1802, according to the statistics published in Ricardo Caillet-Bois, 'Mendoza en los comienzos del siglo XIX', *Boletín del Instituto de Investigaciones Históricas* (Buenos Aires), vol. IX (1928), p. 109.
15 A detailed analysis of the situation in San Juan can be found in the admirable report of José

Notes to the text

Godoy Oro to the Consulado of Buenos Aires in 1806, A.G.N., IX, 4-6-5, fos. 38 ff., published by Germán Tjarks, in *Boletín del Instituto de Historia Argentina y Americana* '*Dr. Emilio Ravignani*' (Buenos Aires), year 2, vol. II, nos. 4-6, pp. 203-37. For the difficulties encountered in deciding the rate of tax due, see the report of Larrechea, from Santa Fe, regarding the authorisation granted to Don Clemente Navarro, a citizen of San Juan, to open a shop to sell the consignment of *aguardiente* he had brought with him, A.G.N., IX, 4-6-4, fo. 104.

16 Reports to the Consulado of Buenos Aires by Juan García de Cossío, 3 November 1797, A.G.N., IX, 4-6-4, fo. 177; Juan José López, 3 June 1803, *ibid*. fo. 211; and Bartolomé Varela y Montoto, 3 August 1804, *ibid*, fo. 220.

17 Enrique Wedovoy, 'Estudio Preliminar', in Manuel José de Lavardén, *Nuevo aspecto del comercio en el Río de la Plata* (Buenos Aires, 1955), pp. 15-20.

18 Quirse Pujato to the Consulado of Buenos Aires, Santa Fe, 12 August 1802, A.G.N., IX, 4-6-4, fo. 128.

19 In 1813, according to the registries of the district of Matanza (contiguous to Buenos Aires), there were 41 owner-farmers and 165 tenants, but one must bear in mind, on the one hand, the close proximity to the capital and, on the other, the fact that the proportion of holders of title to properties is not equivalent to that of the land-surface covered by such properties. The relative abundance of slaves (219 out of 1,691 individuals registered) and of adult males who are not owners of rural properties suggests that some of the latter were absorbing a relatively numerous wage-earning and slave labour-force and were, therefore, more extensive. See the registries dated 24 August 1813, in A.G.N., X, 8-10-4.

20 The dispatch of urban workers to help with the harvest is continually mentioned in the Resolutions of the Cabildo of Buenos Aires. The arrival of workers from the interior provinces, for example, is mentioned in a message from the Viceroy to the Intendant of Salta, guaranteeing that the migrant workers coming from his jurisdictional area – especially from Santiago del Estero – would be exempted from military service, 19 October 1805, A.G.N., IX, 5-7-4.

21 E.g. Félix Weinberg, in his otherwise excellent 'Estudio Preliminar', in Vieytes, p. 23.

22 Hipólito Vieytes, *Semanario de Agricultura*, 8 September 1802, reprinted in Vieytes, p. 396.

23 Diary of Juan Francisco de Aguirre (1781-1798), in *Anales de la Biblioteca Nacional* (Buenos Aires), vol. IV (1905), pp. 171-3.

24 Miguel Lastarria, *Colonias orientales del Río Paraguay o del Plata*, in *Documentos de Historia Argentina* (Buenos Aires, Facultad de Filosofía y Letras, 1914), vol. III, 159-63.

25 Félix de Azara, *Viajes por la América meridional* (Madrid, 1923), vol. II, p. 174.

26 Accusation (among many others) in *Correo de Comercio*, 4 August 1810, reprinted in Manuel Belgrano, *Escritos económicos* (ed. Gregorio Weinberg, Buenos Aires, 1954), p. 180.

27 According to the report of Captain Jorge Pacheco, publ. in Juan José Pivel Devoto, *Raíces coloniales de la revolución oriental de 1811* (2nd ed., Montevideo, 1957), pp. 271 ff.

28 Current accounts of Anchorena, A.G.N., VI, 4-1-1, file 7, fos. 254 ff.

29 Register of the most wealthy citizens of Buenos Aires in 1776, in Archivo de Indias (Seville), V, 125-4-14, publ. by José Torre Revello in *BIIH*, vol. VI (1928), pp. 498-9.

30 Emilio Ravignani, *Asambleas constituyentes argentinas* (Buenos Aires, 1937), vol. II, pp. 906-7 (Session of 13 March 1826).

31 Report to the Consulado of Buenos Aires, 27 July 1801, quoted in Wedovoy, p. 22.

32 Hipólito Vieytes in *Semanario de Agricultura*, ño. 1, 1 September 1802, reprinted in Vieytes, p. 204.

33 Ch. A. Fischer, *Beiträge zur genaueren Kenntnis der Besitzungen in Amerika* (Dresden, 1802), p. 81, quoted in Manfred Kossok, *El virreynato del Río de la Plata. Su estructura económico-social* (Buenos Aires, 1959), p. 73.

34 Salvador de Alberdi, report to the Consulado of Buenos Aires, Tucumán, 10 September 1805, A.G.N., IX, 4-6-4, fos. 69-71.

35 These are the figures given by José Godoy Oro in his 1806 report quoted above, A.G.N., IX, 4-6-5, fos. 38 ff.

Notes to the text

36 See José Luis Moreno, 'La estructura social y demográfica de la ciudad de Buenos Aires en el año 1778', *Anuario del Instituto de Investigaciones Históricas* (Universidad Nacional del Litoral, Rosario), vol. VIII (1965), pp. 151-70.
37 Observations collected in Nicolás Besio Moreno, *Buenos Aires. Puerto del Río de la Plata. Capital de la República Argentina. Estudio crítico de su población* (Buenos Aires, 1939), pp. 283-4.
38 Proceedings of the trial of Don José de Oro, in Museo Mitre, *Papeles de D. José de Oro* (Buenos Aires, 1911), vol. I, pp. 209 ff. The characterisation of Bustos as a noble was made by Régulo Martínez, in R. Martínez to Mitre, Famatina, 30 December 1862, *Archivo Mitre*, vol. XII, p. 262.
39 *Actas Capitulares de Santiago del Estero*, year 1773 (Buenos Aires, 1946), vol. III, pp. 339 ff., concerning the entry of merchants into Indian villages; year 1783 (Buenos Aires, 1946), vol. IV, p. 251, concerning depopulation caused by emigration to lower-lying provinces.
40 The scandal affecting the Capuchins of Buenos Aires is described by Paul Groussac in a note to the Diary of Aguirre, p. 163. The requirement of purity of descent was not abolished in the University of Córdoba until 1855.
41 J. de Hormaechea to the Consulado of Buenos Aires, 4 January 1800, A.G.N., IX, 4-6-7, fos. 36 ff.
42 Salvador de Alberdi to the Consulado of Buenos Aires, 9 May 1803, A.G.N., IX, 4-6-4, fo. 52.
43 Accusation by the merchants of San Juan submitted to the Consulado of Buenos Aires, 9 November 1804, A.G.N., IX, 4-6-5, fo. 25.
44 Mariquita Sánchez, *Recuerdos del Buenos Aires virreynal* (Buenos Aires, 1953), p. 61.
45 Azara, *Viajes*, vol. II, p. 151.
46 Speech of 25 October 1868, in Bartolomé Mitre, *Arengas parlamentarias* (Buenos Aires, 1889), p. 283.
47 Alexander Gillespie, *Gleanings and Remarks: collected during many months of residence at Buenos Ayres, and within the Upper Country...*(Leeds, 1818), pp. 144-7 and 174.
48 Azara, *Viajes*, vol. II, pp. 168-9.
49 A.G.N., IX, 5-7-4.
50 Sánchez, pp. 41-52.
51 Prostitutes in the Franciscan hostel in Santiago del Estero and a mulatto accused of assault in the Mercedarian convent in the same city, protected against the secular authorities, *Actas Capitulares de Santiago del Estero*, vol. III, pp. 342 ff. (30 September 1773).
52 *Cartas pastorales del Ilustrísimo y Reverendísimo Señor D. Fr. Joseph de San Alberto* (Madrid, 1793), p. 3.
53 According to Régulo Martínez the women of the Ángel family were directing operations hostile to the Mitre régime in the valley of Famatina, in La Rioja. See Martínez to Mitre, La Rioja, 14 January 1863, *Archivo Mitre* (Buenos Aires, 1911-14), vol. XII, p. 265.
54 Caillet-Bois, p. 109.
55 Juan Alfonso Carrizo, *Cancionero popular de La Rioja* (Buenos Aires, 1942), vol. I, p. 119.
56 The reference is to those who accompanied and murdered the Portuguese Bartolomé de los Santos. See Larrechea to the Consulado of Buenos Aires, 12 April 1798, A.G.N., IX, 4-6-4, fo. 108.
57 Jules Huret, *En Argentine. De Buenos Aires au Gran Chaco* (Paris, 1912), p. 263.
58 Azara, *Viajes* vol. II, pp. 78-9.
59 The figures for the Interior are those suggested by José Torre Revello in *Historia de la Nación Argentina* (2nd ed., Buenos Aires, 1940), vol. IV, 'Sociedad colonial. Las clases sociales. La ciudad y la campaña', pp. 360-1. For those for Buenos Aires, see Besio Moreno, pp. 278-84.

Notes to the text

Chapter 2 Revolution and the dislocation of the economy

1. Accounts of Don José de Rodrigo y Aldea, merchant of Jujuy, A.G.N., Biblioteca Nacional MSS., no. 6609.
2. General José María Paz, 'Diario de marcha', 14 July 1824, in A.G.N., *Diarios de marcha del General José María Paz* (Buenos Aires, 1938), p. 141.
3. *Ibid.* pp. 15–20.
4. Return of the quantities of silver brought to the Rescate Bank in Potosí (1778–1807 and 1807–1826), Parish to Palmerston, *separate*, in F.O. 6/32, fos. 149–51. The average for the years 1788–97 was $3,451,178 per annum; for 1798–1807, $2,819,411 per annum; and for 1817–26, $1,249,957 per annum.
5. (Enthusiastic) news bulletin on the minting of money in Mendoza, in the *Argos* (Buenos Aires), 3 July 1823. For a detailed account of the process, see Silvestre Peña y Lillo, *Gobernadores de Mendoza* (Mendoza, 1937), pp. 147 ff.
6. Withdrawal of Güemes's coinage in La Rioja, *Archivo del Brigadier General Juan Facundo Quiroga* (Buenos Aires, 1957), vol. I, pp. 90–2.
7. For minting in Santiago del Estero, see letters (also enthusiastic) in the *Argos*, 2 August 1823. For the withdrawal of Federal pesetas in Santiago del Estero, see *Actas capitulares de Santiago del Estero* (Buenos Aires, 1945), vol. VI, p. 812, session of 11 September 1823.
8. For the activities of Burgoa, who set up in business with capital supplied by Juan Facundo Quiroga, there is abundant material in the Archive of the latter, e.g. Burgoa to Quiroga, San Juan, 1 February 1825, *Archivo Quiroga*, copy in the Instituto de Historia Argentina y Americana 'Dr. Emilio Ravignani' (Buenos Aires), file VIII, doc. 1147; also, Burgoa to Quiroga, 26 February 1825, *ibid.*, file VIII, doc. 1159.
9. For passages from López's letter, see Agustín Rivero Astengo, *Juárez Celman, 1844–1909. Estudio histórico y documental de una época argentina* (Buenos Aires, 1944), p. 14.
10. Order of Artigas to José de Silva, Governor of Corrientes, ordering the closure of the port to trade with Buenos Aires, A.G.N., VII, 13-1-1, fo. 7.
11. See text of the proclamation convoking the Legislature, 14 September 1820, and note to Estanislao López, 7 October 1820, in Ernesto H. Celesia, *Federalismo argentino; apuntes históricos, 1815–21. Córdoba* (Buenos Aires, 1932), vol. II, pp. 213 and 219–20.
12. F.O. 97/50.
13. Quiroga to Burgoa, La Rioja, 23 May 1827, *Archivo Quiroga*, file X, doc. 1619.
14. *Archivo Urquiza*, A.G.N., VII, 13-1-1, fos. 19–20.
15. For the situation in Catamarca, see the letter from the refugee Eusebio Gregorio Ruzo to Quiroga, La Rioja, 2 April 1826, *Archivo Quiroga*, file IX, doc. 1377. For traffic tariffs in San Luis, see Peña y Lillo, p. 66.
16. For detailed itineraries see the above-mentioned report of José Godoy Oro, A.G.N., IX, 4-6-5, fos. 38 ff.
17. Emilio Hansen, *La moneda argentina; estudio histórico* (Buenos Aires, 1916), p. 139.
18. A.G.N., IX, 4-6-16, fos. 42 ff.
19. *Ibid.* fos. 50 ff.
20. *Ibid.* fos. 83–4.
21. *Ibid.* fos. 140 ff.
22. *Ibid.* fos. 158–62.
23. *Ibid.* fos. 131 ff.
24. Consulado to the Congressional Committee, 4 October 1817, *ibid.* fos. 203–4.
25. *Archivo Quiroga*, vol. I, pp. 216, 223 and *passim*.
26. Manuel A. de Castro to San Martín, Córdoba, 18 November 1819, *Documentos del Archivo San Martín* (Museo Mitre, Buenos Aires, 1910–11), vol. IX, p. 326.
27. Oro to Dorrego, Bajada del Paraná, 11 April 1828, in *Papeles de D. Domingo de Oro* (Buenos Aires, 1911), vol. I, pp. 21–2.
28. Zapata to Oro, Bajada del Paraná, 4 July 1828, *ibid.* vol. I, p. 21.

Notes to the text

29 Oro to Dorrego, Bajada del Paraná, 11 April 1828, *ibid.* vol. I, p. 21.
30 Dorrego to Oro, Bajada del Paraná, 20 May 1828, *ibid*, vol. I, p. 33.
31 Oro to Dorrego, Bajada del Paraná, 11 April 1828, *ibid*. vol. I, p. 21.
32 General José María Paz, *Memorias póstumas* (Buenos Aires, 1954), pt. VIII, ch. XV (on his activities in Córdoba in 1829), and pt. I, ch. VIII (on Borges).
33 Emilio Ravignani and Humberto A. Mandelli, 'La gestión económico-financiera de la Liga del Norte contra Rosas: el papel moneda del Banco Hipotecario', *BIIH*, vol. XXV (1941), pp. 192-202.
34 'Relación de lo que se cree hacer falta para la expedición a los indios' (rough draft), in Ernesto H. Celesia, *Rosas, aportes para su historia* (Buenos Aires, 1954), pp. 389 ff.
35 Aníbal S. Vázquez, *Caudillos entrerrianos. I. Ramírez* (2nd ed., Paraná, 1937), p. 163.
36 Bustos to Quiroga, Córdoba, 28 May 1827, *Archivo Quiroga*, file X, doc. 1620.
37 On 27 October 1807 Joaquín de Obregón Cevallos, the agent of Juan Estaban Anchorena, informed the latter from Potosí that all prices had fallen and nobody was willing to buy, and that, knowing the 'immense smuggling' taking place from Potosí, 'many individuals had gone to Montevideo to make their purchases'. A.G.N., VII, 4-1-4.
38 A.G.N., IX, 4-6-16, fo. 16.
39 *Ibid.* fo. 10.
40 *Ibid.* fo. 15.
41 *Ibid.* fo. 28.
42 The earliest proposal for the reimposition of the restrictions is included in a report of the Consulado, 5 February 1812, A.G.N., 4-6-16, fos. 72 ff.
43 Ravignani, vol. I, pp. 18 and 73-4.
44 There are numerous instances of this in the commercial accounts of the firms of Anchorena and Santa Coloma, both in A.G.N., room VII.
45 A.G.N., IX, 4-6-16, fo. 15.
46 *Ibid.* IX, 29-1-6, fo. 32v.
47 *Ibid.* IX, 4-6-16, fos. 14v, 37v and 40v.
48 Reports of the Consulado deputies in Corrientes, A.G.N., IX, 4-6-4, fos. 177, 211 and 220. For the Banda Oriental, the illegal activities of the merchants in the North and their economic function, see Pivel Devoto, *passim.*
49 A.G.N., IX, 4-6-16, fos. 130 ff.
50 Public Record Office (London), Customs, 4/7 ff.
51 Samuel Haigh, *Sketches of Buenos Ayres, Chile, and Peru* (London, 1831), p. VII.
52 For the figures, see Public Record Office (London), Customs, 4/7 ff.
53 Archives du Quai d'Orsay, Comm. Buenos Ayres 3, fos. 121-5. Lurde to Guizot, comm. no. 6, 31 March 1843.
54 Collected in the series of Campaign Reports (Police); reports of rural commissaries and justices of the peace, in A.G.N., room X.
55 In the famous chapter 'La historia de mi madre', in Domingo Faustino Sarmiento, *Recuerdos de provincia, Obras Completes* (2nd ed., Buenos Aires, 1948), pp. 126-38.
56 *Diario de sesiones de la Cámara de Diputados* (Buenos Aires), year 1873, pp. 261 ff.
57 This report has been published in R. A. Humphreys, *British Consular reports on the trade and politics of Latin America, 1824-1826* (London, 1940), pp. 27 ff.; for an analysis of the final destination of these British imports, see *ibid*, pp. 48-52.
58 See, for example, the declarations of Du Graty in the Chamber of Deputies of Paraná, session of 27 June 1826, in Carlos Alberto Silva, *El poder legislativo de la nación argentina*, vol. I, *Organización nacional 1854-1861* (Buenos Aires, 1944), pp. 308 ff.
59 H. B. Poucel, 'La province de Catamarca', *Bulletin de la Société de Géographie* (Paris), series 5, vol. VII (March 1864), pp. 267 ff. After describing the decline of the cotton business, he observes (p. 278): '...les mêmes causes auraient produit des effets identiques dans le tissage des laines, si les objets de laine avaient subi une baisse aussi forte que ceux de coton'.
60 See those of the Deputy Villanueva, the representative of Mendoza, in the General Constituent Congress, session of 4 March 1826, in Ravignani, vol. II, p. 868.

Notes to the text

61 Woodbine Parish, *Buenos Ayres and the Provinces of the Rio de la Plata...* (2nd ed., London, 1852), p. 327.
62 A.G.N., IX, 4-6-16, fos. 130 ff.
63 *Ibid.* fo. 220, and Juan José Cristóbal de Anchorena, *Dictamen sobre el establecimiento de una compañía general de comercio de las Provincias Unidas del Río de la Plata* (Buenos Aires, 1818).
64 Ricardo Caillet-Bois and Enrique Popolizio Jr., 'La corrupción administrativa durante la Revolución', *BIIH*, vol. V (1926), pp. 228-53.
65 Felipe A. Espil (ed.). *Once años en Buenos Aires. Las crónicas diplomáticas de John Murray Forbes compiladas, traducidas y anotadas por...*(Buenos Aires, 1956), pp. 68-9.
66 *Ibid.* p. 44.
67 *Ibid.* p. 205.
68 José Torre Revello, 'La casa y el mobiliario en el Buenos Aires colonial', *Revista de la Universidad de Buenos Aires*, 3rd series, vol. V (1945), pp. 59-74. See, especially, Plates 8, 10 and 12.
69 A.G.N., IX, 4-6-16, fo. 73v.
70 *Ibid.* fo. 63.
71 John Parish and William Parish Robertson, *Letters on South America...* (London, 1843), vol. I, pp. 52 and 174-9.
72 Juan Álvarez, *Temas de historia económica argentina* (Buenos Aires, 1929), p. 103.
73 Public Record Office (London), Customs, 4/7 ff.
74 H. M. Brackenridge, *Voyage to South America, performed by order of the American Government in the years 1817 and 1818* (London, 1820).
75 Copies of the reports of Mackinnon to the Foreign Office, in A.G.N., VII, 17-6-2.
76 Miron Burgin, *Aspectos económicos del federalismo argentino* (Buenos Aires, 1960), p. 67. *Registro Estadístico de la Provincia de Buenos Aires*, 3 (Buenos Aires, 1822).
77 Decree of 22 July 1817, *Gaceta*, 26 July 1817.
78 Tulio Halperín Donghi, 'La expansión ganadera en la campaña de Buenos Aires, 1810-1852' *Desarrollo económico* (Buenos Aires), vol. III, nos. 1-2 (1963), pp. 57-110.
79 A.G.N., X, 10-3-3.
80 A.G.N., X, 22-2-6, partially reprinted in Alfredo J. Montoya, *Historia de los saladeros argentinos* (Buenos Aires, 1956), pp. 50-4.
81 As early as 1811 Mackinnon was referring to Sarratea as 'our friend Don Manuel de Sarratea' (Mackinnon to Strangford, Buenos Aires, 7 November 1811, copy in *A.G.N.*, VII, 17-6-2). According to confidential remarks made by Pueyrredón, exiled in Montevideo, to Rear-Admiral Jurieu, British influence favoured the persecution of the supporters of the Directory by Sarratea (*Archives du Quai d'Orsay, Correspondance politique Argentine*, 2, fos. 84-94. Extract from a report of Rear-Admiral Jurieu to the Admiralty, Maldonado, 14 November 1820).
82 Iriarte, vol. III, pp. 35-6.
83 *A.G.N*, Paz, *Diarios*, p. 189.

Chapter 3 The crisis of the colonial order

1 'Autobiografía', in Belgrano, pp. 48-9.
2 Vieytes, pp. 148 and 268.
3 Belgrano, pp. 49-50.
4 Azara, *Memoria*.
5 *Correo de Comercio*, 23 June and 4 August 1810, in Belgrano, pp. 158 and 177-8.
6 'Modo de sostener la buena fe del comercio', *Correo de Comercio*, 15 September 1810, *ibid.* pp. 204 ff.
7 *Archivo del doctor Gregorio Funes* (Buenos Aires, 1944), vol. V, p. 68. The letter from 'Francisco' is dated 15 April 1794.
8 San Alberto, pp. 198 and 201.

Notes to the text

9 See Boleslao Lewin, 'La "conspiración de los franceses" en Buenos Aires', *Anuario del Instituto de Investigaciones Históricas* (Universidad Nacional del Litoral, Rosario), vol. IV, (1960), pp. 9–57.
10 Juan Canter, 'Las sociedades secretas y literarias', in Academia Nacional de la Historia, *Historia de la Nación Argentina* (2nd ed. Buenos Aires, 1941), vol. V, sect. I, pp. 206–10.
11 Resolution of the War Committee of 17 July 1797, approved by the King 4 May 1798, in Juan Beverina, *El virreinato de las provincias del Río de la Plata. Su organización militar* (Buenos Aires, 1935), pp. 190 ff.
12 Belgrano, p. 52.
13 John Lynch, 'Intendants and Cabildos in the viceroyalty of the Río de la Plata, 1782–1810', *Hispanic American Historical Review* (Durham, N.C.), vol. XXV (1955), pp. 337–62.
14 Matías de Cires to the King, Buenos Aires, 20 April 1809, *Mayo documental* (Universidad de Buenos Aires, Facultad de Filosofía y Letras, Instituto de Historia Argentina 'Doctor E. Ravignani'. Documentos para la historia Argentina, 29– , 1961– .), vol. VIII (1960), p. 227.
15 Diego Ponce de León to Floridablanca, Montevideo, 10 February 1809, *ibid.* p. 11.
16 Report of the Cabildo of Buenos Aires, 15 October 1808, *ibid.* vol. VI, p. 334.
17 Juan Manuel Beruti, *Memorias curiosas*, in Senado de la Nación, *Biblioteca de Mayo* (Buenos Aires, 1960), vol. IV, p. 3815.
18 Belgrano, p. 53.
19 Ignacio Núñez, *Noticias históricas, políticas y estadísticas, de las provincias del Río de la Plata* (Buenos Aires, 1952), vol. II, p. 11.
20 Belgrano, Beruti, Castelli and Rodríguez Peña to the Infanta Carlota, 20 September 1808, *Mayo Documental* (Buenos Aires), vol. III, pp. 104–5.
21 Reports of the Legal Officers of the Cabildo of Buenos Aires to the Central Junta, Buenos Aires, 22 January 1809, *ibid.* vol. VII, p. 208.
22 Felipe Contucci to Rodrigo de Souza Coutinho, Rio de Janeiro, 16 November 1808, *ibid.* vol. IV, pp. 196–9.
23 José Manuel de Goyeneche to the Supreme Junta, Buenos Aires, 14 September 1808, *ibid.* vol. III, p. 74.
24 *Ibid.* p. 74.
25 For a balanced account of this complex attitude, see Roberto Etchepareborda, 'Felipe Contucci y el carlotismo (1808–1810)', *Anuario del Instituto de Investigaciones Históricas* (Universidad Nacional del Litoral, Rosario), IV (1960), pp. 59–155, 86.
26 Among these, Dr Roberto Marfany has emphasised the statistically minority character of the sectors active in the Revolution, as compared with the population as a whole; see his *El pronunciamiento de Mayo* (Buenos Aires, 1958).
27 A.G.N., *Acuerdos del extinguido Cabildo de Buenos Aires*, series IV, vol. IV (Buenos Aires, 1957), pp. 119 ff.
28 Belgrano, p. 61.
29 See A.G.N., *Acuerdos del extinguido Cabildo*, *loc. cit.*, pp. 173–4.

Chapter 4 The Revolution in Buenos Aires

1 *Gaceta*, 27 December 1810.
2 *Ibid.* 23 January 1811.
3 *Ibid.* 5 July 1812.
4 *Ibid.* 12 July 1810.
5 *Ibid.* 30 May 1811.
6 Archbishop of Charcas to the Supreme Governing Junta, 26 February 1811, *ibid.* 4 May 1811.
7 José María Mariluz Urquijo, *Los proyectos españoles para reconquistar el Río de la Plata* (Buenos Aires, 1958).
8 Supreme Junta to the Bishop of Buenos Aires, Buenos Aires, 21 November 1810, *Registro Nacional de la Provincia de Buenos Aires* (Buenos Aires, 1879), vol. I, p. 89.

Notes to the text

9 *Ibid.* vol. I, p. 47.
10 H. M. Brackenridge, *Voyage to South America, performed by order of the American Government in the years 1817 and 1818...* (London, 1820), vol. I, p. 244.
11 *Ibid.* p. 302.
12 Beruti, p. 3789.
13 Enrique Williams Álzaga, *Cartas que nunca llegaron* (Buenos Aires, 1967), p. 76.
14 Beruti, pp. 3834 and 3838.
15 *Ibid.* pp. 3830 and 3834.
16 *Registro Nacional,* vol. I, p. 94.
17 Beruti, p. 3800.
18 Juan José Echevarría, 'Diario con referencia a los sucesos de Buenos Aires del 5 al 6 de abril de 1811 y las elecciones de septiembre del mismo año', *Biblioteca de Mayo,* vol. IV (Buenos Aires, 1960), p. 3624.
19 J. Graham to John Quincy Adams, Buenos Aires, 5 November 1818, in William R. Manning (ed.), *Diplomatic Correspondence of the United States concerning the Independence of the Latin American Nations* (New York, 1925), vol. I, p. 513.
20 In *Biblioteca de Mayo,* vol. VII, p. 6139.
21 Juan Martín de Pueyrredón, *Memoria,* in *Biblioteca de Mayo,* vol. III, p. 2148.
22 Thomas Bland to John Quincy Adams, 2 November 1818, in Manning, vol. I, p. 429.
23 *Registro Nacional,* vol. I, p. 24.
24 *Gaceta,* 23 August 1810.
25 *Ibid.* 16 August 1810.
26 *Ibid.* 28 March 1811.
27 *Ibid.* 11 July 1811.
28 Beruti, pp. 3284-5.
29 *Gaceta,* 12 April 1817.
30 Brackenridge, vol. I, pp. 244 and 258.
31 Presidential decree abolishing titles, in Mariano Moreno, *Doctrina democrática* (Buenos Aires, 1915), p. 231.
32 Gervasio A. de Posadas, *Memorias autobiográficas* (Buenos Aires, 1910), p. 22.
33 *Registro Nacional,* vol. I, p. 28.
34 Beruti, p. 3796.
35 *Registro Nacional,* vol. I, p. 33.
36 *Ibid.* vol. I, p. 131.
37 Beruti, p. 3914.
38 *Ibid.* p. 3868.
39 Juan Martín de Pueyrredón, p. 2150.
40 *Gaceta,* 19 October 1811.
41 Beruti, p. 3822.
42 *Registro Nacional,* vol. I, p. 89.
43 Adolfo P. Carranza (ed.), *Archivo General de la República Argentina* (Buenos Aires, 1894), vol. V, pp. 129-32.
44 *Ibid.* p. 242.
45 *Ibid.* p. 247.
46 *Ibid.* p. 76.
47 *Ibid.* pp. 96, 106, 163 and 249.
48 Rómulo D. Carbia, *La revolución de Mayo y la Iglesia* (Buenos Aires, 1945), p. 48.
49 Beruti, p. 3853.
50 Carbia, p. 82.
51 *Ibid.* p. 29.
52 Beruti, pp. 3844, 3871 and 3899.
53 José María Sáenz Valiente, *Bajo la campana del Cabildo* (Buenos Aires, 1952), pp. 208-9.
54 Francisco H. Romay, *Historia de la Policía Federal Argentina* (Buenos Aires, 1958), vol. I, pp. 228-34.

55 *Ibid.* p. 187.
56 *Gaceta*, 13 September 1810.
57 *Registro Nacional*, vol. I, p. 28.
58 *Ibid.* vol. I, p. 117.
59 *Ibid.* p. 131.
60 Beruti, pp. 3863 and 3866.
61 Manuel Antonio Pueyrredón, *Memorias* (Buenos Aires, 1942), p. 25.
62 Beruti, pp. 3868-9 and 3877-9.
63 *Gaceta*, 10 October 1811.
64 *Registro Nacional*, vol. I, p. 28.
65 *Ibid.* p. 72.
66 Pueyrredón to San Martín, 9 October 1816, in Carlos Alberto Pueyrredón, *La campaña de los Andes* (Buenos Aires, 1942), facsimile appendix, p. 52.
67 *Registro Nacional*, vol. I, p. 28.
68 *Ibid.* pp. 79-80.
69 Archivo General de la Nación, *Tomas de razón de despachos militares, cédulas de premio, retiros, empleos civiles y eclesiásticos...1740 a 1821* (Buenos Aires, 1925).
70 Beruti, p. 3859.
71 Jean Adam Graaner, *Las provincias del Río de la Plata en 1816* (trans. José Luis Busaniche, Buenos Aires, 1949), pp. 75-6.
72 *Registro Nacional*, vol. I, pp. 181-2.
73 *Gaceta*, 17 October 1811.
74 Brackenridge, vol. I, pp. 245-8.
75 Enrique Udaondo, *Diccionario biográfico argentino* (Buenos Aires, 1938); Instituto Argentino de Ciencias Genealógicas, *Hombres de Mayo* (Buenos Aires, 1961); A.G.N., *Tomas de razón*; in all cases *sub voce*.
76 For examples, see *Gaceta*, 25 April and 31 May 1817.
77 Juan Martín de Pueyrredón, p. 2141.
78 *La Lira Argentina*, p. 38, facsimile copy in *Biblioteca de Mayo*, vol. VI, p. 4738.
79 Juan Martín de Pueyrredón, p. 2148.
80 Colonel Francisco Saguí, *Apuntes de familia*, in *Biblioteca de Mayo*, vol. III, p. 2193.
81 Brackenridge, vol. I, p. 285.
82 Juan Canter, 'Las sociedades secretas y literarias', *Historia de la Nación Argentina* (2nd ed., Buenos Aires, 1941), vol. V, sect. I, p. 293; *San Martín*, vol. X, pp. 489-91.
83 *La Lira Argentina*, p. 35, in *Biblioteca de Mayo*, vol. V, p. 4735.
84 Beruti, pp. 3864 and 3870.
85 José María Mariluz Urquijo, 'Manuel José García, un eco de Benjamín Constant en el Río de la Plata', *Journal of Inter-American Studies* (Miami), vol. IX (1967), p. 3.
86 Juan Martín de Pueyrredón, vol. III, p. 2148.
87 *Gaceta*, 13 July 1817.
88 Decree published in the *Gaceta*, 27 August 1817.
89 Sáenz Valiente, p. 194.
90 Brackenridge, vol. I, p. 267.
91 *Gaceta*, 3 May 1817.
92 *Ibid.* 6 December 1817.
93 John Parish Robertson and William Parish Robertson, *Letters on South America...* (London, 1843), p. 62.
94 *Gaceta*, 6 December 1817.

Notes to the text

Chapter 5 The Revolution in the country as a whole

1 Adolfo P. Carranza, *Archivo General de la República Argentina* (Buenos Aires, 1894-9), vol. I, pp. 242-3.
2 Tristán to Balcarce, 3 December 1810, *ibid*, vol. I, pp. 245-8.
3 Supreme Junta to Castelli, 12 September 1810, *ibid.* vol. II, p. 5.
4 Supreme Junta to Castelli, 18 October 1810, *ibid*, vol. I, p. 43.
5 Julio César Raffo de la Reta, *Historia de Juan Martín de Pueyrredón* (Buenos Aires, 1948), p. 149.
6 *Registro Nacional*, vol. I, pp. 115-16 and 121.
7 Graaner, p. 39.
8 *Gaceta*, 24 January 1811.
9 Ceferino Garzón Maceda, 'La Revolución de Mayo y la Universidad de Córdoba', *Revista de la Universidad Nacional de Córdoba*, series 2, year 2 (1961), nos. 1-2, pp. 9-33.
10 Ricardo Levene, *Ensayo histórico sobre la Revolución de Mayo y Mariano Moreno* (2nd ed., Buenos Aires, 1925), vol. III, pp. 195-9.
11 *Gaceta*, 6 September 1810.
12 *Archivo Funes*, vol. II, pp. 136-7.
13 *Ibid*. p. 145.
14 *Ibid*. p. 149.
15 *Ibid*. p. 211.
16 *Ibid*. vol. III, p. 124.
17 *Ibid*. p. 156.
18 *Ibid*. p. 183.
19 Carranza, vol. I, p. 215 and vol. II, pp. 174-201.
20 For details of contributions from Catamarca, see Antonio Zinny, *Historia de los gobernadores de las provincias argentinas* (Buenos Aires, 1882), vol. III, p. 475; for those from Santiago del Estero, see *Gaceta*, 27 April 1818.
21 Ambrosio Funes to the Dean, 29 January 1811, *Archivo Funes*, vol. II, p. 125.
22 *Ibid*. pp. 135 and 156.
23 Ambrosio Funes to the Dean, December 1815, *ibid*, p. 215.
24 Ambrosio Funes to the Dean, 19 February 1816, *ibid*. p. 235.
25 M. I. Molina to the Dean, Mendoza, 5 May 1821, *ibid*. vol. III, p. 7.
26 M. I. Molina to the Dean, 23 November 1821, *ibid*. p. 15.
27 Dean Funes to Bernardo Monteagudo, 1 January 1822, *ibid*. p. 23.
28 Mariano Serapio Funes to the Dean, 25 November 1821, *ibid*. p. 18.
29 T. Montano to the Dean, 17 February 1818, *ibid*, vol. II, p. 262.
30 T. Montano to the Dean, 15 April 1822, *ibid*. vol. III, p. 35.
31 Ambrosio Funes to the Dean, 8 July 1823, *ibid*. p. 86.
32 Ambrosio Funes to the Dean, 21 December 1823, *ibid*. p. 147.
33 Mariano Serapio Funes to the Dean, 23 June 1823, *ibid*. p. 80.
34 Mariano Serapio Funes to the Dean, January 1824, *ibid*. p. 155.
35 Ambrosio Funes to the Dean, 21 July 1824, *ibid*. p. 273.
36 Peña y Lillo, vol. II, pp. 11-13; Damián Hudson, *Recuerdos históricos sobre la provincia de Cuyo* (Buenos Aires, 1898), vol. I, p. 424.
37 Diego Barrenechea to J. F. Quiroga, La Rioja, 27 January 1820, *Archivo Quiroga*, vol. I, p. 118.
38 Lieutenant-Governor of La Rioja to J. F. Quiroga, 19 April 1818, *ibid*. p. 87.
39 J. F. Peñaloza to J. F. Quiroga, 10 March 1816, *ibid*. p. 54.
40 Decree of the Lieutenant-Governor of La Rioja, 26 August 1817, *ibid*. pp. 74-5.
41 Protest by the merchants of Jujuy against the exodus decreed by Belgrano, 12 August 1812, A.G.N., IX, 4-6-16, fo. 56.
42 B. Frías, *Historia del General Güemes y la provincia de Salta* (Salta, 1902), vol. I, pp. 389-90.
43 Dámaso de Uriburu, *Memorias*, in *Biblioteca de Mayo* (1960).

Notes to the text

44 Roger M. Haigh, 'Martín Güemes; a study of the power structure of the province of Salta, 1810–1821' (University of Florida unpublished dissertation, August 1963), p. 74.
45 *Gaceta*, 18 February 1811.
46 John Street, *Artigas and the Emancipation of Uruguay* (Cambridge, 1959), p. 299.
47 Artigas to the Cabildo of Montevideo, Paysandú, 9 July 1817, in A.G.N., *Correspondencia del General José Artigas al Cabildo de Montevideo, 1814–1816* (Montevideo, 1946), p. 16.
48 Artigas to the Cabildo of Montevideo, Paysandú, 4 August 1815, *ibid.* p. 28, and 29 October 1815, Headquarters, *ibid.* p. 40.
49 Artigas to the Cabildo of Montevideo, Paysandú, 12 August 1815, *ibid.* p. 23.
50 Artigas to the Cabildo of Montevideo, Headquarters, 2 May and 13 June 1815, *ibid*, pp. 6 and 9.
51 Artigas to the Cabildo of Montevideo, Paysandú, 8 August 1815, *ibid.* p. 22.
52 Street, p. 305.
53 Julio Carlos Rodríguez, Lucía Sala de Touron and Nelson de la Torre, *Artigas, tierra y revolución* (Montevideo, 1967).
54 Pedro Ferré, *Memoria...octobre de 1821 a diciembre de 1842...* (Buenos Aires, 1921), vol. I, p. 10.
55 Promulgated in Corrientes, 29 September 1820; reprinted in Martín Ruiz Moreno, *Contribución a la historia de Entre Ríos* (Buenos Aires, 1919), vol. I, pp. 101–33.
56 Artigas to the Cabildo of Corrientes, 31 January 1816, in Hernán F. Gómez, *El General Artigas y los hombres de Corrientes* (Corrientes, 1929), p. 143.
57 Artigas to Juan Bautista Méndez, 29 March 1814, *ibid.* p. 42.
58 Artigas to José de Silva, Paysandú, 6 July 1815, *ibid.* p. 93.
59 Artigas to José de Silva, Concepción del Uruguay, 2 July 1815, *ibid.* p. 91.
60 Artigas to José de Silva, Paraná, 9 April 1815, *ibid.* p. 82.
61 Artigas to the Cabildo of Corrientes, Headquarters, 19 January 1815, *ibid.* p. 72.
62 Artigas to J. B. Méndez, Headquarters, 26 January 1815, *ibid*, p. 73.
63 Artigas to José de Silva, 9 April 1815, *ibid.* p. 82.
64 Artigas to the Cabildo of Corrientes, 29 October 1815, *ibid.* p. 107.
65 Hernán F. Gómez, *Historia de Corrientes. II. Desde la Revolución de Mayo hasta el Tratado del Cuadrilátero* (Corrientes, 1929), p. 180.
66 Artigas to José de Silva, 4 February 1815, in Gómez, *Artigas*, p. 75.
67 Gómez, *Historia*, vol. II, p. 251.
68 Artigas to the Cabildo of Corrientes, Headquarters, 21 and 25 September 1819, in Gómez, *Artigas*, p. 209.
69 Gómez, *Historia*, vol. II, pp. 111–12.
70 Artigas to the Cabildo of Corrientes, Purificación, 18 November 1816, in Gómez, *Artigas*, p. 167.
71 Artigas to the Cabildo of Corrientes, 12 January 1817, *ibid.* p. 174.
72 Candioti to Álvarez Thomas, Santa Fe, 28 July 1815, in José Luis Busaniche, *Santa Fe y el Uruguay desde la Revolución de Mayo hasta la constitución de la República oriental* (Santa Fe, 1930), pp. 36–7.
73 Artigas to Barreiro, 30 November 1816, in Gregorio F. Rodríguez, *Historia de Alvear* (Buenos Aires, 1913), vol. II, p. 596.
74 See Manuel M. Cervera, *Historia de la ciudad y provincia de Santa Fe* (Santa Fe, 1907), vol. II, appendix, p. 6.

Chapter 6 The dissolution of the Revolutionary order

1 Artigas to Barreiro, 30 November 1816, in Gregorio F. Rodríguez, vol. II, p. 596.
2 Universidad Nacional de Tucumán, *Documentos tucumanos. Actas del Cabildo*, vol. II (Tucumán, 1940), p. 30 (session of 4 March 1817).
3 *Ibid.* p. 194 (session of 14 November 1819).
4 *Ibid.* p. 208 (proceedings of 7 January 1820).

Notes to the text

5 *Ibid.* pp. 31 and 236.
6 *Ibid.* p. 398.
7 Hudson, vol. I, p. 279.
8 Cabildo of San Juan to the Supreme Director, San Juan, 24 January 1820, *ibid.* p. 293.
9 *Archivo San Martín*, vol. X, p. 271.
10 General Gregorio Aráoz de Lamadrid, *Memorias* (Madrid, 1922), pp. 218-20.
11 Carlos S. Segreti, 'La gobernación de José Javier Díaz en 1820', *Humanidades* (Córdoba), vol. I (1960), pp. 57-93.
12 Paz, *Memorias*, pt. II, ch. XI.
13 Celesia, *Federalismo argentino; apuntes históricos, 1815-21. Cordoba*, vol. II, pp. 257 ff.
14 27 February 1825, *ibid.* vol. III, p. 193.
15 Provisional regulations of 1821, ch. 25, arts. 11-14, *ibid.* vol. III, p. 402.
16 A characteristic event was the considerable participation of troops from Córdoba – formerly part of the National Army – in the formation of the Army which took part in the war against Brazil. See Juan Beverina, *La guerra contra el Imperio del Brasil* (Buenos Aires, 1927), pp. 154-5.
17 Ch. 29, art. 3, in Celesia, *Federalismo Argentino*, vol. III, p. 410.
18 *Actas capitulares de Santiago del Estero*, vol. VI, pp. 662-7.
19 *Ibid.* pp. 123, 151, 514 and 551.
20 P. I. Caraffa, *Hombres notables de Cuyo* (2nd ed., La Plata, 1913), p. 171.
21 Hudson, vol. I, p. 375.
22 Published in Santiago Moritán, *Mansilla, Ramírez, Urquiza* (Buenos Aires, 1945), pp. 19-99.
23 *Gaceta*, 3 February 1819.
24 Beruti, p. 3933 (2 October 1820).
25 Governor of Buenos Aires to the Governor of Córdoba, 19 April 1820, A.G.N., X, 5-4-1.
26 Beruti, pp. 3922 and 3924 (26 March and 2 April 1820).
27 Jurieu to the Admiralty, Maldonado, 14 November 1820, *Archives du Quai d'Orsay, Politique Argentine*, II, fo. 86.
28 Iriarte, vol. III, p. 80.
29 *Registro Oficial de la Provincia de Buenos Aires* (Buenos Aires, 1873), vol. I, pp. 88-9.
30 *Ibid.* vol. II, pp. 40-44.
31 *Ibid.* p. 85 (19 April 1822).
32 *Ibid.* vol. I, p. 31.
33 *Ibid.* pp. 36-7.
34 *Ibid.* vol. II, p. 86 (19 April 1822).
35 *Ibid.* vol. III, p. 19 (28 February 1823).
36 *Ibid.* vol. III, pp. 63-4.
37 *Ibid.* p. 98.
38 *Argos* (Buenos Aires), 26 March 1823.
39 Rivadavia to Dean Zavaleta, 23 March 1823, *Argos*, 26 March 1823.
40 *El Republicano* (Buenos Aires), 8 and 15 February 1824; Montoya, p. 63.
41 *El Centinela* (Buenos Aires), 9 February 1823, *Biblioteca de Mayo*, vol. IX, p. 8369.
42 *Ibid.* 22 December 1822, *loc. cit.* p. 8255.
43 *Ibid.* 29 December 1822, *loc. cit.* p. 8280.
44 *Registro Oficial*, vol. I, p. 13.
45 *El Centinela*, 29 December 1822, *loc. cit.* p. 8280.
46 Iriarte, vol. IV, p. 81.
47 Núñez to Rivadavia, 21 January 1825, in R. Piccirilli, *Rivadavia y su tiempo* (2nd ed., Buenos Aires, 1960), vol. II, p. 564; for the list, see *Argos*, 12 January 1825.
48 José Esteban Antonio Echeverría, *Ojeada retrospectiva*, in *Obras completas* (Buenos Aires, 1873), vol. IV, p. 36.
49 R. Piccirilli, *San Martín y la política de los pueblos* (Buenos Aires, 1957), p. 359.
50 Núñez to Rivadavia, *loc. cit.* n. 21.
51 *El Centinela*, 23 November 1823, in *Biblioteca de Mayo*, vol. IV, p. 9002.

Notes to the text

52 John Murray Forbes to Adams, 15 August and 12 September 1823, in Forbes, *Once años en Buenos Aires. Las crónicas diplomáticas de...compiladas, traducidas y anotadas por Felipe A. Espil* (Buenos Aires, 1956), pp. 253 and 259.
53 Forbes to Adams, 2 June and 5 November 1823, *ibid.* pp. 247 and 265.

Chapter 7   The legacy of the Revolution and the war, and the political order of independent Argentina

1 Ignacio Núñez to Woodbine Parish, 2 January 1825, F.O. 354/7.
2 Estanislao López to Woodbine Parish, 13 June 1824, F.O. 6/5 fo. 37.
3 Bustos to J. P. Cisneros, 1 May 1820, in Celesia, *Federalismo Argentino*, vol. II, pp. 199–201.
4 *Ibid.* pp. 317 and 323.
5 Pueyrredón to Soler, 23 December 1814, in Street, p. 398.
6 Street, p. 402.
7 Frías, vol. I, p. 396.
8 Beruti, p. 3885.
9 Iriarte, vol. III, pp. 34–5, 351 and 400; vol. IV, pp. 14, 17–18, 64 and *passim*.
10 Robertson, letter 56, vol. III, pp. 159–78.
11 Juan Manuel de Rosas to the House of Representatives, 2 July 1821, in *Acuerdos de la H. Junta de Representantes...1820–1821*, ed. Ricardo Levene (La Plata, 1933), vol. II, pp. lxi–lxiii.
12 *Ibid.* pp. li–lix.
13 Celesia, *Rosas*. pp. 392–3.
14 For Salta, see the report of F. A. Chiclana, for December 1810, in Levene, *Ensayo histórico*, vol. III, pp. 195–9; for Mendoza, see Hudson, vol. I, pp. 22–3.
15 For example, A. R. Bazán, 'La Rioja en la época de la Independencia', *Trabajos y Comunicaciones* (La Plata), no. 15 (1966); Roger M. Haigh, p. 1963.
16 Frías, vol. I, pp. 401–2.
17 22 March 1827, *Archivo Quiroga*, vol. X, p. 1607.
18 3 February 1825, *ibid.* vol. VIII, p. 1149.
19 For example, that of 17 May 1827, *ibid.* vol. X, p. 1617.
20 Ibarra to Paz, 13 May 1829, in Alfredo Gargaro, *Paz e Ibarra* (Santiago del Estero, 1942), p. 57.
21 Ibarra to Paz, 16 May 1829, in Gargaro, p. 61.

BIBLIOGRAPHY

A. *Manuscript sources*
Archivo General de la Nación, Buenos Aires.
Archives du Quai d'Orsay, Paris.
Public Record Office, London. (Customs)
Public Record Office, London. (Foreign Office)

B. *Contemporary newspapers*
NOTE. *The title of each publication is followed by the number of issues, the dates, and the name or names of the editor(s). All newspapers were published in Buenos Aires.*

El Argos
El Centinela
El Correo de Comercio
La Gaceta
El Republicano
El Semanario de Agricultura

C. *Books and articles*
NOTE. Unless otherwise stated, all works in the following list were published in Buenos Aires.

Academia Nacional de la Historia, *Historia de la Nación Argentina*, 2nd ed., 1939– .
Acuerdos de la Honorable Junta de Representantes de la provincia de Buenos Aires, 1820–1821, 2 vols., 1932–3.
Aguirre, Juan Francisco de, 'Diario', *Anales de la Biblioteca Nacional*, IV, 1905, p. 171.
Álvarez, Juan, *Temas de historia económica argentina*, 1929.
Anchorena, Juan José Cristóbal de, *Dictamen sobre el establecimiento de una compañía general de comercio de las Provincias Unidas del Río de la Plata*, 1818.
Aráoz de Lamadrid, (General) Gregario. *Memorias*, Madrid, 1922.
Archivo del doctor Gregorio Funes, 1944– .
Archivo General de la Nación, *Acuerdos del extinguido Cabildo de Buenos Aires*, 47 vols., 1907–34.
Archivo General de la Nación, Montevideo, *Correspondencia del General José Artigas al Cabildo de Montevideo* (1814–1816), Montevideo, 1946.
Archivo General de la Nación, *Tomas de razón de despachos militares, cédulas de premio, retiros, empleos civiles y eclesiásticos...1740 a 1821*. 1925.

Bibliography

Archivo del General Mitre, 1911–14.
Azara, Félix de, *Memoria sobre el estado rural del Río de la Plata y otros informes*, 1943.
Azara, Félix de, *Viajes por la América meridional*, 2 vols., Madrid, 1923.
Bazán, A. R., 'La Rioja en la época de la Independencia', *Trabajos y Comunicaciones*, 15, La Plata, 1966.
Belgrano, (General) Manuel, *Escritos económicos*, ed. Gregorio Weinberg, 1954.
Beruti, Juan Manuel, *Memorias curiosas*, Senado de la Nación, *Biblioteca de Mayo*, IV, 1960, p. 3815.
Besio Moreno, Nicolás, *Buenos Aires. Puerto del Río de la Plata. Capital de la República Argentina. Estudio crítico de su población*, 1939.
Beverina, Juan, *La guerra contra el Imperio del Brasil*, 1927.
Beverina, Juan, *El virreinato de las provincias del Río de la Plata. Su organización militar*, 1935.
Brackenridge, H. M., *Voyage to South America, performed by order of the American Government in the years 1817 and 1818...*, 2 vols., London, 1820.
Buenos Aires, *Registro Estadístico de la Provincia de...*, 27 vols., 1854–80.
Burgin, Miron, *Aspectos económicos del federalismo argentino*, 1960.
Busaniche, José Luis, *Santa Fe y el Uruguay desde la Revolución de Mayo hasta la constitución de la República Oriental*. Santa Fe, 1930.
Caillet-Bois, Ricardo, 'Mendoza en los comienzos del siglo XIX' *Boletín del Instituto de Investigaciones Históricas BIIH*, vol. IX, 1928, p. 109.
Caillet-Bois, Ricardo and Popolizio (Jr.), Enrique, 'La corrupción administrativa durante la Revolución', *BIIH* vol. V, 1926, p. 228.
Cámara de Senadores, *Biblioteca de Mayo*, 1960– .
Cámara de Diputados, *Diario de sesiones de la....*
Canter, Juan, 'Las sociedades secretas y literarias', *Historia de la Nación Argentina*, 2nd ed., V, sect. I, 1941, p. 206.
Caraffa, P. I., *Hombres notables de Cuyo*, 2nd ed., La Plata, 1913.
Carbia, Rómulo D., *La Revolución de Mayo y la Iglesia*, 1945.
Carranza, Adolfo P. (ed.), *Archivo General de la República Argentina*, 14 vols., 1894–9.
Carrizo, Juan Alfonso, *Cancionero popular de La Rioja*, 3 vols., 1942.
Celesia, Ernesto H., *Federalismo argentino; apuntes históricos, 1815–21. Córdoba.*, 3 vols. 1932.
Celesia, Ernesto H., *Rosas, aportes para su historia*, 2 vols., 1954–68.
Cervera, Manuel M., *Historia de la ciudad y provincia de Santa Fe*, 2 vols., Santa Fe, 1907.
Concolorcovo, *El Lazarillo de ciegos caminantes desde Buenos Aires hasta Lima*, 1946.
Cornejo, Atilio, *Introducción a la historia de la propiedad inmobiliaria de Salta en la época colonial*, 1945.
Documentos del Archivo de San Martín, Museo Mitre, 12 vols., 1910–11.
Echevarría, Juan José, *Biblioteca de Mayo*, IV, 1960, p. 3624.
Echeverría, José Esteban Antonio, *Ojeada retrospectiva. Obras completas*. 5 vols., 1870–4.
Etchepareborda, Roberto, 'Felipe Contucci y el carlotismo (1808–1810)', *Anuario del Instituto de Investigaciones Históricas*, IV, Rosario, 1960, pp. 59 and 86.
Ferré, Pedro, *Memoria...Octubre de 1821 a diciembre de 1842...*, 1921.
Fischer, Ch. A., *Beiträge zur genaueren Kenntnis der Besitzungen in Amerika*, Dresden, 1802.

Bibliography

Forbes, John Murray, *Once años en Buenos Aires. Las crónicas diplomáticas de...compiladas, traducidas y anotadas por Felipe A. Espil*, 1956.
Frías, B., *Historia del General Güemes y de la provincia de Salta*, Salta, 1902.
Funes, Gregorio, *Archivo del doctor...*, 1944– .
'Gálvez, Víctor' [Vicente G. Quesada], *Memorias de un viejo*, 1942.
Gargaro, Alfredo, *Paz e Ibarra*, Santiago del Estero, 1942.
Garzón, Maceda, Ceferino, 'La Revolución de Mayo y la Universidad de Córdoba', *Revista de la Universidad de Córdoba*, series 2, year 2, 1–2, Córdoba, 1961, p. 25.
Gillespie, Alexander, *Gleanings and Remarks: collected during many months of residence at Buenos Ayres, and within the Upper Country...*, Leeds, 1818.
Gómez, Hernán F. *El General Artigas y los hombres de Corrientes*, Corrientes, 1929.
Gómez, Hernán F. *Historia de Corrientes. II. Desde la Revolución de Mayo hasta el Tratado del Cuadrilátero*, Corrientes, 1929.
Graaner, Jean Adam, *Las provincias del Río de la Plata en 1816*. trans. José Luis Busaniche, 1949.
Haigh, Roger M., 'Martín Güemes; a study of the power structure of the province of Salta, 1810–1821', University of Florida unpubl. dissertation, 1963.
Haigh, Samuel, *Sketches of Buenos Ayres, Chile, and Peru*, London, 1831.
Halperín Donghi, Tulio, 'La expansión ganadera en la campaña de Buenos Aires, 1810–1852', *Desarrollo Económico*, III, 1–2, 1963, p. 88.
Hansen, Emilio, *La moneda argentina; estudio histórico*, 1916.
Hudson, Damián, *Recuerdos históricos sobre la provincia de Cuyo*, 2 vols., 1898.
Humphreys, R. A., *British consular reports on the trade and politics of Latin America, 1824–1826*, London, 1940.
Huret, Jules, *En Argentine. De Buenos Aires au Gran Chaco*, Paris, 1912.
Ibarra de Roncoroni, Graciela, 'Un aspecto del comercio salteño, 1778–1811', *Anuario del Instituto de Investigaciones Históricas*, VIII, Rosario, 1965.
Instituto Argentino de Ciencias Genealógicas, *Hombres de Mayo*, 1961.
Iriarte, (General) Tomás de, *Memorias*, 11 vols., 1944–69.
Kossok, Manfred, *El virreynato del Río de la Plata. Su estructura económico-social*, 1959.
La Lira Argentina, Biblioteca de Mayo, VI, 1960, p. 4738.
Lastarria, Miguel, *Colonias orientales del Río Paraguay o del Plata*, in *Documentos de Historia Argentina*, III, 1914, p. 159.
Lavardén, Manuel José de, *Nuevo aspecto del comercio en el Río de la Plata*, 1955.
Levene, Ricardo (ed.), *Acuerdos de la H. Junta de Representantes ...1820–1821*, 2 vols., 1932–3.
Levene, Ricardo, *Ensayo histórico sobre la Revolución de Mayo y Mariano Moreno*, 3 vols., 2nd ed., 1925.
Lewin, Boleslao, 'La "conspiración de los franceses" en Buenos Aires', *Anuario del Instituto de Investigaciones Históricas*, IV, Rosario, 1960, p. 9.
Lynch, John, 'Intendants and Cabildos in the Viceroyalty of the Río de la Plata, 1782–1810', *Hispanic American Historical Review*, XXV, Durham, N.C., 1955, p. 337.
Mandelli, Humberto A., *See* Ravignani, Emilio.
Manning, William R. (ed.), *Diplomatic Correspondence of the United States concerning the Independence of the Latin American Nations*, 3 vols., New York, 1925.
Mayo documental, (Universidad de Buenos Aires, Facultad de Filosofía y Letras, Instituto de Historia Argentina y Americana 'Dr. Emilio Ravignani'. Documentos para la historia Argentina, 29–, 1961– .)

Bibliography

Marfany, Roberto, H; *El pronunciamiento de Mayo*, 1958.
Mariluz Urquijo, José María, 'Manuel José García, un eco de Benjamín Constant en el Río de la Plata', *Journal of Inter-American Studies*, IX, Miami, 1967, p. 3.
Mariluz Urquijo, José María. *Los proyectos españoles para reconquistar el Río de la Plata, 1820–33*, 1958.
Mitre, Bartolomé, *Arengas parlamentarias*, 1889.
Montoya, Alfredo J., *Historia de los saladeros argentinos*, 1956.
Moreno, José Luis, 'La estructura social y demográfica de la ciudad de Buenos Aires en el año 1778', *Anuario del Instituto de Investigaciones Históricas*, VIII, Rosario, 1965.
Moreno, Mariano, *Doctrina democrática*, 1915.
Moritán, Santiago, *Mansilla, Ramírez, Urquiza*, 1945.
Núñez, Ignacio, *Noticias históricas, políticas y estadísticas, de las Provincias Unidas del Río de la Plata*, 2 vols., 1952.
Oro, José de, *Papeles de D...*, 2 vols., 1911.
Parish, Woodbine, *Buenos Ayres and the Provinces of the Río de la Plata...*, London, 1839, 2nd ed., enlarged, 1852.
Paz, (General) José María, *Diarios de marcha del...*, 1938.
Paz, (General) José María, *Memorias póstumas*, 3 vols., 1917–30.
Peña y Lillo, Silvestre, *Gobernadores de Mendoza*, Mendoza, 1937.
Piccirilli, R., *Rivadavia y su tiempo*, 2 vols., 1943.
Piccirilli, R., *San Martín y la política de los pueblos*, 1957.
Pivel Devoto, Juan José, *Raíces coloniales de la revolución oriental de 1811*, 2nd ed., Montevideo, 1957.
Popolizio (Jr.). Enrique, *See* Caillet-Bois, Ricardo.
Posadas, Gervasio A. de, *Memorias autobiográficas*, 1910.
Poucel, H. B., 'La province de Catamarca', *Bulletin de la Société de Géographie*, series 5, VII, Paris, 1864, p. 267.
Pueyrredón, Carlos Alberto (ed.), *La campaña de los Andes*, 1942.
Pueyrredón, Juan Martín, de, *Memoria. Biblioteca de Mayo*, III, 1960, p. 2148.
Pueyrredón, Manuel Antonio, *Memorias*, 1942.
Quesada, Vicente G. *See* 'Gálvez, Víctor'.
Quiroga, (Brigadier General) Juan Facundo, *Archivo del...*, 1957– .
Raffo de la Reta, Julio César, *Historia de Juan Martín de Pueyrredón*, 1948.
Ravignani, Emilio, *Asambleas constituyentes argentinas*. 6 vols., 1937–9.
Ravignani, Emilio and Mandelli, Humberto A. 'La gestión económico-financiera de la Liga del Norte contra Rosas: el papel moneda del Banco Hipotecario', *BIIH*, XXV, 1941, p. 192.
Registro Nacional de la República Argentina...1810–1891, 1879–91.
[Some vols. have title: *Registro Oficial*.]
Rivero Astengo, Agustín, *Juárez Celmán, 1844–1909. Estudio histórico y documental de una época Argentina*, 1944.
Robertson, John Parish and William Parish, *Letters on South America...*, 3 vols., London, 1843.
Rodríguez, Gregorio F., *Historia de Alvear*, 2 vols., 1913.
Rodríguez, Julio Carlos; Sala de Touron, Lucía; and de la Torre, Nelson, *Artigas, tierra y revolución*, Montevideo, 1967.
Romay, Francisco L., *Historia de la Policía Federal Argentina*, 3 vols., 1963–5.
Ruiz Moreno, Martín, *Contribución a la historia de Entre Ríos*, 2 vols., 1919.

Bibliography

Sáenz Valiente, José María, *Bajo la campana del Cabildo*, 1952.
Saguí, (Colonel) Francisco, *Apuntes de familia*. Biblioteca de Mayo, III, 1960, p. 2193.
Sala de Touron, Lucía. *See* Rodríguez, Julio Carlos.
San Alberto, (Bishop) Joseph de, *Cartas pastorales del Ilustrísimo y Reverendísimo Señor D. Fr. ...*, Madrid, 1793.
San Martín, (General) José de, *Documentos del Archivo San Martín*, Museo Mitre, 12 vols., 1910-11.
Sánchez, Mariquita, *Recuerdos del Buenos Aires virreynal*, 1953.
Sánchez-Albornoz, Nicolás, *La extracción de mulas de Jujuy al Perú. Fuentes, volumen y negociantes*. (Estudios de Historia Social, vol. I), 1965.
Sánchez-Albornoz, Nicolás, 'La saca de mulas de Salta al Perú, 1778-1808', *Anuario del Instituto de Investigaciones Históricas*, VIII, Rosario, 1965.
Santiago del Estero, *Actas capitulares de...*, 6 vols., 1941-51.
Sarmiento, Domingo Faustino, *Recuerdos de provincia*, 2nd ed., 1948.
Segreti, Carlos S., 'La gobernación de José Javier Díaz en 1820', *Humanidades*, I, 3, Córdoba, 1960, p. 57.
Silva, Carlos Alberto, *El poder legislativo de la nación Argentina*, 1937.
Street, John, *Artigas and the Emancipation of Uruguay*, Cambridge, 1959.
Torre, Nelson de la. *See* Rodríguez, Julio Carlos.
Torre Revello, José, *Historia de la Nación Argentina*, 2nd ed., IV, sect. 1, 1940.
Torre Revello, José, 'La casa y el mobiliario en el Buenos Aires colonial', *Revista de la Universidad de Buenos Aires*, series 3, V.
Udaondo, Enrique, *Diccionario biográfico argentino*, 1938.
Udaondo, Enrique, *Diccionario biográfico colonial argentino*, 1945.
Universidad Nacional de Tucumán, *Documentos tucumanos. Actas del Cabildo*, 2 vols., Tucumán, 1939-40.
Uriburu, Dámaso de, *Memorias. Biblioteca de Mayo*, 1960.
Vázquez, Aníbal, S., *Caudillos entrerrianos. I. Ramírez*, 2nd ed., Paraná, 1937.
Vieytes, Hipólito, *Antecedentes económicos de la Revolución de Mayo*, 1956.
Wedovoy, Enrique, 'Estudio preliminar', in Manuel José de Lavardén, *Nuevo aspecto del comercio en el Río de la Plata*, 1955, p. 15.
Weinberg, Félix, 'Estudio preliminar', in Hipólito Vieytes, *Antecedentes económicos de la Revolución de Mayo*, 1956.
Williams Álzaga, Enrique, *Cartas que nunca llegaron*, 1967.
Zinny, Antonio, *Historia de los gobernadores de las provincias argentinas*. 3 vols., 1879-82.

INDEX

Achega, Dr, 184
Agüero, Baltasar, 398
Agüero, Julián Segundo de, 359, 367, 368, 370
Aguirre, Francisco de, 23
Aguirre, Juan Pablo, 147
Aguirre, Juan Pedro, 94, 237, 332, 339, 365
Aguirre, Lucho, 250
Alberdi, Father, 208
Alberdi, Salvador de, 38
Alberti, Manuel, 154
Aldao, 70
Aldao, Francisco, 328–9, 387
Aldao, José Félix, 328–9, 387
Allende, family of, 393
Allende, Tomas de, 249
Alonso, Amado, 59
Alvarado, Major, 316
Alvarez, Felipe, 319, 380
Alvarez, Juan, 4
Alvarez, Julián, 172
Alvear, General Carlos de, 192, 200, 203, 204, 214, 217, 219, 220, 221, 222–5, 227, 228, 249, 263, 266, 339, 340–1, 357, 366, 367, 384, 385
Alzaga, Martin, 30, 123, 132, 135, 140, 149, 164, 165, 216, 393
Alzaga, Félix de, 174
Amenábar, Father, 306
Anchorena, family of, 31, 383
Anchorena, J. J. C. de, 83–4, 93
Anchorena, Tomas Manuel de, 30, 147, 343, 359, 365
Andresito, 298
Aparicio, Manuel, 174
Aráoz, Bernabé, 67, 310, 311, 312, 313, 318, 319
Araoz, Diego, 313
Archondo, Tomás de, 393
Araujo, Francisco, 296
Arias, Manuela, 381
Arroyo y Pinedo, Manuel de, 122, 357, 365, 368
Artigas, Andrés, 298, 384

Artigas, José, 53, 69, 76, 78, 88, 213, 223, 227, 228, 251, 254, 271–4, 275–8, 281–3, 284–9, 290, 291, 295, 296, 297–8, 300–1, 302, 303, 304, 308, 309, 310, 330, 331, 339–43, 384
Azara, Félix de, 50, 52, 54, 59, 116, 278–9, 280
Azcuénaga, Miguel de, 30, 154, 155, 161
Azamor, Bishop, 185

Baigorri, 252
Balbastros, family of, 214
Balcarce, Antonio González, 241, 339
Balcarce, Francisco González de, 199
Balcarce, Juan Ramón, 235, 340
Barreiro, Miguel, 276, 308
Barros, Castro, 229
Basualdo, Blas, 294
Bataillon, Marcel, 58
Bedoya, Francisco de, 320, 380
Belaustegui, 30
Belén, Fr Mariano de, 381
Belgrano, family of, 146
Belgrano, Manuel, 49, 112–19, 125, 130, 132, 137, 138, 148, 154, 155, 180, 181, 201, 203, 207, 265, 271, 311, 316, 380, 393
Benavides, Nazario, 387
Beruti, Juan Manuel, 128, 129, 163, 165, 174, 179, 185, 192, 193, 213, 221, 333
Blanco, Angel Fernández, 296
Bland, Thomas, 168
Borges, 78–9
Brackenridge, H. M., 101, 102, 175, 198, 214
Brizuelas, family of, 261
Brown, 94
Buenos Aires, Bishop of, 180, 182, 196
Bulnes, Eduardo, 251, 252
Burgin, Miron, 102
Burgua, Miguel, 68, 70
Bustos, Juan Bautista, 42, 69, 80, 250, 252, 263, 317–19, 320, 321–2, 372, 379, 387

Cabrerita, 250
Campana, Dr, 186, 187
Campbell, Peter, 17

Index

Candioti, Francisco Antonio, 19, 302–3
Cañete, José Vicente, 150
Canter, Juan, 217
Carranza, José Ambrosio, 192, 389
Carrera, José Miguel, 319, 328, 340–1
Carrizo, Juan Antonio, 60
Castañeda, Father, 355
Castelli, Juan José, 138, 154, 241, 243
Castro, Félix, 365, 368
Cevallos, Viceroy, 199
Charles III, 53, 55, 119, 120
Chiclana, Feliciano Antonio de, 192, 237, 247, 248, 249, 253
Chumbita, 43
Cisneros, Baltasar Hidalgo de, 147–8, 150, 151–2, 177
Concolorcorvo, 7
Coni, Emilio, 4
Constant, Benjamin, 227
Contucci, Felipe, 145, 146
Córdoba, Bishop of, (see Orellana)
Correa, 291
Corro, 316
Costa, Braulio, 70, 109, 397
Coutinho, Rodrigo de Souza, 145
Crespo, Domingo, 305
Cruz, Tomás Godoy, 316, 370, 380
Cullen, Domingo, 70, 385
Curado, Brigadier-General, 135

Del Carril, family of, 15
Del Carril, Pedro, 47
Del Carril, Salvador, d385
Derqui, Dr Santiago, 385
Díaz, Jose Javier, 250, 251
Díaz, 122
Dorrego, Manuel, 77, 341, 342, 343, 344, 357, 366, 369, 379, 380, 381, 385, 386

Echeverría, Esteban, 360, 365
Echeverría, Juan José, 166
Elío, General, 135, 137, 139, 140, 141, 148, 274
Escobar, Angel, 296
Esquivel, 330
Escalada, 214
Escalada, y de la Quintana, Remedios de, 214

Ferninand VII, 165
Fernandez, Major, 221
Fernando VII, 159
Ferns, H. S., 11
Ferré, Pedro, 17

Figueroa, Apolinar, 265
Figueroa, family of, 249
Figueredo, Fr, 222
Fontes, José Martinéz, 199
Forbes, John Murray, 367, 370
Forest, David de, 94
Fragueiros, 256
'Francisco', 120
French, Domingo, 209, 216, 221, 237
Frías, B., 318
Funes, Ambrosio, 120, 246, 250–3, 255–60, 392, 397
Funes, family of, 147, 263, 392
Funes, Gregorio, 120, 246, 249–50, 255, 256, 257, 260, 367, 392
Funes, Ignacia, 259
Funes, Mariano Serapio, 258, 259
Funes, Manuel Serapio, 253
Funes, Sixto, 255, 258

Galisteo, José Elías, 306
Galván, Elías, 300
García, Manuel José, 227, 346, 350, 366, 370
Gillespie, Alexander, 52
Gómez, Gregorio, 122
Gómez, Hernan, 297, 298
Gómez, Valentin, 220, 222
Gondra, Adeodato, 385
González, Major Abraham, 311, 312, 313
Gorriti, family of, 8, 266
Gorriti, Francisco de, 386
Gorriti, José Ignacio de, 386, 387, 31–2
Gorriti, Juan Ignacio de, 386, 387
Goyeneche, Manuel José de, 147, 149
Gurruchagas, family of, 8
Graaner, J. A., 196, 206, 244
Grigera, Tomás, 187
Güemes, Martin de, 67, 78, 264–8, 269, 270, 314, 380, 386
Guido, Tomás, 358
Gutiérrez, Celedonio, 385, 387
Gutiérrez, José Albino, 259, 260, 261, 263, 328, 397
Gutiérrez, José Matías, 85
Gutiérrez, Juan María, 163

Hansen, Emilio, 73
Heredia, Governor, 44, 318
Hereñú, Eusebio, 291, 295, 303
Herrera, Nicolás, 222
Huidoboro, Pascal Ruiz, 133, 135, 141
Holmberg, Baron, 291
Haigh, Samuel, 87

Index

Ibarra, Cayetano, 326
Ibarra, Gov. Juan Felipe, 67, 324, 325-7, 385, 386, 387, 395, 397 400, 401
Ibarra, Francisco, 326
Ibarra, Roman, 326
Inchaurregui, 154
Ingenieros, José, 105
Iriarte, General, 9, 105, 349, 362, 381
Isasa, 251
Isasmendi, Nicolás Severo de, 7
Isasmendi, family of, 249

Joaquina, Princess Carlota, 137, 139, 144
Jordan, Tadeo, 291
Jurieu, Rear-Admiral, 348

Kanki, Pazos, 237

Lacunza, Father, 182
Lamadrid, General, 317
Larrea, Juan, 30, 94, 143, 151, 155, 208
Larrea, Major Ramon, 193
Las Heras, 370
Lastarria, 23
Lavalle, 69
Lavalleja, 270, 271
León, Diego Ponce de, 128, 137
León, Juan de, 284
Lezica, Ambrosio, 30, 68, 95, 212
Liniers, Comte de, 94, 123, 127-9, 130, 132, 133, 134, 135, 137, 139, 141, 142, 143, 147, 148, 151, 153, 165, 181, 216
Llavallol, 30, 212
López, Estanislao, 303, 305-6, 308, 316, 324, 332, 336, 338, 339, 340-1, 372, 379, 380, 385, 395, 396
López, Javier, 9, 313
López, Manuel, 68, 322, 387
López, Vicente Fidel, 90, 220
López y Planes, Vicente, 158, 343, 366
Lozano, 252
Lué, Bishop, 182
Luzuriaga, Toribio de, 315, 316, 328

Maceda, Ceferino Garzón, 246
MacIntyre, Patrick, 82
Mackinnon, Alexander, 101
Mansilla, Lucio, 330
Marfany, Dr, 155
Martin of Tours, Saint, 164
Martínez, Fr, 193
Martínez, General, 123
Martínez, Mariano Victor, 361

Matheu, Domingo, 30, 155, 161, 208
Medina, Francisco, 25
Mejía, Ildefonso Ramos, 341, 384
Méndez, Juan Bautista, 295, 298
Mendizóbal, Mariano, 314, 315, 316
Mitre, General Bartolomé, 51, 217, 220, 313
Molina, Francisco Antonio, 160
Molina, family of, 147
Molina, Manuel Ignacio, 257
Monterosso, José, 384
Moreno, Manuel, 237, 249, 357, 366
Moreno, María Guadalupe Cuenca de, 163, 164
Moreno, Mariano, 49, 117, 123, 143, 151, 155, 160, 172, 186, 208-9, 215-16, 218, 219, 221, 377
Morón, Colonel, 325, 328, 367
Mota Botello, 310, 311
Moussy, Martin de, 58
Moxó, Archbishop of Charcus, 160
Muñoz, Joaquin, 212
Murguiondo, Prudencio, 140

Nieto, Vicente, 148, 169, 170
Núñez, Ignacio, 131, 363, 369, 377, 379

Obligados, family of, 147
Ocampo, family of, 161
Ocampo, Ortiz, 246, 250
O'Higgins, Bernardo, 339
Olañeta, General, 66, 269
Orellana, Bishop of Córdoba, 180, 181, 182, 196, 246
Oro, Domingo de, 77-8, 385
Oro, José Godoy, 39, 47
Otorgués, Fernando, 276, 280, 282-3, 298, 380

Pagola, Colonel, 237, 341, 342, 343
Panelo, Julián, 82
Parish, Woodbine, 87, 377, 379
Paroissien, James, 144
Paso, Juan José, 155, 229
Paz, General José María, 66, 69, 78, 106, 201, 203, 293, 318, 320, 322, 385, 397, 400
Peña, Nicolás Rodriguez, 138
Peñaloza, Juan, 262
Pérez, León, 284
Pérez, Manuel, 284
Perugorría, Genaro, 295, 296
Pezuela, 265
Pinedo, Agustin de, 200
Pinedo, Ambrosio, de, 200

Index

Planchón, José León, 184
Ponsonby, Lord, 168
Posadas, Gervasio Antonio de, 177, 178, 221, 222, 249
Puch, family of, 8
Pueyrredón, family of, 147
Pueyrredón, Juan Martin de, 102, 105, 143, 167, 168, 170, 180, 194, 200, 205, 207, 211, 215, 216, 223, 228, 229, 231, 233, 234, 236, 237, 238, 244, 250, 267, 309, 335, 341, 343, 344, 346, 347, 348
Pueyrredón, Col. Manuel A. 192

Quintana, Hilarión de la, 266, 342
Quiroga, José Prudencio, 60, 261, 394
Quiroga, Juan Facundo, 13, 60, 70–1, 76, 79, 80, 261–2, 263, 324, 326, 385, 389, 394, 397, 398, 399, 400

Ramírez, Francisco, 54, 80, 291–4, 308, 319, 330, 332, 336, 337, 338, 339, 340, 380, 384
Reynafé, brothers, 123, 168, 322
Rezával, 129
Rivadavia, Bernadino, 30, 49, 216, 346, 349, 352, 357, 358, 366, 369, 370, 377
Rivera, brothers, 271
Rivera, Fructuoso, 270, 271, 281, 284, 336
Rivera, Lázaro de, 136
Robertson, brothers, 87, 88, 98, 302
Rodrigo y Aldea, José de, 65
Rodríguez, Canon, 252
Rodríguez, Colonel, 285, 341, 342, 345, 346, 348, 366, 370
Rojas, Juan Antonio, 236
Romero, Esteban, 130, 143
Romero, Tomás Antonio, 34
Rondeau, José, 196, 204, 222, 227, 228, 232, 266, 267, 309, 315, 339
Rosa, Lt.-Gov. de la, 314
Rosa, Juana de la, 315
Rosas, Juan Manuel de, 68, 69, 79, 103, 104, 307, 320, 342, 358, 365, 370, 383, 387, 389, 390, 396, 402
Rousseau, J.-J. 167

Saavedra, Cornelio de, 129, 130, 131, 132, 142, 152, 153, 154–5, 161, 176, 208, 215, 216, 219, 226, 318, 358
Sáenz, Antonio, 184
Saguí, Francisco, 211–12
Sala de Touron, 285
Salta, Bishop of, 180
Samaniego, 291

San Alberto, Bishop, 57, 121–2, 250
San Martín, José de, 76, 87, 88, 200, 201, 203, 214, 217, 221, 222, 227, 230, 232, 236, 254, 257, 260, 263, 266, 315, 327, 335, 358, 380
Santa Coloma, 30
Saráchaga, Dr, 250, 252
Saravia, family of, 47, 249
Sarmiento, 57, 59, 79, 90, 107–8, 220, 402
Sarratea, Manuel de, 105, 237, 339–41, 342, 344, 369
Sarratea, Melchora, 237
Sassenay, Marquis de, 136
Seco, Juan José, 212
Seguí, Juan Francisco, 306
Silva, Governor, 296
Sobremonte, Viceroy, 127–8, 132, 133, 250, 252
Sola, León, 77, 154
Soler, Miguel Estanislao, 193, 224, 339–41, 344
Soler, Hipólito, 184
Street, John, 277

Taboada, family of, 44–5
Tagle, Dr, 233, 236, 332, 348–9, 356, 358
Tarragona, 303
Thomas, Alvarez, 204, 223, 228, 233, 302
Thompson, Martin, 212
Torre, Nelson de la, 285
Torre Revello, José, 96
Trápani, Pedro, 104, 396
Tristán, 241

Udaondo, E., 204, 217
Uriburu, Damaso de, 268
Uriburu, family of, 8
Urien, José Domingo de, 130
Urquijo, José María Mariluz, 160, 227
Urquiza, Isodoro de, 71, 220

Valle, Ortiz del, 251
Vásquez, Ventura, 222, 385, 397
Vedia, Joaquín Pablo de, 199
Vedia, Nicolás, de, 199
Vedia, General, 280
Vedoya, Colonel, 298
Velez, Eustoquio Diáz, 303
Velasquez, Dr Pedro Arias, 266
Vera, Mariano, 290, 291, 304–5, 306
Viamonte, Jaime, 199, 303
Viana, Javia de, 222
Vidal, Fr Pedro Pablo, 222
Vieytes, Hipólito, 22, 115–19, 138, 143

Index

Villafañes, family of, 261
Villanueva, 142

White, William Pius, 94, 123

Yapeyú, 289

Yrigoyen, Miguel, 237

Zambrana, José, 159
Zapata, 77
Zapiola, General, 217
Zúñigas, Garcia de, family of, 147